PERSONNEL
The Management of Human Resources

PERSONNEL

The Management of Human Resources

Third Edition

Donald P. Crane
Georgia State University

Cases Prepared by
Richard N. Farmer
Indiana University

KENT PUBLISHING COMPANY
Boston, Massachusetts
A Division of Wadsworth, Inc.

The first edition of *Personnel: The Management of Human Resources* was published under the title *Personnel Management: A Situational Approach.*

KENT PUBLISHING COMPANY
A Division of Wadsworth, Inc.

Production Editor: *Nancy Phinney*
Text and Cover Designer: *Mike Fender*
Production Coordinator: *Linda Card*

Printed in the United States of America
1 2 3 4 5 6 7 8 9 — 85 84 83 82 81

Library of Congress Cataloging in Publication Data

Crane, Donald P.
  Personnel, the management of human resources.

  Includes bibliographies and index.
  1. Personnel management.   I. Farmer, Richard N.
II. Title.
HF5549.C817 1982   658.3   81-19295
ISBN 0-534-01070-9   AACR2

To my wife, Gerri.

Preface

This third edition of *Personnel* contains several major changes and considerable updates. Recent developments in the field are reflected through coverage of such subjects as stress, quality of work life, sexual harassment, court decisions, personnel management information systems, and personnel careers.

A unified scheme frames *Personnel*. The behavioral aspects of personnel management have been combined with substantive research throughout to provide pedagogical soundness. The situational approach of the second edition has been retained. Many chapters have been recast to emphasize practice so as to equip students with the skills needed to make personnel decisions.

Each chapter opens with a list of learning objectives to focus on major points. A short example follows to excite student interest. At the end of each chapter key terms appear, along with reference notes that serve as pedagogical aids. The terms appearing in boldface in the text are listed in a glossary at the end of the book. The case problems at the end of the chapter are designed to teach students the concepts presented and to help them relate these concepts to the real world.

This edition draws heavily upon the author's own extensive real world experience in personnel as a practitioner, consultant, and arbitrator. To heighten student interest, numerous examples are gleaned from this firsthand experience.

Many individuals have played a significant role in preparing this third edition. I am especially grateful to Paul Muchinsky of Iowa State University and Milo Pierce of Corpus Christi State University for their encouragement and advice during the completion of the manuscript. I thank my reviewers Robert Alexander, James Hester, Mary Hopkins, David Robertson, and Richard Scholl for their able assistance. Their efforts enhanced the quality of this edition. Special recognition goes to Penny Pennington for her devoted, capable, and conscientious efforts in assisting me in the development of this edition. My gratitude also goes to my editor Keith Nave, who gave much encouragement and guidance in the development of the entire project. To Nancy Phinney, a truly professional production editor, my thanks for making the final stages of publishing this text a pleasure. Finally, I thank Richard N. Farmer of Indiana University for devising the cases.

Donald P. Crane
Georgia State University
1982

Contents

Chapter Two: The Personnel Environment and Contingency Thinking 39

Contingency Theory 40
A Frame of Reference for the Situational Approach 42
Situational Analysis 50
Cost-Benefit Analysis 53
Summary 54
Key Terms 54
Review Questions 54
Discussion Questions 55
Case Problems 56
Notes 58

Chapter Three: Personnel Policy 59

Policy Making and the Planning Function 60
Personnel Policy Development 61
Policy Determination 62
Policy Formulation Process 63
Policy Implementation 67
Cost-Benefit Analysis 67
Summary 70
Key Terms 71
Review Questions 71
Discussion Questions 71
Case Problems 73
Notes 77

Chapter Four: Motivation and Commitment 78

Employee Motivation 79
Leadership 89
Communications 93
Cost-Benefit Analysis 99
Summary 100
Key Terms 101
Review Questions 101
Discussion Questions 101
Case Problems 103
Notes 106

Contents

Chapter Sixteen: Performance Appraisal   479

Chapter Seventeen: Career Planning   511

Section Five—Maintaining the Work Force

Section One

PERSONNEL MANAGEMENT: Roles and Concepts

The influence of personnel management on the business organization has increased appreciably in recent years. Much of this increase can be attributed to the growing complexity of human resource management and the issues related to it. The critical nature of personnel problems has given rise to a changed role of personnel—primary responsibility still rests with line management, but the personnel staff provides professional support. The basic objective of personnel management is to create guidelines and programs that foster employee effectiveness through motivation, leadership, and communication. Personnel managers develop policies to help employees meet these goals.

Section I provides a framework for the study of this process. Because there is no one best way to solve personnel problems, concepts and methods of the contingency- or situational-approach to personnel management are also presented here. Specific functions of personnel management are covered in subsequent sections.

Chapter One

Evolving Roles of Personnel Management

Nine Steel Companies Settle for $31 Million in EEO Case
Accidents Cost Industry $27 Billion in '79
Nation's Key Energy Source Sapped by Coal Strike
Pregnancy Disability Pay Bill Passes House

These newspaper headlines and others like them heralded a new era in personnel management. Rapid change in the economy, recent legislation, a new generation of workers, and the greater sophistication of organized labor challenge managers to heed the advice of Delta Airlines's chief executive Tom Beebe: "The name of the game in business today is personnel."[1]

The Challenge of Personnel Management

American business is on the threshold of an era in which **personnel management** will be essential to the survival of organizations. Considering today's human resources problems in organizations, we can see that personnel management has become an exciting and expanding field.

If we trace the development of the personnel function, personnel problems have been of concern to business and society for several centuries. As early as 1800, Matthew Boulton and James Watt recognized the importance of employee welfare to the success of their steam engine company. Formal courses in the field were offered at Dartmouth College as early as 1915. These and other developments have been summarized chronologically in Table 1.1. Notice that the emergence of personnel management as a recognized, viable entity in an organization is a recent phenomenon.

LEARNING OBJECTIVES

1. To recognize why personnel management is a challenging field.
2. To know the reason for the expanding role of personnel.
3. To learn the basic functions of personnel management.
4. To understand how personnel departments are organized.
5. To be aware of the various roles of the people in personnel.

1799	In Philadelphia journeymen cordwainers (shoemakers) negotiated first recorded settlement of a collectively bargained agreement.
1800	Matthew Boulton and James Watt, in their Soho, England steam engine company, instituted modern personnel practices for employee welfare: special entertainment to raise employees' morale, payment of overtime, whitewashed foundry walls to improve working conditions, worker housing, Christmas presents, and a mutual insurance society for the benefit of employees.
1800s	Personnel specialists appeared in private industry to assist with: employment, welfare, rate-setting, safety, training, and health.
1810	Robert Owen, in operating his factories at New Lanark, Scotland, recognized the need for enlightened personnel practices: child-labor minimum age of ten years; an open-door policy to air grievances about rules and regulations; meal facilities, housing, schools, and recreation centers for employees and their families; company training for employees. Robert Owen could perhaps be considered the father of modern personnel administration.
1835	Charles Babbage, *On the Economy of Machinery and Manufacturing*, recommended placing workers according to a hierarchy of skills.
1880s	Personnel activities first grouped together in one department.
Early 1900s	Frederick W. Taylor introduced the scientific management movement, which advocated scientific selection, education, and development of workers and intimate, friendly cooperation between management and workers. He also stressed a developmental attitude toward employees, cash bonuses for useful employee suggestions, and individual recognition for superior performance.
1901	Henry Gantt introduced the task-and-bonus wage incentive system. He was convinced that the human element was the most important aspect in all management problems.
1911	Workmen's compensation laws enacted in several states.
1912	Modern personnel department emerged.
1913	Industrial psychology appeared. Hugo Munsterberg described selection of workers for various classifications in *Psychology and Industrial Efficiency*. Aptitude and mental ability tests introduced to industry.
1915	Dartmouth College offered first college personnel course with a training program for employment managers.

Table 1.1 (cont.)

1917	National War Labor Board established work councils of elected worker representatives to discuss wages, hours, and working conditions with employees.
	U.S. Army used group tests for selecting officers.
1920	First comprehensive textbook in the field, *Personnel Administration* by Ordway Tead and Henry Metcalf, appeared.
1921	Walter D. Scott introduced the concept of the worker in the workplace, emphasizing that the employee is both a social and an economic entity possessing different characteristics in different work situations.
1923	Concept of human relations appeared with Hawthorne experiments. Spontaneous team efforts and group participation were found to affect productivity.
1924	Merrill R. Lott developed a plan to evaluate jobs on the basis of their work characteristics.
1940s	Carl Rogers and other social scientists developed a general theory of behavior, which led to the organizational behavior approach to personnel administration.
1942	Training Within Industry (TWI) program was developed to train supervisors during the Second World War.
1946	Personnel recognized as a profession. Cornell University established a School of Industrial and Labor Relations offering the first professional degree in the personnel (labor relations) field.
1955	Writers, including Herbert Simon, Harold J. Levitt, and Robert Schlaifer, stressed that human behavior in decision making is an identifiable, measurable, and observable process.
1957	Social psychology and human relations in personnel (as well as in organization theory, in general) were emphasized by Rensis Likert and Chris Argyris.
1960s	Concept of personnel administration as encompassing the entire organization led to application of organizational development (OD) and organizational behavior (OB) approaches to personnel practice.
1970s	Influence of personnel in business organizations increased. Line responsibility for personnel administration emphasized. Personnel staff professionalized.
1980s	Personnel professionals become human resource strategists for the organization.

In a discussion with the chief executive officer of a prominent business organization, I asked him to describe his three major management concerns. This was his response:

> Stimulating employees to be more productive is a real problem. Our people don't seem to work as hard as they used to, and it shows up in the declining units produced and delivered per employee.
>
> I'm concerned about the health and safety of our people. The traffic congestion in this city and our aging manufacturing equipment make it harder every day to maintain our fine safety record.
>
> And my third concern, which is not the least of these, is two-fold. How can I see that my women and minority employees rise and succeed in this organization and still provide opportunities and benefits for my long-service employees?

As you can imagine, I was astounded at his answer! I fully expected him to tell me about his concerns regarding company expansion or the financial health of the organization (his background was in accounting). But he didn't.

He explained that the basic business areas of manufacturing, finance, marketing, and so on were second nature to him. But the human-resources aspects of the business were mind boggling.

Though this chief executive's response may have been atypical, it does reflect some basic concerns among business executives. What do these concerns have in common? Each of them relates to **human resource**—people problems—and this is what personnel management is all about. But these concerns also reflect two other phenomena: increasing government regulation in personnel matters and a new breed of employee. Health and safety, affirmative action, and pay and benefits are all governed by federal and/or state legislation. And the employees are different now. For the first time we have black and white, male and female, old and young working together, but vying for an equal share in the pay, benefits, and opportunities available in an organization.

Let us take a closer look at some of the challenges facing personnel management today.

RAPID CHANGE

All aspects of management—economic, social, and political—are evolving so quickly that managers find it necessary to review constantly their personnel decisions in the light of change. Policies, procedures, and methods that were effective in solving problems last year may be inadequate today. Forward-thinking managers *anticipate* change; they do not just react to it.

TECHNOLOGY

In the mid-1960s, a group of young assembly-line workers went on strike at the new, automated Vega (General Motors) plant in Lordstown, Ohio. They were protesting the boredom and demeaning nature of their work, a condition later referred to as the blue collar blues. These younger, better-educated workers shared the feelings of many of their fellow employees throughout industry—that is, advanced **technology** tends to dehumanize work and is often the cause of poor morale and lower productivity.

Productivity seems to be a universal problem, and the subject seems to come up every time the issue of wage increases arises. Management has difficulty justifying increases in compensation when it cannot show a commensurate rise in productivity. Productivity (average output per hour) of all persons rose at a rate of 3 percent between 1950 and 1970, but since 1970, the rate has been lower.[2] Technology is no longer the major variable in productivity, however. This fact, coupled with America's declining world position, places the onus on personnel professionals to demonstrate that their programs have a positive impact on the bottom line.

QUALITY OF WORK LIFE

Problems associated with technology—for example, worker dissatisfaction and declining productivity—have caused management to give special attention to improving the **quality of work life.** Jerome Rosow, president of the Work In America Institute, predicts that factors contributing to or influencing the quality of work life in the '80s will be far greater in number and significance than at any other time in America's history.[3]

Some companies are already experimenting with programs to improve the quality of working life. The Mead Corporation, for example, runs a paperboard plant with self-managed work groups. The group directs its own efforts and disciplines its members. Employees are paid not by the level of skill they achieve, but by the number of jobs they can perform. Because each member of the group is qualified to perform all jobs, the members can rotate assignments at will, and the group can function effectively as a team. Naturally, the teams are responsible for results, and the results have been gratifying. The self-managed plant is significantly more productive—and profitable—than its traditionally run counterpart. The Mead experiment is not a panacea for high-technology organizations suffering from declining productivity or low morale, but the team approach and self-managed work groups are seen as trends for the future.[4]

According to the Work In America Institute the key quality of life issues for the coming decade include:

— Pay
— Employee benefits
— Job security
— Alternative work schedules
— Occupational stress
— Participation
— Democracy in the workplace[5]

(Each of these issues will be discussed in detail in later chapters.)

The development of **socio-technical systems** by many firms is an effort to improve the quality of work life. These systems take the form of workers' advisory councils, self-management work groups and labor-management task forces and committees. Odiorne[6] feels that the development of socio-technical systems will be a major concern of management in the future.

A NEW GENERATION OF EMPLOYEES

Young workers today have been characterized as a new breed because they have values and attitudes substantially different from those of previous generations of workers. Traditional employees were raised on the idea that work is a virtue, and that a steady job with an adequate income is the foundation for a good life. The Depression reinforced the belief that money and the things it could buy were tantamount to fulfillment in life. The economic orientation of these workers emphasized wages, work conditions, and employment stability. To them, the smoke belching from factory chimneys was a symbol of security because it meant there was production and work for the people. In contrast, the new generation views the smoking stacks as a threat to the environment. Their concern for the welfare of their fellow human beings, along with their social consciousness, represents a philosophy different from that of their parents. These young workers' material needs have been provided by their parents, but the state of the world has left them confused, concerned, and even disillusioned. Success and happiness, they realize, cannot be measured in dollars. Young people today are seeking an identity, one they feel they have lost in this society of mass conformity. They feel that jobs must be relevant to society's needs as well as provide opportunities to improve existing conditions. According to Kerr and Rosow, they demand more personal autonomy; insist on the right to participate in decision making; place more emphasis on small and self-chosen friendship groups; seek longer vacation periods and a mixing of education with work and leisure; accept hard work; and insist upon consumer rights and sovereignty.[7]

These differences in values—between the new breed and traditional workers—are due not only to age but to level of education as well. The trend is toward more education among American workers. For example, in 1952 only 43 percent of the labor force were high school graduates; by 1979 this number had increased to 76 percent. And twice as many workers had some college education in 1979 than in 1952. The median educational attainment of workers as of March 1979 was 12.7 years.[8]

But this factor only compounds the problem, because as graduates enter a tight job market they tend to settle for jobs that do not use their full potential and become frustrated and dissatisfied. Taylor and Thompson concluded from their study of value systems of 1,058 workers that "Young workers will be demanding both more job satisfaction and higher income. At the same time, more educated persons entering the labor force are less likely to trust existing institutions to meet their needs. Young managers may have as much difficulty as their older superiors in relating to young workers."[9] In the next decade this challenge will be even more acute because, as the U.S. Bureau of Labor Statistics predicts, **white collar workers** will comprise more than half (51.5 percent) of the work force, and the fastest growth will be among clerical, service, professional, and technical occupations.[10]

Enlightened personnel programs are challenged to provide an environment that can accommodate the social demands of the new generation of employees as well as the economic demands of older workers.

GOVERNMENT INTERVENTION

Personnel managers face a real challenge in complying with state and federal legislation that regulates personnel practices while providing an environment that offers fulfilling work, advancement opportunity, and equitable rewards. There is a clear trend toward greater regulation of personnel activities and business operations. Recent legislation and court rulings on minimum wages, equal employment opportunities, work safety standards, and collective bargaining set limits and demands on the personnel process. For personnel managers, growing government influence is a mixed blessing. Certainly, government regulation will constrain unions somewhat from making spiraling wage demands. However, companies can expect a higher minimum wage, more compulsory arbitration, and stricter equal employment opportunity laws for minority groups and women. A decade from now, personnel managers may work under a clearly defined, all-pervasive framework of federal legislation on labor practices.

ECONOMIC DEVELOPMENTS

Economic changes in the labor market have a profound influence on personnel management. **Unemployment** results from fluctuations in the business cycle and/or from the introduction or increase of technology; it creates concern among workers for job security. The mid '70s suffered from an unemployment rate as high as 8.5 percent, with 7.8 million workers unemployed in 1975. We can expect at least a 5 percent rate during the '80s with substantially higher unemployment in some industries, such as automobile manufacturing. Thus, business organizations are challenged to provide job security for their people. The U.S. Steel Corporation and the United Steelworkers are attempting to solve the problem by incorporating provisions in their labor-management agreement that will afford employees lifetime guarantees of work.

Inflation tends to erode compensation. When total earnings are adjusted by the cost-of-living (**Consumer Price Index**), many breadwinners find their real or take-home earnings less this year than they were last. Consequently, people at work become dissatisfied when their pay increases are less than the inflation rate.

Inflation, unemployment, ecology, and the energy crunch; the combination of these with other factors mentioned has a notable impact on personnel activities. For instance, the high cost of labor induces firms to automate; this in turn results in less employment. However, this trend has slowed because the cost of automated equipment is higher, the cost of capital to buy it is higher, and there is uncertainty as to the energy supply needed to power it. In addition, automated equipment increases working condition problems while contributing to environmental pollution. Furthermore, some think that industry in the Northeast is going to move south to take advantage of the milder weather (less energy is needed) and a more plentiful water supply.

SOCIAL ISSUES

The threat of class action suits by aggrieved employees has challenged personnel managers to find ways to avoid even the appearance of **discrimination** (as well as reverse discrimination). Not only has the cost been prohibitive—AT&T settled two discrimination suits for $38 million and $25 million, and there have been numerous other multimillion-dollar settlements—but such publicity adversely affects recruitment efforts. Business organizations today are becoming socially conscious, especially when it concerns their human resources. The American Society for Personnel Administration reported that of 111 annual (1975) corporate reports it selected at random, 46 percent had a separate section on personnel and social responsibility.[11] But reporting on programs alone does not appear to have the same impact as showing tangible results; for example, women and minorities succeeding throughout the organization, personnel working with civic and community agencies, and workers and managers making positive accomplishments through mutual respect and trust.

An Integrative Scheme for Personnel Management

By now it should be obvious that the personnel function is broader than getting things done with people. Personnel management is indeed concerned with people problems, but it also operates to support the attainment of organizational objectives. In other words, personnel management is basically concerned with the most effective utilization of human resources as a means of reaching organizational objectives.

The following personnel situation at the Atlas Manufacturing Company provides further clarification of the definition of personnel management.

When the Atlas Manufacturing Company opened a new plant in the South, it told the employment manager to acquire employees with the operative and managerial skills that would be needed. As the plant began operation, the general manager faced the problem of training workers and molding an effective management team. Then one day, a year after the opening of the plant, several of the equipment operators alleged that they should have a pay raise to equalize their compensation with their counterparts in the northern plant.

This example points up some of the problem areas relevant to personnel management. First, the employment manager was concerned with acquiring human resources so that the company could open its new plant on schedule. Then the general manager faced the problem of integrating the new employees into the organization and developing an effective work force in order to start up production. The immediate supervisor had to maintain the work force by ensuring the fairness of their pay. The Atlas example illustrates the four basic concerns in personnel management, and these can be incorporated into a concise definition:

Personnel management is the process of supporting the accomplishment of organizational objectives by continually *acquiring* human resources; *integrating* employees into the organization; *developing* employee potential; and *maintaining* the work force

This definition then can serve to integrate the material in this text. Each of the four basic areas of concern represents a major section. The activities associated with each area constitute the chapters within each section. The schematic in Table 1.2 indicates the four basic areas with the associated activities that are designed to support achievement of the organization's objectives. (Note: Section I is an introduction to the text.)

1. *Acquiring.* This includes planning human resource needs within an organization and implementing these through employment activities. Employment encompasses recruiting needed employees, screening applicants

Table 1.2
Personnel Manage-
ment Schematic

Areas of Concern (sections of text)	Activities	Result
I. *Introduction*		
II. *Acquiring human resources*	Human resource planning Employee selection/ placement, testing	
III. *Integrating employees into the organization*	Personnel records and research Counseling and interviewing Discipline Labor relations Collective bargaining Labor-management dispute settlement	
IV. *Developing employee potential*	Human resource development Management and executive development Women and minority development Performance appraisal Career planning/development	Accomplishment of organizational objectives
V. *Maintaining the workforce*	Compensation management Executive compensation Benefits and services Employee health and safety	

for employment, selecting the most suitable candidates, and placing newly hired employees in appropriate job vacancies or training programs.

2. *Integrating.* Employees are made a part of an organizational team through counseling activities and interviews that are designed to gain knowledge about their backgrounds, aspirations, work experiences, as well as their problems in adjusting to work. Should the employees be represented by a labor union, the activity of integrating them into the organization involves bargaining with employee representatives on hours, wages, and working conditions. To help support the organization's objectives, employees must understand what is expected of them, and their behavior, when it deviates from expectations, must be corrected through positive disciplinary action.

3. *Developing.* Development includes all activities for the education, training, appraisal, and planning of careers of employees. This prepares them

for present or future jobs and thereby enhances their value to an organization. Training and educational activities develop skills, improve behavior, and provide information necessary for more effective performance. Performance appraisal informs employees of their progress and aids them in correcting deviations from established performance standards. Career planning blends business needs with personal aspirations to help ensure that human talent is optimally utilized.

4. *Maintaining.*   Programs of compensation and benefits reward people's accomplishments. The human resource is also maintained in a safe and healthy state through safety and hygiene activities. This area serves to maintain an efficient and effective work force, retain valuable talent, and sustain and improve the favorable conditions within the organization.

Personnel as a Management Function

Personnel management is an integral part of the broader field of **management.** Management has been defined as *the process of accomplishing objectives through the efforts of other people within an organization.* Notice that people are key in this definition of management, too. Thus, we can conclude that the role of personnel is critical to managing in general.

Objectives are the starting point of the management process. They give the organization and its people a purpose and direction. Objectives serve to guide managers and employees in their efforts. The statement of objectives will vary among organizations depending on management philosophy and whether the organization is an institution, government agency, manufacturer, or service firm. So an organization's objectives could include: making a certain profit, gaining a specific market share, developing a level of competence in its people, creating a certain image, or any or all of these and a host of others.

MANAGEMENT FUNCTIONS

Another way of viewing management is through the functions managers perform. They commonly perform these functions:

1. *Planning*—determining strategies and programs to help accomplish established objectives.

2. *Organizing*—grouping and assigning activities, staffing the organization, and delegating authority to carry out activities.

3. *Directing*—encouraging human efforts and stimulating accomplishment of objectives.

4. *Controlling*—measuring accomplishments, comparing results with planned objectives, determining causes of deviations, and taking necessary corrective action.

It may be obvious that personnel management is the key to the managerial function of directing, because it involves activities associated with people and the problems of getting work done through their efforts. This is not to say, however, that personnel managers are only concerned with the directing function. As do all other managers, they plan, organize, direct, and control within their respective organizations. The nonmanagement personnel people, however, have a more specialized role, as we shall discover later in this chapter.

THE PERSONNEL LINE-STAFF RELATIONSHIP

Personnel is basically a **staff** function. Staff functions are basically advisory and supportive in nature; they do not contribute directly to the primary objective, for example, producing goods or services, which is a **line** function. Rather, they facilitate and support line work. The personnel staff assists line managers in acquiring the necessary talent for their departments, advises managers in the interpretation of labor agreements, conducts training programs as a service, and so on. The responsibility for personnel work should not be the staff's alone, however. To achieve maximum personnel effectiveness, *all* managers should be personnel managers.

Personnel Management Is Everyone's Responsibility

In reviewing his quarterly performance report, a production supervisor noticed the extremely high turnover and absenteeism rate at the plant. "It's those danged youngsters," he bemoaned. "They just don't have any sense of responsibility like we did. In my day you respected your elders, and you considered yourself lucky to have any job at all. We worked hard for what we got, and we never considered laying out. Why, these kids today just don't care; they'd rather loaf than work! I sure wish those personnel guys would get this situation turned around."

Should it really be up to the personnel department to take the initiative in this situation? Or should line management find the answers? Both line management and the personnel staff share the responsibility for handling people problems. First-line supervisors, however, because they deal directly with people in carrying out their own assignments, have the greatest responsibility for personnel management and the greatest effect on the outcome of a personnel program. Their success is, to a large degree, dependent upon their skills in leading, motivating, and communicating with their subordinates. (These skills will be considered in depth in Chapter 4.) But supervisors are not alone in the administration of personnel programs; they need the firm support of higher management, which can make decisions that will enhance personnel effectiveness. Supervisors can, of course, obtain assistance from the personnel staff.

Line supervisors perform activities that are directly related to the primary objectives of the organization. Staff people provide services to support and assist the line. It is to the advantage of line supervisors to work effectively with their subordinates and to understand the personnel staff services that are available. Considering the complexities of human relations problems, it is obvious that the advice and assistance of a proficient personnel staff can prove indispensable. With the changing role of personnel management during the 1980s, it becomes even more important to emphasize line-staff cooperation.

The staff role of personnel is not an easy one. It is up to the personnel people to establish and maintain rapport with the line. Often, staff specialists resent the fact that they are only advisors to line people and have no real authority. Conversely, line people rebel against staff attempts to tell them what to do. How, then, can the personnel staff resolve this conflict? The experience of successful personnel managers reveals that, by repeatedly demonstrating professional competence in rendering service to the line, they gain the confidence of line managers and thereby attain influence. When line managers consider personnel services indispensable to their own success, they tend to grant responsible staff people more and more authority. For instance, Ron Allen, who is in charge of personnel at Delta Air Lines, by demonstrating his expertise in personnel matters, won the support of line management so that today he is a member of the corporation's board of directors. He not only influences personnel policy, he helps guide the destiny of the entire company! Personnel staffs gain power by performing necessary services in an exceptional manner to the line organization.

We should note at this point the distinction between personnel functions and personnel departments. Functions are the activities (hiring, selecting, training, and so on) performed by the personnel staff. These staff members (personnel department specialists, generalists, and managers) operate within the personnel department, which is the organization that operates to carry out the personnel functions.

ROLES OF THE PERSONNEL STAFF

The personnel staff wears many hats in serving the line organization. The following paragraphs discuss some of the roles the personnel manager may play in dealing with the personnel challenges that face the modern organization.

ADVISOR. Since the personnel staff has expert knowledge in a specialized area, line managers frequently seek its advice. In offering advice, personnel might present ideas, suggestions, alternatives, or consequences of actions. For example, in answer to a query regarding promotion, personnel might advise: "After reviewing the records of the candidates, I'd suggest we consider Smith for the job. She has demonstrated leadership ability, and her experience gives her the technical expertise to function in the new position." Notice that the advice in this case was presented diplomatically and was backed up with facts.

Too often, personnel people become officious in their advisory roles. They issue orders or preempt line authority. "You can't hire so-and-so" or "The job has to be posted before you hire anyone," may be said in good faith, but such statements create resentment and destroy the rapport that is so essential to line-staff relationships.

STEWARD.   The personnel staff also performs services for line departments. Examples include: offering food service, operating medical clinics, performing training, writing job descriptions, recruiting employees, and so on. Line departments usually do not have the resources, the time, or the inclination to perform these activities, and they are happy to be relieved of such headaches. But this can be another opportunity for the personnel staff to gain influence. In performing such services, line organizations delegate functional authority to the staff. That is, they grant authority to conduct a particular service. For instance, an instructor may have authority to direct the activities of a line department's personnel while they are engaged in a training course, or a line department might allocate some of its budget to personnel for the purpose of conducting an accident-prevention program. Personnel staffs sometimes complain that they are inundated with requests for what they consider to be unnecessary services, yet continuous requests for staff services might be viewed as line acceptance of personnel's viability.

CONSULTANT.   Because of the highly complex and technical nature of organizational decisions, the personnel staff can consult with line management in the formative stages of programs. In each of the functional areas of management, the personnel staff can provide positive input. In designing long-range plans, personnel might ascertain the impact on the current work force of anticipated changes, or it might research the effect applicable labor laws could have on such plans. In developing organizational changes, management must know what skills are available in the existing hierarchy and what programs it must initiate to recruit new talent. Problems in directing the work force especially require staff consultation. Supervisors consult with personnel daily on pay problems, grievances, scheduling difficulties, discipline, motivation of workers, and potential collective actions such as strikes. Control of activities also requires staff consultation. In one manufacturing plant, department managers became suspicious that the numerous transfers and promotions of personnel were causing payroll costs to skyrocket. Personnel was consulted and asked to institute a control program. The staff investigation revealed that employees were being misclassified in their new jobs. After three months of controlling personnel changes to ensure proper classification of jobs, the company found that personnel had saved more than $10,000.

ACTIVIST/CHANGE AGENT.   Personnel people can actually influence policy. The changes we cited at the beginning of this chapter call for anticipation of future events; reaction to them may prove too little, too late. Thus, personnel managers have to know the organization's business well enough to be able to contribute to strategic debates and policy formulation. When their advice is adopted by top management it becomes policy. Accordingly, when minimum specifications for a pay grade or a job are set by personnel, line (or other staff) management is not free to ignore these guidelines any more than a corporate officer may ignore the controller's rules for the expenditure of funds. The activist role is also demonstrated in the implementation of innovative programs and the assumption of an initiative or aggressive stance on matters affecting human resources. Personnel managers who engage in conceptual thinking and creative personnel activity epitomize the role of change agent.

MEDIATOR.   Managers with divergent views or those having difficulty communicating with each other can call on personnel to serve as an objective outsider who can bring the parties together. Disagreements and conflicts among managers in organizations are common. The personnel staff serves a valuable purpose when it can mediate such differences and remove or reduce those conflicts that inhibit the attainment of objectives.

AUDITOR.   Especially when compliance with legislative regulations is concerned, the need is clear for someone to investigate activities and determine if their results are in tune with the law. Personnel staffs save an organization money, undesirable publicity, time, and embarrassment when they help ensure that programs are being conducted in accordance with policy and the law. Areas suitable for a personnel audit include:

1. *Affirmative action*—to see if Equal Employment Opportunity (EEO) goals are being met and to discover any discriminatory practices that might exist.

2. *Safety/hygiene*—to ensure that safe work practices are being employed in the plant and offices and to discover hazardous or unhealthy conditions.

3. *Testing*—to see that instruments used in hiring, placement, and promotion are related to the job for which the test is used. Audits can uncover areas or jobs where tests are excluding certain groups, for example, women and blacks.

4. *Compensation*—to ensure that pay practices are competitive and equitable.

5. *Training*—to evaluate the effectiveness of various training programs through cost-benefits analyses.

6. *Career planning*—to ensure that people are gaining the desired exposures and experiences in the organization and that those designated promotable are indeed rising in the organization at an anticipated rate.

SPECIALIST VERSUS GENERALIST.   Personnel people, especially at the lower levels, are required to be specialists. A personnel staff member is supposed to be an expert in a specialized field. His or her knowledge of people and the handling of associated problems is the personnel specialist's stock in trade. Thus, an in-depth knowledge and associated skills in hiring, training, counseling, labor relations, testing, safety, compensation, or any combination of these becomes essential to the survival of a personnel specialist. Yet, a personnel manager is expected to be a generalist first. Essentially, he or she should be equipped to manage an area of responsibility the same as any line manager—and in this respect the personnel generalist *is* a line manager. In addition, the personnel manager needs to have a broad perspective of the operating problems of the organization. So, given the fact that personnel people need to be specialists in their field and have generalist managerial capabilities, what are their characteristics and how are they expected to behave?

Functional Roles of Personnel Departments

The principal objectives of personnel departments are to manage and deploy employees to further the organization's objectives; to enhance human resource effectiveness by developing programs in response to changing employee needs and expectations; to ensure and maintain a high level of employee productivity; to ensure compliance with legal mandates in personnel-related manners; and to review and update these policies and systems.[12]

The rapidly increasing cost of the people side of business has prompted organizations to involve personnel in the development of their strategy and long-term plans. Personnel departments, then, keep the human resources area healthy through functions (activities) such as training, compensation, selection, and safety.

Characteristics of Personnel People
TRADITIONAL VIEWS

Traditionally, personnel managers have not been accorded the status that their function deserved.[13] They were considered reactors to, rather than anticipators of, personnel problems.[14] This unfortunate image was due mainly to the fact that personnel departments have been a dumping ground for managerial misfits or executives who were put out to pasture to serve out their time in order to become eligible for a pension. This unfavorable situation is worsened by the lack of power of many personnel departments: top management rarely seeks their advice. A study of 101 personnel managers revealed that the personnel field is relatively lacking in talent compared to other managerial components. The cause, according to the research findings, is that "at the present time we are caught . . . in a perpetually reinforcing cycle whereby the managerial deficiencies of the personnel job attract and retain individuals with lesser amounts of managerial talent, who are then used as evidence that the job should not be given more managerial clout."[15]

In contrast, another study, although it found some managers of the type described here, identified others who were energetic, dynamic, and professionally oriented.[16] This is the type of individual personnel must and, in my opinion, will attract in future years.

NEW CORPORATE HEROES

Perhaps the personnel challenges facing today's organizations have shed new light on the personnel function and reversed the line manager's perception of personnel people. The opinion of James A. Henderson, president of Cummins Engine Co., has been echoed by many other chief executive officers in recent years:

I have always viewed top management and the personnel function as a partnership. At Cummins the personnel head has always reported to the senior operating officer and has been a part of all major decisions. He is one of our most important officers and is paid accordingly. I believe this will be the only way a company can operate efficiently in the future. The personnel head must be one of the very best people in the company— confident, courageous, warm, and perceptive.[17]

Positive views such as this have fostered some movement of personnel people to top positions in organizations. The most prominent examples are Herb Lyon, in charge of personnel at Dow Chemical, and Ron Allen, senior vice president and head of personnel at Delta Air Lines. Both are members of their company's board of directors, and they exercise considerable influence on long-range planning and corporate administration. Similarly, in almost every one of the Fortune 500 companies, the head of personnel is usually a vice president reporting to the chief executive officer and often he or she sits on the board of directors.[18]

Furthermore, personnel managers are beginning to see themselves as *managers* first, with responsibilities for personnel. Some of these positive attributes are confirmed by research findings. Trice and Ritzer, for instance, ascertained from a survey of 419 personnel managers that they were decisive and preferred to use independent action, that is, to reach a decision in a role-conflict situation that is autonomous and therefore largely different from other alternatives available.[19]

Miner recommends that the personnel job be made more intrinsically satisfying to those who enjoy managing and are good at it. He advocates a major restructuring of authority relationships so that personnel managers will have the same role with regard to human resources that controllers do with regard to financial resources.[20] This is a good way to ensure that the personnel function will continue to be dynamic and viable in the future.

Professionalism in Personnel

The challenges to personnel management call for the highest degree of professionalism; mishandling people problems has dire consequences for the entire organization as well as for the personnel staff. Academic preparation produces specialized, in-depth knowledge, which is the personnel staff's stock in trade. Personnel associations publish literature on current issues and developments in the field, sponsor meetings and seminars to provide a forum for discussing personnel problems, and promulgate codes of conduct that enjoin members to uphold professional standards and observe ethical practices. Most prominent among these are the American Society for Personnel Administration (ASPA), the Industrial Relations Research Association (IRRA), and the International Personnel Management Association (IPMA was formerly Public Personnel Association). The addresses of these and other professional personnel associations are included in the Appendix at the end of Chapter 7. **Accreditation** of personnel generalists and specialists was a recent move (1976) by ASPA to enhance the professionalism of practitioners.

Accreditation of Personnel People

The Personnel Accreditation Institute (PAI) is an independent non-profit organization established for the purpose of accrediting professionals in the field. It was formed by ASPA following a three-year task force study.[21] Accreditation seeks to enhance the personnel profession through:

1. The development of a body of knowledge required for successful practice in the various areas of personnel;
2. The provision of guidelines for the development of young personnel practitioners as professionals; and
3. The encouragement of senior practitioners to update their knowledge.

One becomes accredited by gaining relevant experience and demonstrating detailed knowledge of the field through a written test. PAI accredits various levels of professionals—specialists, generalists, managers, executives, and diplomates. The author became certified as an Accredited Personnel Diplomate (APD) by passing a written comprehensive examination and demonstrating that he had more than ten years relevant experience in personnel work. Every three years he must be reaccredited, but can qualify by taking or teaching courses in the field and by researching and publishing. Accreditation is worthwhile because it provides an incentive to keep current on developments in the field and focuses personal development efforts; every three years one must account for certain teaching and research activities in order to be reaccredited.

Critics of accreditation claim it could restrict the supply of personnel people, it does not ensure quality performance of practitioners, and the field is not a profession anyway. Nevertheless, the steady growth in the number of personnel people who become accredited attests to the perceived value.

Personnel as a Career

According to the *Occupational Outlook Handbook* the number of personnel people is expected to grow faster than the average for all occupations during the 1980s.[22] Competition for these openings will be keen, however. The best prospects, according to the handbook, will be for college graduates who have specialized in training in personnel management.

In the present market, salaries range from $12,000 per year for inexperienced personnel specialists to $22,600 for experienced people (job analysts). In the public sector, the federal government starts personnel employees from $11,000 to $14,500 a year. Personnel managers in the private sector average $23,600; public sector supervisors average $16,200 to $21,600, and State personnel directors earn $31,000 to $36,000.[23] Many industrial personnel executives earn in the six figures.

A class of students interested in careers in personnel administration recently asked a corporate vice president of personnel how he made it. He confessed that he was luckier than most, because with a minimum of changes he had attained his present status at the relatively early age of forty-two. After graduating from college, he was offered a trainee position in the industrial relations department of a large manufacturing concern, which gave him a broad perspective of the company's industrial relations program. After a year, he was promoted to industrial relations representative, where his principal duties centered around grievance handling and job evaluation. Several years later he was put in charge of the college-recruiting program when its manager retired. While performing successfully in this capacity, he was offered an opportunity to organize an industrial relations department in another company. The accomplishments of his department in the new company earned him a promotion to industrial relations director of the company's largest division. Ultimately he was elevated to his present position of vice president of personnel.

From this example, it should be apparent that a number of levels can be defined within the hierarchy of the personnel department. Generally, positions exist at four distinct levels (in addition to the trainee level), as shown in Table 1.3.

The content of personnel positions varies according to the level in the department, the nature of the organization, and the services performed by the personnel department. The summaries of selected positions in Table 1.4 on pages 24–26 will give readers an idea of typical duties performed.

Organization of the Personnel Function

Our discussion so far has focused on the field of personnel and the people in it—their roles, characteristics, and professionalization. Let us now turn our attention to the ways that organizations structure the personnel function to meet the challenges we described at the beginning of this chapter.

There are a wide variety of organizational designs in personnel. Most of the existing structures fall into one of the following basic patterns.[24]

1. *Corporate personnel unit* (most prevalent).   The corporate staff provides all personnel services to the organization.

Table 1.3
Personnel Career Ladder

Level	Typical positions
Executive	Vice president, industrial relations vice president, human resources director of employee and public relations personnel director
Managerial/supervisory	Human resources manager manager, personnel and industrial relations employee services manager employment supervisor employee benefits supervisor wage and salary administrator management development administrator
Generalist	Industrial relations representative personnel assistant generalist: labor relations
Specialist	Training specialist personnel research specialist job analyst employment counselor benefits and services specialist

2. *Corporate and plant level units.*   In addition to a corporate unit, there are personnel units in one or more *plants* or similar installations. The personnel function outside the corporate headquarters reports to the installation head.

3. *Corporate and division, or functional operating units.*   In addition to the corporate staff, these organizations have personnel staffs that report to operating *division* general managers. (Examples of divisions are manufacturing or product A, B, or C. Divisions would have plants reporting to them.)

4. *Corporate, division, or functional operating units and plant level units.*   This pattern contains units at all levels. It incorporates the elements of 1–3 above.

5. *Adjunct or split unit.*   In the smallest companies the number of workers is insufficient to justify a personnel staff. Consequently, another function, often the controller, handles personnel as an adjunct or collateral duty.

Companies with 1,000 or fewer employees generally have only corporate staff functions. Those with personnel units at various levels (patterns 2–4) are usually larger than 1,000 employees.

TYPES OF STRUCTURES

The patterns just described can be structured in a variety of ways.

The *functional structure* emphasizes the service role of personnel and is perhaps the most traditional approach to its organization. This type of structure includes units for each of the activities: labor relations, compensation, safety, training/development, planning, employment/records, and so on. But many companies and institutions have modified their functional structures to address specific problems. The *geographic* structure enables the provision of personnel service to a unit or geographically contiguous units. Another variation is the department organized by *types of employees*—separate units for clerical/technical or production/maintenance personnel, for example. An interesting modification in personnel organization is the *matrix* or *program management* structure. This is more in evidence today as a complement to the traditional structure. It allows additional support personnel to report to a program that does not have all the people or activities necessary to do its work. Under this structure, people are assigned on a temporary basis to a program in the personnel department. They would perform their regular duties on such an assignment. Activities such as equal employment opportunity (EEO), health and safety (OSHA), pension administration (ERISA), are most suited to the matrix structure. An EEO program operating under a matrix structure might have a planner from the planning department, a legal advisor from the legal department, a programmer from data processing, an interviewer from personnel, and the EEO officer who would

Table 1.4
Descriptions of Personnel
Career-Ladder Positions[25]

Position	Description
Personnel Director (Alternate titles: director, industrial relations industrial relations advisor manager, industrial relations personnel relations administrator director of human resources)	Organizes, directs and coordinates industrial relations activities of the organization. Assembles and analyzes data concerning problems, such as turnover, absenteeism, and employment of physically handicapped and women. Conducts surveys on living costs and wage rates. Studies current labor laws and regulations, arbitration decisions, collective bargaining contracts, and other labor relations trends. Formulates, interprets, and recommends manpower policies concerning recruitment, selection, placement, wage and salary administration, collective bargaining, maintenance of personnel records, and educational, health, safety, and incentive programs. Develops company policies concerning layoffs, performance reporting, and employee rating. Participates in collective bargaining negotiations or advises other company representatives. Consults with legal staff to insure adherence to laws, regulations and contracts.
Educational Director (Alternate titles: training director staff training officer training coordinator)	Organizes, administers, and coordinates training and educational programs in commercial plant or establishment for the purposes of management and promotional development, on-the-job training, and orientation of employees regarding company policy and routine. Confers with management and line supervision to determine outline and scope of programs. Applies knowledge of plant processes, job breakdowns, safety rules, supervision techniques, and related information to formulate training program curriculum. Organizes lectures, training manuals, examinations, visual aids, reference libraries, and other training implements. Trains instructors and supervisory personnel in proper training methods and techniques and assigns them to specific programs. Maintains records of training

Table 1.4 (cont.)

Position	Description
	activities and evaluates effectiveness and application of programs. Coordinates established training courses with technical and professional programs offered in public schools and universities. May represent company at vocational educational meetings. May screen, counsel, test, and recommend employees for company educational programs or for promotion or transfer.
Safety Supervisor	Plans and administers training programs in health habits, accident prevention, fire prevention and protection, and other safety procedures for employees of an industrial organization. Prepares educational materials for instruction of employees and advises and assists various departments in developing safety practices. Procures information relative to causes of fires and accidents from the Safety Engineer in order to plan instruction procedures. Directs conducting of fire drills. May inspect plant machinery, equipment, and working areas to detect hazardous conditions, and recommend corrective measures. May inspect physical examination reports of applicants and determine acceptability or rejection of applicant for hazardous work. May issue permits for testing for toxic fumes or explosive gas-air mixtures.
Job Analyst (Alternate titles: occupational analyst)	Collects, analyzes, and develops occupational data concerning jobs, job qualifications, and worker characteristics to facilitate personnel, administrative, or information functions in private, public, or governmental organizations. Consults with management to determine type, scope, and purpose of analysis, and compiles staffing schedules, flow charts, and other background information about company policies and facilities to expedite study. Studies jobs being performed and interviews workers and supervisory personnel to ascertain physical and mental

Table 1.4 (cont.)

Position	Description
	requirements of jobs in relation to materials, products, procedures, subject matter, and services involved. Writes job descriptions, specifications, detailed analysis schedules, and narrative and statistical reports, reflecting such data as physical demands, working conditions, skills, knowledge, abilities, training, educational, and related factors required to perform jobs. Conducts related occupational research, utilizing publications, professional and trade associations, and other media to verify or standardize data. Submits written reports pertaining to personnel policies, morale, absenteeism, turnover, job breakdown and dilution, organization, staffing, and related items. Utilizes data to evolve or improve wage-evaluation systems, counseling and interviewing aids, training and testing programs, and other personnel practices. May write descriptions or monographs of jobs, processes, and industrial patterns or trends for publication.

direct the program. At the conclusion of the program the people would return to their permanent assignments in their respective departments.

DECENTRALIZATION

Some personnel departments operate decentralized units (as in the patterns that have plant and divisional units). The feeling is that it is better to have this function closer to the action, so that personnel people learn to understand the needs and pressures of the line people and become actively involved in working with line managers to meet their goals. The other side of the picture, however, is that from a corporate standpoint, the decentralized groups tend to operate independently, which tends to make coordination of efforts difficult.[26]

In a **decentralized organization,** policy, planning, and control are usually centralized, while implementation and routine administration are decentralized. Since the audit function checks on the activities of personnel units, it is usually separated from those units. When the auditor is required to report to the person whose operations are being audited, he or she would naturally be reluctant to be critical of the supervisor who evaluates performance and makes compensation and promotion determinations.

The organization chart in Figure 1.1 depicts the corporate personnel organization at Becton, Dickinson and Company. Note that the head (vice president of industrial relations) reports to an executive vice president who, in turn, reports to the president. In some larger organizations, the head of personnel reports directly to the president. McFarland's studies of personnel departments showed that in smaller organizations, the top personnel officer is either an assistant to an administrative officer or reports to an operations manager. But in larger organizations the function usually achieves equality with other operating departments.[27]

STAFF-STAFF RELATIONS

Where there are corporate and division and/or plant units, problems arise in the relationship between lower level staff and corporate personnel. Essentially, the problem for lower level staff is defining who is in charge. These lower level units report to plant or division managers, yet they must maintain close relationships with corporate staff. The latter may investigate and make studies irrespective of operational or divisional wishes; they may require that information be supplied or that their recommendations be heard. Some of this dual-reporting function has been eased by establishing clear corporate personnel policies (the subject of personnel policies will be covered in Chapter 3) and objectives that clarify the roles and responsibilities of the corporate and unit staffs and the line managers.[28]

SPECIAL SITUATIONS

Under certain circumstances separate organizational units, often detached from the personnel department, may be set up to perform traditional personnel functions. For example, under a major reorganization the chief executive may want to have organization planning, human resource planning, and management development close at hand. These functions, then, might be set up as a separate department. Or, the organization that bargains with a single company-wide union could be concerned that labor relations would overwhelm other personnel activities. So, a department is set up separate from the corporate personnel structure. Or, a personnel head who might have little interest in some newer activities such as pension planning, might have them assigned outside personnel so they would get their deserved emphasis. Then, as mentioned earlier, the audit or evaluation function can be separated from the personnel organization.[29]

Cost-Benefit Analysis

In order to receive top management's support of its activities and cooperation from line supervision, the personnel department finds it necessary to provide tangible evidence of its effectiveness/efficiency. The continued existence of personnel programs is contingent on their demonstrated

Figure 1.1
Corporate Industrial
Relations Unit,
Becton, Dickinson
and Company

Source: The Conference
Board, *The Personnel
Function: Changing Ob-
jectives and Organization*
(New York: The Confer-
ence Board, 1977). Repro-
duced with permission: The
Conference Board.

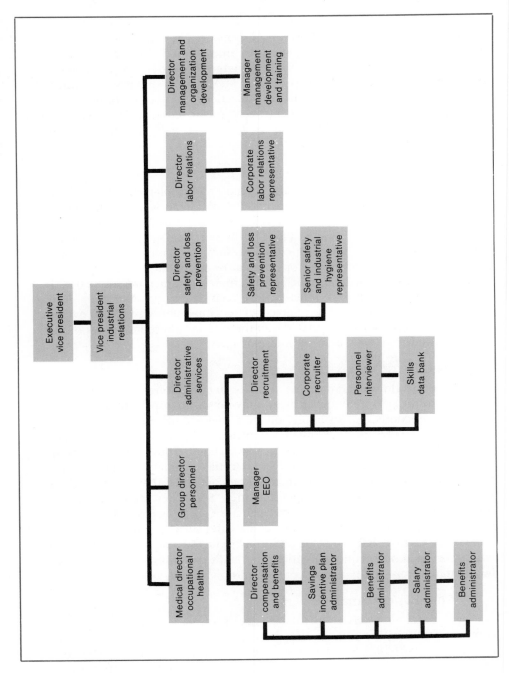

effectiveness, which can be measured in terms of costs versus benefits. Toward this end, each of the chapters in this text discusses the standards for analyzing the costs versus the benefits of programs and activities.

In assessing the effectiveness of the personnel function in an organization McConnell[30] recommends periodic audits. He suggests evaluating:

1. *The department organization,* its objectives, internal relationships, structuring, and relationships with other departments.
2. *Department personnel,* their capabilities, training and motivation.
3. *Security* of documents and facilities.
4. *Facilities,* their location, arrangement and physical condition.
5. *Documentation,* their preparation, storage, and degree to which they comply with legal requirements.
6. *Key activities* (labor relations, training, and so on) and how well they contribute to the overall objectives of the total organization.

He also suggests performing various analyses of operating costs, for example, percentage of personnel costs relative to total operating budget of the company, actual annual operating cost of the personnel department. The audit should also include perceptions of the personnel department's effectiveness by both outsiders and members of the department.

The ratio of personnel staff to total employees may also reflect the department's effectiveness. On the one hand, the use of a smaller staff to carry out personnel programs might be indicative of an efficient operation brought about through computerization or simply through improved staff productivity. On the other, it could also be the result of staff reduction caused by budget cutbacks. The trend seems to be toward larger personnel staffs, because of government regulations and the paperwork these involve. Generally speaking, a major survey of personnel executives reveals that larger companies generally have a lower ratio of personnel staffers to total number of employees (more employees per staff member). For manufacturing companies with under 500 employees the ratio is 96 employees for each personnel staffer; with 5,000 or more employees the ratio is 352:1. This usually means that the personnel department is large enough for specialization.[31]

Fitz-Enz[32] urges that, after completing an audit or any other type of results-oriented study, personnel managers report the findings to top management. This provides a clear picture of the contributions the personnel department is making to the organization.[33]

Summary

Personnel management's greatly expanded influence can be attributed to top management's realization that the ability to work with people is critical to the success of an organization. Advanced technology, a new breed of employee, and other developments present challenges and require greater sophistication in handling personnel situations. The primary responsibility for personnel management now rests with line management; staff specialists provide line management with professional services.

In supporting line activities, personnel staff people play a variety of roles, and they gain influence with line managers by acting professionally and exhibiting distinctive competence in their area of specialization. Personnel organizations also can be structured to be responsive to the requirements of an organization.

When line management effectively handles day-to-day personnel matters and is supported by the personnel staff in *acquiring, integrating, developing,* and *maintaining* human resources on a long-range basis, the organization is in the best position to achieve its stated objectives.

Key Terms

personnel management	Consumer Price Index (C.P.I.)
human resource	discrimination
technology	management
productivity	staff
quality of work life	line
socio-technical systems	delegate
white collar workers	accreditation
unemployment	decentralized organization
inflation	

Review Questions

1. Describe the values of the new generation of American workers. How do these values correlate with your own?

2. What are some of the problems that unemployment creates for personnel management?

3. Explain why personnel directors have become the new corporate heroes.

4. As a career for you personally, what would be the rewards and the drawbacks of personnel management?

5. What are some of the ways a personnel staff can serve the line organization?

6. Is personnel a profession? What are personnel managers doing to enhance their professionalism?

7. Describe various patterns of personnel organization.

8. How was personnel management defined in this chapter? Show how the definition serves as a basic frame of reference for the text.

Discussion Questions

1. Assume you are the personnel director for a large corporation. How would you convince top management that your (personnel) function is vital to the organization and that the company should invest more money in personnel activities? Specifically what would you say to top management?

2. In considering applicants for a starting position in personnel management, what elements in their background would you consider most important? Why?

3. How can the personnel staff gain influence within the organization?

4. Describe the ideal development of an individual for a personnel career. (Include academic preparation, job experiences, and professional affiliations.)

5. In what ways may contemporary developments in technology, energy, and ecology affect employment? How will these developments affect personnel departments?

Case Problem 1

FOUR PERSONNEL SITUATIONS

Situation 1

Your advice is sought on the justification for discharging an employee for chronic alcoholism. The employee has 25 years of service, is 51 years old and married. In the past several years, he has received several written warnings about his use of alcoholic beverages. Five months ago, a recommended discharge was reduced to a 30-day suspension following a hearing in which the employee agreed to abstain from drinking and attend AA meetings on a regular basis. Yesterday, his supervisor saw him intoxicated. When confronted, he responded in a hostile manner with the statement that what he does with his life is his business.

1. What is the overriding problem in this situation?
2. Which facts need to be clarified and what additional information, if any, is needed?
3. What is your recommendation and what are the reasons therefor?

Situation 2

One of your managers who has been on the job for six months approaches you saying he would like to move ahead in the organization and wonders what he needs to do to get a better job in the future. He is an above average performer in his present job.

1. What information would you require before answering the employee?
2. What are the implications for performance appraisal of this employee's inquiry?
3. Specifically, what will you tell the employee?

Situation 3

Sam Johnson, an electrical engineer with your company, has been performing an outstanding job for the past year. He graduated in 1979 from Georgia Tech near the top of his class with a BSEE. You hired him as an engineer trainee at $1550/month. Within six months he was promoted to electrical engineer at $1650/month and on the basis of merit he received an increase six months later (last week) of $100.00.

An expansion of business activities gave rise to the need for additional engineers. Sam recommended his fraternity brother, Jack Tull, who was graduating from Tech in May. After several interviews, you decided to offer him a starting position. But the going rate for EEs this year was $1725/month, which Jack required to accept an offer.

1. Should you offer Jack $1725?
2. If you do offer Jack the job, how do you explain the situation to Sam? Or should you even be concerned about the possible inequity?
3. Can a compensation policy be devised that would accommodate the eventuality described above?

Situation 4

A black female supervisor claims she was discriminated against because she was not selected for promotion to a higher level opening. She feels she is more qualified than the white individual who was selected because she had served more time with the company and as a supervisor. Furthermore, she feels her experience and her performance were at least as good as those of the successful candidate. She threatens to file a complaint with the Equal Employment Opportunity Commisssion.

As the employee's manager:

1. What facts would you attempt to establish?

2. How would you handle her complaint?

3. Should she receive any special consideration because she is black? Because she is a woman?

Case Problem 2

THE JORDAN COMPANY

The Jordan Company manufactures automobile piston rings, pistons, valves, and related products. The plant is located near South Bend, Indiana. The company is relatively small, employing 350 production workers in addition to 125 office and sales employees and executives. Growth has been rather rapid—from an initial 12 employees to the present number in 11 years. (See Exhibit 1.1.)

The founder and president, Thomas Jordan, also holds the title of sales manager in his company. Before organizing the Jordan Company, he had been the sales manager of a large automobile parts manufacturer. Believing that his extensive contacts in the automobile industry and his proven sales ability would enable him to own his own company, he went into business for himself, after obtaining additional capital from two friends, each of whom owns 20 percent interest in the firm.

Jordan never gave much attention to the production aspects of business. In fact, he devoted about 25 percent of his time to contacting important customers and the manufacturers' agents representing the company in the southern and western states. Frank Elliott, his plant manager, started with the company at the time of its organization. He laid out the plant, established production and quality standards, and hired all the production executives under him as well as several of the first production workers.

It was the practice of the company to allow each foreman and office supervisor to hire, discipline, transfer, promote, and otherwise make his own decisions about personnel matters within his department.

Jordan observed that as the company grew in number of employees, morale appeared to degenerate. He commented to Elliott that "the one big happy-family spirit that pervaded our people during the first few years of the company disappeared

Exhibit 1.1
Jordan Company
Organization Chart

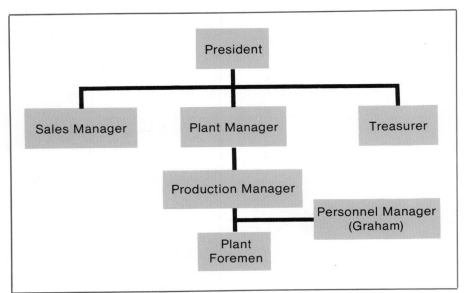

during the past two years." Consequently, Jordan decided that the company should employ a personnel manager.

John Graham, chief cost accountant, learned of Jordan's plans through one of the secretaries with whom he had lunch in the plant cafeteria. John had wanted to get into personnel work for some time. As he put it, "I always did prefer working with people to working with numbers."

John had worked with the Jordan Company for seven years. He joined the company in the bookkeeping department immediately after graduating from college. Since the company was small and work was not highly departmentalized, he had many contacts with people in both production and sales. Elliott and Jordan both believed that he was an alert conscientious employee who "generally is well liked by all."

John applied for the position of personnel manager, and he was selected for the job.

After much debate it was decided to make the personnel manager part of the production management section, the manager of which reported to the plant manager.

John was given an office near the entrance to the plant, and a secretary was assigned to him. The president told him at the time of his appointment that "the scope and success of the personnel department's activities will be pretty much what you make them."

John immediately sent a memorandum to all foremen, over the signature of the production manager, advising them that "the personnel manager will hire all new employees in the future." In addition, the memorandum stated that the personnel manager would henceforth initiate all transfers and changes in pay and that all disciplinary action and other personnel decisions must be approved by the personnel manager before being acted on.

On receiving the memorandum, several foremen expressed considerable resentment against this organization change. They agreed that John had the "bighead."

After a short time the production manager began to receive complaints from foremen to the effect that "new employees aren't what they were when we hired them." On one occasion when he questioned a foreman about a drop in production, the foreman said that his hands were tied: he could not hire, discipline, or otherwise control his men. And, if he could not control his men, how could he be expected to get out production?

One day an employee came into John's office and protested that her foreman had just discharged her "for no reason at all." John telephoned the foreman and the following conversation took place:

> *John:* Hello, Jim. This is John Graham. What's the story on Linda Ralfing?
>
> *Foreman:* I fired her.
>
> *John:* Yes, I know, but why?
>
> *Foreman:* I don't like her.
>
> *John:* But that's no reason. You know that you can't fire her without an OK from my office.
>
> *Foreman:* Well, I did it.

John: But you can't. Jim. There has to be a good reason, and. . . .

Foreman: I don't like her—that's reason enough.

The foreman hung up.

John presented the matter to the production manager who finally insisted that the employee be reinstated. Soon the number of complaints concerning the hiring of poor workers and the lack of control over personnel began to increase. The foremen agreed to stay clear of the personnel department as much as possible.

Finally, the production manager advised the plant manager that he did not believe the firm was large enough to warrant a personnel department. He further recommended that the company return to the former plan of having foremen make their own personnel decisions. Finally, he urged that John be returned to his former job.

The plant manager thought about the production manager's recommendations for a few days and then passed them on to the president, recommending that they be accepted.*

Problems

1. How could the Jordan Company have gained the acceptance of a personnel function by the production foremen?

2. Do you think the personnel function was properly situated in the organization? Why, or why not?

3. Was John Graham a good choice for the personnel job? Why, or why not?

4. As president of the Jordan Company, how would you act on the production manager's recommendations?

---

* Raymond L. Hilgert et al., *Cases & Policies in Human Resources Management* (New York: Houghton Mifflin, 1978), pp. 9–11. Reprinted by permission.

Notes

1. Herbert E. Meyer, "Personnel Directors Are the New Corporate Heroes," *Fortune,* February 1976, p. 88.

2. Jerome Mark, "Productivity Trends and Prospects," in Clark Kerr and Jerome M. Rosow, eds., *Work In America: The Decade Ahead* (New York: Van Nostrand, 1979), pp. 190ff.

3. Jerome M. Rosow, "Quality-of-Work-Life Issues for the 1980's," in Kerr and Rosow, *Work In America,* p. 157.

4. William Abbott, "Work in 2001," *Worklife,* December 1976, p. 21.

5. Jerome M. Rosow, "Quality-of-Work-Life Issues for the 1980's," in Kerr and Rosow, *Work In America,* pp. 157–58.

6. George S. Odiorne, "Personnel Management for the '80's," *Personnel Administrator,* December 1979, pp. 77–80.

7. C. Kerr and J. Rosow, *Work In America,* pp. xiiff.

8. Anne McDougall Young, "Trends in Educational Attainment Among Workers in the 1970's," *Monthly Labor Review,* July 1980, pp. 44ff.

9. Ronald N. Taylor and Mark Thompson, "Work Value Systems of Young Workers," *Academy of Management Journal,* December 1976, pp. 535–36.

10. U.S. Bureau of Labor Statistics, *U.S. Workers and Their Jobs,* Chart 12, and *Educational Attainment of Workers, March 1976* (Special Labor Force Report 193), p. 1.

11. American Society for Personnel Administration, *PA/IR Potpourri,* June 1976, p. 1.

12. William B. Wolf, ed., *Top Management of the Personnel Function* (Ithaca: New York State School of Industrial and Labor Relations, Cornell University, 1980), p. 76.

13. Meyer, "Personnel Directors Are the New Corporate Heroes," p. 84.

14. Robert M. Frame and Fred Luthans, "Merging Personnel and OD: A Not-So-Odd Couple," *Personnel,* January–February 1977, p. 12.

15. John B. Miner, "New Concepts of the Personnel and Industrial Relations Function," unpublished, January 1978, p. 22.

16. Dalton E. McFarland, *Cooperation and Conflict in Personnel Administration* (New York: American Federation for Management Research, 1962), p. 12.

17. J. A. Henderson, "What the Chief Executive Expects of the Personnel Function," *Personnel Administrator,* May 1977, p. 42.

18. Fred R. Edney, "The Greening of the Profession," *Personnel Administrator,* July 1980, p. 28.

19. Harrison Trice and George Ritzer, "The Personnel Manager and His Self-Image," in Mary Green Miner and John B. Miner, eds., *Policy Issues in Contemporary Personnel and Industrial Relations* (New York: Macmillan, 1977), pp. 46ff.

20. Miner, "New Concepts," pp. 19ff.

21. Neil A. Palomba, "Accreditation of Personnel Administrators: Theory and Reality," *Personnel Administrator,* January 1981, pp. 37–40.

22. U.S. Bureau of Labor Statistics, *Occupational Outlook Handbook,* 1980–81 Ed. (Bulletin 2075), March 1980, p. 129.

23. Ibid. (Salary figures from 1978 surveys.)

24. Information taken from The Conference Board, *The Personnel Function: Changing Objectives and Organization* (New York: The Conference Board, 1977), pp. 51ff.

25. These descriptions were excerpted

from the U.S. Department of Labor's *Dictionary of Occupational Titles*, 4th ed. (Washington, D.C.: U.S. Government Printing Office, 1977).

26. Fred K. Foulkes and Henry M. Morgan, "Organizing and Staffing the Personnel Function," *Harvard Business Review*, May–June 1977, pp. 147ff.

27. Dalton E. McFarland, *Cooperation and Conflict in Personnel Administration* (New York: American Foundation for Management Research, 1962).

28. The Conference Board, *The Personnel Function*, pp. 56–57.

29. Ibid., pp. 64–65.

30. John H. McConnell, "How to Audit the Personnel Function," *Personnel Administrator*, August 1980, pp. 67–71.

31. Prentice-Hall Editorial Staff, *The Personnel Executive's Job* (ASPA/Prentice-Hall Survey), (Englewood Cliffs, N.J.: Prentice-Hall, 1977), pp. 7–9. Reprinted from Prentice-Hall, *Personnel Management: Policies and Practices*.

32. Jac Fitz-Enz, "Quantifying the Human Resources Function," *Personnel*, March–April 1980, pp. 41–52.

33. A useful checklist for auditing the personnel function is found in Appendix III of Robert H. Desantnick, *The Expanding Role of the Human Resources Manager* (New York: AMACOM, 1979).

Chapter Two

The Personnel Environment and Contingency Thinking

Pinson Manufacturing, Inc. produces quarter panels and small parts under contract for one of the Big Three auto companies. (The quarter panel is the successor to the fender and is the part most often damaged in accidents.) The panels are made on hydraulic presses that stamp the panels out of metal blanks.

On the morning of August 15 the plant manager received a report that three of the four machines were putting out an excessive number of rejects. In an emergency meeting, the management group went over the circumstances surrounding the rejects. It seems the machines started burring the panels shortly after the 10 o'clock break. Ray Charles, the personnel manager, overheard the press operators complaining about the rough treatment supervisor Nat Berger was giving his people. Yesterday he had suspended the vice president of the local union, Sam Cook, for allegedly drinking on the job. There was no real evidence, but Berger had caught him at it once before, so this time he gave Cook a real tongue-lashing and sent him home for the remainder of the week. It seems that the atmosphere was emotionally tense, anyway, with contract negotiations coming up and the union under pressure to "get a big settlement, or else."

In the meeting, the plant engineers confirmed that the presses had been checked out thoroughly, and they couldn't find anything wrong. The dies and the hydraulic system were both "AOK." The new blanks from Premium Metals had been checked earlier that morning, and they ran perfectly in the test. It just could be that the union operators were hot under

LEARNING OBJECTIVES

1. To understand contingency theory.

2. To be able to recognize the variables essential for analyzing personnel situations.

3. To appreciate how the environment (outside influences) affects the personnel situation.

4. To know how people individually and collectively cause changes in any given situation.

5. To learn the ability to analyze personnel situations.

the collar about the treatment of Sam Cook. "It doesn't take much to get those fellas riled up these days," Ray Charles exclaimed. The engineer suggested it might be an operator problem; just a slight mispositioning of the blanks can cause a reject, it seems.

"Why those ——— ———! It must be sabotage!" Berger exclaimed, and he went storming out of the meeting to confront the operators.

The next morning seven of the eight operators called in sick. At quitting time the night before the operators had met together. Their attitude was "This company doesn't give a hang about us. Every time something goes wrong, it's the employees' fault."

When the operators returned to the job a few days later they found that the problem had been corrected. It seems that the new blanks were of a slightly different compound, which caused them to burr when being stamped. A minor adjustment in the die and the stamping pressure corrected the problem. But the personnel problems will probably take a much longer time to work out.

This example illustrates how traditional approaches to work problems, especially when people are involved, are no longer viable. Rapid change and the complexities of organizations and the environments in which they operate have given rise to a new way of thinking: contingency management.

Contingency Theory

Contingency theory operates on the premise that there is no one best way to handle problems. The manager's job becomes one of determining which technique or approach will work best, given a set of circumstances. As the physician diagnoses a patient's condition to determine the appropriate treatment, the manager analyzes the situation before deciding on the appropriate approach. But this is easier said than done because factors (and their relationships) inside an organization are diagnosed in the process. Then factors external to an organization that constitute its environment must be considered in terms of the restraints they place on a situation.

CHARACTERISTICS OF THE CONTINGENCY APPROACH

The contingency approach to personnel management has been hailed as the dominant management model, the conventional wisdom of this era. It has been practiced for many years, but only recently has it been conceptualized as an operating school of thought. Mockler introduced managers to the notion that decision making requires the examination of contingencies in what he termed the *situational approach*.[1] Several years earlier Albert Speer, the architect of the Third Reich, employed organized improvisation to mold Germany into a smooth-running war machine. In response to the needs of the day, he attempted to utilize participative techniques (directive committees and development commissions) in a plan of industrial self-responsibility, and he expended considerable effort to reform the bureaucracy, which he characterized as an "outmoded, tradition-bound and arthritic organizational system."[2] Cammann and Nadler coined the term *informed choice* for the process of choosing the right strategy for an organization.[3] Several writers have examined the relationship of the organization to its environment and added to contingency theory the notion that success of the organization is predicated on matching its structure with the requirements imposed on it by the environment.[4]

With the historical development of contingency thought in mind, let us explore the basic characteristics of this approach.

1. *Integrative.*   Harold Koontz recognized the fragmentation of thought in the management movement. Behaviorists, systems theorists, engineers, and functionalists each tried to explain management from a different perspective. Koontz referred to this division of thought as the "management theory jungle."[5] Contingency theory attempts to integrate the diverse schools of thought and effectively links theory to practice.

2. *Pragmatic.*   The one best way or prescriptive approach espoused by the other management theories is replaced by a more practical approach that recognizes that whatever works for a particular situation is correct. Contingency management accommodates a variety of appropriate strategies depending on the characteristics of a situation.

3. *Change-oriented.*   As we noted in Chapter 1, the environment of personnel management is dynamic. Whatever strategy worked in a situation yesterday might not work today. Personnel managers who are successful today have learned to be flexible and to cope with change. Contingency theory is particularly conducive to managing in a turbulent environment.

4. *Systems perspective.*   Contingency management recognizes the interdependence and the relationships of variables that constitute the management process. It is a new and more sophisticated look at the nature of cause and effect. And it takes a multidimensional rather than linear perspective.[6]

5. *Multidisciplinary.*   Contingency theory draws from all of the other management disciplines. Decision sciences provide methods of dealing with the uncertain environment of personnel. Motivation and leadership theories developed by the behavioral approach help describe the kinds of psychological and sociological factors that may be related to high performance in different kinds of organizations. **Systems theory** helps explain the relationships among variables that constitute a particular situ-

ation. This characteristic of contingency theory has made successful modern managers aware of the need to keep abreast of developments in all of the management disciplines.

APPROPRIATE THEORY FOR PERSONNEL DECISION MAKING

Personnel problems, in particular, are not amenable to prescribed, preset solutions; the individual attributes of people, the organizational climate, and the environment in which the organization operates are constantly changing. When two or more factors combine, they form a situation that is unique and complex, necessitating a system of analysis that will facilitate decision making. The contingency approach accommodates these phenomena because managers consider each of the elements in a situation and their relationships to each other along with the impact of environmental factors before finalizing a decision. Thus, there may be a variety of right solutions to personnel problems. For this reason, the contingency or situational approach was selected as most appropriate for presenting personnel management. The text material will be oriented toward the contingency approach so that present and future personnel managers can gain a contingency perspective of human resource problems.

We should note at this point that there is a difference between the contingency approach and those that can be characterized as wishy-washy or seat of the pants. In the contingency approach there are a multitude of strategies that may be pursued in a situation, depending upon the occurrence or level of certain (contingency) factors. That is, there is some method to the madness. A wishy-washy approach is characterized by a lack of systematic plan; what-gets-done-when is left up to chance or capricious factors. Both approaches recognize the principle of no one best way. However, the former is based upon a formal strategy (albeit complex), while the latter is not. (NOTE: In this text the terms *contingency* and *situational* are used essentially in the same sense.)

A Frame of Reference for the Situational Approach

Since this text is based on the contingency or situational approach, it might be useful to describe the elements of a situation and how they individually and collectively function to influence the decision-making process.

ELEMENTS OF THE SITUATION

All situations consist of **variables** (or components)—any factors that change. Two or more variables present at the same time form a **situation.** The relationship between variables within a situation is called **interaction.** As the number of variables in a situation increases arithmetically, the number of interactions increases geometrically. For example, the number of inter-actions between variables A and B is two. When one more variable, C, is added, the number of interactions increases to six.

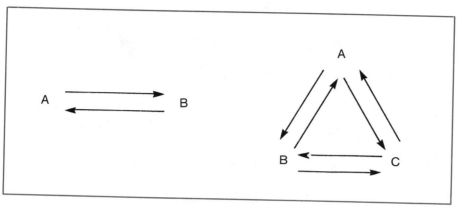

The geometric increase of interactions creates such complex situations of continuous change that there is no single right answer to a personnel situation. A proper solution today may not have the same outcome tomor-row, even under similar circumstances. The complexities created by such interactions call for innovative approaches to the management of human resources.

The schematic in Figure 2.1 is a graphic representation of the variables in situational or contingency management. Variables within the organization (personnel as individuals and groups, physical factors, and functions) interact with each other. But factors that comprise the organization itself, other than the internal variables (philosophy/purpose, nature of the business, and or-ganizational structure) also affect the situation created by internal variables. Finally, variables external to the organization comprise the environment in which an organization operates. Environmental variables interact with each other, but they also constrain and/or influence variables and interactions within the organization. The example at the beginning of the chapter might serve to illustrate the dynamics of Figure 2.1.

A union officer, Sam Cook, had been disciplined, and his fellow workers reacted. So far we have a situation involving personnel interactions only: Sam Cook, an individual, and a single foreman with a group of union members. Personnel then interact with technology—something in the pro-duction system is causing burred panels. It could be the presses, blanks, panels, dies, or the process itself. The introduction of an additional variable, a new type of blank, further complicates the situation. Personnel who happen to be union members operate the equipment, and a supervisor with an

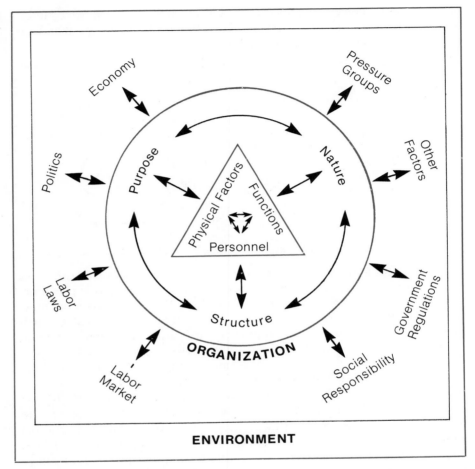

arrogant style of managing creates a conflict. When the organizational variable (auto parts manufacturing) interacts with the environmental variables, emotional pressure increases. The company is a parts manufacturer for one of the Big Three, and this is a critical period because new model cars are about to be introduced. From this illustration of a basic set of variables, we can see how complicated a situation can become. This is so primarily because of the unlimited possibilities for interactions among internal variables, between organizational and internal, organizational, and environmental ones. The arrows in Figure 2.1 indicate major interactions, but if all the possibilities were shown, there would be so many interconnecting lines that the diagram would become indecipherable.

This text is based on the contingency approach. Much of the subject matter will incorporate situational analysis. The analysis and understanding of personnel situations will be more meaningful if we have a familiarity with the basic variables that comprise our frame of reference (Figure 2.1) and we understand how their interaction affects a personnel situation. The discussion will also serve as a departure point for an explanation of situational analysis at the end of this chapter.

INTERNAL VARIABLES

1. *Personnel.*   People are the key to any personnel situation. They are viewed as individuals or as members of a group, as managers or as rank-and-file employees. Individuals are unique; they differ in an almost infinite number of respects, including physical attributes, intelligence, personality, and character. We tend to take these individual differences for granted, yet they influence personnel-management decisions more than any other factors. Individuals bring to a job certain skills, knowledge, abilities, and attitudes which become the basis for their selection, training, promotions, and so on. Pinson Manufacturing (in the example at the beginning of this chapter) could not attempt to produce auto parts without crafts people to fashion the dies, operators to run and maintain the machines, and managers to direct the operation. Thus, the recognition and identification of individual differences become essential to an analysis of personnel situations.

But how can individual differences be identified? One classification system that is probably the most widely adopted includes three major categories: mental capabilities, manual and response capabilities, and interpersonal skills and personality.[7] Another scheme to classify differences among individuals would include factors that contribute to unsatisfactory job performance. Factors would include:[8]

> *Intelligence and Job Knowledge*
> > Verbal ability
> > Special abilities—numerical, spatial, mechanical
> > Organizational and specific job knowledge
> > Capabilities for judgment and memory
>
> *Emotional Characteristics*
> > Emotionality with regard to anger, anxiety, excitement, etc.
> > Emotional health as distinct from neurosis, psychosis, and alcohol and drug problems
>
> *Motivational Characteristics*
> > Motive strength with regard to success and failure, dominance, conformity, and social interaction

Methods used to satisfy motives as related to job re-
quirements
Level of personal work standards
Generalized work motivation

Physical Characteristics
Physical health and illness or disability
Physical health as distinct from disorders of emotional
origin
Physical characteristics such as height and weight
Muscular and sensory abilities and skills

All these factors or variables differentiate people as individuals.
They comprise their unique and personal identities. Personnel in groups
present an additional dimension: demographic factors such as race, sex,
age, culture, religion, and nationality differentiate groups of people. Informal groups such as the grapevine or the coffee break social have an
impact on a situation, but they are less readily distinguishable. But we
can identify a *group* as having the following characteristics: interaction
among individuals, the development of shared perceptions, the presence
of emotional ties, and the development of interdependence and ties.[9] The
union machine operators who collaborated in the sick call in our case
of the burred panels seem to meet these criteria for a group. The interactions of this variable (personnel in groups) are analyzed throughout
the text: minorities, handicapped (in Chapter 6); women and minorities
(in Chapter 15); unions (in Chapters 10–12); and older workers (in
Chapter 8).

2. *Physical factors.*   This category of variable includes every physical condition impinging on a situation. Environmental aspects such as temperature, visual appearance, and audible sounds can affect a personnel situation. Also included here are production techniques; advanced technology;
types of equipment, methods, and procedures; space and location of the
physical plant; and the nature of the work itself. Time also affects this
variable: the pace of the work, the sequence of events, the specific moment
when a problem arises (in terms of the seniority or experience of the
individuals as well as the stage of a project's completion).

High **technology** organizations call for skills among workers who
must be trained to engineer, operate, and maintain equipment. Accelerating technological change causes rapid obsolescence of technical skills
among computer programmers, engineers, and scientists. These people
find that continuing education in their skill areas becomes an economic
necessity. And the technology syndrome—a fear of displacement by automation—creates emotional and morale problems among employees.

Technology was the basic cause of the problem at Pinson Manufacturing, where the new-type blanks caused the panels to burr.

But technology can also have beneficial effects on a personnel situation. It can provide the impetus for upgrading worker skills; it can raise the comfort level of a work place—pleasant color schemes, air conditioning, improved nonglare lighting are a few examples. It can also produce efficiencies in operations that translate into improved working conditions as well as providing for compensation increases.

3. *Functions.* Functions refer to the tasks or activities of a particular individual or group. As we discussed in Chapter 1, managers perform the functions of planning, organizing, directing, and controlling. The style they use (e.g., dictatorial versus participative) in carrying out these functions affects employees' response. Conversely, the functions of others, both inside and outside the organization, are constraints on the effectiveness of managerial functions. For instance, a union-management agreement might place specific limitations on managerial prerogatives: limits on the extent and kinds of work that a foreman can perform; restrictions on hiring and firing; strict definitions of who can perform what work, and so on. Also, the policies that organizations design may be constrained by other groups. For example, legislation regulates the kinds of employees hired and dictates minimum standards for health and safety in an office and plant.

Tasks are activities performed by people in an organization. They might be categorized by organizational function: procurement, engineering, production, distribution (marketing), finance, and personnel; or by the degree of skill involved; or the extent the task involves working with people, things, and information. Interactions among tasks, people, and technology alone create complex situations. Take, for instance, the socio-technical considerations of the interactions between tasks and machine operations. Harmonizing the skills and abilities of machine operators with equipment, to produce a particular item, takes a high degree of human and technical knowledge. Knowledge of job design and analysis, human engineering, and motivation (discussed in detail later) are useful in channeling tasks toward goal accomplishment.

Each of these activities and its interactions can severely restrict personnel functions and greatly increase the complexity of a situation.

THE ORGANIZATION ITSELF

Organizational variables include the purpose of the organization, the nature of the business or institution, and type of organization.

1. *Purpose.* The fundamental purpose of an organization is its reason for being. "What *is* our business?" and "What *should* our business be?" are

questions to ask in determining the purpose of an organization. But the answers to these simple questions are not as obvious as they appear. Many organizations have failed to define their purpose, or they have the misconceived notion that their sole purpose is to make a profit. In reality, all organizations have multiple purposes, as indicated by the variety of their objectives. Some of the possible organizational purposes and objectives are shown in Table 2.1.

We can see that organizations generally will have a variety of compatible objectives. The basic purpose and objectives of an organization provide guidelines for its continued operation. The purposes of an organization largely determine its tasks, structure, and functions. When the objectives of individuals and groups within an organization are in opposition to its purpose, there is unrest, inefficiency, and protest.

2. *Nature of business or institution.* The type of product, the size and the nature of an organization—for example, manufacturing or service, private or public—have a significant influence on personnel decisions. The extent that labor represents a portion of the total cost of doing business is another aspect of the nature of an organization. Some firms such as garment manufacturers are **labor intensive**—labor represents a substantial proportion of the total cost of operation. Others are capital intensive—labor is only a small proportion of total operating cost. Companies in the steel, auto, or metal mining industries are capital intensive.

3. *Type of organization.* There is considerable variability among types of organizations that may result in differences in the way people are handled.

Table 2.1
Possible Organizational
Purposes and Objectives

Purpose	Definitions/Examples
Fundamental	Service, social responsibility, profit, education, recreation, etc.
Operational	Improvement of production facilities; increase in production capacity; extended research and development; increase in market share; increase in revenue; reduce costs.
Economic	Productivity; growth; profit; cost reduction; return on investment, on assets, or on equity.
Human Resource	Improvements in: employee satisfaction, grievance, absenteeism, safety, training, promotional opportunities, labor costs.
Social Responsibility	Conduct of activities: loaned executives, hard-core employment, pollution abatement, financial contributions.

Social mores, tradition, or the philosophy of the owners have an impact. The dress code at IBM was strictly adhered to by anyone who wanted to remain with the company, because the president felt it was an essential part of its image. Employee ownership and representation on the board of directors was part of the philosophy of the late John J. Eagan, owner of American Cast Iron Pipe Company, who perpetuated this practice with a clause in his will.

Organizational structure depends on tasks, people, and functions. The nature of the structure will vary according to the basic purpose of an organization, the nature of its activities and tasks, and its size. In Chapter 1 we discussed alternative structures for personnel organizations. The same considerations and constraints would apply here.

ENVIRONMENTAL VARIABLES

Factors external to an organization interact with internal and organizational variables to affect personnel situations. Following are some of the myriad factors outside an organization that can have significant impact on its personnel policies and practices.

1. *Economy.* The labor market (supply and demand of labor), inflation, and unemployment have varying impact on personnel situations.

2. *Government regulations.* Laws and regulations affect practically every aspect of personnel management, from the hiring of workers to the physical conditions of a plant or office.

3. *Labor laws.* State and federal labor legislation and their definitive guidelines, and court rulings attempt to protect the welfare of employees and are intended to be beneficial to society in general. Later chapters will discuss laws that affect employment, influence training programs, regulate wages and benefits, establish standards for a work environment, and govern the administration of unions and their relationships with employers.

4. *Social responsibility.* Prevailing social values influence management to assume a socially responsible posture. Many company-sponsored programs contribute to the economic and social welfare of the community.[10] The personnel department plays a significant role here because it helps select executives who are loaned to civic projects and social agencies. It administers programs to hire and train the disadvantaged. Personnel is responsible for helping an organization achieve a standard of work-life quality and of maintaining high moral and ethical standards for workers, managers, and executives.

5. *Pressure groups.* Environmentalists, the civil rights movement, feminists, aging citizens, and a variety of other special-interest groups bring pressure upon organizations to support their causes. The way in which organi-

zations respond can affect the way workers feel about management. If an organization has an image of being responsible, moral, and supportive of the community, its employees are generally proud to identify with it. Industry has been spending billions of dollars to abate pollution, remove health and safety hazards from the work place, and preserve the natural state of areas surrounding plants and offices. Even though 19,250 jobs have been lost because of environmentally related plant shutdowns, EPA figures report that 65,000 new jobs have been created from the production of environmental equipment.[11]

Finally, consumer groups have influenced drastic changes in some production methods to make products safer, less costly, and more reliable. The consequent alterations in the production process, materials, and marketing can introduce new job classifications and change present job methods.

6. *Politics.* Variables stemming from factors associated with politics have definite implications for the personnel situation. Government-business partnerships, for example, require an organization's conformity to more stringent government guidelines on personnel practices. The letting of government contracts is also a function of politics. When the C-5A contract was awarded to Lockheed in the early 1960s, employment in the company almost doubled. Conversely, Congress's decision to abandon the B-1 bomber project resulted in the layoff of many Boeing employees.

Situational Analysis

Personnel problem analysis is basic to the decision-making process. Managers who are responsible for accomplishing objectives with workers need to understand the variables and interactions that comprise a personnel situation. **Diagnosis** of a situation becomes a matter of defining the problem; developing factual information as well as opinions and feelings; deciding which alternatives provide the most appropriate solution by blending intuition with objective analysis; and implementing the decision by considering alternative techniques, management style, and interpersonal relationships. The problem-solving technique described below will be useful in analyzing cases and situations in this text, but it also can be applied to real-life situations.

PROBLEM DEFINITION

Decision makers find it useful to isolate a problem or to frame an issue before proceeding with an analysis. As an **arbitrator** of labor-management grievances, the author generally gets the parties to specify the issue on which he is to rule. His job is to act as an impartial judge and to decide on the issue. Generally, the issue or problem is stated as a question to facilitate evaluation and decision. So, in an arbitration the issue could be framed as: "Was the discharge of Herman Smith for just cause?" or "Did the company violate the agreement by denying Mary Smith her choice of vacation?" A clear statement of the problem at the outset can set the stage for systematic diagnosis.

Another aspect of problem definition is the identification of the over-riding or priority problem. Usually several interrelated problems are evident, but one can be identified as overriding, and the others will appear as subordinate. The nature and outcome of the subsequent steps in an analysis are predicated on problem definition. Let us consider, for example, the problem in the burred panel case at the beginning of this chapter. From the perspective of the plant manager, we might frame the problem as: "What is the cause of the burrs?" We would then focus on the equipment, the dies, the blanks, and the sabotage variables as initially happened in this case. But what if, instead, we consider "How can the company meet the customer's need for panels?" One of the alternatives would still be the correction of the burrs condition, but we would, also, weigh the possibility of subcontracting (temporarily, of course) the panel production, or even patching the burred panels.

One additional aspect of problem definition should be noted. The framing of the issue depends on the perspective of the problem solver. While *several* perspectives should be considered in later stages of a situational analysis, the plant manager would take an overall view of a situation while, for example, the personnel manager might view the problem as: "How can we regain the goodwill of the employees?"

DEVELOPING THE SITUATION

At this stage it is important to gain as much insight into a situation as possible. A situational decision maker develops an appreciation for the complexity of an organization and its human relationships; observes concrete events and relationships; and distinguishes between hard facts and perceptions or feelings.[12]

In a personnel situation we tend not to see the forest for the trees. As managers, we are so intimately involved with people that we tend to take the human factor for granted. Part of understanding a situation involves gaining insight into the feelings and perceptions of the people involved. If one does a thorough job here, he or she would interview the participants in a situation and listen to both the words and the feelings being expressed. The purpose of this is to gain an understanding of the participants' interpretation of the circumstances. And, by listening to participants on both sides of an issue, we can recognize that people perceive similar events differently. Had supervisor Nat Berger done this, perhaps the technical problem at his plant could have been solved sooner, and the personnel matter surely would have been less explosive.

Fact-finding is the heart of the development process. Most of us overlook an obvious yet simple method for gathering facts. Why not determine if someone else has encountered the same or a similar problem? Most libraries afford ready access to research findings or case write-ups that might have analyzed a parallel situation. Others in the same organization or elsewhere may have resolved the same problem you are investigating. One word of caution, however: the situations may be parallel, but they are seldom exactly alike. There are dangers in freely adopting someone else's solution to a similar problem. Reviews of records, observations, interviews, and surveys are included in fact-finding.

Key to situational fact-finding is the identification of the variables relevant to a situation. In this respect the schematic (Figure 2.1) can be useful because it serves as a checklist of variables in the personnel situation. Environmental, organizational, and personnel variables all merit consideration.

ANALYZING THE SITUATION

Situational analysis takes account of the interactions among variables, determining the effect each variable has on others. In this respect it is important to examine relevant organizational policies (they are the guidelines that emanate from and support an organization's purpose). Policy statements often imply or direct one to a solution to a problem. In more complex situations, the interactions are too numerous to allow analysis of all of them, but it is still possible to consider different aspects or perspectives of them. In this respect, we are seeking the who, what, when, where, and why of the interactions. Objectivity is essential here, for prejudices and other biases only inhibit the fact-finding process.

An essential element of developing facts is consideration of the implications of those facts. Who and what areas of the organization will be affected by the outcome of this situation? What are the short- and long-term consequences? What are the cost implications? Would a wrong decision here place my job in jeopardy? What is the probability of making a wrong decision? How widespread will the impact of this situation be? The answers to these questions provide insight into the magnitude and consequences of the decision that are given by the facts. The question might be asked, "Is it worth going to all this trouble?" Well, it depends. If the facts show inconsequential implications, a right or wrong decision may have little significance. But if the answer to these questions indicates a critical need for a positive determination, the time and effort expended in this process becomes worthwhile.

Deciding the most appropriate approach to a problem consists of weighing the facts and considering a variety of alternatives. This process calls for blending rational thinking with **intuition**. The hard facts and the feelings and perceptions of participants may give clear indication of an appropriate course of action. But common sense and a gut feeling for a situation are crucial to an ultimate decision. The manager lives with a situation day in and day out, so he or she should have better insight into it than anyone else. There is no substitute for an intuitive sense for what will and will not work.

Successful situational decision makers consider alternative solutions in order to arrive at a decision that accommodates the uniqueness of each case. They weigh the pros and cons of each alternative and evaluate them. Then they determine the one that is best suited to the defined problem and map out a plan of action based on the chosen alternative.

IMPLEMENTING A PLAN OF ACTION

Plans are useless unless they are translated into action. The plan for rectifying a situation needs to be communicated to, and accepted by, those who will be responsible for carrying it out. Follow-up procedures are needed to ensure effective implementation of any decision.

In the action stage of situational analysis the implementing managers select the techniques appropriate to a situation. Translating the decision into action becomes a function of the technical and interpersonal skills of this team and the leadership style and relationship of the manager with his or her people (leadership styles are discussed in detail in Chapter 4).

The foregoing scheme of situational analysis makes it obvious that this approach requires considerable effort. Such expenditure of time and energy may not be worthwhile in all situations. However, situational analysis incorporates a scientific thought process that, if adopted, will add materially to line and staff people's effectiveness as decision makers. Consistently applied, situational analysis becomes second nature.

Cost-Benefit Analysis

While situational analysis is useful for solving personnel problems per se, some attempt must also be made to measure the efficiency/effectiveness of each of its activities. The continued existence of personnel programs is contingent on their demonstrated effectiveness. Toward this end, each of the chapters in Sections II–IV contains a discussion of the criteria for analyzing the costs versus the benefits of programs. Obviously, the value of benefits received from a program should exceed the costs of it in the short and long run. Measurement of costs is generally more straightforward than measurement of benefits. Personnel costs might include wages and salaries, or time lost from work, or medical expenses, and so on. But the benefits derived from a training program or the value of morale improvement may prove difficult to measure. Nevertheless, we will attempt to describe criteria for analyzing the cost/benefit relationships of each of the personnel activities.

Summary

Contingency theory is the conventional wisdom of modern management thought, and it is particularly applicable to personnel management. The underlying concept of the theory is that there is no single best approach to personnel problem solving. Thus, each situation must be viewed as unique and analyzed accordingly.

A frame of reference for contingency management suggests that variables and their interactions need to be considered when analyzing a situation. Variables appropriate to a personnel situation include those inside the organization (personnel, physical factors, and functions; organizational variables, purpose, nature, and structure), and a myriad of external variables that comprise the environment within which the organization operates.

The process of analyzing personnel situations involves: a) developing the situation, b) analyzing the situation, c) deciding, and d) implementing a plan of action.

This approach calls for considerable effort, so it is not appropriate to all situations. But it does blend scientific analysis with common sense and, if it is consistently applied, the decision maker's effectiveness will be enhanced.

Key Terms

contingency theory	organizational structure
systems theory	diagnosis
variables	arbitrator
situation	fact-finding
interaction	intuition
labor intensive	

Review Questions

1. Describe at least five variables in a typical personnel situation.

2. How do environmental factors affect the personnel situation?

3. Discuss the advantages and disadvantages of the contingency approach to personnel management.

4. What is the significance of interactions in the contingency process?

5. Discuss the various classifications of distinguishing among people.

6. What is the significance of organizational variables to a personnel situation?

7. Describe the basic process for contingency decision making.

Discussion Questions

1. From the standpoint of the personnel manager, what advantages does the contingency approach have over traditional decision-making models?

2. What is the logic behind taking a situational approach in personnel problems? Given that the situation dictates the approach, how would you handle each of the following problems under each of the two different situations shown below?

Personnel Problem	Situation
a. Hire production employees	1. All jobs are technical. 2. All jobs are unskilled.
b. Conduct a training program	1. Trainees are midlevel managers. 2. You are under a contract with the U.S. Department of Labor to train disadvantaged people.
c. Develop a policy on handling grievances	1. There is no union in the company and you must prepare an employee handbook. 2. The union has demanded substantial improvements in supervisor-worker relations for their new agreement.

3. From the example of Pinson Manufacturing Company at the beginning of this chapter, identify the variables that are personnel, organizational, and environmental, and describe as many of their interactions as you feel are relevant to the basic problem. Then discuss how you would deal with the operators who called in sick.

Case Problem 1

FIRE THE BUM

''Jason, we just have to fire Jack,'' Andy said. ''He's just too big a risk.''

''Relax, Andy. After all, Jack hasn't done anything wrong. In fact, he's the best bank teller we have.''

''Come on, Jason. Sure, he's a good teller, but the way he's been carrying on off the job recently is just too much. This is a small town, and we only have two banks. First National is already beginning to pick up our customers because of Jack.''

''So he bought a sports car—so what?''

''For $22,000 cash?'' Andy replied. ''Where does a small town bank clerk making $9,200 a year get that kind of money?''

''He says that his aunt left him some money,'' Jason said.

''Did he tell you about his poker winnings, too?''

Jason looked startled. ''No. Did he win?''

''That's what he says. Big game over in Kansas City last month, or so he says.'' Andy began to pace the floor. ''You're the president, Jason, and I'm just a board member, but for heaven's sake, everyone in town is talking about it. And that new blonde girl friend of his—well, bank tellers just don't live that way.''

''Well, Jack's work is excellent. Really, he's about the best teller we've ever had. We certainly can't complain about that. And remember, Andy, we're living in tolerant times. You can't control your workers' lifestyles anymore.''

''I suppose that you're right, Jason, but darn it, this is a bank! Our tellers handle literally millions of dollars of our customers' money every day. You have to have special standards to be a teller!''

''The way the law is now, Andy, I doubt that we even could fire him.''

''Forget the law! Every time Jack runs down Main Street in that 400 horsepower bomb of his, we lose about five conservative customers! When his girl friend's with him, we lose ten. People like their bank tellers conservative, cautious, and colorless. I'll bet you that we get a couple of special audits shortly, just because of this. Bankers just are different than other people.''

Problems

1. What should Jason do? Why?

2. Should a company worry about its employees' lifestyles off the job? Why or why not?

3. Consider various people you have to rely on (often literally for your life), such as policemen, firemen, doctors, and airline pilots. Do you, as a user or consumer of their goods or services, have any right to judge the off-duty lifestyles of these people? Why or why not?

Western State University has long had a good state pension plan for its professors. The state law on which this plan is based states, among other things, that the plan be actuarially sound—that is, that the pension fund be built up by professor contributions and state payments to a level that guaranteed the continuation of payments to pensioners.

One result of this law was that female professors paid more into the plan than males, because females live longer than males. Because they do, they receive pension benefits longer, and hence they need to pay more.

A group of women professors threatened to sue the university on this issue. They pointed out that unequal payments were discriminatory, and hence probably illegal under federal equal-rights legislation. They suggested that the men pay somewhat more, while the women pay somewhat less, so that the pension payments would be equal.

When news of this leaked out, a male faculty group threatened to sue. They pointed out that such a plan was discriminatory, since it required men to pay for something they would never receive.

The university's legal counsel checked with the state attorney general, who noted, after long study, that the university must observe the state law. If it did not, its president and other officers would be criminally liable for deliberate violation of a state statute.

But the legal counsel also checked with the federal equal rights people, who pointed out that in all likelihood, the women would win their lawsuit. However, they also noted that many reverse discrimination suits were now being filed, and they really could not predict the outcome of the men's suit.

The president of Western State was perfectly willing to follow the law. But, as he pointed out, no one could give a clear interpretation. No matter what he did, someone was going to be unhappy.

Case Problem 2

WHO PAYS?

Problems

1. What is the correct solution to this problem? Why?

2. Is the fact that women do live longer than men discriminatory? To whom?

3. What should the president do in this case? Why?

Notes

1. Robert J. Mockler, "Situational Theory of Management," *Harvard Business Review*, May–June 1971, pp. 146–55.

2. Albert Speer, *Inside the Third Reich* (New York: Avon Books, 1970), pp. 274–86.

3. Cortlandt Cammann and David A. Nadler, "Fit Control Systems to Your Managerial Style," *Harvard Business Review*, January–February 1976, pp. 65–72.

4. See, for example: T. Burns and G. Stalker, *The Management of Innovation* (New York: Tavistock, 1961); P. R. Lawrence and J. W. Lorsch, *Organization and Environment: Differentiation and Integration* (Cambridge, Mass.: Graduate School of Business Administration, Harvard University, 1967); C. Perrow, *Organizational Analysis* (Belmont, Calif.: Wadsworth, 1970); P. Selznick, *TVA and the Grass Roots* (Los Angeles: University of California Press, 1949); and J. Thompson, *Organizations in Action* (New York: McGraw-Hill, 1967).

5. Harold Koontz, "The Management Theory Jungle," *Academy of Management Journal*, December 1961, pp. 174–88.

6. Leland M. Wooton, "The Mixed Blessings of Contingency Management," *Academy of Management Review*, July 1977, pp. 431ff.

7. L. W. Porter, E. E. Lawler, and J. R. Hackman, *Behavior in Organizations* (New York: McGraw-Hill, 1975).

8. John B. Miner, *The Challenge of Managing* (Philadelphia: W. B. Saunders, 1975).

9. Lawrence S. Wrightsman, *Social Psychology*, 2nd ed. (Belmont, Calif.: Wadsworth, 1977), pp. 551ff.

10. See, for example, Lloyd L. Byars and Michael H. Mescon, *The Other Side of Profit* (Philadelphia: W. B. Saunders, 1975). It is a compendium of factual descriptions of what certain businesses are doing for society.

11. "The Environmentalists Try to Win Labor Over," *Business Week*, October 3, 1977, p. 104.

12. A. Zaleznik, *Foreman Training in a Growing Enterprise* (Boston: Harvard Business School, Division of Research, 1951), pp. 221–22.

Chapter Three
Personnel Policy

A midwestern insurance company was reviewing its vacation policy because of the problems arising from its implementation. The guidelines stipulated that employees who left the insurance company were not entitled to vacation pay even if they had earned it prior to termination. The vacation policy aroused considerable resentment among employees, and in the long run was costly to the company. Most of the workers who anticipated leaving the organization took their vacations before resigning, frequently giving little or no notice.

This is just one example of the effect personnel policies can have on an organization. Generally speaking, personnel policies support the needs of an organization, but in today's society it is especially important that they address themselves to the issues of the times. **Policy making,** therefore, must anticipate and accommodate human resource needs. For instance, **equal employment opportunity** laws require management to treat all employees fairly; properly formulated and implemented policy serves this goal. Special recruitment efforts are essential when companies seek to hire minorities. Furthermore, management's intent to act affirmatively for all employees, including women and minorities, must be stated explicitly in personnel policy and conscientiously disseminated. *Affirmative action* policy and its implementation are such an important personnel issue that they are discussed in detail in Chapter 15.

LEARNING OBJECTIVES

1. To know the relevance of policies.

2. To learn how policies are formulated.

3. To know the criteria for effective policies.

4. To understand the methods for insuring personnel policy effectiveness.

5. To be able to define policy, principle, rule, practice.

Policy Making and the Planning Function

Policies are guidelines for action. They emanate from business objectives and implement the intent of the formulators. Business writer R. C. Davis points out that business policy basically consists of two parts: first, a **principle** or a group of related principles, and second, a **rule** of action.[1] Together, these two parts support the stated objectives.

PRINCIPLES

A principle is a significant truth that is usually stated as the ultimate source or cause or as a belief or an essential. Years of experience with personnel problems have led to generalizations about administering them; these generalizations have become the principles that channel personnel activities. The principles a manager adopts are based on his or her knowledge or assumptions about human behavior. (The discussion of leadership styles in Chapter 4 is particularly relevant to this point.) Principles in organizations increase efficiency and crystallize the nature of management, but most important, they explain the intent of policy. Some examples of principles related to personnel administration might include:

1. Clear descriptions of positions and their requirements facilitate objective selection of candidates.

2. Employees perform better when they have a voice in determining matters that affect them.

3. The authority, duties, responsibilities, and relationships of everyone in an organization should be clearly and completely communicated in writing to all, so that employees can direct their efforts toward a common goal.

4. Employees' compensation should be related to their contribution to organizational objectives, thereby providing a reward for achievements and an incentive for continued performance.

RULES

When policies are implemented in the form of rules and procedures, their principles are only implied. If the reason behind a rule is not explained, it becomes an edict. As the work force expands its ranks with younger, better educated employees who refuse to obey orders blindly, companies must explain the reasons behind policy statements; employee understanding and acceptance of the meaning of rules are essential in eliciting cooperation. A statement of principle can clarify the meaning of a rule. Take, for instance, this rule on safety: "All employees must wear hard hats in designated areas. Employees who fail to do so will be told to leave the area immediately."

Such a matter-of-fact announcement is sure to elicit hostility from workers. However, if the personnel staff or line supervisors explain the principle behind the rule, voluntary conformity is much more likely to result. Consider this version of the rule: "All employees must wear hard hats in designated areas. At any construction site there is always a possibility of objects accidentally falling from above. The company has found that wearing hard hats significantly reduces injuries from falling objects. If employees do not follow hard-hat rules, they will be told to leave the area for their own safety."

BUSINESS OBJECTIVES

The purpose, **philosophy,** and **objective** of an organization is established before policies are instituted. General objectives provide a sense of direction for a personnel management effort by enumerating the results that they must work toward and the methods they must use.[2] Furthermore, a personnel organization needs specific objectives to provide a direction for its own activities.

To function efficiently organizations plan for the future on the basis of their unique situations and forecasted contingencies. Then they devise the strategies that will most effectively implement their stated purpose.

Personnel Policy Development

The personnel objective that transcends all others is that concerned with optimizing **personnel effectiveness.** To attain this objective, personnel managers must plan in the present for the future. They must recognize emerging personnel patterns that signal problem areas and develop effective strategies and policies to meet these challenges. **Social consciousness** among workers and business people alike is a growing condition, with strong implications for personnel policy. For example, as employees become more involved in community and civic projects, management must establish guidelines on employee release time—including sabbaticals—for such activities. In addition, managers must devise policies on hard-core hiring and development programs for minorities and women. As attention focuses on youth, there will be problems concerning promotion criteria (e.g., should the seniority system continue, giving priority to older workers?). With increased emphasis on young workers, there will also be problems with senior employees which will require policy decisions on matters such as early retirement and benefits programs.

Personnel policies that are effective in achieving these goals usually meet the following criteria:

1. *Congruency.* They support and derive from the overall objectives of an organization. Everyone involved in the personnel process is guided by

organizational policies in general and personnel policies in particular. Consequently, effective personnel policies solidify relations between a line organization and its personnel staff and facilitate the achievement of organizational objectives.

2. *Compatibility*.   Effective personnel policies are compatible with each other; that is, they are all directed toward a common goal. Invariably, some individual units within an organization establish policies that operate at cross-purposes and inhibit progress. Much of the reason for establishing broad, general policies before departmental and functional ones is to avoid this conflict. In addition, many companies have a centralized authority that reviews new policies to ensure that they support and are compatible with existing ones.

3. *Clarity*.   Policies are clearly stated, written, and communicated, so that everyone affected will understand their meaning. The true measure of clarity is whether practice equals intent.

4. *Stability/flexibility*.   Finally, effective personnel policies are stable, yet flexible. In this regard, they respond to fundamental changes in the objectives and characteristics of an organization, yet they must not change so frequently as to introduce uncertainty and thereby depress morale. Personnel policies need to accommodate new situations by being open to revision. Though present emphasis is on policies that treat all employees of a group alike, contemporary workers prefer to be treated as individuals, and strive to maintain their own identity. Enlightened personnel policies are sufficiently flexible to accommodate individual differences among employees.

Policy Determination

Many organizations operate under the misconception that a personnel policy manual will guarantee effective human resource management. Often they hire an outside consultant to draw up an impressive array of personnel policy statements. Cost-conscious firms sometimes adopt another organization's manual, not realizing that many of the policies are inapplicable to their immediate situation and objectives; this approach usually works to their detriment. Policies of another firm may contradict organizational philosophy or conflict with objectives previously established, because employees, processes, organizational structure, and the desires of policy makers are usually dissimilar. Consequently, policies should be determined on the basis of their relevancy to a particular company's situation and be individually tailored to it.

Organizations should not formulate personnel policies just to have them. They should devise policies on the basis of need, as in the following circumstances.

1. *Situations that affect many employees.* Typical examples are safety and health rules: specific policies protect employees' physical well-being.

2. *Situations that recur often.* An example is absenteeism: daily decisions are made on recording attendance irregularities and appropriate disciplinary measures are taken.

3. *Situations that have significant impact on an organization.* A typical example of this circumstance is a drug policy. Even though the percentage of drug-using employees may be low, a problem such as this has many ramifications and must be confronted early.

Policy Formulation Process

When it is determined that a personnel policy is required, policy makers can begin to formulate one. Formulating effective personnel policies is a problem-solving, decision-making process. Personnel managers devise policies that will help achieve an organization's objectives. Because of the myriad variables that interact in every policy-making situation, this process is highly situational. Thus, the situational-analysis scheme proposed in Chapter 2 is an appropriate tool in formulating policy. The following sections identify the situational variables of policy formulation, define the respective roles of line and staff in this process, and describe some of the more widely applied approaches to policy formulation.

SITUATIONAL VARIABLES IN POLICY FORMULATION

The philosophies, objectives, and interests of personnel-policy formulators are influenced by a number of constraints. A few of these are:

1. *Forces external to the organization.* Personnel legislation regulates practically every aspect of this function. Equal employment opportunity laws set standards and guidelines for hiring, selection, promotion, and even discipline. The Federal Privacy Act regulates the way personnel records are kept. Other laws regulate physical conditions of work, the relationships between labor and management, the management of compensation and benefits, and other personnel activities. One example of a company's response to federal legislation is IBM's butting out policy whereby it removed questions from employment applications dealing with marital status, age, nationality, arrest records, and whether any relative worked for IBM. Also, the policy encourages employees to inspect their personnel files and challenge any apparent inaccuracies.[3]

   Special-interest groups outside an organization may, for example, successfully pressure the firm into considering pregnancy a compensatory disability, or to have it increase its pollution abatement efforts, and so on.

2. *Constraints imposed through industry practice.*   Unions, for example control admission to apprentice training, oversee grievances and seniority clauses, which preclude promotion of employees on the basis of qualifications alone. The existence of unions or the threat of one organizing employees, for instance, might prompt a policy on **job posting** to ensure the consideration of all qualified employees for a vacancy. Or, the **open-door policy** or grievance procedure, associated with a policy of open communication, is a direct result of union activity.

3. *Internal factors.*   Collective action by groups of employees acting on their own can also influence policy. **Flexible work hours** policies or a modified form of work schedule can result from employee demands for more convenient arrangements in this area.

Beneath all policy decisions are values or utilities. Often (but not always) management's values operate in internal policy issues. A large midwestern service organization has a policy not to hire the spouse of an employee. This policy is quite unpopular with the employees, especially given the apparent benefits of dual incomes, combined transportation to work, and having the same work hours. This policy was drafted because the company management felt it would have fewer problems without both parties working than with both of them together in the same company.

In most organizations, especially business firms, the philosophies of the highest-ranking officers have more influence on personnel policies than any other single variable. Their attitudes on getting along with employees will largely determine personnel policy and the programs that emanate from it. An excellent example of this is the Haloid Company. The heads of that company believed that their people were the company's most valued asset. They had a policy of expending considerable effort to retain employees. For example, early in this company's life, a young engineer who had recently been hired was proving sadly inept at his job. In any other company he would have been fired, but the president of Haloid thought it the company's fault for placing the man in the wrong job. This people-oriented philosophy pervaded the organization and fostered an esprit de corps within a company that today is one of the world's most successful enterprises—the Xerox Corporation.[4]

The above are situational variables, the interactions of which influence and shape personnel policies. The complexities of each situation exclude any one basic procedure in the formulation of policy that would be common to all organizations. Policy formulation is a combination of strategies and personalities acting under the combined influences of internal and external factors.

LINE-STAFF ROLES IN POLICY FORMULATION

Policy effectiveness is predicated on the coordinated efforts of line and staff managers at all levels of an organization. The personnel staff's role in formulation ranges from being key decision maker to having policy imposed on it and being responsible for its implementation. At Delta Air Lines, for example, personnel is intimately involved in corporate policy implementation. During the 1973–74 fuel shortage (fuel consumption in the month of January 1974 had to be reduced by more than 11 million gallons as compared to January 1973), many of its people were not needed. In the effort to avoid furloughs, the personnel and line staff, working together, were able to reassign almost 500 flight attendants and 200 pilots to ground positions. Leaves, vacations, and other time-off policies played a key role here, too. And, when Delta merged with Northeast Airlines, the personnel staff coordinated the development of policies on seniority arrangements, rescheduling, reassignment of personnel, and so on.[5]

Not only does the personnel department play an important role in formulating policy but also it has the primary responsibility to oversee its implementation. A large industrial manufacturer had opened a small assembly plant in a rural midwestern community. It hired a nucleus work force and encouraged employees to recommend friends and relatives for employment. Because of the congenial atmosphere of the organization, employees were eager to refer applicants. The company soon found that its work force had a disproportionate share of relatives, to the exclusion of other applicants from the community. So top management reacted with a nepotism policy requiring that applicants not be immediate family members of present employees. As soon as employees were notified of the new policy, it became apparent to the personnel staff that the company, by its action, had created a severe employee problem. Through its monitoring activities, the staff influenced line management to modify its stand.

Line management, too, plays a key role, because line managers implement policy. In formulating policy, their opinions are sought because they know which policies are sound and which are in need of revision. Final approval of personnel policies rests with top management, whose wholehearted support is necessary for the policies to be effective.

Policy makers turn to personnel staff specialists to provide research information relevant to policies being considered for adoption. Sound policy requires careful consideration of a wide variety of factors and variables prior to its formulation. The personnel staff's most important role here is in achieving uniform understanding and consistent application of policy. Through training sessions and communication programs, the staff seeks the cooperation of line supervisors. As the latter gain an understanding of the principles behind policies and the basis for their implementation, they are more likely to view these in a positive light (i.e., as an aid to supervision rather than a limitation on their freedom to manage). One major food-products manufacturer has been especially successful in this respect. Top-management representatives introduce new policies in small conferences where open dialogue is encouraged. The follow-up briefing is afforded through video cassettes viewed by individuals or small groups. Finally, the personnel staff offers advice and counsel to line management to promote consistent application of policies.

POLICY FORMULATION METHODS

Although individual situations exclude the universal application of specific techniques, several general ones have gained wide acceptance in this area and are worthy of note. Formulating policy is the responsibility of all managers in the organization. Specific policies should be generated by the manager directly responsible for their implementation, though he or she can, of course, seek the advice of others or even delegate the task.

In generating policies, it is common practice to involve employees from several departments. Employees participate in an analysis of a situation, and a manager can make a final determination. Other, more participative methods utilize groups of employees from different levels of an organization; the use of committees and boards, both standing and ad hoc, to develop policy is an example of this **participative approach.** A few enlightened companies such as Polaroid include representatives from all levels in committees that recommend new policies and changes to top management. Many organizations formulate policy in regularly scheduled staff meetings, and some even assign project work teams to develop specific policies. The project team concept has the advantage of drawing ideas from a variety of talents to focus on a problem; it also encourages people to work outside their functional areas. For example, formulating compensation policy is usually the concern of the wage and salary administrator. But a project team could draw upon the expertise of the benefits administrator for information on services and fringe benefits and upon the controller for the economic ramifications of compensation policy.

It is true that involving many people in policy making is expensive in terms of time, but there are offsetting advantages. Obviously, lower-level employees, on the basis of their day-to-day experiences, can often devise sound policies. When employees participate in determining policies that will affect them, they are more likely to commit themselves to successfully implementing the policies. Such involvement also serves as an excellent means of developing the decision-making abilities of managers, because the policy formulation process is the essence of decision making.

On the other hand, several shortcomings of the participative approach need to be circumvented if it is to be used successfully. Conflicts are likely to occur, especially when diverse interests are present in a group. Consequently, a consensus may be the product of the most vocal, but not necessarily the most knowledgeable, members. All this activity is time consuming, possibly frustrating to individuals in a group, and may not produce desirable results. Also, when groups such as these help formulate policies, they may not be as serious about their responsibilities as they would be if they were held accountable for the results. Thus, clearly defining what is expected of a group and holding it responsible for its actions are means of overcoming some of the disadvantages of participative policy formulation.[6]

Policy Implementation

The personnel program is more effective if an up-to-date **policy manual** is given to everyone with personnel responsibility. This means that there must be existing policies on employment, training and development, compensation, employee services, labor relations, and discipline. And these policies should be reviewed periodically and revised as circumstances warrant.

The sample policy statements in Table 3.1 include governing principles and the guidelines that derive from them. It should be emphasized that the policies provide guidelines for decisions, but they are not a substitute for sound judgment. Employees usually receive a handbook of such basic personnel policies in an abbreviated form, while those responsible for implementation are given a detailed manual of policies and supporting procedures.

Cost-Benefit Analysis

Policy control is concerned with determining the effectiveness of policies and the degree to which practices conform to them. The true test of personnel policy is the practice that derives from it. There may be other reasons for ineffective performance, but policies do set the stage. As mentioned previously, the personnel staff must constantly survey policy administration to ensure consistent application.

An example of inconsistency occurred in the case of a production worker who was discharged for improperly carrying out an order. When the case was appealed, the arbitrator ruled against the company and ordered the employee rehired with repayment of lost wages. It was the employee's first offense, and past practice had been to issue a written reprimand. Inconsistent punishment cost the company a large sum of money, but more significantly, the man's supervisor lost face by having to reinstate an employee he had fired. An organization cannot be too careful in assuring complete understanding of its personnel policies.

The personnel staff can employ a variety of methods to control the

Table 3.1
Sample Policy Statements

Relationships with unions (mining company)

Principle: The company recognizes the important part that labor organizations perform in the relationship between the company and its employees and acknowledges them as spokesmen for employees in many matters concerning company-employee relationships.

Rule: Because labor organizations are such an important factor in company-employee relationships, it is essential that these organizations be democratically organized and administered and be responsible for their actions. Management will encourage union members to take an active part in union affairs to insure democracy and responsibility.

Promotion from within (office products manufacturer)

Principle: The company makes every effort to promote from within.

Rule: Employees with the experience and abilities needed for an opening will be considered for advancement.

Rule: While promotion from within is usually the most desirable way to fill openings, the company's rapid growth sometimes requires it to hire qualified personnel from outside, to bring the company the special talents it needs.

Safety (public utility)

Principle: The study and practice of accident prevention is one of the most important employee activities. Safety is important to the individual in terms of health and well-being. Knowing and applying safe working methods are fundamental parts of every job.

Rule: For their own protection and in the interest of fellow workers, employees must learn and follow all established safety practices and avoid taking any chances that might result in injury. They should consult with their supervisor when in doubt.

Ethical standards (computer company)

Principle: The company strives to maintain a high standard of business ethics, which it believes is in keeping with good industrial citizenship. Employees' adherence to these standards while carrying out their jobs is vital.

Rule: Regular employees may hold outside employment except when such employment adversely affects their performance on the job, competes with the company, or involves a possible conflict of interest.

Table 3.1 (cont.)

Drug dependency (insurance company)

Principle: We believe drug dependency is an illness and should be treated as such. The objective of this policy is to retain employees who have developed a drug dependency and to help them arrest its advance before the condition renders them unemployable.

Rule: If employees with a drug dependency are willing to seek and cooperate in treatment, they will be given company assistance in locating and securing admission to appropriate treatment services.

Employment (beverage manufacturer)

Principle: The employment policies of this company have, for a long time, been nondiscriminatory as to race, creed, sex, age, physical handicap or national origin.

Rule: All job applicants and all employees will be accorded equal treatment in consideration for employment, pay, assignment to a job, and selection for promotion. There must be no discrimination against an individual because of his or her race, creed, sex, age, physical handicap, or national origin.

Compensation (building-products manufacturer)

Principle: The company wants to pay a fair wage. Employees' pay compares favorably with the wages paid employees in other building-products plants who are doing the same kind of work.

Rule: The amount employees are paid depends on:
1. The kind of work they are doing.
2. Their work performance—the quality and quantity of the units they produce.
3. The number of hours they work.

Pregnancy disability (heavy equipment manufacturer)

Principle: Pregnancy is viewed as a compensable disability. A maternity leave of absence may be granted by the company for temporary medical disabilities caused by pregnancy.

Rule: The employee shall notify her supervisor of the anticipated date of delivery as soon as pregnancy is known. The company may, at any time, request the employee to furnish a physician's certification that the employee is physically able to continue working. Otherwise, the point at which the maternity leave commences is a matter for the employee and her physician to determine. At least two (2) weeks notice of intent to commence maternity leave shall be given by the employee.

policies it promulgates. In the field, it can observe practices and actually **audit** activities generated by its policy. In evaluating policies, the following questions are asked:

1. Is there consistent policy understanding among supervisors and managers?
2. Are policies applied consistently?
3. Do the policies contribute to organizational objectives? Do they aid the management process or encumber it?
4. Are policies up to date, or do they need revision?
5. What is the relationship between the cost of administering policies and the benefits derived from them?
6. Do the policies comply with federal, state, and local regulations?

Answers to these questions can be substantiated by factual information. Staff members can evaluate specific policies by observing their implementation, but they should also seek the opinions of managers and gather quantitative data from department records. Analyses of absenteeism, turnover, grievances, and medical claims are just a few examples of objective information that can support findings on policy effectiveness. As a result of an audit or analysis, a personnel staff may decide to revise and reformulate some policies.

Since personnel policies affect all other personnel activities, Driessnack[7] recommends that their financial impact on the company's profits be assessed. Payroll, benefits, and related taxes are often the heaviest contributors to overall expenses, so it makes good sense to analyze these costs and attempt to control them. Personnel policies, when properly formulated and implemented, offer an excellent opportunity to save, or even make profit dollars for the organization.

Summary

Modern personnel policies consider future trends in the management of human resources. Emerging patterns in work force composition, social responsibility, employee attitudes, labor legislation, and union-management issues necessitate innovative planning of objectives and strategies. Policies provide guidelines for practices that will enable organizations to meet these changes and achieve their objectives.

Policies are only as effective as their application: improperly implemented, they are certain to yield negative results. And most assuredly, unsound policies cannot produce effective results.

Successful personnel practice follows and generates clear, flexible policies that are based on organizational objectives and understood by all employees affected by them. Implicit in this statement is the point that top management must believe in and support personnel policies and programs. Halfhearted approval of miscellaneous programs that are not an integral part of an overall strategy can only lead to disaster. Well formulated policies provide clear guidelines for personnel programs that elicit employee support.

Policies are developed through the application of problem-solving skills; it is a decision-making process. When the situational approach is used, the interacting variables of personnel problems can be considered and more realistic policies and solutions reached. Top management's people philosophy, federal labor laws, unions, special interest groups, and other variables affect both the form of policies and the manner in which they are applied.

Certain criteria govern the ultimate soundness of policies. Forward-looking personnel policies are necessary to accommodate anticipated future changes. They must support company objectives by providing clear guidelines that are readily understood by those responsible for their implementation. And they must be flexible in order to consider the individual nature and character of workers. Policies that meet these requirements have the best chance of supporting the personnel function.

Key Terms

policy making	social consciousness
equal employment opportunity	job posting
principle	open-door policy
rule	flexible work hours
philosophy	participative approach
objective	policy manual
personnel effectiveness	audit

Review Questions

1. Describe the criteria for effective personnel policies.
2. Why does the personnel staff influence policy formulation?
3. How can the personnel department control policies?
4. Describe at least four variables that affect personnel policy.
5. Why is line-staff coordination important to personnel policy making?
6. Discuss the roles of line and staff in personnel policy formulation and implementation.
7. Distinguish between principles and rules as they apply to personnel policy.

Discussion Questions

1. It has been argued that worker participation in policy making is a waste of time because the manager makes the decisions anyway. Defend or dispute this contention.

2. Does a clear-cut policy statement make supervisors any less accountable for their actions in a particular situation? Does the policy guarantee they will make the correct decision?

3. Should personnel departments be concerned with problems of ecology, politics, or social issues?

4. Is it possible to maximize personnel effectiveness? What type of policy statements would best support such an objective? What variables constrain optimum worker performance?

5. What general criteria should be used to measure the effectiveness of personnel policies? What specific evidence would you seek in evaluating policies on a) absenteeism, and b) equal employment opportunity?

"What have they got you up to this time, Pete?" Jake asked. Pete was personnel director for the First National Bank, and Jake was the company statistician and Pete's lunchtime pinochle partner.

"Oh, the bosses are upset because so many people are cutting corners on coffee breaks and not coming in on time. I'm supposed to figure out what to do about it."

"Hey, that's a good idea, Pete. I see lots of people coming at 8:15 or even later and the jam up around the coffee machine is something else from 9:30 to 11. I bet half of the 200 people we have don't put in a six-hour day, let alone eight."

"You should talk, Jake—you don't get in at 8:15 most days yourself."

"Yeah, but you know how tough it is to commute down the Westside Freeway, Pete. Can I help it if some nut ties up two lanes with a skid?"

"Every day?"

"Well, there are other things. Besides, hardly anyone else ever complains about the amount of work I do."

Pete sighed. "I know. Lots of people goof off because they just don't have that much to do, or because they work faster—when they work, which is seldom—than some of the others."

"I know what you mean. Some days I'm up to my ears in stuff, and others I could just sit around and goof off for hours. But then no one ever knows when some top brass will want a load of new data."

"You know, Jake, this is a funny business. We have some real goof-offs, and we all know who they are. They're more interested in beating the game than in working. But a lot of the others just do their work in less than eight hours. They finish up, then wander around fouling up other people. Like you, for example, right now."

"Hey," Jake said, "I'm working hard, helping you think."

"We talked about putting in time clocks and tightening up, but for the kinds of professionals we have, that seems pretty drastic."

"Not only drastic, but silly," Jake said. "If you did that, guys like Studs Ballantine, over in the computer section, would spend all their time figuring out how to gimmick the time clocks. He'd work it out, too, and you'd have to hire a guard just to keep track of what was really happening." Jake thought a bit. "I'd quit, since I don't like that stuff, and I bet a lot of the others would too. I punched a clock once, when I was working in college, and I'm not about to punch one again."

"How about posting some rules? I could write up some stuff and put it everyplace."

Jake laughed. "I don't even read the No Smoking signs. If you think that I'm going to read a bunch of rules about doing something that silly, forget it."

"Well, we have to do something," Pete said.

"Why? Are we falling behind in work?"

"Well, no, but the sight of all you bums hanging around that coffee machine drives the boss nuts."

"Maybe you should figure out what's really needed to get a job done, Pete. I mean, don't you guys figure out work standards and things like that?"

"We do. But your job is typical—we have to have a statistician, even if we can't keep him busy every hour of the day. We could dock pay, I suppose."

Jake snorted. "Dock *my* pay? Try it—every time you docked me, you'd get a report that much later. Two can play at that game. Besides, you'd need a police system and a grievance committee to fight out all the arguments. You'd have everyone so mad that they'd spend all their time trying to beat the system, and if they couldn't, they'd just goof off some more."

Pete sighed and fiddled with his pencil. "Well, we have to do something, because Mr. Baxter wants it. And what vice presidents want, they get."

"Yeah, I saw him come in at ten this morning," Jake said. "And he left at two yesterday. He's a great one for keeping us wage slaves on the job. Hey, will you be at the game at lunch today?"

Problems

1. What is the real problem here?
2. Should the personnel director be the one to set this policy on working hours and rules?
3. Would it make sense for the personnel director to use a group approach to setting policy in this case? If so, who should be in the group?
4. How difficult is it to set work standards for professional or creative people as compared to routine workers? Is this a problem here?
5. Draft a policy statement for Pete on working hours and rules.

The Massive Corporation has over 26,000 employees in the United States. They work in sixteen different states in 21 plants and 42 sales offices. Historically, the company was predominantly white; Jews, blacks, Puerto Ricans, Chicanos, Indians, and Orientals were not hired very often. In 1962, the company had 126 minority employees on its payroll. One, Dr. Chen, was a world-famous nuclear physicist employed in Massive's main research and development laboratory; no other minority person was above pay grade 2 on a 14-grade hourly scale (with 1 being the lowest grade).

Massive had serious racial problems in 1969. Several sales offices were picketed; two black organizations conducted a fairly successful boycott against the company's consumer products; and four fair employment suits charging racial discrimination were filed in two states with fair employment laws. Early in 1970, Massive's board of directors, concerned about the negative image the company seemed to be acquiring, agreed to a major policy change on hiring. They decided to use completely nondiscriminatory hiring practices, starting immediately.

In mid-1970, in spite of the new policy which had been put into effect, Massive was still in trouble with various minority groups. The number of minority employees had climbed to 275, but 270 of these were still in pay grade 2 or lower. One black engineer had been hired, together with one Chicano personnel clerk and two black salesmen. The minority race representatives pointed out that this was not enough. Since about 15 percent of the U.S. population are members of minority groups, the representative stated that it is logical to expect 15 percent of Massive's work force to be minority group members. The representatives contended, moreover, that the 15 percent should be proportionally distributed throughout the skill range and the management force.

Massive's personnel director replied by noting that the company turnover was only 4 percent per year. Adding about 1 percent more for work force growth, only 5 percent, or about 1,300 employees, were hired each year. The company tried to get about 15 percent of these from minority groups, but it was very difficult to find people with the proper skills, education, or work experience. Turnover also was very high. To get one black engineer, the company had to hire five. As soon as they obtained valuable experience, some other company would lure them away at a higher salary.

The minority group organizations argued that Massive had been remiss in the past for not hiring blacks and others and that it now had to make up for the lost time. Virtually all its new employees for the next few years should be minority group people, until the 15 percent level was reached. Moreover, it was Massive's duty to upgrade minority employees as rapidly as possible. For decades, these people had suffered from inadequate schooling, job discrimination, and inability to gain experience. The company could not reasonably expect to find many such people with proper qualifications.

While this debate was going on, several black organizations staged a demonstration against Massive in a midwestern city. The demonstration developed into a minor riot; Massive's sales office was burned, several employees were hurt in the scuffle, and the company's name was prominently featured in the press for several days. Editorial comments were not friendly to the company, particularly since the black organizations handed out the employment statistics to the press.

Case Problem 2

EMPLOYMENT
PROBLEMS

Problems

1. Massive's board was scheduled to meet a few days after this incident. Do you feel that they should do anything about it at the board level?

2. What are Massive's obligations here?

3. Do you feel that members of minority groups have fewer educational opportunities than whites? Does any corporation have the obligation to do anything about this, or is it a public problem?

4. What should Massive do?

Notes

1. Ralph C. Davis, *The Fundamentals of Top Management* (New York: Harper & Row, 1951), pp. 173ff.

2. See Peter F. Drucker, *The Practice of Management* (New York: Harper & Row, 1954). The management-by-objectives approach was originally suggested in this book.

3. "Butting Out," *Newsweek*, November 10, 1975, pp. 95–97.

4. From John H. Dessauer, *My Years with Xerox: The Billions Nobody Wanted* (New York: Doubleday, 1971), pp. 60–61.

5. Interview with Ron Allen, senior vice president, Delta Air Lines, Atlanta, Georgia, November 3, 1977.

6. Donald P. Crane, "The Case for Participative Management," *Business Horizons*, April 1976, pp. 15ff.

7. Carl H. Driessnack, "Financial Impact of Effective Human Resource Management," *Personnel Administrator*, December 1979, pp. 62–66.

Chapter Four

Motivation and Commitment

Three stone masons were working on a cathedral. When asked what they were doing the first replied, "I am toiling for a living." The second answered, "I am laying stone for a building." And, the third exclaimed, "I am raising a temple in honor of our Lord!"

As this tale illustrates, some people see work as drudgery, a demeaning burden, and an economic necessity. Work in our industrial, technological world has become complex. It can mean physical effort, mental skill, or some combination of these; it can be a highly skilled job or merely a routine task. To the educated and sophisticated new breed of employees work must be more than a means for economic survival; they will expend diligent, sustained effort only when a job promises achievement and self-fulfillment. Old formulas (higher pay, job security, benefits, company picnics, etc.) for motivating people no longer get the same results they used to. Understanding why people work and knowing how to get them to perform are essential to managing any organization. Managers, especially personnel managers, recognize that people are their most valuable resource, and a knowledge of the methods that have proven effective in gaining their commitment is essential to achieving personnel effectiveness.

Motivation, leadership, and communication are basic behavioral topics. These subjects and their associated skills are keys to attaining employee effectiveness. An understanding of these can help managers influence people to perform their jobs effectively—that is, to direct their efforts toward the goals of the organization. The following sections describe the practical aspects of these subjects.

Motivational activities stimulate employees to become more productive and help gain their commitment to the objectives of the organization.

Employee Motivation

There are as many reasons why people work as there are people. External as well as internal forces affect **motivation;** behavior on a job rarely stems from a single motive. Workers themselves may not even be able to explain their motives. Consider the example of the 58-year-old die-cutter in a small family-owned company. The man's children were grown and his wife worked, so he was financially comfortable. Yet he continued to work overtime on Saturdays. His supervisor puzzled over this until he realized that the Saturday crew consisted of five of the original workers hired during World War II; these men were a very close-knit group. Furthermore, since supervision on Saturdays was minimal, the men were on their own. The die-cutter, then, was not working so much for money as for camaraderie and the satisfaction of being his own boss. Usually, workers' motives are not this clear. Nevertheless, an understanding of what motivates them is necessary to achieve good employee performance. Perhaps the following discussion will provide a basis for understanding motivation and how it operates to affect human behavior.

MOTIVATION DEFINED

The term *motivation* is derived from the Latin word *movere, to move.* But this would hardly suffice as a definition. Others have referred to motivation as:

. . . a process governing choices made by persons or lower organisms among alternative forms of voluntary activity.[1]

. . . an inner state that energizes, or moves (hence, "motivation"), and that directs or channels behavior toward goals.[2]

. . . the steering of one's actions toward certain goals and to commit a certain part of one's energies to reaching them.[3]

. . . a restlessness, a lack, a yen, a force. Once in the grip of a motive, the organism does something. It most generally does something to reduce the restlessness, to remedy the lack, to alleviate the yen, to mitigate the force.[4]

In these definitions we find several common features that characterize motivation: (1) an inner state of restlessness that creates a need or desire to *activate* behavior; (2) the behavior itself, or the *drive;* (3) the goal achievement that *sustains* the behavior; and (4) a form of feedback that *reinforces* or *modifies* the behavior. These could be construed as variables that interact in the motivation situation shown in the model in Figure 4.1.

A more detailed description of the model should provide further insight into the motivation process. Human beings constantly strive to satisfy a multitude of *needs* and *desires* that vary in strength among individuals. They may, for instance, have a high need for additional income or a strong desire to be accepted by their peers. These are the activators of the process and create a restlessness within individuals that they will try to reduce or remedy. These needs and wants are generally associated with a belief that certain actions will lead to a satisfaction of needs, for example, goal attainment. As individuals begin to work toward these goals they receive information or cues either from within themselves or from the environment that reassures them that their behavior is correct or dissuades them from their present course of action. The result is that they may continue with their present behavior or they may modify or discontinue it altogether.

An example that may clarify our description of the motivation process follows. A salesperson has a strong desire to win a sales trophy (*need* for recognition), so she works long hours calling on prospects (*behavior*) in order to place first in the sales contest (*goal*). If she were to have her sales territory reduced (*negative feedback*) she might seek other goals. Winning the trophy (*positive feedback*) would probably motivate her to continue to work to increase her sales.

This model of the motivation process appears to be fairly basic and straightforward, but it cannot possibly incorporate all the complexities of the process. *First,* motives are not obvious or apparent from behavior. Several motives can be expressed in any given act and different behaviors can be a manifestation of the same motive. For instance, a person may work harder because of a need for money, a desire to be recognized, and a need for self-esteem or pride. Similarly, that pride can be the motive to work hard as well as to express dissatisfaction about certain working conditions. *Second,* complications stem from the fact that a person at any given time may have numerous needs and desires, which are constantly changing and often in conflict. A job requirement to travel in order to excel as a salesperson may

Figure 4.1
The Basic Motivation
Process

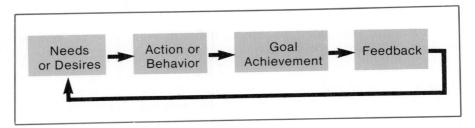

conflict with one's desire to spend more time with one's family. *Third,* individual differences exist among employees that affect the manner in which they select goals and how they pursue them. A salesperson with a high need for achievement might close a big sale and then coast while turning his or her attention to other needs. For another salesperson the same goal might be the impetus to strive for an even bigger sale. Finally, gratification of certain needs and desires might diminish the intensity of a need, or it might serve to increase the strength of a motive. Promoting an employee to a higher, more challenging position might satisfy a desire for promotion or intensify the drive to work harder in anticipation of the *next* promotion.[5]

PRACTICAL APPLICATION OF THE MOTIVATION MODEL

Organizations have gone to great lengths to create an environment that will strengthen motivation and enhance job satisfaction. The concern for productivity improvement has caused many organizations to formalize activities that address this concern. Quality of work life programs often focus on increasing productivity. Employee values and attitudes are major factors considered in creating a motivational work environment. The following sections will discuss the specifics of the practical applications of motivation theory in the work place.

WORK DESIGN AND JOB SATISFACTION.   Herzberg[6] suggests that work can be designed so that the work itself can be enriched through the introduction of motivator factors. Their inclusion in the work environment, he claims, can motivate people to perform better. **Job enrichment** implies that the responsibilities of the job are increased along with the level of difficulty or complexity. In work design, these motivator factors, according to Herzberg, should be included:[7]

1. *Knowing more.*   Employees know more about their jobs as evidenced by their achievements.

2. *Understanding more.*   Employees understand what needs to be done without being told.

3. *Creativity.*   Employees combine knowledge and understanding of the *work itself* to produce new solutions to job problems.

4. *Effectiveness in ambiguity.*   Employees take responsibility for their work and make good decisions despite the ambiguity of the situation.

5. *Individuation.*   Employees develop unique expertise that would qualify them for advancement.

6. *Real growth.*   Employees act ethically and responsibly in their dealings with others.

These motivator factors might also be viewed as variables that have an effect on job satisfaction.

In a similar vein, certain resources have been identified as being relevant to work performance. When they are unavailable, or only partially available (inadequate quantity), or are of poor quality they adversely affect performance. Hence, Peters and O'Connor[8] have described situational resource variables relevant to performance. They contend that these variables are necessary for task performance, but that when their quality or quantity is restricted they constrain performance. These variables include:

1. *Job-related information* from various sources (supervisors, policies, peers, etc.) necessary to do the job.
2. *Tools and equipment* needed to perform assigned duties.
3. *Materials and supplies* needed to carry out the job.
4. *Budgetary support* including financial resources (phone calls, travel, wages and salaries of others who help accomplish the job, and so on) to complete the assignment.
5. *Required services and help from others.*
6. *Task preparation,* meaning the personal preparation, formal education, company training, and work experience relevant to the particular job.
7. *Time availability* to do the job taking into consideration meetings, interruptions, delays, etc.
8. *Work environment*—the physical aspects and surroundings of the job.

Many organizations have reduced performance constraints with innovative, but common-sense approaches to *work design.*

Pehr Gyllenhammer, president of Aktievolaget Volvo (a Swedish automobile manufacturer), reports success with a unique **work design,** combined with a participative management style and improved technology, that was instituted at his Kalmar plant. A hierarchy of works councils encourages worker participation in decision making and opens communications channels. Supervisors are trained to be information gatherers, aides to employees, teachers, and consultants, rather than bosses (environment encourages effort). The work is organized into teams, with each responsible for the assembly and inspection of a specified component of the car. The employees designed a job-rotation system that encourages individuals to learn all the jobs and lessens the monotony of repetitive tasks (improves skills). A carrier or conveyor incorporates a tilting device that eliminates the need to work on the underside of the cars from pits (technology to improve performance).[9]

At American Velvet, a small, family-owned textile firm in Stonington, Connecticut, worker participation is combined with a profit-sharing system.

The unionized employees feel that open communications is the key to making work-place reforms work. Employees are kept informed of the company's profitability, and they are encouraged to ask questions and recommend cost-saving changes.[10] Similar schemes have been adopted by Donnelly Mirrors of Holland, Michigan, where all 450 workers are salaried and belong to work teams; Lincoln Electric company, which operates an Incentive Management Program (profit sharing); and Ralston Purina Company, which consults with employees on job redesign ideas. The team approach helps provide a work environment that encourages effort and integrates formal and informal work structures. All these companies report positive productivity gains as a result of their job-reform efforts.[11] These schemes are not panaceas; there are just as many failures as successes. But these examples show that innovative approaches to employee motivation can be made to work.

PRODUCTIVITY IMPROVEMENT.   Motivation research suggests that high performance and productivity improvement is a function of basic, sound management practice. Factors like better planning, improved job procedures, improved communications, improved goal setting, better leadership, and improved technology are viewed as important to enhancing productivity.[12] Research on the utilization of human resources suggests that employees perform better when:

1. All tasks performed by employees are related to organizational objectives.
2. Most of the employees' work time is devoted to performing these tasks.
3. Employees are working at their maximum-skill levels.
4. The work environment encourages the high expenditure of effort by the majority of employees.
5. Work flow in each unit is structured to minimize wasted or duplicated effort.
6. There is an integration of formal and informal work structures and technology that improves task performance.[13]

In recent years productivity improvement has been motivated by **quality circles,** a practice copied from the Japanese. Quality circles consist of small groups of employees that meet regularly and are trained to detect and correct production problems in their areas. The functioning of the quality circles is relatively simple. A plant steering committee composed of management and labor (quality circles have also been formed when there is no union in the organization) decides which area of the organization would benefit from the services of a circle. Eight or ten employees make up a circle and meet once a week on company time with a personnel representative and the immediate supervisor. The personnel specialist trains the group on basic data gathering and analyzing techniques, management principles, and the basics of presenting their ideas to management. When a circle believes it has arrived at a solution to a problem, it makes its recommendations to management.

Benefits to both management and the employees are significant. One company felt it was getting at least a two-for-one return on the cost for maintaining its circle.[14] One manufacturer, for example, realized a $22,000 annual savings resulting from a circle's suggestion that a single worker come in 15 minutes early each morning to start up the machines. Even more impressive is the $636,000 a year savings that a purchasing department circle effected by recommending that suppliers who were shipping more than was requisitioned be informed that the company would either keep the extra materials (and not pay) or charge for returning the overage. General Motors's Tarrytown, New York, plant cited a marked reduction in employee grievances, a two-thirds decrease in absenteeism, less worker turnover, and a distinctly improved discipline situation as a result of its quality circles.[15] The productivity improvements that resulted from quality circles have prompted 65 companies (as of 1980) to start them. This is an increase over 1979, when there were only 15.[16]

Employees benefit, too. Many organizations give cash awards or shares in the additional profits resulting from the quality circles' suggestions. The satisfaction resulting from solving a work problem is considered a definite plus by the workers, who also appreciate the recognition they get from management for their efforts. "It gives you a feeling of accomplishment when a solution your circle thought up is enacted by management," exclaimed one circle participant. She said she felt rewarded because, "You feel you can put in your two cents worth."

Quality circles are an example of the quality of work life initiatives of many organizations which seek to create a work environment conducive to motivation.

QUALITY OF WORK LIFE (QWL) PROGRAMS.   QWL programs attempt to bring about fundamental changes in organizational and labor management relationships. Essentially, they attempt to innovate means for restructuring work in order to improve organizational effectiveness. Purposes of QWL programs vary from organization to organization. Some focus on productivity improvements, others are dedicated to the enhancement of work satisfaction and the personal development of employees, while others strive to harmonize labor-management relationships. Goodman[17] reported in 1980 that initially QWL programs experienced modest success, but many were discontinued over time. Perhaps some of the problem originated from organized labor's fears that the resulting improvements would manifest themselves in employee layoffs and that worker participation in QWL programs made them less inclined to join unions. Some programs were discontinued because of a lack of total management commitment coupled with a decrease in government financial support.

A recent study at Volvo concluded that there are certain criteria for the operation of a successful QWL program.

1. Redesign strategies must be unique to the organization and should not be copied from another.

2. When management has a true understanding of the local organization's characteristics there is a better chance of success.

3. There must be an active and positive management attitude toward change.

4. Management must be sensitive to the fact that the change process will affect social organizational levels.

5. Change requires freedom of action and time.

6. Management development will increase the capacity for change.

7. Change initiatives must come from the line and not from staff specialists.

8. The staff should serve as catalysts.

9. A multifaceted approach should be used. Delegation, job rotation, participative decision making, and other methods must be fully integrated with a system of joint consultation.

10. Many changes are undertaken spontaneously on the initiative of interested individuals.[18]

One observer of QWL programs concluded that to an assembly line worker quality of work life means good stock, fair treatment, and recognition as an individual. He contended, "What is extremely important for the company, the union, and the workers to understand [and it has become more obvious to me the more I have thought about the situation] is the need to deal with workers as human beings. Workers do not want something for nothing. Most people are interested in making a living; they want to come to work and be treated with the respect normally accorded to adults."[19] This quote perhaps points up the need of managers to be sensitive to employee values when considering methods and programs for gaining commitment.

EMPLOYEE VALUES AND THEIR EFFECT ON MOTIVATION

The programs we have been discussing represent the initiatives of organizations to overcome the deepening discontent of American workers as a consequence of changing employee values. A recent survey concluded that in the past 25 years employee values have changed and their dissatisfaction with their work situations has increased to the extent that management should be concerned.[20] For example, the study revealed that most employees feel their company is as good a place to work as it once was; they do not consider their treatment equitable, especially in terms of advancement; and they don't consider their companies to be responsive to their problems or complaints.

Redesign of work and QWL programs attempt to address this problem. Prior to initiating any formalized programs it might be wise to assess workers' values and attitudes. Then, programs can be tailored to accommodate these values and improve these attitudes.

Attitude surveys attempt to measure the perceptions of employees about various aspects of the organization at a given point in time. When they are conducted at regular intervals, trends can be detected. As an initial step in designing motivational programs it is a good idea to take a reading of employee attitudes toward the organization as a whole or toward any aspect of its operations (e.g., recent changes, quality of supervision, physical conditions). Those experienced with attitude surveys caution that they should not be undertaken unless management is prepared to address each of the issues and problems cited in the responses.

The author conducted an attitude survey for a client for the purpose of determining employee perceptions of the reorganization of the marketing function. The company's president agreed to report the results to the employees and discuss any indicated changes or improvements with them. The form, shown in Figure 4.2, was designed to include issues of special concern (changes brought about by the new marketing department) as well as questions to elicit opinions of specific work issues (supervision, opportunities for advancement, pay, etc.). The wording of the form was considered critical because we wanted all employees to understand the questions and interpret them the same way. So the form was tested on a sample of employees before conducting the survey.

In order to achieve the maximum possible response rate, employees in each department were assembled. In the meeting (on company time, of course) employees were asked to fill out the questionnaire (survey form) and they were provided *blank* envelopes to enclose their responses. This was done to preserve anonymity.

The responses were compiled by departments and the results were fed back to employees for their reactions and responses. Some responses were negative, but most of the problem areas were improved after top management discussed them with the employees and then took steps to make appropriate changes. In fact, one of the changes resulted in the removal of some key managers.

Not all attitude surveys are handled in this manner. Sometimes they are conducted by outside independent organizations, or by the company

Your answers to this survey will help us understand how our employees feel about the company and our effectiveness in working with people. It is completely anonymous. *YOU DO NOT HAVE TO PUT YOUR NAME ON THIS QUESTIONNAIRE.*

Directions: After reading each question, circle the letter (a), (b), (c), (d) or (e) next to the response you most closely agree with. Feel free to add any comments you wish.

1. How do you feel about the work you are doing?
   (a) Very pleased   (b) Somewhat pleased   (c) No feeling particularly one way or another   (d) Somewhat displeased   (e) Very displeased
   Comments: _____
   _____

2. How would you rate the fairness of the way employee promotions are handled?
   (a) They are very fair   (b) They are fair enough   (c) They need to improve a *great deal.*
   Comments: _____
   _____

3. How do you feel about your manager's handling of discipline?
   (a) He/she does this *very fairly*   (b) He/she does this *fairly*   (c) He/she is *about average* in this respect   (d) He/she does this *poorly*   (e) He/she does this *very poorly.*
   Comments: _____
   _____

4. How much trust and confidence do you have in your manager?
   (a) A great deal   (b) Quite a bit   (c) Some   (d) A little   (e) Very little or none
   Comments: _____
   _____

5. Do you know what is expected of you in your job?
   (a) I know *exactly* what is expected   (b) I have a very good idea of what is expected   (c) I have a fairly good idea of what is expected   (d) I have some idea of what is expected   (e) I don't know what is expected.
   Comments: _____
   _____

6. How do you feel about the cooperation between departments in the company?
   (a) Cooperation is excellent   (b) It could be improved   (c) There is no cooperation.
   Comments: _____

Figure 4.2
Employee Opinion Survey

Figure 4.2 (cont.)

7. Compared to last year, how do you feel about your job?
   (a) Improved a lot   (b) Improved some   (c) About the same   (d) Not as good   (e) Much worse
   Comments: _____
   _____

8. How free do you feel to tell your supervisor how you think?
   (a) Completely free   (b) Somewhat free   (c) Depends on *what* (the subject)   (d) *Not* free at all   (e) I'm afraid
   Comments: _____
   _____

9. Compared to last year, how do you feel about the Company?
   (a) I am proud to work here   (b) This is a pretty good place to work   (c) I am not sure   (d) It is not as good   (e) I wish I didn't work here.
   Comments: _____
   _____

10. How well do you understand the various fringe benefits provided by the Company?
    (a) Very well   (b) Fairly well   (c) Somewhat   (d) Not very well   (e) Not at all
    Comments: _____
    _____

11. Please complete this sentence:
    I think the Company's effectiveness in working with people could be improved if:
    _____
    _____

12. Any additional comments:
    _____
    _____
    _____

itself, usually the personnel department. Often, attitude surveys are conducted by mail, but then the low response rate (frequently less than 50%) becomes a problem.

There are other ways of measuring employee attitudes and values. Paper and pencil instruments have been used to develop profiles of group values so that they can be considered in assigning employees to supervision. Considering new breed values to be an important aspect of motivation, Jackson and Mindell suggest profiling employee values and management style as a means of matching up managers and work groups.[21]

It should be obvious from reading this section that leadership behavior has a significant influence on the work situation in creating a motivational environment. The supervisor or manager exercises leadership skills in getting employees to perform at their best. Let us see how this important skill affects employee behavior and how formalized leadership programs operate.

Leadership

The various theories of **leadership effectiveness** suggest that there is a relationship between *leadership style*[22] and productivity. But many variables may affect leadership efforts: the attitudes, personality, experiences, skills, and power of leaders; the nature of the group being led; and the particular circumstances (e.g., the pressures of full capacity operations versus slack production; strike conditions versus labor-management cooperation; economic boom versus depression). Our discussion of contingency theory in Chapter 2 underscored the concept that there is no prescribed method for handling personnel situations. Similarly, with leadership, the situational variables and their interactions are the determinants of leadership behavior and its effectiveness in getting employees to perform as expected.[23] Figure 4.3 presents a contingency model of leadership and illustrates the variables and their interactions that make up the leadership situation.

Various studies have attempted to demonstrate that there is a relationship between leadership style and employee productivity. The mixed results have led to a controversy about the viability of a particular style.

THE PARTICIPATION CONTROVERSY

Studies of participative-leadership approaches are not conclusive that productivity improves with an increase in work-group participation. Powell and Schlacter, for example, found that pay for performance must be tied to participative techniques for them to be effective.[24] (The various uses of pay as an incentive for performance are discussed in Chapter 18, "Compensation Management.")

Questioning 318 executives on their opinions of the characteristics of participative leadership, Larry Greiner found agreement among them that the participative approach was effective, but he also found differences in the approaches managers took to involve their people.[25] Greiner's study suggests that participative management be presented as a general model so that a variety of participative-leadership styles can be utilized to involve employees in the decision-making process. Whatever style one uses, it is important to recognize some of the inherent disadvantages of the participative approach.

Participative leadership is plagued with many of the disadvantages of group involvement. Conflicts are likely to occur, especially when diverse interests are present in a group. Consequently, a consensus may be the

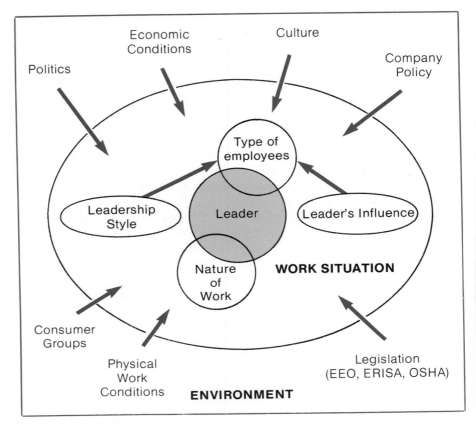

Figure 4.3
Contingency Model
of Leadership

product of the most vocal, but not necessarily the most knowledgeable, members. All this activity is time-consuming, may be frustrating to individuals in the group, and may not produce desired results. Also, when groups make decisions, if the desired outcome does not materialize, there is a tendency to pass the buck rather than accept responsibility. In addition, many managers do not use the participative model because they have neither the necessary skills nor the inclination. The boss-centered approach tends to yield quicker short-term results and confirms to employees the authority of the boss.[26]

A model worker-participation plan at General Foods Corporation's Topeka, Kansas, plant ran into trouble when management and staff personnel saw their positions threatened because the workers were performing well without needing any direction from their supervisors. Too many key decisions, the managers felt, were being made by workers, so the company's organization reverted to a traditional system.[27]

USING THE PARTICIPATIVE APPROACH SUCCESSFULLY

A survey of the highest ranking officers in seventy of the *Fortune* 500 companies on their opinions of participative leadership revealed that most of them favored this style, but few practiced it to any meaningful degree. Those who reported success with the participative technique seemed to employ the following guidelines.[28]

1. *Define objectives clearly.* Employees involved in decision making should know the group's goals. For instance, if a group is a production unit, its goal could be stated in terms of a certain number of units of production per unit of time, with a designated quality index. The employees then might decide how to accomplish the output given the resources of the group.

2. *Provide a system of rewards.* Especially with production situations, economic rewards must be tied to outcomes. If the production unit employees recognize that their efforts yield tangible rewards, naturally they will strive for optimum productivity. Other situations are not so clear-cut. The employees who restructured sales territories for an office products company, for instance, received rewards in the form of more equitable territories. The reward need not always be economic, but there must be a clearly defined outcome of the participative effort.

3. *Make groups accountable.* Companies that experienced success with a participative style suggested that decision-making groups be held accountable for their actions. When a grievance review board composed of union and management members rendered a decision on a grievance, each and every member of the board accepted the answer as if he had made it alone. And in the same vein, the group established reasonable time limits within which it agreed to operate. This self-imposed pressure helps ensure that problems are not stalled in endless debate and never reach an action stage.

4. *Ensure a receptive attitude on the part of top management.* Unless all key executives are convinced of the merits of participative leadership, efforts to involve employees are destined to failure. Lip service alone will not do. The hierarchy must be receptive to suggestions and recommendations from below; their willingness to adopt reasonable proposals is vital to the success of participative leadership. Results of this study clearly showed that most employee groups were limited to making recommendations. Respondents stated that group members become frustrated when their recommendations are not followed. By the same token, there must be

two-way communication; all recommendations should be listened to all the way up the ladder, and higher management's opinions of them should be fed back.

5. *Introduce gradually.*   Organizations cannot expect to move from autocratic management to participation over night. Although executives may be convinced of the validity of this modern style, the transition should occur gradually. A change to participative leadership will certainly be met with skepticism by those who had to function under the former style, and hard-nosed managers will resent having to reverse their approach; they would probably be totally incapable of performing the turnabout. Consequently, the participative style should be introduced gradually, preferably through training of both operative employees and managers.

SITUATIONAL APPROACHES TO LEADERSHIP

CONTINGENCY THEORY.   Situational or contingency leadership theory suggests that **leadership effectiveness** depends upon (is *contingent* upon) the leader's style, the type of work being performed under the leader's direction, the nature of the employees in the work group, and a host of other variables that impinge on the situation, for example, culture, economy, policy, and so on. Figure 4.3 illustrates these factors and their interactions. This theory states that leadership effectiveness varies according to the leader's style and situation. It suggests that task-oriented authoritarian leadership is most effective in situations that are either very favorable or very unfavorable to the leader. A favorable situation is one in which the leader's influence is high, relations with the work group are good, and the task is highly structured, such as machine operation. In an unfavorable situation the leader has little influence, relations are poor, and the task is unstructured and unpredictable, for example, sales. Situations of an intermediate tendency are better handled through more participative, people-oriented approaches.[29]

In his study of 260 senior managers of fifteen large American companies, Frank A. Heller concluded that the extent of power sharing (participation) between bosses and subordinates was contingent upon the job situation.[30] He also found that managers do not employ one particular influence/power style in different situations. Similarly, Woodward found that technology and the nature of the process (batch, continuous flow, etc.) also affected leadership style.[31]

APPLIED LEADERSHIP.   Organizations have devised formal leadership programs to elicit and maintain a high level of employee commitment. In this section we discuss the process of **organizational development** as an example of applied participative leadership.

Organizational development (OD) attempts to bring about organizational change and effectiveness by involving employees in problem solving and planning. OD depends on the support of employees who understand how the manager wants to change. It is a continuous and overall effort that increases organizational effectiveness by integrating individual desires for growth with organizational goals. Managers systematically plan and implement change by sharing power. Specifically, OD locates problem solving as close to the grass roots as possible, builds trust and creates harmony through collaboration, encourages employees' self-direction and self-regulation, and introduces a system to reward the attainment of individual and organization goals.[32]

Formal processes are implemented in OD to create social conditions that encourage employee contribution to organizational objectives. Such methods include: team building activities, such as intradepartmental problem solving meetings; intergroup sessions to discuss changes or to work out common concerns; action research involving data gathering; corrective action, and feedback; training programs, such as laboratory (sensitivity) training; development of specific skills such as decision making, or development of positive attitudes; feedback on survey responses; and activities among groups for problem resolution or training.

Several years ago an eastern hospital implemented an OD system that contained many of the elements described here. Initially, it conducted a dialogue between management and employees to gain both commitment to and involvement in the program. The hospital used a paper and pencil instrument as a vehicle for measuring participants' perceptions on how their department looked the previous year, its present state, and a realistic assessment of future expectations. Next, management and supervisory personnel were brought together in an intensive four-day seminar on personnel and organizational development which focused on team-building and behavioral skills. Then questionnaires and interviews were used to collect data about the organization. The information gained from this process formed the basis of a report to management listing problem areas and their causes, and recommendations for change. Finally, OD teams of employee representatives from major job classifications and first-line supervisors developed an action plan that identified problem areas and recommended cost-effective strategies to improve operations. Involvement of the organization's resources was the key to the process.

Communication

Effective leadership and motivation depend on communications for their effectiveness. In leading the work group and creating an environment conducive to motivation, managers issue instructions, listen to problems and suggestions, and exchange ideas and feelings. Progressive organizations provide training for their managers in these skills. (For a discussion of management training, see Chapter 14.)

Communication is the means of exchanging information, ideas, feelings, and attitudes among people within an organization to coordinate activities and channel personnel toward common objectives. Day-to-day supervision of employees requires continuous, effective communication. The decisions resulting from situational analyses are translated into action through proper communication. And the policies, programs, and procedures needed to direct the efforts of human resources call for accurate communication so that these can be effectively implemented. The personnel department plays a key role in seeing that employees and managers are kept informed of policy changes and relevant developments in the organization. This section will cover the principles of effective communication and the specific methods for getting information to employees and soliciting their inputs and responses.

PRINCIPLES OF EFFECTIVE COMMUNICATION

Effective communication depends on the sending of a clear message, the consideration of a receiver's reaction(s) to the message as well as the basic principles of the process. The following principles incorporate techniques that can help make communication effective.

FEEDBACK.   The single most important aspect of communication is **feedback.** It is the reaction from those receiving a message that can be used by the sender to evaluate the message. In one-way communication, which lacks feedback, senders have little assurance that their message was received, and receivers can place little reliance on its validity.

In the military, a standing joke is that enlisted men have the last word—"Yes, sir." Orders are a form of one-way communication; troops are conditioned to respond without hesitation to the orders of their commander—an absolute necessity in battle. But to make one-way communication work, a lot of two-way communication—and a fair amount of discipline too—goes into the training of troops. In industrial settings employees are disinclined to obey orders barked at them. Without dialogue, there is little hope that an intended action will result. Feedback not only confirms for senders that information is accurately received, but it also makes receivers confident that their action or behavior is correct.

A number of techniques will elicit feedback. Observing facial expressions in face-to-face communication enables communicators to determine whether receivers are paying attention and whether they understand the information being conveyed. Asking recipients to repeat or summarize a message ensures that it was received correctly and also reinforces it. Also, having receivers demonstrate the application of a message (instructions) guarantees that the communication was understood.

SIMPLICITY.   A good rule of communication is to keep it simple. Simplicity helps ensure understanding. Muddled, obscure, and complex communication usually results in misunderstandings and a failure to respond as intended. Recipients of confusing or complex messages rarely respond enthusiastically. Articulate messages are clear, relevant, and appropriate to a situation and particularly to those receiving them. When receivers clearly understand a message as it was sent, it is usually because it was simple.

MULTIMEDIA.   The more senses a message can appeal to, the more likely it is to be received and acted upon. Oral media combined with written methods have proven more effective than either used alone. When a message can be heard, seen, and experienced (through touch or smell for example), the impact is even greater. The power of multimedia communication is demonstrated in the following example. In an arbitration hearing over a disputed job classification, a company spokesman was attempting to prove that there was a substantial difference in the skills required to operate a forklift hoist and those needed for an overhead crane. The company had taken great pains to describe the operation of each piece of equipment, and the arbitrator was supplied with the respective job descriptions. To dramatize the difference in the equipment, the company had the arbitrator operate the forklift hoist by loading metal bars into a bin six feet off the ground. Next, the arbitrator was taken to the cab of the overhead crane, 40 feet off the ground. After a very short ride, the difference in skill requirements became obvious to the slightly shaken arbitrator, and the company won its case.

SENSITIVITY.   Sensitivity to the feelings and reactions of others certainly enhances communication effectiveness. When communicators empathize—put themselves in other people's places—they can understand them better and are more likely to be understood in return. Especially today, when the labor force contains workers of diverse backgrounds, values, cultures, and feelings, communicators' sensitivity to the world of the receivers is critical.

The increased number of women at work has given rise to a sensitivity to statements that might offend them. Communication barriers are formed between a male employee and the modern woman who has been sensitized to respond negatively to what she may interpret as a sexist statement. Remarks that stereotype women, imply that a female's appearance is more important than her credentials, or imply subservience are likely to be ill received. Hence the statement, "That's a good job for a woman" or "Take your coat off so I can see what you look like" (to a job applicant) would be considered sexist or in poor taste.[33]

LISTENING.   An important part of feedback is **listening**. In fact, without it, there can be no feedback. But most people are poor listeners, even though they are often good talkers. After several weeks of negotiations, union and management representatives had worked out the terms of a new contract for workers at a large transistor plant. But the two sides could not agree on the language of the contract. Union representatives claimed that it was intended to humiliate the union, while management insisted that they refused to be a party to a face-saving whitewash of labor. After another week of fruitless argument, the workers went on strike. Perhaps the differences could have been narrowed, if not resolved, had each party made more of an effort to listen to the basis for the other side's demands.

Listening skills can be sharpened. Good listeners conscientiously encourage other people to talk. They ask questions and probe for answers. And people respond eagerly, because they know they're being heard. Good listeners affirm their interest and understanding by restating the speakers' feelings. They might say, "You seem to feel strongly about . . ." or "You think this will happen if. . . ." Furthermore, they exercise patience. Rather than talk to fill a moment of silence, they may pause to give someone else a chance to say something. Finally, skillful listeners hear with a third ear. That is, not only do they hear the words that are spoken, but they understand the connotations, feelings, and emotions that are expressed with them. Listening is indeed an art; it must be carefully nurtured.

As an arbitrator of union-management grievances, the author is paid to listen. The parties (labor union representatives and management representatives) present oral arguments. Not only do these representatives debate an issue, but witnesses tell (they testify) facts about the case. Our job is to form an opinion about which side is right. Because eye movement and body language can say more than the words spoken, a witness who looks at the floor when answering a critical question will lose credibility. Voice inflection, too, may give meaning to what is being said. Words spoken loudly might be a reflection of the witness's anger or short temper while the same words spoken calmly could have a different meaning. Through many years of *listening* to grievances we develop an ability to gain an understanding of and a sensitivity for the issues behind the issue.

COMMUNICATION IN PRACTICE

A constant flow of information and feedback up, down, and across an organization can go a long way toward accomplishing objectives. Some of the current vehicles for communicating with employees are outlined below.

GRIEVANCE PROCEDURES.   Progressive organizations, whether union-ized or not, encourage employees to express their complaints, questions, or job problems; insist they be given a fair hearing; and give them a timely answer. Such **grievance procedures** should also contain some basis for appeal above employees' immediate superiors. Though the basic approach is similar in all grievance procedures, companies usually title them differently (Speak Up, Open-Door Policy, and Operation Feedback are examples).

Xerox Corporation utilizes a formal open-door policy that allows em-ployees to appeal complaints as high as they feel they need to. Employees are asked to put their complaints in writing and present them to their supervisor first. The company strives to make a thorough, expeditious, and objective assessment of all complaints, identify their cause, investigate cor-rective action, and render a prompt answer to the employee.[34]

And, at the Bank of America even frivolous complaints are heard at any level of the Let's Talk It Over program.[35]

MEETINGS WITH EMPLOYEES.   Employee discussion groups or open meetings, in which employees or their representatives (selected by manage-ment) are encouraged to express their problems and concerns, often facilitate upward communication. At General American Life Insurance Company, for example, RAPP (reach-all-people-promptly) sessions serve as listening posts for top management.[36] Delta Air Lines reverses the process by sending top managers (senior vice presidents for operations and personnel) to quarterly employee question-and-answer sessions.[37] And at Norton Company, a major abrasives manufacturer, specially trained workers serve as in-plant counselors to listen to employee problems and make recommendations to someone in management who can solve them.[38]

A client of mine (head of a middle-sized manufacturing company) has established Employee Discussion Groups (EDGs). Each department su-pervisor holds monthly discussions with his or her employees. Managers and supervisors have been trained to stimulate upward communication so that EDG participants feel free to express their feelings and concerns. Then once a quarter, representatives from each department are selected to attend a session with the company president. These representatives express the group's concerns and get a response from the president. The representatives then report back to their group the results of the meeting. These dialogues between the employees and managers make for an open communication system.

BULLETIN BOARDS.   Bulletin boards are an effective means of dissem-inating announcements and news of an immediate nature. Also, to keep employees informed, companies post reminders and information concerning plant rules on bulletin boards.

READING RACKS.   Racks contain pamphlets of general and personal interest and may occasionally include basic company information. Reading material covering a wide variety of subjects is readily accessible in racks and can provide entertainment during off hours. It can influence employees on a social, political, or economic issue, or inform them about a particular subject.

HOUSE ORGANS.   Company newspapers and magazines used to inform employees of the organization's plans and activities are useful communication channels. House organs also include articles of personal and local interest.

COMMUNICATION AND CONFLICT

Conflict and differences of opinion arise in healthy, dynamic organizations. As a matter of fact, such differences can aid progress and innovation. But unresolved conflict can impede progress and may prove dysfunctional. Communication plays a key role in making conflict constructive. An entire chapter (Chapter 12) is devoted to union-management conflict resolution, so our remarks here will be limited to the specific use of communication in managing conflict situations.

Communication-related conflict stems from a variety of sources, some of which are described below.

AMBIGUITY.   Vague and complex communication causes misunderstandings and uncertainties. An ambiguous directive creates conflict when people do not fully understand its meaning and they read into it what they want. Clearly, simply written directives that are straightforward in their spelling out of responsibility minimize the possibility of misunderstandings that lead to conflict.

PERCEPTUAL DIFFERENCES.   When one employee perceives that another is out to get him, a conflict can arise. Dissimilar groups (black-white, young-old, line-staff, union-management) tend to develop misconceptions about each other. Huseman[39] suggests that resolution can best be achieved through problem solving sessions which enable the conflicting parties to see broader opportunities for resolution. Frequently, keeping both groups informed and involved in the organization can stimulate cooperation. Hacon[40] suggests communication training to alleviate conflict caused by perceptual differences. He maintains that this type of training will help modify opinions and attitudes that may hinder understanding between the opposing parties. Kahn[41] espouses an approach he labels "making the system work," which utilizes group communication to clarify role structure and clear up irrational sources of conflict. Then he suggests the institution of training groups outside the organization's influence.

ROLE CONFLICT. Role conflict occurs when there are multiple reporting relationships, especially within large organizations. Role conflict can be prevented by providing policies to those who might become involved in a conflict situation. For instance, if an employee receives orders from multiple sources, the extent of conflict will depend upon the degree to which the orders are incompatible. A clear policy can guide the employee in determining which demand should take precedence. If this same policy has also been communicated to the demand makers, the probability of conflict will be substantially reduced. In addition, managers might hold frequent communication and review meetings with those whose positions are likely to expose them to role conflicts.[42]

SUPERVISOR-EMPLOYEE. Supervisor-employee conflicts arise out of many sources. Personality clashes, the boss feeling threatened by the employee ("He's out to get my job"), a lack of respect for each other, unclear organizational goals, and many others. Such conflicts can often be overcome through open communication. If the supervisor can make the employee feel he or she wants to help, supports development, recognizes accomplishments, discusses goals and performance standards, gives feedback on how he or she is doing, keeps the employee informed of new developments, and welcomes suggestions and criticism, trust and cooperation are likely to ensue.

Cost-Benefit Analysis

The results of motivational programs are measurable. Productivity trends can be measured in terms of efficiency ratios (cases per employee produced or distributed; ton/miles per work hour of mineral that is mined, milled, smelted, refined; the number of units produced compared to a standard or quota). One could also compare readings of absenteeism, turnover, and complaints filed before and after the program was instituted. QWL benefits can be measured similarly, but surveys of employee opinions can yield an indication of their perceptions of the program's effectiveness. Leadership effectiveness manifests itself in cost savings which can be ascertained from cost accounting records. Such savings as decreased downtime, lower scrappage, fewer quality defects result from effective leadership. Communication benefits manifest themselves in better informed and educated employees. Attitude survey responses and employee discussion groups provide a vehicle for ascertaining the degree of satisfaction with communication. Also, the degree of understanding of company policy between top and lower level managers can be determined by asking each level for its interpretation

of a particular policy. When the interpretations are different, or even opposite, communication is lacking.

Costs of motivation and commitment programs are the employee,
staff, and management time to train employees and work with them in
groups. Materials, supplies, and physical facilities to conduct these programs
also represent costs. Salary increases, profit shares, bonuses, and suggestion
awards are cost items, too.

Summary

The new generation of employees, no longer content to work for
monetary reward alone, seeks jobs that are relevant and challenging. Their
performance effectiveness is a function of motivation, leadership, and
communication.

Motivation is viewed as goal directed behavior and is a highly complex
phenomenon. Organizations create work environments conducive to motivation and job satisfaction. Work is enriched through the inclusion of
motivation factors. Productivity improvement is emphasized in quality circles,
which analyze work problems and present ideas to management. And quality
of work life programs attempt to innovate means for restructuring work so
that organizational effectiveness will be improved. Changing values of workers and their rising discontent make it incumbent upon management to
survey employee attitudes, assess the responses, and strive to correct deficiencies. In gaining employee commitment, leadership becomes a determinant of personnel performance, because leaders can provide factors in the
work environment that help to satisfy needs and goals. They can also stimulate employees' desires to achieve. The effectiveness elicited by leaders
depends to a large degree upon their style of leadership and their attitude
toward people. Leadership effectiveness is a function of a leader's style, the
characteristics of a work group, and the nature of the task(s) being performed.
In applying leadership principles organizations devise programs that involve
employees in problem solving and planning. Participative approaches are
encompassed in programs of organizational development.

Communication is closely allied to leadership in attaining high performance. Job information must be communicated to employees, and there
must be feedback to evaluate results. But the communication process requires
a conscientious effort to overcome barriers. To ensure that information is
received as it was transmitted, communicators must keep messages simple,
obtain feedback to ascertain understanding by recipients, and utilize the
proper media for transmission. Truly skilled communicators are also good
listeners, a rare talent among human beings. Personnel departments implement communication through employee meetings, house organs, bulletin

boards, reading racks, and programs to encourage employees to express their complaints and offer suggestions. But poor communication can cause conflict, just as clear and accurate communication can reduce or rectify it.

Key Terms

motivation	organizational development
job enrichment	communication
work design	feedback
quality circles	listening
attitude surveys	grievance procedures
leadership effectiveness	conflict

Review Questions

1. Define motivation and show how individual behavior is influenced by personal needs or desires.

2. What are the variables that affect leadership effectiveness?

3. Discuss the pros and cons of a participative-leadership style.

4. Describe the communication process.

5. What are four methods for implementing upward communication in an organization?

Discussion Questions

1. In every work group there is a wide range of individual motives at work. How can managers accommodate individual differences and still be effective as group leaders?

2. One of the criticisms leveled at achievement-motivation is that an economic setback would deny high achievers the means to demonstrate their newly learned abilities. What arguments could you advance to counter this statement?

3. The nature of work groups influences their leaders' effectiveness. What effects (positive and negative) can each of the following have on leadership effectiveness in a work group?

   a. A union

   b. Highly creative work

   c. Assembly-line operation

   d. Friendly, congenial work atmosphere

   e. What the company's product is critical to (Use national defense as one example.)

4. Companies seek to motivate employees to perform more effectively and increase production. If higher productivity is realized, eventually fewer workers will be needed, and the very employees who were instrumental in attaining these goals will be laid off. Assuming that workers recognize this eventuality, what can management do to motivate them to continue to perform effectively? What form should communication on this subject take?

5. Do you think that informal communications channels such as rumors and the grapevine represent a failure on the part of management to communicate? Why or why not? What measures can managers take to minimize the negative impact of informal communications channels and yet utilize them to advance the organization's objectives?

A major aerospace company once got into very deep trouble on a major space probe contract. Work quality was erratic and a key engineering division was falling months behind schedule in doing certain highly technical design work, causing the whole project to drop far behind schedule. NASA was so concerned that it threatened to cancel the contract for cause, which it could do, given the record.

The manager of this division had an excellent record for getting the work out, and his superior was puzzled as to what was happening. For this project, he had hired over 600 highly trained engineers, so manpower quality was obviously not the issue. But the boss was in a spot, so he transferred his seasoned manager and brought in a younger engineer to supervise the division.

Nothing much happened for a few weeks, and then productivity began to take off. Within a month the division was ahead of schedule. The company eventually won the highest commendation from NASA for outstanding performance. Yet the changes did not cost the company anything. Actually, it saved money, because only 500 engineers were needed to do three times as much work.

The younger engineer who had accomplished all of this once explained how he did it:

"This division had been a bunch of draftsmen historically, and it was structured that way. All 600 engineers came to work at 7 A.M., punched a time clock, and went to work in a huge hangar-like room. The big-boss's desk was actually on a two-foot platform at one end, overlooking everyone. No one could leave the room without permission, and ten minute coffee breaks occurred every two hours. If an engineer did not get back to his desk on time, he was docked. Turnover was enormous, averaging 15 percent per month, so projects lost continuity as people left.

"I took a close look at who left, and it was obvious that all the good people left first. The ones who liked working this way and stayed were typically pretty unimaginative. So all I did was to get rid of the time clock and build partitions all over the place so that various engineers were in small offices where no one could see them, in groups of from one to five depending on the job. I got off the podium myself and hid out in a small office back in a corner.

"People still kept quitting, but now these were the unimaginative ones. We didn't replace them, because the others began to go to work. The ex-manager forgot that he was dealing with a group of very responsible and well-educated professionals, not a bunch of semi-literate manual workers. When I made professionals professionally responsible, I got superb work.

"I also got increases in absenteeism, tardiness, and lots of goofing off, which drove my boss crazy. But productivity kept going up, since the engineers could easily take up the slack."

Case Problem 1

OVERPAID AND UNDERWORKED

Problems

1. How could such simple changes make any difference to professionals?

2. What work environment would you prefer—the old or the new one in this situation? Why?

3. Does the educational and professional level of employees matter when considering work rules and conditions? Why?

Case Problem 2

DIRECTING AND MOTIVATING THE INDIVIDUAL

For each of the individual cases discussed here, specify and justify the following:

1. The dominant technique and pattern of manager-employee relationship that would be best for directing and leading the individual—for example, consultative (participative), autocratic (authoritarian), or free-rein.

2. Select from the following and list in order of importance the three conditions or inducements that you feel would be most likely to motivate each individual to better performance:

   a. Threat of discharge

   b. Raise in salary

   c. More fringe benefits

   d. Less supervision

   e. More recognition for achievement

   f. More status—for example, title, own office

   g. Group profit-sharing plan

   h. Individual incentive plan

   i. More participation in managerial decisions

   j. Job enlargement—for example, opportunity for creativity, wider range of activities

Case A

Alice Brown is office manager for a medium-sized firm. She is 41, unmarried, and lives in a downtown apartment. She has been office manager for three years, and she earns about $29,200 per year. She started in the mailroom and has been with the company for nearly 20 years.

Case B

John Gordon is technical director in a major division of a large aerospace firm working on technology for the space shuttle. He is 33, married, and has four children, whose ages are eleven, eight, five, and four. He is currently earning about $42,500 per year. He lives in Newport Beach, a fairly plush community near Los Angeles. John Gordon has been with the company for about nine years; he started as an engineer at a salary of about $9,500. Within four years, he became chief engineer in his division; last year, he was promoted to his present position. He has a master's degree in aeronautical engineering.

Case C

Jack (Red) Smith is an insurance investigator for a company whose main line is automobile insurance. He is 58 years old, widowed, and has three married children. His annual salary is about $25,000 per year. He has been with this company for 11 years. Previously, he worked for two other insurance companies—as an investigator in one and as a salesman in the other.

Case D

Lila Ray is West Coast sales manager for a perfume company. She was transferred two years ago from the midwestern region where she was a sales manager for one year. Prior to this, she was a salesperson with the company's Detroit office for two years; and before that, she was a salesperson with a major competing firm for three years. Her present basic salary is $26,500; for her previous job, it was $21,000. She also gets a percentage override on the total sales for her region. Last year, this came to an additional $6,000. This amount was considerably more than she ever earned from this source as midwestern sales manager. Lila Ray is 36, married, and has three children, who are 13, 11, and 8 years old. She lives in a large rented house for $625 a month.

Case E

Pat O'Brien is a welder with a company that manufactures pipes and plumbing fixtures. He is 63, married, and has six grown children, four of whom are married. He has been with the company as a welder for 31 years. His basic salary is $13,500; however, with overtime work, he usually earns an additional $1,500 to $2,500 annually.

Case F

Richard Ryder is assistant purchasing agent for a small machine tool company. He is 27. He started with the company four years ago as a shipping clerk. After one year, he became a material requisition clerk; last year, he assumed his present position under Tom Garvey, the purchasing agent, who is 42 years old. Richard Ryder is now earning about $12,500 per year. He is getting married next month.

Case G

Howard Fredman is a research chemist for a large chemical company. Upon graduating with a B.S. degree from a leading university three years ago, he joined this company. He is 25, married, and has no children. His present annual salary is $20,100.

Case H

Sandra Priestly is vice president of finance for a large airline. She is 53, married, and has one married daughter and two sons who attend Yale University. Before she was married, her daughter was one of the debutantes at the major coming-out ball in the city. Sandra Priestly has held this position with the company for seven years. Her current salary is $82,000 per year. Top-level executives of this company share in company profits through a bonus system. The size of bonus payments is linked to the base salary of the top executives. The base salary for the president is $95,000; for the vice presidents of operations and sales, the figures are $75,000 and $65,000, respectively.

Notes

1. Victor H. Vroom, *Work and Motivation* (New York: John Wiley, 1964), p. 6.

2. Bernard Berelson and Gary A. Steiner, *Human Behavior* (New York: Harcourt Brace and World, 1964), p. 240.

3. Saul W. Gellerman, *Motivation and Productivity* (New York: American Management Association, 1963), p. 7.

4. R. H. Sanford and L. S. Wrightsman, Jr., *Psychology* (Belmont, Calif.: Brooks/Cole, 1970), p. 189.

5. Richard M. Steers and Lyman W. Porter, *Motivation and Work Behavior* (New York: McGraw-Hill, 1975), pp. 8–9.

6. Frederick B. Herzberg, *Work and the Nature of Man* (New York: McGraw-Hill, 1966).

7. Frederick B. Herzberg, "Maximizing Work and Minimizing Labor," *Industry Week*, September 15, 1980, pp. 61–64.

8. Lawrence H. Peters and Edward J. O'Connor, "Situational Constraints and Work Outcomes: The Influences of a Frequently Overlooked Construct," *The Academy of Management Review*, July 1980, pp. 391–397.

9. Pehr G. Gyllenhammer, "How Volvo Adapts Work to People," *Harvard Business Review*, July–August 1977, pp. 102ff.

10. Paul Dickson, "Humanizing the Work Place," *MBA* March 1975, pp. 31ff.

11. Ibid.

12. See Mildred E. Katzell, *Productivity: The Measure and the Myth* (New York: AMACOM, 1975), p. 12; and Greg R. Oldham, "The Motivational Strategies Used by Supervisors: Relationships to Effectiveness Indicators," *Organizational Behavior and Human Performance*, February 1976, pp. 66–86.

13. Edward J. Giblin and Oscar A. Ornati, "Optimizing the Utilization of Human Resources," *Organizational Dynamics*, Autumn 1976, pp. 18–33.

14. "U.S. Firms Worried by Productivity Lag, Copy Japan in Seeking Employees' Advice," *The Wall Street Journal*, Thursday, February 21, 1980, p. 48.

15. "Stunning Turnaround at Tarrytown," *Time*, May 5, 1980, p.87.

16. *Wall Street Journal*, p. 48.

17. Paul S. Goodman, "Quality of Work Life Projects in the 1980's," *Proceedings of the 1980 Spring Meeting of the Industrial Relations Research Association* (April 16–18, 1980), pp. 487–494.

18. Berth Jonsson, "Corporate Approaches to the Quality of Work Life: A Personnel Journal Conference Report," *Personnel Journal*, August 1980, pp. 632–638.

19. John F. Runcie, "'By Days I Make The Cars'," *Harvard Business Review*, May–June, 1980, p. 115.

20. M. R. Cooper, et al., "Changing Employee Values: Deepening Discontent?" *Harvard Business Review*, January–February 1979, pp. 117–125.

21. Lauren Hite Jackson and Mark G. Mindell, "Motivating the New Breed," *Personnel*, March–April 1980, pp. 53–61.

22. For discussion of leadership style see: Douglas T. McGregor, *The Human Side of Enterprise* (New York: McGraw-Hill, 1960); Renis Likert and William C. Pyle, "Human Resource Accounting: A Human Organizational Measurement Approach," *Financial Analysts Journal*, January–February, 1971, pp. 75–84; and Robert Blake and Jane Mouton, *The New Managerial Grid* (Houston, Texas: Gulf Publishing, 1978).

23. Contingency leadership writings

include: Fred E. Fiedler, *A Theory of Leadership Effectiveness* (New York: McGraw-Hill, 1967); Frank A. Heller, *Management Decision Making* (London: Tavistock, 1971); Joan Woodward, *Industrial Organization: Theory and Practice* (London, Oxford University Press, 1965), pp. 39ff.; Victor H. Vroom and Philip W. Yetton, *Leadership and Decision Making* (Pittsburgh, Pa.: University of Pittsburgh Press, 1973); and Robert J. House, "A Path-Goal Theory of Leader Effectiveness," *Administrative Science Quarterly*, September 1971, pp. 324ff.

24. Reed M. Powell and John L. Schlacter, "Participative Management: A Panacea?" *Academy of Management Journal*, June 1971, pp. 165–73.

25. Larry E. Greiner, "What Managers Think of Participative Leadership," *Harvard Business Review*, March–April 1973, pp. 111–17.

26. Donald P. Crane, "The Case for Participative Management," *Business Horizons*, April 1976, p. 16.

27. "Stonewalling Plant Democracy," *Business Week*, March 28, 1977, p. 78.

28. Crane, "The Case for Participative Management," p. 20.

29. Fred E. Fiedler, *A Theory of Leadership Effectiveness* (New York: McGraw-Hill, 1967).

30. Frank A. Heller, *Managerial Decision Making* (London: Tavistock, 1971).

31. Joan Woodward, *Industrial Organizations: Theory and Practice* (London: Oxford University Press, 1965), pp. 39ff.

32. For detailed information about OD see: W. Warner Burke, editor, *The Cutting Edge: Current Theory and Practice in Organizational Development* (La Jolla, Calif.: University Associates, Inc., 1978).

33. Betsy Stevens, "Improving Communication with Clerical Workers: The Non-Sexist Directive," *Personnel Journal*, April 1977, pp. 170–72.

34. The Conference Board, *Non-Union Complaint Systems: A Corporate Appraisal*, Conference Board Report #770 (New York: The Conference Board, 1980), p. 12.

35. An interview with A. W. Clausen, "Listening and Responding to Employees' Concerns," *Harvard Business Review*, January–February, 1980, p. 104.

36. John R. Huntley, "Listening Posts," *Personnel*, July–August 1976, pp. 39–43.

37. "Delta's Flying Money Machine," *Business Week*, May 9, 1977, p. 88.

38. "Norton Delegates Personnel Affairs to the Workers," *International Management*, June 1975, pp. 48ff.

39. Richard C. Huseman, "Interpersonal Conflict in the Modern Organization," in Huseman et al., *Readings in Interpersonal and Organizational Communication*, 2nd ed. (Boston: Holbrook Press, 1972), p. 193.

40. R. J. Hacon, *Conflict and Human Relations Training* (Oxford: Paragon Press, 1965).

41. Robert H. Kahn and Elise Boulding (eds.), *Power and Conflict in Organizations* (New York: Basic Books, Inc., 1964), pp. 75–76.

42. Robert J. House, "Role Conflict and Multiple Authority in Complex Organizations," *California Management Review*, Summer 1970, pp. 53–60.

Section Two

ACQUIRING HUMAN RESOURCES

An organization can only be as effective as the people who run it. Personnel effectiveness at all levels depends upon the skills of employees who are dedicated to a common purpose. Acquiring human resources involves forecasting and locating required skills and placing individuals where their talents can be utilized most effectively.

Through planning, the human resource needs of an organization are forecast. Job analysis is then utilized to identify the relevant duties, skills, and requirements of each job to be filled. Recruitment, selection, and placement programs emanate from human-resource plans. Through these, the personnel staff tries to select the best available people and place them in jobs for which they are best suited.

Testing and interviewing can be aids to acquiring human resources. It is important to note that Equal Employment Opportunity guidelines require that selection devices be specifically job-related and that they not be used to exclude any category of people, for example, blacks, women, or the handicapped.

Chapter Five
Human Resource Planning and Recruiting

Manufacturing's going to have to beef up its engineering complement if we take on the Corson project.

I wonder if we have the talent to staff the reorganization.

If we do go public we'll have to get more depth in management.

We have three years to be in compliance. Somehow or other we need to find women and minorities who can move up fast!

These quotes typify concerns that executives express for anticipating future personnel requirements, and finding and developing people to staff their organizations. In response, human resource planners project the size and composition of the work force for the future. The organization then trains employees to fill many of the forecasted vacancies and, when internal resources are insufficient, recruiters acquire outside personnel. Although there appears to be only limited use of formal, human resource planning programs in organizations today, there is definitely a heightened interest and the trend is toward a significant growth in these programs in the near future.[2]

Human Resource Planning

The basic purpose of planning in personnel management is to select courses of action best suited to meet objectives. More specifically, human resource planning has been defined as "the process by which an organization ensures that it has the right number of people and the right kind of people, at the right places, at the right time, doing things for which they are eco-

LEARNING OBJECTIVES

1. To know the components of human resource planning.
2. To be familiar with the basic techniques of forecasting and the tools for human resource planning.
3. To know the Equal Employment Opportunity legislative requirements for recruiting.
4. To be able to cite the various recruiting sources and to be familiar with the recruiting process.
5. To know how affirmative action relates to the planning and recruiting processes.

nomically most useful.''[3] This definition may be a bit broad, although human resource planning does involve anticipating needs and implementing plans. But the education and development programs implicit in this definition, though interwoven with human resource planning, are separate and distinct. This planning process contains two basic components: the total needs of an organization and the number and qualifications of employees available internally. The difference between these components constitutes the recruiting need. In this chapter we shall discuss the use of **forecasts** to determine *total human resource needs* and the methods used to determine availability of the *right kinds of people internally,* for example, skills inventories and career plans. The discussion here focuses on private-sector (nongovernmental) planning programs. Federal programs such as the Comprehensive Employment and Training Act (CETA) are broader in scope and are concerned with more than planning (CETA covers training, placement, and related activities). (Government manpower programs will be discussed with training and development in Chapter 13.)

   Recruiting acquires individuals with the necessary skills, but because many talents are scarce, organizations must often develop their own human resources. This takes time; therefore managers, with the assistance of the personnel staff, must anticipate requirements so that resources are available when needed. The lead time between acquisition and actual need enables organizations to train their talent. This concept, of course, is theoretical, because it assumes that organizations can accurately predict human resource requirements and locate and develop the requisite skills. Nevertheless, the scarcer the skill, the greater the need to anticipate its requirement. For example, with the tremendous emphasis now placed on preserving the environment, organizations are competing for pollution-control experts. These specialists are a scarce resource, and firms that have anticipated this need are more likely to acquire them. Human resource planning has other advantages. With the current emphasis on attainment of **affirmative action** goals, organizations plan career paths that facilitate the upward movement of minorities and women in all areas of an organization (see Chapters 15 and 17). Affirmative action policies have had more direct influence on planning and recruitment than any other single influence in recent times. Human resource planning also provides a basis for controlling labor costs; it insures that people are in positions best suited to contribute to the fulfillment of objectives. Finally, this planning process supports the retention of desirable employees. Because plans are future-oriented, they make managers aware of organizational changes so that promotional opportunities can be discussed with capable employees who might otherwise be lured away by other employers.

Human resource planning is not without its problems. It requires forecasting—the prediction of future manpower needs, though experience has shown that the longer the period predicted, the less accurate the prediction is. Further complications can arise because there are many variables beyond a firm's control. During the planning period, major economic conditions can change; business cycles, fluctuations in the supply of labor, and changes in prices and interest rates affect human resource planning, but are difficult to anticipate. Furthermore, sophisticated planning processes are expensive.

Most organizations take an informal approach to estimating future needs through periodic checks with department heads. The larger organizations that use a formal approach employ the services of planning departments. But this function is too broad to be carried out exclusively by a specialized human resource planning unit. The personnel department plays a central role in the process, and line and staff managers at all levels are involved in formulating and implementing human resource plans.

The importance of such planning is borne out in the following situation, which occurred at the national headquarters of a major religious group. This denomination had decided to restructure its organization in order to mobilize its members more effectively. The new organization was conceptually sound; it eliminated duplicate efforts and provided a vehicle for efficient functioning. However, insufficient attention was paid to planning needs for people: job requirements were not adequately detailed, there was little advance preparation to find and develop candidates, and budget recommendations were made too late to provide funds for the positions. Consequently, results were less than satisfactory. Incumbents, anxious to know what their status in the new organization would be, showed signs of frustration and later, consternation. Effective operation of the new organizational structure took a long time and proved much more costly to implement than was originally anticipated. Certainly, careful attention to human resource planning could have reduced or eliminated these problems.

The Elements of Human Resource Planning

The human resource planning process is shown in Figure 5.1.

The process starts with the provision of basic human resource information; then forecasts, which may be formal or informal, of future total human resource needs are prepared. In conjunction with these forecasts, various operating departments, with the assistance of the personnel staff, take a **human resources inventory** to ascertain the availability of needed skills for present and future job vacancies. The personnel staff then develops and coordinates various human resource programs with other planning ac-

Figure 5.1
The Human Resource
Planning Process

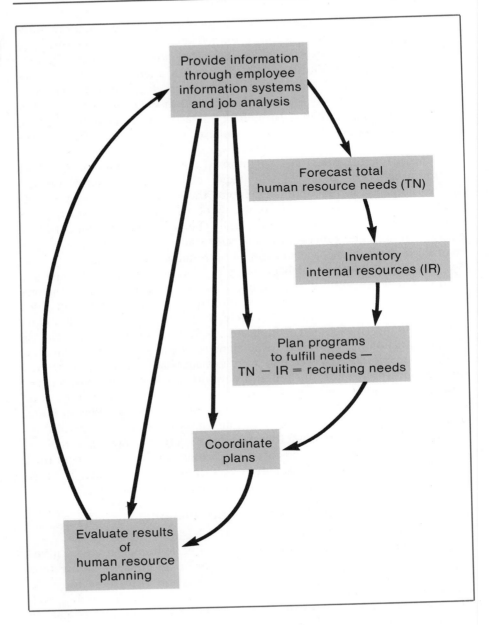

tivities to best meet forecasted needs. The staff implements these programs through recruiting, training and development (see Chapters 13 and 14), and career development (Chapter 17). The relationship between human resource planning and these other activities is critical. As we shall discuss in this chapter, the numbers and classifications of employees to be recruited require careful planning. And only through careful analysis of the anticipated human resource needs can an organization assure accomplishment of its affirmative action plan. Then selection activities can be designed to ensure that the anticipated mix of skills, experience, race, sex, and so on are selected. Through training and development, promotion systems, and career development activities, the numbers and types of people included in the human resource plan should arrive in the right places, at the right time and be qualified to perform their assigned function.

Finally, the personnel staff evaluates the results to improve future human resource planning efforts. Each of these elements in the planning process relies on data supplied from **employee-information systems** or from basic personnel records.

PROVIDING HUMAN RESOURCE INFORMATION

Data for each of the elements of the human resource planning system allow planners to make rational decisions. Information such as **turnover** experience; employee skills; payroll data; and employee training, work experience, and education, can be found in personnel files and related records. Organizations that utilize computers often have employee-information systems that store, manipulate, and retrieve a variety of data on human resources. The advent of the minicomputer has enabled even small companies to create employee information systems. (The subject of computers in personnel is discussed in Chapter 7, "Personnel Records and Research.") **Job analysis** provides information basic to the human resource planning process. It identifies the relevant duties, skills, and requirements of each job in an organization. In fact, it is the basis for designing tests that meet Equal Employment Opportunity Commission guidelines (see discussion of validating selection devices in Chapter 6); it also enables compensation managers to determine the relative value of jobs so that wage rates can be assigned to them (see Chapter 18), and provides tools for the training and development of employees.

JOB ANALYSIS

Job analysis identifies job activities, tasks, and behaviors. It involves compiling a detailed description of duties and responsibilities; ascertaining the relationship of the job to tools, equipment, and related technology; and studying the knowledge, education, experience required to do the job, the accountabilities, and other related requirements. Job analysis also includes the identification, collection, and classification of task statements (i.e., the specifics of what is done in the job) and job behaviors. The listing of task statements offers a detailed analysis of what the incumbent does in the various job activities. A detailing of job behaviors differentiates between acceptable or unacceptable performance; it can even be a basis for establishing performance standards which can later be used in performance appraisal.

Organizations utilize a variety of procedures to collect, analyze, and record data for the analysis. They include:

1. Interviewing the worker or groups performing the job and the supervisor who directs their activities;

2. Observing the job while it is being performed;

3. Preparing questionnaires to be completed by the incumbents themselves and/or the supervisor;

4. Recording job activities as they are performed by the incumbent.

A client company of the author realized substantial benefits from involving its employees in the job analysis process. Employees in the same classification met in groups to complete job analysis questionnaires. A personnel specialist compiled a working draft of the job description, which the group reviewed and revised as they deemed appropriate. Final copies of the description were approved by the supervisors and department managers, who reviewed them with each employee. The manager and employee agreed on expectations (standards) for job performance and these were later used as a basis for evaluating accomplishment. Involvement of the employees made them better informed of their job duties and the managers' expectations of their performance. This resulted in significant improvements in employee performance both individually and collectively.

Job analysis consists of three basic elements: (1) identifying the job; (2) determining its content (including tasks, duties, responsibilities, working conditions, and ascertaining the skills and characteristics required of workers to perform it successfully); and (3) writing a job description and specifications.

1. *Identifying the job.* The usual situation calling for job analysis involves re-identifying the job. Most organizations have **job classifications** already established, but changes in organization, procedures, work force, etc., result in changes in job content that necessitate reidentification.

An important source for identifying jobs—and for obtaining job information on them as well—is the *Dictionary of Occupational Titles*,[4] commonly referred to as the DOT. The DOT contains a classification system for identifying jobs, as well as brief descriptions of more than 35,000 jobs. The DOT system permits jobs to be grouped into occupational classifications, which facilitates the exchange of job information among organizations. The **occupational code** consists of six digits. For example, the job of automobile mechanic (garage mechanic) has a code: 620.281.

The first three digits are a combination of the field of work, purpose of the job, material, product, subject matter, service, generic term, and/or industry. Thus, the first three digits (620) of the auto mechanic's job cited above stand for automotive service. The first digit of the occupational code represents the occupational category, for example, 6 is for machine trades. The first digit of the code can represent any of the following major job categories:

0/1. Professional, technical, and managerial occupations

2 Clerical and sales occupations

3 Service occupations

4 Farming, fishery, forestry, and related occupations

5 Processing occupations

6 Machine trades occupations

7 Bench work occupations

8 Structural work occupations

9 Miscellaneous occupations

The second digit adds specificity to the occupational code. For example, in the clerical category: 2 represents clerical and sales occupations; 20 would further narrow the category to steno and typing occupations. 201 would identify secretaries.

The middle three digits of the occupational code indicate the job's relationship to data, people, and things. The Department of Labor, in conducting research for the DOT, ascertained that every job requires eight levels of difficulty in working with data, people, and things, as shown (in ascending order of difficulty) in Table 5.1.

The last three digits of the occupational code indicate the alphabetical order of titles within the six-digit code groups. They serve to differentiate a particular occupation from all others since several occupations may have the same first six digits. The final three digits are assigned in alphabetical order of titles in multiples of four (010, 014, 018, 022, and so on). Thus, in our example, a legal secretary's code would be 201.362-010; medical secretary's, 201.362-014; and membership secretary's, 201.362-018.

Table 5.1
Difficulty Levels

Data (4th digit)	DOT Occupational Code People (5th digit)	Things (6th digit)
0 Synthesizing	0 Monitoring	0 Setting up
1 Coordinating	1 Negotiating	1 Precision working
2 Analyzing	2 Instructing	2 Operating-controlling
3 Compiling	3 Supervising	3 Driving-operating
4 Computing	4 Diverting	4 Manipulating
5 Copying	5 Persuading	5 Tending
6 Comparing	6 Speaking-signalling	6 Feeding-offbearing
7 N/A	7 Serving	7 Handling
8 No significant relationship	8 No significant relationship	8 No significant relationship

Source: U.S. Department of Labor, Manpower Administration, *Dictionary of Occupational Titles*, Vol. 1, *Definitions of Title*, 4th ed. (Washington, D.C.: U.S. Government Printing Office, 1977), p xviii.

2. *Obtaining job information.* Preliminary to preparing job descriptions and specifications, job analysts gather information on the nature of the work, surroundings, workers' skills, and job requirements. Here analysts are seeking factual information about a job as it exists at the time of the study. Data-gathering methods depend on a situation as well as on the analysts' preferences, but in general, they include questionnaires, personal interviews, and observation. Analysts must be certain that their methods are tailor-made for their organization—detailed enough to produce complete information and capable of providing comparable data for each job analyzed. Figure 5.2 is an abbreviated job-analysis questionnaire used by a large eastern bank.

3. *Writing the job description.* Figure 5.3 is an example of a job description. It contains three parts typical of most job descriptions: a summary statement of duties, responsibilities, and working conditions; the details of the key tasks and responsibilities; and the qualification requirements for employees in that job. Organizations must make certain that job descriptions are clearly and concisely written, and that the information is complete and accurate. When job descriptions are criticized for being overly formal and for containing meaningless detail, the comment is more than an attack on poor writing technique; it admonishes job analysts to make descriptions relevant. One writer[5] recommends spelling out, in the description, the results expected from an employee on the job. This would

1. List in detail the duties you perform daily with the approximate percentage of time for each.

2. List secondary duties performed periodically, such as weekly, quarterly, etc., and state frequency of performance.

3. a. What kinds of previous job experience are required of employees starting in your job.
   b. Where and on what jobs would they get this experience?
   c. How long would it take to obtain this experience? _____ years, _____ months.

4. To what extent are you expected to use your own judgment and take independent action on decisions involving:
   a. Work procedures.
   b. Equipment.
   c. Personnel.
   d. Expenditures.

5. Describe the kind of supervision you give to subordinates in terms of your accountability for:
   a. Assigning and scheduling work.
   b. Outlining work methods.
   c. Checking subordinates' work progress, errors, and production.
   d. Handling exceptional cases or difficulties referred by others.

6. What personal contacts does your work require:
   a. Within your department? Indicate nature (phone, correspondence, or personal meeting), frequency, and purpose of contacts.
   b. Outside your department? Indicate nature and purpose of contacts.
   c. With persons other than bank employees? Indicate nature and purpose of contacts.

7. a. Circle the highest grade of formal education employees assigned to your job should have completed.
      Grammar school   1 2 3 4 5 6 7 8
      High school   1 2 3 4
      College   1 2 3 4 5 6
   b. What specialized knowledge or skills does your

Figure 5.2
Selected Questions from a Bank's Questionnaire for Obtaining Job Description Data

Figure 5.2 (cont.)

job require (accounting, tabulating methods, shorthand, calculating machine operation, etc.)?

8. a. Are your work procedures and methods
    _____ Standard or well structured?
    _____ Determined solely by you?
    _____ Determined by your supervisor?
    _____ Determined by you but in terms of general bank policies?

    b. Are performance standards and results to be accomplished
    _____ Determined by standard practices?
    _____ Determined by your supervisor?
    _____ Determined by you?

    c. Is your work progress and accuracy checked?
    _____ Yes
    _____ No
    If yes, how often? _____
    By whom? (Job title) _____
    What kind of check? _____

9. a. Might the company suffer financial loss as a consequence of errors made on your job?
    _____ Yes   If yes, maximum loss $_____
    _____ No

    b. How long would it take to find such an error? (Work hours) _____

10. Which and how many employees do you supervise?

| Directly | | Indirectly | |
Number	Job Title	Number	Job Title
_____	_____	_____	_____
_____	_____	_____	_____

11. a. List machines or equipment operated as a part of your job.

    b. Indicate any unusual dexterity requirements of your job.

12. Indicate the kinds and nature of confidential information you come in contact with or have access to in the normal course of your work (confidential files, customer bank balances, credit files, etc.).

13. Indicate any unusual working conditions required by your job (occasional or constant travel; irregular working hours, etc.).

certainly clarify the role of a job description and provide a basis for orienting new employees and evaluating their accomplishments.

As Figure 5.3 illustrates, the job analyst should include a declaration such as the following so that workers will not think their duties are restricted to those detailed in a job description: "The above statement reflects the items considered necessary to describe the principal functions of the job identified, and shall not be construed as a detailed description of all the work requirements that may be inherent in the job."

RELATIONSHIP OF JOB ANALYSIS TO OTHER PERSONNEL FUNCTIONS

Job analysis impacts on almost every area of personnel. The courts have favorably viewed methods for making personnel decisions which are based on job analysis. Job analysis helps managers understand the duties and responsibilities of the jobs under their jurisdiction and, in turn, enhances their effectiveness in directing their efforts. Specifically, job analysis has a significant relationship to the following personnel functions.

HUMAN RESOURCE PLANNING.   Job analysis is used to determine the kinds of job vacancies that will occur in the future. By knowing the details of the skills that will be needed in the future, managers are in a better position to plan continuity in staffing their organizations. When a large mining organization, for example, performed a job analysis, it recognized that a conversion to computers in the clerical pool of the personnel department would require the employment of programmers and systems analysts. Although some of the present clerks could be trained for promotion to these positions, the company had to plan to recruit several with degrees in information systems (programming and systems analysis).

EMPLOYEE SELECTION.   In order to select candidates who are qualified to fill a particular job the employer needs to have a clear understanding of the work to be done and the criteria for successful job performance. Job analysis provides details for all jobs so that when vacancies occur recruiters can know what qualifications to seek and those hiring can match specifications against applicants' capabilities.

TRAINING AND DEVELOPMENT.   A detailed job description provides insight into the specific duties and responsibilities of a job. This description enables the supervisor to orient the new employee to the job and it serves as a guide for training the employee in the skills, knowledge, and abilities necessary to perform proficiently.

Figure 5.3
Technical and Office
Job Description

Communication Center Clerk

Occupational Summary

Receive and transmit security-classified coded messages between the company and other facilities in a government electronic communications systems network; act as custodian of and destroy classified material in accordance with government regulations; and otherwise maintain and be responsible for security of a classified communications center.

Work Performed

Check security-classified messages prior to transmission for priority and security designations and completeness of address information; add date-time group and operate keypunch equipment with card reader to cut messages into cards or tapes; proofread cards, tapes, or printed copies of messages to be sent. Similarly receive and transmit unclassified messages processed through communications center. Set up encoding-decoding control attachment and activate control panel of electronic communications system transmitter-receiver with scramble attachment in a manner consistent with message routing and security designation. Transmit classified messages in accordance with indicated priority schedule; and check control panel to ensure receipt of messages transmitted.

Similarly receive classified messages transmitted from other locations on same network and read for clarity of printing and to ensure that coded messages are unscrambled. Prepare classified messages for delivery and destroy classified cards, tapes, manuals, and other materials in accordance with government security regulations.

Prepare and maintain logs of messages received, transmitted, and delivered; logs of personnel entering restricted work area; reports detailing message identification, data, and status of classified cards and tapes; and other related records and reports. Make minor repairs and adjustments indicated by standard test procedures. Perform duties of the teletypist classification when required. Cooperate with agents responsible for periodic security inspections.

Knowledge and Ability Required

Knowledge of applicable encoding and decoding procedures and government security regulations covering classified material. Ability to operate electronic communications system equipment, type sixty words per minute, and operate keypunch machines at a speed equivalent to that required in the keypunch-operator classification.

The above statement reflects the general details considered necessary to describe the principal functions of the job identified, and shall not be construed as a detailed description of all of the work requirements that may be inherent in the job.

PERFORMANCE APPRAISAL. When employees understand what is expected of them they are more likely to perform well. Descriptions developed from job analysis serve as a basis for discussing performance expectations. Performance results can then be compared with these expectations to appraise employee performance. In this manner job analysis adds a dimension of objectivity to the appraisal and enhances the process of developing proficiency in employees.

COMPENSATION. Job descriptions form the basis for job evaluation used to determine the comparable worth of jobs. Jobs requiring greater skill, ability, and/or responsibility are evaluated at a higher level and thereby receive more pay.

PERSONNEL'S ROLE IN JOB ANALYSIS. The personnel department in conjunction with line management is responsible for job analysis. Personnel essentially prepares and coordinates job analysis procedures. Job analysts employed by the personnel department prepare job descriptions and job specifications. Often the employees themselves have been involved in writing their own job descriptions under the guidance of the job analyst. Line managers then review and approve the descriptions. Personnel is usually responsible for evaluating jobs to set employees' pay. Here problems may arise when line managers attempt to get the jobs of their employees evaluated higher so that their employees can be paid more. It thus becomes incumbent upon personnel to analyze all jobs in the organization accurately and evaluate these jobs correctly so that pay inequities do not occur. And, personnel managers can also institute job classification control systems as an attempt to keep evaluation and pay relationships in line. Finally, the personnel department reviews and assists line managers in maintaining job descriptions and specifications in a current state.

FORECASTING

Forecasting attempts to predict factors that are within an organization's control. Changes in organizational structure, such as the content and number of jobs, can be predicted with some accuracy for one, five, or even ten years in the future. Introducing new jobs and realigning responsibilities should not be hastily undertaken; they should be carefully planned far in advance. Sometimes, changes such as automation reduce the number of workers; employees must then be transferred and retained, or laid off. A personnel staff that anticipates these changes greatly reduces the efforts required of all departments.

Technical changes within an organization can be predicted and controlled. While research and development activities result in new and changed products, engineering design creates better methods for performing the work.

Consequently, different numbers of employees with different skills will be required. For instance, the development of xerography changed the Haloid Company from a small producer of photo products into the Xerox Corporation; this growth required employees with varied skills different from those formerly utilized. Forecasters keep in close contact with other departments to be aware of new developments that will influence future human resource needs. Furthermore, they evaluate external influences such as business cycles, interest rates, and labor supply. These factors, beyond the immediate control of an organization, affect its future and its need for human resources.

FORECASTING TECHNIQUES.   Planning for anticipated contingencies involves predicting future events, evaluating courses of action, and selecting the best alternatives. Forecasting the future is the starting point in this process. Basic forecasting techniques are widely used in organizations, but long-range planning and computer modeling are not commonly used.[6] The more accepted forecasting techniques are examined below. The two general classifications into which the various techniques can be grouped are intuitive forecasting and mathematical projections.

1. *Intuitive forecasting.*   This technique relies heavily on the experience, training, and judgment of the individual forecaster or members of forecasting groups. Estimates of future human resource needs made by department heads are usually based on intuition.

   Individual forecasting, or the *genius approach* as it is sometimes called, is the least sophisticated, but most widely used, method. There is considerable merit in predictions made by an individual who is an expert in his/her special area and has both technical understanding and a synoptical overview.[7] However, committees can assemble and review a great deal of information. Members present all the facts they know about a subject, and the group reaches a consensus forecast. A number of factors can inhibit the effectiveness of this method: costs, the influence of members on each other, the reluctance of some members to contribute, and the emphasis on group conformity. But the **Delphi technique** overcomes some of these drawbacks. This technique consists essentially of a series of intensive interrogations of experts who independently and individually respond to a series of questions. An intermediary gathers the experts' responses, summarizes them, and reports the results back to each expert. This continues until the experts' estimates tend to converge, typically after five rounds. The technique is designed to avoid or, at least, minimize interaction among experts in order to stimulate independent thought and allow gradual formulation of considered opinion.[8]

2. *Mathematical projections.*   Mathematical projections are based on quantitative data of the area under study (e.g., production, turnover, or labor-

market composition). Mathematical projections assume that the trend of the past will continue in the future. Of course, unforeseen events can alter past trends, but with a good history of past performance and no evidence of unexpected future changes, mathematical projections can provide reliable forecasts. The significance and utility of mathematical forecasts rely on judgment factors (which are based on the forecasters' experience and must be considered in a final determination of human resource needs). The projection of turnover is a good case in point. If forecasters know from past experience that a certain percentage of employees leave the payroll each year, they can use these turnover figures to product future needs. However, forecasters must be aware of factors that could alter a trend, for example a new plant that draws employees away, or an economic recession that causes a tightening of the job market and makes workers less mobile, thus in effect reducing the turnover rate.

When no historical data are available, forecasters can use **trend correlation,** a statistical technique that assumes that the change in a dependent variable can be measured or projected by the change that occurs in two or more independent variables.

For example, forecasters might be faced with estimating the number of safety engineers (dependent variable) needed by a company that has never before had a safety program. Although there is no direct way to estimate this requirement, there is a relationship between the number of safety engineers required and the number of productive hours lost due to job-related illnesses and accidents (independent variables). The National Safety Council provides statistics on the hours lost due to illnesses and accidents in firms of related size and classification. The forecasters could then estimate the number of safety engineers required.

To be more specific, here are some of the more common mathematical techniques for human resource forecasting:

a. *Time series analysis.* A relatively simple approach, time series analysis is appropriate when past data can be used to predict future events. Here the forecaster would look at a series of past employment figures for a month, quarter, or year. The data would then be graphed to show trends and variations from these. The graph would be corrected for the variations either through visual inspection or by a variety of mathematical techniques. Then, the trend line on the graph can be extended freehand or mathematically. Time series analysis, though simple and easy to explain, has the disadvantage of not considering future events that may have a significant impact on the number and kinds of employees that will be needed.

b. *Regression analysis.* Human resource levels are usually dependent on other factors, for example, sales. When there is a high, positive relationship (correlation) between these factors and the level of human resources, the relationship can be quantified and the other factors can be predicted accurately, and then it becomes a simple matter to forecast human resource needs. The problem with regression analysis lies in the difficulty of finding variables that correlate with human resources. In addition, historical information on these variables must be available to perform the analysis.

c. *Ratio analysis.*   When several kinds of employee groups need to be forecast, ratio analysis may be appropriate. For example, a forecaster might predict the need for key employee groups that are directly related to the volume of business, such as, production, sales, maintenance, using statistical techniques. Then, needs for other groups such as personnel, accounting, and purchasing can be forecast by calculating the ratios to these key groups. When historical relationships between these and other key groups are stable, forecasts are more likely to be accurate.

This is not meant to elaborately describe statistical techniques for human resource forecasting, but to indicate that quantitative methods are available to lend objectivity to the predictive process. For anyone engaged in human resource forecasting, there are helpful sources that elaborate on intuitive and mathematical approaches. Most prominent among them are:

1. Benton, William K. *Forecasting for Management.* Reading, Mass.: Addison-Wesley Publishing Co., 1972.

2. Bramham, John. *Practical Manpower Planning.* New York: Institute of Personnel Management, 1975.

3. Burack, Elmer H. and Nicholas J. Mathys. Human Resource Planning: A Pragmatic Approach to Manpower Staffing and Development. Lake Forest, Ill.: Brace-Park, 1979.

4. Walker, James W. *Human Resource Planning.* New York: McGraw-Hill Book Co., 1980.

5. Wheelwright, Stephen C., and Spyros Markriderkis. *Forecasting Methods for Management.* New York: Wiley-Interscience, 1976.

HUMAN RESOURCE FORECASTING PROCESS

Human resource planners forecast human resource needs, assess available skills, and implement plans. They also coordinate human resource plans with organizational plans and give special consideration to recruiting and assimilating members of minorities and women. Each of the steps in the forecasting process is discussed below.

SELECTING A PREDICTOR OF HUMAN RESOURCE NEEDS.   A business factor is a variable related to the number and types of workers required. When forecasters can isolate such factors, they gather historical data on these as a basis for calculating trends. For example, a direct relationship often exists between the productivity of a firm and the number of workers needed. Hence, for a given number of production units, a certain number of workers is required; as production increases, the labor requirement increases proportionately. For instance, in the production of copper, the final product is a copper ingot. There appears to be a relationship between the tons of copper produced each day and the number of workers required: 16,000 tons using 2,000 employees; 22,500 tons using 2,800; and 28,600 tons using 3,150. If productivity were the only business factor affecting human resource requirements, it would be simple to forecast the number of employees required. But this is an unwarranted oversimplification. There is not always a direct relationship between human resources and productivity. A 10 percent increase in employees may not always be followed by a corresponding rise in production. If improved technology or better work methods increase efficiency, the relationship between productivity and the size of the work force could change.

Logically, the need for human resources appears to be a function of productivity, sales, revenue, and so on, but these variables do not represent the same effect for every firm. Forecasters should exercise caution both in selecting business factors and in calculating them for predictive purposes. Managerial judgment will play a vital role in projecting human resources needs. Thus, historical relationships, though indicative of trends, are not completely reliable for predicting the future.

CALCULATING RATIOS. The relationship between a selected factor and the number of employees is called the **manpower coefficient.** The coefficient can be calculated for previous years from historical data on the business factor and the number of employees. The longer the historical period, the more accurate the coefficient.

PLOTTING AND EXTENDING THE TREND LINE. Forecasters can plot the calculations of manpower coefficients on a graph and, using a simple mathematical formula,[9] fit a trend line. Taking into consideration predicted developments both internal (technology, changes in product mix, etc.) and external (competition, market conditions, etc.), they can extrapolate the trend line to the target year of the forecast.

DETERMINING HUMAN RESOURCES AVAILABLE WITHIN AN ORGANIZATION. A skills inventory, including an audit of employee effectiveness, is the basis for determining the availability of human resources within an organization. The inventory will be discussed later in this chapter as an element of human resource programming.

DETERMINING RECRUITING NEEDS. The projected total human resource needs minus the estimated available skills give us recruiting needs. When human resources must be found outside the organization, information about future conditions of the labor market can prove valuable. Human resource specialists seek statistics on the supply of labor by occupation, age group, educational level, race, sex, and geographic area. The Bureau of Labor Statistics issues data on almost every aspect of the labor market. In addition, human resource projection studies are published by the Engineering Manpower Commission; the Office of Education and the Public Health Service of the Department of Health and Human Services; and the National Science Foundation. The U.S. Employment Service prepares labor-market information on specific localities.

Human resource specialists compare company recruiting needs with the availability of manpower in the labor market. When comparisons reveal a shortage of available resources, they suggest intensified recruiting efforts. For example, the high demand for black college graduates has made companies realize that special efforts are needed to recruit them.

As an economic factor, labor costs are of primary concern to human resource forecasters. Projected wages and salaries are important because they are the price of attracting needed talent. Wage trends and future estimates are calculated similarly to projections of human resource requirements. But the accuracy of forecasts is limited by such unpredictable factors as fringe benefit changes, union wage negotiations, tax structure changes, and fluctuations in the composition of the work force.

COORDINATION WITH OTHER PLANS

Forecasters cannot formulate human resource plans without considering the plans of other functional areas. The activities of other departments bear directly on the number and categories of employees needed, their wages and salaries, and their training requirements. Human resource goals must be coordinated with the planning of other departments. For instance, salaries and wages are dependent on budgets established by the finance department. Research and development conceive new products and modify old ones, thus requiring new and different talent in an organization. Sales determine production demands, which in turn influence human resource requirements. Thus it can be seen that human resource plans depend heavily upon the planning activities of other areas of an organization.

HUMAN RESOURCE PROGRAMMING

Another element in the planning process is **human resource programming.** This involves the application of employee data and forecasts in the planning of programs to meet future human resource needs. It includes taking stock of talent within an organization, identifying promotables, and planning for individual development.

In planning for future human resource requirements, forecasters must, of course, consider qualified personnel presently on the payroll. They can make an inventory of the existing skills to determine which vacancies can be filled from within and which require outside recruiting. Planners base their estimates on the evaluations of employees' supervisors, admittedly an unreliable predictor of potential. Fortunately, organizations seriously committed to human resource planning employ more objective techniques. Companies such as J. C. Penney, AT&T, and IBM, who have utilized the **assessment center** approach (described in detail in Chapter 6, "Employee Selection and Placement"), have reported positive results in its application in evaluating employees. Many organizations also predict the *need* for specific skills and talents. They anticipate organizational change by projecting as much as ten years into the future. The Union Oil Company, for example, developed a computerized Organizational Change Model (OCM) that predicts what the organization and all of its components will be like during the next five years.[10]

A *skills inventory* (also called *manning table*) generally includes demographic information such as age, date of employment, sex, present position, work history, promotion potential, and training development needs. The inventory also shows the number of classifications of employees presently and potentially qualified for promotion. Planners then combine the forecasts and the skills inventory with an analysis of turnover to arrive at an estimate of human resource needs. When lack of existing skills and loss of personnel through attrition indicate a need for additional human resources in the future, planners know recruitment activity is necessary. On the other hand, when research activity shows that there will be a labor surplus in an organization, planners must work toward a reduction of employees.

The identification of promotable talent allows planners to determine internal availability of candidates able to fill anticipated new positions or succeed to openings created by attrition. Traditionally, backup or **replacement charts** have been used to identify successors to each position. The charts show age, appraisal of performance, length of service, and other data on the incumbent and one or more backups. The latter are usually selected by unit managers with personnel staff assistance, with little consideration of the specific requirements for the position and few, if any, hard criteria for the determination of promotability. To overcome these shortcomings, organizations are replacing these charts with intensive sessions on succession programs, during which top management discusses job requirements and compares them to carefully considered facts on promotable candidates' skills, experience, aspirations, and accomplishments.[11]

A natural extension of succession planning is **career development,** a program whereby the career progression of individuals is planned, based on their aspirations within the context of the organization's forecasted human resource needs. (Career development is discussed in detail in Chapter 17.)

SPECIAL CONSIDERATIONS IN HUMAN RESOURCE PLANNING

Prior to implementing human resource plans, organizations often must consider special circumstances. In 1979 the Office of Federal Contract Compliance Programs (U.S. Department of Labor) delineated Affirmative Action Guidelines in a Revised Order Number 4 under Executive Order 11246. (The provisions of the executive order are covered in Chapter 6.) Revised Order Number 4 calls for determining the availability of minorities and females for each job group in order to avoid underutilization. The goal is to have minorities and females currently employed in proportion to their general availability. Good faith compliance with the guidelines would call for an organization's employing the same percentage of minorities and females as are represented in the local labor market. For example if the local labor force contains 30 percent females, the organization's ultimate goal should be 30 percent female representation in *all* job groups.[12] How, then, can an organization achieve this goal and avoid underutilization? First, it would establish minority and female hiring and promotion goals consistent with its forecast. Then it would develop specific timetables for achieving the goals. Table 5.2 is a timetable for achieving hiring goals for a small staff office of a health care service organization. Note that this organization anticipates only ten openings in the next ten years. Most of the openings would be filled by minorities and/or females. All of their office and clerical openings would be filled by females (100%) and two of them would be female minorities (40%).

Finally, plans would be developed to recruit minority and female applicants. Each organization's approach toward employing these applicants as well as members of other ethnic, cultural, and national groups, the hand-

	Anticipated Openings	Minority		Female	
		No.	%	No.	%
Officials and managers	5	1	20.0	1	20.0
Professionals	0	0		0	
Office and clerical	5	2	40.0	5	100.0
Totals	10	3	30.0	6	60.0

Table 5.2
Summary Hiring Goals
7-1-78 to 6-30-79

icapped, and the aged is a policy matter. Developing and implementing these policies is a special problem for the personnel department. (There is a more detailed discussion of recruiting and its Affirmative Action implications later in this chapter. Subsequent chapters in this section deal with the challenges of selecting, placing, and promoting these special groups.)

Organizations must also consider the possibility of reducing the work force. Business recessions are an economic fact, and companies must plan in advance which employees will be retrained and the type of retraining that will be required. Should it become necessary to lay off employees, companies must decide in advance which skills to retain and the basis for the retention (e.g., seniority versus performance). Often, companies cut production and pay, in lieu of laying off employees. Offsetting the economic advantages of this solution are drawbacks such as employee resentment, lower morale, and higher turnover. However, some organizations can retrain and transfer enough employees to eliminate the necessity of layoffs. In this regard, IBM is unique; it has not laid off a single employee in the past 25 years despite economic fluctuations and product changes. It has stabilized its work force through retraining programs, transfers, and careful human resource planning.

The nature of the organizational structure often calls for special approaches to human resource planning. For example, the Martin Marietta Company, an aerospace manufacturer, designed a computerized system called TOSS (Technical Operations Special System) that is tailored for the peculiarities of a matrix or **project organization.** With this type structure, people from various functional areas, for example, engineering, manufacturing, finance, and so on, are assigned to a specific project on a temporary basis, usually for its duration. TOSS indicates to management where people of various skills are, what they are doing, how long they are expected to remain on an assignment, and where they will be needed in the future.[13]

IMPLEMENTING HUMAN RESOURCE PLANS

Human resource plans are implemented through recruiting, selecting, hiring, and placing, which are described in this and the following chapters.

Development activities are a natural adjunct of human resource planning. In recent years, authors of textbooks in personnel and the behavioral sciences have integrated human resource planning with management development, in an approach known as **organizational development** (OD). The organizational development concept views the company as a system of human activities that coordinates their efforts toward a common goal. Through OD, a participative approach is taken in planning human resource needs and to developing individuals and groups within an organization. As a consequence, the entire organization develops into a cohesive working force that accomplishes specified goals. (Because this text takes a functional approach in describing each activity of the personnel department, OD is discussed in a later chapter as an aspect of executive development and it was introduced as an example of participative leadership in Chapter 4. The following examples of human resource planning in the Exxon Corporation and the J. C. Penney Company illustrate the application of the process just described.

EXXON CORPORATION.   With world-wide operations ranging from petroleum exploration to retail service stations and with 125,000 employees, Exxon considers its human resource decisions as critical to its business as its investment determinations. Human resource planning at Exxon is a coordinated effort of the employee-relations staff and operating managers. The process encompasses all aspects of personnel administration, from the initial projection of needs through the utilization of human resources. Long-range human resource projections are a small but crucial part of the process that includes setting objectives, auditing, activating, and controlling human resource programs. Exxon's procedures for making long-range (two to ten years) projections are worthy of detailed description.

As part of its annual business-planning review, each regional organization of Exxon submits to corporate headquarters an analysis of its manpower outlook and plans, including projections of human resources requirements. Exxon staff groups have devised procedures that utilize both statistical analysis and managerial judgment to assist the regions in developing their projections. A key element in these procedures is the selection of a relevant business factor for each significant function or subfunction of operations. For example, the refinery operation uses the intensity-adjusted capacity (IAC) for measuring projected human resource needs. Exxon selected this factor because it includes the elements of refinery operations to which human resource levels are sensitive and because it is not affected by external economic influences such as inflation. The historical IAC data and employment figures including contract labor (contract labor means people who work under an employment contract, usually on a temporary basis) are used to calculate a manpower coefficient. This coefficient is essentially a measure of productivity indicating the number of employees required per thousand barrels of product refined per day. In the hypothetical calculation of the manpower coefficient in Table 5.3, it is readily apparent that productivity has improved over the years. The coefficient is then charted and projected on a long-term trend line as shown in Figure 5.4. At this point, operating managers adjust the long-term trend to take into account factors (such as major technological changes and shifts in the product mix), which they believe will influence human resources in the future. The derivation of projected human resource needs then becomes a simple matter of multiplying the adjusted manpower coefficient for the target year by the intensity adjusted capacity for the same year.

	Effective Fuel Products Employment		Intensity Adjusted Capacity (MB/CD)		Manpower Coefficient (Men per MB/CD/AC)	
1955	9240		1630		5.66	
1958	5577		1835		3.04	
1960	5005		1950		2.56	
1962	4077	Actual	1950		2.10	Calculated
1964	4019		1990		2.02	
1965	3908		1985		1.96	
1966	3940		2030		1.94	
1970	3930	Calculated	2550	Outlook	1.54	Projected
1975	3380		3075		1.10	

Table 5.3
Hypothetical Calculation of Manpower Coefficient

MB/CD: Thousand barrels per calendar day
AC: Adjusted capacity
Reprinted with permission. Exxon Corporation.

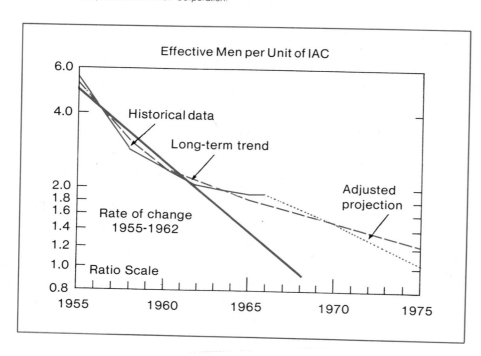

Figure 5.4
Hypothetical Projection of Manpower Coefficient

Reprinted with permission. Exxon Corporation.

Separate projections are made for MPT (managerial/professional/technical) manpower as this is a critical segment of the work force and the trend at Exxon is toward an increase in the proportion of MPT employees in relation to its total employment. MPT requirements are projected by plotting the ratio of MPT to total employment, which will show the rate of change in MPT employment.[14]

J. C. PENNEY COMPANY.   The J. C. Penney Company, one of the nation's leading retail merchandisers, plans its human resource programs from information supplied by each retail store. Penney's develops five-year consumer-demand projections for each position in its organization from data on approved organization forms (Figure 5.5), which are completed annually by all store managers. Corporate personnel procedures designate the approved numbers of people for each classification based on a store's sales.

Human resource needs are supplied primarily by promotion, due in part to low turnover and clearly defined lines of progression. The company recruits recent college graduates as trainees for low-level management and staff positions. Penney associates—all J. C. Penney Company employees are called associates to give them a sense of belonging—are evaluated on their potential for promotion during the succeeding five-year period. Penney's uses these evaluations to compile a corporate-wide inventory of the human resource supply available to fill forecasted vacancies. A computer matches projected vacancies with available qualified personnel in order to locate blocks in promotion paths and discover shortages of qualified backups.

EVALUATING HUMAN RESOURCE PLANS

Organizations that are engaged in human resource planning view objective evaluation of their programs as important. Line managers insist on cost-benefit analysis and audits to ascertain the effectiveness of a program and each of its elements. As line managers become more involved in the human resource planning process, they seem to be more directly concerned with receiving tangible benefits from its application. But the implementation of these planning programs requires a substantial financial investment, especially when computers are used. Yet relatively few objective evaluations have been made of the benefits versus cost of these programs. However, subjective assessments have been favorable and indicate a definite desire for intensified efforts toward evaluating human resource planning programs objectively.[15]

Recruiting: Filling Human Resource Needs

Recruiting is the first and major step in implementing the staffing process. Its primary objective is to acquire qualified applicants to fill vacan-

APPROVED ORGANIZATION

FOR APPROVAL TO USE LISTED POSITIONS

6200-92A REV. 12/1/71

THIS IS NCR PAPER. NO CARBON NECESSARY. **USE TYPEWRITER ONLY.**
IMPORTANT: MAIL ALL COPIES TO DISTRICT WITH ONE COPY OF
ORGANIZATION CHART.

Figure 5.5
Approved Organization
Form

Reproduced with permission. J. C.
Penney Co.

REGION	DISTRICT	STORE NO.	STORE LOCATION

STORE TYPE: ▶ ☐ SMALL ☐ SOFT ☐ MODIFIED ☐ LIMITED ☐ FULL LINE

	POSI-TION NO.	POSITION TITLE	LAST YR. TOTAL SALES VOL. (000)	THIS YR. EST. TOT. SALES VOL. (000)	NUMBER			
					(A) CRITERIA*	(B) PRESENT	(C) PROPOSED	(D) APPROVED
MANAGEMENT	180	Automotive Center Manager						
	160	Custom Decorating Manager – in Store						
	324	Custom Decorating Workroom Manager						
	321	Customer Service Manager						
	017	Department Manager						
	087	Home Improvement Manager						
	116	Merchandise Manager						
	132	Operations Manager						
	206	Personnel Manager						
	012	Sales and Merchandise Manager						
	239	Sales Promotion Manager						
	360	Security Manager						
	323	Small Store Management Trainee						
	050	Stockroom Manager						
	010	Store Manager						
	024	Management Trainee						
	025	Merchandise Management Trainee A						
SELLING	178	Department Head – Appliances and Electronics						
	302	Department Head – Curtain and Drapery Shop						
	192	Department Head – Family Shoes						
	250	Department Head – Fashions						
	249	Department Head – Lawn and Garden						
	226	Department Head – Men's Clothing						
	274	Department Head – Paint and Hardware						
	272	Department Head – Photography Shop						
	273	Department Head – Rec. Equip. and Apparel						
	248	Department Head – Western Shop						
	337	Fine Jewelry Supervisor						
	026	Merchandise Management Trainee B						
		Enter 026 Merchandise Department Assignments Below:						
		STORE PROPOSED TRAINEE DEPARTMENT ASSIGNMENTS						
		REGION APPROVED TRAINEE DEPARTMENT ASSIGNMENTS						
	217	Selling Supervisor						
SALES SUPPORT	063	Advertising and Display Supervisor						
	194	Credit and Layaway Supervisor						
	045	Display Supervisor						
	081	Maintenance Supervisor						
	033	Merchandise Records Supervisor						
	038	Office and Personnel Supervisor						
	032	Office Supervisor						
	096	Security Supervisor						
MDSE. HANDLING	052	Stockroom Supervisor						
SERVICES	056	Alterations Supervisor						
	183	Automotive Service Supervisor						
	150	Beauty Salon Supervisor						
	195	Drapery Workroom Supervisor						
FOOD SERVICE	311	Food Service Manager						
	261	Food Service Supervisor						
CATALOG	221	Catalog Sales Supervisor						

MANAGER'S SIGNATURE	DATE / /	REGION INITIAL	DISTRICT INITIAL

* Consult criteria on Position Descriptions.   **DISTRICT COPY**

cies. Specific considerations within the recruitment process vary with a situation, but the steps described in this chapter are common to most organizations.

SITUATIONAL ASPECTS OF RECRUITING

Particular situations can affect the manner in which a company recruits employees. Organizations experiencing low turnover promote and transfer from within, in which case, outside recruitment is negligible. In high-turnover situations, companies actively solicit new applicants through advertising and intensive recruiting activities. Also, the nature of the product often influences recruiting. In primary industries such as mining, an undesirable location usually makes it necessary to hire and train local residents since it is difficult to attract outside resources. In that company location has a bearing on recruitment, many businesses have their headquarters in areas offering an adequate supply of skilled or highly educated employees. Furthermore, company image significantly affects recruiting success. Companies such as Coca-Cola, IBM, Xerox, and Kodak project such a favorable image that applicants are continually seeking employment, thus providing a steady flow of candidates for all possible vacancies. Legislation has a significant impact on recruiting. EEO regulations emphasize the need for organizations to utilize available sources of minority members and women for positions. Other variables that affect recruiting include the state of the labor market; the types of jobs that become available; the relationship between workers and management; and company personnel policies, such as promotion and transfer, fringe benefits, educational opportunities, training programs, and so on.

THE RECRUITING PROCESS

Recruiting consists of a number of related steps and starts with the determination of recruiting needs. These steps relate to both operative and management personnel.

DETERMINING RECRUITING NEEDS. As previously defined, recruiting needs are the net difference of forecasted total human resource needs minus the people available within an organization. Recruiters can group the number of employees needed, by classification, to facilitate the search effort. For example, if it is determined that three machinists, a mechanic, and a utility person will be required, recruiters can direct search activities toward employing five machinists or five mechanics with interests or experience appropriate to the specific openings. In lower-level jobs, there may be several positions that can be filled by individuals with the same general background, especially when specific experience is not critical. A high school graduate might be equally suitable as a production worker or as a clerk, and a recent business administration graduate might qualify as a production supervisor, a personnel assistant, or a sales trainee. Finally, recruiters must be thoroughly familiar with the position. We have already seen that job analysis provides recruiters with detailed knowledge of each job or position. The more they know about an organization's needs, the better **screening** job they can do.

RECRUITMENT SOURCES. Applicant sources depend on the extent and nature of experience required. In general, applicants might be furnished through internal promotion, friends and relatives of employees, applicant files, help-wanted advertisements, colleges and universities, private employment agencies, and miscellaneous sources.

1. *Promotion from within.* In filling positions above the entry level, many companies first consider promoting present employees. This not only improves morale, but encourages employees to prepare themselves for transfer or promotion. Companies are in a much better position to evaluate their own employees than applicants from outside the organization. Furthermore, employees may require less training than other applicants because they are already familiar with the company and possibly with the position.

   Complete and accurate personnel records can greatly assist the utilization of internal sources by identifying employees with requisite skills, education, and experience. This identification process is greatly facilitated by computer personnel data systems such as skills inventory, which can sort and retrieve relevant information on performance rating, length of service, salary, experience history, and skills.

   Sometimes, however, people within an organization do not possess the requisite skills, knowledge, or abilities, or are unable to develop them. If needed talent cannot be found within an organization, recruiters must look for outside candidates. In fact, some companies consider it essential to recruit outsiders on occasion. New blood can bring different ideas and fresh approaches to company problems.

2. *Employee referrals.* An organization's own employees are an excellent referral source. A friend or relative may have the background required for a particular opening. Employees are flattered when asked to make recommendations, and they generally recommend only those people they feel are qualified. Furthermore, applicants usually want to work where they have friends. Employee referral can help correct underutilization of minorities and females and increase the applicant flow of these groups.

To stimulate referrals, one West Coast organization has an award system that pays an employee 50 dollars for any minority or female referred and hired (and retained for at least three months).[16]

3. *Applicant files.* Previous applicant files can be a valuable source for candidates. Organizations often receive inquiries about employment opportunities from individuals with a variety of backgrounds and qualifications. Even though these applicants were not previously hired, they might maintain an interest in a company for several years following their initial contact. By screening the application files, recruiters can uncover some prime candidates for existing or anticipated vacancies.

4. *Advertising.* A help-wanted ad, with a brief description of a job's duties and the qualifications needed, can be an effective means of attracting applicants. Because responses to ads are forwarded by many who are unqualified, recruiters may use a blind ad, where applicants reply to a newspaper box number. Although this has the advantage of eliminating the necessity for contacting every applicant, whether qualified or not, it has an inherent disadvantage. The name of a well-known organization will often attract qualified applicants, but blind ads preclude the use of a company name or logo. Fair employment practice codes prohibit the statement of preferences (male only, age 35 preferred) which exclude applicants because of race, color, creed, sex, age, or national origin.

5. *Colleges and universities.* Traditionally, the college campus has been a popular source for recruiting management prospects. Organizations that have active campus recruiting programs regularly inform the college placement director of job opportunities in an organization. They also strive to maintain a favorable image on campus through class lectures by organization officials; plant tours; scholarship awards; summer or part-time hiring of students and faculty; and by providing information to teachers on the organization and its operations. The recruiting itself is usually performed by teams consisting of a personnel administrator and one or more line managers with similar positions. The teams interview students and invite the most promising to visit the plant, where tours and second interviews are conducted. Following detailed screening procedures, the organization offers jobs to the best candidates. College recruiting usually produces management candidates (discussed in detail under "Management and Executive Development," Chapter 14).

   Figure 5.6 is an example of a candidate rating form for applicants in college.

6. *Private employment agencies.* In seeking experienced personnel, many organizations use private employment agencies or search and recruiting firms. Some are no-fee agencies, which means that the employers pay

1 Outstanding
2 Good
3 Average
4 Low
5 Unsuitable

Figure 5.6
Candidate Rating Form—
College Recruitment Program

1. *Appearance*
General impression, cleanliness, neatness.

   Comments 1 __ 2 __ 3 __ 4 __ 5 __

2. *Self-Expression*
Can the candidate articulate ideas clearly? Logically? Directly?

   1 __ 2 __ 3 __ 4 __ 5 __

3. *Poise, Self-Confidence*
Is the candidate confident in answering? Forceful in presentation? Or ill at ease and nervous?

   1 __ 2 __ 3 __ 4 __ 5 __

4. *Maturity*
Do the candidate's ideas show thorough reasoning? Are the candidate's plans for the future realistic?

   1 __ 2 __ 3 __ 4 __ 5 __

5. *Interest in Job With Company*
What does the candidate know about the company? About the job? Do the candidate's questions show an interest in the company?

   1 __ 2 __ 3 __ 4 __ 5 __

6. *Technical Grasp of Field*
Does the candidate have a general grasp of his/her specialty?

   1 __ 2 __ 3 __ 4 __ 5 __

7. *Knowledge Gained From Work Experience*
Does the candidate reason practically? What has he/she learned about people? Can he/she communicate his/her knowledge?

   1 __ 2 __ 3 __ 4 __ 5 __

Figure 5.6 (cont.)

8. *Personality*   1 __ 2 __ 3 __ 4 __ 5 __
   Is the candidate's personality
   suitable for the job?

9. *Ambition*   1 __ 2 __ 3 __ 4 __ 5 __
   How high does the candidate
   want to go? Does he/she have
   the drive necessary to reach
   his/her goal?

10. *Potential*   1 __ 2 __ 3 __ 4 __ 5 __
    Given all your above ratings,
    can this candidate, with train-
    ing and experience, reach top-
    level management in this
    company?

General Rating:

1. The outstanding prospect who is far above the normal
   run of college graduates.   _____

2. The above average candidate who appears competent
   and more than just suitable.   _____

3. The candidate who is average.   _____

4. The candidate who is a little below average and leaves
   some doubt as to his/her competence.   _____

5. The candidate who is incompetent and unsuitable.   _____

Remarks:

Recommendation: Hire _____ Reject_____

                                              Signed _____

the fee instead of the applicants. A request for service, or a job order, to an agency includes a description of the job duties, starting pay, and necessary qualifications. Of course, organizations are not obligated to hire the applicants referred by an agency, but they should inform it when the job has been filled. Executive recruiters and search firms, on the other hand, contract with employers to search for needed talent. Organizations compensate the search firm for its services, even if they do not hire a recommended candidate. Because there are so many employment agencies and search firms and such a wide range of competence among them, organizations must select agencies carefully.

7. *Employment services.*   Public employment services are maintained in major cities throughout the country. Employers who are public contractors are required by law to register their job needs with the State Employment Service (also called the **Employment Security Commission**). More important, the public employment offices can provide an excellent source of candidates for employment. Each office attracts large numbers of available candidates when they register for unemployment benefits. In addition, the employed job seeker as well as the unemployed are attracted to these offices by the placement services offered. Skilled employment interviewers advise people on job-search strategies and help them match their abilities and experience to available openings. In addition, the public employment service maintains job banks (exhaustive listings of job openings) in 74 cities.

8. *Miscellaneous sources.*   Labor unions can be a principal source of applicants for certain jobs, particularly blue-collar. In some industries, unions supply particular types of labor through their apprenticeship (training) programs. Skilled workers in construction and unskilled workers in other industries are hired more-or-less exclusively through the hiring hall.

Many professional organizations and societies operate placement services for the benefit of their members. Their journals list job openings and applicants seeking positions. Also, recruiters often attend regional and national meetings of these professional organizations to search for applicants.

In recruiting employees, it is important to check with several minority groups—racial and ethnic, women, older workers, and the handicapped—that can provide valuable and skilled employees.

With the enactment of Title VII of the Civil Rights Act of 1964, many organizations have instituted affirmative action programs to make a concerted effort to employ, train, and promote women and minorities. Minorities include blacks, Chicanos, Orientals, Puerto Ricans, and American

Indians. Affirmative action programs have gained momentum not only because they are required for federal contracts, but because they are also a good business practice. Organizations that overlook women and minorities in hiring and promotion ignore 70 percent of the population. An employment pool of white males forces organizations to find all their employees among a mere 30 percent of the work force. The Employment Security Commission (located in cities throughout the nation), Neighborhood Youth Corps, and equal employment opportunity groups can make minority applicants available to employers. In addition, agencies closely allied with the black community can be helpful in locating minority applicants; these include the Urban League, Equal Employment Opportunity Commission, National Association for the Advancement of Colored People, and Southern Christian Leadership Conference. To aid in recruiting minorities, women, and other "special category" groups, the EEOC prepared *A Directory of Resources of Affirmative Recruitment,* available from the U.S. Government Printing Office, Washington, D.C. 20402.

More and more organizations have found that women make valuable contributions to organizations, both as workers and managers. Currently, about 51 percent of the work force is composed of women (44 million women).[17] Many of the sources applicable to minorities also refer to women applicants. In particular, the National Organization of Women (NOW) has been helpful in locating female talent for interested employers. Interest in the issue of women and minorities has attracted such wide interest that a separate chapter of this text (Chapter 15) is devoted to its discussion.

Two more groups that can provide capable applicants are older workers and the handicapped, yet many firms fail to take advantage of their skills. The retirement plans of some organizations are making many older people available, and a number of these retired and older workers are still productive. Furthermore, they are usually more reliable, experienced, and accurate than younger employees. These candidates can often be found through companies with compulsory retirement policies; the State Employment Service; and nonprofit organizations for older workers such as the Golden Age Club, Over Forty, Forty-Plus Club, and Senior Citizens of America.

When properly placed, handicapped workers make outstanding employees. They are usually very conscientious and have low absenteeism and turnover rates. The following groups are sources for handicapped employees: state vocational rehabilitation agencies; the Office of Vocational Rehabilitation of the Department of Health and Human Services; veterans' organizations and VA hospitals; social-service agencies; and employ-the-handicapped committees. (A more detailed discussion of employment of the handicapped appears in Chapter 15.)

LEGISLATIVE GUIDELINES FOR EMPLOYMENT

Federal and state governments regulate the employment process, including recruiting activities. Employment laws are generally restrictive and are primarily directed toward eliminating discrimination based on sex, age, race, or religion. Following is a synopsis of federal legislation pertinent to the employment process (state laws generally reinforce federal laws).

Title VII, Equal Employment Opportunity of the *Civil Rights Act of 1964* (Public Law 88-352), provides the basis for fair employment practices. The law specifically forbids covered employers to discriminate in hiring or in any term or condition of employment on the basis of race, religion, sex, color, or national origin. The act defines covered employers as those engaged in industries affecting commerce and employing 25 or more workers in a year. The Equal Employment Opportunity Commission has the authority to enforce the provisions of the act, but it encourages voluntary compliance. The act specifically prohibits discrimination through the use of tests, applications, and interviews, and it requires employers to **validate** such selection devices before they are used. (There will be a more detailed discussion on this aspect of the law in Chapter 6.) In addition, help-wanted advertising cannot indicate preference, limitation, specification, or discrimination based on sex unless sex is a bona fide occupational qualification for a job. (Women's dress designers may legally hire only female models, for example.) Newspaper ads with the stipulations ''male'' or ''female'' or ''white only'' are specifically prohibited by the law. All employers are required by the act to submit annual compliance reports to the commission. Personnel departments keep the records used to prepare the reports; these should be kept separate from other personnel information so that their racial and ethnic data cannot influence personnel decisions.

In making purchasing decisions, the federal government can choose its vendors and contractors and fix the terms and conditions of a contract. As a supplement to Title VII, *Executive Order 11246* (amended by EO 11375 to cover sex discrimination), bars discrimination by government contractors and requires that all bidders on federal contracts must formulate and submit affirmative action programs. Affirmative action plans specify the steps contractors will take to guarantee job opportunities for members of minority groups. In checking compliance with the executive order, the commission examines evidence of minority employment at all levels and in all departments. When discriminatory practices were uncovered at Bell Telephone, the federal government awarded $15 million in back pay to women and minority employees. The company also agreed to set goals and timetables for their promotion to skilled jobs and management positions.

The Equal Employment Opportunity Act of 1972 amended Title VII by greatly expanding its coverage (it now covers educational institutions, state governments and joint labor-management committees) and substantially increasing the enforcement powers of the Equal Employment Opportunity Commission. As a result of the 1972 amendment, the Commission may now bring civil suit in a federal district court on behalf of an employee who has been discriminated against. This dramatic change in the law has created a problem for the Commission; it is now more than 22 months behind in the processing of cases.[18] The law is not meant, however, to grant preferential treatment to any employee(s) in order to rectify a racial, religious, sex, or national origin imbalance.

The Civil Rights Act of 1964 contained a provision that directed the Secretary of Labor to study the problem of age discrimination. Out of these studies, the *Age Discrimination in Employment Act of 1967* was enacted to prohibit arbitrary discrimination in employment and to help employers and workers find ways to deal with age-related problems in employment. Consequently, employers can no longer refuse to hire applicants because of advanced age. Also, the Secretary of Labor directs a continuing program of education and information designed to encourage the employment of older workers. Although many companies have a **mandatory retirement** age of 65 (which in itself is not an unlawful practice), such policies cannot be the basis for failing to employ older workers who might not be able to qualify for retirement benefits. However, should older workers seek admission to an apprenticeship program, one in which age would preclude completion before mandatory retirement, companies can lawfully deny them employment. The protected age group under the act was increased to 70 by Congressional action in 1978.

Section 503 of the *Rehabilitation Act* as amended calls for affirmative action in the employment and advancement of handicapped individuals by government contractors. (Affirmative action programs for the handicapped are covered in detail in Chapter 15.)

Congress has enacted protective labor laws, and additional legislation on wages and hours, child labor, labor-management relations, and union administration. (Several of the following chapters cover these laws in more detail.)

Enforcement of equal employment opportunity legislation is coordinated by the Office of Federal Contracts Compliance Programs (OFCCP), connected with the U.S. Department of Labor. Actual enforcement is the responsibility of the specific contracting agency. For example, Social Security enforces compliance with insurance carriers, the Department of Defense with military contractors, and so on. The logic behind this arrangement is that the specific contracting agency is more likely to know the industry.

Cost-Benefit Analysis

Few, if any, organizations perform cost-benefit analyses of the planning function probably because of the difficulty in estimating the benefits directly attributable to this activity. The recruiting and training efforts become more effective as a result of planning, and so yield better utilization of personnel. There is little doubt that having the right people, in the right places, at the right time, is a benefit to an organization, but a realistic assessment of its value is difficult, at best. Obviously, failure to plan can result in substantial losses in terms of not having the right people, or maybe not having any people to produce the goods or services normally generated by an organization. It is possible, however, to calculate the expenses of planning. They include the salaries, materials, and the facilities of the planning staff (and the equipment—often computers—used by them). A significant proportion of the planning cost is often the result of increased computer time, that is, the actual time for the computer to run forecasts and related planning reports.

Costs and benefits of the recruiting activity can be measured fairly precisely. Cost comparisons help determine the efficiency of the recruiting effort. One method of doing this is to compare the cost of hiring a particular individual through an employment agency with that of hiring him or her through use of the recruiting staff. Because information on agency fees is readily available, this comparison is simple to make. If other organizations' costs are known, they can be useful bases for comparison, especially when the organizations are in the same industry, are of similar size, and hire the same classifications of employees.

Analyses can also be made of the comparative yield of various recruiting sources. Where are we locating most of our candidates? Which media sources attract the most applicants? Where are our *best* employees coming from? The answers to these questions are rather straightforward, and maintaining careful records and later reviewing them can provide necessary data. Employment managers will obviously want to concentrate their efforts on sources yielding the required quality and quantity of candidates. Also, analyses of performance reviews, turnover and absenteeism reports; calculation of the time required to fill a vacancy; and comparison of the number of "hires" by recruiters are indicators of recruiting effectiveness.

Summary

The quality of its work force is a major determinant of company effectiveness. The employees who manage the business, operate the machines, and record the progress of operations guide the destiny of an organization. As businesses move through various stages of growth, their human resource needs change. Organizations are at a distinct advantage if they anticipate future human resource needs and plan recruitment, selection, and development activities in advance.

Human resource planning consists of forecasting human resource needs, auditing existing skills, and implementing recruitment and development programs. Planners can forecast human resource requirements on the basis of managerial intuition alone or from mathematical projections that utilize quantitative models modified by personal judgment. The current trend in organizations is toward the latter, more sophisticated approach, as human resource planning becomes increasingly important. In projecting human resource needs, forecasters select a business factor that correlates closely with manpower and has a functional relationship with the size of the work force. They then gather historical data on the business factor and employment. After plotting the data, the forecasters fit a trend line and extend it to a specific year in the future. Then they adjust the forecast, taking into account labor-market studies, anticipated internal and external business conditions, and organizational changes. The adjusted calculations become the total human resource needs for an organization.

Prior to developing the number and type of personnel to be acquired from outside the company, recruiters must discover the projected available supply of talent within it. For this purpose, they usually conduct an audit to determine the availability of skills and the number of promotable personnel. In conjunction with the audit, job analysts determine the duties, skills, and related specification of each job so that recruiters will understand the requirements of the jobs they are seeking to fill. Then they recruit to acquire the resources that will not be available internally. In the recruiting process, organizations must be careful to comply with federal and state regulations governing employment practices. They cannot discriminate on the basis of race, sex, age, creed, or national origin. And where federal contracts are awarded, organizations must make special efforts to locate candidates from disadvantaged groups. In this respect, affirmative action plans include goals for utilizing females and minorities throughout the organization, and timetables for achieving these goals.

Key Terms

forecasts	turnover
recruiting	job analysis
affirmative action	job classification
human resources inventory	*Dictionary of Occupational*
employee-information systems	*Titles* (DOT)

occupational code
Delphi technique
trend correlation
manpower coefficient
human resource
   programming
assessment center
replacement charts

career development
project organization
organizational development
screening
Employment Security
   Commission
validate
mandatory retirement

Review Questions

1. Discuss the advantages and disadvantages of human resource planning.
2. Describe three techniques of forecasting human resource needs.
3. How can one determine the resources available within an organization?
4. Describe the human resource forecasting process.
5. Discuss the various sources available for recruiting.
6. Discuss the formula for calculating recruiting needs.

Discussion Questions

1. Discuss the effect each of the following could have on a recruitment program: a) company image, b) computers, c) type of industry, d) company location.

2. An executive of a large corporation voiced his objections to human resource planning by arguing that there are too many uncontrollable variables affecting human resource needs to make projections meaningful. What is your opinion of this comment?

3. What circumstances would make the following policy feasible: "Promotion from within is a good idea, but once in a while it benefits the organization to hire an outsider."

4. What measures can organizations take to recruit the best available talent and yet conform to EEOC guidelines?

5. Labor Department forecasts of employment trends are readily available to human resource planners, and they are usually accurate. However, there are dangers in organizations adopting these projections as their own. Cite some of the risks in using these figures as an organization forecast.

Case Problem 1

HUMAN RESOURCE PLANNING

Dick Baxter shuffled the mass of paper around his desk. He had been assistant personnel manager only three days, and already he felt the work was swamping him. Nobody told him that he would be doing this sort of thing! Dick had to develop a five-year human resource plan for his company. He dug into the stack and came up with the list of key factors he had to consider. It read like this:

1. Retrieval Systems had 1,100 production and maintenance workers, 190 administrative and clerical employees, 105 supervisors and managers, 50 salaried technical personnel, and 30 salesmen.

2. Turnover had averaged 4 percent per year in recent years, and there was no reason to expect any change in this rate. The rate differed between groups somewhat—production workers turned over at 8 percent, while managers and technical personnel turned over at 3 percent.

3. Planned expansion would lead to a 10 to 15 percent increase in clerical workers and salesmen. Technical personnel would increase by 5 or 6 percent, while supervisors and managers would remain about the same. Production and maintenance workers would increase by 5 percent.

4. There had been considerable government pressure on the company to hire minority group workers and women. All salespeople and supervisory and managerial personnel were men, and only one salesperson and two technicians were from minority groups. One engineer was female. Eleven percent of the production and maintenance workers were minority group or female, concentrated in the lowest job categories such as laborer and assembly-line operator.

5. Since Retrieval Systems had many government contracts, it seemed likely that the company would have to present an affirmative action plan for minorities and women within the next few years to retain these contracts. Such a plan might run into union problems, because advancing these groups could conflict with the strict seniority rules currently in the union contract.

6. Retrieval Systems had never tried systematically to recruit women or minority group personnel, although any such persons who did apply were treated fairly.

Dick was supposed to present a detailed human resource plan to his boss next Friday—and already it was Tuesday. The report was supposed to include such things as the organization chart for Retrieval Systems in the next five years; an affirmative action program; and the number of outside hires the company would have to make.

Dick scratched his head and pushed the piles of papers idly around his desk. Friday! The man was mad!

Problems

1. List the key factors Dick should consider in making his plan.
2. What kind of recruiting program does Dick need here?

3. Retrieval Systems has some interesting new products in the area of recycling garbage. Sales could take off and double in five years. What would this increase do to Dick's forecasts? What contingency plans should Dick propose?

4. What alternative techniques could Dick use to calculate projected human resource needs?

Case Problem 2

DIVERSIFIED CHEMICAL CORPORATION

The Diversified Chemical Corporation has achieved the results shown in Exhibit 5.1 in critical areas during the last five years. Several members of the company's board of directors were disappointed by the firm's results in the last two years. They feel that the corporation's policy of promotion from within, which has been followed quite rigidly for more than a decade, has been a significant constraint on the firm's performance in recent years. They would like to fill most managerial jobs, especially at higher levels, with outside people. But a number of board members advocate that the promotion from within policy be continued and argue that general market conditions and competition—particularly more aggressive foreign competition—have been the major constraints on company performance. There are also several board members who feel that a thorough appraisal of both company personnel and outside prospects should be made before staffing key managerial positions.

Problems

1. Discuss what you consider the likely advantages and disadvantages of the three different staffing policies proposed by Diversified Chemical's board of directors.

2. What staffing policy do you think would be best for Diversified Chemical to follow at this time in filling existing job openings and newly created executive positions?

Exhibit 5.1

Year	Net Profits (millions of dollars)	Rate of Return on Investment (%)	Sales (millions of dollars)	Market Share (%)
1977	52	15	570	14
1978	60	17	610	14
1979	66	16	690	15
1980	61	13	640	12
1981	65	14	650	13

Notes

1. Human resource planning has been commonly referred to as manpower planning. The author has chosen the former term as being more descriptive of this concept.

2. Bureau of National Affairs, *ASPA-BNA Survey: Manpower Programs, Bulletin to Management* (Washington, D.C.: Bureau of National Affairs, December 14, 1972), pp. 1ff.

3. Thomas H. Patten, Jr., *Manpower Planning and the Development of Human Resources* (New York: John Wiley, 1971), p. 33.

4. *Dictionary of Occupational Titles* (Washington, D.C.: Department of Labor, 1977).

5. John W. Gehm, "Job Descriptions—A New Handle on an Old Tool," *Personnel Journal,* December 1970, pp. 983–85.

6. *Corporate Manpower Planning: A Study of Manpower Planning Practices in 220 Major U.S. Business Organizations* (Philadelphia, Pa.: Towers, Perrin, Forster, and Crosby, 1975), p. 4.

7. Marvin J. Cetron and Thomas J. Monahan, "An Evaluation and Appraisal of Various Approaches to Technological Forecasting," *Technological Forecasting for Industry and Government,* James R. Bright, ed. (Englewood Cliffs, N.J.: Prentice-Hall, 1968), pp. 145–46.

8. Richard J. Tersine and Walter E. Riggs, "The Delphi Technique: A Long-Range Planning Tool," *Business Horizons,* April 1976, pp. 51ff.

9. The least-squares method is used to fit trend line to data. The technique is described in all basic statistics texts.

10. William E. Bright, "How One Company Manages Its Human Resources," *Harvard Business Review,* January–February 1976, p. 84.

11. James W. Walker, "Human Resource Planning: Managerial Concerns and Practices," *Business Horizons,* June 1976, pp. 56–57.

12. David A. Brookmire, "Designing and Implementing Your Company's Affirmative Action Program," *Personnel Journal,* April 1979, pp. 232–237.

13. Robert A. Sylvia, "TOSS: An Aerospace System That's GO for Manpower Planning," *Personnel,* January–February 1977, pp. 56–57.

14. The information in this section was adapted from *Manpower Planning: Evolving Systems* (New York: The Conference Board, 1971), pp. 7ff.

15. *Corporate Manpower Planning,* pp. 6ff.

16. Brookmire, "Designing and Implementing Your Company's Affirmative Action Program," p. 237.

17. U.S. Bureau of Labor Statistics, *Employment in Perspective: Working Women* (Washington, D.C.: U.S. Department of Labor, Second Quarter 1980), p. 2.

18. *The Equal Employment Opportunity Act of 1972* (Washington, D.C.: Bureau of National Affairs, 1973), p. 3.

Chapter Six

Employee Selection and Placement

In 1965 a major utility company decided that any employee who sought to be promoted from the labor pool to the operating department of its steam-generating stations must have a high school diploma, a score on the Wonderlic Personnel Test that equaled or exceeded the median score for high school graduates, and a minimum critical score on the Bennett Test of Mechanical Comprehension. A suit brought by black employees in the labor pool charged that these requirements were arbitrary and therefore discriminatory because blacks generally do not score well on such tests. The Supreme Court decided (in *Griggs* v. *Duke Power Co.*) that neither the high school requirement nor the general intelligence test bore a demonstrable relationship to successful job performance. The court also maintained that both were adopted without a meaningful study of their relationship to job performance ability.

This is an example of the kind of problem organizations encounter in selecting employees. Although the law does not bar the use of tests and related selection devices per se, it does require that employers prove that they are directly applicable to job performance. Thus, when organizations require specific educational credentials and a designated level of achievement on tests, they must be able to show that these requirements are necessary for successful job performance.

The objective of a **selection** program is to choose the best individual for a particular job from the available candidates. **Placement** is concerned

LEARNING
OBJECTIVES

1. To learn how interviews are used in employee selection.
2. To understand the application of tests in the selection process.
3. To know the various types of validation of selection methods.
4. To understand the effect of the Uniform Guidelines on Employee Selection Procedures.
5. To be familiar with the activities applicable to the placement process.

with assigning people to the jobs available; it seeks to match the right person with the appropriate job. The selection process requires a reservoir of qualified applicants and clear definitions of the duties and requirements of the unfilled jobs. In this chapter we shall explore the selection and placement processes and consider various approaches that support *rational* selection decisions and conform to legal requirements as well. The elements of the selection process—application forms, interviews, tests, assessment methods, background checks, and assignment to the job—are discussed in detail.

The Selection Process—How It Works

The selection process is a series of steps starting with preliminary screening and culminating in the assignment of newly hired employees. Figure 6.1 is a flow diagram depicting this process; each step is discussed below.

INITIATION OF THE SELECTION PROCESS

Recognizing future human resource requirements is the starting point in the selection process. The department manager who needs an employee usually requests candidates. For example, at Chase Manhattan Bank, managers who requisition candidates must supply explicit information as to the skills and related requirements that are essential to the actual task to be performed. The personnel department then accumulates the requisitions and groups job openings into occupational clusters—groups of jobs with similar requirements. This provides interviewers with comprehensive information about each job vacancy and achieves bank-wide consistency in hiring standards.[1]

In filling openings above the entry level, most organizations first search for qualified candidates within the organization by checking promotion lists, requests for transfer, management recommendations, and performance appraisal data. When it becomes necessary to find outside candidates, the recruiting program takes over.

PRELIMINARY SCREENING OR INTERVIEWING

The preliminary **interview,** the applicant's first personal contact with the organization, is used to screen out unsuitable and uninterested applicants. Coupled with an abbreviated **application form,** this screening device can elicit information on prospective applicants' basic education, experience, background, and abilities. However, the major drawback of this approach is the relative inexperience of preliminary interviewers; they may eliminate some desirable applicants. Some of this overscreening can be averted by using highly structured interviews, with specific instructions on the screening criteria being used. Following this preliminary screening, applicants who are

Figure 6.1
Steps in the Selection
Process

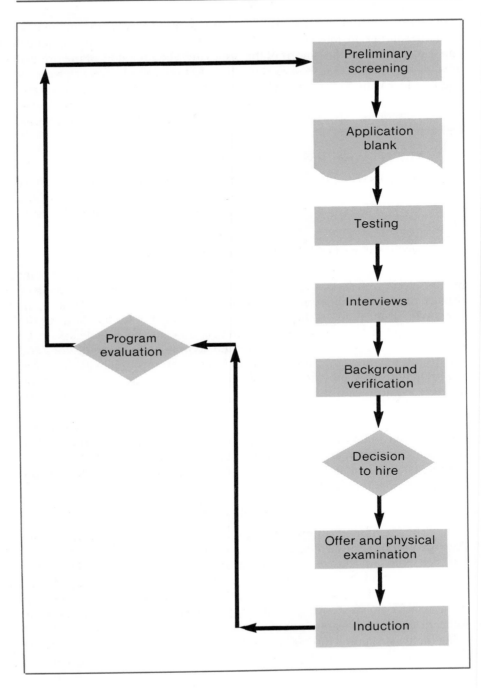

still potential candidates complete a more detailed application form prior to in-depth interviews.

APPLICATION FORMS

There is a wide variety of application forms for gathering information from candidates. The amount of information may vary from the basic name, address, and phone number, to a detailed description of education, work history, and personal data.

Employment applications essentially have two purposes. First, they provide information that can be used to screen candidates. In this respect they are a type of highly structured interview in which standard questions have been developed in advance. Second, they are a source of information for personnel records should the candidate be hired.

Information to be included in the application form is contingent upon its use and legal constraints. Certain questions are prohibited by law, for example, EEOC and Privacy of Information regulations restrict certain questions. (Data allowed and prohibited by law are detailed in Table 6.1.) The Southern Bell Telephone and Telegraph Company application, Figure 6.2, is a good example of a form that is well designed, simple to use, and conforms to equal employment opportunity guidelines.

Properly applied to the selection process, the application form can be one of the better selection devices available to a personnel manager. The weighted application blank and questionnaire are examples of more effective types of applications.

THE WEIGHTED APPLICATION BLANK. Studies have shown that the **weighted application blank** can be a useful tool in selecting employees.[2] Certain items in an applicant's personal history (education, marital status, number of dependents, previous work experience, earnings, etc.) may be predictive of future success on the job. For instance, an insurance company found that prior salary and the number of dependents can be correlated with the sales production of life insurance agents.[3]

Developing a weighted application blank is relatively simple.[4] For example, a company may wish to reduce the turnover rate for a particular position. First, it identifies groups of long-tenure and short-tenure employees who were hired at about the same time. (Short-tenure employees are those who left the company after a brief period of employment.) The person performing the validation then selects data on the application blank that distinguish one group from the other, and weights these items according to the magnitude of difference. Next, a scoring key consisting of those items is developed. Recruiters then use the scoring key to select employees who will probably stay with the company.

Table 6.1
Guide to Fairness of
Selection Practices

Selection Practice	Fair	Unfair*
Testing	To use for selection when tests have been validated for the position.	To use when no direct relationship exists between test and position.
Reference checks	To inquire about work experience and qualifications for job.	To request clergyman's recommendation. To check with present employer without applicant's written consent.
Use of application, advertisement, or interview		
Name	To ask whether applicant has ever worked for this company under a different name or to request information relative to a change of name, assumed name, or nickname necessary to enable a check on work record.	To ask original name of applicant whose name has been changed by court order or otherwise. To ask maiden name of a married woman. To ask names and dates if applicant has worked under another name.
Sex	None.	To make pre-employment inquiry which expresses any limitation, specification, or discrimination about sex unless based on bonafide occupational qualification.
Age	To require proof of age, after hiring. To require work permit for school-age employees.	It is unlawful to discriminate in preference for applicants under 40.
Birthplace		To ask birthplace of applicant.
Marital status	To ask marital status after hiring, for insurance purposes.	To ask marital status or spouse's employment prior to hiring.
Children	To ask numbers and ages of children after hiring, for insurance purposes.	To ask whether applicant has children, who cares for them, or whether applicant plans to have more.

Table 6.1 (cont.)

Selection Practice	Fair	Unfair*
Religion		To inquire into an applicant's religious affiliation, church, pastor, or holidays observed.
		To ask applicant if the organization is Catholic, Jewish, Protestant, etc.
Relatives	To ask name and address of next of kin or relatives already employed by the company.	To inquire, prior to hiring, if parents or spouse are native born.
Race		To inquire into race, creed, or national origin in application or interview.
Physical characteristics	To explain manual labor, lifting, or other requirements of job. To show how job is performed. To require physical exam.	To ask height or weight.
Citizenship	Whether applicant can provide proof of citizenship, visa, etc. after hiring.	Any inquiry into citizenship that would attempt to reveal applicant's lineage, descent, or national origin.
Organizations	To request information on organizations except those indicating race, sex, creed, or national origin.	To require applicant to list all organizations and clubs to which he or she belongs.
Character	To inquire about convictions for crimes (time, place, and disposition).	To inquire if applicants have ever been arrested.
Education	To inquire into the academic, vocational, or professional education of an applicant and the schools he attended.	To require a high school diploma or other educational attainment when no direct relationship exists between the requirement and successful job performance.
Language	To inquire into languages applicant speaks and writes fluently.	To inquire into how applicant acquired ability to read, write, or speak a foreign language.
Disability	To ask if applicant has any impairment, physical or	To ask whether an applicant has a disability or has had

Table 6.1 (cont.)

Selection Practice	Fair	Unfair*
	mental, which would interfere with his/her ability to perform the job for which he/she has applied. To ask if there are any positions or types of positions for which he/she should not be considered or if there are job duties he/she cannot perform because of a physical handicap.	any of a list of diseases. To ask whether any member of his/her family ever had any of a list of diseases.
Military experience	To ask if an applicant has ever been a member of the armed services of the United States or in a state militia. To ask whether military experience has any relationship to the job for which he/she has applied.	To inquire into an applicant's general military experience or type of discharge.
Economic status, house or automobile ownership, or credit rating	To ask how an applicant can be contacted.	To ask if applicant owns his/her home, rents, or lives in an apartment or house. Names and relationships of persons which whom applicant resides.
Photograph requirement	To require for identification purposes after hiring.	To request photographs prior to employment.
Records on racial identity	To maintain records on racial and ethnic identity of employees for purposes of reporting, if files are kept separate from personnel forms or other records available to those responsible for personnel decisions.	To identify by race, creed, or national origin in personnel files or payroll records.
Exclusion because of race, religion, sex, or national origin		Any practice or inquiry that intentionally or unintentionally discriminates against applicants because of race, sex, creed, or national origin.

*Note: These questions are not unfair, per se, but if they have an adverse impact or unequal consequences for minorities, females or other protected classes, they might be construed as illegal.

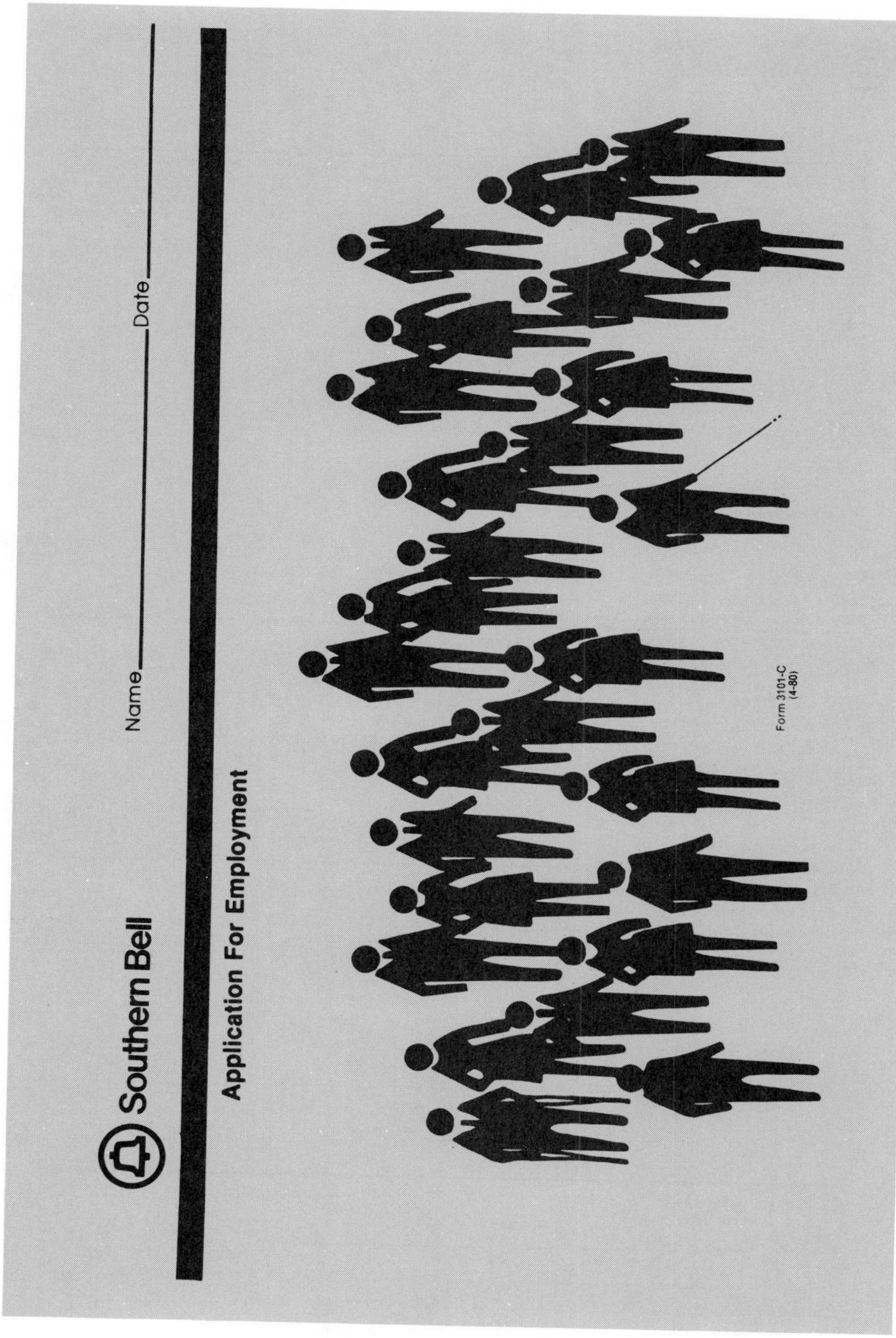

Figure 6.2

Reproduced with permission,
Southern Bell Telephone and
Telegraph Company.

**Figure 6.2
(cont.)**

Southern Bell   Application Record

An Equal Opportunity Employer. Discrimination against all individuals, including disabled veterans and veterans of the Vietnam era regardless of race, sex, color, religion, national origin, or physical or mental handicap is prohibited. The Age Discrimination in Employment Act of 1967 prohibits discrimination on the basis of age with respect to individuals who are at least 40, but less than 70 years of age. If you believe you have been discriminated against, you may notify the Equal Employment Opportunity Commission, the Federal Communications Commission, the Employment Standards Administration or other appropriate federal or state agencies.

It is Southern Bell Policy to insure that all personally identifiable information is held in confidence, properly safeguarded and the use of such information is limited to valid Business Regulatory or Legal Requirement.

Personal Data   PLEASE PRINT

Name _____   Date of Application _____
        (Last)   (First)   (Middle)

Present   Social Security
Address _____   Number _____
         Number/Street   City   State   Zip Code

Home   Present
Address _____   Telephone _____
(if different) Number/Street   City   State   Zip Code

If you are not a U.S. citizen, what is your Alien Registration or Visa Classification Form Number? _____

Were you ever an employee of a Bell System Company?   ☐ Yes   ☐ No

If "Yes", complete the following:

Name of Company _____   Dates of Employment: From __/__/__

Title(s) _____   To __/__/__

Location _____

Have you previously applied for a job with our Company? ☐ Yes ☐ No

Work Preference

Type of Work Desired _____

Kind of Work Sought   ☐ Full Time   ☐ Part Time   ☐ Summer   ☐ Temporary   ☐ Other _____

Work Location/Geographic Preference _____
                                        1st Choice   2nd Choice

Date Available to Start Work _____

Employment &   (Indicate all permanent, cooperative, summer and voluntary work including Bell System employment.
Business Experience   List most recent job first.)

Name and Address of Firm	Nature of Work	Name And Tel. # Of Supervisor	Reasons For Leaving	Salary	Dates (Mo.&Yr.) From	To

Your Last Name If Different: _____

Military Experience   (Do not include ROTC)

Branch of Service _____   From _____ To _____   Grade or Rank At Discharge _____

Occupational Specialization _____   Special/Technical Training _____
                                                (Show Dates; Names and
                                                Addresses of Schools)

Figure 6.2
(cont.)

Education (Include all periods of schooling beginning with high school)

Name and Address of High School, College(s) or other Schools	Dates of Attendance				School Years Completed	Major Field	Degree Received or Expected (if applicable)	
	From		To				Degree	Date
	Mo.	Yr.	Mo.	Yr.				

Scholastic Record (College Only)

Undergraduate: Grade Point Average _____ Cumulative To _____ Yrs. Out of Possible _____ Pts. Rank in Class   Top Qtr. ☐ 2nd Qtr. ☐ 3rd Qtr. ☐ 4th Qtr. ☐

Graduate: Grade Point Average _____ Cumulative To _____ Yrs. Out of Possible _____ Pts. Rank in Class   ☐ ☐ ☐ ☐

Activities   Schools, campus, professional, and/or community (you need not list any organization or activity, the name of which indicates the race, sex, color, religion or national origin of its members).

What Special Training Or Skills Do You Possess ? (e.g., 1st Or 2nd Class Radio License, Programming, Typing, Steno, Keypunch, etc.)

Additional Information

Do you have a valid driver's license? ☐ Yes ☐ No   Number _____ State _____

Have you ever been convicted of or are you awaiting trial for a violation of the law, other than a minor* traffic violation (*Minor — a non-moving violation such as a parking ticket)? ☐ Yes ☐ No   **The fact that you are awaiting trial or have a record of conviction will not necessarily bar you from employment.**

If "Yes", explain: _____

It is the policy of the Bell System to treat qualified handicapped individuals, disabled veterans, and veterans of the Vietnam era without discrimination and to fulfill its commitment to equal employment opportunity and the provisions of Section 503 of the Rehabilitation Act of 1973 and Section 402 of the Veterans' Readjustment Assistance Act of 1974. Both Acts require federal contractors to maintain affirmative action programs for applicants and employees covered by these Acts. They also require that all applicants be afforded the opportunity to voluntarily identify themselves as being handicapped individuals, disabled veterans and/or veterans of the Vietnam era.

This information is to be kept confidential and in accordance with the laws. Applicants who do not wish to provide the information will not be subject to adverse treatment.

Do you consider yourself to be handicapped? ☐ Yes ☐ No	If a veteran, did you serve on active duty more than 180 days any part of which was between August 5, 1964 and May 7, 1975? ☐ Yes ☐ No
If yes, what is the nature of your handicap? _____	Were you discharged or released with other than a dishonorable discharge? ☐ Yes ☐ No
Do you possess any special skills which would allow you to perform a job that you might not otherwise be able to do because of your handicap? _____	If yes, were you released from active duty within the past 48 months? ☐ Yes ☐ No
	Are you entitled to disability compensation under the laws administered by the U.S. Veterans Administration for a disability rate of 30% or more? ☐ Yes ☐ No
What accommodations would you need to perform a job properly and safely? _____	Were you discharged or released from active duty in military service of the United States because of a disability incurred or aggravated in the line of duty? ☐ Yes ☐ No
	If yes, was any of your active duty between August 5, 1964 and May 7, 1975? ☐ Yes ☐ No

**Figure 6.2
(cont.)**

Form 3101-C
(4-80)

AS AN APPLICANT YOU AGREE TO AND UNDERSTAND THE FOLLOWING:

1. Employment is Conditional Until Results of your Pre-Employment Physical are Known and Until Information Given by you Has Been Verified.

2. You must meet Minimum Age Requirements of Applicable Laws.

3. Your eligibility for a Bell System pension is based on the requirements set forth in the Company's Pension Plan, the provisions of which will be described in company publications which will be provided to you upon your employment.

    However, if you are employed after age 60 you are ineligible to participate in the Pension Plan. Additionally, if you do not satisfy the service and age requirements provided by the Plan you will not be eligible to receive a pension.

4. The Company May Conduct Investigations Including Verification of Prior Employment History and Education. By Signing This Application You Authorize the Company to Make These Investigations, and You Indicate Your Awareness That False Statements or Failures to Disclose Information May be Sufficient to Disqualify You for Employment, or if Employed, May Result in Your Dismissal.

Signature
of Applicant _____ Date _____
              FIRST   MIDDLE   LAST

For office use only.

Although the weighted application has not been widely used, the **biographical questionnaire,** which stems from early work on the weighted application, is a promising development in selecting managerial, technical, and sales personnel.[5] This instrument, which is usually constructed and validated by a trained psychologist, is a statistically weighted list of questions about an applicant's personal history. It asks an applicant to select one of several responses for each question. The interviewers then score and interpret the completed biographical questionnaires as if they were tests.

A WORD OF CAUTION.   The weighted application blank and biographical questionnaire can be quite effective in employee selection when many employees perform the same work and when adequate records are available. However, it should be emphasized that success criteria vary from job to job, and organizations must, by law, validate the factors they use as predictors. Organizations must also revalidate their scoring key periodically, since it may not remain accurate indefinitely. Finally, organizations should not hire or reject applicants solely on the basis of one or two answers on an application or biographical questionnaire but, instead, should base their decision on an overall evaluation of their abilities.

TESTING

Properly developed and administered **tests** can be invaluable in the selection process. Some employers test candidates prior to interviewing because the interview often costs more than testing, and the effectiveness of the interview as a selection device varies with the skill of the interviewer. Because of its relative importance and the controversy surrounding testing, a separate section of this chapter is devoted to it.

SELECTION INTERVIEWS

The interview remains the most widely used method for selection.[6] The higher the position, the greater the need for interviewing. In the more important areas, organizations do not make decisions on candidates until after a series of interviews.

In interviewing, an organization's representatives observe and talk with applicants to evaluate their potential value to the organization. Interviewers appraise applicants' mental, physical, emotional, and social qualities; the comprehensiveness of these questions depends upon the nature of the job and the special skills and personality traits needed for it. Interviewers want to match personal qualifications with job requirements in order to find the right person for the job. In addition, they explore any questionable information on a candidate's application blank. Interviewers also supply information to applicants to help them evaluate the company. Finally, interviewers make a subjective assessment of applicants based upon factual information and general impressions. They then decide to hire, reject, or recommend some for further interviews. (The interview process and its techniques are discussed in detail in Chapter 8.)

ASSESSING THE APPLICANT

Following the interviews and tests, the personnel staff decides if applicants are acceptable. Effective interviewers accumulate a great deal of information about applicants to use in evaluations. And test scores can provide an additional dimension in assessment. A method that has proven popular for assessing new, as well as promotable, candidates is the **assessment center.**

Assessment centers differ from conventional selection procedures in that specially trained line managers at a higher level than the candidates, but not their immediate superiors, use multiple exercises to evaluate six to twelve individuals at the same time. The candidates for employment, promotion, or development participate in a comprehensive assessment procedure that includes: personal interviews, management games, leaderless group discussions, individual presentations, mock interviews, written exercises, paper-and-pencil tests, and personality and interest inventories. During a typical three-day assessment that simulates job conditions, specially trained management evaluators observe and evaluate candidates. These evaluators then spend an additional two days estimating potential ranging from nonemployable to vice presidential or presidential caliber. The evaluation report, which may be shared with the candidates, generally summarizes their strengths and weaknesses and makes recommendations on their suitability for employment or promotion.

Although AT&T pioneered in this selection method, at least 300 other organizations have run assessment centers, and the number is growing steadily.[7] Sears, IBM, Standard Oil of Ohio, J. C. Penney, and General Electric are a few of the large firms reporting success using this method. Even small companies have utilized assessment centers. York Graphic Services, with 300 employees, reported success with the program in hiring proofreaders, page make-up personnel, electronic technicians, and certain managers.[8] One advantage they cite is that the team of trained assessors, which is not associated with the candidates but is familiar with job requirements, makes valid, unbiased selections. The fact that no assessment center has ever been challenged on its legality is a prime consideration in its adoption.[9] The contributing factors are the high inter-rater reliability (consistent ratings among assessors) and the impressive predictive validity (assessment centers measure what they purport to measure).[10] An additional advantage is that all candidates, tested under similar conditions for needed skills and abilities, have equal opportunity to display their abilities. Another favorable aspect of these is that talent that might otherwise go undetected can be recognized. Ford's Autolite Division reported the case of a middle-management candidate, with no college degree and no office experience, whose analytical abilities as revealed in their assessment center made him a prime candidate for promotion. Had he not participated in the exercises, management probably would not have noticed his potential.[11]

Assessment centers are used for initial selection as well as for promotion. For promotion decisions or to identify managerial potential, assessment center results are usually combined with interviews conducted by managers and performance appraisal results. When used to make hiring decisions, assessment center data are used in conjunction with information obtained from background investigation, application forms, and selection interviews. In each case, Byham[12] contends that the assessment center is part of a complete decision-making system. In this system, valid job analysis is the key because it provides the dimensions (i.e., descriptions under which behavior can be reliably classified. Assessment dimensions might include oral communication skill, job motivation, initiative leadership, judgment, analysis.) on which a selection system can be built, the rationale for the assessment center exercises, and the rationale for the other components (appraisal data, interviews, etc.) of the system.

There are several drawbacks to the assessment center approach. The process is time-consuming; it takes from one to four days to assess candidates, and additional time is needed to evaluate the results. The success of the assessment center is dependent upon the training of assessors who must be familiar with the work to be performed and the administering of tests. In addition, the center requires the commitment of considerable resources, particularly the time of supervisory and managerial personnel.

BACKGROUND INVESTIGATION

A **background investigation** is usually conducted prior to the actual offer of employment. The background check consists of verifying information from the applicant and obtaining additional information from references and previous employers. The check gives the organization definite evidence of an applicant's previous job performance and investigates the reasons behind his job change. The prospective employer, however, is required by law to secure an applicant's permission before checking references or verifying previous employment.[13]

For a small fee, outside organizations also perform background investigations. Local credit bureaus and organizations like Equifax can provide relatively accurate, detailed information on an individual's work history, financial condition, and character.

A few organizations use less conventional methods such as the **polygraph** (lie-detector) to verify employment information. Although its use is limited due to restrictive state laws and the requirement that polygraph operators be specifically trained and licensed, it can be a viable supplement or alternative to the traditional background check.[14]

From the writings on polygraph use and judicial opinions in polygraph cases, certain criteria for using the results of polygraph tests seem to emerge. They include these conditions that are applicable to employee selection:

1. The test should be administered by a qualified examiner;

2. The test should be voluntary;

3. The examinee must agree to the presentation of results to the prospective employer regardless of their outcome *before* submitting to the test;

4. The examinee should be medically certified to be in proper condition. (A blood test and urinalysis are usually administered to determine if there is a presence of sedatives or tranquilizing drugs in a person's system.)

Also, writers on the subject of the polygraph cite the fact that results can vary depending on the competence and experience of the examiner and this is the major drawback.

The following information on applicants is usually gathered in the background investigation:

1. Verification by former employers of an applicant's dates of employment, job duties, earnings, and reason(s) for leaving.

2. Assessment by their immediate supervisor(s) (or someone familiar with their performance on previous jobs).

3. Assessment of the applicant's character, including the reason(s) for recommendations. A general recommendation is of little value; employers need to know specifically why references recommend the applicants and consider them suitable for the job.

4. Verification of all credentials listed in the application. This can be difficult to do. If a prospective employee cites an academic degree, a certified transcript should be supplied, or the company can contact the registrar at the school.

THE OFFER

After considering all the information gathered in the selection process, the organization may decide to make an offer of employment. At this point, line managers and personnel representatives confer on the amount of compensation and other elements to be offered (relocation expenses, employment agency fees, and so on).

The timing of the offer is significant. Undue delay can result in an applicant's losing interest, but an organization needs sufficient time to consider an applicant's viability for the job and to complete their investigation. Once a determination to hire has been made, an offer enumerating the details should be made promptly and in writing. A warm, friendly invitation to join the organization, with a request for a reply within a specified period of time, generally elicits a favorable response.

Not everyone will accept an offer. The *acceptance ratio* will vary among organizations and by type of job. But acceptance ratios can be determined from historical data, with some modification to reflect variations in the economy. If an organization has the experience that one out of three of its offers to mechanical engineers has been accepted, it should make 30 offers in order to hire 10.

PHYSICAL EXAMINATION

Offers are usually made subject to the successful completion of a physical examination. These examinations can be conducted by a company physician or a doctor outside the organization; some large firms have their own clinics. The objective is to screen out individuals whose physical deficiencies might be expensive liabilities and to place people in jobs they can handle without injury or damage to their health. Physical examinations also protect companies against unwarranted worker's compensation claims by detecting ailments or impairments. However, physical exams do not guarantee that serious medical problems (e.g., cancer, back injuries, or others) will be detected. Only a comprehensive physical, at prohibitive cost to the employer, can increase the likelihood of uncovering such problems. The alternative is to have applicants attest to the accuracy of a questionnaire on health, and sign a release of information from their physicians.

EVALUATION OF THE SELECTION PROCESS

Follow-up studies and information-gathering activities determine if selection programs are effective. Decisions to hire are based on candidates' expected performance as indicated by applications, interviews, tests, and background investigations. If these expectations are borne out in actual experience, then the selection procedure is valid and successful. Conversely, if work experience contradicts selection predictions, the process has failed. There is little sense in expending funds on selection and placement without knowing how effective the programs are. For example, a small midwestern manufacturer of farm machinery abolished an adequate personnel department and went back to the prior catch-as-catch-can method of hiring, which resulted in more goofs and higher turnover, but only cost an estimated $15,000 per year in terms of mistakes made in hiring. Though these would have been caught by the more sophisticated system, its cost would be closer to $50,000 per year.

Testing

Tests can be invaluable supplements to interviews, applications, and background checks in the effective selection of employees. Properly developed and administered, tests improve the accuracy of selection by measuring individual differences in physical attributes, skills, abilities, motivation interests, and aptitudes. Schmidt and his colleagues[15] concluded from their research that the impact on workforce productivity of valid selection procedures is considerably greater than had been believed previously. From the results of their study using the Programmer Aptitude Test (PAT) to select new computer programmers they estimated that hundreds of millions of dollars could be saved by increasing the validity of selection decisions in the computer programmer occupation alone and that there are likely similarities between this occupation and others.

VALIDATION OF SELECTION DEVICES

The methods used to select employees (applications, interviews, tests, background checks, and other related devices) are required by law to be valid. **Validity** is the degree to which a selection device is a good indicator or predictor of success for the job performance in question. More precisely, validity has been defined by the American Psychological Association as, "the degree to which inferences from scores on tests or assessments are justified or supported by evidence. It should be noted that validity refers to the inferences made from the procedure, not to the procedure itself".[16] Valid selection methods are able to predict performance on a specific job. Federal guidelines now require organizations to provide documented evidence that their selection devices are valid and that they in no way discriminate against people required to take them. Selection devices must have validity for the job in question. For example, a mechanical aptitude test may accurately measure mechanical aptitude, but the test results cannot be used to select for a job unless successful performance on that job depends on mechanical aptitude.

UNIFORM GUIDELINES ON EMPLOYEE SELECTION PROCEDURES

In 1978 the federal regulatory agencies concerned with selection procedures (Equal Employment Opportunity Commission, Civil Service Commission [currently the Office of Personnel Management], Department of Labor, and the Department of Justice) jointly adopted the **Uniform Guidelines on Employee Selection Procedures.** The relevant aspects of the guidelines are described below.[17]

1. Selection devices construed as tests were defined as any paper and pencil or performance measure used as a basis for any selection decision, for example, selection for hiring, promotion, demotion, training, transfer, and retention among others.

2. A selection method or procedure would be considered discriminating if it had an adverse impact on classes of people protected by Title VII of the Civil Rights Act. The selection procedure may be justified, however, despite its adverse impact, if business necessity can be demonstrated. Also, if the inferences made from the procedure are highly correlated with success on the job, as shown by hiring people with a broad range of scores, and the trait being measured is a bona fide occupational qualification (BFOQ) the procedures used might be justified. For example, tall people over a certain height are precluded from being selected as flight attendants because of the restricted (overhead) size of aircraft cabins.

3. A fundamental principle underlying the guidelines is that employment practices which tend to limit (i.e., have an adverse impact on) groups protected by Title VII of the Civil Rights Act are illegal. To ascertain whether an adverse impact exists the agencies which are parties to the guidelines use a rule of a thumb called the *four-fifths rule*. Essentially it compares a given group (e.g., blacks, females) to the group with the highest rate of employment in the organization. To be in compliance, the protected class should show a selection rate at least 80 percent (4/5) of the group with the highest rate. Using the four-fifths rule of thumb, the regulatory agencies compare the participation rates of nonminorities, minorities, and females to determine if there is an underutilization and thus an adverse impact on one of the protected classes of employees.

4. Tests should be validated according to procedures of the American Psychological Association's *Standards for Educational and Psychological Tests and Manuals*. Acceptable forms of validation include content validity, construct validity, and criterion-related validity. In cases where content or construct validity is used, relevance must be demonstrated through job analyses.

5. Evidence of the test's validity should consist of empirical data demonstrating that the test is predictive of, or sufficiently correlated with, essential elements of the particular job for which the candidate is being evaluated.

TYPES OF VALIDATION

CRITERION-RELATED VALIDITY. A selection device has criterion-related validity when test scores and some objective measure of job performance (number of units produced, salary, units sold) are closely related, that is, there is a high **correlation** for the same individuals. EEOC guidelines require that, where feasible, these relationships be shown separately for groups by race, religion, sex, and age. The purpose is to assure that the tests apply with equal fairness to members of these groups.

CONTENT VALIDITY.   Specific duties that are representative of the skills, knowledge, and abilities required to perform the job form the basis of the test. Tests that are content valid might include standardized typing tests containing material that would typically be typed on the job, and have appropriate speed and accuracy scoring; tests in which actual job duties such as welding, carpentry, or computer operation, are performed.

CONSTRUCT VALIDITY.   A test is developed to measure a trait or ability that is related to successful job performance. Guidelines require that the test does, in fact, measure the trait and that it is truly related to successful performance of the job.

CROSS-VALIDATION.   Cross-validation demonstrates statistically whether a decision or set of weights derived in one sample remains as effective when this decision is applied to another sample (a different group of people independently drawn from the same population as the validation sample) of people. Cross-validation provides an independent check on the validity of predictive measures (a test).

THE VALIDATION PROCESS

The Uniform Guidelines define the process that should be followed to validate selection measures. When a measure or device is validated according to the following steps it is said to have *predictive validity*.

Step 1. Perform *job analysis*. The techniques for job analysis were outlined in Chapter 4, "Human Resource Planning." For validation purposes it is necessary to study the job or job cluster to identify distinguishing characteristics and the requirements for successful performance of it. These might include personality factors, specific skills, intellectual abilities, job knowledge, kinds of prior experience, or other measures that can be taken before job placement.

Step 2. Decide on the specific predictor measures to be used, and the instruments and devices that will test them. For example, sales personality can be determined from a paper-and-pencil test or an interview. Not only should the test device be selected, but the specific type to be used should also be decided.

Step 3. Select a research group. EEOC Guidelines require that the group be representative of the normal or typical candidate group for the job(s) in question. It must also be representative of the minority population in the local job market. The guidelines also require that a minimum of 30 individuals be included in the group. This obviously would preclude small companies from performing validity studies, but the EEOC suggests that groups of employers with the same types of jobs can use their combined present employees or applicants as the research group.

Although the use of present employees as the research group has cost advantages, it has, from a scientific standpoint, drawbacks. Present employees have already been screened, and those who have failed on the job have left voluntarily or have been discharged. Thus, the research group may not be representative of the typical candidate group. Consequently, this approach, referred to as *concurrent validity*, may not be as desirable from a scientific standpoint as the *follow-up* or *predictive-validity* method. Under this approach people are hired without considering any of the measures obtained at this step. At a later date, these employees are tested and the results are correlated with their job performance. The drawback is the lengthy delay before the test can be validated.

Step 4. Gather **criterion** data—the standard of judgment—on the research group. Information such as units produced, training time required to become proficient, regularity of attendance, number of rejects, units or dollar volume of sales, and so on could be used to measure the work behavior or adequacy of these employees. The data would not be suitable as criteria until the employees had been on the job long enough to stabilize their levels of performance.

Step 5. Calculate the degree of relationship between the predictor values (Step 2) and the criterion measures (Step 4). The predictor should be closely and positively related to the criterion to be considered valid. Statistically, this can be accomplished by calculating the coefficient of correlation (any basic statistics text describes the method).

Usually it is desirable to use several predictors to measure a variety of characteristics in combination. In this case alternative statistical procedures, for example, multiple correlation, are available to perform the calculations.

Step 6. If Step 5 yields a relatively good predictive validity, the study should be repeated with the same job using the same predictors and criteria, but with a different group. This is called *cross-validation* and serves to add confidence that the relationship between the predictor and the criterion measures can be relied on for future employment selections.

EVIDENCE OF VALIDITY

The burden rests with the employer to prove that its selection methods are valid. Generally, selection devices that are validated in accordance with the steps described above will prove acceptable. The best evidence of validity is that the people selected are indeed performing on their jobs as the tests predicted they would. In addition, if an organization contains the number of minorities and women employees at various levels, proportionate to the local labor market, the selection program probably would not be challenged.

However, to ensure that evidence of validity is present, court-proof selection systems usually meet these criteria:

1. Selection devices have predictive validity. They have been validated for each minority group with which they are used, and any differential rejection rates are relevant to performance of the jobs being filled.

2. Predictive data are correlated with criteria relevant to successful job performance.

3. The test has been validated for each job for which it is used. However, when there are no significant differences between jobs and applicant populations, evidence that the test is valid for one unit or company can be used for jobs in other units or companies in the same industry.

4. Tests are administered under controlled and standardized conditions, with safeguards against unauthorized or premature access. If a candidate has prior knowledge of a test the results will be biased. By the same token, test scores not properly interpreted might color judgments of a candidate's acceptability.

5. Performance criteria should be relevant to job success, and they must represent major or critical work behaviors as revealed by job analysis. The most acceptable criteria are objective in nature—units of output, attendance. Subjective criteria such as supervisory ratings need to be carefully developed to minimize rater bias. Too often, low performance ratings are the result of supervisor prejudices, which can unfairly depress the scores of minority groups.

6. **Cutoff scores** need to be reasonable and consistent with normal expectations of proficiency within the study group (the groups used to perform the validation study).

REQUIREMENTS OF A GOOD TEST

We have already discussed the requirement of a test to measure what it purports to measure—*validity*. But a good test[18] must also have **reliability**. A test instrument is considered reliable if the individual taking the test on several occasions scores approximately the same. The most obvious method for establishing reliability is to administer the same test to the same group of individuals on different occasions (the test-retest method). Or the individuals can be given one form of the test on a first occasion and an alternate, comparable form on a second (the alternate-form method). A third approach compares scores on two halves of the same test (the split-half method). The test is divided into halves, that is, odd-numbered questions are compared with the results of the even-numbered to ascertain the degree of reliability.

Classification of Tests

The simplest and most prevalent classification is by function or purpose—namely, mental ability, aptitude, proficiency, interest, personality, and performance. Each of these tests is discussed below. (A list of test publishers is appended to this chapter.)

MENTAL ABILITY OR INTELLIGENCE TESTS

The **mental-ability test** is widely used in selection as a measure of general learning ability. It has proven useful in predicting training potential as well as success in managerial, supervisory, sales, and some clerical and skilled jobs. Some of the more widely used intelligence tests are discussed here. The popular Wonderlic Personnel Test (E. F. Wonderlic and Associates) is a 12-minute individual or group test (this flexibility makes it particularly attractive to industrial users). Its highest validity is in selecting clerical workers. But the Wonderlic has a serious limitation—because of its widespread use, many people have taken the test before, so its reliability is low. The twenty-minute Thurstone Test of Mental Alertness (Science Research Associates, or SRA) measures language and arithmetic problem-solving abilities and yields verbal, quantitative, and total scores. Its greatest validity is in sales and clerical areas. The Adaptability Test (SRA) was designed specifically for personnel placement. It is a 15-minute test used primarily to select clerical workers and first-line supervisors.

APTITUDE TESTS

Generally, the term **aptitude test** refers to any test that is useful in predicting job or training success. An aptitude test either estimates the extent to which an individual will profit from training, or forecasts the achievement level of an employee in a new assignment. Aptitude tests are classified as either multiaptitude or special aptitude.

MULTIAPTITUDE TESTS. These test batteries measure the individual's standing in a number of traits. Instead of a total score or IQ, each trait is scored separately. For example, the three-hour Differential Aptitude Test, or DAT (Psychological Corporation), is a series of eight tests covering verbal reasoning, clerical speed, abstract reasoning, numerical ability, space relations, mechanical reasoning, spelling, and sentences. Each test in the DAT is useful by itself. Other examples of multiaptitude test batteries include the Flanagan Industrial Tests (SRA) and General Aptitude Test Battery.

SPECIAL APTITUDE TESTS. The problem of matching job requirements to specific patterns of abilities led to the construction of special aptitude tests (e.g., clerical, mechanical, dexterity, and sensory).

Clerical Aptitude Tests are among the most widely used. The most effective clerical tests are brief and depend on speed of perception rather than complex reasoning. Most involve spelling, arithmetic, name and number comparisons, vocabulary, copying, verbal and numerical reasoning, and immediate memory. Among the more widely used are the Minnesota Clerical and Short Employment Test (both from Psychological Corporation) and SRA Short Tests of Clerical Ability.

Mechanical aptitude appears to be a combination of spatial visualization, mechanical knowledge, and perceptual speed and acuity. Because of the specific nature of job traits, companies should identify the requisite traits through job analysis and then conduct research to select the mechanical-aptitude tests that will most effectively measure these traits. Mechanical-aptitude tests have been found useful in selecting apprentices and workers in skilled mechanical trades as well as technical employees (engineers, technicians). Examples of mechanical aptitude tests include the Bennett Test of Mechanical Comprehension and the Minnesota Paper Form Board (both from the Psychological Corporation) and the SRA Mechanical Aptitude test.

Dexterity tests measure speed, coordination, and other characteristics of movement response. Most are concerned with manual dexterity. They have been used to select assemblers, production workers, packers, machine operators, and so on. The Purdue Pegboard and Crawford Small Parts Dexterity Test (both from the Psychological Corporation) are examples.

Success in certain jobs requires physical attributes such as visual acuity, color vision, and good hearing. Research indicates that sensory handicaps adversely affect the quality and quantity of some types of work. Some of the more widely used instruments for testing vision include the Ortho Rater (Bausch and Lomb) and Keystone Telebinocular (Keystone View Co.).

ACHIEVEMENT OR PROFICIENCY TESTS

Achievement tests are concerned with what people have already learned or what they can already do; they measure how well applicants know what they claim to know. Tests such as the SRA Typing Skills, Seashore-Bennett Stenographic Proficiency Test (Psychological Corporation), and Purdue Tests for Machinists and Machine Operators (SRA) are widely used to measure proficiency.

INTEREST INVENTORIES

These instruments have not been widely applied in industry and are primarily used in vocational counseling. Although the test results may indicate if a person likes a particular job, the results are not necessarily related to his success on the job. Another major drawback with interest inventories is their susceptibility to faking. Applicants tend to gear their responses to what they think is the accepted pattern of response in the company administering the test.

The Strong Vocational Interest Blank (Stanford University Press) is the oldest inventory test on the market. The form contains 400 questions of the like-indifferent-dislike variety. Scoring is done by correlating the applicant's responses with those of individuals working in a specific vocation (if a person gives responses on the SVIB similar to those of social workers, then it is inferred that his interests resemble theirs). The Kuder Preference Record (SRA) presents test items in triads; applicants choose the one they like best or the one they like least in each triad. The results form a profile of their interests in ten major fields: outdoor, mechanical, computational, scientific, persuasive, artistic, musical, literary, social service, and clerical.

PERSONALITY INVENTORIES

Personality inventories measure motivational, emotional, interpersonal, and attitudinal characteristics. Several have been developed for industry, but they are frequently characterized by low reliability and validity; hence, their accuracy and usefulness have been questioned. Personality tests can be classified as self-report inventories and projective tests. A self-report inventory generally involves a response in terms of how much the individuals being tested agree with a statement, or how well it describes them, or which of the alternatives they prefer. The California Psychological Inventory (Consulting Psychologist Press), Edwards Personal Preference Schedule (Psychological Corporation), and the Minnesota Multiphasic Personality Inventory, or MMPI (SRA), are self-report inventories. Industry's use of the MMPI has been slight because this well-known inventory is essentially a clinical instrument, the proper interpretation of which calls for considerable psychological sophistication. However, the MMPI has served as a basis for the development of other widely used inventories such as the California Psychological Inventory.

A **projective test** is an unstructured task that induces people to reveal certain aspects of their personality during the process of responding. Projective methods originated in clinical settings and remain predominantly a tool for clinicians. In the Rorschach, one of the more popular, the examiner presents a series of ten inkblots and asks a subject to state freely what he sees. The examiner, who must be trained in this technique, then analyzes the results. Scoring is based on the type of response—whether the subject reports movement, human figures, animate or inanimate objects, and so on. The Thematic Apperception Test is another well-known projective test. It presents a series of pictures to subjects who are asked to tell an extemporaneous story about each picture. The examiner analyzes the themes of the stories to reveal dominant drives as well as conflicts and inhibitions. As with the Rorschach, special training is needed to administer and interpret this test.

PERFORMANCE TESTS

Performance tests allow candidates to demonstrate their ability to perform a given skill or task. They have a clear bias in favor of the experienced employee, but solve problems for the small employer who does not have the means of providing extensive or long-term training.

Similar to the performance test is the *trade test* (used extensively by the armed services and some large employers). This type of test relies predominantly on knowledge of specialized terms and procedures that are more-or-less exclusive to the trade or profession in question. Instead of the applicant cooking a batch of biscuits (performance test), he/she is asked questions about the kind and proportion of ingredients, mixing procedure, temperature used, and so on.

These types of tests have high *face* validity and practical utility. But neither will inform an employer as to a candidate's potential for exceptional performance.

Test Scoring

Test scoring itself deserves careful consideration. A score represents an individual's measure of achievement or level of accomplishment on a particular test. The total number of answers that agree with the scoring key is known as the **raw score**. But his score alone has little meaning until it is compared to the scores of others who took the same test. The **average** (mean) or **norm** is one basis of comparison, but a **percentile** rating is more specific. For example, if a person had a raw score of 70 and the average for the group taking the test is 65, we would conclude that he or she scored slightly above average. If the score was at the 60th percentile it would mean that 60 percent of the people taking the test had scored lower. The raw score of 70 would have been more favorable had it resulted in percentile equivalent of 90 or better. Finally, the **cutoff score** is the minimum score an applicant must achieve to be considered. If the cutoff score were 75, the person achieving a raw score of 70 would be rejected. Many organizations have applied variable cutoff scores to applicants in order to "screen in" larger numbers of minority groups who might otherwise be rejected.

Areas of Test Application

Test programs are most applicable to blue-collar and clerical positions because these represent the greatest number of jobs in the labor market, and their duties are similar within a given job classification. Consequently, companies utilize a wide variety of intelligence, ability, and aptitude tests in selecting personnel for these positions.

However, the same degree of usefulness does not hold true for managerial, sales, and scientific positions. The wide range of requisite abilities needed in these areas makes it difficult to obtain criteria to validate tests. Intelligence tests for managerial positions, and biographical and interest inventories for sales personnel, however, have proven to be somewhat effective in employee selection. Biographical inventories have also proven useful for some scientific positions.

Placement Activities
INITIAL JOB PLACEMENT

Candidates who successfully complete all the steps of the selection process are finally matched with a job and placed in a department where their talents could be utilized. Cascio[19] describes several classification strategies for placing employees in jobs.

1. The *vocational guidance* strategy calls for placing each employee according to his or her best talent. The drawback to this approach however, is that, assuming there are several vacancies in the same job classification, one would be filled by an overqualified person and the others would contain unqualified employees.

2. *Pure selection* involves filling each job with the most qualified person. This strategy offers maximum payoff to the organization (obviously, the vocational guidance strategy maximizes payoff to the individual), but its impracticality lies in the fact that it leaves many unplaced or underutilized.

3. The *cut and fit* strategy according to Cascio combines the first two approaches by placing workers so that all jobs are filled by those with adequate talent. This strategy allows people to be placed on jobs which make the best available use of their talents. Employees can be considered for successively less important jobs until their qualifications fit one of them.

Following initial placement the new employee is oriented to the organization and trained for the specific job he or she will perform. The personnel staff can be of significant service to the line supervisor by providing detailed information on the new employee. Unfortunately, the traditional practice has been to withhold basic employee information because the personnel staff assumes line management is incapable of utilizing the data discreetly. This practice defeats the very purpose of gathering details of an employee's background, experience, and abilities in the first place.

PROMOTION

In an effort to comply with EEOC requirements, many organizations have been giving minorities special consideration in the **promotion** process. In some instances they have even circumvented the **seniority system** to allow minorities to become more upwardly mobile and to protect them against premature layoff. The consent decree between the United Steelworkers (Union) and nine steel companies restructured the seniority system to provide freer movement from job to job and paid minorities $30.9 million in damages for reduced promotion opportunities. Until 1977, courts had generally ruled that job seniority systems—seniority is measured by length of service on a particular job—tended to discriminate against minorities. Hence, the courts ordered companies to implement systems of plant-wide seniority unless employers could demonstrate an overriding legitimate business purpose for using job seniority.[20] But in June 1977, the U.S. Supreme Court overturned these rulings in a key decision involving TIME, D.C., Inc. (a trucking company) and *The Teamsters Union* v. *EEOC*. It ruled that discriminatory intent, not merely result (the locking of racial minorities and women into lower-paying jobs while white males moved up a separate seniority ladder), must be proved. This removed the EEOC's advantage of taking a pattern approach to seniority discrimination cases and forced it to prove discrimination on a case-by-case basis.[21] The Supreme Court ruling, in effect, preserves existing seniority systems as a basis for promotion.

JOB POSTING

To reinforce policies of promotion from within, many organizations utilize a procedure known as *job posting*. Its proponents cite reduced recruitment costs, discovery of hidden skills within the firm, and increased morale as major advantages to it. More specifically, the Bank of Virginia Company reported outstanding results with its job posting program because it enhanced the career development of its employees and complemented affirmative action efforts. The bank explained that each job posting candidate receives career counseling, and those rejected for promotion are told the reasons and are guided in their efforts to improve their qualifications for future opportunities. Often, applicants are reassessed by their current department managers, and are promoted within their own departments. The bank reported that 53 of 59 recent promotions have been women or minority members, which enhanced its EEO efforts.[22]

Drawbacks of job posting include the cumbersome paperwork necessary to keep track of applicants; it encourages job hopping, which creates instability in an organization; and it requires extra time to fill a job vacancy. To overcome these shortcomings experts in the field have made these recommendations:

1. Employees should be precluded from bidding until they have been in their present position for six months or more.
2. Bulletin boards, PA systems, and handouts can be used to announce openings.
3. The job announcement should contain *specific standards* for selection, and these should be valid as specified in EEOC Guidelines.
4. The posted opening should be based on human resource plans.
5. Unsuccessful bidders should be counseled as to the reasons they were not accepted.[23]

REDUCTION IN FORCE—LAYOFF

Organizations have a variety of methods for selecting employees for layoff when conditions necessitate a reduction in the labor force. Usually, economic setbacks or seasonal fluctuations necessitate cutbacks, but a relocation of plant or offices, a strike, or the restructuring of an organization can have the same impact. When workers are to be laid off, the most common approach used is seniority: last hired, first fired. But this often has the effect of creating inordinate hardships for minority and women employees because they are invariably the last hired. To remedy such situations organizations have devised alternative systems of work sharing to distribute available work among all employees.

During slack periods in industries that practice **piecework**, for example, garment, textile, and leather, available work is distributed among the available employees in lieu of layoff. The most common form of **work sharing** in primary metals, communications, and transportation industries is reduction in the hours per shift or the number of shifts per week. Where these forms of work sharing may be impractical, as in continuous process operations or in service industries where hours of operations depend on customer demand, a rotation of employment scheme, with employees sharing, through rotation, the job slots to be filled, is the predominant approach used.[24] The concept of applying inverse seniority as an alternative to work sharing may be given serious consideration during future recessions. The program would give optional leave to senior workers within affected job classifications, thus leaving room for the last hired to be retained. The program could work best if senior employees could be induced to elect layoff with attractive pay—optional leave or layoff benefits would have to be set about two-thirds of normal pay. In addition, senior workers would have to be free to use the available time as they saw fit without having to appear weekly at unemployment offices.[25] (The topic of seniority is covered in more detail in Chapter 11.)

The concept of **outplacement** as a device to soften the blow of layoffs has gained wide acceptance lately, especially among terminated executives. Outplacement calls for training separated employees for new positions and guiding them in their search for new opportunities. The Lockheed-Georgia Company, which experiences unstable employment conditions because of phasing in-and-out of aerospace contracts, has reported favorable results with its outplacement program. Not only are laid off employees grateful for the help, but local employers who hired them began to view Lockheed as a company interested in all its employees.[26]

Job stability continues to be a major concern of employees. Unions and employers have addressed his concern by negotiating Supplemental Unemployment (SUB), Guaranteed Annual Wage (GAW) programs, and lifetime security plans. (These are described in Chapter 20.)

Situational Factors in the Selection Process
LEGAL

Discriminatory selection practices are illegal, and the government monitors minority and female selection and promotion in affirmative action programs. In this regard, minorities are groups of individuals who represent a small proportion of the labor force, usually less than 15 percent. Blacks, Chicanos, American Indians, and Orientals are considered minorities. Although women represent a significant percentage of workers, they are also classified by the government as a minority. Any methods that tend to exclude specific groups of candidates from being hired or promoted are forbidden by law. The **fair-employment practices** regulate the use of interviews, applications, tests, and other selection devices used for screening purposes. Table 6.1 on pages 156–58 lists selection and placement practices and shows lawful and unlawful uses.

Title VII of the Civil Rights Act of 1964 prohibits employment practices that artifically discriminate against individuals on the basis of test scores. Out of this legislation grew the Equal Employment Opportunity Commission (EEOC) testing guidelines, which require that companies be 95 percent confident that each test they use for employment purposes does distinguish between successful and unsuccessful candidates. The EEOC guidelines were upheld by the Supreme Court in *Griggs* v. *The Duke Power Company* (cited at the beginning of this chapter) and in *Albermarle* v. *Moody*. In the latter case the Supreme Court ruled that the company's selection tests had been inadequately validated because no job analysis had been performed and questionable performance criteria, for example, supervisor ratings, had been used. The *Albermarle* decision is significant to employers because the court ordered the company to make restitution to the litigants to make them whole for "injuries suffered on account of unlawful employment discrimination." As a result, back pay has become a standard remedy where victims of discriminatory practices have been identified.[27] Then in 1976 the U.S. Supreme Court decided, in *Franks* v. *Bowman Transportation Co.*, that employees who can prove past hiring bias can be granted retroactive seniority. These rulings strictly interpreted EEOC guidelines and severe sanctions were issued to defendants. However, in the case of *Washington* v. *Davis*, the U.S. Supreme Court found acceptable testing procedures (they were requirements for a police training program) that did not strictly adhere to EEOC guidelines. The Uniform Guidelines, however, clarified much of the previous ambiguity by specifying how to validate job relatedness of selection instruments. The result may well be a more consistent judicial support of agency enforcement of Title VII.

The experience of the steel industry's first consent decree (Consent Decree I, 1974) had some beneficial results that may have implications for organizations committed to affirmative action. The steel companies, the unions, and the courts negotiated a system that proved beneficial to all people regardless of race, sex, and age by providing steelworkers an opportunity to better themselves if they wish. The consent decree made choices available that were not there before and all parties—management, the unions, employee groups (and the courts) were parties to the system's design. The details of how the system works are not as important as the realization that it can be made to work if those affected want it to work. Through sound human resource planning and affirmative action the spirit as well as the letter of the law can be accommodated.[28]

SEX DISCRIMINATION AND SEXUAL HARASSMENT.   These are now illegal. As we have already discussed, women are now grouped with minorities under the protection of Title VII. In addition the EEOC issued guidelines dealing with sexual harassment in March 1980. They state:[29]

Unwelcome sexual advances, requests for sexual favors, and other verbal or physical conduct of a sexual nature constitute sexual harassment when (1) submission to such conduct is made either explicitly or implicitly a term or condition of an individual's employment, (2) submission to or rejection of such conduct by an individual is used as the basis for employment decisions affecting such individual, or (3) such conduct has the purpose or effect of substantially interfering with an individual's work performance or creating an intimidating, hostile or offensive working environment.

Employers are considered fully responsible for any such act committed by supervisors. In addition, employers are required to take immediate and appropriate corrective action for known acts of sexual harassment in the work place. The EEOC guidelines describe preventive measures including affirmatively raising the subject, expressing strong disapproval, establishing sanctions, developing methods to sensitize employees and supervisors, and informing people of their right to raise the issue of harassment. The guidelines also make it clear that harassment on the basis of color, race, religion, or national origin is unlawful. In response to the guidelines, many organizations are addressing the harassment issue in their EEO training.

Numerous court cases have focused on the sexual harassment issue. In one particular case, *Tompkins* v. *Public Service Electric and Gas Company* (1976), the appellate court found for the plaintiff and clarified the bases for an employer's liability in sexual harassment cases. The case came to court after an employee (the plaintiff) was sexually approached by her supervisor during a discussion about job advancement. The employee turned down her supervisor. Following the incident she was threatened with demotion or layoff and eventually she (Ms. Tompkins) was fired. In making its judgment, the court used the following test of liability:[30]

1. The harassment must somehow be linked to the victim's job status.
2. The employer must have had knowledge of the supervisor's conduct.
3. The employer has a defense if prompt remedial action is taken on learning of the behavior.[31]

The Guidelines on Sex Discrimination also cover pregnancy discrimination (Title VII was amended in 1978 to cover this aspect of discrimination). Organizations offering employees hospital, medical, surgical insurance and disability or leave benefits must provide the same coverage (including leave) as for any other disability. Some companies feared that the cost of providing pregnancy coverage would be exorbitant and they might have to cut back the coverage. But few large companies have actually done so, the Conference Board reports.[32]

The EEOC guidelines on sex discrimination also make it unlawful for employers to make a distinction because of sex on the premium costs or benefits they provide to employees. Decisions of the courts seem to uphold the EEOC. For example in a 1978 case, *City of Los Angeles* v. *Manhart*, the U.S. Supreme Court endorsed the prohibition against charging males and females differently for the same benefit. Because substantial amounts are involved in medical, life, and pension benefits, it would not be surprising to see this issue appear again before the Supreme Court.

AFFIRMATIVE ACTION FOR THE HANDICAPPED. Employing qualified handicapped individuals is the basis of the Rehabilitation Act of 1973 (amended in 1974) which requires public contractors to take affirmative action to hire, train, and promote handicapped persons. Affirmative action with regard to the handicapped means monitoring job requirements to identify work that can accommodate physical disabilities. It also provides for eliminating the architectural barriers that block or endanger the handicapped employee. For example, many buildings today have ramps for wheelchair access; catches were removed from doors so that employees with artificial limbs could enter; braille markers were conveniently placed for ready identification by blind persons; and magnifying devices were placed on TV screens or monitors to allow viewing by the visually impaired. Organizations have numerous ways in which they can adapt their environments to people's physical impairments. The cost is usually small compared to the benefits that can be realized. However, there is a fine line between the handicapped and the high-risk employee. The latter represents a liability, and an improperly selected or placed handicapped individual can become a danger to those in the immediate environment.

Problems of Workers' Compensation, a legislated protection program that compensates employees for job-related injuries or illness (discussed in Chapter 20), arise when a handicapped employee sustains a job injury and becomes totally disabled. Some states maintain in their workers' compensation programs a second injury fund to compensate for this problem.

AGE DISCRIMINATION IN EMPLOYMENT. The 1967 Age Discrimination in Employment Act (amended in 1978) seeks to protect older (40–70 years of age) applicants and workers from job discrimination, and it promotes their employment on the basis of ability rather than age. This act parallels Title VII. Initially, age discrimination was overshadowed by race and sex bias, but with the economic recessions of the mid '70s and companies attempting to create efficiencies by substituting lower-paid young employees for the older, higher compensated ones, there has been a dramatic increase in the number of age discrimination complaints.[33] It seems likely that there will soon be court settlements on age suits on the magnitude of the *Griggs* and *Moody* race discrimination cases.

ACCOMMODATING RELIGIOUS PREFERENCES. Must employers accommodate religious preference, too? Title VII makes discrimination in employment on religious grounds unlawful. But some employees feel that their religious convictions should excuse them from certain types of work or from performing job duties on certain days. An interesting case in point occurred at Meredith Company's printing facility. Several press room and bindery personnel refused to work on printing *Penthouse* and *Viva* magazines because they considered them sexually explicit and therefore contrary to their Christian principles. Management felt it could not adjust its schedules to accommodate them or others who might have similar convictions. When the employees persisted in their refusal to work on the production of the magazines, they were discharged. They filed discrimination complaints alleging violation of their religious beliefs. A court decision is still pending. In a similar case, the Parker Seal Company fired supervisor Paul Cummins because he refused to work on Saturdays because of his religious beliefs. On appeal of his case, the circuit court agreed with Cummins. The principle that emerges from this case is that the employer must make reasonable accommodation to employees' religious needs and that undue hardship on the employer must be proven to justify dismissal of an employee. But just how far an employer must go to make reasonable accommodation of religious preferences still is unclear. For example, in the postal service, the refusal by Seventh Day Adventists and others to work on Saturdays because of religious beliefs was deemed by the courts to be justification for discharge.

The reasonable accommodation issue was clarified by the U.S. Supreme Court in its 1977 decision in *Trans World Airlines* v. *Hardison*. The Court ruled that allowing Hardison the right to be off on the Sabbath would create inefficiencies and create additional costs to the employer. The Court claimed that a ruling for Hardison would be the same as denying some employees their preferences on jobs and shifts, thus depriving them of their contractual rights (TWA and its union had an agreement) in order to accommodate or prefer the religious needs of others. As a result of the Supreme Court's decision, the guidelines on religious discrimination are being revised. The revision will require employers to explore alternatives for accommodating religious preferences. Employers would have to show that each alternative would in fact result in undue hardship of more than a minimal (*de minimus*) cost.[34]

THE REVERSE DISCRIMINATION ISSUE.   If we concluded our discussion of equal employment opportunity and the selection process at this point, one would be left with the impression that employment laws were designed solely for racial minorities, women, aged, and handicapped persons. But there has been white backlash in the employment process. Recent court decisions have ruled that it is against the law to give preference to minorities to the detriment of majorities. Provision 703j of Title VII states that, "nothing contained in this Title shall be interpreted to require any employer to grant preferential treatment to any individual or group on the basis of race, color, religion, sex or national origin."[35]

Selection policies that favor minority applicants over whites are being questioned by the courts. In university programs, especially where quotas for minority applicants tend to exclude more qualified whites, they are often found to be contrary to the intent of the law. This held true in the much publicized Bakke case (U.S. Supreme Court's 1978 decision in *Regents of the University of California* v. *Bakke*). The new medical school of the University of California had instituted a special admissions program exclusively for minority group applicants. The Court held that the special admissions program unlawfully kept Bakke, a white applicant, out of the school. It did say, however, that the school could properly give some consideration to race in its admissions process.

Other reverse discrimination awards have created legal uncertainties about affirmative action selection and promotion procedures. When a Texas transportation company, for instance, fired two whites, but retained a black who was guilty of the same infraction, the court ordered reinstatement of the whites. Although the company was trying to act in accordance with the law, the court felt it had discriminated in reverse. AT&T Long Lines lost a case in its attempt to promote in accordance with a consent decree (an agreement between the company and the courts on affirmative action). It promoted a female over a white male. He sued and the company lost. More recently (1978) in *United Steelworkers of America* v. *Weber* in a reverse-discrimination suit, the U.S. Supreme Court decided that employers could indeed choose to give special job preference to blacks without fear of reverse discrimination reprisals. In this case, Brian Weber, a white laboratory analyst sued both his employer (Kaiser Aluminum and Chemical Corporation) and the Steelworkers Union because half the places in training programs for higher skilled jobs were reserved for blacks. In ruling against Weber, the justices said that employers can give blacks special consideration for jobs that were traditionally all white. The Court concluded that companies could properly use affirmative action to remedy "manifest racial imbalance" in employment.[36]

Personnel managers feel that they are caught in a dilemma. On the one hand they work diligently to ensure that minorities and women are hired and promoted. Yet they must show progress in this area without minimizing the opportunities for the majority. Those experienced with this dilemma suggest that management must conscientiously develop human resource plans that will identify skills within the organization and open up opportunities for all employees.[37]

ORGANIZATIONAL FACTORS

The selection process is also affected by a number of factors inherent in an organization. The *types of positions* vary from organization to organization. Logically, the technical, professional, and managerial positions require a more detailed and sophisticated evaluation of candidates. The *size* of an organization, too, affects the selection process; larger organizations usually have the resources to develop and validate their own selection instruments, while smaller organizations usually rely on less formal devices such as unstructured interviews. Social forces also impact on the selection process. Minority groups, for example, emphasize the potential of applicants rather than their credentials—they stress the notion of qualifiable rather than qualified. Unions emphasize seniority for promotion, while management prefers to select primarily on the basis of skills, knowledge, and abilities.

Since personnel managers cannot study, let alone adequately fill, all jobs simultaneously, the determination of those that are most important must be made. Thus, a priority system that uses the following criteria can be employed:

1. Vacancies that are critical to continued operation (bottleneck jobs, switchboard operator, etc.);
2. Need for key managers (plant manager, operations vice president);
3. Present and anticipated demand for labor;
4. Present and anticipated supply of labor (e.g., if there will be a scarcity of systems analysts we might hire in advance of our needs);
5. Any other difficulties anticipated in filling a job. For instance, one university spent a great deal more time, effort, and money in finding a professor who was proficient in Serbo-Croatian (of which they had one), than in seeking another professor of English (of which they had 104).

Cost-Benefit Analysis

Studies to evaluate the selection program attempt to measure the job performance of the employees who have been hired. Among the best indicators of employees' merit are performance-appraisal results such as productivity rates, length of service, promotion records, attendance records, and employees' attitudes (usually based on supervisors' subjective opinions). Organizations can compare this evidence of employees' success in the work situation with the predictions made at the time of selection. In addition, organizations can determine the cost of the selection process. (Actually, personnel departments should confer on a regular basis with the accounting department in order that proper cost-accounting methods be applied to all aspects of the personnel function.)

Specifically, the costs of selection and placement include the cost of tests and their administration; the time and effort to train interviewers and the actual time the interviewer takes to conduct the interview; costs associated with validating selection devices (consultant fees, additional time of people involved in the process); and the administrative costs associated with various selection and placement activities. In job posting, for example, the posting notice must be typed and posted later; job bids have to be analyzed to select a successful bidder. From the standpoint of tests there is variability in their costs, so the desired results must be weighed against these. The Weschler Adult Intelligence Scale (WAIS), for instance, costs $50 to $75 *per head* to administer, but produces an accurate estimate of the kinds of abilities measured (e.g., verbal and other intelligence abilities). The Otis Quick Scoring Mental Ability Test costs about $3 and tends to distinguish between bright, average, and stupid applicants. As a practical matter, tests of functional literacy, arithmetic, and clerical aptitude might be of more use in lower-level jobs.

The obvious benefits of selection and placement are greater organizational efficiency and effectiveness, but measuring the specific impact of placement and selection is virtually impossible. We can measure the benefits in a negative sense, however. Proper selection and placement avoid the costs associated with EEOC class-action suits and/or consent decrees and the associated adverse publicity and ill will these can engender.

Summary

Employee selection activities seek to match the best individuals available to the jobs for which they are best suited. This process is affected to a large extent by legal and social aspects such as fair employment practice codes and the influence of minority and related groups.

The selection process consists of a series of interrelated steps that emanate from human resource planning and recruiting efforts and culminate in the hiring of employees. First, applicants are interviewed to determine if they are acceptable. Following this initial screening, recruiters analyze completed applications for information that will serve as an objective basis for a selection decision.

Interviews give further insight into an applicant's character, personality, motivation, experience, and background.

Assessment centers have proven a viable means for evaluating applicants. Evaluators utilize a combination of tests, exercises, group discussions, and interviews to determine candidates' suitability for employment or promotion.

After basic information on the applicant is verified through background checks and the candidates passes a routine physical examination, an offer of employment is normally made.

Testing is one of the tools that can assist in selecting candidates for job vacancies. Test results provide necessary information for selection, but they cannot substitute for other factors that may help predict job success.

Tests can provide an objective means of measuring intelligence, aptitude, skills, attitude, personality, and interests. But they have also been widely criticized. Allegations that test requirements discriminate against minorities have led to federal and state legislation and court decisions regulating the use of tests. All selection devices, and tests in particular, must now be related to the job in question and must be valid predictors of job success.

Key Terms

selection	criterion
placement	reliability
interview	mental-ability test
application form	aptitude test
weighted application blank	projective test
biographical questionnaire	raw score
tests	average
assessment center	norm
background investigation	percentile
polygraph	cutoff score
validity	promotion
Uniform Guidelines on	seniority system
Employee Selection	piecework
Procedures	work sharing
correlation	outplacement
job analysis	fair-employment practices

Review Questions

1. Describe the various steps in the selection process.

2. How can the weighted application blank be useful in selecting employees?

3. Quote at least five lawful questions appropriate to pre-employment screening.

4. Describe the process for predictive validation of selection devices.

5. How does the background investigation support the selection process?

6. Discuss the impact of laws and Supreme Court decisions on the selection process.

7. How are test scores interpreted?

8. Describe the various classifications of tests.

Discussion Questions

1. Tests have been criticized for their white, middle-class orientation. How would you go about developing a test that would be free of cultural bias? What problems would you encounter in such an undertaking?

2. Now that the law requires validation of all tests, many organizations have abandoned their testing programs. Do you feel that tests are still worthwhile? If not, what are the alternatives?

3. Can you explain why a person who scored high on a battery of selection tests might fail on the job?

4. Do you think applicants should be given their test results? Even if the company offers them a job?

5. Specify selection criteria for each of the following categories of jobs: a) highly skilled automobile repair; b) construction labor; c) office products sales; d) general clerical supervision.

6. Many firms will select only college graduates with a B average or better. Do you think academic achievement is a valid predictor of job success? Is this a sound criterion?

7. How important are the preferences of line managers in selecting new employees? In the selection process what would be the role of the employment department? Of the line manager?

Case Problem 1

THE MISSELECTION OF MARTIN

Inco, a large multinational manufacturer of electronic components, had been attempting to fill a personnel generalist slot in the industrial relations department. The employment manager, Glen Cunningham, had screened the applicants and presented two candidates to the personnel director, Steve Taylor, for final selection. Their resumes were as follows:

Raymond Collins. Age thirty, BBA degree in management. Seven years general personnel and industrial relations experience. Two previous jobs, both positive recommendations. Interview results: deemed acceptable for employment. Test scores in upper third.

Martin Jackson. Age thirty-one, BS degree in personnel administration. Six years experience in personnel and industrial relations. Two previous jobs in personnel. Both employers verified dates of employment. First employer gave high recommendation. Most recent employer stated policy was only to verify employment. Interview results: deemed acceptable for employment. Test scores in upper third.

After reviewing the information and interviewing the candidates, Steve called Glen into his office and said, "Well, they both look like good candidates. Which one do you think would do a better job for us?"

Glen replied, "After checking their credentials, both seem well qualified. The only thing that bothers me is that Jackson's last employer gave me very little to go on, but I really couldn't find anything negative in his background."

Steve said, "Okay, Glen, but remember, we were both extremely impressed with the way Jackson handled the interview. He has a lot on the ball, and I think I could work with him better."

"Since he'll be working with you, I think it's your choice to make. I'll make him an offer today," said Glen.

Jackson accepted the offer. After six months on the job, it became apparent that he was not performing as expected. He failed to follow through on assignments, which resulted in complaints from line management. It was evident that something would have to be done about Jackson.

Problems

1. Why did the misselection of Jackson occur? How could Inco have developed selection criteria for the position of personnel generalist?

2. How could Glen Cunningham have influenced Steve Taylor to make a more objective selection? What selection techniques would have revealed Martin Jackson's shortcomings?

3. What should the personnel manager do with Jackson?

"Now gentlemen, we have to take up this staffing problem," Mr. Allen said.

"You mean for the comptroller's position?" Mr. O'Connell asked.

"That's it," Mr. Baumgarten replied. "My committee has gone over the applications, and we've narrowed the field down to two candidates."

"I don't have to remind you, Baumgarten, how important this is," Mr. Allen said. He carried his duties as chairman of the board very seriously.

"I know, but we have two excellent men. This John Watkins is a CPA, has spent five years as comptroller for Westport Brass, and is quite highly regarded in the field." Mr. Baumgarten produced a thick personnel folder. "We checked out the candidates most carefully. We even called in a private investigation service for the job." Mr. Baumgarten wiped his glasses. "The second man is a Mr. William Smith. He has had two years experience as assistant manager in the office of the vice-president of finance for Acme Electronics." Mr. Baumgarten produced a much thinner folder. "Mr Smith is a younger man than Watkins; he's 28 while Watkins is 37."

"See here, Mr. Baumgarten," Mr. Allen said, "there doesn't seem to be any contest. Watkins seems to be a much better choice."

"I would agree, Mr. Allen," Baumgarten answered, "except for one thing. This Watkins is more mature, has much more practical experience, and his educational qualifications are better. I might add that his letters of recommendation are far stronger and from better-known people in the field. But I felt that we had to present a choice, and Smith was the next best man we could find. You know how hard it is to find capable men these days, particularly in this field."

"Come on, Baumgarten, get to the point," O'Connell growled.

"Well, it's just . . . his wife."

"What about his wife?" Allen asked. "Is she deformed or something?"

"Oh, no," Baumgarten answered. "And they have three lovely children—14, 11, and 8, I believe. It's just that, well, she probably wouldn't fit into our executive circle."

"Why not?" Mr. Allen asked. "After all, we're not exactly a bad bunch."

"Well, she's quite dark for one thing—Puerto Rican, I believe. And she joins things." Mr. Baumgarten paused uncomfortably.

"I know your wife has joined everything around for years, Mr. Baumgarten," Mr. O'Connell commented. "PTA, Junior League, sororities—."

"I mean, she joins the ADA, the Committee for the Cuban Revolution, the Daughters of the New African Nations . . . things like that. If not red, certainly quite pink." Mr. Baumgarten turned through the file. "Oh, yes, she paints, too—nudes."

"Oh, come, come," O'Connell said. "Are we hiring the man or his wife?"

"Mr. Baumgarten may have a point, O'Connell," Mr. Allen said. "Remember, our comptroller has to deal with our bankers—on the job and socially. Can you imagine what Williams of First National would think if he found out? With him belonging to the Sons of the American Revolution and so on?" He shuddered.

"Mrs. Watkins doesn't believe in dealing socially with her husband's colleagues," Mr. Baumgarten said. "She commented that businessmen were horribly dull—very uncultured."

Mr. Baumgarten wiped his glasses again. "Still, he's an awfully good man."

Case Problem 2

THE WOMAN'S TOUCH

Problems

1. What is your opinion of this company's management-selection criteria?
2. Is a company ever justified in using criteria unrelated to job performance? Why? When?

Appendix

Test Publishers

Bausch and Lomb, Inc.
One Lincoln First Square
Rochester, NY 14601

Consulting Psychologist Press
577 College Avenue
Palo Alto, CA 94306

Keystone View Company
Division of Mast Development
  Company
2210 East 12th Street
Davenport, IA 52803

Psychological Corporation
757 Third Avenue
New York, NY 10017

Science Research Associates
259 East Erie Street
Chicago, IL 60011

Stanford University Press
Stanford, CA 94305

U.S. Employment Service
Washington, DC 20212

E. F. Wonderlic and Associates
P. O. Box 7
Northfield, IL 60093

Notes

1. Benjamin Roter, "Personnel Selection: An Update," *Personnel Journal,* January 1976, pp. 23–24.

2. See Edwin A. Fleishman and Joseph Berniger, "One Way to Reduce Office Turnover," *Personnel,* May–June 1960, pp. 63–69; J. N. Mosel and R. R. Wade, "A Weighted Application Blank for Reduction of Turnover in Department Store Sales Clerks," *Personnel Psychology,* 1951, pp. 177–84; Marvin D. Dunnette and James Maetzold, "Use of the Weighted Application Blank in Hiring Seasonal Employees," *Journal of Applied Psychology,* May 1955, pp. 308–10.

3. Robert Tanofsky, R. Ronald Shepps, and Paul J. O'Neill, "Pattern Analysis of Biographic Predictors of Success as an Insurance Salesman," *Journal of Applied Psychology,* April 1969, pp. 136–39.

4. For a discussion of the development and use of the weighted application blank, see George W. England, *Development and Use of Weighted Application Blank* (Dubuque, Iowa: William C. Brown Company, 1961).

5. R. R. Shepps, R. Tanofsky, and H. Mead, "Life History Information and Success as an Insurance Salesman: The Use of a 'Localized' Salary History" (New York: Metropolitan Life Insurance Company, 1967); W. D. Buel, "Biographical Data and the Identification of Creative Research Personnel," *Journal of Applied Psychology,* 1965, pp. 318–21; T. W. Harrell, "The Validity of Biographical Data Items for Food Company Salesmen," *Journal of Applied Psychology,* 1960, pp. 31–33; H. C. Lockwood and S. O. Parsons, "Relationship of Personal History Information to Production Supervisors," *Engineering and Industrial Psychology,* 2 (1960), pp. 20–26.

6. Prentice-Hall, *P-H/ASPA Survey: Employee Testing and Selection Procedures—Where Are They Headed?* April 22, 1975, pp. 652–53.

7. Steven D. Norton, "The Empirical and Content Validity of Assessment Centers vs. Traditional Methods for Predicting Managerial Success" *Academy of Management Review,* July 1977, p. 442.

8. Edward L. Thigpen, "Pre-Employment Assessment: A Systematic Approach to Selecting New Employees," *The Personnel Administrator,* September 1976, pp. 46–48.

9. Donald J. Willis and Jared H. Becker, "The Assessment Center in the Post-Griggs Era," *Personnel and Guidance Journal,* December 1976, pp. 201–5.

10. Ann Howard, "An Assessment of Assessment Centers," *Academy of Management Journal,* March 1974, pp. 115–34; John R. Hinrichs and Seppo Haanpera, "Reliability of Measurement in Situational Exercises: An Assessment of the Assessment Center Method," *Personnel Psychology,* Spring 1976, pp. 31–40.

11. "Where They Make Believe They're the Boss," *Business Week,* August 28, 1971, p. 34.

12. William C. Byham, "Starting an Assessment Center the Correct Way," *The Personnel Administrator,* February 1980, pp. 27–32.

13. Under the Fair Credit and Reporting Act, an employer who orders an investigative report (one that supplies information on an individual's general reputation, personal characteristics, or mode of living) must notify the applicant of his action. This can be in the form of written notification or a statement on the application blank.

14. David T. Lykken, "Psychology and

the Lie Detector Industry," *American Psychologist,* October 1974, pp. 725–39.

15. Frank L. Schmidt et al., "Impact of Valid Selection Procedures on Work-Force Productivity," *Journal of Applied Psychology,* December 1979, pp. 609–626.

16. American Psychological Association, *Principles for the Validation and Use of Personnel Selection Procedures* (Berkeley, Calif.: Division of Industrial-Organizational Psychology, American Psychological Association, 1980), p. 2. This booklet contains guidance for practitioners conducting validation studies, principles for the application and use of valid selection procedures, and information that may be helpful to personnel managers and others responsible for authorizing or implementing validation efforts. It is available ($4.00 per copy) from Dr. Lewis E. Albright, Kaiser Aluminum and Chemical Corporation, 300 Lakeside Drive—Room KB2140, Oakland, CA 94643

17. Equal Employment Opportunity Commission, Civil Service Commission, Department of Labor, Department of Justice, Uniform Guidelines on Employee Selection Procedures (1978), published in the *Federal Register,* 25 August 1978.

18. Organizations setting up a test program have difficulty locating information about various kinds of tests. One of the best sources is the *Mental Measurements Yearbook* edited by Oscar K. Buros and published periodically by the Gryphon Press. This book contains descriptions and critical reviews of published tests by persons unassociated with the authors or publishers. Test publishers also provide information on their tests.

19. Wayne F. Cascio, *Applied Psychology in Personnel Management* (Reston, Va.: Reston Publishing Company, 1978), pp. 260–62.

20. Barry A. Friedman, "Seniority Systems and the Law," *Personnel Journal,* July 1976, p. 335.

21. "The EEOC Retreats After a Seniority Ruling," *Business Week,* June 20, 1977, pp. 28ff.

22. H. Nathaniel Taylor, "Job Posting Update," *The Personnel Administrator,* January 1977, p. 46.

23. Dave R. Dahl and Patrick R. Pinto, "Job Posting: An Industry Survey," *Personnel Journal,* January 1977, pp. 40–42.

24. Clyde W. Summers and Margaret C. Love, "Work Sharing as an Alternative to Layoffs by Seniority: Title VII Remedies in Recession," *Industrial Relations Law Digest,* Winter 1977, pp. 1–24.

25. Robert T. Lund, Dennis C. Bumstead, and Sheldon Friedman, "Inverse Seniority: Timely Answer to the Layoff Dilemma?" *Harvard Business Review,* September–October 1975, pp. 65–72.

26. J. J. Phillips, "'Outplacement,'" *Training,* June 1975, pp. 30–33.

27. Alfred W. Blumrosen, "Developments in Equal Employment Opportunity Law—1976." *Federal Bar Journal,* Winter–Spring 1977, p. 55.

28. Gopal C. Pati and Darold T. Barnum, "Human Resource Programming: The Experience of Steel's Consent Decree I," *Human Resource Planning,* 4 (1979), pp. 175–85.

29. Equal Employment Opportunity Commission, *Guidelines on Discrimination Because of Sex.* The provisions of 29CFR 1604 (Sexual Harassment) were published on 11 March 1980 and were in effect on an interim basis.

30. Michele Hoyman and Ronda Robinson, "Interpreting the New Sexual Harassment Guidelines," *Personnel Journal,* December 1980, pp. 996–1000.

31. This test is incorporated into the final guidelines issued by the EEOC and published in the *Federal Register* the week of 23 September 1980. They included employees and non-employees in the

Notes

employer's work place.

32. Ruth Gilbert Shaeffer, *Nondiscrimination in Employment and Beyond* (New York: The Conference Board, 1980), p. 33.

33. Donald Shire, "Age Discrimination in Employment," *The Personnel Administrator*, June 1975, p. 30.

34. John D. Blackburn and Kathryn P. Sheehan, "Recent Developments in Religious Discrimination: The EEOC's Proposed Guidelines," *Labor nal*, June 1980, p. 336.

35. The Equal Employme tunity Act of 1972—Public L Sec. 703(j).

36. "What the Weber R *Time*, July 9, 1979, pp. 48—

37. Gopal C. Pati, "Reverse Discrimination: What Can Managers Do?" *Personnel Journal*, July 1977, pp. 334ff.

Integrating Employees into the Organization

Integrating employees serves to mold them into a team that is dedicated to achieving the objectives of the organization. Information about employee skills, experience, aspirations, and performance is recorded so that research can be conducted to improve the effectiveness of the team effort. Personnel reports provide information to the relevant government agencies and are used externally for information and control purposes.

Both line and staff managers are constantly confronted with personal and job-related problems they must resolve through discussions with employees or by referral to professionals. Interviewing skills are utilized to gain insight into these problems and to learn about employees' backgrounds, aspirations, work experiences, and work problems.

If employees are represented by a labor union, integrating them into an organization involves bargaining with their representatives on hours, wages, and working conditions. To help support company objectives, employees must understand what is expected of them. Should their performance deviate from expectations, their behavior is corrected through positive disciplinary action.

Chapter Seven

Personnel Records and Research

Following are some typical requests for information contained in personnel records or that require personnel research:

State Department of Labor

You are hereby requested to supply the following information on the attached forms: turnover (quits, discharges, layoffs, deaths, retirement, and other); offers tendered and accepted by age, sex, race, color, veteran, handicapped—by occupation—for the quarter ending December 31, 1982.

A Local Company

Please complete this salary and benefits survey.

A President's Memo

Please calculate the costs of the following union demands:
$.75 across-the-board wage increase
remove the deductible provision from the medical insurance plan
one additional holiday

Regional EEOC Office

This is to confirm our agreement that you will provide us with evidence of completion of a validation study of your selection tests for insurance underwriters.

Accurate preparation and maintenance of personnel records are essential when organizations use them as data sources in research activities.

This chapter focuses on the types of records that organizations must maintain to support organizational objectives and to comply with legal (governmental) requirements. Personnel research activities are described, and the methodology of conducting research is emphasized in order to highlight an area of personnel that has received too little attention.

The Importance of Records and Research

Records are a primary source of data for evaluating and controlling personnel activities; they also serve as a basis for research by the personnel department. Personnel records provide facts for a myriad of applications, including reports to government agencies and employees; reports on the effectiveness of personnel activities; controls on operating (e.g., absenteeism) and problem situations (e.g., grievances); surveys of wages and personnel practices; industrial relations audits; and explanations of the importance of personnel programs. Today's cost-minded executives require concrete evidence of personnel program effectiveness; properly maintained records can provide preliminary data that, alone or supported by research results, can substantiate effectiveness.

Organizations are using personnel research to gain greater insight into their employees and therefore make better personnel decisions. Very few organizations use behavioral science techniques to counter personnel problems, but an increasing number are engaging in research and sophisticated methodology.[1] Because human behavior is difficult to measure, effective personnel decisions depend upon research methodology to achieve a desired outcome.

Records, when properly maintained, provide the data base for conducting relevant research. The information generated from personnel records enables personnel departments to make more objective decisions about people so that they can better contribute to the organization. Objective information from employment records improves the judgment of management in dealing with organized labor. Essentially, recorded information and the conclusions that can be reached from its analysis help integrate employees more successfully into the organization.

The types of records maintained by the personnel department are largely dictated by management's need for specific information. Federal legislation also has considerable influence, since employment laws and health and safety acts require record keeping. The availability of storage and retrieval equipment also affects record keeping; computers have literally revolutionized this aspect of personnel.

Research-oriented companies (like IBM, GE, and Xerox) are likely to have formal personnel research activities conducted by their own staff of behavioral scientists. Management attitude has a great influence on the utilization of behavioral research; business has not fully accepted the psychologists who usually perform such activities. However, pressures from outside the business sector may result in intensified efforts in the utilization of personnel research. For instance, decisions that formerly were made on the basis of subjective judgment, especially in the areas of selection and testing, now call for strict objectivity backed by tangible evidence.

Records
LEGAL REQUIREMENTS

All organizations with federal contracts or grants-in-aid, as well as most companies employing 25 or more workers, must comply with federal and state reporting regulations. Most of these reports concern employment, but in recent years government regulations in other areas (involving health and safety) have required reports, of which the more pertinent are described below.

EMPLOYMENT RECORDS. Laws governing fair employment practices require organizations to maintain records on race, sex, national origin, and age of all applicants and employees. The Age Discrimination in Employment Act amended in 1978 empowered the EEOC to prescribe whatever reports and supporting records it deemed necessary to enforce the law (to date, it has not called for any specific reports). The Equal Employment Opportunity Commission is authorized under the Civil Rights Act of 1964 to require records on race, sex, creed, and national origin; it requires periodic reports based on these records. The commission recommends keeping these records separate from regular personnel files in order to reduce the possibility of bias in personnel decisions. To administer unemployment compensation programs in each state, the Employment Security Commission requests quarterly reports of turnover from employers. Organizations usually record these data—the number of resignations, layoffs, discharges, deaths, retirements, and hires, as well as work days lost due to labor strikes—on a daily, weekly, or monthly basis. This information is compiled regionally and nationally by the Bureau of Labor Statistics of the Department of Labor to provide valuable research data to companies.

The 1974 **Privacy of Information Act** was the first attempt by Congress to legislate standards for the protection of individual privacy. Its purpose was to guard against the misuse of records and allow individuals ready access to their personal records. Although the legislation was limited to federal agencies, it influenced numerous organizations to be more careful about what goes into personnel files. Many organizations now require documentation for information placed in employee files, and a few have employees sign items so that each employee knows what is placed in his or her file.[2] In addition, some organizations have purged personnel files of irrelevant data and allow their employees, on request, to review the data contained in their files.[3] With more and more companies purging personnel records or greatly reducing their content as a result of interpretation of federal law, fewer personnel records are kept. Ironically, it is those records that personnel researchers use to extract archival data for analysis. Personnel research on archival data may all but disappear as a result of this situation. Regrettably the sensitive information being purged is also usually quite valid for prediction purposes.

LABOR-RELATIONS REPORTS. The purpose of the Labor-Management Reporting and Disclosure Act of 1959 is to "afford necessary protection of the rights and interests of employees and the public generally as they relate to the activities of labor organizations, employers, labor relations consultants, and their officers and representatives." Consequently, if employers make expenditures or arrangements to interfere with, restrain, coerce, or persuade employees about their rights, they must maintain records of such expenditures and report them to the Secretary of Labor. For example, if a company engages a consultant to influence its employees not to join a labor union, the company must submit a record of the consultant's fees and expenses to the Department of Labor.

HEALTH AND SAFETY. Regulations of the Occupational Safety and Health Act of 1970 require employers to maintain records of occupational injuries and illnesses. The records consist of a log and summary of occupational illnesses and injuries that must be retained for at least five years, a supplementary record of each occupational injury and illness, and an annual summary of information contained in the log. In addition, workers' compensation laws in each state usually call for similar reports. (The implications of these laws are covered in Chapter 21.)

RETIREMENT PLANS. Under the Employee Retirement Income Security Act (ERISA), pension plan administrators are required to provide interim reports on their organization's plan on request; submit statements to employees who leave the organization and are eligible for benefits; submit an annual registration report to the Secretary of the Treasury as well as annual reports and report summaries to the Secretary of Labor and all plan participants and beneficiaries.

Other laws that regulate personnel activities (e.g., Fair Labor Standards Act, Walsh-Healy, Davis-Bacon) also have specific reporting requirements. Subsequent chapters will discuss the applicable laws and the reports they require.

TYPES OF RECORDS

As mentioned previously, personnel records provide information to evaluate and control personnel activities. Since situations vary from organization to organization, the types of records and methods of maintenance will likewise vary. It is impossible to describe every type, but Table 7.1 provides a capsule description of a variety of personnel records.

PERSONNEL DATA SYSTEMS

There are a number of systems for maintaining and processing personnel data that companies should consider, depending on the organization's size and needs and the availability of a computer. For example, the McBee Keysort might be appropriate for small employers (less than 500), the punch card might suit medium-sized organizations (up to 5,000), and a computer-based system might be useful to large employers.

Computer applications have recently begun to find wide acceptance in the personnel field. Until recently, operational and financial needs have had priority on data processing sections; and personnel data, except when there was excess computer capacity, had rarely been computerized. But personnel departments, realizing the advantages of **electronic data processing** (EDP), are starting to budget funds for computer time. And with the wider availability of computers, especially with the advent of minicomputers, many organizations have developed **management information systems** (MIS). These systems possess three major characteristics.[4]

1. They use an integrated data base, with large storage capacity and a data base management system.

2. They have a hierarchical information structure, generally serving operating management's needs with scheduled reports and middle management's control needs with demand reports, and may serve top management's strategic planning needs by responding to specific information requests of an unstructured nature.

3. They have a decision-support orientation that provides enough flexibility and comprehensiveness to supply useful and meaningful data at all levels when needed.

Management Information Systems (MIS) in personnel translated into Human Resource Information Systems (HRIS), which were outgrowths of basic computer systems to maintain payrolls and, more recently, skills inventories. HRIS today utilizes computers for applications in human resource planning, EEO, union-management negotiations, training and development, and some other areas.[5] But the rapidly rising costs of hardware (the computing machinery) and software (programs) make it advisable for some

Table 7.1
Description of Selected
Personnel Records

Record Name	Description
Attendance records	For each employee, shows coded absences (reported or unreported, excused or unexcused); disciplinary layoffs; time off due to illness, strike, leave of absence, and vacation.
Turnover records	Lists by name or classification employees leaving the company, with reasons and date of termination. May also show length of service.
Promotion lists	For each occupation, shows names and titles of employees qualified for promotion. Indicates readiness for promotion and position to which promotable. May also include data on age, length of training, and so on.
Application files	All applications and supporting documents are usually separated according to salaried or hourly; active or inactive; and likely to be hired or not being considered.
Apprenticeship agreements	File of agreements between employer and apprentice training for journeyman classification, specifying duration and type of training and pay scales at various phases of the apprenticeship.
Compensation records	For each employee, shows historical earnings data, showing job titles, classification designations, wage or salary rates, dates and amounts of increases, and basis of compensation change (e.g., promotion, cost-of-living adjustment, merit raise).
Performance ratings	Usually filed with other information for individual employee. Original performance appraisal, completed by immediate manager and signed by employee and appropriate reviewers, is usually retained as a record.
Insurance records	Copies of policies, claims filed by employees, designations of beneficiary and others covered by policies; premium rates for group insurance: hospital, medical, surgical; major medical; accident and sickness; accidental death and dismemberment; automobile; homeowners; and life.
Health and accident records	For each employee, details of medical examinations: employment physical, sick calls, first aid, and other job-related health information. Recordings of job-related illnesses or injuries showing appropriate dates,

Record Name	Description	TABLE 7.1 (cont.)
	description of nature or cause, extent of illness or injury, time lost from job, and disposition if claim is involved.	
Suggestion records	List of suggestions submitted, indicating nature of suggestion, disposition by committee (accepted, deferred, or rejected) and amount of award.	
Grievances	Company copies of grievances, showing issue, company and union positions, and final determination. Arbitration awards and supporting documents can be kept with grievances.	
Collective bargaining files	Historical data on contract clauses showing, by clause, union demands, company replies, and final resolution.	

organizations to consider software packages or canned programs designed to deal with specific personnel functions. Although these packages may not be tailored to the particular organization, they may meet a given need adequately.[6]

EDP ADVANTAGES IN PERSONNEL.   The personnel function relies heavily on vast amounts of information for its activities. Gathering, storing, and retrieving data is a record-keeping function that, if improperly administered, can encumber personnel's operating efficiency. EDP can alleviate many record-keeping problems, but computer output is only as good as its input. Below are the principal advantages of EDP.

1. *Speed.*   Computers can compute and retrieve data in a fraction of the time people require to perform the same operation. Because computers can handle so much data in so little time, they decrease the per unit cost of processing information. Even more important, computerized information is readily available and up-to-date. Computers can even monitor activities as they occur by tabulating real-time information.

2. *Space.*   Personnel records, a massive accumulation of documents, require considerable file space. Furthermore, data files must be located in an area designed to meet security and protection specifications. The sheer volume of information can delay the personnel staff in locating and later refiling requested information. On a comparative basis, computer memory banks have a far greater capacity to store information than conventional filing systems.

3. *Availability.*   Users can easily retrieve information from computers through printouts or visual displays. Remote access is another benefit; terminals at remote points can retrieve information from a centrally located computer.

4. *Decision making.*   Decision makers can use computers to handle large volumes of data and rapidly perform computations. Organizations can use computers to abstract their problems and build mathematical models to help determine solutions. By quantifying and manipulating the information already stored in the computer, personnel administrators can gain new insights into some of their pressing problems. In this manner, records become a vital component of a system, rather than just little-used statistics occupying storage space. But computer output is only as good as the information entered into the system, and people still control the input.

PERSONNEL APPLICATIONS OF EDP.   A survey of personnel departments showed that the most frequent EDP applications were used for employee record keeping and payroll processing.[7] Companies like IBM, Dow Corning, and Xerox, which have personnel data systems, apply EDP to most of the functional areas of personnel, such as manpower analysis and planning, employment and recruiting, personnel records, manpower development, compensation and benefits, personnel simulation, and personnel statistics. The computer services performed in each of these areas are described below.

1. *Human resource analysis and planning.*   For more effective selection and placement and to analyze human resources, organizations compile data on absenteeism and turnover, assemble manpower data, and isolate success-predicting variables. In human resource planning, organizations also assemble and maintain data bases for analyses of manpower trends.[8]

2. *Employment and recruiting.*   Data systems supporting these activities improve speed, accuracy, significance, and timing in handling relevant information. IBM markets a software package (a computer program) called IRIS (IBM Recruiting Information System), which locates candidates for employment or promotion by matching job requirements with a file of employees' qualifications. Honeywell offers a similar system that also maintains current status reports on all job applicants. Union Oil has developed a system that stores and handles historical records on applicants, measures source effectiveness and recruiter efficiency, analyzes recruiting data, and provides programmed communication with applicants regarding their status.[9]

3. *Personnel records.*   To maintain employee records, organizations must store, update, and compile information in various forms. Computer systems afford ready access to this data while, of course, maintaining the

confidentiality of private information. These systems are also a simple and rapid way to update records and they provide a variety of alternative displays or printouts that can serve as reports. Carefully designed forms allow the input of large quantities of relevant data. A typical employee record form is shown in Figure 7.1.

4. *Affirmative action.* Computer-based systems can provide organizations with standard reports and special request information on their affirmative action programs. They also permit identification of problems and provide information for corrective action so that affirmative action can be achieved instead of merely monitored. Such systems generate reports required by government agencies for compliance reviews. Information readily available through such a system includes the number of people by race, sex, and EEO category, who were referred to individual departments, received an offer, were rejected, or accepted an offer. In addition, the affirmative action system can provide the current job status of each employee along with a variety of analyses pertinent to EEO.[10]

5. *Human resource development.* Computerized inventories of human resource capabilities and replacement charts keep an organization informed of available skills, employee performance, and individual career motivation. Analyses of the system strengthen selection and training programs and help ensure competent backups for critical jobs.

6. *Compensation and benefits.* Dow Corning's insurance department reduced manpower costs 10 percent by using computers to prepare the reports required by the corporation's insurance carriers and actuaries.[11] Other savings to Dow included reduced clerical time in supplying wage-survey data; replacement of manual tickler files for salary-action notification; reduced clerical time in the service-award program; and improvement of job evaluation, leave-of-absence reviews, draft deferment expirations, and retirement-program administration. Computers can assist compensation and benefit-cost analysis in the following areas: cost determination of benefit variants (such as increased life insurance coverage); computation of proposed wage or salary costs by mathematical constants (for 5, 6, or 7 percent increases); salary policy control through pay lines and charts; and monthly salary and wage tracking.

7. *Personnel simulation.* **Simulation** reflects real life situations. Simple or complex models can simulate environments that may occur at a later time. Changes made in the simulated environment will yield outcomes that can be used as a basis for making future decisions in the real world. Personnel people have applied computer-simulation models in a number of situations: to evaluate alternative manpower plans under varying conditions; to ascertain the best mix of skills to meet changing technology;

Figure 7.1
Personnel Action Form

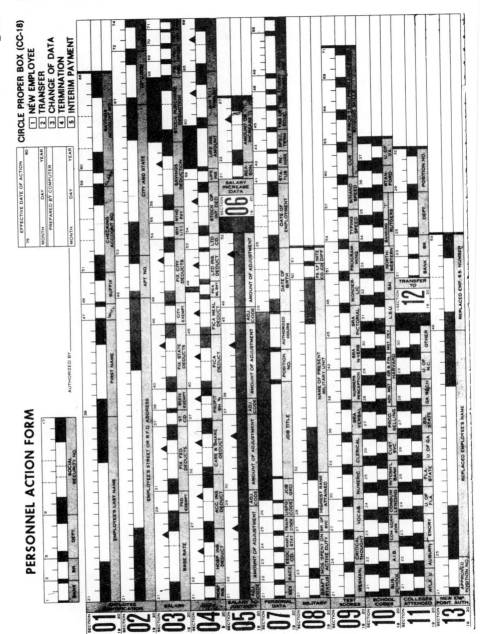

to help predict the reaction of employees to policy changes; and to experiment with decisions or strategies on personnel problems without the risk of real life consequences.

8. *Personnel statistics.* Organizations continuously record statistical data on employee performance to provide a variety of reports on absenteeism, turnover, insurance claims, seniority, grievances, and so on. Computerized data files enable rapid retrieval of information in final report form. The computer can even be programmed to print out a report whenever an input involves a variation from policy or an exception from norms (e.g., when an employee's absences exceed the specified limit).

9. *Comprehensive employee information systems.* Few comprehensive systems are evident in personnel and most of them are reportedly of poor design compared to other application areas.[12] Possibly the most sophisticated system is in use at the Coca-Cola Company. Called CHRISP (Comprehensive Human Resources Information System Project), it utilizes a central data base that contains a continuous history of significant events and changes relating to an employee from employment to retirement. Information is obtainable from remote stations via ordinary telephone lines. New data can be programmed into the system in plain English (a special computer language is not necessary), so personnel files can be updated easily, and authorized users can request an unlimited variety of information on employees including salary data, turnover rates, human resource forecasts, available skills, and so on.

Personnel Research

Personnel activities should be designed and evaluated in terms of their contribution to organizational objectives. Research is the only meaningful basis for developing and evaluating personnel activities. The purpose of the following section is to provide an appreciation for the importance of personnel research through a basic familiarity with its nature and techniques.

LEVELS OF RESEARCH

Research can be categorized as pure, basic, or applied. **Pure research** is conducted to provide knowledge for the sake of knowledge—it does not necessarily involve a concern for the immediate, practical application of its results. **Basic research** is long term, and its findings have wide, rather than specific, interest and applicability. For this reason, it is seldom conducted in the personnel area. Universities and government agencies perform basic research, with industry providing support in the form of funds, facilities, and subjects. Typical basic research studies might be on the effect of working conditions on productivity, or on methods of improving training effectiveness. A few companies undertake extensive basic social science research. For instance, the social science research department at Bell Labs has been studying why and how people join groups, and General Electric conducts in-plant studies on manager motivation, risk-taking behavior, and creativity, for use in GE training programs. **Applied research** is intended to solve immediate, practical problems of a limited nature. Almost all personnel research in business is applied.

TYPES OF APPLIED RESEARCH PROJECTS.   There are three types of applied research projects: descriptive, predictive, and controlled. The **descriptive study,** perhaps the most common in personnel research, is intended to describe a situation (e.g., union activity, severity and incidence of accidents, or turnover analysis). The purpose of the **predictive study** is forecasting. It examines the relationship between variables but does not establish cause and effect. An example of this type of study would be the validation of a specific selection test. In the **controlled study,** which is the most difficult but also the most definitive, researchers design an experimental situation from which they can quantify the cause-and-effect relationship between variables. The evaluation of a training program is an example.[13] In a controlled study, the minimally appropriate design incorporates pretests and posttests along with control-group procedures. That is, in the most elementary model, one group is exposed to training while another, comparable group is not. Both groups are measured against preestablished criteria prior to and following training. **Statistical analysis** then indicates if the training has resulted in a significant change in behavior.

USES OF APPLIED PERSONNEL RESEARCH.   As personnel managers have become increasingly aware of the uses of investigations in decision making, research technology has spread to most activities of the personnel department. Quantitative techniques can test, analyze, and control many aspects of the personnel function, thus enabling managers to be more effective in utilizing human resources. Some of the more common uses of applied personnel research include:[14]

1. *Selecting and placing employees.*   Applied research helps employers understand the meaning of applicant information and helps them validate tests and interviews, so they know how various factors relate to job success.

2. *Determining employee opinions and attitudes.*   Organizations frequently conduct surveys to obtain feedback on employee attitudes and opinions. When scientifically designed and analyzed, an **opinion survey** can provide an abundance of valuable information. However, there is little value in using surveys unless management is willing to take positive action on

problems cited. Figure 4.2 (Chapter 4) presented a sample selection of survey questions from a typical opinion survey.

3. *Appraising employees.* Although performance appraisal is discussed in Chapter 16, some aspects of appraisal are relevant to personnel research. If personnel practitioners merely applied the existing knowledge and techniques that have proven successful, they could realize tangible benefits with minimal expenditure of money and effort.

   Research continuously seeks ways to improve appraisal methods. Studies have resulted in training programs for reviewers, and research activity has explored ways to reduce bias in appraisals, maintain consistency of ratings among raters, improve the accuracy of ratings, and find relationships between ratings and job-related data (such as the size of a work group and the nature of work).

4. *Training and developing employees.* Training programs benefit organizations by improving employee attitudes, skills, and knowledge. Training directors want to show that desired changes occur as a direct result of the training, which will justify the expenditure of time, effort, and money. Research activities can uncover problem areas that indicate training needs. They can evaluate and help develop instructional methods and techniques that will enhance teaching effectiveness. Finally, research provides objective methods to evaluate the impact of training programs. (Specific techniques for evaluating training effectiveness are treated in Chapter 13.)

A RATIONAL APPROACH TO RESEARCH

Those who conduct research usually follow the scientific method. It is not the purpose of this chapter to teach students how to conduct research—textbooks on this subject are readily available—but the following outline should familiarize students with the rational approach, which includes these eight steps.[15]

1. *State the problem.* What is the problem? Why is it a problem? What is to be determined from the research?

2. *Develop hypotheses.* A **hypothesis** is a tentative proposition that researchers can confirm or reject. The hypothesis might be based on the researchers' intuition or possibly on pure speculation. The hypothesis being tested is usually referred to as the **null hypothesis.** If the null hypothesis is rejected, researchers apply an alternative hypothesis. For example, one might seek to determine if there is a difference in productivity between male and female assemblers. The null hypothesis would be stated as:

   H_o: There is no significant difference in the number of units produced by male and female operators in the final assembly department.

3. *Perform background search.*   To gain insight into a problem, researchers investigate as many sources of information as possible: books, periodicals, or published results of similar research describing or discussing the same problem. (Some periodicals and associations either directly or indirectly concerned with personnel problems are listed in the appendix to this chapter.)

4. *Design the experiment.*   In order to test a hypothesis, researchers devise a scheme to collect and analyze data in a meaningful manner. Experimental design involves selecting or developing methods that can reasonably be expected to evoke answers to the questions of the problem-formulation step. Many basic statistics texts cover the subject of experimental design.

5. *Collect the data.*   Up to this point, researchers have primarily been engaged in planning the experiment. They now collect the data through any of a variety of methods including interviews, observation, questionnaires, or some combination of these.

6. *Analyze the data.*   At this point, researchers analyze the data to test the hypothesis and find a solution to the problem. One method of analysis is the situational approach described in Chapter 2, but for research purposes, statistical analysis is preferred. (Here, again, students should consult a basic statistics textbook for analytical techniques.)

7. *Report research findings and recommend action.*   Reports of personnel research findings are all too often dry and confusing. Researchers tend to forget that someone else has to read the report. A good research report is concise, but thorough; includes figures, tables, or charts to summarize an abundance of data; and is clearly written.

8. *Take action.*   Although researchers are seldom responsible for implementing their research findings, they still have a vested interest in seeing that their recommendations are carried out. Research reports often lead to changes in methods or even to a revamping of the organization. Research findings backed by concrete data and based on sound methodology can initiate positive change in personnel management.

Cost-Benefit Analysis

Costs associated with preparing and maintaining personnel records and conducting research include the salaries of the employees performing these functions and the facilities (offices), equipment (files, calculators, computers, copiers), and supplies. The cost of the time of employees from whom data are gathered and the cost of obtaining information from outside sources must also be calculated. Additional cost calculations can be made, such as the average time required to process a new hire, transfer, promotion, and so forth multiplied by salary and benefit costs of the processing clerk.[16]

The benefits of records and research activities are realized in terms of the availability and speed of information that enhances decision making. Record-keeping efficiency can be measured and compared to alternatives, for example, manual versus computer records. Periodic audits of the records system can help maintain efficiency. Forms tend to become outdated or, as is more often the case, too many forms and reports are allowed to remain in the system. The audit can uncover unnecessary or outdated reports that can be eliminated or consolidated. Reports should be spot-checked periodically to ensure their accuracy.

Summary

Research is probably the most significant step toward making the personnel function more sophisticated. The impetus for expanded personnel research in the future comes from requirements to validate selection instruments, the need to establish objective measures of performance, and the importance of substantiating the personnel department's contribution to corporate objectives.

Conscientious personnel managers familiarize themselves with the tools that can increase the effectiveness of their activities. Computer technology provides the means for storing and retrieving human resource data and facilitates the manipulation and calculation of quantitative data, thus increasing the objectivity of personnel decision making. The effectiveness of research activity is contingent upon a carefully maintained record-keeping system. The quality of the computer output depends entirely on the information input, the basis of which is the raw data recorded by personnel workers.

The rational approach is used to research factors affecting complex situations and to determine objectively whether these are truly or only apparently significant. Situations too complex to permit absolute certainty can nevertheless be accurately indicated by statistical descriptions, and the likelihood of assertions being correct can be precisely assessed.

Key Terms

Privacy of Information Act
electronic data processing
   (EDP)
management information
   systems (MIS)
simulation
pure research
basic research

applied research
descriptive study
predictive study
controlled study
statistical analysis
opinion survey
hypothesis
null hypothesis

Review Questions

1. Describe the steps in the scientific method of personnel research.

2. What are the various quantitative techniques available to analyze research data?

3. Describe the various types of applied personnel research projects.

4. What are the inherent advantages and drawbacks of EDP in personnel record keeping and research?

5. Discuss the various records and reports required by law.

Discussion Questions

1. What are the components of an absentee control system? How can companies determine if they should be concerned about the absentee rate?

2. What alternatives for conducting personnel research are available to a company too small to support its own research staff?

3. Personnel departments are often regarded as paper mills because they generate so many forms and records. What are some possible causes of this criticism? How important are personnel records? What can be done to improve record-keeping efficiency, while keeping the number of forms and records to a minimum?

4. If EDP is really increasingly necessary in personnel work, how could a personnel manager justify to line management the relatively high cost of converting to a computerized system?

5. Some organizations employ outside consultants to perform personnel research. What are the advantages and disadvantages of this arrangement?

"I don't care what those women say, I need that information!" Joe Maxwell said.

"You may be head of personnel for Lockwell, but I don't think you're going to get it much longer," John Brown, the office manager and his coffee drinking companion said.

"Why not? Look, John, all I need to know is whether or not a woman is married and living with her husband. Is that so weird?"

"It has nothing to do with the job," John said.

"It has everything to do with the job, John. You agree that absenteeism and the quit rate are critical to our costs?"

"Sure," John said. "And you've done a nice job in getting those rates down in the past two years. The boss appreciates it. Boy, a few years ago, before you came, we were being killed."

"But that's the point, John. I figured out exactly what to look for. For those assembly-line jobs, and even for the typing and filing work, I discovered that married women quit less often and aren't absent as much. And now they want to take away my predictor!"

"The union says that the only personnel data we should get from a job applicant should be relevant to the job. Period. It looks like that will get written into the next contract. The women are upset. You've refused to hire a lot of women who were qualified, except that they were single, divorced, or separated. You just can't do that anymore."

Joe moodily sipped his coffee. "I figure that out of a hundred new employees, about 11 percent of the married women will quit in the first year. About 33 percent of the others will quit. That's an expensive quit rate for us."

"But it's probably discriminatory not to hire qualified people just because they're not married, Joe. You just can't play the game the old way any more. Oh, you could talk to the boss and try to get our bargaining team to fight for rights, but I doubt that they would go along. There are other items up for bargaining that are more important."

Case Problem 1

THE PREDICTOR

Problems

1. Suppose Joe's data are correct, and suppose that it costs about $1,300 to hire and train an employee. Do you think that Lockwell should fight for his right to have these data included on their employment forms? Why or why not? (The difference in a quit rate of 11 and 33 percent is about 135 employees per year.)

2. Do employees and potential employees have any rights here? Is it any of the boss's business to know what one's family situation is? Why or why not?

3. Are these family-status data for women relevant to job performance? Why or why not?

Case Problem 2

AN OBJECTIVE
EVALUATION

At Nordik Development Company, both the personnel research department and the training and development department report to the personnel director. Jim Dyson, the manager of personnel research, is a close friend of Sam Barge, training and development manager. Personnel research had just completed an evaluation of a recent eight-week supervisory training course. Sam Barge was proud of this course because he had a personal hand in its development. But when he read the evaluation report from Jim Dyson's research people, he was infuriated. Their study concluded that there was "no significant behavioral change as a result of the training program." Barge argued with Dyson, saying, "The tests your researchers used were not a proper measure of training effectiveness; the evaluation was poorly planned; thus, the results are invalid. This is a helluva way to treat a friend. It'll sure make me look bad in the boss's eyes. Anyway, the supervisors said they loved the course!"

"But we tested your participants before and after the course, Sam, and compared to the control group our figures showed that there wasn't a great enough change to be significant. Why don't we approach this constructively and take another look at the content and at the way the course was taught. I'll bet we can find something to make the program more effective," Jim answered.

"But just the same, Jim, the supervisors really enjoyed the program, and isn't that what should count?" asked Sam.

Problems

1. Is it more important to produce a truly objective evaluation or to maintain the training program's credibility with the personnel director?

2. How should the company use the research conclusions in this situation?

3. Did Jim Dyson follow the scientific method of conducting research?

4. What measures could be taken to test the results of the research findings?

Appendix

Personnel Research Sources

The Academy of Management Review
P.O. Drawer KZ
Mississippi State University
Mississippi State, MS 39762

Across the Board
845 Third Avenue
New York, NY 10022

Administrative Science Quarterly
Graduate School of Business and Public
  Administration
Cornell University
Ithaca, NY 14850

Advanced Management Journal
Society for the Advancement of
  Management
135 West 50th Street
New York, NY 10020

American Behavioral Scientist
Sage Publications
275 Beverly Drive
Beverly Hills, CA 90212

The Arbitration Journal
American Arbitration Association
140 West 51st Street
New York, NY 10020

British Journal of Industrial Relations
London School of Economics and
  Political Science
Houghton Street
Aldwych, London WC2A 2AE,
England

Business Horizons
Graduate School of Business
Indiana University
Bloomington, IN 47405

California Management Review
Graduate School of Business
  Administration
University of California
Berkeley, CA 94720

The Canadian Personnel and IR Journal
Council of Canadian Personnel
  Association
Suite 602
222 Yonge Street
Toronto, Canada

Compensation Review
American Management Association
135 West 50th Street
New York, NY 10020

Employee Benefit Plan Review
222 West Adams Street
Chicago, IL 60606

Employee Relations Law Journal
Suite 2310
10 Columbus Circle
New York, NY 10019

Harvard Business Review
Graduate School of Business
  Administration
Soldiers Field
Boston, MA 02163

Human Relations
Plenum Press
227 W. 17 Street
New York, NY 10011

Human Resource Management
Graduate School of Business
  Administration
University of Michigan
Ann Arbor, MI 48104

Human Resource Planning
P.O. Box 2553
Grand Central Station
New York, NY 10017

Industrial Engineering
American Institute of Industrial
    Engineers, Inc.
25 Technology Park/Atlanta
Norcross, GA 30092

Industrial and Labor Relations Review
New York State School of Labor and
    Industrial Relations
Cornell University
Ithaca, NY 14853

Industrial Medicine and Surgery
Medical Publication for Industry
918 N.E. 20 Avenue
Box 7151
Fort Lauderdale, FL 33041

International Labor Review
International Labor Office
CH-1211
Geneva 22, Switzerland

Industrial Relations
Institute of Industrial Relations
University of California—Berkeley
Berkeley, CA 94720

Industrial Relations Law Digest
Graduate School of Business
    Administration
The University of Michigan
Ann Arbor, MI 48109

Industrial Relations News
Enterprise Publications
20 North Wacker Drive
Chicago, IL 60606

Industrial Relations Research Association
    Proceedings
University of Wisconsin
Madison, WI 53701

Journal of Applied Behavioral Science
Institute for Applied Behavioral Science
Box 9155
Rosslyn Station
Arlington, VA 22209

Journal of Applied Psychology
American Psychological Association,
    Inc.
1200 17th Street, N.W.
Washington, DC 20036

Journal of Applied Social Psychology
7961 Eastern Avenue
Silver Spring, MD 20910

Journal of Collective Negotiations in the
    Public Sector
Baywood Publishing Company, Inc.
120 Marine Street
Farmingdale, NY 11735

Journal of Counseling Psychology
American Psychological Association
1200 17th Street, N.W.
Washington, DC 20036

Journal of Human Relations
Central State University
Wilberforce, OH 45384

Journal of Human Resources: Education,
    Manpower, and Welfare Policies
University of Wisconsin Press
P.O. Box 1379
Madison, WI 53701

Journal of Industrial Relations
P.O. Box 2260
G.P.O.
Sydney, Australia 2001

Journal of Occupational Psychology
British Psychological Society
St. Andrews House
48 Princess Road East
Leicester, LEI 7DR, England

Journal of Vocational Behavior
111 Fifth Avenue
New York, NY 10003

Labor Law Journal
Commerce Clearing House, Inc.
4025 West Peterson Avenue
Chicago, IL 60646

Management Review
135 West 50th Street
New York, NY 10020

Manpower
Department of Labor
Room 2212, Main Labor Building
Washington, DC 20001

Michigan State University Business Topics
Graduate School of Business
   Administration
East Lansing, MI 48824

Monthly Labor Review
Bureau of Labor Statistics
Department of Labor
Washington, DC 20212

Monthly Review of Management Research
P.O. Box 4
Dolton, IL 60419

National Safety News
National Safety Council
444 North Michigan Avenue
Chicago, IL 60611

Occupational Health and Safety
Stevens Publishing Corporation
3700 West Waco Drive
Box 7573
Waco, TX 76710

*Organizational Behavior and Human
   Performance*
Academic Press, Inc.,
111 Fifth Avenue
New York, NY 10003

Pension World
Communication Channels, Inc.
6285 Barfield Road
Atlanta, GA 30328

Personnel
American Management Association
135 West 50th Street
New York, NY 10020

The Personnel Administrator
American Society for Personnel
   Administration
19 Church Street
Berea, OH 44017

Personnel and Guidance Journal
5203 Leesburg Pike
Falls Church, VA 22041

Personnel Journal
Box 2440
Costa Mesa, CA 92627

Personnel Literature
Office of Personnel Management Library
Washington, DC 20415

Personnel Management Abstracts
Bureau of Industrial Relations
University of Michigan
Ann Arbor, MI 48104

Personnel Psychology
Personnel Psychology, Inc.
P.O. Box 6965
College Station
Durham, NC 27708

Public Administration Review
American Society for Public
   Administration
1225 Connecticut Avenue, N.W.
Washington, DC 20036

Public Personnel Management
International Personnel Management
  Association
1850 K Street, N.W., Suite 870
Washington, DC 20006

Public Productivity Review
445 West 59th Street
New York, NY 10019

Sloan Management Review
Sloan School of Management
Massachusetts Institute of Technology
50 Memorial Drive
Cambridge, MA 02139

Studies in Personnel Psychology
Public Service/Canada Commission
Ottawa K1A OM7 Canada

Supervisory Management
American Management Association
135 West 50th Street
New York, NY 10020

Training
Lakewood Publications, Inc.
731 Hennepin Avenue
Minneapolis, MN 55403

Training and Development Journal
American Society for Training and
  Development
P.O. Box 5307
Madison, WI 53705

University of Michigan Review
Graduate School of Business
  Administration
The University of Michigan
Ann Arbor, MI 48104

**PROFESSIONAL PERSONNEL
ASSOCIATIONS**

American Management Association
135 West 50th Street
New York, NY 10020

*American Personnel and Guidance
  Association*
1607 New Hampshire Avenue, N.W.
Washington, DC 20009

*American Society for Personnel
  Administration*
30 Park Drive
Berea, OH 44107

*American Society for Training and
  Development*
P.O. Box 5307
Madison, WI 53705

Center for Management Development
(American Management Association
  Affiliate)
135 West 50th Street
New York, NY 10020

*Employment Management
  Association*
20 William Street
Wellesley, MA 02181

Human Resource Planning Society
P.O. Box 2553
Grand Central Station
New York, NY 10017

*Industrial Relations Research
  Association*
7226 Social Science Building
University of Wisconsin
Madison, WI 53706

*International Association for Personnel
  Women*
150 West 52nd Street
New York, NY 10019

*International Industrial Relations
  Association*
International Labour Office
c/o Leg/Rel
CH-1211
Geneva 22, Switzerland

*International Personnel Management
  Association*
1850 K Street, N.W., Suite 870
Washington, DC 20006

*National Employment and Training
  Association*
250 East Fifth Street
Salt Lake City, UT 84111

*National Society for Performance
  Instruction*
1126 16th Street, N.W.,
Suite 315
Washington, DC 20036

Planning Executives Institute
5500 College Corner Pike
Oxford, OH 45056

**SERVICES FOR PERSONNEL
RESEARCH**

Bureau of National Affairs, Inc.
1231 25th Street, N.W.
Washington, DC 20037

Bureau of Labor Statistics
U. S. Department of Labor
Washington, DC 20212

Commerce Clearing House
4025 West Peterson Avenue
Chicago, IL 60646

Prentice-Hall, Inc.
Englewood Cliffs, NJ 07632

Notes

1. William C. Byham, *The Uses of Personnel Research,* AMA Research Study 91 (New York: American Management Association, 1968), p. 14.

2. Mary Green Miner, *Selection Procedures and Personnel Records,* Personnel Policies Forum Survey No. 114 (Washington, D.C.: Bureau of National Affairs, 1976), p. 20.

3. T. Michael Jackson, AEP, "The Personnel File—What and Whose?" *The Personnel Administrator,* February 1977, pp. 41–42.

4. J. Hugh Watson and Archie B. Carroll, *Computers for Business: A Managerial Emphasis* (Dallas: Business Publications, 1976).

5. H. W. Hennessey, Jr., "Computer Applications in Human Resource Information Systems," *Human Resource Planning,* 4 (1979), pp. 206–13.

6. Stephen R. Ruth, "Personnel and EDP in the 1980's," *MSU Business Topics,* Summer 1980, pp. 51–52.

7. Edward A. Tomeski, B. Man Yoon, and George Stephenson, "Computer-Related Challenges for Personnel Administrators," *Personnel Journal,* June 1976, pp. 300–301.

8. Benjamin Roter, "Personnel Selection: An Update," *Personnel Journal,* January 1976, p. 24.

9. William E. Bright, "How One Company Manages Its Human Resources," *Harvard Business Review,* January–February 1976, p. 83.

10. Robert T. Graver, "An Automated Approach to Affirmative Action," *Personnel,* September–October 1976, pp. 37–44.

11. Kent Granat, "After Personnel System Installation, Then What?" *Personnel Journal,* November 1971, pp. 868–69.

12. Tomeski et al., "Computer-Related Challenges," p. 300.

13. Warren S. Blumenfeld and Donald P. Crane, "Opinions of Training Effectiveness: How Good?" *Training and Development Journal,* December 1973, pp. 42ff.

14. For an excellent discussion of applied personnel research see William C. Byham's research study on this subject in *The Uses of Personnel Research.*

15. A useful guide to research and experimentation in personnel and related areas is Stephen Isaac and William B. Michael, *Handbook in Research and Evaluation* (San Diego, Calif.: EDITS Publishers, 1977). For an excellent text on experimental design see William Mendenhall, *The Design and Analysis of Experiments* (Belmont, Calif.: Wadsworth, 1968).

16. Jac Fitz-Enz, "Quantifying the Human Resources Function," *Personnel,* March–April 1980, p. 48.

Chapter Eight
Interviewing and Counseling

Walter Perkel, a senior design engineer with Hansen Industries (manufacturers of electronic components) for the past eight years, had submitted his resignation two weeks ago. This is the essence of his final interview (exit interview) with Randy Parker, the company's personnel manager.

Randy: Well, Walt, I guess this is your last day. The people in your department sure did give you a nice sendoff.

Walter: Yeah, Randy. It kinda makes me sad to leave.

Randy: I sure hope they appreciate you over at Jasper. We feel we're losing a valued employee. (NOTE: Jasper is a competitor located a few miles north of Hansen.)

Walter: Thanks for the compliment, Randy; I'm confident they'll do right by me.

Randy: O.K., Walt. I guess we'd better let you get on your way. Here's your final paycheck. Are there any questions I can answer for you?

Walter: No, none that I can think of. I appreciate your help, Randy. It's been nice knowing you.

Randy: So long, Walt. And good luck on your new job.

This interview between Randy and Walt displays the characteristics of an interview situation, and it also demonstrates the failure of some interviewers to take into account the total situation.

We might define the **interview** as a medium of exchange of infor-

LEARNING OBJECTIVES

1. To know the applications of directive versus nondirective approaches to interviewing.
2. To know the steps in the interview process.
3. To understand the uses of counseling in personnel management.
4. To be familiar with the problems giving rise to counseling.
5. To know the relationship of counseling to productivity.

mation from one person to another. The interview has a specific *context* (The setting, sequence, and objectives), *content* (subject matter around which the conversation centers), and *roles* (various behaviors intended to accomplish the objectives of the interview and provide certain responses). In the interview cited above, the exchange of information took place when Randy confirmed that Walt was leaving the company; in return Walt received his final paycheck. The interview was probably conducted in the personnel office (setting); it included the communication of the company's regret over Walt's leaving and the determination that Walt had made all the necessary arrangements to leave the company (sequence), and it resulted in Walt's receiving his final paycheck. Randy viewed his *role* as playing the good guy and facilitating Walt's exit from the company; Walt saw his role as employee/interviewee, and he merely wanted to leave on a positive note.

Situational Considerations of Interviewing

Felix Lopez emphasizes, "An interview is not an isolated event but rather is embedded in a complex social matrix and constitutes but one of a sequence of events. As an interviewer, therefore, you cannot perform very effectively if you fail to take into account the total situation and your immediate objective."[1] Randy did not achieve the full purpose of the interview when he merely wished Walt good luck and sent him away with his final paycheck. He would have accomplished far more had he delved into the reasons why Walt was leaving and his attitudes about the company, its policies, and practices.

Lopez's quote suggests that each interview situation is unique. The perceptions, motivations, attitudes, emotions, previous experiences, roles, and so on of each party in the interview are unique. When these factors interact, they form a highly complex situation. For example, had Walt perceived that Randy would withhold his paycheck until he imparted certain information, Walt may have become reluctant to be open with Randy. Similarly, the personalities of the parties may dictate the approach to be taken by the interviewer. The use of a directive versus a nondirective approach is often a function of the personality of the interviewer and his or her perception of the interviewee. Personality and other personal characteristics also influence the way questions and responses are interpreted. Ideally, both parties exchange information freely and openly, and the process achieves its intended purpose. In reviewing the literature on the employment interview, however, Arvey[2] concluded that situational bias or unfairness existed to a greater degree than might be expected. He found that:

1. The interview is vulnerable to legal challenge which makes future litigation in this area probable;

2. Researchers do not clearly specify the processes and mechanisms that contribute to bias in the interview;

3. Research on resumes demonstrates that females tend to receive lower evaluations than males, but this varied with the job and other situational variables;

4. There is little evidence to suggest that blacks are evaluated unfairly in interview contexts;

5. Few studies have been conducted to investigate interview bias against the elderly and handicapped; and

6. No evidence concerning the differential validity of the interview for minority groups appears to exist.

Alderfer and McCord also investigated situational variables in the interview. Their studies sought to identify the effect of various interview factors on applicants' decisions to accept a job.[3] Interview content is a significant situational variable. The context and roles are significantly different in a disciplinary interview than they are in an orientation interview. In the former, the interviewer is firm, possibly even stern, in seeking to correct the other person's behavior. In an orientation interview there is a friendly, receptive atmosphere where an exchange of information takes place. To simplify discussion of interviewing, we have classified interviews according to their basic purpose: *information exchange, decision making,* and *problem solving.*[4] The **information exchange interview** is the most elementary because it involves the simple acquisition or dissemination of information. Fact-finding, attitude survey, employee orientation, and job-skills coaching are a few examples of this category of interview. They are usually given by line supervisors who, hopefully, have been given training offered by the personnel department. The **decision-making interview** requires the gathering of information and related data, comparing it to some established criteria, and drawing a conclusion or making a determination. Employment/recruiting interviews are of this category, and they are usually performed by employment specialists and/or specially trained line managers. The **problem-solving interview** serves the purpose of resolving some type of employee problem and may call for conflict resolution or motivating behavioral change. Counseling interviews fall into this category, and because they are so varied and complex, they are explored in detail in a special section of this chapter. Usually, line supervisors detect a problem requiring counseling and refer their employee to a certified counselor for help. But in cases requiring discipline, the line supervisor or manager will decide on a final course of action to be taken, for example, warning, discharge, referral, or some other measure. Interview researchers have generally found that employment interviews have low validity and reliability.[5] Nevertheless, interviews have remained popular in personnel activities.

Following a discussion of the techniques of interviewing, we will explore the different types of interviews.

Techniques of Interviewing
INTERVIEW PLANNING

Advance preparation allows interviewers to determine which factors should be emphasized and maintain control of an interview. Careful development of an objective or purpose of an interview can help assure its full utilization. Had Randy established an objective for the interview with Walt he probably would have obtained some valuable information that could have helped in improving personnel practices and retaining valuable employees. Also, an interviewer might frame the questions to be asked and anticipate likely responses. A conscientious interviewer might even role-play an interview in order to practice particular techniques or to gain familiarity with the more difficult aspects that might arise. This strategy is most appropriate in appraisal interviews, in which a manager seeks to correct some aspect of an employee's performance.

THE INTERVIEW SETTING

Privacy, in a location free from distractions or interruptions, is essential to an effective interview. Such an environment is conducive to a free exchange and creates an impression that what the interviewee has to say is important.

As the interviewee responds to questions, an interviewer decides if the responses are appropriate. If not, or if they are incomplete, further questions may be in order. Sometimes an interviewer may have to delve into a response by probing to get deeper into an issue. In this respect, an interviewer has to be a skilled listener, aware of the meanings behind statements, and sensitive to voice inflections, eye contact, and mannerisms.

To create a favorable environment and to put an interviewee at ease, interviewers try to establish rapport with them. Randy put Walt at ease at the outset of their interview when he said, ''The people in your department sure did give you a nice sendoff.'' This form of banter created a feeling of good will in Walt and encouraged him to respond more openly to further questions.

APPROACHES TO INTERVIEWING

Interviews are directive (structured), nondirective, or a combination of the two. It is unlikely that one type of interview is appropriate for all situations.[6]

In the structured, or **directive approach,** interviewers determine in advance the questions and their sequence. They then systematically proceed down a list of questions, recording the responses. The directive interview does not utilize open-ended discussion, which makes the approach relatively straightforward. Thus, situations like the following would be most conducive to the directive approach:

1. Basic information needs to be imparted or gathered.
2. Both people in the interview think alike and have similar perceptions of the subject involved.
3. The purpose of the interview is to:
   a. orient the person to a new way of performing the job.
   b. discipline a person where there needs to be an abrupt facing of facts.
   c. summarize information that has been discussed previously.
4. The interviewee likes to know specifically what is expected of him or her.
5. The interviewer wants to get a reaction to an idea or some facts.
6. The interviewer wants to remain in control and feels more comfortable with such a style.

Figure 8.1 is an example of a guide that is used in a directive interview.

The **nondirective interview** is guided by how the interviewee sees the situation. The interviewer asks an open-ended question such as, "Tell me about yourself," and listens carefully. The nondirective interview encourages expressions of feelings, opinions, and ideas, and it permits interviewees to emphasize what they believe is relevant and important. The interviewer makes comments or asks questions to stimulate thinking and free expression. A typical question might be, "How do you feel about your

Name of applicant _____ .
What do you know about our organization?
To date, what have been some of your more important work responsibilities?
What is your previous work experience?
What were your duties in your previous job?
What are your feelings about leaving your present job?
What are your career objectives?
What are your salary requirements?
Why do you want to work for this company?
What can you contribute to this organization in the way of abilities, personal characteristics, and experience?
What kinds of work do you like best? Least?

Figure 8.1
Structured Interview Guide

new job?" Or a comment such as "You seem to feel that your work is causing you stress," would be an example of a nondirective approach.

Situations such as the following are most appropriate to the nondirective approach:

1. The interviewer needs to ascertain feelings, opinions, and attitudes as well as facts.
2. The interviewee needs to gain insight into the causes and related factors affecting his or her situation.
3. The situation involves self-development of the person being interviewed.
4. The two parties need to reach an understanding.

There are several advantages to the nondirective approach. There is better feedback, and an interviewer gains insight into the interviewee's motives, feelings, problems, perceptions, and so on. This approach affords an interviewer an opportunity to develop understanding, reduce conflicts, tensions, and resentments. It is conducive to eliciting acceptance and cooperation on follow-up activities because an interviewee becomes more involved and feels more a part of the process. On the other hand, the nondirective approach requires greater planning and skill on the part of an interviewer, as well as considerably more time than the structured approach.

THE IMPORTANCE OF SKILLED INTERVIEWERS

Expertise in interviewing is essential, yet few organizations give any consideration to selecting and training interviewers. Traditionally, entry-level personnel people are assigned as interviewers. This use of untrained and inexperienced interviewers can lead to such undesirable results as failure to obtain desired information; selection of unqualified applicants; the loss of potentially valuable candidates; incorrect discipline procedures; or faulty diagnosis of a personnel problem.

Previously, it was assumed that interviewing experience helped people become effective interviewers. However, research suggests that experience alone does not make good interviewers. One study found that managers who conducted different numbers of interviews over the same period of time benefited very little from day-to-day experience.[7]

Organizations with successful interview procedures believe that training interview personnel is a key element. These organizations provide systematic training in the theory and application of interviewing techniques as well as in-company policy and procedures. They use role-playing sessions, during which trainees assume the roles of interviewers and applicants. A qualified instructor observes these sessions and provides constructive criticism. These companies also use audio and video recordings of interview situations to help trainees evaluate their own style and technique.

Techniques also vary with the type of interview. Let us explore the various types of interviews and the appropriate techniques for each type.

Types of Interviews

DECISION-MAKING INTERVIEW

Since the employment (selection) interview is the primary form of decision-making interview, our discussion will focus on it.

In an employment interview, organizational representatives observe and talk with applicants to evaluate their potential value to an organization. Interviewers appraise applicants' mental, physical, emotional, and social qualities; the comprehensiveness of these questions depends upon the nature of the job and the special skills and personality traits needed for it. Interviewers want to match personal qualifications with job requirements—to find the right person for the job. In addition, they explore any questionable information on the application blank. They also supply information to applicants to help them evaluate the company. Finally, interviewers make a subjective assessment based on factual information and general impressions. They then decide either to hire, reject, or recommend further interviews.

Employment interviewers first acquaint themselves with the duties and requirements of a position. Larger organizations use job descriptions and job specifications to provide much of this information, but reading descriptions is not sufficient. Interviewers must observe the functions associated with a job. They must analyze job requirements to determine which factors to measure with tests and reference inquiries, and which to evaluate in interviews.

Second, interviewers analyze completed application forms and resumes to get a feel for applicants' personal characteristics, skills, education, and background; this analysis can raise questions that will be clarified during an interview. Interviewers notice the manner in which an application is filled out; legibility, thoroughness, and writing style can indicate a great deal about an applicant.

Third, interviewers outline in advance the topics to cover and their order of importance; they also allot sufficient time for thorough coverage. The length of interviews depends upon the responsiveness and articulateness of the interviewees, the types of positions to be filled, and the amount of time available.

GUIDELINES FOR EMPLOYMENT INTERVIEWING. Questions requiring a yes or no limit applicants' replies, but broad, general inquiries can elicit ideas that are most important to applicants. Such responses provide valuable clues to candidates' values and personalities. Interviewers then probe areas needing expansion or clarification. For instance, if an applicant says he or she resigned from several jobs, an interviewer can delve into the reasons and circumstances. As applicants respond to questions, interviewers decide if their responses add to or detract from their acceptability. In this respect, interviewers must be skilled listeners, aware of the meanings behind statements, sensitive to voice inflections, eye contact, and mannerisms. Interviewers can learn as much about candidates from the way they reply as from the words they use.

Interviewers also provide information that will give applicants a favorable opinion of the company. Such information covers basic job duties, training, working hours, compensation, supervision, benefits, prospects for advancement, characteristics of the organization, the work environment, and so on. Interviewers can promote good will for their companies even when applicants are not hired.

Stronger enforcement of EEOC guidelines makes it advisable for interviewers to be alert in handling questions from minority and female applicants, who expect straightforward, honest answers to questions such as the following:

1. How many blacks (or women) are in line positions in your organization?

2. In what position is your highest ranking woman (or black)?

3. What is the company's affirmative action plan for improving opportunities for blacks (or women)?

4. What is the affirmative action officer's rank in the organization?

5. Is your firm really committed to affirmative action?[8]

An interview ends when an employment interviewer has a good idea of an applicant's basic qualifications and the latter is aware of the opportunities offered by an organization. If there is mutual interest, further interviews and tests are arranged. If there is no interest, interviewers should tell applicants that a prompt decision will be forthcoming.

EMPLOYMENT INTERVIEWS—HOW GOOD? Numerous studies have questioned the effectiveness of interviews in the selection process.[9] Some of the deficiencies of interviews are the fault of the individuals performing the task; as previously mentioned, most interviewers are largely untrained to handle this responsibility. One criticism of interviews points out that under controlled conditions, interviewers usually arrive at different evaluations of the same applicants. Other studies conclude that even if interviews were a reliable selection device, there remains the question of validity—how well they predict future job success. Only a few studies show interviews as a meaningful predictor.

An interviewer's biases will distort evaluations and reduce reliability. Also, interviewers are more influenced by unfavorable than favorable information about applicants. Along this line, most interviewers are taught to establish a benchmark for evaluating applicants. Interviewers learn to determine which applicants are marginally acceptable and marginally rejectable; they then reject those who make a less favorable impression and accept those who appear to be better qualified. Unfortunately, interviewers' benchmarks are often preconceived stereotypes of good and poor candidates.

One might also suspect that the degree of structure affects the reliability of selection interviews: whether the structured or nonstructured approach is more desirable is still debatable. However, research in this area indicates that structured interviews generate more consistent evaluation[10] (although consistent evaluations are not necessarily accurate in predicting job success).

Despite the negative implications of research findings, interviews remain a widely used tool in the selection and placement processes; to date, no one has devised a better alternative, though interviews can be made more effective by applying research data. Personnel departments should make interviews one element among many in the over-all selection procedure, but the employment interview should be tailored to the job or the family of jobs for which people are applying.[11] Aids such as structured question guides and standardized evaluation and prediction forms are useful in this regard. The interview guide shown in Figure 8.2 is considered a valuable tool in employment interviews. Also, interviewer training is a necessity if interviews are to be an important device in selection and promotion.[12]

INFORMATION EXCHANGE INTERVIEW

Information exchange interviews consist of two types: information-getting and information-giving.

Information-getting interviews have the purpose of obtaining desired data on subjects such as reasons for turnover, employee attitudes and morale, workers' opinions, training needs, evaluations of employee desires, or demand for specific activities, for example, credit union, and many others. Planning for this type of interview is critical. It assures that questions do not suggest answers. For example, "Do you think your supervisor knows his job?" suggests the answer. "What do you think of your supervisor?" would be a more appropriate question. Also, questions should be phrased so they are clear and not misleading. "Is our open-door policy satisfactory in your mind?" might confuse the interviewee and result in mixed or biased responses. The question, "Tell me what you think of our open-door policy," is clearer and gives less of an impression of interrogation. In accordance with sound research practice, it would be appropriate to field test the questions on a sample of people in order to avoid errors that even the most careful planning may not avoid. The attitude survey questionnaire in Figure 4.2 is an example of a useful aid for an information gathering interview.

Figure 8.2
Interview Guide

Source: Henry H. Morgan and John W. Cooger, *The Interviewer's Manual* (New York: The Psychological Corporation, 1973), pp. 46–47. Reproduced with permission.

INTERVIEWING

INTERVIEW GUIDE

LISTEN	COMMENT	INQUIRE
Be Receptive and Responsive	Make Conversation	Probe: What? How? Why?

Keep Questions Open-Ended

INTRODUCTION

Cover:
Greeting
Small talk
Opening question
Lead question

Look for:
Appearance
Manner
Self-expression
Responsiveness

WORK EXPERIENCE

Cover:
Earliest jobs,
    part-time, temporary
Military assignments
Full-time positions

Ask:
Things done best? Done less well?
Things liked best? Liked less well?
Major accomplishments? How achieved?
Most difficult problems faced? How handled?
Ways most effective with people? Ways
    less effective?
Level of earnings?
Reasons for changing jobs?
What learned from work experience?
What looking for in job? In career?

Look for:
Relevance of work
Sufficiency of work
Skill and competence
Adaptability
Productivity
Motivation
Interpersonal relations
Leadership
Growth and development

EDUCATION

Cover:
Elementary school
High school
College
Specialized training
Recent courses

Ask:
Best subjects? Subjects done less well?
Subjects liked most? Liked least?
Reactions to teachers?
Level of grades? Effort required?
Reasons for choosing school? Major field?
Special achievements? Toughest problems?
Role in extracurricular activities?
How financed education?
Relation of education to career?
Consider further schooling?

Look for:
Relevance of schooling
Sufficiency of schooling
Intellectual abilities
Versatility
Breadth and depth of knowledge
Level of accomplishment
Motivation, interests
Reaction to authority
Leadership
Team work

(over)

Figure 8.2 (cont.)

EARLY YEARS (OPTIONAL)

Cover:
Family and home
Guidance and discipline
Individual and group
    activities
Neighborhood and
    community

Ask:
What did father do for a living?
Describe parents' interests? personalities?
How about brothers and sisters? Contrast
    with self?
Parents' expectations? How strictly raised?
How spend time? play? chores? organizations?
How describe neigbhorhood? community?
Effect of early influences?

Look for:
Socio-economic status
Parental examples
Attitudes toward achievement,
    work, and people
Emotional and social
    adjustment
Basic values and goals
Self-image

PRESENT ACTIVITIES AND INTERESTS

Cover:
Special interests and hobbies
Civic and community affairs
Living arrangements
Marriage and family
Finances
Health and energy
Geographical preferences

Ask:
Things like to do in spare time?
What social activities?
Extent involved in community?
Describe home? and family?
Opportunities to build financial reserve?
What kind of health problems? physical check-up?
Reaction to relocation?

Look for:
Vitality
Management of time,
    energy, and money
Maturity and judgment
Intellectual growth
Cultural breadth
Diversity of interests
Social interests
Social skills
Leadership
Basic values and goals
Situational factors

SUMMARY

Cover:
Strengths
Weaknesses

Ask:
What bring to job? What are assets?
What are best talents?
What qualities seen by self or others?
What makes you good investment for employer?

What are shortcomings?
What areas need improvement?
What qualities wish to develop further?
What constructive criticism from others?
How might you be risk for employer?
What further training, or experience, might
    you need?

Look for:
PLUS (+) AND MINUS (−)
Talents, skills
Knowledge
Energy
Motivation
Interests
Personal qualities
Social effectiveness
Character
Situational factors

CLOSING REMARKS

Cover:
Comments regarding interview and applicant
Further contacts to be made
Course of action to be taken
Cordial parting

Employee orientation is the primary form of an *information-giving* interview. The content is initially one-way communication, with the interviewer telling or briefing the new employee about details of the work, benefits, rules, company history, and so on. But a checklist such as the one shown in Figure 13.1 can determine how much of the information the employee felt he or she absorbed. (The subject of employee orientation is discussed in Chapter 13.)

PROBLEM-SOLVING INTERVIEWS

Problem-solving interviews encompass performance appraisal, which is covered in Chapter 16, career guidance, covered in Chapter 17, and employee counseling, which will be discussed here and in a separate section of this chapter.

COUNSELING METHODS AND SKILLS.   In employee counseling, the nondirective approach is more appropriate, because individuals are in the best position to solve their own problems if they can gain greater insight into them. The nondirective approach helps people accept their problems and gain a better understanding of themselves—of their strengths and weaknesses.

In the counseling interview it is important to create a climate of mutual understanding so that employees with problems will talk freely about them. Encouraging an employee to talk about the problem is important, but since the problems being discussed are often highly personal, trust-building is also very significant. Such a climate can only be realized in a private setting, where both parties can be relaxed and feel assured that the conversation will be confidential. Listening is a basic communication skill that is key to all types of interviews, but it is especially important in problem-solving ones. The counselor who actively listens shows care and respect for the employee with a problem. But active listening isn't easy; it takes considerable concentration and an avoidance of distractions. By listening carefully, the counselor is able to utilize a basic technique of counseling—**reflection.** Reflection is a counseling technique whereby feelings are clarified by their restatement by the counselor. Here the counselor reflects feelings and, thereby, clarifies them and reflects meaning to help the employee gain a clearer understanding of what he or she is actually stating. The following examples will clarify this technique. The employee (an equipment repair person) complains, "Those guys in sales are always promising performance that our equipment just can't deliver." And the counselor reflects (feelings): "You feel angry about this situation." Or, the counselor might reflect meaning by stating: "You're saying these salespeople are overstating the capabilities of our products." Both content and feeling reflections are needed to clarify the employee's problem and provide an avenue to a solution. To encourage an employee to talk and to convey support and build rapport, a counselor might use a variety of verbal and nonverbal responses. Comments such as "Tell me more," "I see," "Go on," are examples. A nod of the head communicates (nonverbally) that his or her words are being understood.[13]

At this point a counselor guides an employee to the solution of a problem. The counselor might make an observation from his or her perspective. For example, consider the salesperson who is in a slump and can't seem to close any sales. After listening to the salesperson's problems, an interpretation response by the sales manager (counselor) might be, "You're frustrated and upset with yourself because you're not closing sales. Maybe this is because you're not making enough sales calls and asking for enough orders." If the employee can arrive at his or her own solution to the problem the results are likely to be far more effective than if the answers are spelled out by the counselor. The process of leading an employee to a solution, however, takes considerable patience and skill on the part of a counselor. Finally, after an employee has identified the problem and the real solution, a counselor is challenged to gain commitment to execute, to make the change necessary to correct the problem. The same process of leading, reflecting, assuring, questioning, and listening applies to this final step.[14]

Several situational variables affect the development of each counseling interview. It depends on the judgment of the counselor, his or her insight into the personal relationships involved, and the attitudes of the employee being interviewed. Other people involved, for example, managers or employees, may be cooperative, indifferent, evasive, or openly hostile. The counselor should gauge these factors along with the nature of the problem and direct the interview to maximize the prospects for an appropriate solution.[15]

Employee Counseling

Employee counseling as an industrial practice stemmed from the Hawthorne studies at Western Electric Company. These studies were conducted to determine the effects of various physical factors in the work environment. The investigators discovered that it was not the physical conditions of the job that were crucial, but how the employees felt about their jobs, their fellow workers, and management in particular. These results led to the introduction of an interviewing program in the plant as a new attack on human relations problems.[16]

The need for employee counseling became most apparent, however, when the rapid industrial expansion and high production pressure of the Second World War created complex employee problems. Many manufacturing companies set up counseling programs to handle these problems. After the war, they discontinued most of these programs. Today, more companies are turning to counseling programs as a means of keeping employees productive (and loyal to the organization). The costs of recruiting, selecting, training, et cetera, seem to far outweigh the costs of counseling. Ten to fifteen years ago the prevalent management attitude (for all but key employees) was "if they are 'bad' let them go." Even with this changed attitude full-time counselors are rare in business and industry and counseling is usually handled by first-line supervisors.

At one time or another all employees have problems; many are work-connected, and some are not. If an organization provides counseling, line supervisors, assisted by the personnel staff, play a significant part. Supervisors often have no choice about counseling—their subordinates come to them with problems they cannot avoid even if they wish to. Therefore, the supervisors' role in counseling requires a sensitivity to employees' needs and an attitude that encourages workers to consult them about problems. Also, supervisors must be alert for signs that employees are experiencing difficulties.

Most employee problems can be identified by a supervisor, and many can be resolved without additional help. But after consulting with a troubled employee, a supervisor may find that the problem requires the attention of a specialist. Alert, sensitive supervisors learn to recognize problems beyond their capability, and they know to whom to refer troubled employees. In referring subordinates, they do not divest themselves of the ultimate responsibility for solving a problem—through cooperation with specialists and follow-up on the job, supervisors can maintain a continuous, active interest in an employee. Although various resources are available to handle counseling programs, the personnel department is, for supervisors, the logical referral point because of its familiarity with such matters.

Problems Requiring Counseling

Employees' personal problems fall into two general classes: (1) those arising from job-related situations such as performance appraisal (covered in Chapter 6), discipline (covered in Chapter 9), job adjustment, vocational planning, and retirement; and (2) those arising from situations unrelated to employment, but which nevertheless affect employees' abilities to perform their jobs effectively, such as health care, emotional illness, family relations, and financial problems. Each of these problems is described as it relates to job performance. Detection and resolution of problems are viewed from the standpoint of personnel representatives and line supervisors, and are generally applicable to all business situations.

JOB-RELATED COUNSELING PROBLEMS

JOB ADJUSTMENT. Generally, the employee's immediate supervisor is responsible for the employee's **job adjustment,** the orienting and instructing of him or her in the functions of a job. Supervisors not only see that new employees are properly instructed in performing their job duties, but they ensure that they are familiar with the organization, its benefits and policies, and that they know how their job fits in with others. These same supervisors frequently have to reorient seasoned employees to changed conditions or because they have developed poor habits or a different attitude toward their work. But some employees have more trouble adjusting to the job than others. Perhaps an employee is not suited to the work, or perhaps he does not get along with his peers or his supervisor. Organizations cannot ignore such problems. Counseling with these employees can identify problems, while further counseling and instruction by immediate supervisors can improve and often correct situations. Sometimes, alternative measures such as transfer or discipline become necessary.

Counseling employees to help them adjust to the work situation is especially critical with former hard-core unemployed workers. (Hard-core unemployed refers to individuals who are poor and at least one of the following: under 22 or over 45; handicapped; high school dropout; or subject to special obstacles to employment, i.e., being a minority member.) The following description of a program developed by the author is representative of the counseling for disadvantaged workers in government-sponsored programs.

Counseling will consist of one group session followed by individual meetings. The group session will orient the employee to the work world, allow him or her to develop positive attitudes toward work and, through various assessment techniques, evaluate vocational desires and potential. General areas to be covered in group sessions include: avoiding consumer pitfalls, interpreting test scores, role-playing, and getting along with fellow workers; getting along with supervision; working out personal problems.

Supportive activities will include a "buddy" system, which will pair a mature sympathetic worker with each new employee. The "buddy" system will be screened and care will be taken to see that he or she is sincere in the desire to help a new employee. He or she will also be given a period of training in assisting in personal matters.

The counselor will also serve as an advisor to the new employee, visiting with the employee and his or her foreman on the job frequently to ensure that the employee is adjusting to the job. When necessary, home visits by the counselor to encourage continued attendance by the employee will be made. The counselor will work closely with the administrator and supervisors and will make them aware of problems the employee might be experiencing both on and off the job.

RETIREMENT AND PROBLEMS OF AGING. The issue of **retirement** is an emotional one. On the one hand it is viewed as an abridgement of individual rights. To require a person to leave the job, give up an important role, and accept a substantially reduced income because the mandatory retirement age has been reached seems blatantly unfair. On the other hand, the opportunity to retire is sought by many workers in order to enjoy the fruits of their labor. They tolerate work in order to earn money, have social status, and accumulate enough worldly goods and benefits to have the right to leisure, with its peace and comforts, in their twilight years.[17] When we consider the growth in the number of retired persons in this country—the ratio of persons 65 and over to those 20–65 is projected to rise from 19 percent in 1970 to about 28 percent by 2050—the issue of retirement is a major one.[18]

Given the fact that American workers are aging, many are concerned about improving their economic situation when they retire. Consequently, receiving increased Social Security benefits is a primary concern of retired people. Given the various sources of retirement income—public assistance, personal savings, charity, social security, insurance, and pension plans—the economic reality is that the working population must produce whatever the retired population consumes. This gives rise to the problem of fewer workers having to produce more for the growing aging and retired segment of the population.[19]

Determining Retirement Age.   Organizations face the problem of determining the age at which their employees must retire. Some maintain a flexible policy of permitting employees to retire anytime after they accumulate a combination of service years plus age (e.g., an aerospace manufacturer allows full retirement when 80 points are accumulated, e.g., a 51-year-old employee with 29 years of service). Others allow their employees to work as long as they are physically sound and reasonably effective. There is medical evidence that thanks to better nutrition and improved medical care employees can be productive even beyond age 75; that age does not cause a significant decline in learning ability; and that the older worker generally exhibits more mature judgment and more reliable attendance than his or her younger counterpart. A 1974 Harris Poll found that nearly 40 percent of the American retirees would prefer to work.[20] In fact, 750,000 Americans are still employed after age 71.[21] However, the prevailing practice is to establish a compulsory age at which employees must retire. The usual mandatory retirement age was raised from 65 to 70 by Congress in 1978. The bill (an amendment to the Age Discrimination in Employment Act) does not force people to keep working beyond 65 (they can still begin collecting maximum Social Security benefits at that age), but it does require employers to give them the option. On the one hand, the mandatory retirement practice uncomplicates the process of removing loyal employees who may no longer be viable; and it opens promotion opportunities for upwardly mobile younger persons. On the other, forcing an employee to retire may cost an organization a person with valuable skills and talent who could continue to make substantial contributions. Firms have overcome this drawback in several ways. They extend, by invitation, employment on a year-to-year basis. As an alternative, some phase their employees into retirement by allowing them to work a reduced schedule for a specified period of time prior to full retirement. Some retain post-retirement-age employees full-time or part-time as consultants.

Early retirement has become increasingly attractive to both organizations and employees. Inducements to encourage retirement have grown. Unions have bargained successfully for early retirement provisions. The United Electrical Workers Union, for example, signed a pact with a Dayton, Ohio, foundry that includes a 30 and out full pension with $250 extra until Social Security payments begin, or $730 a month after 30 years.[22] Another factor is the liberalization of Social Security benefits before age 65. U.S. corporations are using early retirement as a means to cut costs, realign top-heavy organization charts, and build younger management teams. Many offer liberal benefits, e.g., full salary or a retirement supplement to those with sufficient service who opt for early retirement. If the experience at General Motors is any indication there is a clear trend toward earlier retirement. In 1954, the average G.M. hourly paid worker retired at 67 and the salaried employee at 63; today they both retire at 58 or 59.[23] The phenomenon appears to stem from the wider career interests of some younger people, or their desire to find another job where the chances of advancement are better, or simply a wish to stop working altogether. Even among executives, the same drives that took them to the top of their organizations may also cause them to leave, because once at the top they may find that their personal needs are not being satisfied.[24]

Should the trend toward early retirement continue, a major social problem will surely result. Considering our aging work force coupled with early retirees, it may take 60 workers to support 40 retirees. This will mean higher payroll taxes which, in turn, would create a financial disincentive to work, leading more people to conclude, "Why not retire early?"

An alternative might be a **flexible retirement** system or what also has been termed *transition retirement*. Best[25] points out that longer life expectancy produces several problems: longer years of non-income-earning retirement, an erosion of savings and pension income due to inflation, and further draining of pension revenues. Thus, retirees find it increasingly difficult to maintain an acceptable living standard. Flexible retirement programs, though few in number, attempt to address this problem. Older workers under these programs opt to work a reduced schedule, either a reduced workweek or a reduced work year. Under the reduced workweek option, retirees who have reached a certain age (say 60), are near normal retirement (e.g., two years), and have a minimum service with the organization (say, five years) become eligible to work a reduced schedule (such as four days a week the first year and three days after that). Under this arrangement many choose to continue working beyond normal retirement age.[26]

Regardless of the retirement age of an employee, there are many adjustments to be made, which include time, finances, health, friendships, leisure time, and others.[27] Some find it impossible to adjust, others are able to develop a lifestyle that blends past experiences with future needs.

Views of Retirement.   An understanding of the variety of ways some employees come to terms with retirement can help older employees make the transition from an active work life. They include:

1. *Maintenance*—continuing work to satisfy the same needs as before retirement.
2. *Withdrawal*—adopting a new lifestyle in order to engage in leisure activities.
3. *Changed activities*—satisfying preretirement needs by engaging in new activities.
4. *Changed needs*—having time "to do what I've always wanted to do."[28]

Retirement Counseling.   Employees about to retire face many anxieties. Their supervisors, in conjunction with the personnel department, can ease the adjustment period prior to retirement. Line supervisors do not have the time and training to advise their employees on all the problems of retirement. But they can lend a sympathetic ear and help employees find answers to their questions about retirement by referring them to the personnel department.

An organization's retirement plans provide a **pension** based on earnings and years of service. Most retirees also receive Social Security benefits (their offices in most major cities can closely estimate the benefits employees are entitled to). In addition, working people generally have accumulated some savings, investments, and real or personal property that can be converted into income. The trust officers of local banks can provide good advice on financial planning for retirement.

After retirement many people have difficulty filling up the hours that were formerly taken up by work. Hunting, reading, cooking, and tinkering around the house cannot replace the work schedule of active people. Prior to retirement, employees need to develop purposeful interests that will keep them interested in life through their retirement years. Supervisors must take the responsibility of influencing employees nearing retirement age to change their life patterns and actively prepare for retirement.

Old age brings health problems. Employees approaching retirement worry that their insurance will not cover their medical bills as health wanes. Organizations can dispel this apprehension by explaining hospital, medical, and surgical benefits available through company and government health programs. Low-cost health insurance can supplement these sources. It is the personnel department's responsibility to provide information of this nature to retiring employees. Also, numerous handbooks and pamphlets on retirement are readily available commercially, through company retirement programs, insurance companies, financial institutions, and the federal government. Since retirement programs are considered a fringe benefit, a more detailed discussion of the elements of such programs is included in Chapter 20.

Preretirement Education.   There appears to be a marked growth in the field of preretirement education and an awakening excitement about the programs among a wide range of professionals in both education and industry.[29] In addition, ERISA (Employee Retirement Income Security Act of 1974) requires employers to communicate retirement benefits in laymen's language. The problem is that most organizations do not have personnel who are trained to counsel employees about retirement. Some organizations have rectified this condition by contracting with outside consultants to perform preretirement education services.[30]

The ideal characteristics of the educational function are described below. Professionals suggest that employees join an educational program ten years prior to retirement, allowing sufficient time to deal with the issues of finances, health, and use of time.[31] They also recommend that co-planners or spouses be involved in the retirement planning process.[32]

The specific topics that can be covered in a preretirement educational program are outlined in Table 8.1.

PERSONAL COUNSELING PROBLEMS

HEALTH-RELATED PROBLEMS: ALCOHOLISM AND DRUG ADDICTION. **Alcoholism** and **drug addiction** are the most prominent health problems identified with the work force. They have received the widest attention because they have such a noticeable, negative effect on job performance and because they are widespread and growing.

The American Medical Association identified alcoholism as a serious, complex disease as early as 1956. The National Council on Alcoholism estimates that the alcoholic employee in the United States costs industry over $25 billion a year. For an individual company these losses are estimated at an average of 3 percent of payroll dollars; plus increased health insurance premiums; higher worker's compensation payments; and the intangible costs

I.   Individual Needs
   A.   Feelings about retirement
   B.   Factors in retirement—satisfactory and unsatisfactory

II.   Finances
   A.   Social Security
      1.   Earnings restrictions
      2.   Provisions for widow(er) and disabled
      3.   Medicare registration and benefits
   B.   Pension benefits
   C.   Financial planning
   D.   Consumer education
   E.   Community agencies
   F.   Insurance and investments
   G.   Estate planning and wills

III.   Health
   A.   Hospital and insurance benefits
   B.   Physical examinations
   C.   Mental health—coping with retirement
   D.   Effect of aging on health

IV.   Changing Roles
   A.   Planning for leisure time
   B.   Retirement adjustment—T groups
   C.   Death and dying

V.   Living Arrangements
   A.   Housing
      1.   Repairs
      2.   Mortgages
      3.   Rent or buy
      4.   Relocation considerations

VI.   Leisure Time
   A.   Part-time work
   B.   Travel
   C.   Hobbies
   D.   Volunteer work
   E.   Joining clubs
   F.   Meaningful use of time

of lower morale, higher turnover, and absenteeism. Recognizing this problem, over 1,000 organizations covering several million employees have adopted alcohol recovery programs.[33] Furthermore, nearly three out of four companies with more than 50 employees have a serious drug problem.[34] Among the drugs fashionable among employees are: caffeine, nicotine, ethyl alcohol, and amphetamines. An increasing number of younger employees use hallucinogens (i.e., LSD), marijuana, and hard drugs (such as heroin). In large urban areas in particular, marijuana is the new bootlegged socializing drug, just as ethyl alcohol was the smart set's plaything during Prohibition. These newer drug trends are bound to have an impact on job behavior similar to that of alcoholism.[35]

Alcoholism and drug dependency are highly complex illnesses according to the American Medical Association. They are chronic diseases characterized by repeated excessive drinking or drug use that interferes with a person's interpersonal relations, health, or ability to earn a living. Alcoholism and drug dependency can be fatal if untreated. Definitions of alcoholics indicate that they are persons in serious trouble with themselves and everybody else because of their excessive, repetitive, uncontrolled drinking. Much the same can apply to drug abusers, although their problems are complicated by legal aspects. Both of these problems can be categorized as **chemical dependency (CD).** Chemical dependency rehabilitation (CDR) has become nationally recognized as the best available means to attack such problems effectively.[36] CDR programs emanate from company policy and include methods of identifying the problems and detailed procedures for referral and treatment.

Company Policy. Kemper Insurance Companies policies on drug dependency and alcoholism provide a model for industry. They are quoted below, with the term *chemical dependency* (CD) covering both alcoholism and drug dependency:

In accordance with our general personnel policies, whose underlying concept is regard for the employee as an individual as well as a worker:

1. We believe CD is an illness and should be treated as such.

2. We believe that the majority of employees who develop CD can be helped to recover and the company should offer appropriate assistance.

3. We believe the decision to seek diagnosis and accept treatment for any suspected illness is the responsibility of the employee. However, continued refusal of an employee to seek treatment when it appears that substandard performance may be caused by an illness, is not tolerated. We believe that CD should not be made an exception to this commonly accepted principle.

4. We believe that it is in the best interest of employees and the company that when CD is present, it should be diagnosed and treated at the earliest possible stage.

5. We believe that the company's concern for individual drinking and drug practices begins only when they result in unsatisfactory job performance.

6. We believe that confidential handling of the diagnosis and treatment of CD is essential.

The objective of this policy is to retain employees who may develop CD by helping them to arrest its further advance before the condition renders them unemployable.[37]

In addition to Kemper's specific policy on chemical dependency, the company also recognizes the legal implications of narcotics traffic.

Employees convicted of illegal drug traffic charges will be terminated immediately. Also, employees found to be involved in such traffic on company premises or during working hours will be terminated and reported to the proper civil authorities.[38]

Detection and Referral.   The supervisor's role is solely one of CD detection and referral. Supervisory personnel should not attempt to analyze the problems of employees having CD. This diagnostic function is not within their province. Medical practitioners now have a reliable method—a specific blood test—to detect chronic alcoholism.[39] The Firestone Tire and Rubber Company provides its supervisors with a guide for detection and referral, "How to Confront a Troubled Employee," which is reproduced in Figure 8.3.

Users of any drug can be classified under the following categories: (1) drug experimenters and infrequent users; (2) steady and regular users; and (3) drug abusers and drug-dependent persons. CD is a progressive disease, because deviations from normal behavior appear gradually, and increase in frequency and intensity. Hence, the illness is generally thought of in stages of development. In the case of alcoholism, there is a prealcoholic stage, first stage, middle stage, and third stage, reflecting the fact that deviant behaviors are multiplying and deepening in their destructive, deteriorating effects. CD is often difficult to detect because afflicted employees become adept at camouflaging the effects of their condition. The effects of CD manifest themselves in job disorders (such as absenteeism) at different stages, depending on the type of job. For instance, the absenteeism of operative workers will be obvious earlier than that of their CD counterparts in management. Figure 8.4 provides some of the common signs that supervisors might observe in blue-collar workers.

Once CD problems have been detected, the personnel department should consider referral. But the best medical or psychological care is to no avail unless employees recognize that they have a problem. If company officers attempt moral persuasion or advice, they will probably be resented and may reinforce the dependency. Organizations can sometimes stimulate employees to seek help by telling them that they must improve their job performance. Organizations should unhesitatingly support workers who make a concerted effort to seek rehabilitation. Benefit plans often pay all or most of the cost. In this situation there are many groups offering treatment services. A sampling of these includes:

1. The local Alcoholism Information Center or local Council on Alcoholism, or the National Council on Alcoholism, 2 Park Avenue, New York, NY 10016.

2. The local Central Office of Alcoholics Anonymous, or Alcoholics Anonymous, Box 459, Grand Central Station, New York, NY 10017.

3. The Al-Anon Family Groups Headquarters, P.O. Box 182, Madison Square Station, New York, NY 10010.

4. The Family Service Agency in the community.

5. The state agency concerned with alcoholism or drug abuse. It may be an independent commission or a division within the state Department of Public Health or Department of Mental Health.

6. Local AFL-CIO Community Service Committee, or AFL-CIO Community Service Activities, 815 16th Street, N.W., Washington, DC 20006.

7. State or federal Bureau of Narcotics and Dangerous Drugs.

8. Pastor, priest, or spiritual advisor.

9. Doctor, psychiatrist, or hospitals. In many instances, physicians and clergymen may have had special professional training and experience with the disease of alcoholism or drug abuse.

10. Volunteer groups, halfway houses.

Discipline—A Last Resort.   Finally, if efforts to rehabilitate the CD employee fail, Dr. Harrison Trice, an authority on alcoholism, recommends:

Stringent disciplinary methods should be used, such as curtailment of fringe benefits, layoffs, and finally discharge. Unless the threat of final separation remains real, the alcoholic will discount the danger and any therapy will fail. Such action removes his last defense, that of an intact job, and acts to offset the emotional rewards of drinking. The confrontation thus reduces the value of alcohol to the alcoholic.[40]

MENTAL AND EMOTIONAL ILLNESS.   The stress and strain of our fast-paced society, coupled with the pressures of work, can cause fatigue and

Figure 8.3
How to Confront a
Troubled Employee

1. ESTABLISH levels of work performance you expect. How much irresponsibility will you tolerate? What is acceptable and unacceptable to you?

2. RECORD all absenteeism, poor job performance, etc. Specific behavioral criteria are necessary.

3. BE CONSISTENT — Don't tolerate more with one employee than you would with another because you feel sorry or inadequate.

4. Don't be an "ARMCHAIR DIAGNOSTICIAN." Avoid labeling.

5. Base the confrontation on JOB PERFORMANCE — not alcoholism, drug addiction, schizophrenia, etc.

6. BE FIRM — But tell him you are there to help. Try to gain his trust.

7. BE HONEST — Don't hedge; speak with authority. He'll respect you for it.

8. BE READY — to cope with the employee's resistance, defensiveness and even hostility. An effective method of overcoming his defensiveness would be for you to talk about your own feelings first. Tell him how this situation makes you feel — without moralizing. Once you've done this, then go to the specific impaired job performance. Never jump to the job performance first; that creates hostility, resistance and defensiveness.

9. ACCEPT NO EXCUSES for failure. If you accept excuses, you don't really care and he'll know it. If he uses excuses, go back to the specific job criteria you expect him to perform.

10. Try to GET HIM TO ACKNOWLEDGE the problem (or admit that he has a problem). Then work from that.

11. SET UP A PLAN FOR IMPROVEMENT — a Progress Slope, so that you both know if he's making progress or not. Evaluate his performance periodically *together*.

ACCEPTABLE JOB PERFORMANCE

6 weeks

4 weeks

2 weeks

JOB PERFORMANCE

(Design your own progress scale with the employee. The time periods will vary from individual to individual depending upon his abilities and the severity of the impaired job performance.)

12. Don't make VALUE JUDGEMENTS — Better to say: "I don't like this or that" than "I think you are wrong." Rely on your own feelings and specific job performance criteria.

13. DON'T MORALIZE. Avoid the appeal to "shoulds" and "shouldn'ts." (Don't tell him what he should do or shouldn't do. This creates hostility. Better to tell him what you expect.)

Figure 8.3 (cont.)

14. Never ask WHY do you do this or that, or why do you drink so much, etc. Why serves as an excuse for him. Remember, he is responsible for his own behavior *always*.

15. Try to get the EMPLOYEE to tell what his problem is, even if you know. Avoid saying so, if he resists. Indicate you are willing to get involved — or — indicate your concern and desire to get the problem worked out for his own sake.

16. If he says he is "SICK" — or makes other excuses, let him know that there is *no* excuse for prolonged impaired job performance. He is responsible for his own behavior.

17. Don't let him "BOX or CORNER" you. Hold fast to your contention that it's *his* responsibility to improve job performance by seeking help. Yours is a therapeutic and legitimate argument, his isn't!

18. Don't let him play you against higher management and/or the union — you're not in the middle here — he is. NO UNION EVER PRAISED POOR JOB PERFORMANCE. Many times the union can be of valuable assistance in motivating the employee and a combined labor-management effort increases his chances for improvement.

19. Get a COMMITMENT from him and monitor it. Set down specific work criteria which employee agrees to work for during certain time period. RECORD.

20. DON'T MAKE IDLE DISCIPLINARY THREATS — Follow through with your warnings. (Use specific time intervals, day, week, certain number of shifts, etc.)

21. WHEN CONFRONTING a problem drinker or other troubled employee, be specific about the behavior you are referring to when you point to his job performance. A legitimate and very effective approach would be one similar to the following: "It is possible that personal problems may be contributing to your impaired job performance. Therefore, I strongly urge you to contact the Employee Assistance Program in the Medical Department. Whether you do or not, I will be contacting you again at a specific time and day to consider more severe disciplinary action if there is no significant improvement." To avoid employee defensiveness put yourself into your statements.

22. Take the responsibility to intervene. Don't be afraid to interfere or get involved. You have a legitimate right to interfere when his behavior is interfering with job performance. Remember, it is highly probable that a troubled employee's performance (both on and off the job) will improve if he's confronted constructively and consistently. It is a fact that he may get worse if he's ignored or just warned occasionally.

Monitor — Be Consistent — Follow Through

(Above material courtesy R.C. Wayne, Columbiana, Ohio)

Figure 8.4
Performance Patterns of
Blue-Collar CD Workers

Source: Kemper Insurance Group,
"Detour, Alcoholism Ahead" (April
1971), pp. 8–10. The behavior described here also applies to white-
collar workers, although these workers show slightly different performance pattern disruption.

Last Half of Early Stage	First Half of Middle Stage	Second Half of Middle Stage
1. Occasional drop in work quality or quantity on part of previously steady employee.	More pronounced spasmodic swings in work production.	Swings in work pace become greater and more frequent.
2. Occasional attendance problems; tardiness, failure to report on or off, subtle changes in former attendance pattern.	Attendance problems, if present, continue to worsen. Absentee excuse pattern develops. Increase of minor illnesses causing absence.	Chronic absenteeism may appear. If so, excuse pattern for absences become more elaborate and often bizarre.
3. Minor decline in overall performance may appear.	More pronounced decline in performance.	Overall performance quite unsatisfactory.
4. Minor accidents on the job may increase.	Frequency of on-the-job accidents, if present earlier, may decrease, while off-the-job accidents, causing lost time, may increase.	Off-the-job accidents may increase in frequency and, if so, may be expected to increase in severity and lost time.
5. Changes in grooming and dress; the employee either becoming more careful about appearance or less neat.	Personal appearance occasionally sloppy, and showing signs of hangover on the job.	More frequent hangovers on the job.
6. Subtle changes in personal relations on the job may appear.	Begins to avoid boss or associates, or goes out of the way to please the boss.	Either avoidance of associates or belligerent and grandiose behavior becomes evident.
7.	Employee's supervisor tends to evaluate the employee's performance on the basis of its peak periods.	Supervisor stops believing the alibis but is likely to report to his own superior, "He's one of the best in the crew — when he's sober."

Figure 8.4 (cont.)

Last Half of Early Stage	First Half of Middle Stage	Second Half of Middle Stage
8.	Employee neglects details formerly attended to.	Lapses and careless-ness become more fre-quent, occasionally causing damage to equipment or material or creating a safety haz-ard.
9.	Increased trips to water cooler and taking other rest breaks.	Sleeping on the job.
10.	Beginning of financial problems; garnishment, etc.	More severe financial problems.
11.		Reporting for work in-toxicated or drinking on the job. Use of breath purifiers.
12.		Marked increase in nervousness and occa-sional hand tremors may appear.
13.		Behavior and excuses that may result in marked increase in la-bor grievances.
14.		Marked increase, in some instances, of hos-pital—medical—surgical claims, often involving off-the-job accidents, gastric disorders and conditions commonly associated with lack of proper diet.

eventual breakdowns. Nervous breakdowns and related mental disorders can and do occur among workers at all levels. Various studies estimate the annual cost to industry of **mental illness** as between $3 and $12 billion. Add to this the fact that two of the most prevalent illnesses—heart disease and alcoholism—are attributable to mental stress and strain, and the significance of mental illness becomes obvious. There is a myth about executive ulcers that result from the pressures of top-level decision making. In reality, this malady is not exclusive to the executive suite; in fact, it is more prevalent among operative workers. Any employee can experience frustration, mental strain, anxiety, and the many other contributors to mental and emotional illness. When job performance is affected, organizations approach employees exhibiting mental disorders in much the same manner they would with CD workers. As a matter of fact, emotional disturbances often manifest themselves in alcoholism and drug abuse. When it has been determined that the mental illness is job-connected, a reassignment to another department or retraining for a different classification might help alleviate the condition. An increasing number of group insurance plans now are paying all or a portion of the cost of out-patient psychiatric care for employees.

Stress is closely allied to mental and emotional problems. Up to a point it can be productive but beyond that it becomes disastrous.[41] Medical researchers have studied stress and the body's reactions to it as far back as 1936. They point out that the body and mind react to stress and mobilize defenses against its continuance. But, if the causes of stress persist or the defenses prove to be inadequate, energy becomes depleted and exhaustion often accompanied by mental and/or physical breakdown results. DeVries[42] identifies various sources of stress and claims that their interaction forms the stress situation. *Organizational factors* contributing to stress include the physical work environment (noise, heat or cold, long hours of work, hazardous job conditions, shift work, repetitive work); technology; role pressures (role ambiguity, role conflict), work overload; *interpersonal variables* such as leadership style, absence of group cohesion, lack of participation, and responsibility for people; and *career variables* including occupation, occupational levels, status of career (demotion, stagnation, obsolescence), and stage of career (the most stressful stages are entry, mid-career, and retirement). Also affecting the stress situation are the individual's personality, socio-cultural background, and nonwork environment. Counselors can be sensitive to these variables when working with clients who suffer from stress. Specific remedies that have been suggested by various writers on stress range from psychotherapy at one extreme to exercise and various relaxation techniques (i.e., transcendental meditation, zen meditation, autogenic training, and biofeedback). When employees have participated in dealing with substantive issues (as opposed to ritualistic nonessential forms) the result has often been a reduction of stress.[43]

FAMILY RELATIONS. Divorce, separation, and maladjusted children are growing problems among American families. A certain percentage of any organization's employees are bound to experience a family problem that will ultimately affect their job performance. The teenager who leaves home to become a hippie, the unmarried daughter who gets pregnant, the spouse who abandons the family—any one of these situations takes its toll on an employee's ability to do a job. With almost half of all marriages failing, any organization is bound to have employees who suffer the pains of divorce. Where family situations are involved, the best advice is no advice. Supervisors or personnel representatives can let troubled employees unburden themselves by lending a sympathetic ear, but the analysis and treatment of such problems are best left to qualified counselors experienced in handling family relations.

FINANCIAL PROBLEMS. Even if organizations pay their employees well, they cannot assume that all their workers properly handle their personal financial affairs. This country's society encourages overspending; no matter how large an employee's income, none are immune from overextending themselves. Despite admonitions to save for a rainy day, few people budget their financial resources, and fewer still are rational in their spending habits. Gambling is not restricted to horse racing and card games; frivolous spending and speculative investments have equally serious consequences. Such situations are not conducive to high productivity. In these circumstances, supervisors, with the support of the personnel department, can offer advice and counsel. In periodic meetings with employees, supervisors should stress the importance of living within a budget. They can also inform employees of the details of compensation and benefit plans. The personnel department can offer literature and related information on financial matters to all employees. Local banks and savings and loan associations have the resources available to provide financial advice and services. When employees have financial difficulties, organizations can help them identify the problems and obtain assistance from within through the accounting department, credit union, or personnel department, or externally through the proper financial institution.

DEHIRING. The economic recessions of the mid-1970s brought with them a rash of management firings and the attendant agony and humiliation that naturally results. In response, a new breed of management consultant called *outplacement specialists* emerged and successfully counseled and relocated thousands of dehired (fired) managers. In **dehiring** their initial task is to counsel the fired individual to adjust to the psychological trauma and the loss of personal esteem that stems from a job loss.[44] Counselors then help an individual assess career plans, identify past mistakes, overcome initial feelings of worthlessness, form a new identity, and renew self-confidence.

Finally, they guide an individual in a campaign to find a new job, in which they have been 95 percent successful in doing within two to six months.[45] Outplacement programs, either in-house or through outside consultants, seem to be a trend.

DISCIPLINE. In an effort to correct work behavior that is not acceptable, supervisors counsel employees to conform to policies. When employees fail to respond they are usually disciplined for the purpose of correcting their behavior. This subject is covered in detail in Chapter 9.

Special Considerations for Small Organizations

Small organizations concerned with counseling problems might follow the pattern established by the Connecticut Gas Company, which employs fewer than 600 persons. It contracts with outside agencies to provide counseling services. Supervisors refer troubled employees, depending on their problem, to the state Alcoholic Council or the Mental Health Association; one of a number of United Way social service agencies; family service agencies (Family Services of America, Inc., has more than 300 affiliates through the U.S. and Canada); or to a private counselor who is under contract with the company.[46]

Cost-Benefit Analysis

The costs and benefits of interviewing were analyzed in Chapter 6, so our discussion here will focus on counseling.

Costs of counseling include the salaries and expenses of the counseling staff and any related materials such as psychometric instruments and pertinent testing devices. Many organizations compare the feasibility of in-house counseling services to outside agencies, and the trend seems to be toward the latter.

The costs of counseling problems in terms of lower productivity, higher accident rates, poorer quality work, inept decisions, tardiness and absenteeism, deterioration of employee morale (attitudes), lost sales, conflict among employees, and damaged plant and equipment can be measured. The extent to which these costs are reduced are the tangible benefits of counseling. Subjective evaluation of intangibles, for example, good will of employees who feel the company cares, enhancement of an organization's image of being socially responsible, and an additional beneficial service to employees, can help justify the cost of the program in the eyes of top management.

Summary

Interviews are a medium of exchange between people. They are a complex array of social interactions calling for careful situational analysis.

The perceptions, motivations, attitudes, and emotions of the interviewee; the content of the interview; and the setting and the personality of the interviewer are some of the variables in the interview situation. The situation will determine whether the directive or nondirective or a combination approach is most feasible. Alternative interview techniques can be applied to various classifications of interviews: *information exchange,* when information is either given or gotten; *decision making,* when a conclusion is drawn or a determination made such as in employment interviews; and *problem solving,* to resolve some sort of employee difficulty, especially as applied to counseling situations.

Employees' personal problems, whether or not they are job-related, can adversely affect productivity. Not only do employees fail in their jobs, but other employees in their job area suffer. Therefore, detecting and correcting employee problems becomes a primary responsibility of supervisors. In their role as counselor, supervisors can gain the respect of their employees by showing a sensitivity to problems and a willingness to listen. However, diagnosing and treating behavioral disorders must not be performed by supervisors, but by skilled practitioners in psychology or psychiatry. Organizations should refer employees to the appropriate agencies, where proper care and attention can be given to their problems.

Problems directly involving an employee's job include performance appraisal, job adjustment, and preparation for retirement.

Problems not directly related to the job are usually personal in nature and include alcoholism and drug addiction, mental illness, family problems, and financial difficulties. Rapid technological change, the fast pace of living in today's society, and the innumerable pressures of work itself create emotional and related personal problems in employees. Each problem is unique, but supervisors must take corrective action to maintain personnel effectiveness. Alcoholism and drug addiction are among the most damaging problems to both employees and companies, and many organizations are developing counseling programs to deal with them. When emotional problems are detected, supervisors must work with the personnel staff to help employees recognize that they have problems and to assist them in seeking professional help. As far as the work situation is concerned, alternative remedies include reassignment or retraining; discipline, even to the extent of discharge; retirement; or possibly rehabilitation through continuous counseling.

Key Terms

interview
information-exchange
  interview
decision-making interview
problem-solving interview
directive approach
nondirective interview
reflection
employee counseling

job adjustment
retirement
flexible retirement
pension
alcoholism
drug addiction
chemical dependency (CD)
mental illness
dehiring

Review Questions

1. Discuss the various classifications of personnel interviews.

2. Distinguish between the directive and nondirective techniques of interviewing.

3. Describe the steps in the counseling interview.

4. What is the supervisor's role in CD problems?

5. Discuss the elements of preretirement education.

6. Describe the performance patterns of blue-collar CD workers in the second half of the middle stage of alcoholism.

7. How does outplacement serve to help the dehired employee?

Discussion Questions

1. How far should supervisors go in counseling their employees? What facilities are available to assist them in their efforts?

2. What types of interview situations are most conducive to the directive approach? The nondirective approach? Why?

3. How can an organization validate an employment interview?

4. "The company considers alcoholism a disease. Alcoholics will be given the same consideration as employees suffering from any other illness." If this were your company's policy, how would you react to it? Does this mean that employees caught drinking or intoxicated on the job should not be punished? What are the implications of this policy for absenteeism control?

5. Since employees' activities off the job can affect their work performance, does management have a right to concern itself with employees' private affairs? Should supervisors counsel employees whose problems off the job affect their performance at work? Should supervisors refuse to become involved with employee problems that have no relationship to the work situations?

Case Problem 1

THE ADDICT

"Well, that confirms it," Pete said. "Mike's definitely a heroin addict." He tossed the letter over to Jack, his assistant.

"Gee, and he seems like such a nice guy," Jack said, as he read the letter. "I guess that this Martha is his girl friend?"

"Right. She's been under treatment for a while now. I wondered about Mike, Jack. Sometimes he acts kind of strange on the job. Sort of out on cloud nine."

Jack thought for a moment. "Say, Pete, that machine he's working on could be dangerous. Fifty thousand pounds per square inch of pressure on those dies. We do have the safety catch, but he could cause real trouble."

"Well, I guess we have to fire him," Pete said.

"It's funny, though, Pete. This letter says that Mike's been an addict for over five years, and he's worked here most of that time. He never has given us any trouble, has he?"

"None at all. Actually, he's been one of our better employees. Let's see. . . ." Pete leafed through Mike's file. "Almost never absent, and never without an advance notice. Never been sick, except one year he had a cold and was out for two days. Spent some time in the Far East with the Army—must have picked up the habit then. Hell, he's one of our most reliable production employees, when you get right down to it. No accidents at all. But he sure acts weird sometimes."

"Don't we all," Jack mused. "You're kind of weird too, some days."

"Still, policy is policy, Jack. You know the rules—any employee using an illegal drug is subject to immediate discharge. We also should notify the authorities."

"Still," Jack said, "He's an awfully good man."

Problems

1. Should an employee be fired in this way, even though he or she is functioning well on the job? Why or why not?

2. What other options does Pete have here? Should a company have such an absolute policy regarding the use of illegal drugs?

3. Consider the legal aspects of this incident. Does a letter from a girl friend of an employee alleging the use of illegal drugs serve as total proof? What other information might you want before you fired Mike? How might you get it?

A large but geographically isolated university sometimes hired highly qualified professionals without job interviews. This was particularly true in the past, when budgets for travel were tight. In other cases, similar professionals were hired after various types of interviews. Like most organizations, this university never bothered to train interviewers, and potential professional employees often had quite diverse experiences in the interview process.

Since professional qualifications are quite easy to verify by mail, the university never had any trouble along these lines. But in analyzing the success of its hiring process, one personnel specialist discovered that if an employee had been interviewed by anyone in any way, the probability of obtaining a successful and productive person was about five times greater than if the person had been hired without any interviews. Those hired without interviews were much more likely to create job problems; they caused endless difficulties with their peers and superiors, and they were terminated much more often, and quit much more often than those interviewed.

Case Problem 2

INTERVIEW EFFICIENCY

Problems

1. Consider various types of interviews. What goes on in these that is common to all?

2. Do you think that any interview, regardless of type, is preferable to no interview?

3. Suppose that a business professor is to be hired by your school. What kinds of interviews would you think might work best? Why?

Notes

1. Felix Lopez, *Personnel Interviewing*, 2nd ed. (New York: McGraw-Hill, 1975), p. 8.

2. Richard D. Arvey, "Unfair Discrimination in the Employment Interview: Legal and Psychological Aspects," *Psychological Bulletin*, 86:4 (1979), pp. 736–65.

3. C. P. Alderfer and C. G. McCord, "Personal and Situational Factors in the Recruitment Interview," *Journal of Applied Psychology*, 54 (1970), pp. 377–85.

4. This classification scheme was adapted from Felix Lopez, *Personnel Interviewing*.

5. See for example, M. D. Dunnette and W. C. Borman, "Personnel Selection and Classification Systems," *Annual Review of Psychology*, 1979, pp. 477–525.

6. J. M. Frazer, T. M. Higham, and J. Chapman, "The Ultimate Interview," *Personnel and Training Management*, 12 (1967), pp. 22–26.

7. R. E. Carlson, "Selection Interviewing Decisions: The Effect of Experience, Relative Quota Situation, and Applicant Sample on Interviewer Decision," *Personnel Psychology*, 20 (1967), pp. 259–90.

8. Jean L. Rogers and Walter L. Fortson, *Fair Employment Interviewing* (Reading, Mass: Addison-Wesley, 1976), p. 67.

9. See R. Wagner, "The Employment Interview: A Critical Summary," *Personnel Psychology*, 2 (1949), pp. 17–46; L. Ulrich and D. Trumbo, "The Selection Interview Since 1949," *Psychological Bulletin*, 63 (1965), pp. 100–16; E. C. Mayfield, "The Selection Interview: A Reevaluation of Published Research," *Personnel Psychology*, 17 (1964), pp. 239–60.

10. R. E. Carlson, D. P. Schwab, and H. G. Heneman, III, "Agreement Among Selection Interview Styles," *Journal of Industrial Psychology*, 5:1 (1970), pp. 8–17.

11. James G. Goodale, "Tailoring the Selection Interview to the Job," *Personnel Journal*, February 1976, pp. 62–65ff.

12. Robert E. Carlson, Paul W. Thayer, Eugene C. Mayfield, and Donald A. Peterson, "Improvements in the Selection Interview," *Personnel Journal*, April 1971, pp. 269–75.

13. Richard J. Walsh, "Ten Basic Counseling Skills," *Supervisory Management*, July 1977, pp. 5–7.

14. Ibid., pp. 8–9.

15. U. S. Civil Service Commission, *Equal Opportunity Counseling: A Guidebook*, Personnel Methods Series No. 19 (Washington, D.C.: U.S. Government Printing Office, 1976), p. 10.

16. W. J. Dickson and F. J. Roethlisberger, *Counseling in an Organization: A Sequel to the Hawthorne Researches*, (Boston: Graduate School of Business Administration, Harvard University, 1966).

17. Richard A. Kalish, *The Later Years: Social Applications of Gerontology* (Monterey, Calif.: Brooks/Cole, 1977), p. 128.

18. James H. Schulz, *The Economics of Aging* (Belmont, Calif.: Wadsworth, 1976), pp. 4–5.

19. Ibid.

20. "Retirement: Later Rather Than Sooner?" *The Morgan Guarantee Survey*, January 1977, p. 1.

21. "Unretiring Workers: To These Employees, The Boss Is a Kid," *Wall Street Journal*, December 7, 1977, p. 1.

22. "Early Retirements on the Increase in the U.S.," *New York Times*, July 10, 1977, p. 22.

23. Ibid.

24. "Don't Call It 'Early Retirement,'"

Harvard Business Review, September–October 1975, pp. 103ff.

25. Fred Best, "The Future of Retirement and Lifetime Distribution of Work," *Aging and Work,* Summer 1979, pp. 173–80.

26. Gail S. Rosenberg and Maureen E. McCarthy, "Flexible Retirement Programs in Two U. S. Companies," *Aging and Work,* Summer 1980, pp. 210–214.

27. Leland P. Bradford, "Can You Survive Your Retirement?" *Harvard Business Review,* November–December 1979, pp. 103–9.

28. Charles A. Ullman, "Preretirement Planning: Does It Prevent Postretirement Shock?" *Personnel and Guidance Journal,* November 1976, p. 118.

29. Murray H. Reich, "Limited Survey of Developers and Users of Preretirement Education Programs and State Agencies on Aging," unpublished, 1976.

30. Don E. Pellicano, "Overview of Corporate Pre-Retirement Counseling," *Personnel Journal,* May 1977, p. 236.

31. Murray H. Reich, "Group Preretirement Education Programs and Whither the Proliferation?" *Industrial Gerontology,* Winter 1977, p. 32.

32. Pellicano, "Overview," p. 235.

33. Stanley E. Kaden, "Compassion or Cover-Up: The Alcoholic Employee," *Personnel Journal,* July 1977, p. 357.

34. S. J. Mayer, "Employee Dependency on Drugs and Alcohol," *The Personnel Administrator,* November–December 1971, p. 19.

35. Lewis F. Presnall, *What About Drugs and Employees?* (Chicago: Kemper Insurance Companies, 1971), p. 6ff.

36. Herryman Mauer, "The Beginning of Wisdom," *Fortune,* May 1968, p. 176.

37. Kemper Insurance Companies, "Management Guide on Alcoholism and Other Behavioral Problems," August 1971, pp. 5–6.

38. Presnall, *What About Drugs and Employees?*

39. Lawrence K. Altman, "A New Test Detects Chronic Alcoholism," *New York Times,* November 28, 1976, p. 1.

40. Harrison M. Trice, "Alcoholism and the Work World," *Sloan Management Review,* Fall 1970, p. 73.

41. Herbert Benson and Robert L. Allen, "How Much Stress Is Too Much?" *Harvard Business Review,* September–October 1980, pp. 86–92.

42. Manfred F. R. Kets de Vries, "Organizational Stress: A Call for Management Action," *Sloan Management Review,* Fall 1979, pp. 7ff.

43. Ibid., p. 9.

44. William J. Morin, "Outplacement Counseling: What Is It?" *Personnel and Guidance Journal,* May 1977, p. 553.

45. Patricia Aburdine, "Executive Outplacement: The Fire-For-Hire Business," *The Washington Monthly,* June 1977, pp. 53ff.

46. Robert W. Reardon, "Help for the Troubled Worker in a Small Company," *Personnel,* January–February 1976, pp. 50–54.

Chapter Nine

Discipline: Dealing with the Difficult Employee

The Western Metal Equipment Company manufactures railroad boxcars, a competitive business that requires a high level of employee efficiency. In fact, the company's concern for efficiency is specifically stated in the union-management agreement. Bobby K. Stevens was a production worker assigned to rivet various areas of the boxcars. On several occasions he had been asked to move from one position to another on the roof. He refused and was warned. His behavior was discussed prior to each warning with Bobby and the union representative in attendance. Early in the afternoon of December 14, 1981, foreman George Bennett (Stevens's supervisor) approached Bobby, who was then riveting on the roof, and read to him a warning for his refusal to accept work assigned to him in the morning. Stevens tore up the warning slip, threw it in the supervisor's face, and voiced his objection to the action in a profane manner. As a consequence, Bobby Stevens was discharged.

The efficiency of an organization depends on sound **discipline.** If employees were free to do as they pleased, the productive capabilities of an organization would suffer and employees and employer would be at a disadvantage. Thus, the right of management to discipline becomes a prime requisite for the successful operation of an organization. On the other hand, discharge or lesser forms of punishment represent the loss of a person's immediate livelihood, and the stigma of discharge often makes it difficult for that person to find other employment.[1]

In the absence of a union there are few limitations placed on man-

LEARNING OBJECTIVES

1. To understand the differences between the concepts of punitive and corrective discipline.
2. To know the steps in the discipline process.
3. To know the criteria for proving just cause.
4. To be familiar with the measures for controlling absenteeism.
5. To understand the concept, *duty of fair representation.*

agement (laws being the exception) with regard to the manner of discipline and the penalties that it can impose on employees. Once a union has been certified to represent the employees, management's right to discipline employees becomes severely restricted by the collective bargaining agreement. However, when management maintains reasonable standards of behavior and strives to *correct* deviations, the interests of safety, morale, and the general well-being of employees are generally best served. This chapter will focus on corrective approaches to discipline and the methods for establishing and implementing disciplinary procedures that are conducive to the support of organizational objectives.

Responsibility for Discipline

Management establishes and communicates policies and procedures for discipline. Because these policies need to be understood by supervisors and their employees, sound management practice dictates that they be clear and that they delineate responsibilities for carrying them out. Also, these guidelines will usually spell out the specific procedure for carrying out disciplinary action and list rules or infractions and the appropriate penalties. Most disciplinary procedures distinguish between major infractions, for example, theft, sabotage, drinking on the job, which call for immediate discharge, and lesser infractions that carry less severe penalties. Table 9.1 is a disciplinary procedure used by a primary metals producer that meets these criteria.

The supervisor is of primary importance in the discipline process. He or she works with employees on a day-to-day basis, and thus is in the best position to observe unsatisfactory performance or behavior that violates organizational rules. The supervisor can counsel employees to determine the reasons for their failure to comply with a particular rule, to explain the reasons for the rule, and to reach an understanding regarding expectations of the employee's future behavior. Discipline is used only as a last resort.

Personnel's function in discipline consists of advising supervisors on policies affecting discipline, ensuring conformity to policy, assisting supervisors in handling specific cases, providing data on past practices, indicating legal implications of the particular disciplinary action, providing sources of referral for counseling or medical assistance and so on, and acting as a sounding board to help supervisors ascertain if the discipline is appropriate, that is, fair, consistent, and impartial.

The Corrective Approach to Discipline

Basically, there are two approaches to discipline: **punitive** and **corrective**. However, few organizations subscribe to the punitive approach to discipline whereby persons who deviate from the prescribed standard of

Table 9.1
Discipline Procedure

STATEMENT OF POLICY: (NOTE: This company has a union.)

It is the policy of the company to establish and maintain fair, just, and reasonable discipline among its employees. Such discipline must be as consistent as circumstances permit. The company believes that failure to maintain such discipline can only result in discriminatory and unequal treatment to employees, with a subsequent deterioration of employee relations and loss of efficiency.

1. *PURPOSE AND SCOPE*
   1.1. To establish a procedure to assist all Supervisors in handling discipline cases.
   1.2. This procedure will be followed by all Supervisors who have employees under their jurisdiction.

2. *OBJECTIVES TO BE GAINED*
   2.1. The establishment of a procedure to insure uniform, reasonable, fair, effective and prompt handling of all discipline cases that involve written warning, layoff or discharge.

3. *GENERAL INFORMATION*
   3.1. The following constitutes the more prevalent causes for disciplinary action:
      a. Insubordination, such as:
         1. refusing to carry out orders;
         2. using abusive language to one's supervisor; and
         3. threatening or striking one's supervisor.
      b. Drinking or being under the influence of alcohol on the job
      c. Sleeping on the job
      d. Fighting on the job
      e. Theft
      f. Leaving the job without supervisory permission
      g. Distributing literature without permission
      h. Insufficient work or "gold-bricking"
      i. Violation of conduct, safety, or operating rules
      j. Absenteeism
      k. Habitual tardiness
      l. Careless or deliberate damage to equipment or materials
      m. Violation of safety regulations
      n. Horseplay
      o. Other offenses of similar nature
   The following forms of disciplinary action may be taken:
   (a) written reprimand; (b) Layoff without pay for prescribed period; and (c) discharge. However, an employee may not be laid off without pay nor discharged without a hearing. He may, however, be suspended pending the hearing.

Table 9.1 (cont.)

3.2. Except in cases of gross breaches of rules and regulations meriting discharge, the company's attitude is that discipline should be corrective in nature.

3.3. All cases of discipline sufficiently serious to involve possible discharge of an employee or employees shall be discussed with the General Manager prior to final decision.

3.4. Rules and regulations relating to employee conduct shall be conspicuously posted on bulletin boards throughout the company and shall be subject to review on an annual basis to guarantee applicability.

3.5. Every case of discipline may result in a grievance and is filed in the offender's personnel record. Because of this, it is important in every case to thoroughly investigate and determine all the facts upon which a fair and reasonable decision can be made and justified.

3.6. Every case of discipline is a very serious matter to the employee involved and to the company. Both have a considerable investment in each other. It is, therefore, very important that discipline cases be handled impartially and with judicious consistency.

4. *WHEN A SUPERVISOR IS CONFRONTED WITH A NEED TO DISCIPLINE AN EMPLOYEE*

4.1. He/she shall either issue the employee a written warning or suspend him or her pending a hearing, depending upon his judgment of the seriousness of the offense.

4.1.1. In case of insubordination, drinking on the job, sleeping on the job, fighting on the job, stealing, leaving the job without supervisory permission, and other offenses of such nature, where layoff or discharge is indicated, supervisors shall suspend the employee or employees pending a hearing to determine the facts.

4.1.2. In cases of less serious nature that nonetheless merit discipline, supervisors shall either issue written warnings or suspend—depending upon either the seriousness of the offense or the accumulated number of minor offenses committed by the individual.

4.2. If either a written warning or suspension is given it shall immediately be signed by the supervisor, and given to the offender.

4.2.1. Copies of the disciplinary action shall be sent immediately by the supervisor to his/her Department Head and the Industrial Relations Supervisor.

4.2.2. The Industrial Relations Supervisor shall promptly reproduce the warning or suspension and send copies to the Assistant General Manager, the union, and the Comptroller. In cases of warning or suspension for violation of a safety rule, a copy shall be sent to the Safety Director.

Table 9.1 (cont.)

4.3.   For all discipline cases involving suspension, there shall be conducted a hearing by the Department Head of the suspended employee in order to determine the facts.

    4.3.1.   For all suspension cases the Department Head involved will discuss the case (prior to and after the hearing) and before he or she makes a decision with the Superintendent and the Industrial Relations Supervisor.

    4.3.2.   Because a decision must be reached as soon as possible following the suspension hearing, it is of major importance that the Department Head make every effort to thoroughly investigate and ascertain the facts in the case so that a fair and equitable decision shall result.

    4.3.3.   The proper union representatives, the supervisor involved, and the necessary witnesses (both company and union) shall attend the Department Head's hearing of the case. Upon request from the Department Head, an Industrial Relations Representative will also attend.

    4.3.4.   Following the hearing (and within the time limits of the applicable contract) the Department Head shall render his decision in writing to the employee or employees involved and to the union. The decision shall clearly state the employee's offense and the penalty levied.

    4.3.5.   Copies of the Department Head's decision and copies of the minutes of the hearing shall be sent by the Department Head to the Superintendent and Industrial Relations Supervisor.

    4.3.6.   The Industrial Relations Supervisor shall reproduce the decision and minutes of the hearing and distribute copies as outlined in 4.2.2. to all supervisors down to and including Department Heads.

behavior are automatically punished. Here the motivating factor is fear, and individuals supposedly adhere to strict rules in order to avoid punishment, which is meted out arbitrarily according to a schedule that matches sanctions with infractions. The punitive approach has yielded such negative results that there is little evidence of its application.

The philosophy of the corrective approach states that the purpose of discipline is to correct rather than punish. It operates on the premise that consistent, impartial, and humane discipline is conducive to high morale, safety, and well-being of employees. It emphasizes counseling, a system of **progressive discipline,** and penalties that are commensurate with the offense. To illustrate, when the work quality of a production employee appeared to be falling off, the supervisor conferred with him to identify the problem. The employee blamed the raw material being used on the job. But the supervisor explained that he was using the same stock as other employees and further questioned the employee to see if there could be other reasons. At that point the employee explained that he had personal problems at home. The supervisor offered his help but cautioned the employee to improve his performance. Despite the supervisor's attempt to understand the employee's problem, his performance did not improve. Thus, the supervisor met with the employee again and cautioned him that more severe discipline would result from a failure to improve.

With the corrective approach, each instance of misconduct is judged individually. It calls for the analysis of the variables and their interactions in the discipline situation. These variables include:

1. *The seriousness of the offense.* Offenses involved might be major or secondary in nature. Major offenses are sufficiently serious to warrant summary discharge. Examples of such offenses would be assault on a supervisor or other employees, drinking on the job, insubordination, theft, sabotage, leading an unauthorized strike, or selling drugs on company property. Secondary offenses cover most of the violations to which corrective discipline apply. For example, negligence or incompetence, for example, failure to perform required work, personal misconduct such as disloyalty, absenteeism, distributing literature without permission, and using abusive language fall in the category of secondary offenses.

2. *Mitigating circumstances.* The employee's previous record, length of service and the past conduct might deserve consideration in determining the appropriateness of discipline. For instance, the organization would likely be more lenient with an employee with many years of service who had few previous infractions, than it would with one who had repeatedly violated rules and had been employed for a short time.

3. *Extenuating circumstances.* In arbitration cases we often find that the employee was intimidated or provoked to violate a rule by a supervisor. Under such circumstances there may be a lesser penalty or none at all. In one arbitration case, a supervisor and employee became involved in a fight. Because the employee punched the supervisor in the nose, he was discharged immediately. In the arbitration hearing the evidence was clear that the supervisor had provoked the assault by intimidating the employee and referring to him in a derogatory manner (the extenuating circumstances). The arbitrator felt the supervisor was equally at fault and ordered the employee returned to his job.

4. *Extent of training.* Investigation may reveal that the employee failed to comply principally because he or she did not have the necessary skill or

ability. These cases reveal a deficiency in training, and discipline would be inappropriate. An employee in a small manufacturing plant had worked as an assembler for 19 years. Adverse economic conditions resulted in the company's imposing more stringent production standards, which this particular employee could not meet—she was often a few units short of standard. After a month of substandard performance, she was discharged. An arbitrator hearing her case was astonished to learn that she had never received any training—not even after the company discovered her production was below standard. Obviously, the discharge was unfair and improper under the circumstances. However, when it is determined that the employee has adequate training and still fails or refuses to comply, discipline is in order. But we should note that orientation and training serve even more as a preventive approach than as a corrective one.

5. *Precedent.*   What has been done in the past under similar circumstances will influence the present course of action. If employees had generally been warned for leaving the job without permission on a first offense, it would be inconsistent to discharge the next employee given the same factors.

6. *Just or proper cause.*   To avoid arbitrary and capricious action in discipline, there should be *proof* that the discipline is just. This subject is so essential to corrective discipline that it is covered in a separate section of this chapter.

The Discipline Process

Once a problem has been classified as a discipline situation and has been analyzed, it becomes the supervisor's obligation to explore and deal with the causes of it. When it has been determined that discipline is in order, the supervisor discusses the matter with the employee and assesses the appropriate discipline.

INTERVIEW

During the disciplinary interview, the supervisor explores the causes of the problem, informs the employee of the rule that was violated, and the problem caused by the violation. The supervisor will also discuss expected improvements in future behavior and may offer assistance in correcting the situation. The tone of the interview is critical to a successful outcome. The goal is to have an employee cooperate in improving future actions. To elicit a positive response the supervisor must be sincere, criticize performance rather than attack an employee's character, and try to project a positive attitude.[2]

DISCIPLINARY MEASURES

Under corrective discipline for secondary or lesser offenses, employees are first cautioned or reinstructed during counseling interviews. Repeated or more serious infractions result in a sequence of penalties, with increasing severity (progressive discipline), such as:

1. oral warning with a notation in the employee's record
2. written reprimand
3. short suspension—three days to one month
4. demotion or withholding of merit increase
5. long suspension—30 days to 6 months, with loss of seniority
6. discharge—the most severe penalty

JUST CAUSE AND BURDEN OF PROOF IN DISCHARGE. Because discharge cases can be tested through arbitration (if a union represents the employee), in court, or by one of several state and federal agencies, organizations need to ensure that there is **just cause** for discharge. A universal definition of the term just cause does not exist, but the criteria stated by arbitrator Harry Platt are enlightening. He equates just cause with, ". . . what a reasonable man, mindful of the habits and customs of industrial life and the standards of justice and fair dealing prevalent in the community ought to have done under similar circumstances and in that light . . . whether the conduct of the discharged employee was defensible and the disciplinary penalty just."[3]

When a discharge is appealed, the burden of proof is placed on an organization to show that it had just cause to discharge an employee. Employers often lose discharge cases in arbitration because the evidence they present fails to prove their case. This may result from inadequate preparation or inadequate proof. Our system of justice presumes a person innocent until proven guilty. In a disciplinary case involving an employee's alleged poor attitude and insubordination, the key witness refused to appear at the arbitration hearing. He had ordered the discharge and was the only person who could testify against the employee. Without this evidence, the company had no case; it was unable to prove that the employee was guilty as charged. For this reason, the arbitrator granted the employee's grievance and ordered her reinstated.

CRITERIA FOR PROVING JUST CAUSE. As an arbitrator of numerous discipline cases, the author has personally observed effective and ineffective presentations to support an organization's case for discharge. The following guidelines have been gleaned from these disciplinary hearings. In essence they consist of five questions that should be answered in the affirmative before a decision is made to discharge.

1. Did the employee violate a rule?
2. Did the employee know the rule?
3. Was the employee properly warned, cautioned, or reinstructed?
4. Did the employee have a fair hearing?
5. Was the punishment:
   a. Consistent with past practice?
   b. Fair in light of the circumstances?
   c. Administered within a reasonable time?

Arbitrators differ in their application of the degree of proof that is required in discipline cases. Sometimes proof beyond a reasonable doubt has been required. But in other cases a lesser degree such as a preponderance of the evidence, or clear and convincing evidence, or evidence sufficient to convince a reasonable mind of guilt is called for. When the case involves alleged misconduct that carries the stigma of social disapproval or involves moral turpitude or criminal intent, arbitrators are more stringent in the degree of proof they require.

Let us look at the basis of proof for each of these questions cited above.

1. *Rule violation.*   An appeal agency or an arbitrator would expect to see evidence to prove that the employee violated a particular rule. Sometimes an organization proves that the employee did violate a rule, but not the rule for which he or she had been discharged. Take for instance the case of Mildred G., a deli clerk in one of the grocery stores of a major chain. Mildred had sliced a pound of baked ham ($1.99 per half-pound) for a friend and she marked the package "4⁶/". The mismarking was detected by the checkout clerk who called the matter to the attention of the store manager. When he discussed the matter with Mildred she insisted she had made an honest error, that she was distracted and mismarked the package. The store manager, on the other hand, considered the mistake intentional and discharged her for dishonesty. In the arbitration hearing, the company proved that Mildred had violated company policy (she should have marked the price with dollar and cents signs), and she was careless in her work (the proper price was $4.02). Both of these offenses were just cause for discharge, but the company failed to prove she was dishonest in mismarking the package. Because of the seriousness of the dishonesty charge that would impugn her character, the arbitrator felt

the evidence must be compelling. There was sufficient doubt in his mind that Mildred had performed a dishonest act, so she was reinstated. A simple investigation of the discharge situation would have made it clear that the company did not have a good case for a dishonesty discharge. Thus we can see that a technicality—charging an employee with violation of the wrong rule—can cause an organization to lose a discipline case.

2. *Knowledge of rule.* Often employees violate rules because they misunderstand them. Clear, concise statements of rules go a long way to rectify this problem. When employees understand the reasons behind rules, they are more likely to accept and support them. In one discipline case, the arbitrator ordered an employee reinstated with back pay (despite the employee's failure to obey an order he considered unreasonable) because management never explained *why* he should obey the order.

   The fact that the rules were explained on the first day, and that the employee signed a statement attesting that he or she understood them is not sufficient to prove knowledge of a rule. Who could possibly remember everything that occurred the first day on a new job? However, a written statement or even a notation in the supervisor's calendar or notebook that he or she had been counseled about the rule infraction on a specific date is appropriate evidence.

3. *Proper warning.* Preliminary to discharge on secondary offenses, the guidelines for just cause call for a warning statement. In corrective discipline the employee usually receives an oral warning followed by a written one. A proper warning should include a statement of the rule, with the exact nature of the violation and the consequences of continued deviant behavior. A warning statement that says, "your continued absence will result in more serious discipline" would not meet the standards for a proper warning because the nature of the violation is loosely stated, and the employee is not informed of the consequences. A statement such as this is unfair because an employee does not know what to do to correct the improper behavior. On the other hand a statement that reads: "You have been absent unreported or unexcused three times in the past month. You must improve your attendance. One additional unreported or unexcused absence in the next two months will result in your discharge." The statement is clear and direct, and it leaves no question in the employee's mind as to the *action* that must be taken and the *consequences* for failing to do so.

4. *Fair hearing.* When an employee has had an opportunity to express his or her side of the story, the resulting discipline is more likely to be correct. Consequently, it is good practice to conduct a hearing with the employee and, if possible, a representative of the employee to air the circumstances

of the case. Frequently, extenuating or mitigating circumstances can alter the outcome. If the food store manager had held a hearing in Mildred's case, he would have realized that the charge of dishonesty would not hold up in arbitration. The approach to a hearing outlined in the discipline procedure in Table 9.1 can help assure fair treatment of employees in discharge cases. Also, arbitrators look favorably upon the fact that an organization has investigated the case and/or conducted a hearing.

When an organization has a union, the law now requires an employee to have a union representative present at any hearing or investigatory interview if there is reason to believe that disciplinary action might be taken. The U.S. Supreme Court upheld this right in the Weingarten case.[4]

5. *Reasonable punishment.* Arbitrators generally apply the rule of reasonableness to determine if punishment was commensurate with the violation. They consider reasonable to include consistency and impartiality. Reasonableness is illustrated in the hot stove rule indicated in Table 9.2.

APPEALS FROM DISCHARGE. Employees represented by a union generally have recourse to appeals through the grievance procedure and ultimately to arbitration. (The subject of arbitration is covered in Chapter 12, "Labor-Management Dispute Settlement.") Federal civil service laws and regulations of many state and local agencies provide comprehensive review procedures for dismissals. Federal legislation protects people from improper discharge due to age, race, creed, color, or national origin, and it provides for appeal through specific agencies and/or the courts. The Equal Employment Opportunity Commission, for example, offers legal recourse to fight discriminatory dismissal due to race, creed, or color. Also, the Occupational Safety and Health Act protects employees from dismissal as a result of reporting an employer for unsafe or unhealthy working conditions.

Absenteeism: A Case in Point

A disciplinary problem that can illustrate the application of the corrective approach is absenteeism. The problem exists in practically every organization and is sufficiently serious in most cases to warrant a detailed discussion here.

Table 9.2
Hot Stove Rule

1. The burn is *immediate*. There is no question of cause and effect.

2. There was *warning*. If the stove is red hot, people know what will happen if they touch it.

3. The discipline is *consistent*. Everyone who touches the stove is burned.

4. The discipline is *impersonal*. People are burned not because of who they are, but because they touch the stove.

Absenteeism ranks as one of the most serious of discipline problems. Costs in terms of lost wages have been estimated to run as high as $20 billion per year—the average employee takes from 7 to 12 unscheduled days off each year.[5] Absences also represent a cost to organizations in terms of production disruptions, the need for additional personnel to fill in for absent workers, and the expense to train the additional personnel. Surveys show absence rates running from 2.8 percent to 3.37 percent on the average, with banks experiencing the lowest and manufacturers the highest percentage of absences.[6]

The conditions that give rise to poor attendance can include illness, personal problems, supervisor's failure to enforce standards, deterioration of the work ethic, job dissatisfaction, child-care problems, liberal benefits, transportation problems, alcoholism and drug abuse, and a host of others. Considerable research has been conducted in an attempt to pinpoint the cause or causes of absenteeism, but, to date, the results have been inconclusive. Some studies, for example, show a high positive correlation between attendance at work and job satisfaction, others yield conflicting results.[7] One thing is clear, however; any given absence may take a multitude of forms and may be caused and constrained by a host of diverse factors—the employee, the variables in the work place, and the outside world. Hence, definitive research on absenteeism will need to look at this behavior in greater depth, for example, the systematic comparison of absence-prone and absence-free individuals, over longer periods of time, for example, in longitudinal case studies.[8]

Researchers have, however, investigated the predictability of absenteeism. For example, Blumenfeld[9] and others were able to predict absenteeism behavior of employees through biodata. Garrison and Muchinsky[10] found that paid absences (e.g., sick leave) were unpredictable, but unpaid absences could be correlated with certain variables (e.g., number of children and job satisfaction) to predict absenteeism. Their findings suggest that employees who are more dissatisfied with their job situation and who have several children are more likely to experience higher levels of absenteeism.

The control of absenteeism clearly depends on a program to encourage employees to work every scheduled shift and to bring up to standard the attendance of employees whose absenteeism results in loss to themselves and the organization. Such a program would consist of clarification of expectations, recording absences, counseling employees with irregular attendance, and disciplining persistent offenders.

CLARIFYING EXPECTATIONS

When orienting a new employee to an organization, it is typical to explain the various benefits of employment, especially holidays, vacations, and sick leave. It is only natural that he or she would be left with the impression that the organization offers considerable free time, and that the employee should take advantage of these opportunities. Supervisors who desire regular attendance of their employees will have to take special measures to counter this impression. They will have to stress that they *expect* their employees to be on the job, giving their best effort *every* day. They should emphasize that it is the employee's *obligation* to attend work regularly.

Nevertheless, some employees will still feel they have a right to be absent for such appropriate reasons as illness, especially when they present medical certification. However, even this type of unavoidable absence can only be tolerated to a point. Sporadic absences that become chronic require that the employee correct the problem or suffer the penalty. Employees do have options. Medical or psychological help or rehabilitation should restore regular attendance, but there is also the possibility of alternative forms of employment either within the present organization or elsewhere that might accommodate a person's condition. There is also the option of disability retirement should the condition be serious enough to warrant the classification of permanently and totally disabled. The author arbitrated a case in which an asthmatic employee became a chronic absentee. She was a shipping clerk in a food-products warehouse. Evidently her condition was aggravated by her job, and she constantly suffered disabling asthma attacks as certified by her physician. Her absences became so frequent that the company counseled her about the problem, later warned, and finally discharged her for failure to improve. The company argued that it could not tolerate her poor and deteriorating record—she missed 88 work days (in one- to three-day absences) the first year and 132 the second year. The union countered that she had a *right* to be absent because she had a medical excuse. It was clear from the evidence that the company had bent over backwards in its effort to reform this absentee and that her record worsened despite counseling and repeated warnings. The author found no alternative but to sustain the company's action.

RECORDING ABSENCES

Maintaining daily attendance records for each employee enables supervisors to identify absence problems and take timely action to correct them. It is advisable to distinguish between absences that are reported and those that are not. Most organizations require employees to report an absence prior to or soon after the start of the workshift. Usually an employee reporting an absence will give a reason for it, and it is at this point that the supervisor can determine whether or not to record the absence as excused or unexcused. Obviously, an unreported absence would be unexcused, and chronic absences, even for bona fide reasons, would eventually be recorded as unexcused. If an employee reports the absence and offers a reason, it is up to the supervisor to decide whether the reason, balanced against the requirements of the operation, justifies granting an excuse.

Recording not only distinguishes the types of absences, but it also reveals patterns. A prolonged absence due to illness or injury will be evident on the record and probably can be tolerated. But sporadic, consistent absences will stand out in a record and will signal the need for counseling. Organizations vary in their application of the term chronic. One may consider chronic three unexcused absences in one month or ten absences in six months for any reason. Another might go as far as allowing three work weeks a year.

COUNSELING ABSENTEES

The purpose of counseling in cases of absenteeism is to encourage an employee to have regular attendance. Generally, calling an employee's attention to his or her record and citing it as a problem will be sufficient to elicit a positive behavioral change. Sometimes, however, it requires more. In such cases, the supervisor can apply the counseling techniques used in the problem solving interview described in Chapter 8. There would be a mutual exploration of the problem and its causes, a discussion of the necessity to have regular attendance from the viewpoint of both the employee and the organization, and a mutually acceptable plan for corrective action. Should the initial counseling fail to correct the problem, subsequent sessions would include sterner measures—cautioning or warning the employee of the need to improve and the consequences of failing to do so.

DISCIPLINING

Often, a warning will suffice to correct a situation, but with employees who persist in frequent absences, it may become necessary to resort to suspension or even discharge (discipline is progressively severe for repeated violations). Some organizations have discarded time-off-without-pay (suspension) measures because employees view them as nonpunitive; they welcome the free time in that it is construed as a reward and merely serves to reinforce their deviant behavior. Because of the severity of discharge, it is used as a last resort after all corrective measures have failed.

ENCOURAGING ATTENDANCE

Interest is gaining among organizations to stimulate improved attendance. Rewards and incentives are being used to complement disciplinary measures in an effort to control absenteeism. A study by Pedalino and Gamboa used a lottery incentive program as a **behavior modification** measure to reduce absenteeism at a manufacturing/distribution facility. Each day an employee reported to work on time he or she was allowed to choose a card from the deck. At the end of the week a person would have five cards to make up a poker hand. The highest hand in each department would win \$20. This incentive system decreased absenteeism 18.27%.[11]

A program for absenteeism control that has been used successfully to train supervisors is outlined in Table 9.3.

Table 9.3
Keys to Absenteeism
Control

At least 50 percent of absenteeism can be controlled. Applying the following methods can help you reduce absenteeism in your department.

1. *Stress good attendance.* Let your employees know that you expect them to be at work *every day.* A fair day's pay deserves a fair day's work, and an employee has to be on the job to do any work at all.

2. *Require employees to call in when they have to be absent.* First, inform every employee of this rule. Then, make it simple for employees to report—calling you at work within a half-hour should do. But make sure they understand *why* and *how* you want them to call in.

3. *Request reasons for absences.* If an employee has to be off, ask for a reason. But don't accept any excuse; no alibis are excusable.

4. *Record attendance daily for each of your employees.* A running record will help identify chronic absentees.

5. *Discuss individual attendance records with employees on a regular basis.* Praise regular attendees. Counsel those who find it difficult to come to work to try to help them toward regular attendance. Work out a plan for improvement with the employee. Be sure to set time limits for improvements.

If, after you've made an honest effort to get the employee to improve attendance, and he or she fails to improve . . .

6. *Caution the employee of the consequences of continuing to be absent.* Emphasize the importance to you and to him of regular attendance. You may have to issue a warning that further absences will result in suspension or even discharge. Keep a record of the conversation.

7. *Follow up.* On call-ins it sometimes pays to check on the employee at home—by phone. A genuine concern is appreciated by the employee who is ill, and it's uncomfortably embarrassing to the one who isn't. Check with the employee who is trying to improve and offer encouragement for continuing.

8. *Chart the department's attendance.* When you can show that the entire department's attendance is improving it becomes an incentive to come to work regularly.

As a rule of thumb . . . WHEN IT'S HARDER TO STAY OFF THE JOB THAN IT IS TO COME TO WORK, EMPLOYEES WILL HAVE REGULAR ATTENDANCE.

Cost-Benefit Analysis

Lack of discipline can be costly to any organization. When employees feel they can get away with murder, morale suffers, absenteeism skyrockets, production declines, and employees adopt a devil-may-care attitude. The application of disciplinary procedures is far less costly than laxity. Employers incur costs associated with supervisory and managerial time spent in counseling sessions and investigations of rules infractions. There are also costs in processing appeals through grievance procedures or adjudication processes, for example, EEOC, the courts, labor hearings, and so on. Attorney fees, transcript expenses, time off for employees who serve as witnesses are other costs associated with the disciplinary procedure.

Fair but firm discipline has its benefits, however. Most employees want to know where they stand and subscribe to principles of fair play. Hence, all the elements of employee effectiveness, for example, higher morale, improved productivity, better attendance, and so on accrue from consistently and fairly applied disciplinary procedures.

Organizations can test the effectiveness of discipline by recording the number of disciplinary cases that result in corrected behavior, the trend of discipline cases appealed beyond the internal system, for example, to arbitration or the courts; calculation of ratio of arbitration cases or court rulings made in favor of the organization. Direct measurements can be taken of absence trends, incident rates of accidents, and the adherence to or violation of various rules.

The costs associated with absenteeism have already been cited in this chapter, but organizations might profit from computing some of the following detailed costs of absenteeism:[12]

1. Total work hours lost to absenteeism broken down by blue-collar, clerical, managerial/professional

2. The weighted average hourly wage/salary plus benefits for the various occupational groups that were compensated for absences during a given period

3. The estimated total supervisory hours lost to absenteeism for a given period

4. An estimated cost of premium (overtime) hours or temporary help needed to fill in for absentees

5. An estimate of machine downtime, production losses, quality deficiencies, delays that are directly attributable to absences

Summary

Discipline serves to maintain order and promote efficiency in an organization. Toward this end policies and procedures are promulgated that spell out rules, consequences of their violation, and methods to correct offenders.

The corrective approach to discipline adopts the philosophy that discipline should be humane, consistent, and impartial and should emphasize correction rather than punishment. It incorporates counseling to determine the cause of the problem and plans corrective action with the employee. Discipline then is applied only as a last resort, and a system of progressive discipline is utilized whereby repeated or more serious violations result in a sequence of penalties of increasing severity.

Should the most serious penalty, discharge, result from the process, organizations are challenged to show just cause for their actions. Proof that the discharge is proper can be based on evidence that the employee knew and violated the rule, received proper warning to correct the deviant behavior, was given a fair hearing, and received punishment conmensurate with the violation.

Absenteeism appears to be the most common discipline problem. Although the causes of absenteeism are varied and complex, specific measures can be taken to control it. Emphasizing regular attendance, recording absences, counseling absentees, and disciplining chronic offenders have had positive results in stabilizing regular attendance.

Key Terms

discipline	extenuating circumstances
punitive	just cause
corrective	absenteeism
progressive discipline	behavior modification
mitigating circumstances	

Review Questions

1. Distinguish between the punitive and corrective approaches to discipline.
2. What are the criteria for a policy on discipline?
3. Describe the steps that can be taken to control absenteeism.
4. Discuss the guidelines for proving just cause in discipline cases.
5. What is the "hot stove rule" and how does it apply to discipline?

Discussion Questions

1. Why do you suppose it is important for employees to understand the *whys* of rules?
2. Fear of reprisal is sometimes used to maintain discipline. What are the pros and cons of this approach?

3. What is the rationale for having a schedule of discipline for various violations of rules?

4. If illness is considered a legitimate excuse for absence, how can management determine its tolerance limits on this type of absence?

5. Should employees in a nonunion organization have recourse to appeal from discharge? Support your position.

Case Problem 1

DILLER DALLIES

John Kemper had just finished leading a seminar in management education for a group of engineers. The seminar was part of a two-week, intensive program offered by a large eastern university. Allan Clement, one of the participants, came up to Professor Kemper and said, "John, we were just discussing leadership, direction, and motivation. Now, I have a problem, and I don't see either how to solve it or how the problem fits into the framework of management. It concerns an engineer, Jim Diller, who has worked for me for the past 18 months, ever since I took over the department. Jim has been on the same job for over four years. The problem looked simple at first, but I haven't been able to make any headway at all. Jim persists in coming to work late every morning. He is always 30 minutes late, more usually 40 minutes to an hour. And he doesn't work overtime. I am at my wit's end. I have tried everything I can think of—private discussions, written reprimands, threats, sarcasm, and more. He just doesn't change. He still is late every morning. He won't give me any real reason, just that he doesn't feel that promptness is part of his job."

Professor Kemper spoke. "I have a question or two. First, does he do his job? That is, does he finish all his assignments in the seven hours or so that he works?"

"Well, that's hard to say. His is not the sort of job that lends itself to direct measurements, like a draftsman's for example. He is more or less a troubleshooter—consultant might be a better word, perhaps. My general impression is that he is doing an average or slightly below average job. His output seems satisfactory to the other divisions in our company. I guess you could say that his job is being done in a passable fashion. But I sure would have a hard time trying to document either satisfactory or unsatisfactory performance."

"Another question," said Professor Kemper. "What effect does his behavior have on the rest of the office?"

"I know that work stops and everyone watches him as he goes through to his own office. I feel that morale is deteriorating. But I can't prove it. The office gets its work done, but we don't generate or control our own work."

"Allan, if you're not fully satisfied and if Diller's work is only average, it should be easy to get rid of him. Why haven't you fired him and gotten a replacement who keeps better hours?"

"I don't have the authority to do that," answered Clement.

Problems

1. In your opinion, what is the problem? What were its causes?

2. What should Professor Kemper advise Clement to do?

3. What should Clement do?

A prestigious college had a long tradition concerning cheating. The rule was simple: anyone caught cheating on any course exercise and found guilty by a special student court was expelled. Moreover, any student who was aware that another student was cheating and did not report it, was also guilty, and if found so by the student court, was also expelled. There were no exceptions to this rule, which was published in the student handbook given to all entering students.

The student court held a hearing if requested by an accused student. The student could not have counsel.

A junior once stole a paper from a senior who lived down the hall in the same dormitory. This senior discovered that his paper was missing, but he did nothing about it, since he was pretty smart (A-average), and he had a copy anyhow. Later, a friend of his told him that the paper was used by the junior in another course, but he didn't bother much about it.

The junior was discovered, confessed, and was expelled. The senior was accused and ordered before the student court to determine guilt. He refused to attend, and he was found guilty and expelled as well. This upset him, to put it mildly, since he didn't even know the person who had stolen his paper. But the court argued that he was guilty because once he knew about the theft and the paper's use, he was bound to report the incident.

The senior then sued the college for $5 million. His attorney argued that (a) this senior was not guilty of anything, including the cheating charge; and (b) the student court was illegal, since the accused was denied counsel, and since there was no avenue of appeal. In the United States, if somebody deprives one of valuable property (such as a college diploma), one has the right to due process, and there was no due process here.

The college president was pretty upset too. He felt that the "hot stove rule" applied here. There was warning: the punishment was immediate; discipline was consistent; and it was impersonal. Hence the senior really had no case.

Case Problem 2

HOT STUDENT STOVES

Problems

1. Who is right here? Why?

2. In this case, a student was denied something rather important—namely his college diploma. Does the punishment fit the crime here? Why or why not?

3. Do you think that accused students in such situations should have a right to counsel? Why or why not?

4. Do you think that students found guilty by a student court should have a right of appeal? Why or why not?

Notes

1. Arthur A. Sloan and Fred Whitney, *Labor Relations,* 4th ed. (Englewood Cliffs, N.J.: Prentice-Hall, 1981), pp. 426–27.

2. Wallace Wohlking, "Effective Discipline in Employee Relations," *Personnel Journal,* September 1975, p. 492.

3. Arbitrator H. H. Platt, *Riley Stoker Corporation,* 7LA 764, quoted in Maurice S. Trotta, *Arbitration of Labor-Management Disputes* (New York: AMACOM, 1974), p. 236.

4. *N.L.R.B. v. J. Weingarten,* U. S. Supreme Court No. 73-1363, February 19, 1975.

5. Frank E. Kuzmits, "Managing Absenteeism," *Personnel,* May-June 1977, p. 73.

6. See *BNA's Quarterly Report on Job Absence and Turnover* (Washington, D.C.: Bureau of National Affairs, 1960), and *Absenteeism and Lateness: How Much Is Too Much?* (Englewood Cliffs, N.J.: Prentice-Hall, 1973), p. 12.

7. Daniel R. Ilglen and John H. Hollenback, "The Role of Job Satisfaction in Absence Behavior," *Organizational Behavior and Human Performance,* June 1977, p. 148.

8. Nigel Nicholson, Colin A. Brown, and J. K. Cradwick-Jones, "Absence from Work and Job Satisfaction," *Journal of Applied Psychology,* December 1976, p. 735.

9. Warren S. Blumenfeld, Aprile M. Holland, and Marilyn Edwards, "Predicting Employee Absenteeism From Biodata: An Application of the Weighted Application Blank Paradigm in Public Sector Personnel Administration," *Proceedings of the Tenth Annual Meeting of the Southeast Section, American Institute for Decision Sciences,* February 20–22, 1980, pp. 113ff.

10. Kathleen R. Garrison and Paul M. Muchinsky, "Attitudinal and Biographical Predictors of Incidental Absenteeism," *Journal of Vocational Behavior,* 10 (1977), pp. 221–30.

11. Ed Pedalino and Victor U. Gamboa, "Behavior Modification and Absenteeism: Intervention in One Industrial Setting," *Journal of Applied Psychology,* Vol. 59:6 (1974), pp. 694–98.

12. Frank E. Kuzmits, "How Much is Absenteeism Costing *Your* Organization," *The Personnel Administrator,* June 1979, pp. 29–33.

Chapter Ten

The Personnel Manager and Labor-Management Relations

Since 1963 the Textile Workers Union of America (TWUA) had been trying to organize the southern mills of the J. P. Stevens Company. As a consequence of the company's tough anti-union tactics the union was successful in organizing only one of its locations—Roanoke Rapids, N.C. Realizing that there is strength in numbers and that an aggressive campaign was needed to increase its membership in the South—only about 10 percent of 650,000 textile workers were organized as of December 1977—and at J. P. Stevens in particular, the textile union launched its "Southern strategy."[1] First, the two major textile unions, the Amalgamated Clothing Workers and the Textile Workers Union of America merged to form the Amalgamated Clothing and Textile Workers Union (ACTWU) with 525,000 members. The ACTWU then launched a $15 million crusade for social justice through a boycott of Stevens' products and a publicity campaign designed to win public support of its efforts to get Stevens to relent in its strong resistance to unions.[2] Through rallies, multimedia presentations, testimonials of public and civic leaders, and worker accounts of what is alleged to be a climate of fear and intimidation, the union openly attacked the company.

Stevens was cited 15 times by the National Labor Relations Board (which oversees the federal labor law governing union-management relations) for unfair labor practices. At Roanoke Rapids, N.C., the Board charged that only surface bargaining had taken place, so there was still no contract after two years of negotiations. The company had refused to give in to what it considered to be unrealistic demands. The union claimed that Stevens was

LEARNING OBJECTIVES

1. To be familiar with the personnel manager's role in labor relations.
2. To understand the differences in relationships between the personnel staff and employees with and without a union.
3. To know the various issues of labor relations policies.
4. To be familiar with various types of union organization.
5. To be familiar with alternative union security arrangements.

heartless. A former employee testified that the company fired her and her husband for union activity. She said, "They told us if any of us was goin' to get any work we would have to leave town to do it, because nobody here would hire us."[3]

The company steadfastly resisted union organizing attempts. It felt its actions were justified because the employees had consistently voted against unions. Stevens insisted that its employees have "rejected the idea of dealing through an outside union hierarchy. Union presence has historically led to strife and discord over issues that can be settled amicably when the relationship is based on mutual respect."[4]

Then on October 19, 1980, the Amalgamated Clothing and Textile Workers Union and J. P. Stevens Company signed a two-and-one-half-year collective bargaining contract covering 3,500 employees in four plant locations. The agreement ended seventeen years of strife between the parties and was expected to "lay a foundation for a harmonious and productive relationship."[5] In the settlement the ACTWU agreed to call off the consumer boycott and both parties agreed to settle or terminate existing lawsuits and to refer unresolved grievances to an arbitrator.

This example points up a number of concerns that personnel managers must contend with. Labor relations are part of the environment in which the personnel manager must operate when integrating employees into an organization. Whether the organization operates with a union or strives to maintain nonunion status, emerging patterns in labor relations present a new challenge to personnel managers. Employees—including professionals—are being attracted to unions for reasons that are not always obvious. Union-management relations are now broader and more complex, and handling problems in this area has become a sophisticated task that calls for professionals. A basic familiarity with the motivations for forming unions provides a background for understanding collective bargaining and the administration of union-management relations.

The Personnel Manager's Role in Labor Relations

Labor relations experts have claimed that "unions are the fault of poor management." Whether or not this is an accurate statement (experience shows that the size of the organization is a significant factor), there is little question that a lack of sensitivity to employees' needs and feelings has served as an impetus to seek remedies through union organization. Without a union, management is relatively free to operate as it chooses, but with one, the direction of the work force is dictated by the terms of a contract. The personnel manager then is confronted with the challenge to ensure fair treatment of all employees, guide their efforts toward the objectives of the organization, and either maintain a union-free environment or promote harmonious relations between the representative of the employees (union) and management. In a nonunion situation the personnel manager serves as a liaison between employees and management, perhaps even being an advocate of the employees. Once the company has been organized, however, the personnel manager becomes essentially an advocate of management. The following discussion suggests some of the reasons why organizations such as J. P. Stevens may resist union-organizing attempts.

RESTRICTIONS ON MANAGEMENT PREROGATIVES

The union represents an infringement on management's unilateral right to direct its work force. The agreement between the union and management is restrictive in nature. It specifies hours of operation, and requires management to pay a premium for deviations from stipulated procedures. The manner of scheduling work; the amount of pay for specific kinds of work; the assignment of people to jobs; the methods for transferring, promoting, and laying off employees, and many other provisions are spelled out in detail and restrict the right of an employer to manage. J. P. Stevens and other textile manufacturers have resisted organizing attempts because they felt a union would have an encumbering and costly effect on them. The personnel manager plays a key role in situations like this by advising line management on details of the contract's administration.

CHALLENGES TO MANAGEMENT DECISIONS

One benefit of being a manager is having the authority to make decisions independently. Unions, almost without exception, insist on a formal grievance procedure whereby managers' decisions can be challenged even to the extent of a review and judgment by a third party. The grievance procedure can be construed by management as a threat to its autonomy. But from an employee standpoint, a grievance procedure can represent protection from arbitrary or unfair treatment. For example, a union could have appealed management's action and might have won reinstatement of the employee who was fired by J. P. Stevens. Organizations that practice open communications and encourage employees to challenge what they perceive to be unfair, capricious decisions usually overcome the hostile attitudes that build up when feelings and opinions are suppressed. The personnel manager can advise line managers on specific matters dealing with grievances and, even without a union, can facilitate smoother communications between employees and management through training and by monitoring the entire process.

A QUESTION OF LOYALTY

A major public utility became concerned when top management observed that its employees were giving their allegiance to the union instead of the company. Workers looked to the union representatives rather than their supervisors for leadership, and any improvements in compensation and working conditions (the company had the best in the state) were credited to the union. This is a serious enough condition when the union becomes a certified representative of the employees, but during organizing campaigns the modus operandi is to characterize management as lawless; exploiters of labor; using unsafe, unhealthy work practices; and heartless. The aim of the Amalgamated Clothing and Textile Workers Union was to have the public believe these terms applied to J. P. Stevens. The personnel manager is faced with the problem of developing an attitude of employee loyalty toward the organization. Employee orientation, training, and communication will support this effort, but unless supervisors are developed to be *effective* leaders the other activities will have minimal impact.

CONSTRAINTS ON EFFICIENCY

Unions, in their efforts to preserve the job security of their members, push for practices that can have a negative impact on productivity. Insisting that people be selected and assigned to jobs solely on the basis of seniority; precluding management from contracting work outside the organization; restricting supervisors' performance of union employee work; regulating the composition of work crews; preventing people from performing work that is "outside their job classifications" are some of the practices that detract from efficiency and increase the cost of operations. Unions are not the primary cause of inefficient utilization of human resources; management practices themselves often contribute to low productivity. The union may often become a partner with management to enhance efficiency, and the personnel manager as the organization's primary contact with the union can do much to build a continuing cooperative relationship. (Cooperative union-management efforts to increase productivity will be discussed in Chapter 11.)

UNION-FREE MANAGEMENT

The personnel manager may be commissioned to maintain the non-union status of an organization. Employers such as J. P. Stevens view unions as contrary to the best interests of their organization. Consequently, companies take great pains to frustrate any and all efforts to organize their employees. Unfortunately, such tactics have led to bitterness that will delay any constructive type of relationship with their employees. And the anti-union campaign may, in the long run, create the very condition that the company fought so hard to avoid, unionization of its own plants as well as those of smaller textile manufacturers. Nevertheless, the personnel manager plays a key role in devising and coordinating the campaign to keep the organization nonunion.

An organizer for one of the country's largest unions spoke to the author's personnel class. He stated that the strongest deterrent to union organization is "just plain good human resource management." He said that companies that pay attention to their employees and treat them with respect usually don't have to worry about a union. He claimed that his union doesn't "knock on company doors to organize employees, they come to the union hall and ask us to get them in the union!" Why do employees join unions? There are many different reasons and some of them are discussed below.

Labor Issues and Policies

A standard motto of the labor movement is, "In union there is strength." Labor organizations want to increase their membership roles to remain financially and politically viable. Their effectiveness in influencing legislation depends to a great degree on sizable memberships that solidly support their leadership.

WHY EMPLOYEES ORGANIZE

Higher wages and shorter hours might, at first glance, appear to be the most obvious incentives for workers to organize. But surveys fail to verify these as primary reasons why workers join unions today.[6] Recent studies conclude that dissatisfaction with working conditions, particularly job security and wages, and frustration in attempts to exert influence on management were prime reasons why workers vote for a union.[7] Following are some of the situational inducements to join unions.

JOB SECURITY.   Employees want to be confident that the jobs they have today will definitely exist in the future. They do not want their jobs to be jeopardized by economic fluctuations, and they need to know they will be treated fairly and will not be discharged without just cause. This is a basic need that can be satisfied by efforts to stabilize employment.

GOOD WORKING CONDITIONS.   A safe and healthy place to work, coupled with high quality standards in both product and job environment are important to workers. Organizations can help meet these needs by conscientiously adhering to OSHA guidelines.

OPPORTUNITY TO ADVANCE.   Employees want to be certain their organization will consider them for promotion to higher paying, more responsible jobs. Organizations can satisfy this desire by instituting a fairly administered policy of promotion from within based on seniority and qualifications. Also, they can communicate to employees that opportunities for advancement increase as the organization grows. Job-posting practices (described in Chapter 6) help satisfy this desire.

IMPORTANCE OF THE WORK.   Work itself is important to employees. They want to feel that their efforts are making a contribution; they want to know where their job fits in the overall picture. They also want to feel that their work is relevant—that the work they are doing will help improve the world or some part of it. Repetitive, routine tasks, especially assembly line work, present the greatest difficulty in this respect, and the nature of this kind of work induces workers, who become bored and feel they have no identity, to seek unionization. Job-enrichment programs can make the work itself more meaningful.

OPPORTUNITY TO BE HEARD.   Perhaps one of the strongest motives for joining a union is that it provides a vehicle for employees to express their dissatisfactions and disagreements with particular job matters. Many organizations realize that it isn't necessary to have a union to install a grievance procedure or an open-door policy. Organizations can train supervisors to listen to employees and try to resolve their problems.

NEED TO BE RECOGNIZED.   Well-done jobs deserve recognition, and exemplary performance calls for an occasional word of thanks. Workers do not expect anything special for doing their jobs, but recognition of meritorious work serves to reinforce positive behavior.

NEED TO BE RESPECTED.   Employees want to be treated as human beings. Supervisors and workers can show mutual respect and treat each other in a courteous manner. Supervisors do not need to be distant and authoritarian to win the respect of their employees. The supervisor's commendation for a job well done serves to build an employee's self-esteem.

NEED TO BELONG.   People need to associate with other human beings and feel they belong. Unions meet these needs by offering an organization of people with common interests. Through meetings, educational programs, social events, and other activities designed to involve members, unions build a strong bond of brotherhood. Companies that have expended the same sorts of efforts have gained the loyalty of their work force. Many workers join a union because it gives them a means of expressing their leadership aspirations. The labor movement provides numerous opportunities for employees to be trained for and to assume leadership responsibilities. Companies, too, have created work environments that are conducive to socializing and/or feeling a sense of belonging.

MONEY.   Employees want to receive a fair day's pay for a fair day's work. They are most concerned with receiving wages that are competitive in the community and commensurate with the work they are performing compared to other jobs within a plant. One theory of motivation is that employees can be induced to perform when they can reasonably expect to be rewarded with a valued outcome. Money sometimes serves that end.

If management would apply the basic principles of worker motivation to satisfy these needs, there would be little incentive for workers to join unions. Is it possible, then, that unions are the fault of management? Perhaps. Supervisors' failures to apply motivation theory in work situations result in worker dissatisfaction and frustration, and employees turn to unions to fulfill their wants. As a general rule, workers join unions over some dissatisfaction with the way management runs the organization. In a broader sense, there are several major issues that affect the unionization of employees and exert an impact on the labor-management relations situation. Let us explore these policy issues.

CURRENT LABOR POLICY ISSUES

To attract and retain members, the union movement has concentrated its efforts on issues that significantly affect workers. Generally speaking, labor is currently concerned with the economic issues of unemployment and inflation; social issues of minority employment, poverty, and related aspects; quality of life issues such as health care and housing; and administrative issues such as regulation of internal union affairs and the right to work. A number of issues representative of current labor policy matters are discussed below.

TECHNOLOGY AND UNEMPLOYMENT. To remain competitive, organizations search for ways to increase production; technological change has been the primary approach to accomplishing this end. But technology has dislocated large numbers of workers, many of whom are union members. The resulting membership loss originally led unions to resist technology that would displace labor. As it became obvious that only improved productivity could justify wage increases, however, unions changed their policy on technology; currently they are supporting productivity improvement while working for measures to minimize its impact on workers. Productivity improvement, unions realize, can result in noninflationary compensation increases for their members and will improve the position of American products in foreign trade and, thereby, stabilize domestic employment. To minimize the impact of technological change, unions have bargained for compensation to workers displaced by technology, that is, **supplemental unemployment benefits,** retraining for workers whose skills were eliminated by automation, relocation assistance for laid-off workers, and distribution to workers of monetary gains from productivity improvements. The Steelworkers' demand for some form of guaranteed career-employment security resulted in a provision in the 1977 agreement that allows certain employees with 20 or more years of service to retire on a regular pension plus a $300 supplement should a plant be shut down.[8]

MINORITY GROUPS.   Traditionally, the labor movement has supported the principle of equal rights for all people regardless of race, creed, or national origin. Because organized labor itself employs more than 110,000 people, it faces the problem of eliminating discrimination. Like any other employer, it must comply with the provisions of Title VII of the 1964 Civil Rights Act. Furthermore, some unions allied themselves with the Civil Rights movement in their organizing efforts. In the West, equal opportunity for Chicano migratory farm workers was the rallying point for organizing efforts of the United Farm Workers Union. And now the AFL-CIO is supporting the Equal Rights Amendment for women.

QUALITY OF LIFE.   Improving the **quality of life** for all Americans is a basic union aim. The enactment of a national health security act to improve health care is a major legislative goal of the AFL-CIO's efforts. Labor has pointed to the high cost of health care, inefficient use of resources, inadequate or unavailable care, and the shortage of doctors as creating the need for national health care legislation.

Organized labor, in supporting the fight against poverty, advocates a guaranteed minimum standard of living for everyone through recommended reforms in welfare programs, manpower policies, housing development, and care for the aged. Some might criticize the approach as socialistic, but organized labor insists its stand is based on social responsibility, which is the obligation of all citizens. (Union-management quality of life initiatives are described in Chapter 11.)

INTERNAL UNION AFFAIRS.   Irregularities in the administration of some unions, the failure of rank-and-file workers to ratify agreements, and members' insistence on a greater voice in union affairs have caused organized labor to correct and improve itself. The Labor-Management Reporting and Disclosure Act (LMRDA, also referred to as the Landrum-Griffin Act) of 1959 provided much of the impetus for regulating the conduct of union internal affairs. (This act applied to management as well.)

Under the LMRDA, the government has been given surveillance power over union internal affairs in an attempt to eliminate and prevent irregularities and in particular to protect members against the embezzlement of union funds by officials. The government exercises its power by requiring unions to file copies of their constitutions and bylaws and reports on their administrative policies and finances with the Secretary of Labor; these reports then become public record. In addition, LMRDA guarantees union members certain rights, including safeguards against union disciplinary actions; access to policy and financial information; the right to vote, nominate, and debate issues, regulations, and candidates; and the right to appeal union hearing procedures and violations of specific provisions of the act.

Prior to the enactment of LMRDA, the United Auto Workers, at their 1957 constitutional convention, established the UAW Public Review Board. It represented the broadest grant of authority over internal affairs ever voluntarily given by a labor organization to an outside body. The board is composed of impartial and distinguished citizens who review appeals from the internal hearings procedure. It reviews alleged violations of members' rights and of ethical practices codes. Jack Stieber, reporting to the Center for the Study of Democratic Institutions, concluded:

> Perhaps the Board's greatest contribution has been the creation of an increased awareness and respect, on the part of the UAW leadership, for the importance of due process as set forth under the union's own constitution. The international executive board has tended to regard the Public Review Board as a super appeals body which would double-check union decisions in appeals cases to make sure that members were not treated unfairly.[9]

UNION SECURITY.   Union strength lies in its dues-paying membership. Unions believe that the people they represent have an obligation to participate in union activities and to support the union financially by paying dues. The various forms of union security arrangements include: **union shop,** which requires employees to join the union within a specified time after hiring as a condition of employment; and **agency shop,** which requires nonunion workers to contribute to the union, usually an amount equivalent to union dues. The *closed shop* and its requirement that all workers be union members at the time of their hiring was made illegal by Taft-Hartley. (Union security is discussed as a bargaining issue in Chapter 11.) It is understandable, then, why unions consider the **right-to-work laws** of various states a threat to their security. Section 14b of the Taft-Hartley Act permits states to enact laws that prohibit agreements making union membership a hiring condition or a requirement for continued employment. As of 1981, 20 states had right-to-work laws. Union efforts to repeal Section 14b have been unsuccessful, but the negative impact has been somewhat reduced through agency-shop clauses in a few contracts.

FUTURE PROSPECTS FOR THE LABOR MOVEMENT.   In an essay appearing in the *Harvard Business Review,* A. H. Raskin admonished the labor movement for its failure to keep abreast of existing problems. He argued that ". . . it is evident that the policies and programs which unions have carried over virtually intact from the Great Depression more than 30 years ago are irrelevant or positively distasteful to a membership gone middle class."[10] Raskin's contention is substantiated by public opinion. In a national survey, the Roper Organization, which measures public confidence in leaders, found a strong belief that union leadership was doing only a fair to poor job of meeting its responsibilities to the public; 52 percent of the general public expressed this sentiment, and more significantly, almost half of union members shared the same negative opinion. In addition, four persons in ten see top labor leaders as ruthless, and only 39 percent view organized labor as basically sound (this compares to 52 percent in a 1974 poll). And 51 percent have serious reservations about the way labor is organized (up from 39 percent in the previous poll).[11] Kochan's survey of American workers found both positive and negative perceptions of unions.[12] On the one hand they viewed unions as requiring members to go along with leaders' decisions and as having leaders who do what is best for themselves. On the other, they saw unions as effective in protecting members against unfair practices of management, improving job security and wages of members, and giving dues-paying members their money's worth. How then, can unions build on the positive aspects of their image, regain popular support, and revitalize themselves? The labor movement must open opportunities for the deprived. It must become politically sensitive to the trends of our society and initiate appropriate legislation. It must support efforts to increase productivity in factories and to improve living conditions in the cities. The most crucial problems that have sapped much of labor's political power (the 1980 landslide election of a presidential candidate it opposed attests to this fact) have been cited as: the inability of unions to organize a greater proportion of the nation's workers, and a widening gap between the workers and top union officials. Union leaders seem to be taking great pains to get themselves and their members on the same political wavelength in order to present a unified front in future election years.[13] Whether the labor movement gains in size and significance in the future depends upon its effectiveness in mustering the forces of change.

MEMBERSHIP. In 1978, at latest official count, there were 20.24 million union members in the United States, a slight increase over the previous high of 20.19 in 1974.[14] But the expansion did not keep pace with the growth of the non-farm labor force, traditionally the chief area of labor organizing. Figure 10.1 graphs this relationship from 1930 to 1978. About 24.0 percent of that workforce is unionizing today, as against 27.3 percent in 1970.[15]

Shifts in demand to new products and services, technological advances, and the increased emphasis on services, all affected membership

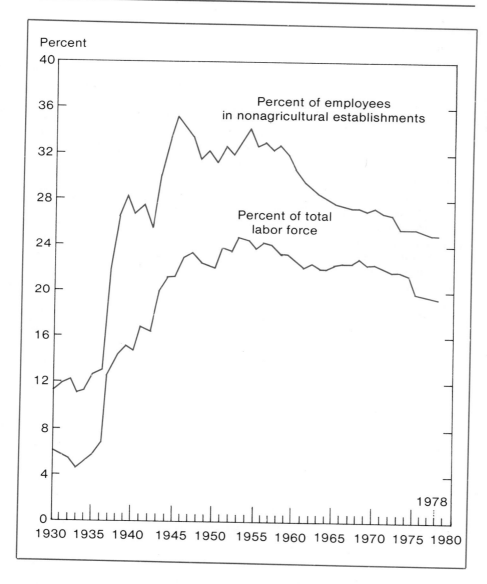

Percent

Figure 10.1
Union Membership,
1930–78[1]

Source: U.S. Department of Labor,
Bureau of Labor Statistics, *Directory
of National Unions and Employee
Associations,* 1978, Bulletin No. 2079
(Washington, D.C.: U.S. Govern-
ment Printing Office, 1979), p. 60.

Percent of employees
in nonagricultural establishments

Percent of total
labor force

1978

gains and losses. Unions that have benefited the most from these shifts in
the private sector represent service employees (the Service Employees Union
increased their membership almost 61 percent in the past decade and Communications Workers increased about 42 percent). The most significant advances by far were made in public sector unions and teachers' associations;
their growth figures range from 180 to 203 percent—which is extraordinary

compared to the figures tallied for private sector. Table 10.1 lists the unions that gained 100,000 members or more.[15]

WHITE-COLLAR AND PROFESSIONAL UNIONS.   A combination of elements has given rise to a surge of organizing activity among white-collar and professional people. Teachers and college professors—disturbed over their diminishing influence in school administrative matters and concerned about infringements on their academic rights—have formed associations or joined existing ones, some of which have affiliations with labor organizations. Many of the nation's engineers, upset by persistent unemployment, have moved toward unionism. Secretaries, clerical workers, and technicians, who have traditionally resisted union overtures, are provoked by management's unresponsive attitudes and are now ripe for unionism.

In March 1975 more than 2,000 New York City physicians went on strike for four days. As legitimate union members (they were members of the Committee of Interns and Residents) they contended that work weeks of 100 hours and more were harmful to their patients. Encouragement for health care professionals to form labor organizations may have been provided in the 1974 amendment to the National Labor Relations Act that extended coverage to some 2 million people in hospitals and nursing homes. It is interesting to note that even the established, private-practice physicians join unions (the Service Employees International Union has 1,200 doctors in locals across the country). The union assists them in dealing with third parties, for example, the federal government, insurance companies, and hos-

Table 10.1
Unions That Gained 100,000 Members or More, 1968–78 (numbers in thousands)

Unions	Membership			Increase 1968–78*	
	1968	1976	1978	Number	Percent
State, county employees	364	750	1,020	656	180.2
Teachers	165	446	500	335	203.0
Service employees	389	575	625	236	60.7
Retail clerks	552	699	735	183	33.2
Teamsters (Ind.)	1,755	1,889	1,924	169	9.6
Steelworkers	1,120	1,300	1,286	166	14.8
Communications workers	357	483	508	151	42.3
Electrical workers	897	924	1,012	115	12.8

* Includes several unions where a portion of the membership gain was due to a merger with one or more other unions. Excludes merged unions where the membership of the smaller organization represented a significant proportion of the total and the combined membership did not increase by 100,000.

Source: U. S. Department of Labor, Bureau of Labor Statistics, *Labor Union and Employee Association Membership—1978*, news release, September 3, 1979, p. 6.

pital administrations. Over 27,000 dentists and physicians belong to the American Federation of Physicians and Dentists, which seeks to negotiate with government units and insurance companies that finance medical care. On a broader base, the American Nurses Association represents 201,000 members, of whom more than a third are covered by collective bargaining agreements.[16] Professional and technical employees, who include public school teachers, college professors, musicians, actors, journalists, engineers, and the health-care professions are the fastest growing segment of the work force. They may well represent significant expansion potential for American unions in the future. They are becoming increasingly dissatisfied with inadequate technical support, insufficient opportunity to pursue interesting ideas, excessive interference by superiors or outside agencies, and lack of sufficient input to project assignment decisions. This type of dissatisfaction has led to over 420 college campuses being organized by their professors in the past decade.[17]

White-collar workers often feel they have sufficient bargaining power to control their careers or their jobs effectively. An interesting illustration of this condition comes from the ranks of middle management. By 1985 the 30- to 34-year-old group is expected to be 45 percent larger than it is today. This is the executive entry age group and such growth will almost certainly curtail promotional opportunities for many. As middle managers become disillusioned with career prospects, they are likely to engage in self-interest collective bargaining with an executive union as their agent! In Arch Patton's opinion, "Too many aggressive young executives are aware of what organized self-interest has accomplished for other groups to assume that they will long ignore this potent weapon where their own interests are at stake."[18]

PUBLIC SECTOR UNIONISM.   Public employee unions and associations are not a recent phenomenon, but their rapid growth in the past decade occurred while union membership in the private economy was declining. Most government union members have joined since 1962, the year President John F. Kennedy issued Executive Order 10988, which established the basis for collective bargaining among federal government employees (subsequently the Executive Order was amended by EO 11491 and later, in 1975, by EO 11838, which focused on unit consolidation, scope of negotiations, and grievance and arbitration procedures). That executive action provided the impetus for the burgeoning growth of public-sector unionism among federal employees. By 1978, 1.4 million employees of the federal government had joined unions, as had 2.2 million state and local government workers; one of every five public service employees belonged to a union in 1974. Employee associations claimed an additional 2.5 million government employees as members, virtually all at the state and local levels.[19] About 40 states have enacted collective bargaining laws, and 21 have comprehensive statutes covering state and/or municipal employees. Five states even permit the limited right to strike.

One of the best examples of public union growth is the American Federation of Government Employees (AFGE), which doubled in size between 1962 and 1972. It ranked nineteenth in size in 1972, while a decade earlier it was forty-third. Similarly, the American Federation of State, County and Municipal Employees (AFSCME), with 700,000 members, and gaining 7,000 each week, was fifth in 1975, an improvement from twenty-first thirteen years earlier.[20]

The administration of public sector labor relations is governed by the Civil Service Reform Act of 1978, which codified into law most of the principles established by EO 1149 (amended by EO 11616). Under the Act the duties of the Civil Service Commission were assumed by the Office of Personnel Management and responsibility for handling union-management relations was assigned to the Federal Labor Relations Authority.

Traditionally, issues handled by public unions centered around wages, hours, and benefits. (It should be noted, however, that most federal employees and their unions are not permitted to bargain for wages.) But more recently employee representatives have pressed for discussion of promotional and educational opportunities, standards of conduct and performance, rights of employees in disciplinary matters, and changes in civil service regulations on labor legislation. Probably the dominant issue in public sector labor relations is whether all public employees should be allowed to **strike.** The question has been tested repeatedly in the courts, which have held that except in proprietary services (schools, libraries, parks, etc.), they do not have a constitutional right to strike—reasoning that public employees have a higher obligation to ensure uninterrupted functioning of government in the interest of public health, safety, and welfare.[21] Nevertheless, the record indicates numerous incidents of open defiance by public unions that engage in strikes or other forms of job action. The 1981 strike of air traffic controllers (PATCO) is a case in point.

POLITICAL INFLUENCE.   Labor's impact through legislation has grown significantly in the past several years. The labor movement believes it has great influence on the Congress and will continue to seek its ends—increase in the minimum wage, labor law reform, national health insurance, economic recovery, right-to-work repeal, and others—with ever-increasing frequency through the legislature.[22] The efforts of unions to maintain their political influence take the form of lobbying, voter education, and active campaigning (including financial support) for candidates who support labor's position.

ORGANIZATIONAL STRUCTURE. In 1935 the Convention of the American Federation of Labor (a federation of national unions and the dominant force in the labor movement at the time) debated the issue of craft versus industrial unionism and those supporting the organization of mass-production industries were narrowly defeated. (A **craft union** consists of workers in a single craft, such as carpenters, machinists, or painters. An **industrial union** includes all occupations—crafts and unskilled workers within a company or industry, for example, auto workers, machinists, assemblers.) This issue led to a schism in the labor movement that lasted until 1955. One consequence of the division was the formation of the Congress of Industrial Organizations (CIO) composed of eight unions suspended from the AFL. The need for a united front to promote social and political reforms and to strengthen membership led to the merger of the AFL and the CIO in 1955. The American labor movement is composed of about eighty thousand local unions, most of which are affiliated with national or international unions. These national and international unions have similar structures. Since about 70 percent of union members belong to unions associated with the AFL-CIO, an examination of its organization should explain the general structure of most international unions. Figure 10.2 is a chart of the AFL-CIO structure.

The AFL-CIO is a federation, a loosely knit league of affiliated national and international unions. The chief characteristic of the AFL-CIO is that it has almost no formal power or control over its affiliates. The nationals and internationals remain completely autonomous and decide on their own policies and programs. However, in practice, affiliates usually follow the AFL-CIO's policies.

The biennial convention is the legislative arm of the AFL-CIO. Each member, national, or international union is represented at the convention by delegates (the number of delegates is proportionate to the amount of per capita tax paid by the affiliate). The convention has supreme authority over the organization, and its decisions are final. Between conventions, the executive council—consisting of the president, secretary/treasurer, and twenty-seven vice presidents—directs the affairs of the AFL-CIO. The executive committee of six vice presidents advises the federation's officers. Then, a general board—composed of the executive council and an officer from each international union and affiliated department—meets annually to decide on policy matters referred by the executive officers of the council.

As shown in the chart, the organization receives technical advice and assistance from an extensive staff. The labor lobby in Congress needs expert support on political matters, because political involvement is a crucial aspect of the AFL-CIO's activities. The staff also has experts on fair employment practices, social security, workmen's compensation, unemployment insur-

Figure 10.2
Structure of the AFL-CIO

Source: U.S. Department of Labor, Bureau of Labor Statistics, *Directory of National Unions and Employee Associations, 1979* (Washington, D.C.: U.S. Government Printing Office, 1980), p. 17.

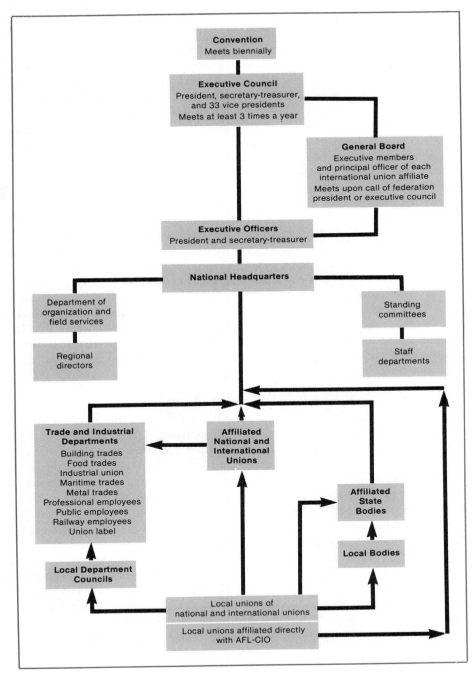

ance, and other matters of concern to union members. In addition, it provides information and advice on organizing activities, which are critical to the progress of affiliates.

The six trade and industrial departments unite national organizations whose members are likely to work in the same trade or on the same kind of job. The basic purpose of these departments is to add cohesiveness to the organization, because the most critical problems arise out of jurisdictional disputes. Consequently, the departments carry out joint organizing campaigns, and they are commissioned to prevent and settle jurisdictional disputes. State and local central bodies influence legislative bodies and the public on matters of local or regional concern; membership in these bodies is optional.

Lane Kirkland, the current president of the AFL-CIO, made a significant break with tradition when he announced at the February 1980 meeting of the executive council that he was reserving two seats on the council, one for a woman and one for a minority. Up to this point only presidents of affiliated organizations were elected and they were rarely, if ever, female or black.

MERGERS.   The future will see a trend toward conglomerate unions; a combination of economy and strength will provide the impetus. **Union merger** is the expressed desire of AFL-CIO President Lane Kirkland and AFL-CIO officials have encouraged some unions to merge, but they have refrained from taking an activist role. The reason behind the encouragement is that at least 50 AFL-CIO affiliates have less than 50,000 members. This small membership is insufficient to provide adequate services, accumulate the financial resources for effective organizing campaigns, or bargain with management on an equal footing. Prospects point to more mergers. Since the AFL and the CIO joined forces in 1955 there have been more than 20 mergers, and since early 1972, at least a dozen more unions have made advances toward mergers.

Now that the Steelworkers (the most active union in mergers) has united with District 50 of the Allied and Technical Workers (a former subsidiary of the United Mine Workers), it represents workers in all basic metals industries from mine to mill. Potentially, teachers could have one of the biggest unions in the nation; large units of the National Education Association have been breaking away and affiliating with trade unions, principally the American Federation of Teachers.[23] The merger of the two largest textile unions into the Amalgamated Clothing Workers and Textile Workers Union is another example of a merger for the purpose of gaining power—in this case the goal will be to organize southern textile plants, as noted at the beginning of this chapter.

By all indications, the trend to merge will continue. In fact, Kirkland has stated that he wants to strengthen the labor movement by bringing disaffiliated and other independent unions under the banner of the AFL-CIO. He has extended invitations and the Teamsters are exploring the issue. The Auto Workers could ratify reaffiliation as early as 1983.[24]

The Legal Environment

The labor relations situation is significantly affected by federal and state legislation, which governs *union organizing campaigns,* the **certification** of union elections, **decertification** elections, rights of employers and employees under collective bargaining relationships, methods of dispute resolution, internal union administration, and related aspects of union-management relations. Although appropriate sections of labor laws are found in the chapters dealing with this subject, the summary of the basic laws of labor relations in Table 10.2 (pp. 300–301) should serve as a handy reference.

Cost-Benefit Analysis

Many organizations prefer to remain nonunion because, as Beavers estimates, the increase in labor costs due to unionization range from 25 to 30 percent.[25] However, there are also costs associated with maintaining nonunion status. Direct costs include those associated with staff time to campaign against union organizing attempts and the fees of lawyers retained to give advice. The indirect cost in terms of potential employee ill-will and negative public sentiment is probably impossible to calculate. When a union represents an organization's employees, the costs associated with maintaining harmony between employer and employees are based, primarily, on the time employees and managers need to administer the collective-bargaining agreement (a discussion of costs associated with collective bargaining is included at the end of Chapter 11).

The advantages of maintaining a continuing relationship of cooperation between employer and employee are too numerous to describe here, and will be noted in other chapters. Suffice it to say that substantial benefits accrue to organizations when there are good labor-management relations.

Summary

Recently, the area of labor relations has witnessed dramatic change. Developments such as the entry of minorities and women into the labor force, quality-of-life bargaining issues, and legislation regulating the administration of union affairs, are presenting a challenge to unions as well as management. Personnel management's role is either to develop and maintain harmonious relations with the union or to manage the work force in such a manner that unionization will not be sought by the employees.

Unions rely on a growing and active membership for their survival. The absolute number of organized workers is increasing, although the unions' share of the active work force is declining. Thus, organized labor is seeking new avenues to expand its ranks. White-collar, professional, and technical workers and public sector employees show the highest propensity toward organization at present. The reasons workers join unions have changed over the years, too. Initially workers formed associations to improve working conditions and protect each other from unscrupulous employers. Today's employees seek security, opportunity, recognition, fair treatment, and respect. When employers fail to fulfill these needs, workers seek satisfaction through unions.

In recent years, the union movement has exerted considerable financial and political effort to strengthen its influence. Mergers combine memberships and thereby increase union power. Organized labor continues to lobby for bills that it feels are in the best interests of the working class in particular and society in general.

Key Terms

supplemental unemployment benefits

quality of life

union shop

agency shop

right-to-work laws

strike

craft union

industrial union

union merger

certification

decertification

Review Questions

1. What are the underlying reasons behind the tendency of unions to merge?
2. Why are so many white-collar and professional people joining unions?
3. Describe the basic provisions of the federal labor laws enacted since 1949.
4. Describe the organization of the AFL-CIO and discuss the basics of its administration.
5. What are unions doing to accommodate the new breed member?

Discussion Questions

1. Consider the reasons why workers join unions. What steps can management take to satisfy these motivations and perhaps make unions unnecessary in a particular plant?
2. What, if any, needs of blue-collar workers do unions fail to satisfy? Can any of these needs be better met by management? Why and how?
3. Assume you are a white-collar worker in an insurance company, and

Table 10.2
Summary of Legislation Governing Labor Relations

Title of Act	Year of Enactment (or amendment)	Basic Provisions	Enforcing Agency and Powers
1. Railway Labor Act	1926	Railroad workers assured the right to organize and join unions without employer interference.	
2. Norris-LaGuardia Act	1932	Limited restrictions on strikes, picketing, and boycotts. Forbade use of yellow-dog contracts (workers, as condition of employment, had to agree to abstain from union membership). It limited liability of unions and their officers and members for unlawful acts of individual officers, agents, or members.	
3. National Industrial Recovery Act (NIRA)	1935	Guaranteed employees right to join unions and bargain collectively. Declared unconstitutional by U.S. Supreme Court, 1935.	
4. National Labor Relations Act (Wagner Act)	1935	Guaranteed right to self-organization, collective bargaining, and concerted union activities. Created National Labor Relations Board. A number of states passed little Wagner Acts.	National Labor Relations Board: • Prevent and remedy unfair labor practices of employers. • Determine bargaining unit. • Conduct certification elections.
5. Labor-Management Relations Act (Taft-Hartley)	1947	Amended Wagner Act. Added unfair labor practices of unions. Outlawed closed shop provisions and secondary boycotts. Section 146 allowed states to restrict union security clauses (right-to-work laws). Provided rules for national emergency strikes including cooling off period of 80 days. Federal Mediation and Conciliation Service made a separate agency from the Department of Labor. Made it a duty of both parties to bargain in good faith.	National Labor Relations Board: • Same powers as in Wagner Act. • Employers could also appeal to Board. • Certain practices could be penalized by court action and law suits for damages.
6. The Labor-Management Reporting and Disclosure Act	1959	Contains Bill of Rights of members of Labor Organizations: participation in union affairs; protection from unwarranted financial burdens; and the right to testify, be informed of union agreements, and of fair disciplinary actions.	Secretary of Labor can sue in Federal district court to obtain relief and/or damages for the plaintiff.

	Year		
7. Labor-Management Relations in the Federal Service EO 10988	1962	Requires reporting by labor organizations and their officers and employees, and by employers and their labor relations consultants; deals with: standards for union elections; safeguards for labor organizations, and related matters. Permits voting by economic strikers; controls secondary boycotts; limits hot cargo agreements; regulates organizational and recognition picketing; eliminates non-communist affidavits for union officials.	Agency's own management serves as appeal channel.
8. EO 11491	1969	Recognized Federal Employees' right to join unions and bargain collectively. Types of recognition included: informal, formal and exclusive (when 10% of employees of agency are involved and majority of them select union). Agency required to meet and confer regularly on policy, practices and working conditions. Strikes prohibited. Used exclusive recognition only. Set up administrative agencies.	Federal Labor Relations Council decides major policy. Assistant Secretary of Labor for Labor-Management Relations.
9. NLRA (amended)	1974	NLRA amended to extend same rights and protection to health-care employees, for example, nurses, technicians and others.	
10. (EO 11491 amended by: EO 11616, 11636 and 11838)	1975	Expanded scope of EO 11491: consolidation of units, scope of negotiations, and grievance and arbitration procedures.	
11. Civil Service Reform Act	1978		Assistant Secretary of Labor for Labor-Management Relations settles disputes over bargaining unit makeup and representation rights; orders and supervises elections, disqualifies unions from recognition because of corrupt or undemocratic influences. Federal Services Impasses Panel settles disputes during contract negotiations.

a union organizer has just approached you about joining the union. List the benefits and the disadvantages from joining the union. Would you join? Substantiate your reasoning.

4. As a staff employee with the AFL-CIO, you have been requested to outline a national campaign to organize engineers. What are some basic considerations? List some ideas that might be used to carry out the campaign.

5. Why do so few members attend union meetings? Recommend changes in the organization and administration of local unions to increase member interest.

6. What subjects should be included in a training course for local union officials? How should the course be conducted? Who should conduct it, outsiders or union officials? Where should the sessions be held, at the union headquarters or in a separate location? Should the course be concentrated or divided into a series of short sessions? Discuss other aspects of the course's implementation.

Joe Belluci jumped about two feet off his plush chair as he read the telegram. "What are those guys in San Francisco up to?" he shouted.

"What's the trouble, Mr. Belluci?" Al Sneed, his assistant, asked.

"Trouble? Those characters in the San Francisco plant just gave the union an extra 50 cents an hour, that's the trouble!"

"Did they prevent the strike?"

"Of course they prevented the strike! For 50 cents an hour, no union in its right mind would go on strike! Wow—50 cents!" Joe slumped back in his chair. "Al, what's the matter with those guys we have in San Francisco? First, they complain that I stick my nose in their business too much, so I decentralize. They want to make their own decisions, so we let them. First, they get control over production, then sales, then accounting. Finally, they argue that they have to handle labor problems too. With the Teamsters, yet! I must've had rocks in my head to let them handle the negotiations on a local level." He lit his cigar for the fourth time.

"You have to admit that decentralization paid off, Mr. Belluci."

Joe turned around to stare at Al. "Sure it worked—net there was up from $65,000 in 1975 to $242,000 in 1978. The boys are working their pants off—and should, with that bonus system they talked me into in '74. But 50 cents—wow!"

Joe leaned back and stared at the ceiling. "I know the Teamsters man out there—boy, is he tough. We locked horns a couple of times back in the old days. Now, if I had just made sure that I was talking to him. . . ."

"Mr. Belluci, we've been through this a dozen times. You are now president of a firm with 19 plants in 14 cities spread all over the country—one plant in Canada, too, don't forget that. You have 1,800 men working for you. There are about 40 unions representing the men, and the labor law these days is so complex that even our lawyers aren't sure when we're legal and when we're not. You can't expect to sit down with every union man who comes along and negotiate—there aren't enough hours in the day!"

"Yeah, but do we have to turn over bargaining authority to those do-gooders in San Francisco? Boy . . . now that bunch in Newark are different. They are tough, believe me! Remember when the electricians wanted 90 cents last year, plus all those fringe benefits? You couldn't move Jacobs."

"Yes, and he had the plant closed for two months, too."

"Yeah, but he was tough. Remember, they settled for 10 cents. Now we're going to face a whole bunch of demands for 50 cents, all over the place. Those union boys pick up something like this so fast it isn't even funny. The one I really worry about is Smith, up in Seattle. He's chicken, and when those union guys start pushing, he'll cave in early. Let's get a cable off to him saying that 30 cents is tops."

"But that would be against your own policy, Mr. Belluci. Remember what you said last year about decentralization."

"Yeah," Joe sighed, "I remember."

Problems

1. Should labor relations be decentralized? Why or why not?

2. Would you advise Mr. Belluci to send the wire?

3. What would be the impact of sending a wire? Of not sending a wire?

Case Problem 2

STUDENT UNIONS

During the late 1960s there was student unrest on many campuses. All sorts of grievances, real and imagined, were presented as demands to administrations, and frequently campuses had demonstrations, occasional violence, sit-ins, and occupation of administrative offices. Grievances typically revolved around the following points:

1. Demands for changes in student rules, such as curfews, visiting privileges, lockout times in dormitories, and so on.

2. Demands for more student participation in decisions directly affecting them, such as grading, graduation rules, flunking out, new courses, and so on.

3. Civil rights demands, such as new courses in black problems, more black professors, more black students, the end of discrimination in fraternities and dormitories, and so on.

4. Objections to certain types of activities, such as military recruiting on campus, visits by the CIA, and visits by companies making materials for the war in Vietnam.

Some students suggested that they form a union similar to the trade unions to fight for their rights. After all, they argued, most young people nowadays spend at least two years in college, and they should have the opportunity to bargain for their rights, just like industrial workers. Many of these students felt that if a well-financed, well-organized campaign were begun, most students could be unionized very quickly, and students would, at long last, get the rights to which they are entitled.

Problems

1. Do you agree with these students' arguments? What similarities do you see between being a student and being an industrial worker or craftsman?

2. What differences are there between students and workers? Would any of these differences create problems in organizing such a union?

3. In addition to the demands cited in the grievances, what other benefits would you seek if you were the person representing the union?

4. Which of the four demands, if instituted, could be construed as fringe benefits? Which ones are basically nonfringe issues? Why?

Notes

1. Bureau of National Affairs, *Labor Relations Yearbook–1976* (Washington, D.C.: Bureau of National Affairs, 1977), p. 246.

2. "A Boycott Battle to Win the South," *Business Week,* December 6, 1976, pp. 80–82.

3. *Testimony—Justice vs. J. P. Stevens* (New York: Amalgamated Clothing and Textile Workers Union, AFL-CIO, CLC, 1977), p. 10.

4. J. P. Stevens and Co., Inc. *Straightening Things Out* (New York: J. P. Stevens, February 15, 1977).

5. Amalgamated Clothing and Textile Workers Union, "Amalgamated Clothing and Textile Workers Sign National Settlement with J. P. Stevens Co.: Foresee 'Harmonious, Productive Relationship'," News release, October 19, 1980.

6. William F. Gutivein and Rayburn Watkins, *Preventive Medicine in Labor Relations* (Frankfort, Ky.: Associated Industries of Kentucky, 1960), p. 7.

7. See, for example, Jeanne M. Brett, "Why Employees Want Unions," *Organizational Dynamics,* Spring 1980, pp. 47–59, and Thomas Kochan's Department of Labor Study, "How American Workers View Labor Unions," in *Monthly Labor Review,* April 1979.

8. "The 1977 Steel Settlement," *Steel Labor,* May 1977, p. 14.

9. Jack Stieber, "The UAW Public Review Board: An Examination and Evaluation" in Walter Fogel and Archie Keingartner, eds., *Democracy and Public Review* (Belmont, Calif.: Wadsworth, 1968), p. 333.

10. A. H. Raskin, "The Labor Movement Must Start Moving," *Harvard Business Review,* January-February 1970, p. 109.

11. "Labor's Image Slips Further, Even Among Its Own Members, a Poll Shows," *Wall Street Journal,* May 3, 1977, p. 1.

12. Thomas Kochan, "How American Workers View Labor Unions," *Monthly Labor Review,* April 1979, pp. 23–31.

13. "Labor Worries over Decline in Its Influence," *New York Times,* Sunday, January 4, 1981, p. E3.

14. U. S. Bureau of Labor Statistics, *Directory of National Unions and Employee Associations, 1979* (Washington, D.C.: U.S. Government Printing Office, 1980), p. 59.

15. U. S. Bureau of Labor Statistics, News release: *Labor Union and Employee Association Membership—1978,* September 3, 1979, p. 6.

16. "Doctors, Nurses, Teachers—Why More Are Joining Unions," *U. S. News and World Report,* November 10, 1975, p. 61–62.

17. Dennis Chamot, "Professional Employees Turn to Unions," *Harvard Business Review,* May-June 1976, pp. 119–27.

18. Arch Patton, "Ideas and Trends," *Business Week,* May 24, 1976, p. 20.

19. U. S. Bureau of Labor Statistics, *Directory of National Unions and Employee Associations,* pp. 69–70.

20. "Labor's Jerry Wurf: Can He Shut Down Your Town?" *Nation's Business,* March 1975, p. 42.

21. Lee C. Shaw, "The Development of State and Federal Laws," in Sam Fagoria, ed., *Public Workers and Public Unions* (Englewood Cliffs, N.J.: Prentice-Hall, 1972), pp. 22–23.

22. Daniel D. Cook, "Will Labor Fulfill its Destiny?" *Industry Week,* March 14, 1977, p. 53.

23. "Why Unions Have an Urge to

Merge," *Business Week,* July 15, 1977, p. 94.

24. "Kirkland Takes Reins, Urges Key Unions to Join," *The Washington Post,* November 20, 1979, p. A-2.

25. Wiley I. Beavers, "Employee Relations Without a Union," in Dale Yoder and Herbert G. Heneman, Jr., eds., *Employee and Labor Relations, ASPA Handbook of Personnel and Industrial Relations,* vol. III (Washington, D.C.: Bureau of National Affairs, 1976), pp. 7–82.

Chapter Eleven
Collective Bargaining

It was 10:30 P.M. A strike was scheduled for 12:01 if a contract settlement could not be reached. The federal mediator had brought the parties together on all but one major issue—management's right to have repair work performed by outside contractors. The union insisted on sabbaticals for senior employees in return for the freedom to contract out. The company refused. The union went on strike.

The situation described here occurs frequently in bargaining, but it does not encompass all the variables included in a **collective bargaining** situation. What, then, is collective bargaining? How does it function? What issues are involved? In what ways does collective bargaining influence the personnel process? This chapter will focus on the answers to these questions.

Collective Bargaining Defined

Collective bargaining lies at the heart of the personnel process. Whenever employee-employer relationships involve unions, collective bargaining establishes, administers, and enforces agreements between the parties. Harold W. Davey defines collective bargaining as:

A continuing institutional relationship between an employer entity (governmental or private) and a labor organization (union or association) representing exclusively a defined group of employees of said employer (appropriate bargaining unit) concerned with the negotiation, administration, interpretation, and enforcement of written agreements covering

LEARNING OBJECTIVES

1. To know the various types of collective bargaining relationships.
2. To know the process of negotiations.
3. To be familiar with the role of the National Labor Relations Board in collective bargaining.
4. To know the various issues in collective bargaining.
5. To understand the bases for conflict in collective bargaining and the methods of settlement.

joint understandings as to wages or salaries, rates of pay, hours of work, and other conditions of employment.[1]

This definition emphasizes a continuing relationship because collective bargaining is ongoing and dynamic. In this relationship, management (private sector) can bargain on anything it wants to, but it is only required to bargain on wages, hours, and working conditions, which include most *personnel* policy issues, but very few in other areas, for example, pricing, product development, company expansion, market strategy, and so forth. The resolution of problems between union and management is a process of day-to-day living under a negotiated agreement.

A Situational Model of Bargaining Relationships

Figure 11.1 graphically depicts the variables that influence collective bargaining relationships. These variables interact individually and collectively to determine the collective bargaining situation. The model focuses on the parties (union and management representatives) continuously bargaining for advantages through negotiation, contract administration, and enforcement. The strategies of the parties are affected by issues, state of the economy, union-management agreement, precedents, public sentiment, labor laws, politics, and ideologies.

PARTIES

Collective bargaining essentially involves two parties, labor and management. Aside from such factors as individual attitudes and the size, structure, and nature of the respective organizations, relationships between the parties fall into two major classifications, continuing relationships and power relationships.

CONTINUING RELATIONSHIPS.   In day-to-day contract discussions there are four classifications of continuing relationships:

1. Conflict or overt hostility, characterized by constant strife and often accompanied by violence. Few relationships reach this extreme today, though rioting, bloodshed, and property damage have occurred during some strikes.
2. Reluctant toleration, when employers have to recognize bargaining agents, but either no agreement is reached or else concessions are won only after long and costly court battles.
3. Accommodation, when parties take a lethargic attitude of laissez-faire. Employers make concessions to avoid altercations, and unions do not assert their full power.
4. Cooperation, when management and unions work together for mutual benefit. The products of such relationships are prolonged industrial peace,

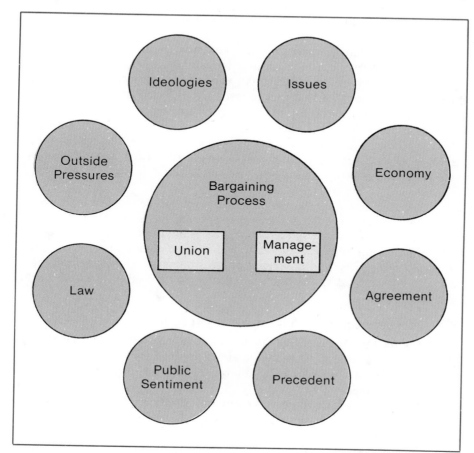

Figure 11.1
Model of Collective
Bargaining

innovative solutions to human resource and production problems, and a high level of good will. The American Motors-UAW agreement is an excellent example. It includes a provision for an American Motors-UAW conference to discuss philosophies, needs, and common responsibilities to the community. In addition, their Progress Sharing Plan compensates employees for improved productivity.[2] The attitude of the parties is that working together is in the interest of both labor and management.

POWER RELATIONSHIPS.   The relative strength of each party helps set the tone of the bargaining relationship. The union's right to strike and the company's prerogative to manage are obvious factors. Strikes have both positive and negative effects on collective bargaining. Though they can do irreparable damage to the bargaining relationship, strikes, or even the threat of them, offer a positive element. Bargaining representatives faced with the curtailment of production are more likely to make a conscientious effort at settlement.

But management maintains the prerogative to run the business, unless it abdicates that right through careless bargaining. A strong **management-rights clause** reserves for management either a list of specific rights, or else the general freedom to manage if not restricted by specified exceptions. Such clauses provide the basis for management's insistence (at the bargaining table) that matters within their authority be excluded from negotiation. Likewise, a clear definition of management's domain guards against union attempts to gain, through other means (e.g., grievances and arbitration), what they cannot win in bargaining sessions.

THE PERSONNEL MANAGER'S ROLE.   Personnel managers are key to the bargaining relationship. Often they represent management at the bargaining table either in the role of spokespersons or as advisors to the management negotiating team (collecting and analyzing data, evaluating proposals, framing counterproposals, and observing union strategies). The personnel manager also advises and assists line management on the administration of the agreement.

COLLECTIVE BARGAINING—THEORETICAL ASPECTS

The bargaining process includes the actual negotiating, which involves interactions between union and company representatives. The methodology and techniques of conducting bargaining sessions are discussed separately later in the chapter.

In their behavioral theory Walton and McKersie identify several sub-processes in labor negotiations.[3] Negotiation whereby the gain of one party represents a loss to the other is called **distributive bargaining.** A joint problem-solving approach, working toward mutually beneficial solutions, is labeled **integrative bargaining.** Attitudes (e.g., trust and fear) and social relationships (e.g., competitiveness and cooperation) are changed and restructured during negotiation.

Goodman and Sandberg[4] have developed a contingency model which, though it is theoretical, does attempt to identify the link between various behaviors involved in labor relations and organizational strategies. The model seeks to predict labor relations strategy (i.e., labor yields to management or vice versa, there is accommodation, or a strike is likely) according to alternative matches of company resources and union aggressiveness. Union aggressiveness, according to the authors, would depend on grievance frequency and settlement ratio, work stoppages and slowdown frequencies. Company resources would depend on existence of mutual-aid pacts within industry, ability of the company to withstand shutdown in terms of short-term debt, fixed costs, inventory depth, vulnerability of substitute goods, and other industry-specific costs of discontinuity. Thus, in applying the model, if there is extreme union aggressiveness that is met by strong corporate resources, a strike is likely. While it is obvious that this model does not consider external variables (e.g., the economy, government policy) it does serve to demonstrate that planning can be applied to the development of collective bargaining (labor relations) strategy.

APPROACHES TO BARGAINING. The particular approach to bargaining the parties take depends on influences too complicated to isolate. Nevertheless, the approach can generally be classified as belonging to one of four major groups.

1. *Crisis bargaining*, the first type of negotiation, occurs when the parties face an impending contract expiration and usually the threat of a strike or lockout. Management and union work frantically in tense bargaining marathons to reach a settlement before the deadline.

2. *Continuous bargaining* is an attempt to avoid crisis situations. As soon as one agreement is signed both parties begin informal study and negotiations on the next one. The major steel producers use this approach through joint committees that meet throughout the contract period and make recommendations to the bargaining spokesmen well in advance of actual negotiations. This approach helps eliminate strikes.

3. In *initiative bargaining* the company makes its final offer at the outset and maintains a firm position. Unless a company can withstand union pressures, including a prolonged strike, this approach is ill-advised.

4. *Joint approaches* truly embody integrative bargaining. They bring parties together through the identification and discussion of common objectives. Essential to the success of such programs is a strong desire on the part of both management and labor to make them work. Joint approaches sometimes use committees to study problems and recommend solutions or employ third parties as mediators, fact finders, or arbitrators.

THE AGREEMENT

The **agreement** between the parties is the result of negotiations, but assumptions about the nature of agreements can influence the behavior of the parties during the negotiations themselves. One view considers the agreement a restrictive document. This residual-rights concept of collective bargaining maintains that management may act unilaterally except as restricted by the contract. Residualists tend to regard collective bargaining as an intrusion on management's prerogative to run the business, and they are often defensive and negative toward unions.

Conversely, unionists view the agreement as a vehicle for consultation with employers. The consultative concept envisions collective bargaining as a joint decision-making process that provides an opportunity for management and labor to work toward solving problems of mutual concern. Proponents of this view believe unions have resources that can help accomplish organizational objectives. Consequently, relationships between parties with consultative attitudes are more likely to be cooperative in nature.

PRECEDENT

Day-to-day working relationships frequently shape the outcome of contract negotiations. Practices in the workshop often set precedents and result in concessions that unions were unable to gain in bargaining. A good example of this occurred on the assembly line of a lighting fixtures manufacturer. Industrial engineers had designed an assembly operation that, for maximum efficiency, required employees to work in a standing position. Shortly after the system's installation, several workers began to sit on crates while they worked. Although sitting reduced production efficiency, supervisors were lax in enforcing prescribed work methods. Eventually, almost all assemblers had crates or benches, and working while seated became an accepted practice. When the union demanded that the company provide stools for assembly workers, the company had no defense, despite the fact that the practice was inefficient, because a precedent had already been established.

Also, settlements in other organizations may establish precedents. In the trades, for instance, a ten percent wage increase and an additional paid holiday for plumbers will serve as a basis for a similar demand by electricians. For the same reason, Chrysler is concerned about the bargaining results at General Motors.

PUBLIC SENTIMENT

Contemporary collective bargaining procedures have been criticized for insensitivity to public welfare. Construction-industry bargaining is a good example. Craft unions and contractor associations have agreed to exorbitant wage increases that result in skyrocketing prices, which consumers have to pay. Historically, whenever labor-management disputes threaten the health, welfare, or security of a large segment of the population, the federal government intervenes through injunctions, jawboning, or even takeovers.

OUTSIDE PRESSURES

Although the influence of elected public officials on collective bargaining is slight, the political pressures from union and management constituencies do have significant impact. Union negotiators are perhaps subject to greater constraints than their management counterparts, since union members elect them and ratify their proposals. In addition, they must answer to the international union.

The company negotiator's performance is determined by the wishes of top management and, to a lesser degree, by the requests of the staff and lower-level supervisors.

IDEOLOGIES

The ideologies and beliefs of the negotiators and the institutions they represent influence collective bargaining. The personal styles of the chief negotiators translate into ideologies and are accepted in that form by other members of the organization. These interacting beliefs affect the outcome of negotiations. Management's ideology has traditionally emphasized its prerogative to guide the destiny of the enterprise. This view naturally clashes with basic union values that consider worker interests and social welfare paramount. But over the years, increased agreement about many fundamental values and issues has contributed to more positive union-management relations. Both parties have been supporting such objectives as minimizing layoffs, increasing efficiency and productivity, softening the impact of pollution-control legislation, fighting imports, curbing inflation, and even urging tax breaks for business. But this cooperative ideological spirit began to fade with the bitter fights on labor-law reform, which management viewed as punitive and labor construed as merely procedural. The defeat of the common-situs picketing bill in Congress in 1977 created animosity between contractors and their unions, and resulted in the breakdown of a number of joint projects.[5] Whether or not other common objectives will override these mounting resentments remains to be seen.

ISSUES

The nature of the bargaining issues also influences the behavior of the parties. The initial exchange of demands includes cover-up or trade-off issues that the parties can offer later as concessions against hard-core issues. The union might initially demand a union shop clause, intending to exchange it later for an additional ten cents per hour. Sometimes negotiators introduce issues solely to facilitate future bargaining; they may introduce a demand without expecting a concession, but hoping to make it seem less outrageous or less novel when reintroduced in subsequent years, thus increasing the likelihood of a concession. Many pension plans and productivity-based compensation improvements evolved in this manner.

Distinguishing between trade-off issues and hard-core demands that could break down negotiations is crucial to the outcome of bargaining. Skill and experience alone do not guarantee that the issues can be separated, because the distinctions are rarely clear cut, even to those who make the demands. As negotiations proceed and the parties debate the issues, the more serious matters solidify. Some insight can be derived from negotiations in the same industry or in other industries with the same union. A pattern of hard-core issues emerges when the bargaining parties consistently push specific issues. Negotiators can greatly reduce the possibility of a breakdown in negotiations by focusing their attention on the hard-core issues.

ECONOMY

The state of the national economy as well as the economic health of the specific company or industry affect the conduct of negotiations and the continuing bargaining relationship. In a tight economy, a concerted push for higher wages is less likely, especially if the pay boost would tend to be inflationary.

Stagflation—a phenomenon that characterized the 1970s, when there was substantial inflation in an environment of stagnating or deteriorating economic activity—provides a case in point. In this kind of economy, workers push for increases that are high enough to preserve purchasing power in the face of inflation, yet are not so high as to aggravate the shaky economy— and thereby cause further loss of jobs.[6] But unions still insist that wages maintain pace with price hikes. And different unions within the same industry are extremely sensitive to compensation improvements won by some and not others. If a segment of the work force they represent falls behind, they will demand in subsequent negotiations that their wages catch up. If the longshoremen get a 10 percent increase, the maritime union will want at least as much. The union must also consider the size of its strike fund and other sources of money that could support the striking members over a prolonged period.

Companies, too, must consider economic conditions, especially in the future, because that is when wages negotiated in the present must be paid. The company must ascertain, based on present economic conditions and the long-term business outlook, its ability to pay. It must also calculate the extent to which price increases can absorb additional labor costs without placing the company at a competitive disadvantage or incurring public wrath. Negotiators must weigh these considerations against the company's ability to withstand a strike. Can other plants take up the production slack? Are finished-goods inventories sufficient to supply customers during a cessation of operations? A company producing a diversity of products in various locations is less vulnerable to a strike than a highly concentrated one negotiating with a single union.

LAW

The final variable in the model is labor legislation. Federal laws in particular govern collective bargaining by directing the parties to negotiate in good faith and to establish ground rules for their continuing relationship. The basic law concerning collective bargaining is the National Labor Relations

Act as amended by the Taft-Hartley Act (Labor-Management Relations Act). The Railway Labor Act contains similar provisions governing air and rail transportation. Related labor laws were summarized in Table 10.2. Provisions of the act cover union certification, **unfair labor practices** of employers and unions, strike regulation, and other aspects such as administration and enforcement.

Uninterrupted production is in the interest of the country's economy. One basic purpose of the Taft-Hartley Act is to achieve this goal. For as its preamble states:

It is the purpose and policy of this Act, in order to promote the full flow of commerce, to prescribe the legitimate rights of both employees and employers in their relations affecting commerce, to provide *orderly and peaceful procedures for preventing the interference by either* with the legitimate rights of the other, to protect the rights of individual employees in their relations with labor organizations whose activities affect commerce, to define and proscribe practices on the part of labor and management which affect commerce and are inimical to the general welfare, and to protect the *rights of the public in connection with labor disputes affecting commerce.* [Emphasis added.]

CERTIFICATION

The NLRA recognized the right of employees to form or join labor organizations and to bargain collectively through representatives of their own choosing. The act specifies a procedure for certifying bargaining units and delineates the actions employers can take during the union's organizing campaign.

UNION ORGANIZING CAMPAIGN.   Within the limits of the law unions follow a typical pattern in their drive to become the elected bargaining representative of an organization's employees. Nonunion organizations will, of course, expend considerable effort to ward off organizing attempts and remain union-free.

Union organizers make initial contact either in response to an employee request or through their own initiative. They try to convince at least one worker from each department to serve on an in-plant committee that contacts other employees and provides overall support for the union drives. Shortly after the initial contact, organizers invite all employees to regular meetings. Here, the union organizers attempt to convince workers that the union can fulfill specific needs and correct work-related problems and concerns. For example, if the organizers have identified a problem of workers being exposed to safety and health hazards, they can highlight the role of the union safety committee and its rights under the law (the Occupational Safety and Health Act). Or, if the organizers determine that workers are concerned with inconvenient or excessive hours they might point out that the union can negotiate specific work schedules with advanced notice requirements and premium pay for work outside the schedule. The organizers also cite general advantages of union membership such as a guarantee of fair treatment, and the satisfactions of associating with an organization dedicated to workers' welfare. This type of meeting is one of the most effective techniques for persuading workers to sign up for a union.

When the union obtains the signatures of at least 30 percent of eligible employees who have indicated their desire either to have the union represent them or to have an election to choose a union, the National Labor Relations Board (the National Mediation Board performs the same function under the Railway Labor Act) acts on the **petition.** During the ensuing period, usually 30 to 60 days, both parties attempt to influence the employees.

EMPLOYER FREE SPEECH. Imaginative employers have considerable latitude in creatively countering union organizing attempts. To counter the union drive, employers have the right to send letters to employees and their families and to talk with workers, individually and in groups, on company time, up to 24 hours prior to the election. They can lawfully express any of the following views, as long as they do not threaten reprisals or force, or promise benefits: (Note: Employer free speech does *not* extend to federal agencies.)

1. They can point out the benefits and advantages the workers presently have. They may even point out that all benefits would have to be renegotiated if a bargaining relationship were established.

2. They can set forth the union's record on violence and corruption (if such is the case) through reprints of news releases or citations of factual data. They can calmly describe the union's philosophy toward integration or other controversial issues when the union's stand runs contrary to the workers' sentiments.

3. Employers may state the costs of union membership including initiation fees, dues, and assessments, and also point out the possibility of fines against union members for failure to comply with union rules and constitutional provisions.

4. Employers may emphatically state that they prefer not to have a union in the plant.

5. They may predict possible consequences if the union wins (e.g., the loss of wages under strike conditions).

THE REPRESENTATION ELECTION. The NLRB conducts secret-ballot **representation elections** according to strict standards that let employees freely indicate if they want to be represented in collective bargaining. Usually, the NLRB regional director decides election details such as time, place, and notification of election, and obtains the agreement of the parties on these matters.[7]

All employees in the bargaining unit who have a substantial continuing interest in their employment conditions are generally eligible to vote. The only stipulation is that the employee must have worked during a certain period, usually the payroll period immediately preceding the day the election is set. But those who vote must be part of the **appropriate bargaining unit,** which is determined in a pre-election investigation and/or hearing conducted by the Board. The appropriate bargaining unit is a grouping of jobs or positions in which two or more employees share common employment interests and conditions and which may reasonably be grouped together for collective bargaining purposes. The NLRB's determination of the appropriate bargaining unit can often influence the outcome of an election. For example, an employer with a facility containing both sales and production employees might wish to combine the two groups if it is felt that the sales people would vote against the union. Each party employs strategy to have the Board designate an appropriate bargaining unit that is most likely to vote for its side. Also, the Board has certain guidelines for designating units. For example, guards are not included in units containing nonguards; professionals are usually not mixed with non-professionals and managerial employees who develop and enforce employer policy are usually excluded from any unit. An interesting case in point is the U.S. Supreme Court's decision involving a Yeshiva University professor who sought union representation. The Court (in NLRB v. Yeshiva University, February 20, 1980) ruled that the professors could not form a union because they exercised absolute managerial authority in academic matters. They decided course offerings, teaching methods, matriculation and graduation standards, and the teaching schedule. This decision will undoubtedly have far reaching consequences for collective bargaining efforts in higher education, but for our discussion here, it clearly points up the strong opposition of the courts to allowing managers to engage in collective bargaining with their employers.[8] In the election employees have a choice of one or more bargaining representatives or no representative at all. To be certified as a bargaining agent an individual (individuals willing to represent employees can be certified) or union must receive a majority of the valid votes cast. A tie results in no union.

UNFAIR LABOR PRACTICES

Section 8 of the Taft-Hartley Act lists unfair labor practices of both employers and unions in the collective bargaining relationship. It prohibits such unfair practices because they are considered disruptive to maintaining labor peace. Consequently, charges of unfair labor practices can be filed against either party. When a complaint is filed the NLRB can conduct a hearing to decide if an unfair labor practice was committed. Then it can issue an order telling the party to cease and desist the practice and take affirmative action to correct the situation.

Employees, companies, and unions are committing an unfair labor practice if they interfere with an employee's right to organize or to bargain; refuse to bargain; or discriminate against employees because of union membership or refusal to join a union. The following are some of the specific activities cited by the law as unfair labor practices.

1. In an attempt to prevent union organization, employers would have employees sign a **yellow-dog contract**—an agreement stating that the employee would not join a labor organization or attempt to assist in organizing one. Such an arrangement has long been outlawed, but the NLRA continues to recognize discrimination for union activity as an unfair labor practice.

2. **Hot Cargo agreements** provide that employees would not be required by their employer to handle or work on goods or materials going to, or coming from, an employer designated by the union as unfair. A 1959 amendment to the Act forbade employers and unions from entering into such an agreement.

3. **Secondary boycotts** are prohibited by the Act. A secondary boycott occurs if a union has a dispute with Conpany A, and to further the dispute it forces Company B to stop handling products of Company A or to cease doing business altogether with Company A. Company A is the primary employer; Company B is the secondary employer, hence the term secondary boycott.

4. The Act also forbids *featherbedding* because it involves an attempt to cause an employer to pay for services which are not performed.

THE ROLE OF THE NATIONAL LABOR RELATIONS BOARD (NLRB)

The principal agency responsible for administering national labor relations is the NLRB. Since its inception in 1935 it has filled two basic functions: investigating, adjudicating, and prosecuting unfair labor practice charges (a regulatory function); and conducting elections to certify bargaining representatives (a service function).

The Board and its policies and practices have constantly suffered severe criticism from both labor and management. Congress intended it to be an impartial, quasi-judicial administrative tribunal, but it sometimes is a far cry from this. Bargaining parties have attempted to influence presidential appointments to the board to increase the likelihood of decisions in their favor. Much of the criticism levied at the NLRB stems from the nature of the law it administers. As Davey characterizes the board, "It is charged with the unenviable task of administering a statute that is in a real sense schizophrenic."[9] The NLRB was initially pro-labor in order to establish employees' rights to bargain collectively. Then Taft-Hartley amended and balanced the act with restraints on unions. Consequently, the Taft-Hartley Act was dubbed a slave-labor law by the labor movement. Thus, the NLRB is in the difficult position of having to administer controversial and contradictory laws under political pressure from all sides.

The Bargaining Process

In **negotiating** sessions both parties bargain for concessions that will help them achieve their objectives—objectives that are often more the personal aspirations of individual negotiators than the goals of their constituents. The procedures they use in arriving at an agreement depend on the situation, since there is no one best way to negotiate a contract. Collective bargaining is an art that demands the talents of skilled professionals. But some of the steps in negotiating are common enough that describing them can provide an overview of the bargaining process.

NOTIFICATION TO REOPEN THE CONTRACT

For existing bargaining relationships, the Taft-Hartley Act requires that parties desiring termination or modification of a contract follow certain steps. Sixty days prior to contract expiration, they must provide written notification of their desire to terminate or modify. They must include an offer to meet with the other party to discuss the terms of a new agreement. If the parties fail to reach an agreement within a specified period of time, the law averts a strike or lockout, temporarily at least, through mediation and a 60-day cooling-off period.

PREPARATION FOR BARGAINING

The importance of careful preparation for negotiations cannot be overstressed. As soon as a contract is signed, both parties should begin preparing for the next one. Management attaches great importance in preparing for bargaining, though there is no single best method of accomplishing the task.[10] The extent of preparation depends on the bargaining requirements of the parties and the resources available for research. Obviously, a small trucking firm dealing with a Teamster's local does not prepare as extensively as General Motors does to negotiate with the UAW. Some of the preparation methods and techniques conmon to both large and small organizations are summarized below.

GATHERING INFORMATION. During the course of a contract, organizations poll staff and line managers for their recommendations on changes. In periodic conferences, managers discuss recommendations, probe the rea-

sons behind them, and synthesize numerous opinions into concrete proposals. In addition, researchers analyze grievances filed during the course
of the contract to spotlight problem areas and gain additional insights into
contract clauses that may be difficult or expensive to administer. And day-
to-day shop practices are often reviewed to uncover difficulties arising from
contract administration and to determine if contract language or specific
provisions are inhibiting efficient production. Substantial data are readily
available for analyses relevant to collective bargaining. Economic forecasts
are published by financial and academic institutions and can help determine
ability to pay. Statistics on unemployment and inflation (the Consumer Price
Index) provide insight on general economic conditions. These and related
data can be obtained from federal agencies (Bureau of Labor Statistics, Commerce Department, and others) and the state government. The information
is valuable for bargaining preparation as well as for monitoring the effectiveness of various clauses and programs previously negotiated.

REVIEW OF CONTRACT CLAUSES.   Labor relations staff people usually
review the agreement article by article to decide which clauses to demand
removal of (especially those that curtail management's rights). Then they
write their proposals in language beneficial to management's position. Too
frequently, employers fail to insist on provisions they previously traded off
or conceded. Unions persist in their demands; management should, too.

ECONOMIC STUDIES.   Bargaining is more objective when the parties
base their arguments on reliable data. Most issues, because of their increasing
complexity, now require more thorough preparation than they formerly did.
Research staffs for unions and companies supply factual material and exhibits
to substantiate their respective positions. Fortunately, a wealth of data is
available from the Bureau of Labor Statistics (BLS), the Federal Reserve
Bank, and numerous academic institutions and research organizations. Particularly valuable to negotiators are BLS surveys on wage rates for selected
occupations, industries, and labor market areas; comparative characteristics
of agreements; schedules of negotiation dates; and a variety of other data.
The more thoroughly the parties prepare, the better equipped they will be
to make and respond to proposals as they approach the coming bargaining
sessions.

EXCHANGE OF DEMANDS

Following notification to terminate or modify the agreement the parties exchange demands. Usually, the union submits a list of proposals to the
company, which weighs each demand in light of its previously gathered
data. Frequently, the union includes an abundance of blue-sky proposals

intended to put the company on the defensive (later the union will trade them for concessions on more practical issues). It is advisable for the company to prepare suitable counterproposals, including a sufficient number of demands to use as trade-offs.

GETTING READY TO NEGOTIATE

Conscientious negotiators specify their objectives, detailing what they wish to gain in the bargaining sessions. The objectives should include optimum and minimally acceptable resolutions for each proposal and for the overall settlement. Using this approach, negotiators clearly understand the parameters acceptable to them and to their constituents.

An integral part of management's objective setting is pricing every union demand and company counterproposal. Analysts must determine a cents-per-hour or overall dollar cost for all items, including subjective ones. Even though it is extremely difficult to determine the value of an arbitration clause or to measure the cost of conceding a union security clause, management must attempt to quantify them. Careful attention to costs adds objectivity to arguments on issues and keeps parties conscious of the relative importance they should place on each proposal.

With the opposing party's demands in hand, negotiators can build their cases against unacceptable proposals and formulate arguments to support their own suggestions. Also, they can determine what concessions they are willing to make. The side making a concession generally makes it clear that it expects one in return. Sometimes, too, negotiators work to remove a concession made in previous negotiations (such as a contract clause that has proven unsatisfactory).

As the first scheduled meeting approaches, both sides muster support. The union holds meetings and uses bulletins and personal contact to build rank-and-file enthusiasm. The company directs its public-relations efforts to winning community support and enlisting employee sentiment by presenting its side of the story. Both parties use clever tactics to influence employees and the public, since their support can be a powerful force in negotiations. For example, during one strike resulting from a bargaining impasse, the local community had become antagonistic toward the union's prolonged strike because it adversely affected the local economy. Community leaders and union members joined forces to pressure the union into a settlement. One day the union spokesman approached the company representative and proposed arbitration of the unresolved issue. The company strongly opposed allowing outsiders (the arbitrators) to determine its destiny. But the union spokesman persisted and offered to allow a three-member arbitration panel consisting solely of business executives to rule on the issue. This was a clever move, for all three arbitrators were customers of the company, and the union representative knew the company would never place its clients in the difficult position of judging one of their suppliers. The following day's newspaper carried the headline, "company refuses union proposal to have businessmen settle strike." The resulting shift in public sentiment forced the company to concede.

BARGAINING SESSIONS

Bargaining is a give-and-take process that has been variously characterized as a poker game, horse trading, power politics, a rational process, and a heated debate. Perhaps there is some of each of these elements in bargaining, yet no amount of description can capture the true flavor of negotiating sessions.

Fundamental to all bargaining is the shifting of positions, which Dunlop has aptly described:

> If the collective bargaining process is to be understood, attention must be directed particularly to the problems involved in changing a position and the process by which these changes are made. Parties starting far apart must change their positions if there is to be any agreement. But changing a position is difficult because it may harden the other side and create the hope, if not the expectation, that the moving party will go all the way and close any gap between the two sides. It is not easy for a negotiator to drop a demand he has been arguing for with great enthusiasm without casting some doubt on positions taken on other issues as well. Changing positions is at the heart of collective bargaining process, and the way in which a negotiator handles these problems distinguishes a skilled veteran from a novice.[11]

Negotiators have individual, yet deliberate styles of bargaining, for example, aggressive, patient, assertive, tenacious, situational, or other; but no particular style seems to be preferred. However, the consensus of negotiators is that patience and avoidance of passive behavior are necessary characteristics for successful bargaining. This is understandable in light of the give and take nature of most sessions.[12]

NEGOTIATING TACTICS.   When the issues are finally whittled down to the hard-core items, the nitty-gritty bargaining begins. At this point a variety of tactics are brought to bear.[13]

Boulwarism was a popular tactic of the General Electric Company in its negotiations with the electrical unions many years ago. Though it is seldom used in major negotiations today (in fact, it is considered an unfair labor practice), there is still some evidence of the application. Usually the company will make no proposal initially. Rather it listens to the union and adds its arguments to the extensive economic analysis it has prepared. Then at a selected time before the deadline, it makes a final offer and refuses to accept proposals that would increase the total cost. This tactic is subject to severe criticism because it sharply curtails the union's role. Similarly, local unions frequently have entered negotiations with money demands and simply sat tight until they were granted.[14]

In *game playing* a few representatives from each side hold a secret meeting prior to the official opening of negotiations, and they reach an agreement on the essential issues. When negotiations begin these same individuals put on a sham battle including table thumping, name-calling, and the usual dramatics of crisis-type bargaining. After both sides of the bargaining committee seem to be properly conditioned, the deal emerges gradually. Even without the game-playing tactics, principal negotiators often sound each other out away from the bargaining table and off-the-record. If a basically sound relationship exists, important matters that might otherwise undermine the negotiations if disclosed too early can be discussed in confidence. Veteran negotiator and mediator William Simkin admonishes that, "No individual is a good negotiator unless he understands the value and necessity of 'exploration in confidence' and of the timeliness in the development and disclosure of constructive solutions."[15]

Bluffing is a standard tactic whereby the negotiator attempts to gain a little more than he or she is willing to settle for—much the same as in poker playing. When haggling over the one fair wage, or the only reasonable length of a work day, or the only efficient way to assign labor, one side is attempting to determine what the other is willing to settle for. For example, management tries to find the irreducible minimum wage increase that labor will accept, and the union attempts to ascertain the absolute maximum increase management is willing to agree on. The union threatens strike action; management pleads inability to pay. As the contract deadline approaches, both parties are forced toward some middle ground between their bluffing positions. If the union negotiator at this point repeats his strike threats, he had better mean them or his members will be working on management's terms tomorrow; if the employer stands firm on his latest offer, he must contend with the prospect of a strike. In essence, all bluffs are called by the contract deadline.[16]

SUBCOMMITTEE EXPLORATION. Throughout the bargaining process small committees usually explore avenues of agreement. Here the parties attempt to ascertain the areas where concessions are possible. They consider alternative packages that might yield a settlement. Perhaps the union will fail to mention some of its original demands, thereby indicating a willingness to drop them, or perhaps the company might express a willingness to concede a point. Then the parties begin moving toward an agreement.

INFORMAL SETTLEMENT.   Despite the popular notion of a smoke-filled room, with a full night of fist-pounding arguments that ends with one side submitting to the other, few contracts are initially settled at the bargaining table. The meeting of the minds usually occurs off-the-record at an informal meeting. A representative in a position of influence or leadership might suggest, over a drink or at a meal, a solution that leads to settlement. Negotiators might indicate that they are personally agreeable, but that they have no official sanction to speak for their committees and that they will try to convince the other committee members on the preliminary settlement. Numerous negotiation impasses have been broken in this way. One in particular comes to mind in which only one issue prevented settlement of a contract. The parties had given up any further attempts to sign an agreement, and the union representatives were returning by bus to their office. Recalling an offhand comment the union spokesman had made in private, the company representative thought of an idea that might settle the issue. He intercepted the bus, which by then was several miles out of town, called the union spokesman out of the bus to propose the settlement, and on the side of the main highway, shook hands in agreement. And sometimes agreements are settled by individuals other than the bargaining representatives themselves. Several years ago when long and arduous bargaining sessions failed to produce an agreement between a major metals producer and the Steelworkers Union, the company president and his long time personal friend, the international president of the union, met across the country and arrived at a settlement.

FORMAL SETTLEMENT.   To formalize the agreement, the organization's legal staff presents the settlement to the negotiating committee for acceptance. A **memorandum of agreement,** briefly listing terms, makes up the settlement. The lawyers explain this package and each of its terms to the committee, which then signs the memorandum, subject to ratification by the union rank-and-file. Later they prepare the contract language and incorporate it into the full agreement.

RATIFICATION.   Finally, the rank-and-file union members approve the terms of the new agreement. The leadership must convince the members to settle. They explain why certain issues were dropped, reasons for changing positions, what gains were won, and what concessions were made. This job is often a difficult task, especially when the union presents an adamant front on certain issues and later backs down. Ratification is a function of the members' confidence in their leaders. When they feel their negotiators have acted in the interest of the union members, there is little difficulty in ratifying the agreement, but the opposite is too often the case. When the membership fails to ratify the agreement, as is becoming more common in recent years, the union negotiators must return to the bargaining table and try to gain additional concessions.

Bargaining Issues

Negotiators can select from an unlimited number of possible issues; however, issues basic to most contracts are management rights, union security; conditions of work, hours, and wages; contract duration; and seniority.

MANAGEMENT RIGHTS

Since an employer's greatest fear is that operating efficiency and profits will be jeopardized by union activities, management negotiators generally demand a management-rights clause in an agreement. Certain subjects cited as management prerogatives are excluded from compulsory bargaining. The size of the work force, the corporate structure, products to be manufactured, production schedules, and direction of employees are subjects not usually discussed with the union.

The importance of the management clause is illustrated by the decision of the Sixth Circuit Court of Appeals in *Timken Roller Bearing Company* v. *NLRB*. In this case, the employer contended that subcontracting was a management prerogative under the terms of the collective bargaining agreement, so the company refused to confer with the union on a dispute about **subcontracting.** The court held that the employer's refusal to confer was not a refusal to bargain, since interpreting a management-rights clause was an issue to be settled by the grievance procedure.[17] The issue of subcontracting is, nevertheless, a negotiable issue.

A strong management-rights clause delineates as many prerogatives as management can secure concurrence on. In addition, it includes a statement to the effect that "the union recognizes these rights and responsibilities as belonging solely to the company, but they are by no means wholly inclusive."

UNION SECURITY

The union, in turn, seeks to protect its position by including union-security provisions in the contract. The Bureau of Labor Statistics, in analyzing 620 agreements covering 2,000 workers or more, found 84 percent contained union-security provisions.[18] Provisions vary from contract to contract and may take any of the following forms.

1. A *union shop* requires all employees to join the union within a specified time after hiring and to remain members as a condition of continued employment.

2. The *modified union shop* is essentially the same as a union shop except

that certain employee groups are exempted. For example, those who had not joined the union at the time the clause was negotiated might possibly be exempted.

3. In an *agency shop*, employees are not required to join the union, but they are required, as a condition of continuing employment, to pay a fixed monthly amount to the union, usually the equivalent of dues.

4. Under a *maintenance-of-membership agreement*, a condition of continued employment is that union members must maintain their membership for a specified period, usually the duration of the agreement.

The Taft-Hartley Act made closed shops unlawful. This type of union security clause had made union membership a condition of employment; applicants had to be dues-paying union members before they could be considered for employment, and they had to retain their membership as a condition of continued employment. Opposition to the closed shop was based on the feeling that making an employee's right to earn a living contingent upon union membership was a restriction of individual liberty.

It is understandable why unions opposed Section 14b of the Taft-Hartley Act, which permits states to pass laws prohibiting companies from requiring union membership as a condition of continued employment. These right-to-work laws, in effect in 20 states, nullify union-security agreements. Such laws guarantee an open-shop arrangement, permitting employees to abstain from union membership or payment of dues. Within right-to-work states, however, a few unions have successfully negotiated union-security clauses that are contingent upon the state's abolition of this law.

An integral part of union security is the **dues-checkoff** provision. Dues are the basis for the union's financial support, and the union administration must collect from the members. The company can alleviate the problem by agreeing to deduct dues automatically from each member's pay and remit the total to the union. Through dues checkoff, the company saves the union the burden of collecting each month from its members and spares it the embarrassment of reminding some members of their delinquency.

WORK CONDITIONS, HOURS, AND WAGES

Hours of work, compensation, benefits, and working conditions usually involve a monetary outlay by the employer and are, therefore, categorized as economic issues. The company's **ability to pay,** the business outlook, and the state of the economy are primary considerations in bargaining on economic issues. Recent changes in public policy (e.g., the 1970 wage-price freeze and OSHA) have influenced bargaining on these issues. Since Chapter 18 covers wages and Chapter 20 discusses benefits and relevant aspects of working conditions, there is little point in repeating them here. In general, compensation and working conditions are primary matters for union-management consideration at the bargaining table, but several new developments regarding hours of work need review at this point.

Countering the unions' push to reduce the work week and thereby spread the available work among more employees, companies have reacted with various schedules of flexible hours, most prominent being the **four-day, forty-hour week.** However, unions have opposed any moves to rearrange the work week without reducing the total hours of work. In any event, a flexible-hours work week seems to be logical for reducing overall working hours. If four ten-hour days result in productivity improvements, without undermining employees' mental or physical health, that is certainly a substantive basis for unions' arguments to raise wages or reduce working hours.

The advent of double digit inflation has caused both parties to make economic demands. Unions continue to push for *cost-of-living adjustments,* which tie automatic wage increases to inflation. Escalator clauses grant wage improvements proportionate to inflation rate (the Consumer Price Index) advances. By the same token, management is concerned with eroding profits and declining markets due to necessary price hikes that are inflation-related. Hence, management is making demands of its own, for example, insisting that workers hold the line on pay increases or face layoff, requiring that benefit plan participants share in premium costs, and so on.

CONTRACT DURATION

Employers want to stabilize production and minimize disruptions due to strikes. Prior to 1948, most agreements were of one-year duration, and companies and unions were constantly involved in contract negotiations and the turmoil and strike activity associated with them. The remedy lay in contracts of longer duration. In their 1948 negotiations, General Motors and the UAW agreed to a two-year contract, setting the pace for U.S. industry. Subsequently, the trend has been toward two- three- and even five-year contracts. The BLS reports that 98 percent of contracts have a duration of two years or more, with the most common being a three-year agreement.[19]

SENIORITY

A basic and long-established precept of the labor movement is that seniority should govern preference in promotions, layoffs, and recalls. Seniority is the length of continuous service in a defined unit, for example, company, plant, department, or classification—plant-wide seniority being the most common basis. Unions insist that seniority is the only objective basis for employee-placement decisions. Companies, on the other hand, contend that management's freedom to operate efficiently depends on the skills and abilities of the work force. Recognizing job performance and abilities, they claim, is an incentive to grow and improve, and is in the best interest of employees.

In contracts, this issue is usually resolved to: "ability and efficiency being substantially equal, seniority shall govern." This means that when there is little difference in the seniority of two employees under consideration, the choice can be made on the basis of a demonstrated difference in skills and abilities. When one employee is substantially senior to the other, however, length of service must prevail. (The EEO implications of seniority provisions were discussed in Chapter 6.)

PRODUCTIVITY

Unions and employers alike are concerned about productivity, because without advances in this area, it becomes difficult to raise the income and living standards of workers, to control inflation and to maintain a competitive edge for U.S. products in world markets. Individual firms have traditionally recorded productivity figures in terms of the volume of output compared to some volume of input, usually employee-hours. The U.S. Bureau of Labor Statistics records these data and compiles productivity measures for American business. Its figures reveal that employee output per hour of work has been slumping—the annual rate of increase averaged 3.1 percent from 1950–1967, but since then it has averaged only 1.6 percent.[20] Experts believe that production will rise an average of 2.4 to 2.7 percent until 1985, but it will take extraordinary efforts on the part of employees and employers to achieve even this small improvement.[21]

Recognizing this problem, the major steel companies and the Steelworkers Union negotiated a contract provision that established joint (union-management) advisory committees on productivity. Their purpose is to work cooperatively to improve productivity in order to meet the challenge posed by foreign competition. The committees discuss and consider such matters as: more efficient use of production time and facilities; reducing equipment breakdowns and delays; improving quality and reducing the need for reprocessing products; eliminating waste and negligent use of materials, supplies, and equipment; reducing excessive overtime; boosting employee morale; improving safety experience; and generally focusing employee awareness on productivity problems and the real threat of foreign competition.[22] The magnitude of the productivity problem is such that it will likely be a major bargaining issue in future negotiations throughout industry.

Initiatives in Labor-Management Cooperation

A study by the Department of Health, Education and Welfare revealed numerous joint union-management efforts to improve the quality of work life in America. Projects, in general, involve worker self-management in autonomous groups responsible for a total project. Jobs are redesigned to enrich the work itself. Work groups set their own goals, and there is open communication on costs, production, sales, and other matters relevant to the work. Employees rotate work assignments, even to the extent of moving from factory to nonfactory jobs, and pay is often based on the number of jobs workers can perform. The results have been gratifying: higher productivity, lower absenteeism, and so on.[23]

These projects emerge from joint discussion of matters of mutual interest that leads to cooperative efforts. Labor needs the job security and better wages that efficient organizations can provide; management needs creative ideas for improvements that people on the job can provide. Encouragement of participation, open communications, an environment of trust, a sense of equity, and individuation (the employees' perceptions of his/her ability to grow in terms of the individual's work situation), are basic to the implementation of quality of work life projects.[24]

An excellent example of such a project in operation is the Bolivar Project at Harmon International (Bolivar, Tennessee). The company is a major manufacturer of automobile mirrors, and the employees are represented by a local of the United Auto Workers (UAW). A joint union-management structure was established to encourage creativity and stimulate a constant two-way communication flow. Figure 11.2 depicts the structure: an advisory committee (the chief executive officer of the company, the

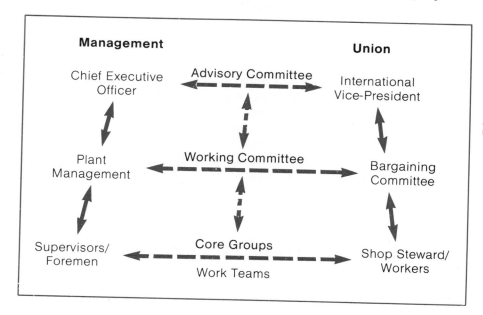

Figure 11.2
Bolivar Project Union-Management Organization Structure for a Quality of Worklife Project

Diagram from: Michael Maccoby, "The Bolivar Project—Productivity and Human Development" (unpublished, December 1977), p. 13.

international vice president of the union, and an outside consultant) reviews recommendations from the working committee (the plant managers and the bargaining committee). The core groups of the supervisors and the union stewards make recommendations, ranging from changes in the work process to group and individual problems, to the work committee, which secures advice and/or approval of the advisory committee. One outcome of the structure in operation is particularly noteworthy. The core groups (work team) were able to effect improvements in one area of the production process so that the operation could be completed in substantially less time. However, the tight economic condition of the company precluded any type of monetary reward. The team suggested that the employees be permitted tc attend training classes in the plant for the period of time that was saved—the nature of the courses was determined by the core groups and ranged from music to the technology of paint—and the arrangement was readily accepted by the higher level committees.[25]

It is apparent that future years will see substantially more of these kinds of union-management cooperative programs designed to improve the quality of work life. In fact, projects have become so widespread that the National Center for Productivity and Quality of Working Life has published a directory of joint committees.[26]

Contract Administration

In the day-to-day administration of contract provisions, personnel people play a key role. As the representatives of management, they advise line management on discipline matters (this subject was covered in Chapter 9), investigate and recommend answers to grievances, and help line supervisors establish working relationships with employees. In essence, the outcome of collective bargaining rests squarely on the shoulders of the personnel staff. In handling grievances personnel people deal with union stewards who usually file grievances on behalf of members or the union-at-large. The number of grievances filed (grievance load) is a major concern of personnel managers. So it is interesting to note that Dalton and Todor's study of grievance procedures found that the number of grievance procedures filed is largely a function of individual differences in union stewards. While other situational variables (supervision, nature of job, climate, policies of the union and management, etc.) affect filing, the manifest needs of stewards are a significant determinant of their behavior. These researchers concluded that there is a significant association between the number of grievances filed and need for achievement, dominance, affiliation, and autonomy.[27]

GRIEVANCE HANDLING

A grievance can be defined as anything about a job that the employee thinks is wrong or unfair—whether the employee is right or wrong. This definition does not include a judgment on the validity of the complaint. Thus, if an employee files a grievance that is absolutely baseless, the supervisor should still handle it in accordance with normal grievance-handling principles. The employee need only think he or she has been wronged or treated unfairly. This in itself does not give the grievance legitimacy, but it certainly makes it a real grievance. Also, there is literally no limitation on the subject matter of grievances, with the exception of matters specified in the management-rights clause. All other matters are proper subjects for grievances. Even the attitude of the supervisor can qualify as an issue.

STEPS IN THE GRIEVANCE PROCEDURE.   Almost without exception, union-management agreements contain a grievance clause. The number of steps and the method of handling grievances vary from contract to contract, but generally follow the pattern described below.

1. Either orally or in writing an employee submits a grievance to the first-line supervisor. A union official (shop steward or committeeperson) usually advises the employee. A written grievance should set forth a complete statement of the grievance, the facts on which it is based, and the remedy the employee desires.

2. If the grievance is not settled at the first step, the employee can appeal. At the next higher step, the employee, with the union representative, discusses the grievance with the appropriate department head. If the matter is not resolved at this step, it continues upward.

3. At this step, the plant manager, with the advice of the personnel department, confers with a committee of union representatives (usually the international representative and several grievance committeemen). As a general practice, all those involved in the initial steps are included in subsequent hearings.

4. If the grievance is not settled at the third step, a labor relations board or a general review board, consisting of high-ranking company and union officials, may conduct a formal hearing and attempt to settle the grievance.

5. The final step in most grievance procedures is **arbitration.** When the parties themselves fail to resolve the grievance, they submit the issue to an impartial third party, who renders a decision that is binding on both parties. (Chapter 12 analyzes the arbitration process in depth.)

PRINCIPLES FOR HANDLING GRIEVANCES.   Most grievances are resolved at the first step. In investigating grievances, personnel people who adhere to the following principles have been most successful in minimizing problems.

1. Every complaint should be taken seriously. Even though a grievance may appear ridiculous on the surface, it is a serious matter to the employee.

Indicating to employees at the outset that their complaints have no merit, or that they are foolish even to think their problems warrant attention can destroy whatever good relations may exist between the company and its employees. The personnel staff must give full attention to any complaint and try to find the source of trouble, obvious or hidden. It must try to determine why there is a grievance. One of the basic principles of good communications applies here: Listen. Attentive and sincere listening allows employees to talk freely. Many grievances solve themselves when employees have the opportunity to express their problems. It is the supervisors' duty to endeavor to settle the grievance at their level and personnel can provide vital information and advice. Experience shows that as a case proceeds through the grievance mechanism, the difficulties in making a settlement multiply, and the original complaint frequently takes on a new face.

2. Personnel people must work with the committeemen or shop stewards. When employees request the presence of their steward (within reason), he or she should be summoned promptly. It helps to have the attitude that stewards can assist in solving problems and are not adversaries who are out to get the company.

3. In written grievances, personnel people must make certain the grievance form is completely filled out. Many employees are not articulate, especially in writing. As a result, grievance statements are often unclear, illegible, incomplete, or otherwise confusing. Written grievances should be carefully checked to ensure they are clear, complete statements of the problem including the remedy sought, with the date of initiation and the employee's signature.

4. When handling a grievance with a union official, personnel people must stick to the issue of the grievance. This is easier said than done, since emotions and side issues tend to be interjected into the conversation. Stewards may attempt to confuse the issue and put management on the defensive by introducing extraneous matters. Personnel people should make every effort to redirect the discussion to the issue at hand.

5. Personnel people must gather all the facts available. Unless an answer to the grievance appears obvious, the time allowed by the contract should be used to investigate the problem, developing as much relevant data as possible: company policy, previous settlements, facts regarding circumstances of the case, and other pertinent information. They should contact sources such as supervisors, workers involved with the situation, witnesses, and when necessary, the department head. Personnel people should develop information as though the case would be appealed to arbitration.

6. The company must adhere to time limits, since procrastination quickly creates disharmony. The contract specifies the maximum amount of time allowed for the company to answer a grievance. If it requires additional time, special arrangements can be made by mutual consent. But as a general practice, management should reply within the time limits established by the agreement. Firms have lost arbitration cases on the technicality of exceeding time limits.

7. Management's answers should include reasons, especially when a grievance is denied. The answer may not be acceptable, but the reasoning behind it can help promote understanding and convince the union not to appeal. Whatever the answer, major criteria for grievance decisions include:

   a. **Precedent**—what has been done before.

   b. Company policy and guidelines.

   c. Reasons behind the complaint—ask the employee why.

   d. Consequences of the decision.

   It should be remembered that the answer to the grievance, if accepted by the union, is a binding, enforceable settlement.

8. Finally, personnel should record all the facts, particularly if the grievance goes beyond the first step. When others (i.e., the department head, personnel director, or arbitrator) rule on a grievance, they need facts to base their decisions on; the record preserves these facts for future reference.

In the grievance-handling process the personnel representative engages in bargaining with *both* the union and management. There is rarely a grievance in which management may not have been technically in error, just as there are few to which the grievant did not contribute. The personnel representative must find out what the grievant will settle for, make a judgment as to the strength of the case, discuss the matter with relevant management officials, secure authorization for an offer of settlement, and get the settlement accepted by the grievant and the union representative.

Regardless of the outcome, both management and the union have a legal obligation to represent employees fairly in grievance matters. This **duty of fair representation** has been enunciated by the U.S. Supreme Court, which ruled that grievants are entitled to all the rights and benefits guaranteed them under the contract. It recognized that unions do not have an obligation to process every grievance to arbitration, but it admonished the parties to ensure that individuals have equal access to the grievance machinery. In addition, the Court said, an individual union member has a right to have his or her grievance settled on its merits. Thus, a union that trades an individual's grievance for settlement of another complaint would violate the fair representation standards. The union may make a good-faith judgment that a particular grievance lacks merit, but it still must exercise reasonable care and diligence in making an investigation before concluding that it lacks merit.[28] As might be predicted, the result of the Court's standards is that fair representation complaints before the NLRB have tripled over the last ten years.[29]

STRIKES AND LOCKOUTS

Most contracts provide for strike and **lockout** bans that assure that production and employment will not be interrupted during the term of the contract due to a labor dispute. An employer-initiated suspension of work is a lockout. Although employers rarely use this tactic, it has proven effective when the contract term has expired, negotiations have reached an impasse, and the employer initiates the lockout before the union strikes. The lockout gives employers a psychological advantage when unions interpret it as a show of economic strength and fail to strike as a result. However, many states allow locked-out employees to draw unemployment benefits, which can dilute its impact. If employees stage a **wildcat strike**—a strike when a nonstrike clause is in effect—the employer may legally discipline the violators. The National Labor Relations Act requires that before a strike or lockout may take place in a dispute concerning modification or termination of an existing collective bargaining agreement, 60 days' notice must be given to the other contractual party. And within 30 days of that notice, federal and state mediation agencies must be notified if no settlement has been made by that time. Federal labor law does not protect workers who strike (except to protest an unfair labor practice) while a no-strike clause is in effect.

BASES FOR STRIKES.   Although 90 percent of strikes occur over disagreements on contract terms (contract strikes), other reasons also account for them. Organizational strikes are attempts to force an employer to accept a union as the bargaining agent of its employees. Presently, an insignificant number of workers are involved in this type of strike. Grievance strikes are called to protest an employer's day-to-day handling of a labor-relations matter. Using arbitration to settle grievances has greatly diminished the incidence of these disputes.

Historically, strikes have been criticized for their disruptive effect on society. They allegedly cause income loss to strikers, with consequent economic suffering to their families; they inconvenience the general public because of disrupted production and services; and they inhibit the firm's economic progress by curtailing its activities. Actually, though, strikes have a minimal direct effect on the economy. Fewer than 4 percent of contracts result in strikes. And according to BLS figures, an average of less than two-tenths of 1 percent of total estimated working time was lost to strikes from 1976 to 1980.[30] In addition, strikes serve a useful purpose as inducements to settle the terms of a contract. According to Chamberlain and Cullen:

> The mere availability of labor's right to strike for its demands, and the countervailing "right" of the employer to take a strike rather than to yield to those demands, weigh heavily in the calculations of both parties as the strike deadline approaches. There lies the primary incentive for the parties to back off from their extreme positions and to inch toward a compromise agreement, most often without resort to an actual strike.[31]

Under certain circumstances, however, the deleterious effect of a strike on the national welfare is sufficient to require special consideration.

NATIONAL EMERGENCY STRIKES.   Sections 206 to 210 of the Taft-Hartley Act provide for **national emergency strikes** where government can intervene when strikes affect "an entire industry or a substantial part thereof," and in the view of the President, "imperil the national health and safety." The law calls for the President to appoint a board of inquiry to investigate and report the facts. At his discretion, the President may also seek an injunction to restrain the strike for 60 days. He can extend this **cooling-off period** an additional 20 days if necessary. During the latter period, employees are polled in a secret-ballot election on their willingness to accept the last offer of the employer. If the strike persists at this point, Congress can take appropriate action. Due to considerable controversy over the national emergency provisions of the Taft-Hartley Act, Congress is still debating alternative proposals.

Similarly, the Railway Labor Act establishes machinery for resolving labor disputes, but this legislation more stringently prohibits strike activity. Taylor and Whitney, in *Labor Relations Law*, assert that "government dominance" of collective bargaining under the Railway Labor Act has seriously impaired successful collective bargaining in the transportation industry. Prohibiting strikes removes a major impetus to resolving labor disputes.[32]

SUPERVISORY ACTION IN STRIKE SITUATIONS.   A basic responsibility of line supervisors is to prevent strikes and work stoppages if possible. During the term of an agreement, strikes or related curtailment of production are in violation of it, and there are specific measures that can be taken. One organization (a major automobile manufacturer) called for the following steps to be taken by its line supervisors:

1. *Be there and stay there.*
   It is extremely important that a member of management be on the job

at such a time; otherwise, the employees will be without management direction, and it will not be possible to record the event.

2. *Notify management and labor relations immediately.*
    Phone or send word by messenger.

3. *Get employees back to work.*

    a. Give positive instructions, tell employees who are involved in the strike or work stoppage:

        1. "You are in violation of the agreement."

        2. "Go back to work."

        3. "Stay on your job."

        4. "Any problems you have can be handled through the grievance procedure if you go back to work."

        5. "This strike is not authorized."

    b. Get any shop steward (a union committeeman). Insist he or she instruct employees to return to work. Keep repeating instructions!

4. *Don't imply permission to go home.*

    a. Never say "go back to work or go home."

5. *Don't bargain or argue the merits of the complaints.*

    a. It is important to remember that the issues should not be discussed while the stoppage is in progress.

    b. Avoid making any agreements in order to get employees to return to work.

6. *Observe everything.*
    Management has the right to discipline any employee for taking part in an unauthorized strike or work stoppage. Facts must be present in order to prove leadership in a strike or work stoppage. Suspicion is not acceptable—management must establish facts by credible evidence, which mainly consists of what members of supervision see and hear.

7. *Evidence of strike leadership.*

    a. To wave or call others off the job.

    b. To shut down lines, machines, or equipment.

    c. To make evident moves such as:

        1. Obvious preparation to leave work.

        2. The first to quit work.

        3. In the forefront of those leaving their job area.

    d. To act as spokesperson for those striking is very definite evidence of leadership *unless* the spokesperson clearly indicates that he is not associating himself or herself with the actions of those on strike and is *only reporting* the situation.

e. To permit or direct picketing.

Observation should include the conduct of union leaders. Committeepersons have a responsibility to see that the employees observe an agreement; therefore, they have an obligation to assist in getting employees back to work when they engage in a stoppage in violation of an agreement. If the union officials (stewards, committeepersons) stand idly by in a stoppage situation, they should be placed on notice that it is their responsibility to assert positive leadership and to tell the employees that they should stay on the job. Committeepersons who fail to take positive action in those circumstances are guilty of at least negative leadership.

8. *Report fully in writing.*
There has never been a report of a work stoppage that contained too much factual information. Everything that can be remembered should be written down as soon as possible after the stoppage is over. If the report contains opinions, indicate that they are opinions. The report should cover:

a. People involved

b. Time of occurrence

c. Sequence of events

d. Distances

e. Locations

f. Details

g. What was said—by whom

Cost-Benefit Analysis

The benefits of collective bargaining are significant because of its alternatives—slowdown of production or strike with a complete cessation of operations. One measure of the effectiveness of the bargaining process, then, is the degree to which it promotes industrial peace. Measures might include recording over time the number of work days lost to labor disputes; the number of grievances settled at various levels, especially the trend of grievances appealed to arbitration; and historical data on the number and kinds of unfair labor-practice charges filed by the union and management. The benefits of initiatives in union-management cooperation can be measured too. The Bolivar experiment which we described earlier in this chapter calculated that the net benefit per employee to the organization was over $3,000. In addition the parties measured a significant improvement in productivity and product quality.[33]

In negotiations management calculates the cost of various economic demands. Because settlement of economic issues represents a continuing expense of doing business, the need for precision in these calculations cannot be overstressed. Bargaining results can be analyzed immediately following negotiations in order to determine which strategies and tactics proved successful and to compare planned versus actual cost of settlement and changes in the agreement demanded by management.

Summary

Collective bargaining is a vehicle for establishing, administering, and enforcing understandings between unions and management. Diverse variables interact to form the collective-bargaining situation.

The parties—labor and management—and the relationships that can exist between them significantly affect the collective-bargaining process. The relationships influence to a great degree the approach the parties will take to bargaining. Regardless of the approach, specific steps in the process can be identified. Both parties must prepare for negotiations by gathering data to support their respective positions. Then, following an exchange of demands, they give and take in bargaining sessions, which it is hoped will result in a signed agreement. In the final step, the union members ratify the settlement.

Precedent influences the outcome of bargaining because demands are often based on past practice within the organization as well as on the negotiated settlements of other contracts. The desires and interests of constituents influence the behavior of spokesmen on both sides in bargaining sessions. Bargaining strategy also considers the present and predicted state of the economy and public sentiment of both parties' positions.

Central to the collective-bargaining process is the resolution of issues. One of the most basic issues is a firm's right to manage its business free from union restraints. In opposition, unions have consistently stated their right to a voice in matters affecting the work force. But the recognition that controversy proves costly to both sides is increasing the trend toward contracts of longer duration, that is, two years or more.

The basic law of collective bargaining, the National Labor Relations Act, as amended by the Taft-Hartley Act, plays a significant role in maintaining uninterrupted production. The National Labor Relations Board administers the provisions of the act by investigating unfair labor practices and conducting bargaining representative certification elections.

In administering collective bargaining agreements, supervisors play a key role. Timely, open-minded, conscientious grievance handling results in sound employee relations. But regardless of efforts to administer contracts properly, disputes are inevitable, and some result in strikes. Unions consider strikes a right and in the public interest. No-strike clauses are becoming more prevalent in contracts, but some disputes between labor and management still can threaten the national welfare. Consequently, union leaders, management associations, and legislators are introducing alternative measures such as arbitration, fact finding, and statutory strikes.

Key Terms

collective bargaining
management rights clause
distributive bargaining
integrative bargaining
agreement
stagflation
unfair labor practices
petition
representation elections
appropriate bargaining unit
yellow-dog contract
hot cargo agreements
secondary boycott
negotiating
Boulwarism

memorandum of agreement
subcontracting
modified union shop
maintenance-of-membership
  agreement
dues-checkoff
ability to pay
four-day forty-hour week
arbitration
precedent
duty of fair representation
lockout
wildcat strike
national emergency strikes
cooling-off period

Review Questions

1. Describe the variables in a collective-bargaining situation.

2. Define collective bargaining and discuss how the bargaining process relates to your definition.

3. Why is a strong management-rights clause important? What elements should be included in such a clause?

4. Describe the alternative continuing relationships in collective bargaining that can exist between the parties.

5. What are the arguments for and against the right to strike? What legal remedies are available for settling national emergency strikes?

6. Discuss the principles for handling employee grievances.

Discussion Questions

1. In a collective-bargaining relationship, management is essentially free to manage its business as it chooses except as specifically modified by an agreement. Does this mean that an agreement is a restrictive document? Discuss why and why not. Discuss how a strong management-rights

clause can give management greater flexibility in running its operations.

2. How essential to effective collective bargaining is the parties' right to strike or lockout when they have had a continuing relationship of co-operation? Describe at least three alternatives to a strike or lockout. To what extent should the government become involved in settling disputes?

3. If you were the principal labor-relations negotiator for a large business firm, what position would you take on common expiration dates for local contracts (the company has four contracts with the same union)? On the intervention of a third party into your negotiations? On advance consultation with union officials about matters not covered by the contract?

4. Labor has traditionally viewed seniority clauses as sacred. Seniority's purpose has always been to add objectivity to selecting, placing, and promoting workers. How, then, can a seniority system be justified to Equal Employment Opportunity administrators, who produce statistical evidence that the preponderance of minority employees are recent hires? How can existing seniority systems be adjusted to accommodate minority employees?

5. If we agree that free collective bargaining must be preserved, and the general public must be protected against strikes that threaten the nation's welfare, what kind of legislation can accommodate both objectives? Describe the elements of a law that would accomplish this end.

Negotiations in 1981 at the Weldon Manufacturing Company were particularly difficult. The eight-member union committee seemed disorganized, which made it difficult to narrow the issues to the most serious ones. Most of the time in bargaining sessions was taken up with discussion of noneconomic issues, primarily because the federal government had imposed severe restrictions on ecomonic improvements.

A basic company strategy was to do its trading on noneconomic issues first, so that it could use these concessions as tradeoffs in the economic phase of the bargaining. In addition, the management team timed their offers. They waited until debate on an issue seemed to be leaning to the management position before introducing their best offer. Management also used the caucus quite effectively to gain team consensus on particular issues. If the spokesman felt one of the members was proceeding down the wrong path, he called a caucus to resolve the difficulty and present a united front.

On the other hand, the union negotiators were poorly organized. On several occasions during the bargaining sessions, they argued among themselves over fundamental differences on issues. Whether by design or because of their disorganization, the union introduced the issue of no compulsory overtime near the contract settlement deadline. Here they presented a united front, and they were adamant that afterhours and weekend work must be on a voluntary basis. But the company insisted that it could not relinquish its right to schedule work. As the deadline approached, the negotiators still had not discussed wages and benefits, and a strike appeared likely.

Problems

1. How could this kind of crisis have been avoided?

2. Did the company's strategy of discussing noneconomic issues first contribute to the crisis?

3. How could the company team have taken advantage of the union's disorganization?

4. What measures could the union have taken to present a more united front in the bargaining sessions?

5. What would be the consequences of giving in to the union's demand on no compulsory overtime?

6. Why do you suppose the union insisted on this demand?

Case Problem 1

AN APPROACH TO NEGOTIATIONS

Case Problem 2

WILDCAT STRIKE AT THE DARBY MINE

Ringo Shelby was the union president of the Associated Mine Workers' Union Local 3 which represented the employees of the Darby Mining Company. Ringo had been a discipline problem to the company because of his poor attendance record; it was so poor, in fact, that he had been warned twice in the past six months that if his record didn't improve he would be discharged. But the company tried to be lenient because of Ringo's influence with employees.

When the company instituted a new absentee control system, designed to reduce the unusually high absenteeism rate, Ringo refused to support the program. He insisted that the program was unilaterally imposed—the union should have been consulted first—and it was an infringement of worker's rights. Ringo was so adamant in his feelings about the new system that he even tried to get employees to interfere with its administration by refusing to call in, giving false reasons for absences, et cetera. Ringo was advised that if he persisted in his "insubordinate actions" he would be discharged. The next day he was overheard by his foreman agitating a group of workers to convince them to torpedo the system. After getting the approval of the superintendent, the foreman fired Ringo.

Within one hour, word of Ringo's discharge spread throughout the mine. Groups of employees congregated on the job to decide what action they should take. Someone shouted, "Let's shut'er down!" All the workers stopped work and left their jobs in protest over Ringo's discharge. The foremen tried in vain to get the workers back to their jobs, telling everyone, "This is an unauthorized strike, get back to work."

Problems

1. Assuming there was a no-strike clause in the contract:

    a. Are the employees' actions protected by law?

    b. What action can legally be taken against the employees?

2. What would have been the proper procedure for the union to follow?

3. What is at stake here?

Notes

1. Harold W. Davey, *Contemporary Collective Bargaining*, 3rd ed. (Englewood Cliffs, N.J.: Prentice-Hall), 1972, p. 2.

2. Edward L. Cushman, "The American Motors–U.A.W. Progress Sharing Plan," in Max S. Wortman, ed., *Critical Issues in Labor* (New York: Macmillan, 1969), pp. 271ff.

3. Richard Walton and Robert McKersie, *A Behavioral Theory of Labor Negotiations* (New York: McGraw-Hill, 1965), pp. 3ff.

4. Jon Prooslin Goodman and William R. Sandberg, "A Contingency Approach to Labor Relations Strategies," *The Academy of Management Review*, January 1981, pp. 145–54.

5. "The New Chill in Labor Relations," *Business Week*, October 24, 1977, pp. 32–33.

6. Michael H. Moskow, "Collective Bargaining Strategies in the Context of Unemployment and Inflation: The Economic Context," *Proceedings of the 1976 Annual Spring Meeting of the Industrial Relations Research Association*, reprinted from *Labor Law Journal*, August 1976, pp. 463–64.

7. National Labor Relations Board, *A Guide to Basic Law and Procedures Under the National Labor Relations Act*, (Washington, D.C.: Government Printing Office, 1978), p. 17.

8. "The Yeshiva Decision," *Academe*, May 1980, pp. 191ff.

9. Davey, *Contemporary Collective Bargaining*, p. 53.

10. Readers can achieve a better understanding of the process from management's standpoint by studying Meyer S. Ryder, Charles M. Rihmus, and Sanford Cohen, *Management Preparation for Collective Bargaining* (Homewood, Ill.: Dow Jones-Irwin, 1966). Also, a valuable tool for management in collective bargaining preparation is *Check Points for Sound Collective Bargaining* (New York: National Association of Manufacturers, 1958).

11. J. T. Dunlop and J. J. Healy, *Collective Bargaining* (Homewood, Ill.: Richard D. Irwin, 1953), p. 55.

12. George E. Constantine, Jr., "The Negotiator in Collective Bargaining," *Personnel Journal*, August 1975, p. 447.

13. There are several good handbooks available on how to negotiate, including: Bruce Morse, *How to Negotiate the Labor Agreement* (Southfield, Mich.: Trends Publishing Company, 1977); Harry J. Keaton, *Drafting the Collective Bargaining Agreement*, Reprinted from *Labor Law For General Practitioners* (Los Angeles: The Regents of the University of California, 1960); and Edward Peters, *Strategy and Tactics in Labor Negotiations* (Los Angeles: Edward Peters, Conciliator, 1976).

14. William E. Simkin, *Mediation and the Dynamics of Collective Bargaining* (Washington, D.C.: Bureau of National Affairs, 1971), p. 170.

15. Ibid., p. 171.

16. Donald E. Cullen, *Negotiating Labor-Management Contracts* (Ithaca: New York State School of Industrial and Labor Relations, 1970), pp. 6–7.

17. *Labor Law Course*, 24th ed. (New York: Commerce Clearing House, 1979), p. 1651.

18. U.S. Bureau of Labor Statistics, *Characteristics of Major Collective Bargaining Agreements* (Washington, D.C.: U.S. Government Printing Office, 1980), p. 16.

19. U.S. Bureau of Labor Statistics, *Characteristics of Major Collective Bargaining Agreements*, p. 8 (calculated from BLS figures).

20. U.S. Bureau of Labor Statistics, *Productivity and the Economy* (Washington, D.C.: U.S. Government Printing Office, 1977), p. 4.

21. "Some Fresh Ideas for Boosting Workers' Output," *U.S. News and World Report,* November 29, 1976, p. 83.

22. United Steelworkers of America, *The Joint Advisory Committee on Productivity: What Does It Mean to You?* (Pittsburgh, Pa.: United Steelworkers of America, 1971), pp. 25–28.

23. Report of a Special Task Force to the Secretary of Health, Education, and Welfare, *Work in America* (Cambridge, Mass.: MIT Press), 1973.

24. "Quality of Work Demonstration Project at Eaton Corporation Plant," in *Recent Initiatives in Labor-Management Cooperation* (Washington, D.C.: National Center for Productivity and Quality of Working Life, February 1976), pp. 37ff.

25. Michael Maccoby, "Work and Human Development," *The Franklin Foundation Lecture Series* lecture at Georgia State University, November 15, 1977.

26. See *Directory of Labor-Management Committees* (Washington, D.C.: National Center for Productivity and Quality of Working Life, October 1976).

27. Dan R. Dalton and William D. Todor, "Manifest Needs of Stewards: Propensity to File a Grievance," *Journal of Applied Psychology,* December 1979, pp. 654–659.

28. Jean T. McKelvey, editor, *The Duty of Fair Representation* (Ithaca: New York State School of Industrial and Labor Relations, Cornell University, 1977), pp. 4ff.

29. "On Trial: A Union's Fairness," *Business Week,* August 13, 1979, pp. 76–77.

30. U.S. Bureau of Labor Statistics, "Work Stoppages" (Washington, D.C.: Bureau of Labor Statistics, News release, Tuesday, December 30, 1980).

31. Neil W. Chamberlain and Donald E. Cullen, *The Labor Sector,* 2nd ed. (New York: McGraw-Hill, 1971), p. 212.

32. Benjamin J. Taylor and Fred Whitney, *Labor Relations Law,* 3rd ed. (Englewood Cliffs, N.J.: Prentice-Hall, 1979), pp. 535–36.

33. Barry A. Macy, "A Progress Report on the Bolivar Quality of Work Life Project," *Personnel Journal,* August 1979, pp. 527ff.

Chapter Twelve

Labor-Management Dispute Settlement

Then two harlots came to the king and stood before him. The one woman said, "Oh, my lord, this woman and I dwell in the same house; and I gave birth to a child while she was in the house. Then on the third day after I was delivered, this woman also gave birth; and we were alone; there was no one else with us in the house, only we two in the house. And this woman's son died in the night, because she lay on it. And she arose at midnight, and took my son from beside me, while your maid servant slept, and laid it in her bosom, and laid her dead son in my bosom. When I rose in the morning to nurse my child, behold, it was dead; but when I looked at it closely in the morning, behold it was not the child which I had borne." But the other woman said, "No, the living child is mine, and the dead child is yours." The first said, "No, the dead child is yours, and the living child is mine." Thus they spoke before the king.

Then the king said, "The one says, 'This is my son that is alive, and your son is dead,'; and the other says, 'No, but your son is dead, and my son is the living one.'" And the king said, "Bring me a sword." So a sword was brought before the king. And the king said, "Divide the living child in two, and give half to one, and half to the other."

Then the woman whose child was alive said to the king, because her heart yearned for her son, "Oh, my lord, give her the living child, and by no means slay it." But the other said, "It shall be neither mine nor yours; divide it." Then the king answered and said, "Give the living child to the first woman, and by no means slay it; she is its mother."[1]

LEARNING
OBJECTIVES

1. To understand why the role of neutrals in collective bargaining is expanding.

2. To know the distinctions between the processes of arbitration and mediation.

3. To be familiar with the general qualifications of mediators and arbitrators.

4. To be familiar with the various alternatives to the strike.

5. To know the various cases involving judicial review of arbitration decisions.

This case may well be the first arbitration case recorded in the Old Testament. Two parties with opposing views (the harlots) mutually agreed in advance to submit their dispute (who is the mother of the child?) to an impartial third party (King Solomon), whose decision would be binding upon both of them.

As both labor and management increase in size and strength, and as the issues of collective bargaining become more complex, the probability of disputes grows even greater. When disputes develop into strikes, such disruptions of normal activity affect labor, management, consumers, and the community.

The attention the press and Congress have given to maintaining labor peace makes the subject of dispute settlement worthy of special consideration. The basic objective of dispute-settlement measures is to minimize the negative effects on the public welfare without jeopardizing the free conduct of collective bargaining. In the description of dispute-resolution mechanisms in this chapter it will become obvious that not all approaches support this objective. Voluntary arbitration and mediation seem to be the most widely accepted forms of dispute resolution, and they have been the most effective approaches to resolving differences between the parties without interfering with negotiating. For these reasons, a detailed analysis of *arbitration* and *mediation* is provided in this chapter.

Voluntary Labor Arbitration

In labor arbitration situations, awards are not always so clear cut as King Solomon's. Arbitrators are constrained in their decisions by the terms of the agreement. Their purpose is not so much to determine the just solution, as to interpret contracts and render awards consistent with contract terms. The awards handed down favor one party or the other, but their nature is not such that all other arbitrators would have ruled the same way. Also, the nature of arbitration cases differs.

Basically, arbitration cases fall into two categories: interest and rights. **Interest arbitration** refers to arbitration over the terms of a new collective bargaining agreement. **Rights arbitration** arises out of grievances on the interpretation or application of the agreement.

ADVANTAGES OF ARBITRATION

As a dispute-settlement mechanism, labor arbitration has several distinct advantages. Because the parties themselves have established arbitration as a means of settling disputes, it becomes an integral part of a system of self-government. Arbitration thus emphasizes mutual consent and is a cooperative effort toward reaching accord. The arbitration process also substitutes reason for strife. The parties submit their differences to a factual test by an impartial observer who looks at the issue objectively and renders a judgment based on the strength of their arguments. Contracts that stipulate arbitration as the final step of the grievance procedure generally substitute it for strike activity, at least during the term of the agreement. Some contracts even prohibit strikes until the parties have exhausted the grievance machinery. The preponderance of grievances—about 90 percent—are settled before arbitration.

Arbitration is preferable to court action, since costly court procedures are time-consuming and not compatible with the peculiarities of labor relations. In arbitration the parties can ensure that proceedings are inexpensive and of reasonably short duration. And arbitrators understand the subtleties of labor-management relations, so their decisions are more realistic.

Most arbitrated cases merely seek an answer to a question arising from a grievance. Some arbitrations settle issues in disputes that occur during contract negotiations or during the day-to-day administration of a contract. Other cases are arbitrated as a matter of political expediency for one of the parties. Take, for example, the case of a union member who claims he has bidding rights to a certain job because of his seniority. The company denies the grievance, and the union agrees confidentially that the grievant is wrong. But he is a staunch union supporter of long standing, so the union refers the case to arbitration in order for an outsider to deny the grievance. In this way, the employee has his day in court, and the union is spared the problem of denying to a member what he considers his legitimate right (and thereby destroying his loyalty).

LEGAL BASIS OF ARBITRATION

Not only is grievance arbitration widely accepted—over 90 percent of all union contracts have arbitration clauses—but it is well established in national labor policy as the preferred method for resolving labor disputes. Fundamentally, arbitration is a product of the contract agreement between the parties. The law has only been concerned with the enforceability of arbitrated agreements and the review and enforcement of arbitrators' awards. Only a small percentage of awards actually find their way to court. From the time an arbitrator is selected, through the hearing and rendering of an award, the parties rarely give much thought to the legal posture of arbitration. In practice, the arbitration process (even though witnesses must be sworn in) is as informal as the parties wish. Arbitrators have no legal power per se, and their awards are binding mainly because the parties previously agreed they would be. (However, the courts have ruled that parties must accept arbitrated decisions if their contracts contain an arbitration clause).

State and federal statutes support arbitration by recognizing it as a viable force for dispute settlement, by establishing administrative machinery to encourage its use, and by promulgating procedural guidelines. Section

203 of the Labor-Management Relations Act (Taft-Hartley) promotes arbitration by declaring that final adjustment by a method agreed upon by the parties is "the desirable method for settlement of grievance disputes over the application or interpretation of an existing collective bargaining agreement." The Railway Labor Act delineates more extensively the steps parties must take in arbitration tribunals to resolve disputes "concerning changes in rates of pay, rules, or working conditions" unresolved in conference or referred by a party.

Legality of the Arbitration Clause

A series of Supreme Court decisions provided legal support for arbitration by consistently ruling that it is a proper alternative to strikes and that courts will enforce the awards of arbitrators. In the celebrated *Lincoln Mills* case,[2] the Supreme Court held that Section 301 of the Taft-Hartley Act authorized federal courts to enforce arbitration clauses in labor-management contracts. The Supreme Court, by its ruling, recognized arbitration as a substitute for strikes.

Of even greater significance were the landmark decisions of the Supreme Court in the Steelworkers' Trilogy. In two of the cases, the Steelworkers requested the high court to order arbitration of a grievance. In its interpretation of Section 301, the court ruled that a party does not have to submit to arbitration if the contract does not require it. Therefore, the courts must confine their inquiry to whether or not the parties agreed to arbitrate the issue. In the second case, *Warrior and Gulf Navigation Company*,[3] the Supreme Court concluded, "An order to arbitrate the particular grievance should not be denied unless it may be said with positive assurance that the arbitration clause is not susceptible of an interpretation that covers the asserted dispute. Doubts should be resolved in favor of coverage." This decision supported the decision in the *American Manufacturing Company* case,[4] when the courts ruled that whenever a party seeks arbitration of a grievance that appears on its face to be governed by the contract, arbitration should be ordered. In essence, these court rulings mean that grievances involving contract interpretation—regardless of their apparent merit, just as long as the subject is covered by the contract—must be arbitrated. Unless the contract expressly precludes arbitration of a particular grievance, the grievance must be arbitrated.

Obviously, these rulings angered companies in that they felt that arbitrators' authority had been unduly expanded to the point that it infringed on management's rights. Managers are firm in their insistence that certain matters are the sole prerogative of management and therefore beyond the scope of arbitration. The court's rationale in these two decisions was that, in agreeing to an arbitration clause in the contract, the parties agreed to settle contract interpretation controversies through arbitration and not through litigation. The Steelworkers' Trilogy thus delineated the authority of the arbitrators and the courts in contract disputes.

Court Review and Enforcement of Awards. In the last case of the Steelworkers' Trilogy, when the Enterprise Wheel and Car Corporation[5] refused to comply with an arbitrator's ruling, the union sued to have the award enforced. The matter was appealed to the Supreme Court, which ordered enforcement and emphasized that courts should enforce awards so long as arbitrators base these on contract agreements. Courts are inclined to uphold arbitrators' decisions except when there is evidence of corruption or partiality; evidence of arbitrators exceeding their power; evident miscalculation of figures; or when the award does not accurately describe people, things, or property. However, the rarity of adjudication of arbitration awards indicates that the parties are usually willing to accept arbitration awards as final and binding. Essentially, arbitration is a private contract matter in which the court's role in deciding and reviewing awards is minimal.

There are, however, several prominent court cases that challenged or limited the arbitrator's authority. Generally, arbitrators use past practice to clarify ambiguous contract language, and they are usually supported by court decisions. However, the courts in both *Porter*[6] and *Torrington*[7] ruled that the arbitrators had exceeded and abused their authority by reading an implied contractual relationship into the contract. Specifically, the court said:

> . . . the mandate that the arbitrator stay within the confines of the collective bargaining agreement requires a reviewing court to pass on whether the agreement authorizes the arbitrator to expand its express terms on the basis of the parties' prior practice. Therefore, we hold that the question of an arbitrator's decision that he has authority should not be accepted where the reviewing court can clearly perceive that he has derived that authority from sources outside the collective bargaining agreement at issue.[8]

Similarly, the concern that arbitrators might not be professionally competent to decide legal issues, especially in claims of employment discrimination, was expressed in *Alexander* v. *Gardner-Denver Co.* by the Supreme Court, which observed:

> The resolution of statutory or constitutional issues is a primary responsibility of courts, and judicial construction has proven especially necessary with respect to Title VII, whose broad language frequently can be given meaning only with reference to public law concepts. Moreover, the factfinding process in arbitration usually is not equivalent to judicial factfinding. The record of the arbitration proceedings is not complete; the

usual rules of evidence do not apply; and rights and procedures common to civil trials, such as discovery, compulsory process, cross-examination, and testimony under oath are often severely limited or unavailable.[9]

And circumstances beyond the control of the arbitrator can cause his/her decision to be overturned by the courts. For example, in *Anchor Motor Freight*[10] the Court held that an arbitrator's decision is subject to reversal by a federal court when a union does not provide fair representation to employees involved in the arbitration. Eight truck drivers were discharged for allegedly submitting false expense reports. The drivers requested the union to investigate the circumstances, but it failed to do so. After the arbitrator sustained the discharge it was discovered that a motel clerk had made false entries in the register and pocketed the difference. Essentially, the Court said that it has authority to reverse an arbitration award when a union commits a gross error in representing the grievant(s).

The NLRB will usually defer to arbitration. Three key cases have established policy on **deferral to arbitration.** In *Collyer Insulated Wire*[11] the Board majority required the party charging an unfair labor practice to resort to agreed-upon grievance and arbitration machinery in disputes that were resolvable under the agreement. In *Dubo Manufacturing*[12] the Board will stay (defer) the hearing of unfair labor practice charges where the charging party is voluntarily pursuing resolution of the matter through the arbitration procedure. Finally, the Board established the Spielberg doctrine in the following majority opinion: "The Board will defer to an arbitration award where the proceedings appear to have been fair and regular, all parties have agreed to be bound, and the decision of the arbitrator is not clearly repugnant to the purposes and policies of the Act."[13] The NLRB strongly reaffirmed its Spielberg doctrine in its decision in *Kansas City Star Company.*[14] Here it dismissed the union's unfair labor practice charge, holding that "the facts and issues involved in the alleged unfair labor practices have been fully and completely decided by an arbitrator pursuant to grievances filed under the parties' bargaining agreement." Thus, there is a high probability that the Board will defer to the arbitrator's ruling when it appropriately considers alleged unfair labor practices.

The Arbitration Process

Orderly dispute settlement is outlined in collective-bargaining clauses that require arbitration of grievances and other contract interpretation matters. Arbitration has been characterized as a quasi-judicial process, and it does incorporate basic legal principles, common law, and established judicial procedures. But there is as much variety in the nature of arbitrators and the conduct of hearings as there is in bargaining relationships. Despite this variation, arbitration is the single most effective process for resolving union-management disputes.

ARBITRATION CONTRACT CLAUSES

With better than 90 percent of agreements containing arbitration clauses, their format is fairly consistent in designating a method for selecting the arbitrator, dividing arbitration expenses, defining arbitrators' jurisdiction, and specifying time limits. Table 12.1 shows a typical clause.

This article is merely an example, and it should not be construed as a model for contract construction. Arbitrators are often plagued by arbitration

Table 12.1
Article 20 Arbitration

A. Any grievance which has not been settled pursuant to steps 1-4 of the grievance procedure of Article 19, and which involves the interpretation or application of this Agreement, shall be referred to arbitration.

B. The procedure for arbitration shall be as follows:

1. The party seeking arbitration must deliver to the other party written notice of such intent to proceed to arbitration within ten (10) working days after the decision has been rendered at step 4.

2. Within five (5) working days of the delivery of such notice, an arbitrator shall be selected by mutual agreement, or the parties shall request the Federal Mediation and Conciliation Service to submit a list of five (5) persons from which the arbitrator shall be chosen. Within five (5) working days following the receipt of such panel from the Federal Mediation and Conciliation Service, the parties shall select an arbitrator in the following manner: The Union and the company shall alternately strike one (1) name from such panel (the right to strike the first name having been determined by lot) until only one (1) person remains and that person shall be the arbitrator.

3. The arbitration hearing shall be started within fifteen (15) calendar days, if practicable, of the selection of the arbitrator and carried to a conclusion as expeditiously as possible. A decision and award by the arbitrator shall be rendered within thirty (30) calendar days of the completion of the hearing.

C. The decision of the arbitrator will be final, and the company and the union agree to abide by such decision.

D. The costs and expenses of the arbitration, including the compensation of the arbitrator and stenographic expenses, shall be borne equally by the union and the company.

E. The arbitrator shall be confined to the subjects submitted for decision, and may in no event, as a part of any such decision, impose upon either party any obligation to arbitrate on any subjects which have not herein been agreed upon as subjects for arbitration; nor may he, as a part of any decision, effect reformation of this agreement, or of any provision thereof.

clauses that were taken from other sources. In negotiations the parties themselves should shape the terms of an arbitration clause to what they want
and in language everyone understands.

NATURE OF THE ARBITRATOR

Arbitrators come from a diversity of backgrounds. Clergymen, lawyers,
civil servants, economists, professors, school administrators, accountants, and
others have been certified to arbitrate labor-management disputes. Occasionally, the parties may specify the qualifications of an arbitrator, but generally speaking, impartiality, integrity, and ability are the essential characteristics of a good one. The parties want to know. ''Will he give us a fair
shake?'' They are concerned with an arbitrator's good judgment and fairness
in rendering a decision, and it is the record of past awards that forms an
arbitrator's reputation. This has been borne out in several studies of the
attitudes of company and union representatives toward arbitrators. The Rezler and Petersen[15] survey revealed that experience was the primary criterion
in selecting an arbitrator. Experience was measured by number of years as
an arbitrator, number of cases handled, number of awards published by
reporting services, and membership in the National Academy of Arbitrators
(a professional organization of arbitrators who have substantial and current
experience). The study also found that professional background had a bearing
on arbitrator selection, though the nature of the issue had a strong bearing
on this factor. Thus legal training was preferred in cases where arbitrability
was being challenged, economists were favored for interest disputes, and
industrial engineers would be chosen for wage incentive cases. Age was a
significant factor in the Boals study.[16] A high proportion (41 percent) of the
respondents preferred arbitrators over 40.

Both studies found that an arbitrator's reputation for being readily
available was an important selection factor. Arbitrators' fees in themselves
seem to have little impact on selection, but survey respondents indicated
that they become upset when the total bill is out of line. In both surveys
the idea of selecting female arbitrators met with some resistance. Women
as arbitrators appear to be faced with the same barriers they encounter in
the work world in general.

The continued acceptability of arbitrators is governed by their conduct
and demeanor. The parties expect the arbitrator to be of good moral character
with sound ethical standards. They expect the arbitrator to conduct an orderly
hearing in a courteous manner. And they insist that the arbitrator's opinion
include an adequate discussion of the case and be reasoned through to a
justified result. They appreciate an opinion that is clearly written so that all
concerned, especially the grievant, can understand how the arbitrator arrived
at his/her decision. And the prompt rendering of a decision is invariably

viewed with favor by both sides. Essentially, the parties believe that if arbitrators understand the problems of contract administration, they will be more likely to recognize the impact their awards will have on the bargaining relationship.

ARBITRATOR SELECTION

Selecting arbitrators is often a difficult matter because each party wants the individual to be objective, yet favorably disposed toward the party's own position. This desire presents a dilemma, since awards always favor one side over the other. The most desirable means is direct selection by mutual agreement. This method is most often employed to choose umpires or impartial chairmen, who are the permanent type of arbitrator employed by large companies and unions in auto assembly, rubber and tire manufacturing, and shipbuilding. As an alternative, an outside agency can supply a list or panel of arbitrators, or appoint them directly. Most prominent among these agencies are the Federal Mediation and Conciliation Service, The National Mediation Board, and the American Arbitration Association. Each certifies individuals as arbitrators and supplies panels at the request of the parties. A more recent development, **expedited arbitration,** has led to the preselection of arbitrators. The Steelworkers and major steel producers have jointly approved a list of arbitrators who are instantly available to hear grievances and render quick decisions.

CONDUCT OF THE HEARING

The parties determine the method of conducting the hearing. Some have the aura and formality of a judicial proceeding, including the swearing in of witnesses and other legal formalities. Others are informal and relaxed. In both situations, each side endeavors to present a clear picture of the circumstances of the grievance along with arguments to support its position. The purpose of the hearing is to allow both parties to present sufficient evidence for the arbitrator to render an objective opinion.

In weighing the evidence in hearings, an arbitrator generally adopts the rule of **preponderance of evidence** in cases of contract construction; the evidence with the greater weight wins the hearing. Disciplinary cases are analogous to criminal law, and an arbitrator applies the rule of beyond reasonable doubt. Since disciplinary grievances relate to human affairs, which are open to possible doubt, the basis for weighing evidence must be carefully selected. It is generally held that the ultimate **burden of proof** rests with the union in contract construction and with the company in disciplinary cases. Another way of stating it is that in arbitration cases the burden of proof rests with the party that initiates the action. Since the party is seeking to alter the status quo, it must establish the validity of its action. Thus, when a company disciplines an employee, it must defend its action by showing how it altered the employee's status. If, after hearing all the evidence, the arbitrator is left with a reasonable doubt about the company's justification for its action, the company (which bore the burden of proof) would lose.

Past practice can often supply evidence to clarify a contract clause or determine if a reserved right of management has become part of the bargain. The everyday conduct of both parties can clarify ambiguous contract language. Consistent past practice tends to remove uncertainties in working relationships, and arbitrators emphasize that it offers the strongest evidence of the parties' intent. On the other hand, when the contract is silent, arbitrators must determine whether past practices constitute implied obligations. For example, arbitrators generally do not consider gratuities a benefit that management is obliged to continue to award. Management can withdraw a unilateral year-end bonus given on a voluntary basis without prejudicing its position, even though the company has given the bonus for several years. However, if the bonus was mutually arranged, management's position is very different. Arbitrator Burton Turkus provides some questions to determine if a practice is binding when there is no contract provision for it.[17] (Affirmative answers tend to make the practice binding on management.)

1. Does the practice concern a major condition of employment?
2. Was it established mutually?
3. Was it administered mutually?
4. Did either of the parties seek to incorporate it into the body of the written agreement?
5. Was the practice repeated frequently?
6. Is the practice a longstanding one?
7. Is it specific and detailed?
8. Do the employees rely on it?

ARBITRATION AWARDS

By mutual agreement arbitration awards are binding on both parties. Since labor and management alike must live with the decisions rendered, it is essential that awards be clearly written and understood by the rank and file most directly affected by them. Arbitrators must draw their decisions from the essence of the contract agreement, which is seldom understood by those most concerned with its administration—supervisors and shop stewards. Since arbitrators write awards for these people, they must couch their decisions in the simplest possible terms to facilitate implementation.

EMERGING TRENDS IN ARBITRATION

Arbitration remains one of the few institutions of justice still credible to its constituency. Although there have been public attacks on the judicial system, arbitration has thus far avoided public scandal. Much of this is probably due to the integrity of the people involved. In addition, the system automatically purges itself of undesirables because parties will only reselect arbitrators who are completely acceptable to both sides. Thus, proper conduct, objective decisions, and timely awards will become even more essential criteria in the future selection of arbitrators.

The cost of processing a grievance through arbitration is high, and the expense is increasing. Using legal assistance to present arguments and prepare briefs adds considerably to the cost. But when either party feels its interests are at stake, cost becomes a secondary consideration. However, arbitration is almost always less expensive to both parties than strikes.

Delays in processing grievances through arbitration continue to be a problem. Some of the difficulty arises from a shortage of seasoned arbitrators; their caseloads are so heavy that they must delay hearings as much as several months. As railroads and the public sector move toward more arbitration, the shortage will become even more critical. But the parties themselves, who often delay the process, are even more to blame. As the grievance load increases, time limits are often exceeded to the point that when a hearing date is finally set, it may be long after the incident causing grievance. To overcome this problem, the Steelworkers and cooperating steel companies, as part of their Experimental Negotiating Agreement (ENA), in 1971, negotiated an *expedited arbitration procedure.* Under this arrangement panels of arbitrators—most of them young men and women, including blacks—are preselected and agree to hear every case within ten days. Hearings are completely informal, and the arbitrators either make a decision at the close of the hearing or in a memorandum within 48 hours. After several years' experience with the instant arbitration procedure, the parties expressed satisfaction and confidence in the success of the experiment. The Steelworkers' official news medium, *Steel Labor,* editorialized on the experience with expedited arbitration: "In addition to cutting local union arbitration costs and helping reduce backlogs which jammed arbitration channels for the more complex cases, the expedited arbitration procedures drastically reduce the time for adjudication of a case since the decision must be rendered within 48 hours after conclusion of the hearing."[18] Perhaps this favorable experience with expedited arbitration led to the pioneering 1973 agreement between the steel producers and the Steelworkers to submit unresolved bargaining issues to arbitration, thus eliminating the threat of a strike in that industry. The American Arbitration Association (a private arbitration service) also offers expedited arbitration as a regular service, with arbitrators selected as cases arise. But some grievants feel they deserve more detailed consideration of their cases and insist on a full-blown hearing instead of the expedited treatment.

Mediation

The purpose of **mediation** is to assist the parties in a dispute (e.g., in an impasse in negotiations) to arrive at their own settlement. Unlike arbitrators, mediators do not rule on issues. A mediator has no authority to impose a settlement, but rather serves as a facilitator. In contrast to arbitration, which is a formal intervention procedure, mediation is a supplement to the negotiation process. While arbitrators serve through mutual selection of the parties, mediators become involved as a matter of law—the National Labor Relations Act calls for mediator intervention when a 30-day strike notice is filed. Mediation is an active role, for when the situation demands, the mediator will interject, suggest possible areas of agreement, and generally guide the parties in a positive direction. **Conciliation** is traditionally used synonymously with mediation, but by its strict definition it involves gaining the goodwill of the parties and creating an atmosphere conducive to agreement. Compared to mediation it is a more passive role.

THE MEDIATOR—ABILITIES AND ROLES

In mediation, the neutral third party (the mediator) is a full-time employee of the Federal Mediation and Conciliation Service or may be a member of one of the city or state mediation boards (the latter are ad hoc). Mediators are selected for their ability to bring two divergent points of view together; they are themselves experienced negotiators, and they are required by the Service to update their skills on a regular basis. Since mediation is considered an art, it must be learned by trial and error through experience in negotiations either as an advocate or as a mediator. As with arbitration, the success of mediation depends on the parties' acceptance of the mediator, based on trust and confidence in him/her. Acceptance is especially important because the mediator must obtain from the parties confidential information which they have withheld from each other. Such information, if not used with discretion, could harm a party's bargaining strategy and, in turn, tarnish the mediator's reputation. So the mediator's services can be of substantial benefit to the parties in reaching an agreement.

There are often alternative solutions to problems that parties do not see because they are completely engrossed by their own position. The mediator, having encountered similar situations, is in a good position to suggest viable alternatives. To illustrate, a situation occurred several years ago in which a mediator was called in to settle a dispute involving a protracted strike—the contract had expired several months before. The mediator was able to assist the parties in resolving all issues except retroactivity. The company was adamant that it had never granted retroactivity previously, and it refused to make an exception now. The union was equally firm in its position that to settle it must have retroactivity. Through adroit questioning the mediator found that the company feared that many of its highly skilled employees would not return after the strike. Recalling a previous situation similar to this one, the mediator suggested that an amount of money approximating the sum each employee would have received had retroactivity been granted, be put aside to serve as a financial inducement for employees to return to work. The mediator also suggested that the sum be paid to employees who returned within three days of settlement and remained with the company for at least 30 days. The mediator's suggested alternative resolved the dispute.[19]

Emotions often run high in bargaining sessions, and the arguments that ensue can significantly hamper progress. Mediators are skilled at defusing such situations by asserting their role as chairperson, redirecting the discussion to less emotional issues, or calling a caucus.

The timing of counterproposals and offers, as we have already mentioned, is critical to acceptance by the other party. The mediator's neutrality places him or her in the best position to assess the suitability of a proposal and advise the parties accordingly. By the same token, one of the parties may want to offer a solution to a problem without making a commitment. The mediator can present it to the other side to test its acceptability; if it is acceptable, it can be formalized; if not, the proposing party has not jeopardized its position.

The order of presentation or the formulation of offers and counterproposals will affect their acceptability. Consequently, mediators urge the party making concessions to lead off with an issue in which the other party has indicated the greatest interest. This helps establish an atmosphere of receptiveness. Also, the mediator can assist parties in couching proposals in affirmative terms even when the meaning is restrictive. For example, if a clause limiting stewards' grievance-processing time were worded, "Stewards may not leave their work stations to process grievances for more than two hours in any day," it would certainly be quickly and adamantly rejected. A more acceptable wording would be, "Stewards have the right to process grievances on company time up to two hours in any shift."

THE MEDIATION PROCESS

When a mediator enters the bargaining process[20] he or she will typically convene the parties in a joint session. After establishing his/her role as chairperson, a mediator will clarify the unresolved issues by first having the parties state these and then by asking for a review in sufficient depth to indicate the scope and complexity of the problems. Next, the mediator will mentally couple or segregate related issues and plan a strategy for solution of some of the issues.

Part of the strategy might include the stipulation of the total agreement, whereby the parties agree that "any concession, modification, or withdrawal of any particular issue made by any of the parties is for the purpose of arriving at a full agreement—if no agreement is reached, either or both parties are free to revert to any position they deem advisable on all the issues." Such a stipulation protects both parties' positions and permits the tentative disposition of issues so that negotiations can progress.

Under certain circumstances the mediator will call a caucus and meet separately with each party to reconcile differences. A caucus will usually be appropriate when:

1. Emotional debate threatens progress.

2. The parties are repeating themselves and no progress is being made.

3. A possible compromise or area of agreement appears.

4. Either or both sides are rigid in their positions.

At the propitious moment when the mediator feels (this is the art of mediation, and it is a sense developed through experience) the parties can agree, he/she may urge a particular solution or approach that would have a maximum impact on negotiations and possibly be acceptable. To maximize the probability of agreement, mediators have the parties at the end of each session summarize (either orally or in writing) the items agreed upon. When the mediator has been shuttling between the parties in separate conferences, he or she will reconvene them in a joint session to state any offers and remove the possibility of misunderstanding.

FUNDAMENTALS OF MEDIATION

Long experience with mediation[21] suggests the following principles (they apply essentially to mediators, but are presented here to provide insight into their behavior):

1. *Understanding and appreciating the problems confronting the parties* based on a mediator's thorough knowledge of labor relations and of the industry and company involved.

2. *Conveying to the parties a feeling that the mediator understands their problems.*

3. *Getting the parties to realize that their positions are not valid.*

4. *Suggesting alternative approaches that may facilitate agreement.* The mediator's

suggestion may not be the final settlement, but it might open an approach that will result in one.

5. *Maintaining neutrality* by not stating opinions on the fairness or quality of a proposal or the legality of a matter before the parties.

6. *Maintaining confidentiality* of information disclosed by the parties, separately or jointly.

Other Alternatives to the Strike

The public's growing concern with strike activity and its negative impact, real or imagined, on the economy, has spurred an interest in measures to settle labor disputes. Congress continues to debate several remedies, the more prominent being **extended injunctions,** seizure, and compulsory arbitration. Other methods, such as **fact finding, advisory arbitration,** mediation, and conciliation, are well established in collective bargaining. Some new proposals such as the statutory strike, arsenal-of-weapons approach, and partial operation, have emerged from experiments similar to expedited arbitration.

NATIONAL-EMERGENCY STRIKE REMEDIES

Congressional proposals and study committee recommendations for legislation include measures to prevent national-emergency strikes from arising and, if they do occur, to minimize their impact. One method is to extend the 80-day Taft-Hartley injunction for an additional 30 days. During the extended cooling-off period, a board of inquiry would continue to mediate the dispute. However, it appears unlikely that injunction alone would produce a settlement.

In the most dire circumstances, the federal government might resort to seizure or executive receivership. Such legislative proposals call for partial or total government takeover and operation of business enterprises involved in a dispute. Companies would lose all claims to the operation during seizure, but would receive recompense in an amount determined by the President. (Companies could sue in the court of claims if they thought the amount unfair.) Likewise, during this period the government would adjust the company's wages, declare further strike activities unlawful, and suspend union security agreements. Such action is unlikely to be taken in the foreseeable future. During the Korean conflict, President Truman seized and operated steel and railroad companies, and his actions met with severe and even bitter criticism. Critics of government intervention believe it inhibits free collective bargaining.

There are two other compulsory arbitration agreements available for dispute settlement. Under both plans, the parties select a panel of neutrals. In one case, the panel hears only the issues in contention and then offers a ruling, which presumably breaks the deadlock. Under the second plan, the President would direct the parties to exchange two final offers with each other. There would then be a limited period of negotiation. If the offers failed to bring about a settlement, the panel of arbitrators would select the fairest, most reasonable offer as the contract. The arbitrators' decision would be based upon the historical relationships of terms and conditions of employment within the firm, and similar terms of comparable collective-bargaining units. Compulsory arbitration would indeed avert a strike, but there is considerable doubt, because of its negative effects on the bargaining relationships, whether it is worth the price.

ESTABLISHED DISPUTE SETTLEMENT PROCEDURES

Fact finding involves the appointment of a respected, neutral third party to study the facts underlying a dispute and to issue a report with specific recommendations for a fair settlement. Fact finding is traditionally preceded by negotiation and mediation efforts to resolve impasses. This method has been used to settle disputes under the Railway Labor Act since 1926 and under the national-emergency dispute provisions of the Taft-Hartley Act since 1947. The process is similar to arbitration except that either party can reject the fact finder's recommendations. This method certainly overcomes the inherent disadvantages of compulsory approaches, but it is not a panacea. Fact finders cannot possibly refrain from urging the parties to accept their reommendations, and the proceedings become more akin to mediation than pure fact finding.

Advisory arbitration is similar to fact finding in its approach. For a number of years it has been successfully employed in settling contract disputes between the United Press and Associated Press and the United Telegraph Workers, AFL-CIO.[22] Advisory arbitration is a modification of traditional arbitration. It is a voluntary process, which occurs after the parties have exhausted their dispute-settlement machinery, whereby an arbitrator renders an advisory opinion that is not binding on the parties. Advisory arbitration has most of the advantages of fact finding, mediation, and arbitration, but its application is limited to impasses over contract issues.

Final-offer arbitration consists of the submission of each party's final position and their arguments to substantiate their respective stands. The arbitrator considers both offers and must select one of them. The award must be one of the offered positions, not a compromise. This form of arbitration has been in existence for more than a decade and has been the source of considerable controversy. It was a method prescribed by President Nixon to resolve public-sector interest disputes and has been applied with variable success. On the positive side the requirement of the arbitrator to accept one position in toto induces the parties to develop their most reasonable position prior to arbitration. There is also an incentive for the parties to negotiate to a settlement because of the sudden death nature of the procedure. On the other hand, the winner-take-all characteristic of final-offer arbitration is a deterrent to the parties to submit voluntarily to the procedure.

POTENTIAL NEW METHODS

One of the methods by which labor and management can voluntarily limit the impact of their disputes is through a **statutory strike,** which in effect is a nonstoppage strike. By this arrangement, each side makes a monetary forfeiture as a substitute for the strike. If a strike vote passes, the workers agree to reduce their earnings by a stipulated amount and this money is placed in a public fund as a strike tax. Production continues during the statutory strike, and negotiators strive to reach agreement—an injunction precludes an actual walkout or lockout. Because the strike tax is permanently lost to the parties, and because they must pay the tax every seventh day of the injunction period, there is a strong inducement to settle. Although the statutory strike is difficult to implement, it retains most of the voluntary and power aspects of collective bargaining without the drawbacks of government intervention and lost production.

There are also proposals that would empower the President to use an **arsenal-of-weapons approach** in national emergency dispute seizures and when both parties are hostile to compulsory arbitration in such situations. Since labor opposes injunctions, management abhors seizures, and both are hostile to compulsory arbitration, the President can hold the threat of the arsenal approach over their heads as a deterrent to major work stoppages. Proponents theorize that the offensiveness of all these weapons, combined with the parties' uncertainty about which unpleasant measures will be inflicted on them, will induce settlements. Further, they argue that different weapons are needed for different disputes, so all of them should be available to the President. This approach is currently in use by the Federal Service Impasses Panel under Executive Order 11491. The success of the panel and the approach is unparalleled. The panel's power to issue a "Decision and Order" has only been used in 4 of over 200 cases; the balance of the disputes were settled either prior to hearing or by resolution based on recommendations for settlement.

The **partial operation approach** might overcome much of the distastefulness of the arsenal's proposed measures. Rather than infringe on the entire bargaining process, the government could alter the few strikes that affect the national welfare by intervening only to the extent necessary to keep minimum goods and services available. A limited injunction might allow reduced production while labor and management bargain under the pressures of a partial stoppage. The partial operation approach has had wide support, at least in concept. However, though it has been a Massachusetts law since 1947 and has been endorsed and praised by labor, management, and neutrals alike, it has rarely been used.

Cost-Benefit Analysis

Costs of dispute settlement vary with the method utilized, arbitration or mediation. Since arbitration costs are more readily controllable by the individual organization, we shall focus on them.

There can be considerable variation in the costs of conducting an arbitration hearing. Arbitrators' fees vary, but usually represent a small proportion of the overall cost. Unless the hearing is conducted at the offices of the company or union, there are meeting-site expenses. Organizations would be wise to weigh the costs versus benefits of a court reporter (transcript) and legal counsel. In addition, the wages or salaries of employees who serve as witnesses as well as the time of the staff members who investigate the grievance and prepare for arbitration, must be considered. If back pay is part of the remedy sought by the union, it represents an additional cost.

But we have already seen the numerous benefits of arbitration. The advantages of a continuous operation far outweigh the costs of the proceedings. Arbitration is also an alternative to civil suit; the delay as well as the legal fees and court costs far exceed the cost of arbitration.

Summary

Continued industrial peace is essential to the nation's economic welfare; hence, efforts to settle labor-management disputes are in the public interest. Alternative dispute settlement approaches strive to curtail the impact of strikes, but only methods that do not disrupt free collective bargaining can ever be truly effective. Voluntary, self-regulatory measures devised by the parties themselves are the most desirable.

Voluntary arbitration meets the criterion for a dispute settlement mechanism that preserves free bargaining. Grievances, contract issues, and other points of disagreement between labor and management can be amicably settled through arbitration. The parties themselves choose a neutral third party who hears both sides of the issue and renders a decision which, they have previously agreed, will be binding.

Supreme Court rulings have consistently supported the legitimacy of arbitration clauses. Under the Taft-Hartley Act, where an arbitration clause appears in a contract, the parties must submit all issues that are not resolved internally to arbitration, unless they have previously agreed to exclude specific items.

Mediation is another viable means for resolving labor-management disputes. Unlike arbitration, it attempts to get the parties to narrow, then resolve their differences. The mediator is a seasoned negotiator who understands the problems and, through joint meetings and separate conferences, helps the parties reach agreement.

Supplemental or alternative approaches such as fact finding and the statutory strike have been employed, experimented with, or proposed with varying degrees of success. If industrial peace is to be preserved, unions and management must find and voluntarily adopt measures to resolve their disputes.

Key Terms

interest arbitration	conciliation
rights arbitration	extended injunctions
deferral to arbitration	fact finding
expedited arbitration	advisory arbitration
preponderance of evidence	statutory strike
burden of proof	arsenal-of-weapons approach
mediation	partial operation approach

Review Questions

1. Distinguish between mediation and arbitration in labor-management dispute resolution.

2. What can supervisors do to help resolve strike situations?

3. Discuss the various court cases that both support and limit the arbitrator's authority.

4. Discuss the various alternatives to the strike (other than mediation and arbitration).

5. What are the principles of grievance handling? Discuss them.

6. Describe the mediation process.

Discussion Questions

1. A dispute is defined as *an argument, debate, quarrel; opposing in any way.* Does a union-management dispute have to end in a strike? What other outcomes might a dispute have? Describe at least two and discuss alternative methods for their resolution.

2. Suppose you were preparing a discipline case for arbitration. Contrast your case if you were the union spokesman and then the company representative. Would there be any difference in your approach if the employee were discharged instead of suspended?

3. This chapter emphasized that imposed dispute settlements are harmful to free collective bargaining. Why is this so?

4. The role of neutrals appears to be expanding in settling union-management disputes. Discuss at least three labor-relations situations in which neutrals might be used. What advantages and disadvantages do you see in using neutrals in union-management dispute settlements?

5. In your opinion, can federal legislation minimize the impact of strike activity on our economy and also preserve free collective bargaining? Describe the elements of a bill that might accomplish this objective.

6. How might worker-employer disputes be handled if the contract had no arbitration clause or if there were no contract as opposed to a situation in which there is an arbitration clause?

"Pete, we just can't do it!" said Mr. Hartley, United Manufacturing Company's manager of personnel relations. "I know that we promised, but we just can't!"

"Look, Mr. Hartley, this whole thing went to arbitration last year. We both agreed to accept the arbitrator's ruling. He ruled that warehouse seven has to be kept at 70 degrees all the time. Now, you have to do it."

"Last year, when that ruling was made, there wasn't any energy crisis, Pete. We were perfectly willing to heat up that place. But that was just after the base period for fuel oil allocations. When we got our allocation, they cut us 10 percent as it is, not even counting the 20,000 gallons it'll take every winter to heat up number seven. Be reasonable!"

"Mr. Hartley, it's cold in that place."

"Yes, but a man only goes in once or twice a day."

"And every time they go in, they stay there for as long as 30 minutes. You can turn blue in that place in 10 minutes, let alone 30. Why, yesterday we took the temperature—it was 37 degrees in there, and Sam had to find some stuff. He damn near froze before he finally located the junk."

"We just use number seven for odd storage, Pete. You know that. No one has to work in there. Besides, we just don't have the fuel. Even if we had it, it costs twice as much as it did when the arbitrator made that award."

"Mr. Hartley, we agreed to accept arbitration, and we aren't moaning. You agreed too. What is going on now is your problem. We want number seven heated. We expect the dump to be up to at least 68 degrees by next Monday—we'll give you that much."

"Oh, fine," Mr. Hartley said. "We save a thousand gallons of oil on that."

"If it isn't, we go to court. None of my men are going to freeze to death just because this cheap company can't keep its buildings warm."

Case Problem 1

UNWINDING ARBITRATION

Problems

1. Is Pete being reasonable here?

2. Is Mr. Hartley being reasonable here?

3. What should Pete do?

4. What should Mr. Hartley do?

5. Under the changed circumstances, is the arbitrator's ruling still binding?

6. Can the parties legally agree to amend the arbitrator's award to maintain a 70-degree temperature?

Case Problem 2

MAY THE BEST MAN WIN

Jack Brown, a black, was hired by the Westwind Manufacturing Company as a mechanic in August 1969. He was the first black this company had ever hired, although the firm had been in existence since 1911.

Mark Wilson, white, was hired in September 1969, by the same company, also as a mechanic. The two men worked together in the shop where they repaired company trucks and other internal combustion powered equipment.

Jack was a tolerable mechanic, but not really all that good. Mark was considered significantly better as a mechanic, and his ratings by his superior (who also supervised Jack) showed this. Mark usually got the tough jobs because he could produce.

This year a vacancy occurred in a shop that the company had recently opened. The job called for a grade 16 mechanic, and at this time Jack and Mark were rated grade 14. The company only used two grade 16 mechanics, since its work did not usually involve this type of advanced mechanical work. Among other things, a grade 16 mechanic did engine rebuilding and re-assembly, a highly skilled craft. A failure here could mean a ruined engine—and truck engines cost over $4,000 each.

The company offered the job to Mark, and he accepted it. Shortly thereafter, Jack filed a grievance under the union contract. He alleged two things: first, since he had seniority over Mark, he should get the grade 16 job, which paid $1.33 an hour more than grade 14. Second, the company was guilty of discriminatory practices, since it rarely hired minority persons, and never promoted them.

The company pointed out that since 1969, it had indeed hired many minority workers, who now amounted to 8.5 percent of its total work force of 388. It further noted that this grade 16 job called for skills that most mechanics did not have, and that it had a right to promote the best person, not the one who had seniority. But at this time the company had no women or minority supervisors.

Problems

1. Who's right here? Why?

2. Suppose that the company is right and that Mark is a superior mechanic, but Jack might be able to do the job. Does this change your answer? Why or why not?

3. When does competence *really* count in promotion situations? When doesn't it matter much?

4. Suppose that Mark and Jack worked for a major airline, and the mechanical work they do is on aircraft that you might fly in some day. Does this make any difference in your answer? Why or why not?

Notes

1. I Kings 3:16–27.

2. *Textile Workers Union v. Lincoln Mills,* 353 U.S. 448 (1957).

3. *United Steelworkers v. Warrior and Gulf Navigation Co.,* 353 U.S. 574, 578–79.

4. *United Steelworkers v. American Manufacturing Company,* 363 U.S. 564, 567–68.

5. *United Steelworkers v. Enterprise Wheel and Car Corporation,* 363 U.S. 593, 596–97.

6. H. K. Porter v. United Steelworkers, 333f. 2d. 596 (3d Cir.).

7. *Torrington Co. v. Metal Products Workers Union,* U.A.W. AFL-CIO, Local 1645, 362F. 2d. 677 (2d Cir.).

8. Ibid. 363.

9. 415 U.S. 36 (S. Ct. 1974) 7EPD 9148.

10. *Henes v. Anchor Motor Freight,* 96 U.S. Sup. Ct. 1048 (1976).

11. *Collyer Insulated Wire,* 192 N.L.R.B. 837 (1971).

12. *Dubo Manufacturing Corporation,* 142 N.L.R.B. 431 (1963).

13. *Spielberg Manufacturing Company,* 112, N.L.R.B. 1082 (1955).

14. *Kansas City Star Co.,* 236 N.L.R.B. 119 (1978).

15. Julius Rezler and Donald Petersen, "Strategies of Arbitrator Selection," *Daily Labor Report,* June 26, 1978, D-1–D-10.

16. Bruce R. Boals, "Attitudinal Survey of Industrial Relations Managers in Tennessee Manufacturing Towards Arbitrators and Arbitration." Copies of the survey results are available from the author, Division of Business Administration, The University of Tennessee at Nashville, Tenth and Charlotte, Nashville, TN 37203.

17. *Jacob Ruppert v. Office Employees International Union,* Local 153 (October 19, 1960), 35 LA 503, 504, Arbitrator Burton B. Turkus. BNA, Inc.

18. "Breakthrough in Expedited Arbitration," *Steel Labor* (Pittsburgh, Pa.: United Steelworkers Union of America, May 1972), p. 9.

19. Walter A. Maggilo, *Techniques of Mediation in Labor Disputes* (Dobbs Ferry, N.Y.: Oceana Publications, 1971), pp. 30–31.

20. Ibid., pp. 47–62.

21. Ibid., pp. 12ff.

22. Ezra K. Bryan, "Avoiding Confrontation by Advisory Arbitration," in Gerald G. Somers, ed., *Arbitration and the Expanding Role of Neutrals, Proceedings of the Twenty-Third Annual Meeting, National Academy of Arbitrators* (Washington, D.C.: Bureau of National Affairs, 1970).

Section Four

DEVELOPING EMPLOYEE POTENTIAL

Human resource effectiveness depends to a large degree on developing the capabilities of employees. Rapid change in all aspects of business, from technology to social interaction, demands constant efforts to keep employees informed of new policies, techniques, and developments in the organization and in the economy. Considering the variegated composition of the work force, management faces a real challenge and responsibility in developing the full potential of every employee. Concepts and techniques applicable to human resource training in general are covered in this section, and specific examples of training programs are discussed. An overall scheme incorporating the essential components of executive development is presented along with a systematic, situational approach to development activities. Special development programs for women, minorities, and handicapped persons are also covered.

Chapter Thirteen
Human Resource Training

Angus Badger was a hard-core unemployed before the president of Metal Cabinet Works, Ltd., agreed to hire him. On his first day on the job he was assigned to the fabrication department as a cutting-machine operator. The department foreman instructed him in operating the machine.

Foreman: OK, Angus, this here machine is real simple. Now just watch me. You take this piece of sheet metal from the pile here and place it on the table. Then you step on the foot pedal like this and you pull the lever. See? Think you can do it?

Angus: Oh, sure.

So Angus repeats the same steps, but the pattern cut is irregular.

Foreman: OK, Angus. Try it again; this time be more careful.

Angus: Yeah man!

Angus tries again with no better result than the first time.

Foreman: I guess some people just can't do anything right! Turning to his assistant—*What do you think we can do with this guy? We can't dump him 'cause the president hired the guy himself.*

Asst.: Suppose we could let him operate the elevator and clean up around the place. But who'll run the cutter?

LEARNING OBJECTIVES

1. To be familiar with the various types of employee training.

2. To know the basic concepts of learning.

3. To know the methods of determining training needs.

4. To know the various techniques for conducting training sessions.

5. To know the methods of evaluating training effectiveness.

Foreman: Don't worry about that, my kid brother just got laid off over at Johnstown
Assembly. He could use the work.

NEXT DAY

Foreman: Putting his arm around his brother—Bo, I'm sure glad we had this
job come open. You don't have to worry about getting laid off here. As
long as you're working for this company I'll look out for you. This is
an important job you have here. Y'know that XL-100 you have home?

Bo: Yeah.

Foreman: Well, I know you're proud of it. That pretty cabinet it sits in starts right
here. See these metal blanks. Your machine cuts them so they can be
made into a cabinet, so you need to be real careful how you work the
cutter. There are a couple of tricks to doing it right, but I'll teach you.

Bo: Thanks, brother.

Foreman: You take this blank—there's a shiny side and a dull side. Ya put the
shiny side up on this here table, it cuts smoother that way. Then ya
slap the table on the side like this, see?

Bo: Gotcha, brother.

Foreman: Then you stomp on this foot pedal and just as you feel it hit and start
to come back up, ya pull this lever. And there's a good cut! Wanna try
it?

Bo: You betcha!

So Bo performs the steps in the operation. And you guessed it, he
does it perfectly!

Human resource training (HRT) incorporates the teaching of the art
and science of performing a job. HRT refers to the process of helping employees improve their effectiveness in present and future jobs. HRT integrates
the training system and techniques with the behavioral aspects of development. This implies that the HRT situation is student-centered; it is tailored
to the individual needs and abilities of trainees. In our example Angus's
needs were not considered (he had never worked before and wasn't familiar
with machine operations), so he failed. Bo's needs were considered, and he
was successful. HRT also means that it is a continuous process, starting with
the introduction of employees to their first jobs and continuing throughout
their careers. But Angus was only told that his job was simple, while Bo
was given the total picture—how his job related to the entire production
process as well as the tricks of performing the job. Organizations that really
want their people to learn adopt the attitude that "to expect a particular

kind of performance from employees, we must *teach* them how we want them to perform.''

In this chapter we shall describe the various types of training (HRT activities) that organizations use and the components and techniques of an HRT system. Much of the discussion applies to any HRT situation regardless of who is to be trained and developed.

Classification of HRT Activities

EMPLOYEE ORIENTATION

Employees' initial impressions of their organizations may shape their attitudes about their work situations and affect their performance long after they are hired. In fact, it is of key importance in integrating them into the organization. Employees' introduction to their new employer, therefore, should attempt to make them feel welcome and needed and present a favorable image of the organization. Most organizations orient new employees by informing them about the nature of their job; history, products, and objectives of the company; rules and regulations; physical situation near their work area; and the names of their supervisors and fellow employees. This information gives new employees a feeling for the significance of the work they will perform and a sense of being a part of the organization. Also, describing job duties during orientation reduces misunderstandings, thus permitting new employees to learn the skills that are required quickly during training.

More specifically, orientation generally consists of three stages:

1. *Preliminary,* which consists of the initial introduction of the new employee to the company;

2. *Pre-duty,* just prior to starting work in the initial assignment.

3. *Continuing,* which is the educational and reorientation process to integrate the employee fully into the organization.[1]

The preliminary stage enables employee/employer relationships to begin on a positive note. Unfortunately, many orientation programs fail to recognize the opportunity to respond to the organization's need for self-aggrandizement. The new employee naturally has personal anxieties about the new or changed work setting. Hence, the need exists to reduce unknowns by helping the new employee learn about his/her job, supervisors, and co-workers. Ideally, this could be accomplished on a one-to-one basis with the supervisor making the new employee feel welcome and taking the time to familiarize the employee with all aspects of the job's performance measures, its requirements, skills, physical aspects, and any other information necessary to assure expected performance.[2] Several problems arise from this approach, however. In order to be successful in the orientation process, supervisors require training in the rudiments of teaching. This takes time and resources that few organizations are willing to commit. Also, supervisors sometimes find themselves too busy to devote the necessary time to inducting the new employee properly. Yet neglecting the details of orientation can have dire consequences in the long run. Employees who are inadequately oriented are more likely to be less productive than expected and they may even become discipline problems. For example, there are many cases of employees failing to obey work rules, claiming the rules were never explained to them in the first place. One method of ensuring that supervisors cover the necessary details is the use of a checklist similar to the one that is shown in Table 13.1.

Table 13.1
Checklist of Information for New Employees

To the New Employee:

We want to help you get off to a good start on your new job. Being fully informed about it will aid you greatly. Please complete this questionnaire and return it to your supervisor today. If you know the answer place a check in the left-hand column: if not, place a check in the right-hand column.

	I clearly understood the explanation.	I would like more information.
DO YOU KNOW:		
1. *How to report for work*		
How to record your time?	————	————
How you should dress for work?	————	————
Where to leave personal property?	————	————
2. *How you are paid*		
Your rate of pay?	————	————
When and how you are paid?	————	————
Days and hours of work?	————	————
Deductions from your pay?	————	————
3. *How to report*		
An absence, accident, your problems?	————	————
Change of address, marital status, number of dependents?	————	————

	I clearly understood the explanation.	I would like more information.	Table 13.1 (cont.)
4. Do you understand			
Smoking, safety, and fire rules?	_____	_____	
Security regulations?	_____	_____	
Rules of conduct?	_____	_____	
Details of your job?	_____	_____	
Plant locations?	_____	_____	
Affirmative Action Program?	_____	_____	
5. Your benefits			
Group insurance?	_____	_____	
Retirement plan?	_____	_____	
Holidays?	_____	_____	
Vacations?	_____	_____	
Workers compensation?	_____	_____	
Social Security?	_____	_____	
Promotion policy?	_____	_____	
6. Names			
Your supervisor's name?	_____	_____	
Your fellow workers' names?	_____	_____	

List below any further questions you may have concerning the company, your job, or anything else.

_____

_____

_____

_____

_____
Employee signature

By the preduty stage, new employees should have a sense of belonging to the organization. At this point, a variety of methods can be employed. Groups of new hires might be briefed on subjects considered to be important (company history, policies, benefits, etc.) and they might be taken on a tour of the facilities. The essential aspect of this phase of orientation is to gain a lasting commitment on the part of the employees. Here they can be made to feel that their services are needed and that the organization can provide opportunity for growth and security. Training professionals are naturally involved in all stages of orientation, but they are the ones who traditionally conduct the preduty stage. Line managers, though, are not excluded from taking an active role as well.

When few new employees are hired together or when hiring is sporadic, the delivery of orientation training becomes a problem. Many organizations have overcome this by utilizing individualized approaches. Parts of the orientation programs are produced on a video cassette that can be played on a conventional television viewer at the convenience of the employee.[3] To reinforce the learning experience the taped presentations can be combined with **programmed-learning** modules of back-up information in manuals or self-study pamphlets.

The continuing stage includes ongoing educational opportunities. Employees are exposed to various training and educational experiences based on their individual needs. In this process, they are gradually weaned from the orientation group and assimilated into the general skill area work force.[4]

VESTIBULE TRAINING

When many employees must be trained quickly, **vestibule training** can provide the answer. Under this arrangement, a training area is set up away from the work area to approximate, as closely as possible, actual working conditions. With the guidance of special instructors, trainees can learn the skills of the job without the pressures of a production schedule. Theoretically, vestibule training permits greater emphasis on proper techniques, and results in more productive workers. But vestibule training does not have the same environment as the actual work place. When trainees assume their jobs, they will have to adjust to the production situation, and this adjustment can inhibit their efficiency. Supervisors at the work place are not likely to give workers the kind of encouragement they received from their instructors (and therefore may cause them to become discouraged). This problem can become particularly acute when the disadvantaged enter the work force. Line supervisors must be keenly aware that their continued attention is necessary, otherwise employees may become discouraged and resign.

ON-THE-JOB TRAINING

The more common **on-the-job training** (in contrast to vestibule or off-the-job training) requires employees to learn skills at their work place by receiving individualized instruction on a one-to-one basis from their instructors. The negative aspect of on-the-job training is that instructors may be poor teachers. Organizations frequently assign training responsibilities to supervisors or seasoned employees without knowing whether they possess teaching abilities. As a consequence, workers develop inefficient or unsafe habits that (if they are ever detected) are difficult to correct. But if the instructors or the teachers are carefully selected and taught how to instruct, this method is a most effective means of training large numbers of workers.

The more highly skilled the work, the greater the need for preparation in training. Today's production methods call for sophisticated machinery that, in turn, requires skilled operators and technicians. Hence, workers of this type must not only have special aptitudes but must be educated in subjects related to their particular skill. For instance, machinists and even some machine operators must learn algebra and trigonometry to calculate tolerances and angles.

RETRAINING AND REFRESHER TRAINING

Rapid change is a phenomenon that organizations will be facing in the future, and that will cause many jobs and skills to become obsolete at an increasing rate.[5] Changed work methods, the introduction of new products, reorganization, and the revision of policy give impetus to programs for retraining.

The speedy advance of technology in this country has resulted in the displacement of numerous skills. The introduction of computers in payroll and accounting departments has mechanized data gathering and posting operations formerly performed by hand. In many instances employees who performed these functions have been retrained in data-processing machine operation, thus upgrading their skills as well as their compensation. Employees who have been displaced by an economic recession or the phasing out of a government contract frequently find their skills unsuited to other organizations. This was the situation when some aerospace contractors eliminated projects or otherwise curtailed production. During one layoff when many aerospace engineers found themselves out of work for long periods, some enrolled in training programs to learn new skills. Also, with the rapid change in methods and technology, companies must often untrain employees in inefficient procedures before retraining them in new techniques and proper equipment operation. The experience of a prosperous manufacturer of soft drinks is a good illustration. Retail sales were beginning to decline, so the marketing director conducted a study to find out why. He discovered that the veteran route salespersons were completing fewer than half the steps they had originally been trained to follow and sales were suffering as a result. Items as significant as rotating the product to ensure that there was a variety of fresh beverages on the shelves, pricing the product, installing point-of-purchase advertising, and asking for increased shelf space were among the items ignored by these salespeople. The introduction of a short refresher program had dramatic results. The program included a one-day classroom reorientation to reacquaint the salespeople with the items on the checklist and to remind them of the importance of completing *all* of them. The managers rode the routes with the salespersons to reinforce the training, and later each sales manager checked a sampling of outlets in each territory on a regular basis to assure that items on the checklist were being completed correctly. Soon afterwards sales revenues (as well as market share) showed significant improvement.

VOCATIONAL REHABILITATION

The current concern with social responsibility in business, coupled with EEOC amendments, has placed considerable emphasis on hiring the handicapped. With **vocational rehabilitation** workers with impaired hearing or sight and amputees with artificial limbs can prove to be as skilled as other employees. Those who have been rehabilitated are highly motivated to succeed. Studies show that these employees usually prove more capable and more loyal than the average employee. Public opinion has changed to the point that the physically handicapped are no longer relegated to second-rate jobs and are now employed in almost every field. Juliette Arthur, in writing on handicapped employment, points out:

> There are over three hundred different jobs that blind men and women are holding in industry and the professions. There are deaf employees doing work as diversified as the sixty or more on the payroll of Lockheed Missile and Space Company, where they work as chemist, clerk, electrical assembler, engineer, inspector, janitor, machinist, sheet metal worker, or welder.[6]

Few training programs for the physically handicapped exist within business organizations but there are numerous agencies and schools especially equipped to teach them new skills. Studies show that not many disabled workers take the initiative in retraining themselves, but companies with such employees can guide and encourage them in training opportunities outside the organization. Worker's compensation systems provide vocational rehabilitation for workers injured on the job. In addition, the Veterans Administration and various state agencies offer programs for the handicapped to develop skills.

APPRENTICESHIP TRAINING

Apprenticeship training is designed to develop specific skills. Apprentices perform useful work while learning a trade, becoming increasingly valuable as they progress in their training. In return for a period of employment, apprentices sign an agreement with an employer to learn a specific trade in accordance with standards certified by an accrediting agency (usually the Department of Labor, Bureau of Apprenticeship and Training, or a state agency recognized by the latter). The agreement also includes detailed standards that govern each apprenticeship program. As an example, a synopsis of the automobile mechanics' standards is included in Table 13.2. Under the guidance of skilled journeymen, apprentices progressively increase their capabilities through on-the-job training supplemented by classroom instruction or correspondence study in related subjects. As they advance in the program, their wages are progressively increased until they reach the journeyman rate.

Properly planned and administered apprenticeship programs can assure companies of an adequate supply of skilled craftsmen. Such programs not only attract high-caliber employees but are also an excellent means of improving employee-employer relations. The author recalls helping negotiate

---

Table 13.2
Standards of Apprenticeship (synopsis)*

Automobile Mechanics

1. Age: At least 18.

2. Term of apprenticeship: 3 years (approximately 6,000 hours).

3. Aptitude for mechanical work plus other selection criteria—established by local apprenticeship committee.

4. Related instruction: 144 hours in classroom or self-study (to be taken on company time).

5. Wages: 55% of journeyman's rate first year following 15 week probationary period to 90% during 3rd year.

6. Periodic examination during apprenticeship.

7. Scheduled work experience specified in the standards includes an orientation period plus a sequence of tasks to be mastered throughout the apprenticeship.

8. Provisions for supervision of on-the-job training.

*U.S. Department of Labor, Manpower Administration, Bureau of Apprenticeship and Training. Washington, D.C., *Standards of Apprenticeship*, 1966.

the first apprenticeship agreement with a particular industrial union. The labor representatives had not been convinced of the program's value until diesel mechanics, who were dues-paying union members, were laid off. During a lengthy period of unemployment they were unable to find work elsewhere in the tight labor market. The experience made these workers realize that if they had been certified journeymen mechanics, they would have received abundant job offers. After working out a few internal problems (i.e., selection procedures and seniority provisions), the company and the union reached an agreement; the apprenticeship program later proved to be mutually advantageous.

The advent of high unemployment and the recent emphasis by the federal government on upgrading the skills of women and minorities have focused attention on apprenticeship programs.[7]

JOB-INSTRUCTION TRAINING

As previously emphasized, the quality of training is only as good as the instructors. Therefore, it is essential that instructors be trained in proper teaching techniques. During the Second World War, the War Manpower Commission developed the JIT (Job-Instruction Training) program for teaching industrial trainers how to instruct. It utilizes the four-step method shown in Table 13.3.

CORRESPONDENCE STUDY

Convenience is the greatest single advantage of correspondence courses, or home study. Also, this form of training allows students to complete a series of lessons at their own pace. After receiving the training

Table 13.3
How to Instruct

	Prepare the trainees. Put them at ease and discuss the specific job. Find out what they know about the job, and develop their interest.
Step 2	*Present the job.* Explain and demonstrate each step, one at a time. Stress key points, especially safety. Present no more than trainees can master at one time.
Step 3	*Try out performance.* Have trainees do the job, explaining each detail in advance. Correct errors and have them do the job again. Continue until they have mastered the task.
Step 4	*Follow up.* Put trainees on their own. Have them assist the instructor in training others. Tell them where to go for help, and encourage questions. Check frequently, but taper off coaching.

materials by mail, students prepare a sequence of assignments in accordance with detailed instructions. As they complete each lesson, they test their knowledge by solving problems, preparing cases, answering questions, or completing a quiz, which they forward to the instructor for grading and critique. The instructor's comments then reinforce the learning process.

Correspondence courses cover a spectrum of subjects ranging from basic arithmetic to sophisticated electronics or from elements of supervision to law. Some colleges and universities even offer courses with credit toward undergraduate degrees. Correspondence study can supplement on-the-job training as in apprenticeship programs, or complement classroom instruction in programs such as basic supervision. In home-study courses, instruction materials must be especially clear because the instructor is not immediately available to answer questions. Also, the better correspondence courses represent significant research and development efforts. Because enrollees do not have to be centrally located and do not have to complete assignments at the same time, many can take the courses. With the high cost of developing content and materials spread over many enrollees, the registration fee is relatively small. These advantages for the students translate into benefits for companies. Employees can develop essential skills at low cost without having to travel to a central location or tie up training facilities. And most correspondence courses can be completed at home on the employee's own time. Private home-study schools are accredited by an independent Home Study Accrediting Commission, which has been approved by the Office of Education as a nationally recognized accrediting agency under Public Laws 82-550 and 85-564.[8]

GOVERNMENT-SPONSORED TRAINING PROGRAMS

The Manpower and Development Training Act of 1962 (MDTA) created and funded a national program to provide manpower research and occupational training for disadvantaged citizens so they can become productive wage earners. Major programs established under MDTA provisions include institutional and on-the-job training. The majority of trainees enrolled in the institutional program receive training in public and private vocational education or technical schools; more recently manpower training centers have been established in larger cities for this program. Although classroom work is included, these programs emphasize shop work. In on-the-job training programs, enrollees are hired and then taught work skills while they are gainfully employed. The programs focus on helping the underemployed upgrade their skills and on equipping the unemployed with the new skills required by a changing job market. Other sections of the act provide for training in basic education and also help workers qualify for and benefit from occupational training. The act also makes special efforts to assist such disadvantaged groups as minorities, handicapped workers, public assistance recipients, and unemployment insurance claimants.

By the end of the 1960s, there were more than seventeen government-funded programs to provide training and employment opportunities for the disadvantaged, underemployed, and unemployed. Each of these so-called categorical programs had a separate organization and funding base. The general dissatisfaction with this patchwork approach led to the passage of the Comprehensive Employment and Training Act (CETA) in late 1973. This legislation established a program to provide comprehensive manpower services throughout the nation. Its purpose is to give financial assistance to state and local governments (prime sponsors) which will, in turn, research, design, and deliver training programs, job opportunities, educational and counseling services, supportive services (e.g., child care, medical services, job information) for people most in need of help (disadvantaged, unemployed, and underemployed). The act also provides funds for hiring unemployed and underemployed persons in public service jobs; special federally supervised programs for Indians, migrant and seasonal farm workers, persons of limited English-speaking ability, youth offenders, and older workers; and the continuation of the Job Corps, which develops disadvantaged young people for gainful employment. Prime sponsors are required to establish advisory planning councils that are representative of the population mix in the area. With these councils the CETA staff prepares programs dictated by the people in their area.[9]

The magnitude of CETA is indicated by the fact that in fiscal year 1979–80 the total CETA budget was $8.6 billion, and a total of 4.5 million citizens were trained to provide services through CETA offices.[10] Yet, a three-year comprehensive study of CETA's impact suggested that those most in need (low-income people and women) received progressively fewer benefits from (CETA) programs.[11] At the time of the writing of this edition the CETA program was being phased out by the Reagan administration.

VOCATIONAL AND TECHNICAL EDUCATION

Recognizing the continuing need for specialized skills development, the federal government appropriates funds to promote vocational education by constructing new facilities (vocational-technical schools), developing necessary curricula, and encouraging citizens to enroll in programs. Vocational education in modern industrial training has been expanded by the appropriation of funds, most prominently through the National Defense Education Act of 1958, the Vocational Rehabilitation Act of 1973, and the Vocational Educational Act of 1963. The wider availability of such training in future years will make it even more vital in developing productive skills. In addition to these government-sponsored schools, technical training is also conducted in proprietary trade schools (about 20,000 exist throughout the country), through vocational-education programs in high schools, in company-sponsored institutes such as General Motors Institute and RCA Institute, and through university extension programs.

HRT As a System

The development of human resources is both costly and time-consuming. Consequently, line management will not hesitate to insist on evidence that its objectives are being enhanced by HRT activities. A systematic approach helps ensure that training and development efforts are directed toward the organization's objectives. Figure 13.1 illustrates the HRT system. While this system is designed expressly for employee training, many organizations have adopted the *Human Resources Development* (HRD) approach. HRD is a set of management practices concerned with optimizing the interaction of people, their work, and the organization so that the entire organization can function as effectively as possible.[12]

In the HRT system (Figure 13.1), analyses are made initially of the organization, operations, and people do determine development needs. Then objectives are prepared that focus on performance standards. They are concerned with the specific skills, knowledge, and abilities a trainee needs to be effective on the job. Next, curricula are created to meet these objectives. This involves the selection, organization, and presentation of subject matter

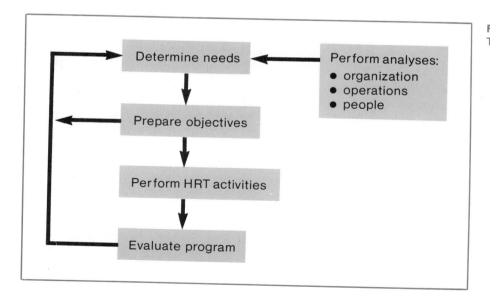

Figure 13.1
The HRT System

within the framework of practical, proven principles of educational psychology. (See the short discussion of learning theory in this chapter.) The use of course outlines, lesson plans, competent instructors, and adequate facilities equipped with audio-visual aids enhances presentations. Finally, each session and the overall course undergo continuous scrutiny. The evaluation process compares training/development results against objectives to ascertain how well organizational needs have been met. Improvements indicated by the evaluation can then be incorporated into subsequent offerings.

Determining Training Needs

Although some organizations still train for the sake of training, enlightened management insists on applying quality control to training just as to any other management process. The effect on personnel people of this insistence has been most fruitful: either they create effective training tools or they are eliminated.

In the HRT system, organizations first analyze specific problems that training can help solve, and they create programs on this basis. If organizations can carefully and specifically define needs, they can write intelligent and clear-cut objectives and later assess a program's performance against them. Evaluation will show management in rigorous and definite terms to what extent training has fulfilled the need for which it was created. The reality of this approach is simple: there is no need for training unless a problem—which training can help solve—exists.

TECHNIQUES FOR TRAINING-NEEDS DETERMINATION

McGehee suggests a scheme for training-needs determination. He recommends an **organizational analysis** to determine which organization training efforts are to be emphasized, **operations analysis** to determine what the training content should be, and **personnel analysis** to find out how employees must behave to perform their job tasks in an acceptable manner.[13]

ORGANIZATIONAL ANALYSIS.   This analysis consists of three major categories. The *personnel audit* involves taking inventory of the skills and talents available in an organization and projecting the kinds and numbers of employees that will be needed in the future. This type of analysis takes into consideration anticipated technological, marketing, and organizational changes so that needs can be anticipated and lead time can be provided to meet those needs. For example, if payroll will be handled by electronic data processing, payroll clerks can be retained in key punch operation, computer programming, and related fields.

Through **organizational effectiveness** analysis various indices are examined to see whether training might improve the performance these indices measure. Statistical reports can be reviewed to uncover problems on production, safety, costs, quality, maintenance, absenteeism, attitudes, morale, or turnover. The difficulty with these indices, however, is that their primary purpose is not to spot training needs, so they probably are biased. Statistics can signal possible problems for training, but the HRT manager will have to investigate the factors that make up the index before accepting it as an indication of training need.

ORGANIZATIONAL CLIMATE ANALYSIS. Organizational climate is composed of the opinions, beliefs, attitudes, and feelings that members have about their organization, others in it, and their own role. It is essentially the organization's value system, and it determines the support any HRT activity is likely to receive. Unless the organization values better performance and rewards it, there is little chance that HRT activities will succeed. Consider, for example, the frustration of the supervisor who has just completed a course in human relations and whose manager remarks, "Just forget that stuff those training guys threw at you and get your people to shape up." Such a statement reflects the manager's attitude that human relations training is a waste of time. If other managers share these feelings, training efforts in this area are destined to fail.

The organizational climate can be analyzed in several ways. Attitude surveys are frequently used to uncover employee concerns and dissatisfactions and can often pinpoint problem areas that training can resolve. Through exit interviews, terminating employees can provide information that might indicate deficiencies in training activities. Review of personnel reports on grievances, suggestions, absenteeism, and so on can also be enlightening in uncovering training needs. Often when the people who will probably be trained have been asked their opinions of needs, they respond more favorably when placed in training programs they recommended. In this regard, training-needs surveys or advisory committees of key people in an organization are appropriate.[14] However, these approaches have built-in biases in that those being trained may not recognize their own deficiencies or other problem areas most needing development.

OPERATIONS ANALYSIS. Although operations analysis utilizes many of the same techniques used in job analysis (Chapter 5 "Human Resource Planning and Recruiting" discussed job analysis), there are differences in the two analyses. Operations analysis is *employee*-centered (rather than job- or task-centered), and it specifies the level of behavior (objectives) and standards of performance (criteria).

Specific questions that might be answered in an operations analysis would include:

1. What is the desired performance?
2. What are the differences between the incumbent's actual versus expected performance?
3. What is the cost of the performance deficiency (assuming one exists)?
4. Could the employee perform properly if his or her life depended on it?
5. Do deficient workers know *what* is expected? *How* and *when* to perform correctly?
6. What are the consequences of performing correctly versus incorrectly?
7. Is the problem a lack of understanding or a lack of skill?[15]

An instrument that has been used successfully in operations analysis is the *Position-Analysis Questionnaire,* which measures, in psychological terms, the inputs an employee must deal with in performing a job and the outputs or results he or she is expected to achieve.[16]

PERSONNEL ANALYSIS. The focus of training is on the behavioral change of *individuals.* Inexperienced employees lack skills, knowledge, and abilities necessary to perform effectively, and experienced employees sometimes develop poor work habits or were improperly trained originally. Thus analyses of work performance can identify individuals whose below-standard performance can be upgraded by training. A personnel analysis also seeks to determine specific deficiencies in skill, ability, knowledge and attitude that training can improve.

PREPARING HRT OBJECTIVES

Objectives provide a framework for organizing a training program. They can delineate the knowledge required in each subject area and guide companies in selecting appropriate teaching methods. They can then evaluate training effectiveness against these objectives. Training directors then break down every major section of the course and write specific objectives for each. A presentation usually has at least three or four very specific objectives. The following criteria are guideposts in defining objectives.

1. Training objectives and corporate goals must be compatible.
2. Objectives must be realistic.
3. Objectives must be clearly stated in writing.
4. Results must be measurable and verifiable.

In writing training objectives, program directors distinguish two basic areas of training. The first involves the development of skills that are mainly physical in nature and usually require conditioned reflexes. Mental activity is present, but the primary goal is some form of physical movement. The second general category, ideation, is the development of knowledge, understanding, attitudes, and conceptual analysis. In both of these areas, skill and ideation, there are three levels of learning, and objectives can be stated in terms of these levels.

SKILLS LEARNING LEVELS. *Level I—The Appreciation Level.* Training at this level merely exposes students to the discipline. Students are taught the skill under the guidance of instructors.

Level II—The Performance Level. Here students are taught to perform the task with only occasional supervision, typically through vestibule training (a classroom training technique that utilizes the essential elements of the job site).

Level III—The Mastery Level. At this level students are not only able to perform the skill but to teach it.

IDEATION LEARNING LEVELS. *Level I—The Appreciation Level.* Instructors present only a general overview of the subject.

Level II—The Performance Level. The instructor's objective is to ascertain that all trainees learn and recall the subject matter. The presentation must be complete and must include repetition and evaluation to ensure that students thoroughly assimilate the material.

Level III—The Mastery Level. Instructors teach not only the structure of the subject but also the significance of each item and the relationship among items. Students should be able to recall the significant points and discuss their own philosophies of the subject.

PERFORMING HRT ACTIVITIES

Determining who will teach and how they will do so is as important as determining what is taught. The type of training system needed is a function of many situational variables such as: the type of industry, company size, customer requirements, technological development, level and variety of employee skills, union relations, legal and government requirements, and company policies. However, the attitude of top management is *the* most significant determinant. As we mentioned in our discussion of organizational climate analysis, when executives believe that training contributes to company objectives, the training function will have a significant impact.

Large organizations usually have a training (HRT) department or division sometimes housed in a separate training center with a full-time faculty and administrators. Course offerings may even include the full curriculum for a bachelor's degree. The staff of a large HRT organization consists of specialists and coordinators supervised by training managers, with line managers as technical advisors and instructors. Staff members research needs, define objectives, establish standards, and develop, conduct, and evaluate programs. Staff specialists also do the actual training, although larger organizations often enlist line operators and supervisors, since they are experts in their area. However, people who are experienced operators are not necessarily capable instructors. Operating a machine and teaching other people how to operate it require very different abilities. Therefore, organizations try to select instructors carefully to ensure that they possess not only the skill to be taught, but also the ability to teach the skill. Organizations must often train instructors to teach, for competent teaching requires a knowledge of the principles of learning. Some of the more commonly accepted learning theories are discussed below.

Regardless of size, many organizations rely, either partially or exclusively, on outside contractors and educational institutions to develop and implement specific HRT programs. Area vocational-technical schools, for example, offer a spectrum of skills-related courses; and academic institutions, through their continuing education divisions, can supply programs from their catalogs, but many also have the capability of delivering tailor-made seminars and courses. And business organizations like IBM, Xerox, Control Data, General Electric, and many others can contract with organizations to bring HRT activities in-house.

Learning Concepts

FEEDBACK

Feedback, or knowledge of one's success, is necessary for learning. People learn faster when they receive immediate, informative feedback on their performance. It enables them to direct their effort toward what they don't know rather than expend it on what they have already learned. Awareness of results not only reinforces acquired knowledge but also encourages more learning. Instructors also need continuous feedback to evaluate the success of their teaching methods. Attentiveness of students, response to instructors' questions, test results, observers' comments, and participants' opinions are feedback that can tell instructors how effective their teaching methods are.

SCHEDULES OF LEARNING

Massed practice is training concentrated into a few long sessions; distributed practice is spread over many short classes. The superiority of distributed practice is probably one of the best-established and best-documented learning principles for both simple and complicated tasks. Almost without exception studies show that short practice periods, interrupted by frequent rest periods, result in more efficient learning.

TRANSFER OF TRAINING

The effect of what is learned in one situation on learning in subsequent situations is called transfer of training. Because few training situations exactly simulate actual job conditions, trainees sometimes encounter difficulty transferring the skill learned in one setting to a somewhat different skill in a different setting. Positive transfer occurs when past learning helps people learn something new; negative transfer occurs when previous learning hinders learning in a new situation. The following techniques enhance the probability of positive transfer.

1. Make the instruction relevant to the students' real-life situations.
2. Present part of the training in a situational context, so that students can practice handling material under a variety of circumstances.
3. Test students under conditions that approximate reality. When trainees can demonstrate their new learning they gain the confidence that they will need to perform well outside the classroom.

PART VERSUS WHOLE TRAINING

Industrial training programs, seeking to raise the level of competence maximally in the shortest period of time, need to find the most efficient training methods. Should the entire operation be taught as one unit (whole training), or should individual segments be taught separately and combined with others when students have mastered them (part training)? Experience has not yet demonstrated the superiority of either, but it appears that a combination of the two (in a whole-part or whole-part-whole sequence) is usually better than either method alone. Instructors first expose students to the entire subject to give them an overview. Then they divide the subject into parts, and students assimilate the segments. Finally, instructors and students review the whole and integrate the parts into a coherent unit.

MOTIVATION

Motivation is essential for learning, and unless instructors ensure adequate motivation, little learning is likely to occur. Instructors can motivate students by convincing them of the personal benefits to be derived from learning. An individual with a strong drive to be a programmer, for example, learns much more effectively than one who sees little benefit in learning programming.

LEARNING CURVES

People learn rapidly during initial training, but level off after a short period. Graphs of trainee progress, regardless of the skills being learned, take the same general form. The flatness, or plateau, can stem from a number of sources such as fatigue, lack of motivation, or ineffective teaching. Although plateaus appear to be inherent in learning, instructors who understand them can minimize their effect by keeping the training relevant, understandable, and interesting.

LEARNING BY DOING

Employees learn technical skills especially from actually performing the work. Repeated practice with guidance from the instructor impresses the trainees with the proper techniques and reinforces correct operating procedures.

Development of Training Courses

Course designers utilize the principles of learning described above so that both curriculum and method contribute to established objectives. They develop courses in three stages: syllabus, outline, and lesson plan. Training specialists usually prepare the syllabus and course outline from which instructors develop a lesson plan. Each of these stages is described below.

THE SYLLABUS

A **syllabus** enumerates the main objectives of a course and outlines the major subject headings in enough detail to indicate the direction and dimensions that a course should take. The syllabus also allots time to each portion of the course. An example of a syllabus is given in Table 13.4.

THE COURSE OUTLINE

The **course outline** spells out specific objectives for each lesson by elaborating the general outline of the syllabus and informing instructors of exactly what material to cover. An accompanying bibliography or list of sources can provide instructors with general background information. Usually the training coordinator or the training specialist prepares the syllabus. The course outline ordinarily suggests methodology and audio-visual aids.

THE LESSON PLAN

Lesson plans are instructors' tools, developed and shaped by instructors to benefit their particular style of presentation. Instructors accept the

Course Title	Hourly-Employee Orientation Course
Course Objectives	Participants should: 1. Understand the company's labor relations philosophy. 2. Know the company's rules and regulations. 3. Be familiar with the overall process. 4. Understand their relationship to the organization.
Course Duration	Eight hours (one work day)
To Be Presented By	Supervisor of personnel administration, assisted by designated members of the technical department
To Be Presented To	All new hourly employees
Information To Be Covered	
Lesson 1 (1 1/2 hours)	1. Welcome 2. Company philosophy 3. Importance of the individual 4. Company history, products, and organization 5. Manufacturing process description
Lesson 2 (1 hour)	1. Pay practices and policies 2. Hours of work 3. Administrative practices
Lesson 3 (1 1/2 hours)	1. Employee benefits 2. Time off 3. Employee services and special programs 4. Training and promotion
Lesson 4 (1 1/2 hours)	1. Plant tour
Lesson 5 (1 1/2 hours)	1. Personal safety 2. Hygiene 3. Clean area rules 4. Protective clothing 5. Rules and regulations
Lesson 6 (1 hour)	1. Summary 2. Questions and general discussion 3. Immediate level evaluation

Table 13.4
Course Syllabus

objectives spelled out by the course outline, but are free to develop their own techniques and approaches to the subject matter within the framework. They research the subject using the bibliography provided by the training staff and develop a lesson plan detailing their strategies. Instructors can add techniques and training aids of their own, establish the timing of the lessons (so long as objectives are met), and use their own particular methodologies to meet existing situations.

This approach puts the burden of presentation directly on instructors. It gives them enough background on a subject to be stimulating and credible, and enough flexibility to be unique and creative. Effective instructors organize their lessons to present their subject matter as a complete learning experience. This experience, which might be termed a cycle of learning, includes:

1. Stimulation of the students' desire to learn.

2. Integration of the subject matter with what they have previously learned.

3. Detailed exposition of the subject matter showing the interrelationships between parts.

4. Summary of the subject matter, including reinforcement of what has been taught and introduction of the material that will follow.

The **job-breakdown sheet** is a type of lesson plan particularly relevant to manual and mechanical operations. The breakdown lists all the steps in sequence of the operation. Instructors study each of the steps to assure their own familiarity with them and to ascertain the correctness of the sequence. The breakdown sheet is divided into two columns, one listing steps, or what the workers must do, and the other specifying key points, or what the workers must know. The initial training units should include tasks that are easily learned; instructors should defer the more complicated steps until later. Table 13.5 is an example of a job-breakdown sheet for a grinding operation.

Table 13.5 Job-Breakdown Sheet		
Part: Engine Cam	Operation: Grind to Thickness
What workers must do. Steps.	What workers must know. Key points.
1. Pick up block.	1. Number of rubs.
2. Place on wheel (face down).	2. Amount of pressure to apply.
3. Pressure and draw rub.	3. Length of draw.
	4. Routines to save time, particularly by reducing the number of times thickness is measured.

TRAINING TECHNIQUES

During the lesson itself all the course development and material preparation are put to the test. The learning that takes place depends to a great extent on the method of presentation. The traditional lecture method is effective for explaining a mass of information but other methods can supplement or replace it for certain types of training. When trainees are active participants rather than passive receptors, they learn better. Consequently, there has been increasing interest in participative or **experiential learning techniques** during the past decade. However, the emphasis on participative techniques in the following paragraphs is not meant to minimize the importance of lectures as a teaching device. The advantages as well as disadvantages of each method are presented so readers can evaluate these techniques.

COACHING.   Learning by doing has particular application to manual and operative skills. Trainees benefit greatly from demonstration, practice, and encouragement, and the technique is conducive to continuous feedback and motivation. Instructors can act as coaches, especially when training individuals or small groups. The disadvantage of the coaching method is that few people with both the expertise in a skill and the ability to train others in it are competent coaches.

ROLE PLAYING.   **Role playing** is essentially acting, performing, and practicing. Individuals and groups can improve their effectiveness not only by talking about problems but by playing parts and roles (either their own or someone else's) in a hypothetical or real situation. Many techniques are used to make the enactment more meaningful, but interaction between people is the core of the method.[17] Instructors can use role playing in training in several ways, for it can increase the effectiveness of learning by letting participants dramatize work situations and portray figures in current events or historical circumstances. It can also develop human relations skills by encouraging people to interact. A unique advantage of role playing is that by decreasing the gap between thinking and doing, it gives trainees an opportunity to practice new behavior. However, participants have a tendency to overplay their roles, which sometimes can add an element of artificiality. Instructors should introduce role playing only after a climate of trust has been established, otherwise the group might resist or misuse the technique.

At the beginning of the session, instructors clearly state the purpose of the psychodrama, the background of the situation, and the basic character of each role. The players project themselves into their assigned roles, making up (improvising) the lines as the play proceeds. Following the dramatization, there is a discussion and critique. The best results are obtained when the discussion is structured by a prescribed format such as an outline of questions.

CASE STUDIES.   The **case study** method is an attempt to inject more realism into training programs. This method teaches broad principles, exposes trainees to situations that will arise in the real world, and develops skills for handling similar situations. It offers the distinct advantage of transferability of learning, but the degree of transferability varies with the realism of the case. In the case method instructors give situations to the trainees, who evaluate them on the basis of previously learned concepts and experiences. Trainees can be objective in their analyses of the cases because they are not personally involved in the outcome; this method emphasizes analysis rather than the decision.[18] The trainees' task is to state the problem, identify its causes, suggest possible solutions, and isolate the best alternative. Lively discussions in subgroups or by the entire group help motivate learning and usually come about when trainees are adequately prepared prior to the discussion period. Classroom experience with this technique reveals, however, that some students fail to prepare for case discussions, relying on others to do the work. The result is that only a few profit from a case study.

IN-BASKET.   The **in-basket** was developed as a device for selecting Air Force officers. However, the method is now used not only for selection but also for classroom teaching and industrial training. The in-basket presents trainees with the sample contents of a manager's in-tray or mailbox. Within a limited amount of time, trainees must decide on the appropriate action for each item in the tray. Then their decisions are discussed in small groups or by the entire class to determine the best action. In-baskets are interesting and involving, and trainees receive feedback on the possible consequences of their actions from members of the group. The involvement is a motivational factor and realism of the items in the exercise enhances the transfer of learning. However, there are several limitations to in-baskets. First, trainees must handle the problems through people they have never encountered before. Second, the interpersonal relationships that would influence their decisions in real life are absent. Also, the exercise may prove difficult for individuals such as foremen and leadmen, who deal with problems face-to-face rather than through correspondence.

INCIDENT PROCESS.   Paul and Faith Pigors have developed a training method for practical problem-solving which they call the **incident process.**[19] (This method is sometimes considered a variant of the case method.) The incident process gives trainees only the bare incident; trainees must seek out pertinent details on their own. The method's chief advantage is that it corresponds more directly to real life than case studies do. The incident-process method teaches trainees analytical thinking and critical decision making (i.e., deciding which facts are pertinent and which are not). The basic purpose of developing the facts surrounding an incident may not be realized unless instructors can draw information out of the group by asking relevant questions. Also, instructors must be thoroughly familiar with the incident under discussion and its possible outcomes.

BUSINESS SIMULATION GAMES.   **Games** that simulate business conditions range from simple problems to complex situations involving a whole field organization, with participants rotating through key roles and dealing with specific situations of the kind they encounter in real life. The more sophisticated games use computer programs to store information, calculate decision data, and provide consequences from the combined results of team decision. Games can be tailor-made for specific companies. Simulation develops awareness of management decision making problems and of the importance of team effort in company success. Business games provide practice in using data that would be available, for example, to a general manager: production schedules, sources of funds, staff and market positions, inventories, resources, fixed and variable costs, and so on.[20] Participants use this information to reach decisions that affect output, costs, and sales. Their decisions create new situations that call for further decisions, and so on, through a number of stages. Several trainees or teams of trainees can compete with each other, using information on the competition's position in considering their next decision. The rapid feedback of results and competition among players help motivate learning.

A possible drawback of business simulation methods is that they emphasize competition too much, thereby detracting from the learning experience. Also, because the effectiveness of the game depends on prompt feedback of results, computer access is desirable, which adds considerably to administration costs.

PROGRAMMED LEARNING.   Programmed instruction can train many students individually and simultaneously. The program is designed to lead students step by step toward a desired objective. It offers advantages to both slow and fast learners. Slow learners, who might drop farther and farther behind in a conventional class, receive the extra instruction they need to grasp a subject. And fast learners, who are often bored or frustrated by the slow pace of typical group instruction, retain interest and progress quickly. A difficulty with programmed learning is that special technical ability, which can represent a significant cost, is required to develop the programs. And it is not advisable for companies to adopt package programs blindly because the information may not be pertinent to their situation.

GROUP DISCUSSION AND CONFERENCES.   The **conference method** is basic to all participative techniques. Here, group members discuss and share common problems. Sharing experiences and pooling suggestions create interest and satisfaction and motivate learners through the involvement of all members. Group discussions encourage analytical thinking, although participants gain little new information. The success of this technique depends on good conference leaders—their role is to stimulate discussion, keep it on track, and summarize the consensus.

PROJECTS.   The project method is similar to the conference method. Trainees are encouraged to learn by doing as well as by talking. They begin with a problem, outline a method of analysis, collect the facts, and reach a conclusion. **Projects** are essentially small research studies that stimulate trainees to learn more about a subject. A limitation of the project method is that it requires an instructor's time to ensure that trainees use proper methodology, gather and analyze data correctly, and study subjects pertinent to the curriculum.

SENSITIVITY TRAINING.   This method helps participants learn about themselves and their ways of relating to others. Participants become aware of the impressions they create in others and sensitive to their reactions and feelings. A training group, or T-group, composed of 10 to 20 members, starts its session without an agenda. There appears to be no leader, since dependence on a trainer is discouraged; the goal is to have the group become self-reliant. Participants are encouraged to examine their individual and group behavior and emotions, and express their feelings and thoughts. The result to be hoped for is that they will break down the barriers that inhibit human relations and establish new behavioral patterns. Sometimes sensitivity groups overemphasize changing behavior; the assumption that everyone's behavior needs some adjustment is not always true.

BEHAVIOR MODELING.   This method is nothing more than demonstrating a behavior which the observer (trainee) learns to duplicate. It includes three steps:[21]

1. *Demonstration of master performance* shows the desired behavior. To be effective the performance must be presented in a clear and understandable fashion; and contain situations that are compatible with the students' real world.

2. *Guided student practice* gives students a chance to imitate the model in a simulated real world situation. Learning research suggests that this practice step is critical to the process to assure correct application back on the job.

3. *Feedback* from instructors and fellow students on the quality of the learner's efforts both encourages and promotes his/her further development. Feedback that is well-timed and appropriate to the student's use of the new skill is sought in behavior modeling.

TRANSACTIONAL ANALYSIS.   Many organizations have experimented with **transactional analysis (TA)** to smooth out internal communications. The technique popularized by Thomas Harris through his book *I'm OK— You're OK* is essentially a translation of psychology into basic layman's terms. TA is a scheme for analyzing interpersonal communications. Harris distinguishes various *ego states* or units of personalities as parent, child, and adult. And he describes *transactions*—units of measure in interpersonal relations—which he classifies as complementary, crossed, or ulterior. In other words, when one person says something to another and the other person responds, a transaction takes place. In a complementary transaction both parties are on the same frequency and there is good communication. In this type of transaction one person might say, "How are you, today?" and the other might answer, "Fine, how are you?" On the other hand, in a crossed transaction one of the parties is turned off by what the other says. In such a case the response to "How are you today?" might be, "None of your business!" In an ulterior transaction, the words being stated have other meanings. An employee might complain, "Oh, I'm just no good at anything," when actually he or she is seeking recognition and/or reassurance from the boss.

Ego states exist in all of us and in each transaction one of the ego states predominates. The parent acts as he or she was taught to (authoritative), the child as he or she feels at the moment (emotional), and the adult after independent thought (rational). By studying transactions, people can determine which ego states others are operating in, and they can respond accordingly. TA can serve to enhance communications and develop more positive relationships among people in organizations. The Bank of America trained 68 of its middle managers in TA and 86 percent of them felt they had improved their ability to solve interpersonal problems.[22]

Behavior Modification and HRT Technology

Recently, many organizations have adopted an approach to employee **behavior modification** that operates on the principle that by rewarding behavior—providing a positive consequence—it is possible to increase its frequency. The opposite effect results from penalties—negative reinforcement. Fred Luthans[23] explains that only the contingent consequence (the one that is most immediate and given attention to by the individual) will cause a change in behavior. For example, the supervisor who observes an employee operating equipment unsafely and bawls him out might cause an increase rather than a decrease in the very behavior he was trying to change. A co-worker's *positive* consequence for the employee's behavior (e.g., "You sure got the boss's dander up that time—good going") overrode the negative consequence and was contingent, thus having impact on subsequent behavior. The process of modifying behavior toward a desired objective includes these steps:

1. Identify the performance-related behaviors that can be changed. Personnel audit techniques can be applied here (see description of personnel audit under *Techniques for Training-Needs Determination* on page 384).

2. Measure and record the frequency of the behavior. Measurements are obtainable from attendance records, time sheets, quality or quantity production reports, or from direct observation.

3. Functionally analyze the behavior by identifying cues that precede the behavior and the consequences that follow the behavior and seem to be reinforcing it.

4. In this action step develop intervention strategies: positive-reinforcement strategies to accelerate behaviors and punishment or extinction strategies to decelerate behaviors. Natural reinforcers include performance feedback and attention or recognition. Initially, **O. B. Mod** (organizational behavior modification) theory suggests, the schedule of reinforcement is continuous and after the behavior is moving in the desired direction it can be intermittent.

5. Finally, evaluate performance improvements to determine the reaction of the personnel involved and the behavior changes that occur as a result of the employment of O. B. Mod techniques.[24]

The O. B. Mod approach was initially implemented by Emery Air Freight, which reported phenomenal results. Subsequently, people involved with the approach at Questor, Ford, United Airlines, IBM, Milliken and Company, and others showed dramatic changes in relevant job behaviors in areas of attendance, quality and quantity of output, following safety regulations, and submitting constructive suggestions. More specifically, at the 3-M Company, where everyone in a plant is trained in this approach, their experience (which was also positive) showed that tangible reinforcers (money, gifts) were less durable than social, intangible reinforcers (attention, praise, affection, granting favors, allowing participation). No action was used to discourage less critical, nonproductive performance, but it elicited quick response when used intentionally, and punishment (criticism, negative statements, and discipline), when viewed as undesirable to the employee, helped reduce or remove nonproductive or counterproductive behavior. The key, according to 3-M, is to have supervisors know their people well enough to avoid situations where well-intended efforts yield undesirable results.[25]

Instructional Aids

Audio-visual aids are an integral part of any training designed to involve participants. These devices make training easier and more effective because they involve several of the participants' senses during a presentation. Studies have shown that a combination of the aural and visual in a training situation enables participants to absorb more material and retain it for a longer period of time. A study conducted by the Socony-Mobil Oil Company revealed that people learn 11 percent through hearing and 83 percent through sight. In addition, students retain 10 percent of what they read, 20 percent of what they hear, 30 percent of what they see, and 50 percent of what they see and hear in combination.

Numerous training aids and audio-visual devices are available to instructors. Companies can purchase them as packages from manufacturers and publishers, or they can produce them internally. The extent and variety of training aids are functions of the training budget, physical facilities, type of training, characteristics and size of the audience, and instructors' preferences.

Aids that can enhance presentations include movies, closed-circuit television, filmstrips, slides, recordings, charts, and mock-ups. These devices, with or without sound, can dramatize events or illustrate points that are difficult to describe in words. A disadvantage, particularly with movies, is that students may think of them only as entertainment. A brief introduction and a discussion following a screening can overcome this drawback. Flip charts, flannel boards and blackboards, opaque projectors, and transparent slides focus students' attention on particular points. They also provide convenient outlines during lectures.

Closed-circuit television can serve many purposes. Remote receivers can present movies and lectures simultaneously in several locations. Furthermore, television monitors at remote locations can enable observers to witness the reactions and progress of selected groups. Participants in role playing, especially of sales presentations, can receive instant feedback of their demonstrations through replay of tapes. Also, students can play back taped presentations at a later date to refresh their memories or study material they have missed because of absence. Video-cassette recordings combined with modules of programmed instruction further increase the uses of television. Similarly, computer-aided instruction (CAI) has been successfully applied in simulation exercises, gaming, and for individual programmed instruction. The computer performs calculations, displays information, asks questions, processes answers, and provides right/wrong information.[26]

Mock-ups of technical equipment (mechanical, electrical, or electronic) provide an interesting means of demonstration. Instructors can isolate sections of equipment to provide a step-by-step demonstration and expose internal components for students to observe. Flying, truck driving, explosives handling, and electronics repair, to mention a few, are skills taught through basic hands-on training with mock-ups, thus freeing operating equipment as well as providing safer training for novices.

Evaluation of Training Effectiveness: Measuring Results Against Objectives

Normally, evaluation[27] is an end-of-the-course process to discover how much students have learned, or think they have learned. This is analogous to the management concept of control, in which performance is measured against a standard and action is initiated to correct deviations from the standard. Traditional evaluations rely on trainee opinions of training effectiveness. The results of one study, however, showed statistically that no systematic relationship exists between trainee perception and concrete evidence of training effectiveness.[28] Using pretest and posttest comparisons also falls short of supplying empirical evidence of training effectiveness because any improvement in test scores could have resulted from factors other than the training. The only way training effectiveness can be truly evaluated is by comparing the change in performance of a group receiving training to the performance change of a comparable group that did not undergo training.[29] And the comparison of the two groups should be made using hard criteria such as better quality of production, increase in the number of operators able to meet job standards; reduction in time required to do a specific job; reduction in breakage or spoilage; decline in absenteeism; lower turnover rates; reduction in operational costs; and higher scores on tests, rating scales, or attitude surveys.[30]

The objections to the traditional evaluation approaches are largely overcome by that proposed in the following paragraphs.

First, instructors establish standards of measurement and criteria for evaluation. The objectives of the course, written as specifically as possible and elaborated in the course outline, guide the development of these criteria and standards. Instructors develop a specific program for evaluating the training simultaneously with the objectives. Evaluation occurs on three levels: immediate, intermediate, and final. The various levels form a complete evaluation of the course and also cross-check each other.

1. *Immediate.*   The immediate evaluation occurs while a course is in progress. It is the instructors' tool for gauging the progress of students, and it permits them to change tactics according to revised needs.

2. *Intermediate.*   The intermediate evaluation takes place just after the completion of a course. At this evaluation instructors examine a course's effect on the trainees' attitudes, behavior, and skills.

3. *Final.*   The final level of evaluation measures the effect of changes in the trainees' job performance on the organization.

THE IMMEDIATE LEVEL

INFORMAL METHODS.   In the past the most common method of evaluating a course has been to ask students for their reactions. Obviously, positive bias is built into this system of evaluation. Students are usually quite relieved that a course is finished and tend to be caught up in the general conviviality that prevails at its completion. However, there are a number of informal methods that can aid in course evaluation.

1. *Internal evaluation.*   The main device for internal evaluation is an instructor's observation and analysis. Experienced instructors will intuitively evaluate their own effectiveness and the class's progress. A strong sensitivity to students' needs and a detailed knowledge of educational psychology are the most important tools needed for this kind of evaluation.

2. *Questioning techniques.*   The question is the instructor's prime tactic for determining student progress. Questioning is a complex and difficult undertaking; the ability to understand and use various questioning techniques is essential to the instructors' ability to evaluate.

3. *Performance critiques.*   If the training is aimed at teaching a skill, instructors watch trainees practice the skill. Then they give a critique of the trainees' performance and evaluate their progress.

4. *Short quizzes.*   These are useful as progress checks. Quizzes need not be elaborate; in fact, elaborate and difficult quizzes may defeat the purpose of internal evaluation. Throughout the course, short quizzes covering major points give instructors an invaluable tool in evaluating class progress. Students should understand that the purpose of quizzes is not to test individuals but to evaluate the progress of the class as a whole.

5. *Outside observers.*   Training supervisors and outside consultants can evaluate both instructors and classes. Their critiques can be simple or complex. For instance, sociometric analysis (a sophisticated statistical analysis of the reactions and interactions of participants) has been used in evaluating a human relations course. But this depth of evaluation is rarely necessary.

6. *Discussions with individual students.*   Instructors often overlook this internal evaluation method. Frank and honest discussions with individual students can help an instructor determine problem areas and weaknesses in the course.

FORMAL METHODS.   Various formal methods traditionally are employed to aid in course evaluation. Following are descriptions of the more common.

1. *Questionnaires.*   Formal measures of student reaction are usually taken by questionnaire or opinion surveys. They ask such questions as, "Was this course worthwhile?" However, yes-or-no questions do not enable students to express their feelings about a course. Analysis has shown that students are more likely to answer positively—on the grounds that some small part was helpful—than negatively. Statisticians agree that questionnaires can be designed to prove almost anything. Properly used, however, they are useful evaluation devices. Evaluators should pretest questionnaires among a sample group to determine whether the questions are ambiguous. Good questionnaires seek to discover not only the positive aspects of a course but also the negative ones.

2. *Tests.*   To design and evaluate tests effectively, the person using them must have a working knowledge of testing. A test devised by an untrained person provides little information in evaluating a course. Tests range from simple forced-choice questions to open-end responses to human relations incidents. All testing devices are subject to evaluation themselves; they must be reliable, valid, and internally consistent.

3. *Learning curves.*   As mentioned earlier in this chapter, a learning curve is a graph of the students' progress over time. Instructors can measure progress in manual skills by the units produced, operations learned, and reduction in waste. In intellectual or human relations subjects, measuring progress is more difficult but still possible. Instructors can use principles from educational psychology (discussed earlier under learning theory) to measure students' progress over a period of time.

4. *Pretests and posttests.*   Instructors can make a more involved but more satisfactory evaluation by giving students a pretest before training, and a similar one after training. The pretest not only establishes a base line from which to measure achievement, but also gives instructors a detailed picture of the training needs of their classes. The main problem with this method is the necessity for tight statistical control. Instructors must use statistical analysis to establish the similarity of pretest and posttest items.

5. *Final performance.*   Instructors find it very useful to administer a final

performance test evaluated by predetermined standards. In a public-speaking course, for example, the final performance test could be a 15-minute address to the class followed by the instructor's and the class's critiques. In vestibule schools teaching manual skills to new employees, final performance tests are essential.

6. *Control-group evaluation.* This technique requires controlled scientific experiments. Prior to training, an instructor tests both the group to be trained and a **control group** of similar individuals. (A control group is a group of individuals similar to the test group—trainee group—and used as a basis of comparison to the test group.) At the end of the course, both groups are tested again. Instructors then attribute the differences in performance to training. For example, several experiments of this nature have been undertaken to prove the effectiveness of formal, on-the-job training; results show that groups receiving formal training progress much more rapidly than control groups receiving no formal training.

However, it is difficult for instructors to isolate training from other factors influencing a group's progress. The control group and the training group must be similar in all other variables. The statistical technique used to establish this similarity is called covariance. Instructors must understand this procedure if they are to do professional evaluations using control groups.

THE INTERMEDIATE LEVEL

1. *Ratings by supervisors and employees.* Supervisors' ratings can be used in evaluating almost any kind of HRT activity in manual skills as well as ideational subjects. Also, subordinates' ratings are especially effective in evaluating supervisory training. Organizations must carefully design and use rating forms to insure that these elicit the necessary information and are not ambiguous or misleading.

A special type of supervisory rating is the performance review. At the beginning of each review period supervisors and their employees meet to establish goals. At the end of the performance period, supervisors analyze subordinates' performance to see if they have, in fact, met their goals. (The performance-review process is very similar to the training system.)

2. *Performance curves.* When learning curves are extended over a period of time, they can fall into the intermediate-evaluation category, especially when the skills are highly complex. For example, to acquire conference leadership skills, an individual must practice for a long period of time; a realistic learning curve in this case might stretch over six months or a year.

3. *Retention over time.* Instructors can send out tests and questionnaires after a certain period of time to test student retention of subject material.

4. *Opinion over time.*   An instructor can also distribute opinion surveys some time after a course in order to establish the effect of subsequent experience on trainees' evaluations of a course.

FINAL LEVEL OF EVALUATION

The final level of evaluation measures the effect of the HRT on the organization. This effect emerges in changes in the trainees' behavior, skills, and attitudes. Statistical analysis is invaluable in this evaluation. Skill improvements can be measured in terms of increases in units produced, delivered, sold; better quality of output; lower cost per unit; etc. And behavior criteria such as attendance (absenteeism), turnover, and grievances are also significant in demonstrating the value of employee training programs. Final evaluation is most useful, but hard to effect because it is difficult for organizations to isolate training as an independent variable.

Cost-Benefit Analysis

For HRT activities to be continued, top management requires justification of the costs. Training costs and benefits are not always easy to measure, yet some attempt to quantify them is essential to the survival of the function. Cost of training per employee-hour of instruction can be calculated and compared between courses and vis-à-vis outside programs. Instructor time; wages or salaries of trainees while they are away from the job; expenses (meals, travel, hotel) of trainees and staff while attending class; cost of facilities, equipment, and materials are all relevant in computing direct training costs. Indirect costs include the overhead of the training staff.

Summary

Human resources training was defined as the process of helping employees improve their effectiveness in present and future jobs. HRT can be viewed as a system in which training needs are analyzed, objectives are established to meet these needs, programs are designed and implemented to effect appropriate behavioral changes, and evaluations are conducted to measure program results against objectives.

Experiential learning techniques are considered appropriate to business-training situations because they incorporate most or all of the basic learning principles of feedback, transfer, retention, motivation, and reinforcement. Organizational Behavior Modification, in particular, has been applied successfully to HRT situations in affecting positive performance behavior.

Key to successful HRT are instructors who thoroughly know teaching fundamentals and understand the materials they present. They are aided by tools of course design: the syllabus, outline, and lesson plan.

HRT program results are judged by line managers who seek hard evidence of effectiveness. The only sound approach—which is a difficult one at best—is to employ an experimental design. Using hard criteria, the training group and a control group are tested before and after training. When test results show differences that are statistically significant between the two groups, training can be considered effective.

Key Terms

human resource training
programmed learning
vestibule training
on-the-job training
vocational rehabilitation
apprenticeship training
organizational analysis
operations analysis
personnel analysis
organizational effectiveness
syllabus
course outline
lesson plan
job-breakdown sheet

experiential learning techniques
role playing
case study
in-basket
incident process
games
conference method
projects
transactional analysis (TA)
ego states
behavior modification
O. B. Mod
audio-visual aids
control group

Review Questions

1. What are the various types of HRT activities?

2. Describe the steps in the HRT system.

3. Discuss the various analyses for determining HRT needs.

4. What are the advantages and disadvantages of each of the following experiential learning techniques: a) role playing, b) case study, c) simulation, d) programmed instruction, e) sensitivity training?

5. How does O. B. Mod attempt to change behavior?

6. Describe the process of evaluating training effectiveness.

Discussion Questions

1. A company's quality-control manager blames poor training for the high rejection rate of products during inspection. Is training necessarily the cause? What other factors might be the cause?

2. How would you justify the cost of a formal training program for an industrial plant?

3. What are some steps an instructor can take to motivate trainees?

4. "Apprenticeship can be used to teach any complicated skill." Assuming this is an accurate statement, could an apprenticeship program be used to develop medical technology skills? What problems might be encountered with such a program?

5. In vocational rehabilitation (skills training for the handicapped) programs, what elements are likely to be different from traditional skills training programs?

"The boys and I are doing fine, Mr. Baxter," Paul Manton said. Paul was a foreman of the group that did some complicated assembly routines on electronic tape cassettes, and Baxter was his boss.

"Well, you may be doing all right, but some improvement can always be made, Paul."

"This way? By going to school with the boys? It's crazy! I haven't been to school for 25 years!"

"It's not school—it's just a few professors in our conference room, with you and the guys."

"It sounds like school to me, and I don't see how it will work. Are these profs experts in electronics?"

"No, they're human relations specialists."

"Human what? How can guys like that tell us how to run our job? We do fine."

Baxter tapped his desk with his pencil. "You know that scrappage rates are way up, Paul."

"Sure, but we got that fixed. I just told Joe and Jack where to go, and they shaped up."

"The record doesn't show it."

"It will, Mr. Baxter. Wait till next week."

"I've been waiting, Paul. Look, you know that the boys are restless. You know that the union contract is up for renewal in three months and already there's plenty of strike talk. You look pretty haggard yourself. Paul—I know it's rough down there, but I also think that you could handle your problems better if you were, well, a little more aware of human relations."

"Hell, I've been doing human relations all my life, Mr. Baxter. I know how to handle men. Besides, having a bunch of eggheads in to probe around won't do much good. These profs spent three days talking to the top brass. They're a helluva bunch to decide what we need. Why don't they come down here and find out what *our* problems are?"

"I'd like you to accept this willingly, Paul. It probably won't work if you fight it."

"You can be sure it won't work if I volunteer either. Just let me yell at those slobs the way I've always done, and things will work out. You'll see."

Case Problem 1

OLD DOGS AND NEW TRICKS

Problems

1. Why is Paul resisting this idea?

2. Do you think that a couple of "egghead" professors who have never worked in this plant can do any good in this situation?

3. Did the company properly determine the training needs for the human relations course?

4. What should be the objectives of this course?

5. How can the company determine the effectiveness of the course?

Case Problem 2

THE ETERNAL JERK

"Okay, fellows, I want you to pay attention," Rex Winsor, the foreman, said as he walked up to the machine. "Spoilage is way up, and it's about time you guys learned how to do this job right."

"Big deal," Joe muttered to Jack, as they stood at the edge of the group. "Old Rex is going to tell us how to do our jobs."

"I think he's drunk with power," Jack mumbled. "They send him off to some quickie training course, and now he knows more than any guy who's been doing the job for the past ten years."

"Shut up and listen, you guys!" Rex yelled. "Now, when you feed the machine—"

"How did a creep like Rex ever get to be foreman, Joe?"

"Beats me, except he is a creep. That's the only kind of foreman this company gets."

"Look at him fumbling with the feed—I could do it better with my eyes closed," said Jack.

"Maybe you should do it with your eyes closed, Jack—you waste more material than anyone around here," said Joe.

"Sure," Jack said. "The company's got plenty of money—they can afford it."

"Boy, if they had any sense, they'd get one of us to go for training. How'd you like that, Jack? Two weeks in Chicago at company expense. But they had to send him, for God's sake. He couldn't thread a machine right if he had to."

"Joe, shut up," Rex shouted. "You're not so hot on this job, you know—your scrap rate is way above the norm."

"Sure, boss, sure," Joe said. "Jack," he muttered out of the corner of his mouth, "doesn't the union have some rule against this sort of hogwash? Do we have to listen to that guy rave?"

"I suppose so," Jack said. "Just grin and bear it."

"With luck, I won't remember a thing," Joe said. "Hey, are you going bowling tonight?"

Problems

1. Why would workers mistrust a foreman to this extent? What's going on behind the scenes?

2. Would it make sense to have a worker go through a training course instead of a foreman?

3. What other kinds of training should this foreman get?

Notes

1. Walter D. St. John, "The Complete Employee Orientation Program," *Personnel Journal,* May 1980, p. 374.

2. Daniel N. Kanouse and Philomena I. Warihay, "A New Look At Employee Orientation," *Training and Development Journal,* July 1980, pp. 35–36.

3. American Society for Personnel Administration and Bureau of National Affairs, Inc., *Bulletin to Management ASPA-BNA Survey No. 32: Employee Orientation Programs,* August 25, 1977, p. 7.

4. Mark S. Tauber, "New Employee Orientation: A Comprehensive Systems Approach," *The Personnel Administrator,* January 1981, p. 69.

5. Gordon L. Lippitt, "Training for a Changing World," *Training,* May 1975, p. 47.

6. Juliette K. Arthur, *Employment for the Handicapped* (New York: Abingdon, 1967), p. 155.

7. James P. Mitchell, "New Directions for Apprenticeship Policy," *Worklife,* January 1977, pp. 2–5.

8. Personnel managers and HRT directors interested in correspondence courses should obtain a copy of *Home Study Courses for Industry Training* and *The Directory of Accredited Private Correspondence Schools* from National Home Study Council, 1601 18th Street, N.W., Washington, DC 20009. Also useful is *A Guide to Correspondence Study in Colleges and Universities,* published by the National University Extension Association, 122 Social Sciences Building, University of Minnesota, Minneapolis, MN 55455.

9. National Academy of Sciences, *The Comprehensive Employment and Training Act: Impact on People and Programs—An Interim Report* (Washington, D.C.: National Academy of Sciences, 1976), pp. 3ff.

10. U.S. Department of Labor, Employment and Training Administration, U.S. Dept. of Labor, general records.

11. Donald C. Baumer, Carl E. Van Horn, and Mary Marvel, "Explaining Benefit Distribution in CETA Programs," *The Journal of Human Resources,* XIV, No 2(?), pp. 177–180.

12. Irving R. Schwartz, "Try this Model HRD System: It matches Individuals and Organizational Goals," *Training/HRD,* November 1979, pp. 52–53.

13. William McGehee, "Training and Development Theory; Policies and Practices" in Dale Yoder et al., eds. *ASPA Handbook of Personnel and Industrial Relations,* vol. V, *Training and Development* (Washington, D.C.: Bureau of National Affairs, 1977), pp. 5–9ff.

14. Donald L. Kirkpatrick, "Determining Training Needs: Four Simple and Effective Approaches," *Training and Development Journal,* February 1977, pp. 22–25.

15. Gary Rummler, "How to Determine What Problems Can—and Can't—Be Resolved by Training," *Training/HRD,* August 1976, p. 18.

16. E. J. McCormick, J. R. Jenneret, and R. C. Mercan, *The Development and Background of Positions Analysis Questionnaire* (Lafayette, Ind.: Occupational Research Center, Purdue University, 1972).

17. Malcolm E. Shaw, "Role Playing," in Robert L. Craig and Lester R. Bittel, eds., *American Society for Training and Development Handbook,* (New York: McGraw-Hill, 1967), p. 206. This handbook is a broad reference source for practitioners developing human resources. Of

particular relevance are the six chapters dealing with description, analysis, and evaluation of participative techniques.

18. William Elenko, "The Case for a More Creative Case Study," *Journal of Business Education,* February 1967, p. 201.

19. Charles A. Myers and Paul Pigors, *Personnel Administration* (New York: McGraw-Hill, 1969), pp. 646ff.

20. For a reference list of business games, see Robert G. Graham and Clifford F. Gray, *Business Game Handbook* (New York: American Management Association, 1969). Also, an evaluation of the current Harvard simulation model, which can be used as a management game, is available in James L. McKenny, *Simulation Gaming for Management Development* (Boston: Harvard University, 1967).

21. Donald T. Tosti, "Behavior Modeling: A Process," *Training and Development Journal,* August 1980, pp. 70–74.

22. "Business Tries Out Transactional Analysis," *Business Week,* January 12, 1974, pp. 74–75.

23. Fred Luthans, "How PF/PR Pays Off for Human Resource Managers," *Training/HRD,* December 1976, p. 17.

24. Fred Luthans and Robert Kreetner, *Organizational Behavior Modification* (Glenview, Ill.: Scott, Foresman, 1975), pp. 70ff.

25. Jay L. Beecroft, "How Behavior Modification Improves Productivity at 3-M," *Training/HRD,* October 1976, pp. 83–85.

26. Patricia A. McLagan and Raymond E. Sandborgh, "Computer . . . Aided Instruction—A Special Report," *Training/HRD,* September 1977, pp. 38ff.

27. Adapted from Lloyd L. Byars and Donald P. Crane, "Training by Objectives," *Training and Development Journal,* June 1969, pp. 38ff.

28. Warren S. Blumenfeld and Donald P. Crane, "Opinions of Training Effectiveness: How Good?" *Training and Development Journal,* December 1973, p. 50.

29. Melton L. Blum and James C. Naylor, *Industrial Psychology,* rev. ed. (New York: Harper & Row, 1968), p. 266.

30. L. G. Lindahl, "How to Build a Training Program," *Personnel Journal,* March 1949, pp. 417–19.

Chapter Fourteen

Management and Executive Development

All passengers and crew aboard a private plane were killed when it crashed on a hillside near Palos Verde. The passenger manifest contained the names of the president, vice-president of operations, and treasurer of one of the country's largest producers of primary metals. They were taking the trip to evaluate an acquisition prospect. Its board of directors searched within the company for suitable replacements but could find no one qualified. After considerable effort they eventually located new officers outside the company, but in the meantime the organization suffered and profits declined. Needless to say, the new management promptly instituted a strong program to ensure management succession in the future.

Organizations today maintain their competitive edge through a succession of capable management teams. Measures to assure that managers and executives are proficient in their present positions and their potential for higher responsibility is identified and nurtured can help prevent the situation that the above company had to face. This chapter focuses on the concepts and methods for developing managers in large and small organizations. It discusses how various interrelated components form a system of management development.

Management Development Defined

Management development is the continuous process of training and developing selected individuals for present and future positions. Its purpose

LEARNING OBJECTIVES

1. To understand the relevance of management development to the personnel function.
2. To understand how succession plans apply to management development.
3. To know how management inventory works.
4. To know the distinctions between management development and employee training.
5. To be familiar with the various activities used to develop managers.

is to provide backup for every management job as well as to build a high level of competence in an organization.[1] The process starts with the selection of candidates with management potential and continues throughout an individual's career. Because of individual differences among managers and among various managerial positions, development efforts must be tailored to individual needs. After reaching executive development, Myles Mace wrote:

> For the purposes of developing executives in individual organizations, no universally applicable list of quantities or qualities was found during the course of this study. The executive capacities and skills required in each situation will vary, and the determination of what is required must be arrived at in terms of the working environment in which they are exercised.[2]

The emphasis on self-development logically follows from these findings. Supervisors provide an environment that motivates employees to grow and organizations provide appropriate opportunities, but individuals must bear the primary responsibility for their own development.

The Purpose of Management Development

In a free enterprise system, the managers of each organization determine its destiny. Management development is the means of securing competent managers to maintain an organization's competitive position. More specifically, management development has four major objectives:

ORGANIZATIONAL CONTINUITY.　Business organizations usually operate for the long run; that is, they plan to exist for an extended period of time into the future. To do this, the enterprise must have a succession of qualified managers who will effectively attain its objectives.

MANAGEMENT SUCCESSION.　Companies need competent replacements for key managerial positions to carry on the functions of the organization. Ideally, for each management position, two qualified replacements should be ready to assume responsibility if the need arises.

COMPETENT MANAGEMENT TEAMS.　Management development seeks to develop competence in individuals, but it also tries to mold a coordinated team from the trained individuals. Thomas A. Mahoney, who first espoused the concept of management-team development, stated that management development "seeks a continuity of performance and a continuous improvement of performance of management functions in all group activity now and in the future."[3] The team concept contributes to management development objectives because all individuals must, naturally, work in the same direction to support organizational goals.

INDIVIDUAL DEVELOPMENT. Building competence in each potential or incumbent manager is the principal aim of management development. After all, the organization is composed of individuals, each making a unique contribution. Therefore, management programs should develop each individual to maximum potential, assuming he or she has substantial potential as well as a desire to grow.

The Importance of Management Development

Management development programs are much in vogue today. Virtually all large organizations in both private and public sectors have formal programs, and even businesses too small to underwrite a full-scale effort have informal programs or plan to in the near future. There are many reasons why interest in management-development programs continues to expand. Several of the more significant factors are briefly mentioned below:

1. The practice of management as a discipline has resulted in a communicable body of knowledge. Management is now accepted as a profession because of the recognition of good management principles and their effectiveness. Associations, journals, and educational institutions now emphasize the professionalization of managers through continuous training.

2. When company executives were drawn off by the military during the Second World War, a shortage of management talent developed. The conspicuous absence of methods to develop competent successors for vacated positions focused attention on the need for management development. The growth of organizations and the advent of technology complicated the job of managing, so that even with the return of managers after the war the shortage of managerial talent continued.

3. Executive turnover is common to all organizations. As long as good managers remain scarce, competitors will promise higher pay and better opportunities to entice executives to change jobs. Retirement and death also account for the loss of managerial talent, especially at higher levels where incumbents tend to be older. Unfortunately, it took the ill-fated plane crash in the example cited to make the board of directors realize the need for a management-development program.

4. Increased acceptance of management development has made its absence conspicuous in those organizations lacking formal programs. Consequently, many firms have adopted such plans just to keep up with competition.

5. Executives realize, since the advent of conglomerates (multi-interest organizations), that managerial talent is highly transferable. The functions of planning, organizing, directing, and controlling are common to all managers and organizations. Therefore, managers competent in performing these functions in one situation can be equally effective in entirely different circumstances. Conglomerate and decentralized operations test the effectiveness of managers in a variety of situations. For example, a company may transfer the head of a service organization to manage an auto-parts plant. Executives may have as many as six to ten different assignments during their careers. Only a concerted development effort can create this kind of flexible and mobile manager. In a negative sense, some executives experience burnout at some stage of their careers. This phenomenon occurs when a manager feels used up after a relatively short time in a position. When there is no longer a challenge to an assignment or when a manager feels frustrated in his/her efforts to succeed, burnout results. Initiatives to broaden the experience of managers and to stimulate their professional growth can forestall burnout.

6. In a recent Opinion Research Corporation survey it was discovered that there is a growing discontent among managers. The evaluators of the survey concluded that growth of businesses will depend on "intact managerial workforce characterized by entrepreneurialism, initiative, and appropriate risk taking."[4] In other words, companies, to stay competitive, are going to have to develop their managers to be innovative and aggressive, and to channel their frustrations into positive energy.

The personnel manager (or training director) plays a key role in management and executive development. This person supplies expert advice on sources of managers, development needs of existing managerial talent; the appropriate methods and sources of development programs; and the systems for recognizing and rewarding management accomplishments. He or she also develops and coordinates the implementation of systems and programs to ensure a succession of competent managerial talent in the organization. All of this is integrated with other aspects of the business and focuses on the support of the organization's goals.

Variables Unique to the Management Development Situation

In Chapter 13 we talked about HRT, which included manager development. Some of the variables that are *unique* to management development include:

1. *Characteristics of the manager.* The strengths and development needs of the manager, individual characteristics such as age, level and field of

education, personality, and potential for growth all help determine developmental approaches.

2. *Organizational structure.* The relationships among physical facilities, human factors, and organizational functions influence the nature of management development. The greater the number of management levels an organization has, the greater the opportunity for advancement it offers; hence, the more involved an organization must be in preparing candidates for greater authority.

3. *The company's unique management style.* Each organization has its own operating style, and to be successful, managers must learn to function intuitively in that style.

4. *Anticipated future need for managers.* Organizational growth and manager turnover are obvious reasons to anticipate a future need for managers. Some organizations require more managers than others, therefore they must exert a correspondingly greater effort in seeking and developing them.

5. *Activities of the management development system.* The actual activities and methods of a management development program influence its success and the positive reactions to it of the managers and the company.

Management Development Activities

Program implementation is not a simple task. Planning and execution of management development activities in themselves require considerable effort. In addition, firms must carefully control individual activities to keep them directed toward the same objective. Finally, unequivocal top management support of each activity as well as the overall program is essential; lip service from management inhibits a program.

The activities can be viewed as components functioning in a coordinated system, aimed at providing an organization with a succession of competent management teams. Figure 14.1 is a flow chart of this system. Each component must be present for the system to operate effectively, and each must be directed toward the attainment of objectives. Each component in Figure 14.1 is described below.

ORGANIZATION PROJECTION

To develop an effective program, organizations find that they must base management development on existing as well as future organizational needs. The lead time required to develop competent managers makes accurate forecasting particularly important for human resource planning. Firms will recruit top-level executives for the year 2000 in the 1980s.

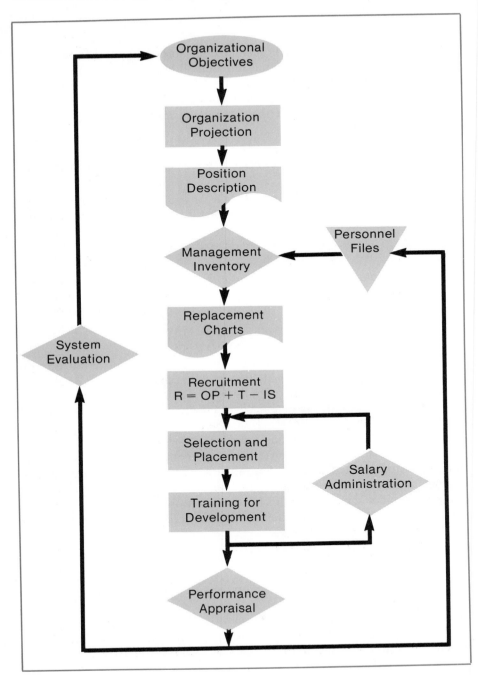

Figure 14.1
Management
Development System

The first step in **organization projection** is to chart the organization's present form, its predicted structure in five years, and its predicted structure in 10 years. The greater the time span covered by the forecast, the less accurate its predictions. Nevertheless, firms must attempt to chart their organization for some time in the future; after all, they commit capital expenditures for plant and equipment as much as 20 years in advance. Organizations should periodically revise their charts as they refine their organizational plans. Projected organization charts should depict an ideal organization.[5] From these, firms can spotlight deficiencies in the existing organization by comparing it with the projected ideal. Among the innumerable considerations in planning the ideal organization are:

1. Plans for expansion, acquisition, or mergers that affect the organization.

2. Product changes from research and development. Introducing new products and phasing out old ones force companies to realign responsibilities and eliminate, restructure, or create departments.

3. Redesigned functions, which result in a demand for new skills. For example, the emergence of computer technology gave rise to management-information systems and the organizational units to implement them. Programming consolidated the record-keeping functions of various departments under one head and offered services previously unavailable.

4. New organizational concepts, which can cause drastic restructuring. When reorganizing under the marketing concept, for instance, the functions of sales, advertising, market research, product design, distribution, and sales service (formerly performed by separate departments), are integrated under a marketing director. New departments usually integrate these separate functions in steps over a period of years. Forecasting is greatly simplified when planners are aware that management intends to adopt new organizational concepts. In a similar vein, decisions to centralize or decentralize affect existing and projected organization charts. Decentralizing establishes new lines of authority, restructures organizational units, and changes staffing requirements. But since firms decide to centralize or decentralize far in advance of the actual event, they can project the organization chart prior to the need for staffing.

5. Detected deficiencies in an organization which companies are likely to respond to by making changes. They might assimilate ineffective or inefficient units into other departments or eliminate them entirely. As an economy measure, firms can discontinue or reduce the strength of some functional areas. Ineffective reporting relationships and overly broad spans of control can also require restructuring. While these deficiencies are difficult to predict, companies can anticipate their possible occurrence and avoid incorporating them into an ideal plan.

Charting the projected organization is only the first step of this component; the second step is filling it with people. The projected chart shows not only relationships of positions in the hierarchy, but also the names and titles of personnel who will fill the positions. From the **management inventory** (see component 3) and replacement charts (component 4), planners can determine which current personnel will be qualified to fill these positions. The remaining vacancies—the positions that cannot be filled from within the organization—comprise the recruiting needs (component 5).

POSITION DESCRIPTION

Position descriptions are written outlines of managers' jobs showing responsibilities delegated to them and their limits of authority in fulfilling these. Position descriptions are used principally as clear definitions of managers' responsibilities, delegation of authority, and cooperative relationships; as bases for standards of performance; as guides for measuring current performance and building personal development plans; and as checklists for training for new assignments. These descriptions are seldom alike, since every management job is unique and changing. Supervisors and their subordinate managers cooperatively tailor-make them and revise them periodically. Techniques for their preparation are the same as the ones described under job analysis in Chapter 5.

On occasion supervisors may find it more convenient to list duties for purposes of appraisal rather than describing them more precisely. While less comprehensive, lists can serve as bases for evaluation and discussion. Like position descriptions, they must not be so specific that managers will feel limited, nor so broad that they will feel unguided.

1. *Common management responsibilities.*   In addition to summarizing and specifying each manager's unique responsibilities, supervision duties, and relationships to others, each position description mentions the activities such as cost control, employee relations, and protection of company assets, that are much the same for all managers. Finally, the description specifies the characteristics, experience, and abilities of an ideal candidate. A sample position description with specifications is provided in Figure 14.2.

2. *Preparation.*   Since managers know their own jobs better than anyone else, they should actively participate in describing their assignments. In that they feel that their work is important, their sense of responsibility can be increased by thinking through and writing out their own position descriptions. There are times, however, when supervisors prepare these descriptions and then discuss them with the managers. This is the case when either the position or the manager is new.

Figure 14.2
Example of a Position
Description

Title: District Sales Manager
Reports to: Regional Sales Manager
Division: Southeast
Classification: 9900-01   Date: December 12, 1981

Summary

Under the direction of the regional sales manager, the district sales manager supervises and controls assigned salesmen's and sales representatives' activities toward achieving the objectives established for the team.

Responsibilities

Plans sales personnel activities toward attaining overall district objectives.
Guides and counsels salesmen in developing sales strategy for maximum account penetration.
Informs regional sales manager of district sales, customer relations, and other sales team activities, new applications of products, and competitors' actions.
Forecasts sales volume of various products for given budget periods.
Trains and develops salesmen in selling skills, product knowledge and applications, and territory management.
Conducts regular training meetings for all salesmen assigned to the district. Teaches team selling methods for greater sales penetration of important or difficult customers and prospects.

Supervision

Supervises the day-to-day activities of salesmen, assuring that maximum potential is obtained from their accounts or territories while maintaining reasonable expense levels.
Appraises performance of salesmen from daily observation, sales and service records, and account visits; recommends to regional manager compensation adjustments and development needs.
Insures that all sales personnel maintain records and submit required reports.
Recruits and selects salesmen and service representatives for the district.

Figure 14.2 (cont.)

Relationship to Others

Assists regional manager in territory layout, territory and account potential, quotas, budgets, position assignments, and related activities.

Coordinates the activities of administrative and staff personnel and salesmen to obtain maximum cooperation in satisfying prospects and customers.

Ensures that all accounts receive adequate sales coverage and technical coverage.

Position Specifications

Four years' sales experience in related product lines. Two years' experience directly supervising sales team, including quota responsibility. Demonstrated ability to forecast sales and analyze sales records.

Education: Bachelor's degree in marketing or business administration. MBA degree preferred.

Must be able to coordinate activities with sales, service, and administrative organizations. Good physical condition and appearance required. Must have assessed potential for regional manager position.

3. *Organizational planning.*   Companies can improve their organizational planning and management orientation by using position descriptions. By distributing organizational manuals, which include a cross section of these descriptions, they provide managers with an overview of a firm's structure.

4. *Accountability.*   Position descriptions list those duties for which managers are accountable. Since they have full authority to carry out their duties, they are responsible for performing them successfully. Yet even in supervisor-subordinate relationships, there may be many areas of uncertainty and confusion about responsibilities. This is just as true at higher levels as at lower. The result is inefficiency, friction, and buck-passing. Properly administered position description programs can clarify the freedom subordinates need if they are to be held clearly accountable for job-related responsibilities.

5. *Performance appraisal.*   Because position descriptions outline job responsibilities, managers can base appraisals on them by carefully evaluating subordinates' performance on each description item. Both managers and their superiors know what is expected and both use the same factors for

measuring results. This keeps appraisals sharply in focus and leads to more accurate evaluations.

6. *Instruments of growth.*   As managers develop and their jobs enlarge, their position descriptions change to reflect this growth. Personal-development plans (discussed in detail in Chapter 16, "Performance Appraisal") are often based on the strengths and development needs revealed by analyzing position descriptions. Evaluations of present performance on position description items are valuable estimates of potential for greater or different responsibilities.

MANAGEMENT INVENTORY

By taking stock of existing personnel, management inventories (sometimes called skills banks, reserve groups, or personnel inventory and capability systems) determine the availability of management talent in the present and for the future. Inventories usually include such information as position title, age, length of service, promotability, and development needs. Frequently they indicate new or anticipated positions for which incumbents qualify. In such cases, the same employees prepare both inventories and replacement charts, so the two can be easily coordinated. Usually, the head of the organization or department decides the details of replacement charts and inventories by using personnel files and performance appraisals to designate likely successors to high positions. Sometimes this function is performed by a management development committee composed of top officials and assisted by the personnel manager.

Table 14.1 shows a simplified, traditional form of management inventory. It lists each employee's name, title, year of retirement, year of employment, replacement positions, and training needs. The first two digits in the retirement year and service column show the year in which the individual will retire at age 65; the last two digits, the year in which the individual was employed by the company. Thus 9049 indicates that the employee was hired in 1949 and will retire in 1990. Note that Doe (industrial relations representative) and Acworth (track foreman) will both retire in 1982. Computers can easily sort incumbents by retirement year and classification, thus accurately forecasting one cause of replacement needs. Training needs are also coded to simplify recording. The letter o, for instance, might stand for report writing and e for principles of supervision. When several managers need the same type of training, the personnel department can organize a group program. When only one individual requires a specific type of training, it is more efficient to rely on resources such as correspondence courses, coaching, or outside seminars. In Table 14.1, employees are grouped into four categories, I through IV, indicating potential for promotion.

Table 14.1
Management-Inventory
Report

| | Division _____ | | | Date _____ | |
Group	Name	Present Position	Retirement Year and Service	Replacement Positions	Training
I	Smith, J. Z.	Industrial engineer	9049	Service general foreman	t,d
	Jones, R. T.	Electrical foreman	9263	Reduction plant industrial engineer	e,g
	Harper, C. D.	Industrial relations representative	9762	Mines plant supervisor of industrial relations	b,g
II	Faircloth, O. C.	Power plant supervisor	8441	Reduction plant engineer	e,t,o
	Doe, John C.	Industrial relations representative	8241	Mines plant supervisor of industrial relations	n,r,t,p
III	French, J. C.	Smelter test engineer	8545	Plant industrial engineer	o,z,t
	Schroeder, A. H.	Service general foreman	8762	Flotation general foreman	w,r
	Acworth, R. W.	Track foreman	8241	Drilling and blasting general foreman	x,z
IV	Brant, C. M.	Engineer trainee	1169	None	o
	Clemmer, A.	Electrical general foreman	8340	None	z
	Burton, T.	Communications director	8459	None	o

Group I is promotable to top-management positions, and groups II and III to middle management. The individuals in group IV may be performing satisfactorily in their present positions, but they have reached their maximum levels and are not considered candidates for promotion.

Organizations that computerize their inventories (computerized inventories are prevalent today) generally include more complete information in their management inventories. In addition to the elements just mentioned, printouts show performance-review data, test results, salary grades, and career interests, and sometimes include nonsalaried employees with management potential. Generally, computer programs integrate inventories with management-succession plans (replacement charts) and the performance appraisal system. Such inventories match skills against validated position specifications developed through job (position) analysis. When inventories contain work-experience data so they can be used for job matching, their effectiveness can be enhanced by translating the employment history into job families or subfamilies. Thus, specific tasks that the manager has performed, regardless of the job title, are detailed in the inventory.[6] Inventories can only effectively aid management development when they are coordinated with other activities. A simple, basic-information form that functions as a working component of the system is better than an extensively detailed information file that defies ready application. Planners must strike a happy medium between detail and workability, although the latter does take precedence.

REPLACEMENT CHARTS

By indicating each manager's retirement data, length of service, qualifications, and readiness for promotion, a **replacement chart** systematically identifies successors (usually at least two) for each position. The scientific approach to selecting successors calls for matching of successor attributes with demands of the position. Such attributes as promotional origin, leadership style, degree of need fulfillment, and successor age, as well as research aspects of multiple successions might be used.[7] Management developers agree that the charts should remain confidential, and that even the replacements themselves should not be told that they are being designated for particular positions, since such information tends to make replacements complacent. Such information stifles the initiative of other aspirants when they learn they are no longer contenders for promotion.

Replacement charts can utilize a company's organization chart or they can merely list all positions in a company (Table 14.2 is an example of this type). For each position, charts generally rate each incumbent's job performance and indicate the position to which the incumbent is promotable; they also designate the readiness of at least two possible candidates for promotion to the position.

Replacement charts are usually maintained at the corporate level by officers of a company. The management development committee, which is the final designator of management replacements, revises the charts on a quarterly, semiannual, or annual basis with new performance appraisal data.

MANAGEMENT RECRUITING

An essential task of management development programs is recruiting an adequate number of candidates, both experienced and recent graduates, for management positions. Such a goal presumes that clear definitions of the requirements for these positions exist. Carefully prepared position descriptions provide a reliable basis for the specifications. (The recruiting process was discussed in detail in Chapter 5, "Human Resource Planning.")

Table 14.2
Management-Replacement Chart

Date: June 25, 1982

Position Title	Incumbent	Retirement and Hiring Dates	Performance	Promotability	Promotion Positions	Replacements Name/Position/Promotability
General material handling foreman	D. S. Crow	8451	2	B	Reduction plant superintendent	M. G. Jackson/shift foreman/B T. N. Murphy/senior industrial engineer/B
Material handling foreman	C. D. Bond	8249	1	D		R. B. Gormley/crusher operator/A T. P. Hull/shift foreman reverberatory/C
General reverberatory foreman	C. B. Laughton	8753	1	A	Smelter superintendent	T. L. Bayard/converter foreman/A N. R. Miles/shift foreman reverberatory/B
Shift foreman reverberatory	C. T. Cummings	8755	5	B	Converter general foreman	S. T. Mattison/test engineer/B Q. V. Maleson/instrument repairman/C
Shift foreman reverberatory	J. T. Black	9758	3	C	Material handling foreman	T. R. Kramer/engineer trainee/A W. B. Post/skimmer/B

Legend

Performance Code		Promotability Code	
1	Outstanding	A	Immediately promotable
2	Satisfactory	B	Promotable within 1 or 2 years
3	Marginal	C	Promotable with 3 or more years' development
4	Unsatisfactory	D	Not promotable
5	New in position		

SELECTION AND PLACEMENT

Whether managers are promoted from within the organization or recruited from the outside, companies must screen, select, and place them before they function. The objective here is to select the best person for the job.

Though related in their objectives, selection and placement are conceptually distinct. The selection process screens out or rejects candidates unsuited for a position, while placement more positively connotes matching individual capabilities with a position's requirements. Regardless of the distinction, both processes identify candidates who will best accomplish staffing objectives.

The selection process measures qualifications, compares them to job criteria, and chooses the most suitable individual. Selecting and placing employees is described in Chapter 6; to avoid repetition, this section covers only those characteristics of the selection and placement processes peculiar to management development.

SELECTION AND PLACEMENT DECISIONS.   Managers base their decisions to select and place individuals on predictions of managerial effectiveness. They glean the criteria for measuring this effectiveness from position descriptions if specifications are included. These criteria describe personal characteristics required for managerial effectiveness: leadership, decision making and communication abilities, intelligence, character, and the desire to become a manager. The degree to which these qualities exist and the extent to which they can be developed are not easily measured. To aid in their assessment of managerial potential, managers observe, interview, and test candidates, and then verify and evaluate their backgrounds. As mentioned in Chapter 6, "Employee Selection and Placement," the quality of selection and placement decisions depends to a large degree on the reliability and validity of the selection devices used. That chapter also discussed the value of assessment centers in selection and placement decisions. As an alternative to assessment centers, and especially for identifying management potential, Bush and Schoenfeldt[8] suggest the *integrated appraisal method.* It emphasizes profiling (via job analysis) the requirements for managerial jobs and continuously assessing their performance on elements of the position that are relevant to (or would predict success in) higher level positions. The process includes the observation, recording, and evaluation of a manager's behavior. A variety of evidence of performance is collected over a longer period of time than in the typical 2–3 day assessment center. The observed performance is then evaluated against the criteria obtained from the job analysis. Trained appraisers then discuss performance results with the incumbent managers. With this method promotion decisions are likely to approach objectivity. Unfortunately, manager promotions are frequently based on soft criteria (e.g., the person the selecting manager happens to like best), which thus have little validity.

Regardless of the selection devices managers rely on, at some point they must make a judgment in every hiring and promotion situation. They must observe candidates under fire in situations similar to the positions for which they are being considered. Occasionally, such trial periods may spotlight deficiencies that immediately render a candidate manifestly unqualified; or a candidate may recognize his or her own inadequacies and disqualify him or herself, or at least become more amenable to rejection. However, as Bennett contends,[9] the data produced by trial-under-fire are more important. Sufficiently developed and properly administered trial periods produce data—from written records, interviews, and observers' testimony—that are invaluable to those who make final promotional decisions.

SOURCES OF MANAGERIAL TALENT.   If a successor is not designated from within an organization, outside sources will be called on to supply managerial talent. The reason for going outside may stem from a desire to bring fresh ideas or new blood into an organization because it is in trouble, financially, technologically, marketing-wise, or for other reasons, or simply because top management feels a particular outsider would be better suited for a position than existing company candidates. An organization may seek outside candidates directly or through its banks or law firm. But most typically, for top management and executive openings, the organization will engage a search firm. Top management changes made through search firms seem to be at an all time high and accelerating. Most of them contact candidates, perform the initial screening, and arrange a series of meetings with the prospective employer. For this effort search firms generally charge 30 percent of the new manager's first year's salary whether or not the organization actually fills the position.[10] Obviously, the hiring organization needs to be highly specific about selection criteria—the character, personality, abilities, background and experience—of the manager they are seeking.

INITIAL-PLACEMENT CONSIDERATIONS.   Break-in periods, with incumbents or other experienced people guiding the newly promoted managers, minimize the possibility of failure during the trial period or that following placement. However, if candidates do not qualify for permanent status, the company must consider whether to demote, discharge, or transfer them. Properly designed development programs answer these questions before candidates are promoted. Many recent college graduates start in operative positions to gain exposure to the business at the lowest rungs. They have to work their way up regardless of educational credentials. This practice of starting at the bottom can be frustrating to the graduate who has visions of applying the high-level knowledge gained in college.

TRAINING FOR DEVELOPMENT

Programs for developing incumbents and candidates, whether individually or in groups, fall into three categories: presupervisory and supervisory; middle management; and executive. Although the basic approach is distinct for each, many of the training activities are common to all three. Formal classroom training courses present concepts and impart basic knowledge, but management developers also emphasize situational exposure. Superiors give recently placed managers new job responsibilities and experiences and, as their abilities improve, expose them to more complex and sophisticated situations. A discussion of activities common to all levels of development follows.

ORGANIZATIONAL DEVELOPMENT. Organizational development, covered in detail in Chapter 4, can also be considered in terms of management development. Traditionally, management development has taken place on an individual basis. *Organizational development (OD)* depends on the support of colleagues who understand how a manager wants to change. OD is a continuous and overall effort that increases organizational effectiveness by integrating individual desires for growth within organizational goals. Managers systematically plan and implement change by sharing power, collaborating, and building personal trust.[11] The need for OD arises from a lack of cooperation between departments or divisions; ambiguous lines of responsibility; labor-management disputes; poor problem solving relationships in project teams; or technological change that redirects company objectives.[12] OD helps individuals and groups maximize their contributions to an organization. More specifically, OD locates problem solving responsibilities as close to the grass roots as possible, builds trust and creates harmony through collaboration, encourages employees' self-direction and self-regulation, and introduces a system to reward the attainment of individual and organizational goals. OD has produced tangible benefits for a number of companies. General Motors' commitment to OD resulted in a change from production- to people-centered management, thereby reducing costs, increasing morale, and improving efficiency and quality.

The OD Process. In OD a change action or intervention follows a diagnosis of the organization. This diagnosis is similar to the one used to analyze training needs described in Chapter 13. It is important to note here that a good organizational diagnosis distinguishes between technology-related problems and people problems. For example, one OD consultant's diagnosis of a newspaper's pressroom found that productivity was low, morale was declining, and there were numerous interpersonal conflicts. The consultant chose to use a series of team building exercises as the change action. Despite the skillful teaching of the consultant and the enthusiastic response of both employees and managers there was no significant improvement. Several weeks later one of the mechanics discovered that the drive mechanism on the main press was out of alignment. When this mechanical problem was corrected productivity improved and the employees returned to a state of satisfaction. This example points up the importance of a thorough diagnosis that considers all factors of the situation: social (people as individuals and groups), technical (machinery, tools, methods, and so on), and the external environment (the economy, governmental influences, etc.). In addition, it should be obvious that organizational problems are complex and, as with most personnel problems, they are not amenable to ready solution. Nevertheless, once the diagnosis is completed the change agent or consultant selects appropriate interventions. **OD interventions** usually are structured activities of selected target groups or individuals.

Dyer[13] suggests several criteria for intervention selection.

Root cause. The intervention should deal with the basic causal factors of the problem(s).

Time frame. Consideration has to be given to the time the intervention should start and when it should be completed to have optimum impact.

Financial resources. Considers the amount of funding available for implementation of a suitable intervention.

Client support. It is critical that the involved parties support the change program in order to have improvements occur and continue.

Change agent skill. Change agents must have the appropriate skills to implement the action. These skills would include the ability to identify problems, select appropriate interventions, and then sequence the interventions to ensure that problems are solved.

Energy level. There must be a high degree of enthusiasm, commitment, and motivation to engage in the change effort for the intervention to be successful.

Types of Interventions.   Organizations have recently been viewed as sociotechnical systems, for example, interactions between people and technology. As a result, organizational change agents or consultants select interventions that impact on both individuals and systems. French and Bell, for example, have identified various target groups and appropriate interventions.[14] Some target groups and a few of the interventions appropriate to them are listed in Table 14.3.

Target Group	Interventions
To Improve the Effectiveness of:	
Individuals	Life/career planning activities; coaching and counseling, sensitivity training, education, job enrichment, transactional analysis, grid OD.
Teams	Team building, survey feedback, process consultation, management by objectives.
Intergroup Relations	Intergroup activities, survey feedback, third-party peacemaking, grid OD.
Total Organization	Technostructural activities such as collateral organizations (task forces), confrontation meetings, strategic planning activities, grid OD.

Table 14.3
OD Interventions for Target Groups

Source: Adapted from Wendell L. French and Cecil Bell, Jr. *Organization Development*, 2nd ed. (Englewood Cliffs, N.J.: Prentice-Hall, 1978), p. 112.

A wide variety of canned interventions are available,[15] but some change agents tailor interventions to the specific needs of a client. Some of the more widely used interventions include:

1. *Sensitivity training.* A training group (T-group) creates a new social system in which participants learn how they relate to others and may change behavior patterns in a way more conducive to cooperative effort.

2. *Team building.* Members of a single workgroup meet to improve interpersonal relationships and task effectiveness.

3. *Role analysis techniques.* Participants clarify their roles, expectations, and accountabilities.

4. *Grid OD.* This multistage approach provides for individual education, team development, interteam problem resolution, and goal clarification and achievement.

5. *Survey feedback.* Survey responses are reported to employees and their managers, who work together to resolve problems indicated in the survey.

6. *Socio-technical system design.* Unit operations analysis is used to map the organization's technology. Then conflicts between the technical and social subsystems are identified and methods are devised to correct them.

7. *Job restructuring.* The characteristics of employees are matched to jobs through job redesign, enrichment, and/or enlargement.

According to a recent survey of professionals who deal with OD interventions, program activities relevant to OD that are expected to increase in the next few years include assertiveness training, behavior modeling, career development, productivity training, quality of work life, team building, and work redesign,[16] all of which are covered elsewhere in this text.

The Role of Personnel in OD.   Although organizations often retain outside consultants to implement OD, many have internal consultants or change agents. Professionals within the organization who are responsible for OD are invariably associated with the personnel function. The change agent or internal consultant is responsible for performing the organizational diagnosis, selecting appropriate interventions, and implementing them. And, as with any change process, the change agent evaluates the effectiveness of the OD initiative. These change agents or consultants utilize their expertise in training and development to introduce change actions to the organization. They work with managers to help them bring about changes that will have a positive impact on the objectives of the organization. Because change agents work between groups and with people at various levels of the organization they function in roles that may be political or diplomatic in nature. For lower level participants these change agents become surrogate participants in decision making, and for higher-level decision makers they act as representatives of the lower-level employees. In another role, the change agent/ consultant may be called on to mediate between organizational groups that are independent but have different vested interests, beliefs, values, and perceptions. The consultant can act as a communications channel by facilitating face-to-face interaction. In this role the consultant can aid the integration of both groups' vested interests while, at the same time, focusing on their interaction.[17] Although some organizations prefer to use outside OD consultants for the objectivity they bring to a situation, the internal consultant understands both the formal and informal nature of the organization and may be able to achieve positive results at a lower cost.

COACHING.   A basic responsibility common to all managers is developing subordinates. In his classic study on manager development, Mace concluded that "the most effective way of providing for the growth and development of people in manufacturing organizations is through the conscious coaching of subordinates by their immediate superiors."[18] **Coaching** refers to the daily guidance given by managers to develop subordinates. Coaching is helping subordinates find their own solutions rather than telling them the answers. The philosophy that pervades management development is that self-development is the only true development. Argyris, however, argues that coaching inhibits self-development because subordinates are molded to conform to their boss's pattern of behavior. He then explains:

Under true development, the individual is taught how to develop and is left alone to produce his own "outputs" from the process; to develop his own ideas of effective behavior. These may or may not jibe with the corporation's. Under these conditions, the range of acceptable behavior is much broader. The probability of conformity is much smaller. The only conformity required is how to grow. The uniqueness of each individual will develop.[19]

The coaching activity espoused by Mace avoids Argyris's criticism by encouraging managers to develop their own responses to problems. Mace states that the coach-employee relationship is analogous to that between the farmer and his wheat crop. The wheat grows by itself, but the success of the crop depends in large part on the farmer's help.[20]

Managers who are effective coaches possess the innate ability and patience to impart their business acumen and managerial skills to others. When coaching talent is identified other managers can profit by observing and adopting the techniques of the successful coach.

COUNSELING. Counseling is an integral part of coaching; it adds a dimension of guided learning. Managers learn how to manage by performing tasks under the guidance of their superiors, who encourage, stimulate, and constructively criticize them. Unfortunately, because of the psychological connotation of counseling, superiors avoid this approach, feeling they are not qualified specialists. Despite this reluctance, they must be encouraged to counsel if they are to develop managers effectively. Methods of counseling range from formal conferences and interviews to casual conversations over coffee. Setting examples is also a counseling technique. Performance appraisal, as a component of the management-development system, provides an excellent opportunity for counseling as supervisors review managers' progress with them. (For a detailed discussion of counseling techniques see Chapter 8.)

DELEGATION. When properly utilized, **delegation** is one of the most powerful management-development tools. Delegated assignments challenge the abilities of neophyte managers, provide relevant learning opportunities, and build confidence. These advantages are especially significant today, when achievement-oriented young people demand meaningful and challenging work—which is sometimes lacking in corporate life. Delegation offers the additional benefit of flexibility; tailor-made assignments can be geared to an individual's development needs and capabilities. In delegating, supervisors ensure that responsibilities are given to those capable of handling them and that assignments are carried out satisfactorily and punctually. Managers must remember that they are accountable for the results and that they cannot excuse substandard performance by subordinates. But despite the initial dangers of inefficient performance, the long-range benefits in developing managers far outweigh the short-term costs.

GUIDED EXPERIENCE.   **Guided experience** is the general term for a host of approaches to individual development. It is epitomized by the rotation, on a formal schedule, of a manager through several jobs in different departments. For example, an individual might first manage a service organization, then a manufacturing operation, and so on. Specific types of guided experience are termed planned progression, flying squadrons, **job rotation,** and work experience.[21] The emergence of conglomerates has increased the importance of guided experience by replacing the acquired company's management with executives who have been put to the test through a series of rotational assignments. A common practice today is to start management trainees at the bottom, initially performing a variety of operative tasks, and later taking on more responsibility as experience is gained. For example, some of the major oil companies start their new college graduates pumping gasoline and doing mechanical work. After this they might assist in managing a service station, and later they will be assigned to a district office.

Every organization in which assignments are made to develop individual managers and meet staffing requirements uses guided experience in one form or another. In its broadest sense, guided experience is merely assigning managers with a view to developing their responsibilities beyond their immediate task. However, if a conscious effort is made to plan the ideal pattern of experiences for advancing and developing managers, coupled with appraisals, coaching, and delegation, the guided approach benefits both the organization and individual managers.

ASSISTANT-TO.   By serving in an understudy position, a staff assistant or **assistant-to** can learn management skills by observing the activities of his or her managers. Many critics have faulted this approach because assistants-to have little authority to manage. However, from a developmental standpoint, these positions can provide opportunities for growth, especially for inexperienced managers who would profit more from observation and study than from the actual exercise of line authority.

MULTIPLE MANAGEMENT. McCormick and Company originated the method of developing managers in decision making committees, or junior boards, with rotating membership. The few organizations that have adopted this method of development consider it effective, claiming that managers develop faster when they help formulate policies broader than their own areas of responsibility.

CONTINUING EDUCATION. As managers progress in an organization, the nature of their work changes. This factor coupled with rapidly changing technology, possible overspecialization of certain positions, and a failure to communicate how well or poorly a manager is performing lead to a phenomenon called **managerial obsolescence.** The term simply means that the manager is no longer up-to-date, which is most common among managers when they reach their late thirties.[22] Obsolescence is a problem viewed in terms of *education*—awareness of new ideas, methods, and techniques, and in terms of experience—effective application of knowledge. Research data imply that once a person has become a manager, experience becomes more important than education in determining his or her relative obsolescence. Thus, to combat obsolescence, organizations should encourage managers to use their talents and to participate in managerial activities so they will develop the capabilities to handle future assignments. Education plays a significant role here, too. When managers are aware of their shortcomings, have definite educational objectives, and are open-minded about change, they can gain optimum results from educational exposures.[23] The use of outside sources for management education appears to be a viable alternative to in-house programs. Organizations engage consultants to conduct internal programs; they purchase training materials such as films, instruction kits, and so on from outside vendors; and they send selected individuals to seminars or to university continuing education or management development programs.[24] Table 14.4 is a selective listing of *organizations* offering management education services.

University continuing education programs are a growing source of management education.[25] Programs range from specific skills building seminars, which usually offer Continuing Education Units (CEU's) based on the number of classroom hours, to a degree program—the **executive MBA.** In the latter a manager is sponsored by his or her organization, which finances the candidate's tuition and expenses (typical costs run from $10–15,000 for two academic years and covers tuition, books, and materials), and allows time off to attend school. Most programs are conducted on weekends to minimize disruption of work schedules. A typical schedule calls for attendance on alternate Fridays and Saturdays. Candidates ordinarily are seasoned man-

Table 14.4
A Sampling of Organizations That Offer Management-Education Services

Organization	Services
American Management Associations	Trains leaders and provides program materials for numerous in-house courses in supervisory and management development. Offerings include: general supervisory development courses, fundamentals of finance for non-financial managers, how to improve managerial performance, and numerous other specific skills-development programs and general management seminars.
Addison-Wesley Publishing Company	Publishes books, audio-cassette programs, filmstrips, programmed texts, video programs, and reference materials.
AMR International, Inc.	Conducts management seminars and in-company programs on a variety of subjects including: management by objectives, successful negotiating, project financing, merging and selling companies, and others.
American Society for Training and Development	Sponsors workshops and seminars in supervisory and management development and publishes directories, workbooks and handbooks on management development.
Battelle Memorial Institute	Offers a subscription program (Technical inputs to planning) designed to bridge the management-technology gap.
Conference Board	Offers management/executive conferences, seminars, publications, custom research, chief executive lunches.
Mantread, Inc.	Is a clearing house for management-training programs and services. Offers evaluation of training programs offered by others.
Sterling Institute	Conducts both standard and custom-tailored management courses either in-house or in outside facilities. Develops training modules for general use.
Strategic Planning Institute	Is a data bank based on information from 150 companies—analyzes data for corporate members.

Organization	Services	Table 14.4 (cont.)
Westinghouse Learning Corporation	Offers numerous courses, workbooks, filmstrips, etc. for individual and group instruction.	
Xerox Educational Systems	Develops custom-tailored programs and offers specialized packaged programs in a variety of managerial areas.	

Note: This list contains only a sampling of organizations offering educational services or materials. A comprehensive list is published periodically by the American Society for Training and Development, Inc., P.O. Box 5307, Madison, Wisc. 53705.

agers with 10 or more years experience including several years in the managerial or senior professional position. The executive MBA offers the advantage of allowing participants to relate concepts learned in the classroom to their work immediately. Also, each class progresses through the program as an integrated group, so they are able to share ideas and problems and form strong affiliations.

MENTORING.   The term **mentor** derives from Greek mythology. Mentor was the dear friend of Ulysses who was entrusted with the care of his son during his father's ten-year odyssey. Modern mentors serve to stimulate protégés (managers) through ideas and information. They usually possess an intimate knowledge of the organization, especially the informal structures and politics. Most frequently mentors are self-appointed and they take on the relationship because they care. Mentors are especially important to the development of aspiring young managers, particularly women managers. But the intimacy of the mentor-protégé relationship often discourages men from assuming this role with women. (Mentoring of women managers is discussed further in Chapter 15). Obviously, when mentors give poor advice or cause the protégé to become dependent, the latter could suffer emotionally and career-wise. Organizations can enhance the mentor-protégé relationship by giving it credence in appraisals and rewarding its positive consequences.[26]

PRESUPERVISORY AND SUPERVISORY TRAINING.   Programs at the supervisory level aid individuals in making the transition from trainee or operative worker to the first level of management. This process develops supervisory skills and shapes attitudes conducive to managing—transforming the techniques-oriented operative into a manager who achieves objectives through other people.

The author, in designing and implementing several supervisory-development programs, has found a number of factors crucial to successful training. For instance, the program must provide a smooth transition in training and in subject matter from operative work to supervision because they are distinct and require different skills. Highly skilled machinists, for example, cannot be given supervisory responsibilities and be immediately effective. Also, trainees want challenging and relevant work that contributes to the organization.[27] In recognition of this desire the training experience gave trainees line responsibility as quickly as possible. Furthermore, trainees were not underemployed; their assignments were relevant to their educational backgrounds, past experience, and interests. The author conducted the training in three phases. Phase I, introduction, familiarized trainees with the organization, the production cycle, and the physical plant. During this phase, which lasted less than a week, trainees attended classes on company policy and procedures. Phase II, orientation, acquainted trainees with operating problems, and developed their supervisory and technical skills through on-the-job training in specific operational areas in conjunction with classroom work in management policies and practices. Typical classes included sessions on managerial economics, report writing, human relations, discipline, union relations, communications, leadership, work scheduling, methods of control, and instruction techniques. During this phase instructors encouraged trainees to develop new methods, ideas, and recommend improvements. Time limits for this phase were flexible, varying from individual to individual and averaging 6 to 12 months. Home-study courses supported by a tuition-refund program supplemented the job experience. In Phase III, internship, trainees assumed their permanent assignments under the guidance of their immediate supervisors, who rotated trainee jobs and gave special assignments on the basis of individual interests and development needs. The duration of this phase depended on the individual's progress, the needs of the organization, and position openings in the trainee's progression path.

The personnel department was responsible for program administration, but line managers played an active role in implementing and evaluating all phases. Middle line managers trained to coach in the area of supervision sponsored the trainees, reviewed the progress reports from trainees' supervisors every six weeks, and submitted reports on their own reactions to the training. Sponsors measured performance against objectives they established jointly with the trainees. The effect of involving the managers of these supervisors created a receptive environment in which to try out their new skills and provide the appropriate reinforcement. The elements of this program are compatible with Byham and Robinson's recommendations for Interaction Management training.[28] After three years the company deemed the program successful because the trainees outperformed their counterparts (the control group) who had not received the same training exposure.

MIDDLE-MANAGEMENT TRAINING. Middle managers often attend seminars, institutes, short courses, and special programs both within the company and off-site.[29] In contrast to supervisory training courses, this type of exposure usually mixes conceptual and practical subject matter. Middle managers aspiring to executive positions digest current articles in administration and study the literature relevant to their specialties and to their industry. An important adjunct of a junior executive's training is affiliation with professional associations. Societies and associations for almost every specialty within management offer technical journals, information exchange, training programs, seminars, and additional stimuli to encourage a professional approach to management. Middle managers who have been identified as comers can be developed in a challenging manner through a succession of planned transfers that expose them to a variety of work experiences. Although it may be a problem to get other divisions or departments to accept transferees, one study found that the effort yields tangible benefits in terms of development and retention of high-potential managers.[30] Specific managerial skills can be developed through repetitive learning from experience. Waters[31] suggests that those types of managerial skills can be identified and can be developed by converting abstract generalizations to behavior tailored to specific situations. *Practice skills* are those for which reasonably specific behavioral descriptions are available (active listening, nondirective interviewing, report writing, appraising performance, etc.), and which are performed over a relatively short time interval. *Context skills* can also be fairly well described (goal setting, work planning, managing time, asserting authority, designing controls, etc.); but their learning takes place over a long period of time, so they are difficult to teach in a training class. *Insight skills* emerge gradually and their learning is less controlled than for the other two skills. Examples of insight skills include: dealing with authority, building trust, working in groups, coping with ambiguity, etc., which are learned indirectly from the training exposure. For instance coping with ambiguity can be developed through encouraging the manager-learners to design their own learning experiences and use the instructor as a resource person.

EXECUTIVE TRAINING. In addition to programs similar to middle-management training, top managers attend development programs offered by colleges and universities. Perhaps the greatest contribution of these programs, and the one most widely acknowledged by participants, is the exposure they provide to the thinking of executives from other industries, companies, functions, and locations. The programs encourage managers to question the patterns of their thinking and techniques built up over a decade or two with their company and its procedures. Their imagination is stirred by discovering that other organizations, facing problems similar to theirs, have used different solutions successfully. Formally and informally, in daytime classes and in nighttime bull sessions, good executive-development programs challenge, stimulate, exercise, and broaden their thinking.[32] Programs vary in length, subject matter, and cost. Perhaps the best known is the 13-week Advanced Management Program offered by Harvard University's Graduate School of Business Administration. Through the case method, supplemented by lectures and readings, top managers absorb an intensive curriculum of business policy, finance, marketing management, accounting and financial policy, business history, problems of labor relations, business and world society, behavior, mathematical concepts, and simulation.[33]

Since the major function of out-of-company resource programs is to excite the minds and challenge the prejudices of managers, the need for participation is greatest for those at the highest levels of management, where habits have become more ingrained.[34] To evaluate executive development programs, management should measure them against the objectives it is seeking. Farnsworth suggests that organizations check with others to ascertain their experience with and perceptions of specific executive programs.[35] Reliable techniques are not yet available for assessing the contribution of these programs to participants,[36] however, performance appraisals of executives who have attended such programs should indicate their effectiveness. Various services are available to aid in the selection of the program that is most compatible with an executive's needs. Most notable is *Bricker's Directory*, which lists general executive programs of two weeks or longer duration. Each program is described in terms of its objectives, content, faculty, class scheduling, methods of instruction, class size, accommodations, method of selection costs, and Bricker's recommendation regarding the relevance of the program.[37]

PERFORMANCE APPRAISAL (THE DEVELOPMENTAL APPROACH)

This component of the management development system appraises developing managers by comparing actual performance with individual performance goals. Variances from objectives indicate strengths and weaknesses. To maintain strengths and overcome deficiencies, managers and their superiors prepare development plans to implement and review at the end of a specified period. This and other approaches to appraisal are covered in Chapter 16, "Performance Appraisal."

MANAGEMENT COMPENSATION

Chapter 19 discusses executive compensation in detail; therefore, this section provides only a few observations on its relationship to management development.

Management development systems would be ineffective without provisions for incentives and rewards. **Management compensation** includes all salaries, incentives, and fringe benefits paid to managers in return for their past, present, and potential services to an organization. Management compensation serves several important purposes.[38]

1. It helps attract competent personnel. Organizations hire employees for existing and forecasted vacancies. By offering competitive salaries, they can attract first-rate talent. Compensation is often the deciding factor in acceptance of a position offer. It is also the factor most easily shaped by an organization to attract prospective employees.

2. It enables companies to retain qualified personnel. Although other factors may become more important after managers are hired, compensation still looms large as a factor in encouraging continued participation in an organization. More important, compensation plans can provide a continuing link between organizational and personal objectives.

3. It provides incentives for performance. Compensation plans can be designed to encourage the type of performance needed by an organization. Improved individual contribution, more effective teamwork, or both, may be developed by the way a plan is devised. For these results to accrue, however, employees must perceive a relationship between their performance and rewards.

4. Theoretically, at least, compensation is commensurate with the individual's contribution to an organization. Organizations sometimes gear pay and benefit improvements to performance. This seems to imply a relationship between performance appraisal and salary administration, thus refuting the previous contention that the two must be separate. It is possible to use the appraisal for development and reward performance separately with advancement and commensurate compensation increases. For as employees develop, they become more qualified; they advance either within their positions or to promotional positions. Under both circumstances, compensation improves.

5. Salary, incentives, and fringe benefits comprise the total compensation package. Salary is of major concern to an organization because it is the largest element of compensation cost and other elements of the compensation package are geared to it.

6. Incentive plans are designed to motivate managers with bonuses, stock options, and profit-sharing plans. Bonuses are usually linked to earnings improvements, so some of the increased profits that result from managers' efforts are passed on to them. Also, stock options and stock-purchase

plans may foster participation in ownership by equating owner and executive interests. There is a wide variety of fringe benefits that supplement compensation and can enhance the attractiveness of a compensation package. These benefits might include: vacation, sick leave, educational assistance, pension plans, insurance, expense accounts, company transportation, executive dining rooms, company-paid memberships in clubs and professional associations, stock options, bonuses, and others.

EVALUATION

To maintain an effective, competitive management team, organizations find they must continuously scrutinize their management development system and each of its components. Constant evaluation makes the system dynamic because it locates the need for change and upgrading. As discussed in Chapter 13, organizations measure their system and its components against established objectives. Performance appraisal provides an excellent vehicle for system evaluation—another reason why it is the key component. In addition, audits conducted by personnel within the firm or by outside consultants can provide excellent analyses of each component; but because audits are a periodic device and because systems need continuous evaluation, they can only supplement other techniques. Hard criteria to evaluate a system can also be provided in performance statistics: profitability, return on investment and assets, growth, numbers and types of promotions, turnover, and so on. Another indicator is the number of times organizations must go beyond their doors to fill important vacancies, since an effective management development system will provide most key personnel. In using performance criteria, the attempt is made to estimate the effects of management development in actual job performance.

In the evaluation of a management development system *both* the research design and the selection of criteria for managerial effectiveness are critical. According to studies conducted on this subject, the confidence that can be placed on evaluation results is predicated on the handling of the criteria and research design. Regarding the latter, its prime concern is to ensure that any changes in managerial effectiveness can be traced conclusively to the program itself. Thus, an adequate design would have to include an experimental group (those included in the program) and a control group (a similar group not included) who are exposed to a test or evaluation before and after development activities, for example, pretest, posttest.[39]

Cost-Benefit Analysis

At this point, students should be convinced that management and executive development programs are essential to the continued viability of a management team. Thus, we are primarily concerned with ensuring that development efforts produce desired results at the lowest possible cost.

A number of criteria could be used to measure results. For example, we could trace the management-replacement experience of an organization. The ratio of management vacancies to qualified replacements available within (not to say that all management vacancies are to be filled within, but inside replacements should be identified and developed nevertheless) is a good indicator of the impact of development activities. Another indicator is the degree of obsolescence of managers in an organization. When it is low, management and executive development programs may be a positive contributing factor. And often, improvement in the appraisals of managers' performance is a reflection, at least in part, of development programs. As we shall see in Chapter 16, appraisals are a key factor in management and executive development.

Summary

A dynamic system of management development consists of components that interact to support organizational objectives. The purpose of the system is to develop and maintain an effective management team, with qualified backup, to assure organizational continuity. Various components of the system and their functions are listed below.

1. A projection of an organization (to forecast human resource needs) aids in planning for successors to key positions.

2. Position descriptions of all jobs in the present and future management hierarchy provide a basis for recruiting and training activities.

3. An inventory of existing human resources identifies management talent in an organization and spotlights potential manpower deficiencies.

4. Replacement charts identify designated successors to management positions and enable top management to detect blocks in promotion paths and deficiencies in replacements.

5. Recruiting needs are then determined from anticipated turnover and from forecasted vacancies that cannot be filled from within.

6. Management vacancies are filled through careful selection and placement to ensure that the best available individuals fill the positions.

7. Employees train to develop capacities to their maximum through programs designed to meet individual needs.

8. In performance appraisal, employees set performance goals jointly with their managers, measure themselves against their goals, and establish personal development plans.

9. Management compensation rewards performance and provides an incentive for growth.

10. Finally, the entire system and each component are continuously evaluated using hard criteria and an adequate research design.

Considerable effort and strong support from top management can help ensure the success of a management development system. The benefit of an effective system is a strong leadership position, which can only be established and maintained through the efforts of a strong management team.

Key Terms

management development	delegation
executive	guided experience
organization projection	job rotation
management inventory	assistant-to
position descriptions	managerial obsolescence
replacement chart	executive MBA
OD interventions	mentor
coaching	management compensation

Review Questions

1. In many organizations, management development consists of miscellaneous training activities. How does a management development system differ from this approach?

2. Specify at least three criteria for measuring the effectiveness of a management development program. Give examples of the techniques that can be used to measure program effectiveness.

3. How are replacement charts used in management development?

4. What is organizational development? Describe some of the team-building techniques used in this activity.

5. What are some of the management development activities available to small organizations?

Discussion Questions

1. Describe how a management development committee can support a management development system. What contributions can the personnel department make to these activities?

2. What are the alternatives to the systems approach to management development? What advantages and disadvantages does a management

development system have compared to the alternatives you described? How can a management development system contribute to the success of an organization?

3. Currently, companies are concerned with the problem of overqualified management candidates. Recently hired college graduates become disillusioned with business when they serve their training period performing routine tasks. What alternatives are available to companies that want to hire the best and also provide opportunities for employees to grow with an organization?

4. Why have management development activities increased in the past decade?

Case Problem 1

THE JUNIOR BOARD OF DIRECTORS OF UNION CORPORATION

The president of Union Corporation, Mr. Ryan, decided to establish a junior board of directors composed of executives directly below his own subordinates. Ryan's direct subordinates were not to be on this board; the members were to be the deputy division managers, assistant functional vice presidents, and some of the deputy managers of the staff and service departments at the corporate level. The board was to have 16 members, with Ryan as chairman, and was to meet at least twice a month.

Ryan's main reason for setting up this board was to get a better firsthand feeling for the people, problems, interests, desires, and apprehensions lower down in the management hierarchy. He felt that the junior board would be excellent for trading pertinent information, improving communication, and for getting things off people's chests and minds. He was also convinced that the board would foster greater initiative and creativity lower down in the organization, promote greater effective decentralization of authority, and be highly beneficial in terms of management development. Ryan felt that a number of his own key deputies were not doing enough in these areas, in spite of his constant prodding, pressure, and encouragement. However, the board would not have any formal decision-making power, so as not to violate the formal chain of command or usurp the authority of Ryan's own subordinates.

Several subordinates were unhappy about and strongly opposed this junior board of directors. Only four of Ryan's ten direct subordinates were on the corporation's board of directors. The other deputy heads and staff specialists of the corporate staff and service departments, as well as a number of other key head-office personnel, were upset because they had not been asked to be on the junior board.

Problems

1. Discuss the likely advantages and disadvantages of the junior board at Union.

2. Do you think Ryan has good ideas about the use of junior boards? In general, under what conditions, for what purposes, and in what ways do you think junior boards might prove effective?

3. Assuming that the junior board at Union is there to stay, what changes would you recommend in its membership and functions, if any?

Case Problem 2

THE WORTHLESS MANAGERS

A famous economist once commented that managers in large, publicly held corporations are like so many interchangeable parts. They think that they are unique, but actually they can be easily replaced.

The economist based this statement on stock-market price reactions when major management changes are announced. "If managers really were valuable, and if they were seen as unique," he stated, "we would expect the price of a firm's stock to rise or fall when a significant management change is announced. Actually, virtually nothing happens, even when a firm like General Motors or Ford gets a new president. The most sophisticated observers of firms' operations just don't react to such changes. This proves that one manager is about as good as another."

Problems

1. Do the above facts *prove* that one manager is just about as good as another?

2. What other interpretations might be placed on the above evidence?

3. Do you know of any cases in which management changes caused significant stock-market price shifts? When? Why?

Notes

1. Jon English and Anthony R. Marchione, "Nine Steps in Management Development," *Business Horizons,* June 1977, p. 88.

2. Myles L. Mace, *The Growth and Development of Executives* (Boston: Division of Research, Harvard Business School, 1959), pp. 22ff.

3. Thomas A. Mahoney, *Building the Executive Team* (Englewood Cliffs, N.J.: Prentice-Hall, 1961), p. 22.

4. Michael R. Cooper et al., "Early Warning Signals—Growing Discontent Among Managers," *Business,* January-February 1980, p. 11.

5. Robert B. Burr, "The Purpose and Extent of Management Development" in Robert L. Craig and Lester R. Bittel, eds., *The Training and Development Handbook* (New York: McGraw-Hill, 1967), p. 367.

6. Ross E. Azevedo, "Missing Ingredient in Skills Inventories," *Journal of Systems Management,* April 1977, pp. 27–28.

7. Insight into the selection of successors to management positions can be gained from the research studies of Donald L. Hemlich on management succession. See his articles "Corporate Succession: An Examination," *Academy of Management Journal,* September 1975, pp. 429–41; and "Executive Succession in the Corporate Organization," *Academy of Management Review,* April 1977, pp. 252–66.

8. Donald H. Bush and Lyle F. Schoenfeldt, "Identifying Managerial Potential: An Alternative to Assessment Centers," *Personnel,* May–June 1980, pp. 68–76.

9. Willard E. Bennett, *Manager Selection, Education and Training* (New York: McGraw-Hill, 1959), pp. 87–88.

10. "Executive Mobility—Why More Companies Look for and Find—Talent Outside," *Business Week,* October 4, 1976, pp. 55–62.

11. Glen H. Varney, *An Organization Development Approach to Management Development* (Reading, Mass.: Addison-Wesley, 1976), p. 7.

12. W. Warner Burke and Warren H. Schmidt, "Management and Organization Development," *Personnel Administration,* March–April 1971, p. 49.

13. William G. Dyer, "Selecting an Intervention for Organization Change," *Training and Development Journal,* April 1981, pp. 64–68.

14. Wendell L. French and Cecil H. Bell, Jr., *Organization Development,* 2nd ed. (Englewood Cliffs, N.J.: Prentice-Hall, 1978), p. 112.

15. One of the most widely used sources of OD interventions is University Associates, 6617 Production Avenue, San Diego, California 92121. This organization publishes an *Annual Handbook for Group Facilitators,* which contains OD interventions and exercises for human relations training.

16. Rob Jones, "A Caution Signal for HRD," *Training and Development Journal,* April 1981, p. 44ff.

17. Anthony T. Cobb and Newton Margulies, "Organization Development: A Political Perspective," *Academy of Management Review,* January 1981, pp. 53–54.

18. Mace, *The Growth and Development of Executives,* p. 108.

19. Chris Argyris, "Do-It-Yourself Executive Development," *Think,* May 1960, pp. 9–11.

20. Mace, *The Growth and Development of Executives,* p. 113.

21. See Mahoney, *Building the Execu-*

tive Team, pp. 224–29; Mace, The Growth and Development of Executives, chap. V; Earl G. Planty and Carlos Marquis, eds., The Development of Executive Talent (New York: American Management Association, 1952); James Morris, Job Rotation: A Study and Program (Chicago: Industrial Relations Center, University of Chicago, September 1957); and James G. Stockard, Career Development and Job Training (New York: AMACOM, 1977).

22. Clayton Reeser, "Managerial Obsolescence: An Organizational Dilemma," Personnel Journal, January 1977, pp. 27–31ff.

23. Richard L. Shearer and Joseph A. Steger, "Manpower Obsolescence: A New Definition and Empirical Investigation of Personal Variables," Academy of Management Journal, June 1975, pp. 263–75.

24. Mary Green Miner, Management Training and Development Programs (Washington, D.C.: Bureau of National Affairs, March 1977), pp. 10ff.

25. John F. Sullivan, "Trends in University-based Continuing Management Education," Training and Development Journal, March 1977, p. 23.

26. The Woodlands Group, "Management Development Roles: Coach, Sponsor and Mentor," Personnel Journal, November 1980, pp. 918–921.

27. See "An Anatomy of Activism for Executives," Harvard Business Review, November-December 1970, pp. 131–42.

28. William C. Byham and James C. Robinson, "Interaction Management: Supervisory Training That Changes Job Performance," The Personnel Administrator, February 1976, pp. 16–19.

29. Robert B. Burr, "The Purpose and Extent of Management Development," in Craig and Bittel, eds., The Training and Development Handbook, p. 391.

30. Robert A. Pitts, "Unshackle Your 'Comers'," Harvard Business Review, May–June 1977, pp. 127–36.

31. James A. Waters, "Managerial Skill Development," Academy of Management Review, July 1980, pp. 449–453.

32. Melvin Ashen, "Executive Development, In-Company vs. University Programs," Harvard Business Review, September–October 1954, pp. 83–91.

33. For a comprehensive survey with detailed outlines of management development programs offered worldwide, see Nancy C. McNulty, Training Managers, The International Guide (New York: Harper & Row, 1969).

34. Bennett, Manager Selection, Education and Training, p. 144.

35. Terry Farnsworth, Developing Executive Talent (London: McGraw-Hill, 1975), p. 18.

36. Some helpful suggestions for evaluating executive development programs are provided in Melvin Ashen, "Better Use of Executive Development Programs," Harvard Business Review, November–December 1955, pp. 67–74.

37. George W. Bricker, Bricker's International Directory of University Sponsored Executive Development Programs (South Chatham, Mass.: Bricker Publications, Compiled Annually).

38. For a discussion of this subject see: David W. Belcher, Compensation Administration (Englewood Cliffs, N.J.: Prentice-Hall, 1974); Richard I. Henderson, Compensation Management (Reston, Va.: Reston Publishing, 1976); and Thomas H. Patten, Jr., Pay: Employee Compensation and Incentive Plans (New York: Free Press, 1977).

39. William J. Kearney, "Management Development Programs Can Pay Off," Business Horizons, April 1975, pp. 81–85.

Chapter Fifteen

Development Programs for Women, Minorities, and the Handicapped

In her classic novel, *Atlas Shrugged,* Ayn Rand gave the following biographical description of the heroine, Dagny Taggart:

> Dagny was nine years old when she decided that she would run Taggart Transcontinental Railroad someday.... It was not a final decision, but only the final seal of words upon something she had known long ago....
>
>   ... She felt the excitement of solving problems, the insolent delight of taking up a challenge and disposing of it without effort, the eagerness to meet another, harder test. She felt at the same time, a growing respect for the adversary....
>
>   ... She was fifteen when it occurred to her for the first time that women did not run railroads and that people might object. To hell with that, she thought—and never worried about it again.
>
>   She went to work for Taggart Transcontinental at the age of sixteen.... Dagny's rise among the men who operated Taggart Transcontinental was swift and uncontested.[1]

Dagny Taggart is a fictitious character and one might conclude that women only act like this in novels. Not so. As we shall see later in this chapter, studies have found that Dagny Taggart is *typical* of successful women managers in today's business world. The problems Dagny faced in her rise at the railroad are similar to those of women in the real world. We will explore the special problems of women in organizations, the programs to develop their skills and abilities, and specific success patterns of women. The

LEARNING OBJECTIVES

1. To know the legislative guidelines for affirmative action.

2. To know the composition of affirmative action programs, in general.

3. To understand the special problems of women, handicapped, ethnic groups, and the aged at work.

4. To be familiar with development programs specific to women, minorities, handicapped, aged, and related groups.

situation for minorities, especially blacks, is similar, so special consideration for their development will also be discussed.

Women at Work

Although the Dagny Taggarts of the working world are few and far between, opportunities for women are expanding. They too seek career opportunities in business and government that will afford them challenging work and economic independence. However, in their quest for advancement they face a host of problems that are associated with sex differences. Fortunately, efforts abound to remove inequalities in the treatment of women at work, and their prospects for the future look bright.

CHARACTERISTICS OF WORKING WOMEN

LABOR FORCE PARTICIPATION.   Almost half the women over 16 years of age are now working. In mid-1980 they represented 51 percent of the entire labor force—40 million women were actively employed. The **labor force participation rate** is the percentage of eligible people who are working. Figure 15.1 shows the increasing participation rate for women.

Figure 15.1
Labor Force Participation Rates of Women and Men, Annual Averages, 1950–76, and Projected Rates for 1980, 1985, and 1990.

Source: U.S. Department of Labor, Bureau of Labor Statistics, *Perspectives on Working Women* (Washington, D.C.: U.S. Government Printing Office, June 1980), p. 2.

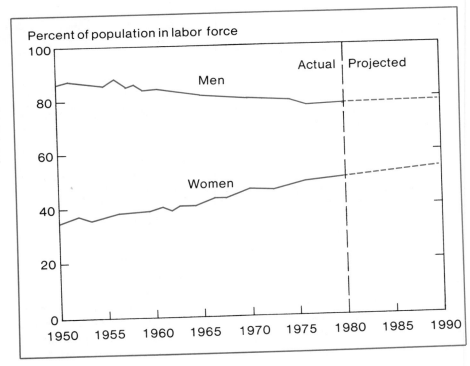

For women, the most significant increase in this rate has been in the 25–34 age group, which advanced by 18 percent between 1970 and 1979. This increase is remarkable because the majority (64 percent) in this age group are married and have children, factors that traditionally have tended to keep women out of the labor force.[2]

Major advances in female employment have been made in the white-collar and professional occupations. For example, 36 percent of the accountants in the United States in 1980 were women as opposed to 15 percent in 1950. Among lawyers and judges, the proportion of women rose from 4 to 13 percent; among physicians from 7 to 13 percent; and among bank officials and financial managers, from 12 to 34 percent. And women managers as a percentage of all managers rose from 13.8 in 1950 to 26 percent in 1980.[3] A recent survey showed changes in jobs held by women in the decade from 1967 to 1976. During this period the number of companies reporting women executives increased 19 percent; at the mid-management level 15 percent more companies reported using females in this capacity; and traditionally male jobs were taken over by women at 41 percent more companies.[4]

On the negative side, unemployment has increased among women. In 1980 the number of unemployed women increased about 400,000 to 3.3 million. Unemployed women are more likely than men to be entering or reentering the labor force.[5]

EDUCATION. Women seem to recognize that educational credentials enhance their chances for success in the work world. Generally, additional education raises the likelihood that they will enter the labor market and remain employed. In addition, the more education they bring to their jobs, the higher they are likely to be paid. During the decade of the '70s female educational attainment showed a substantial improvement. By 1979, 34 percent of women workers had completed at least one year of college (up from 24 percent in 1970). During the same period the number of female associate degree earners nearly tripled. As a result, women accounted for half the associate degrees in 1970 and they nearly equalled men in the proportion completing vocationally oriented science and engineering-related courses. The availability of occupational training at community colleges and their convenient locations have particularly benefited women by providing an opportunity for them to receive paraprofessional training for a variety of occupations. In the bachelor's degree, women have been keeping up with men and their representation among graduates in all degree levels has increased slightly.[6] And the survey by the American Assembly of Collegiate Schools of Business of enrollment trends for 1976–77 showed an explosive growth in the number of female MBAs—there were 14,041 women enrolled in MBA programs in 1976–77. Female graduate school enrollment, in general, jumped from 2,294 in 1967–68 to over 15,000 in 1975–76![7]

PERSONAL CHARACTERISTICS. Just as important as a woman's education are her abilities and aptitudes for a particular line of work. This seems to be particularly true in the area of business management. One study showed that women who are attracted to business exhibit many of the same characteristics of established executives, for example, strong communications skills; an ability to deal with people; a drive toward accomplishment and recognition; and a desire to solve problems and see results.[8] In a study of successful executive women prepared for her doctoral dissertation, Margaret Hennig identified characteristics that were significant for promotability.[9] There are amazing parallels between Hennig's executives and Dagny Taggart. As does Dagny, they also value high achievement and personal responsibility. Even as children they thought of themselves as successful and able, yet somehow frustrated. But they realized that the drive to achieve, an orientation to task, the desire to be respected for one's abilities, the enjoyment of competition, and a capacity to take risks were fundamental to succeeding at anything. They, like Dagny, accept their femininity, but they want to be admired for their accomplishments and abilities; they, too, refuse to identify with the traditional feminine woman.

Each of these women's personal and career goals were integrated enough to allow them to think through a logical career plan. They had all attended college and by that stage of their lives they had learned that it was possible to develop working relationships with men on a basis of competence and intellectual ability. After becoming established in an organization they usually remained, concluding that it was a great deal more difficult for a woman to establish working relationships than it was for a man, so once they had established these it was thought unproductive to move on.

CAREER ASPIRATIONS. Women's changing concept of their own roles and their reduced childbearing expectations contribute to their plans for work or a career. According to an Ohio State University study of women age 30–44, 60 percent of white and 67 percent of the black employees indicated that they would continue to work even if they could live comfortably without their earnings. And their commitment to remain with their present employers was displayed by the fact that 40 percent of the white and 25 percent of the black respondents indicated that they would not leave their present employer even for a substantial pay increase. While this may reflect their perceptions of limited job opportunities for women, the responses nevertheless illustrate their stability.[10]

Another study revealed that women generally have a tendency to gravitate toward preponderantly female occupations. In 10 selected occupations, the study found 9 heavily filled by women (90 percent). The data imply that the social and psychological factors and the additional experiences that affect career aspirations have caused existing employment patterns among women to persist rather than change. As younger women enter the labor force and continue to seek opportunities in "female" occupations, they increase the probability that similar patterns of employment will continue.[11]

The career aspirations of successful managerial women have been similar to Dagny Taggart's; the establishment of goals early in life with a focus on a clear path upward. Unfortunately, most women do not follow Dagny's example. Rather, there is ambiguity surrounding their career decision; they tend not to make a choice until after they are 30 years of age or older even though they may have been working for a number of years. This reluctance to commit themselves to a career also manifests itself in considerably less motivation to manage than there is on the part of men. Miner consistently found this to be the case in groups he studied.[12] Frequently, a woman does not become career-minded until she either feels challenged in a job and is motivated to seek more responsibility or finds that a career is an economic necessity because of divorce or the death of her spouse. By this time her male counterpart has moved ahead of her, and she has to double her efforts to convince her bosses that she should be promoted.

This lack of clearly defined and conscientiously implemented career aspirations coupled with other problems of being female have been deterrents to women who want to work.

Special Problems of Women at Work
PAY INEQUALITY

Is it possible that unequal treatment of women has its roots in Biblical history? In Leviticus, the Lord instructed Moses that the "valuation of a male from twenty years old up to sixty years old shall be fifty shekels of silver" and "if the person is a female your valuation shall be thirty shekels."[13] Coincidentally, the median weekly earnings of women on full-time jobs in 1980 were about 64 percent of those of men. And women's earnings relative to men's have not improved since 1955 (63.9 percent in 1955).[14] Similarly, only 2.3% of managers earning $25,000 or more in 1980 were women.[15]

Much of this pay inequity can be explained by the fact that women are not only concentrated in the lower-paying industries (and in relatively large numbers in nonunionized business enterprises), but in the lower-paying occupational groups, for example, clerical and service work. In addition, even when both sexes are well represented in an occupational group, women's earnings are lower than those of men. Discriminatory pay practices are still evident.

MALE-FEMALE DIFFERENCES

Female occupational distribution and the attendant pay distinction relative to males are the result of a combination of influences that start from childhood. Role differentiation in early life ultimately affects educational and occupational choices, hours and location of work, and related factors that relegate women to lower-level and lower-paying positions.

As children, boys learn many things that equip them for the work world that girls do not: flexibility, how to develop a style intuitively among one's peers, a way of behaving that makes it simpler to get what one wants, assertiveness, and a sense of team competition. Boys are openly encouraged to develop a masculine identity and self-assurance. Consequently, men are more likely than women to have expectations of success, to judge their performance more favorably, and to predict their future performance favorably. Boys are also found to be more gregarious than girls; they associate with peers more often and depend upon the group as a source of activity, for a system of values, for mutual support, and to gain freedom from the structures of authority and adult control.[16]

Girls, on the contrary, are taught to believe that their role in life is based on the concept of femininity: ladylike appearance and behavior, conformity to authority, motherhood and family, and so on. Behavior that results from this upbringing coupled with distortions of judgment in our society lead to stereotypes of women. One study found that respondents characterized women as dependent, subjective, passive, not competitive, not adventurous, not self-confident, and not ambitious. In each instance, people indicated that the traits possessed by males are more desirable in our culture.[17] Further evidence of biased perceptions of women results from another study that showed that in a choice between highly competent males and females, employers indicated a clear preference for highly competent males.[18] Schein found that male managers described men and successful middle-level managers in very similar terms, while women were seen as quite different from the successful manager.[19] Yet, in reality the life history experiences of women in management are more like those of men in management than of other women. This is a major finding in the area of vocational development, which has always had gender-linked norms. One of the consequences of the feminist movement, affirmative action and similar social forces is that they have begun to narrow the gender-based differences between males and females with regard to career aspiration, vocational interests, abilities, and aptitudes. One noticeable result of this is that women are beginning to suffer from more traditional male problems of job stress, peptic ulcers, job-related drinking problems, migraine headaches, and so forth.

The evidence is clear that men and women differ in their concepts of masculinity and femininity and that masculinity is more valued by our society. Furthermore, while there are some indications that these stereotypes are changing, more careful consideration suggests that these changes may only be skin deep.[20] (Note: The Women as Managers Scale (WAMS) was designed to identify and measure stereotypic attitudes toward women as managers and can be a useful tool in sensitizing males.)[21]

The expression, "Vive la différence!" is symptomatic of traditional male attitudes that cause a woman's physical appearance to impede her progress in an organization. Women also have physical limitations that restrict their job choices. A difference in physiological make-up and their lower physical strength often restrict their performance in tasks requiring heavy physical labor.

PROBLEMS IN MARRIAGE

According to the BLS, the number of married women in the labor force tripled between 1950–1979, reaching 48.2 million in 1979.[22] Whether or not this increase in employment among married females has contributed to the dramatic rise in the divorce rate in the past decade has yet to be established. In any event, families with working wives (two-career families) experience substantial emotional pressures. A study of women who were both married and employed in middle-management jobs found that these women experienced conflicts, but they chose to direct their energies primarily toward their jobs. Most of them had to decide which of the two roles should dominate, and they predicted that they eventually would have to give up one or the other.[23] In her study of two-career families, Lynda Holmstrom discovered some of the factors in society that lead to these conflicts. They include: (1) the rigid structures of professions that assumes a career person can change locations, travel at will, and devote massive amounts of time to promote a career; (2) isolation of the modern family, which means that relatives are not in the home to be of assistance; and (3) the equation of masculinity with superiority—the husband is threatened when a wife's career is superior to his.[24] There appears to be no worthwhile solution to these problems. Each family must work out its own way of coping with them. In seminars for women executives, several of the participants stated their individual resolutions. One woman insisted she would forego a promotion (that was imminent) if her husband objected. Another, whose husband was jealous of her success, held career over marriage and had just accepted a substantial promotion with the knowledge that it might lead to divorce. The inevitable role strains that a career brings to marriage are frequently dealt with through counseling. The counselor who has a knowledge of the kinds of problems encountered by married professional women can help them develop effective coping strategies.[25]

Working mothers face additional problems. In addition to the guilt feelings that inevitably result from leaving the care of children to outsiders, women managers are cut off from the after-hours socializing that can lead to promotion. They often have to rush home to relieve the babysitter or care for ill family members, and so on. These responsibilities place constraints on their career progress.

Sexual Harassment

The legal ramifications of sexual harassment were discussed in Chapter 6. In this section, we shall explore some of the causes and cures of **sexual harassment** at the work place. The stereotyped roles of females and male attitudes toward women manifest themselves in actions that are often perceived as harassment. Perceived harassment may not always result from the spontaneous act of a nasty old man. Often a mutual attraction is the principal cause. Nevertheless, the results are similar. The women tend to believe the incidents were their fault because they must have done something to encourage the man's behavior. They feel guilty and demeaned. Consequently, these women worry that they are valued for their bodies rather than their abilities or performance. They become resentful and begin to doubt the value of work and may as a result end their working career.

With the emergence of sexual harassment as an issue, several organizations have been formed to alleviate the problems. For instance, the Working Women's United Institute in New York provides resources for women who are sexually harassed, acts as a clearing house for information for lawyers and others, conducts research on the subject, and presents workshops. And in Minneapolis/St. Paul, Minnesota, professionals from social service agencies organized the Coalition Against Sexual Harassment (CASH) to educate the public about the problem, share information, and offer consultation to victims.[26]

Enlightened organizations have developed policies which identify sexual harassment as unacceptable conduct and provide vehicles for reporting harassment. Women are reluctant to complain, especially when no formal avenue is available, but informing top management that the problem exists is the key to its alleviation.[27] Creating an environment that discourages and censures harassment is imperative and it also makes good business sense. Sensitizing managers to the harassment problem and training them to listen to their employees are obvious measures. And basic to this whole issue is the treatment of women as individuals and the respect for their ability to make a unique contribution to the organization.

Action to Remove Inequities

Despite the impediments to women's progress in the work world the prognosis is hopeful. New laws to protect their rights, stricter enforcement of legislation, an attitude of social responsibility, and the individual and collective initiatives taken by women heralds a new era for the feminist movement. Each of these actions to improve opportunities and remove inequities for working women is discussed in this section.

LEGISLATIVE ACTION

Affirmative action has had an impact on the perceived opportunities for managerial women. A series of federal anti-discrimination laws have been enacted since the Equal Pay Act of 1963 prohibited sex differences in compensation for substantially equal work. Title VII of the Civil Rights Act essentially prohibits employers, unions, employment agencies, and other specified groups from discriminating on the basis of sex (race, color, religion, and national origin are also included). Title VII prohibits discrimination with regard to any employment condition: hiring, promotion, transfer, compensation, discharge, and selection for training. The Equal Employment Opportunity Act of 1972 amended Title VII by expanding its coverage and increased the authority of the Equal Employment Opportunity Commission, which is empowered to receive and investigate job discrimination complaints. When it finds reasonable cause, it first attempts to reach an agreement with the employer (through conciliation) to eliminate all aspects of the discrimination. Should the EEOC fail in this effort, it has the power under the 1972 amendment to go directly to court to enforce the law. With these new powers it seems apparent that EEOC legal actions against violators will increase substantially.

Executive Order 11246 (as amended by Executive Order 11375) was signed by President Lyndon B. Johnson in 1965. It requires that Affirmative Action Programs be established by all federal contractors and subcontractors. For organizations with contracts over $50,000 and 50 or more employees, the law requires the development and implementation of results-oriented programs. Title IX of the Education Amendments Act of 1972 extends the Equal Pay Act and prohibits sex discrimination against employees and students of any educational institution receiving federal aid. In addition to these federal laws, many states and municipalities have regulations prohibiting sex discrimination.

COURT ORDERED ACTION

Where courts have found discrimination, they have consistently ruled that remedies must not only open doors to equal employment, but also must "make whole" and "restore the rightful economic status" of those who suffered discrimination. Often the courts have assessed extreme penalties for back pay (up to two years) prior to the date the charge was filed, for an entire "affected class" (those who have suffered the effects of past discrimination). In a pay discrimination case, Wheaton Glass Company was ordered by the court to pay more than $900,000 plus interest in back wages to 2,000 female employees.[28] In addition, Bell Telephone paid $315 million as a result of a class-action suit alleging *systematic* discrimination, that is, the system in use for job evaluation was biased in favor of jobs typically held by men in the assignment of pay grades.

The law (Title VII) allows unequal treatment only when an organization can show a business necessity for its action. When it can show, for example, that sex is a **bona fide occupational qualification** (BFOQ), discrimination is permitted. The courts have interpreted the BFOQ exemption very narrowly, however. Certain traditional contentions line managers use to rationalize disparate treatment of females, for example, "Our customers won't buy from a female salesperson" or "We'd have to build separate facilities" will not hold up in court.[29]

AFFIRMATIVE ACTION PROGRAMS

The basic purpose of affirmative action is to remedy the underutilization of females and/or minorities in any job category or classification in which it may exist. An employer's employment practices become suspect when the Standard Metropolitan Statistical Area (SMSA) from which the employer recruits is heavily populated with persons of a minority, racial, or ethnic classification, and these persons are not employed at any reasonable level in the organization. Thus, a program of affirmative action would have to include: (1) finding the underutilization, (2) affirmative outreach (recruiting) efforts, and (3) activities to ensure the existence of a nondiscriminatory work force.[30]

The steps in an affirmative action program are specified by the Equal Opportunity Commission. They are outlined below to familiarize students with the breadth and scope of affirmative action programs.[31]

Step 1: Issue written equal employment policy statement and affirmative action commitment. This calls for the issuance of a firm personal commitment from the chief executive officer, including a statement of legal obligation and the importance of EEO as a business goal. The EEOC urges the inclusion of each of these elements:

    a. Equal employment opportunity for all persons regardless of race, creed, color, sex, national origin or age is a fundamental organization policy. EEO is a legal, social and economic necessity for the organization.

b. The equal employment policy will require *affirmative action* throughout the organization to overcome the effects of past discrimination.

c. Therefore, it cannot merely be a neutral policy, but requires new goal-setting programs with measurement and evaluation factors similar to other programs of the organization.

d. Affirmative action assures equal employment opportunity in all policies including:

Recruiting	Compensation
Hiring	Benefits
Transfers	Training
Promotions	Layoff and Recall

e. Responsibility for the **Affirmative Action Program (AAP)** is assigned to a major executive of the organization. All management personnel share in this responsibility and are assigned specific tasks. Management performance of the AAP is evaluated as are other organizational objectives. *Results* are the key.

f. Successful attainment of AA goals accrues positive benefits to the organization through fuller utilization and development of previously underutilized human resources.

Step 2: *Appoint a top official with responsibility and authority to implement the AAP.* Many programs fail because the individuals named to head them do not have sufficient status, authority, time, or staff. Managing AAP requires a major time commitment, so it cannot be a collateral duty. Program success is dependent upon the sensitivity of the responsible person to the varied ways in which discrimination limits job opportunities.

Step 3: *Publicize the AAP.* A multimedia approach lets managers, employees, applicants, suppliers, and the public know of the organization's policy. This can be accomplished through posting the policy statement on bulletin boards; publicizing the program in the organization's newsletters, magazines, employee handbooks, and annual reports; presenting discussion of the AAP in seminars and training programs; issuing policy statements to employees, suppliers, managers, and any interested parties, and by notifying all recruiting sources of the program.

Step 4: *Survey and analyze female and minority employment by department and job classification.* This is the first step toward defining specific AA goals. It includes the identification of present areas and levels of employment as well as the areas of underutilization of females and minority group members. To accomplish this, a model that shows the movement or "flow of women and minorities through each level of an organization" has been proposed.[32] Such models have been used in human resource planning and development, and in compensation planning. In AA planning, the flow approach enables an organization to identify the number of individuals in each category or classification for any year in the future and for any given population group—women, blacks, etc. The predictions result from interactively analyzing the relevant hiring mix, the replacement charts (see Chapter 14 for a discussion of replacement charts), and the present composition of the work force. Computerization can greatly facilitate this process. The flow model produces the minimum yearly hiring distribution for women or any minority group that will most likely result in the achievement of the organization's AA goals for that group.[33] If the flow model is used, unrealistic goals can be avoided if EEO is defined in terms of current hiring rates and current promotion rates rather than in terms of the current management mix. This concept is proposed especially for managerial levels because it often takes at least 25 years to develop senior-level managers. If an organization is committed to hiring and promotion policies that will eventually produce parity in the management mix, the organization should not be chastised for a shortage of women and minorities in the top slots now.[34]

Step 5: *Develop goals and timetables.*   Using the flow model or a conventional approach, the organization can next establish immediate, intermediate, and long-range targets with reasonable timetables for achieving them. The EEOC urges organizations to develop numerical annual targets for hiring, training, transferring, and promoting to reach goals within the indicated time frames. Annual targets will, of course, be contingent upon such factors as anticipated turnover, growth or contraction of the organization, availability of required skills, and job training to acquire skills. Internal factors that produce barriers to the achievement of these goals need to be pinpointed and removed.

Step 6: *Develop and implement specific programs to eliminate discriminatory barriers and achieve goals.*   In addition to removing discriminatory practices and other barriers, organizations can engage in action programs in affirmative action. The recruiting, testing, and selection activities have already been covered in Chapter 6. Table 15.1 lists a sampling of action items for AA. In addition most AAPs include an upward-mobility system with AA records to monitor the system.

Women (minorities, too) in the work force are often a major untapped resource for administrative, technical, managerial, and professional jobs. One

Affirmative Action Program—Action Items		

Table 15.1
Chart of Action Items Included in AAP (large eastern manufacturing company)

Contacts

Minority and female agencies

State employment bureau

Urban League

NAACP—Minority Skills Program

Engineers Joint Council

Society of Women Engineers

Office of Voluntary Programs

Federal Organization for Professional Women

Women's Action Program—HEW

Colleges, universities with minority, female enrollment

Internal assessment/Career counseling

Meetings with management

Training programs to develop minorities and females for upgrades, promotions

Skills and interest inventory
—Salary, nonexempt
—Participation by hourly minorities, females

Develop talent bank for all minorities, females

Job posting system

Communication of Affirmative Action

Luncheons with minorities

Encourage minority referrals

Union/management committee

EEO workshops
—All meadow lands supervision
—Field marketing supervision

Meetings with management to determine goals, timetables

Liaison programs of industry and academic institutions sponsored by National Alliance of Businessmen

Other external programs

Cooperative education programs with minority and female universities

Cooperative education programs with local high schools, career counseling and co-op program

Source: Mary G. Miner, Equal Employment Opportunity: Programs and Results PBF Survey No. 112 (Washington, D.C.: Bureau of National Affairs, March 1976), p. 38. Reproduced with permission.

of the author's clients inventoried the skills of its female employees. There were about 100 in production and clerical jobs. The company was shocked when it found that 10 had college degrees and that 3 of those had taken graduate level work! In addition, 4 others had held supervisory positions in other companies. Within a few months 3 were promoted to salaried sales positions and the remainder have been identified as candidates for higher-level salaried positions. Invariably, in any organization women and minorities can be found with skills and abilities beyond those required by their present job. Job restructuring that separates less-skilled functions or that creates the position of special assistant to an executive offers development opportunities for those women and minorities who may not yet be qualified for higher responsibility. A variety of other approaches to upward mobility are described later in this chapter.

The records that are needed to identify existing barriers and determine needed action for upward mobility include:

1. Promotion, transfer, and termination rates for each minority group and for females, by job category, compared to other employees;
2. Number and percentage of each minority group and of females in apprenticeship and all training programs;
3. Charts showing formal lines of progression.

From these records and the survey in *Step 4* the following analyses are prepared:

1. Identify jobs held by minorities and women (both union and nonunion jobs) in terms of job progression and opportunities for upward mobility compared to other employees.
2. Compare rate of minorities and women referred for promotion but not promoted to that of other employees.
3. Identify seniority and other factors that operate as barriers to upward mobility for minorities and women.
4. Perform job analyses to determine actual requirements for job and time needed to gain work experience for promotion to higher jobs.

INDIVIDUAL INITIATIVES

Women can take a number of steps to help overcome problems of inequality. Margaret Hennig and Anne Jardim suggest these measures for women seeking careers in management.[35]

1. Accept the fact that the residues of problematic male-female differences in assumption, perception, and behavior will remain with you for the rest of your life. Identify these residues and manage them.
2. Decide whether you want a management career. It will require competition with men who understand the system better than you. Understand the true costs and rewards of a management career.

A woman must be able to say with confidence that she wants a career and that she is willing to confront the problems she will inevitably encounter. She must be willing to be far more specific in her planning than the men around her and even more alert at anticipating situations which might accentuate the pressure she will feel or expose the vulnerabilities she will continue to sense. She must in other words be clear on the need to manage her environment and herself concurrently.[36]

3. Ask yourself a series of career questions such as:
   Do I want a working career?
   Do I expect to marry? Have children?
   Where do I want to be five, ten and twenty years from now?
   What skills do I need to develop?
   What skills and abilities do I have now?
   If I work now—which of my skills is the boss unaware of?
   Do I know someone who can help me advance my career?

4. Measure your potential by assessing your prior experience and achievements. Assess your effectiveness, in detail, in each of your previous jobs. Include any experience you have had in volunteer organizations.

5. Seek a mentor, advocate, godmother, or godfather, someone in a more senior management position who can coach, advise, and support you.

6. Set some clear career goals that answer questions like:
   Where do I want to be a year, five years from now?
   What kind of income do I want to earn?
   What specific kinds of work experiences do I want to have?
   What is the nature of the organization with which I want to be associated?

7. Develop relationships in the organization. Establish links with people who will make promotion decisions on you and with other women in the organization.

8. Find a style that will work effectively. Top women managers develop a style early in their careers. It emphasizes competence and task achievement as the major reason for a work relationship. Invariably a capable female will have to form a working relationship with a man who challenges her right to be where she is. When this happens, the appropriate strategy is to focus on the task to be accomplished.

9. Manage your emotions and feelings. Try to understand when and why you become emotional. Women tend to express feelings more directly than men and in doing so they often make men uncomfortable. When you can anticipate your reactions and the reactions of others in emotional situations and think them out beforehand, you will more likely deal with them appropriately.

10. Make a conscientious effort to have other people in your life understand your commitments, their importance, and the time they require beyond your home life.

Three women who seem to have followed this advice are:

1. Katherine Graham, chairwoman of a $309 million media empire, the Washington Post Company that publishes *The Washington Post* and *Newsweek* magazine and operates five TV stations and two radio stations. She proved her executive ability in backing the *Post*'s Watergate investigation despite severe government pressure and in winning a long and bitter strike by the pressmen's union against the newspaper.

2. Sherry Lansing, president of 20th-Century Fox Productions and the first woman studio chief.

3. Joyce Miller, president of the Coalition of Labor Union Women. She was unanimously elected to the executive council of the AFL-CIO and is the first woman ever to serve on this policy-making body.

ORGANIZATIONAL INITIATIVES

Numerous organizations are making special efforts—beyond basic AAP's—to see that their female employees succeed. Women responsible for painting heavy, cumbersome control panels at Westinghouse's industrial equipment division were experiencing difficulty lifting and positioning them. The company installed positioning devices that reduced the physical burden. Montgomery Ward has a flexitime program that permits employees to work their eight-hour shift anytime between 7:00 A.M. and 5:30 P.M. The arrangement facilitates transportation because employees can more easily make carpool arrangements and are able to schedule their travel to avoid traffic congestion. Similar benefits accrue to workers at Hewlett Packard at its Loveland, Colorado plant where six pairs of employees (predominantly women) share jobs on a ten-hour shift. And Xerox Corporation is experimenting with day care centers, hoping to make it easier for working mothers to continue in their jobs. Organizations sponsor programs and activities to develop the managerial talents of women.[37] These programs are discussed in the next section of this chapter.

Developing Women Managers

This section will discuss the various activities and programs that prepare women for management positions and develop their abilities once they are there. Developing women managers includes career planning and development activities that are tailored and vary according to individual needs. Organizational programs are more formal and, although they include individual activities, they are usually group oriented. The broader concepts and activities of management development are covered in Chapter 14, counseling in Chapter 8, and career planning in Chapter 17. The focus here will be on the specific aspects of development that apply to women managers.

CAREER PLANNING ACTIVITIES

We have already discussed the difficulties women face in setting **career goals.** Nevertheless, it is extremely important for women who aspire to management positions to do this. Organizations today are seeking women with managerial talent, but a prime requisite is that they know where they are going and how they plan to get there. Few organizations have formal career planning programs, so the managerial aspirant must plan her own career. The techniques described in Chapter 17 should be useful in this regard.

Through **networking,** women gain support in the effort to be upwardly mobile. Much of this support can come from other women, but personnel staff people and successful men in the organization are also good sources of support. In networking, relationships develop informally and are based on mutual needs. In building a network Bonnie Garson advises women to "pick allies who have a record of being in favor of a woman . . . So, if you can find a good person, male or female, that can set an example for you, you are very lucky."[38] The network can help women to:

1. Gain insight into how to get ahead in the organization;
2. Clarify the kind of support expected; and
3. Communicate those expectations to others.[39]

Career counselors (both private and in organizations) are trained to understand the problems of women. They can help women work out the conflicts associated with entering the job market that formerly was the province of men. They can guide women in their efforts to change their image and improve their self-esteem. Counseling becomes particularly meaningful to women who need to deal with the conflict between career and marriage.[40]

One of the most effective means of helping women toward managerial development is through the use of an informal sponsor or mentor. Hennig and Jardim urge women managers to, "try to pick a winner . . . , a winner who can become a godfather, a rabbi, a sponsor, a patron—who will invest in you, teach you, and speak up for you. If you're right, you'll move with him. If you're wrong—disengage and leave him behind. But find another."[41] This quote implies that the mentor will be a man and more often than not, this will be the case because of the scarcity of women at the top levels of management. It then becomes crucial to establish a *professional* relationship with him, and Jacqueline Thompson offers some guidelines:

Read the signals correctly . . .

A woman who tries to cultivate a male patron creates a problem for herself. Everytime a woman becomes too solicitous, she falls into the traditional female enchantress role. The guy will either get scared and disappear or zero in. The worst thing a woman can do is sleep with a prospective patron. The second worst thing she can do is encourage him and turn him down.[42]

ORGANIZATIONAL PROGRAMS

Organizations can demonstrate their affirmative action commitment to increasing the number of women managers in a variety of ways. These include intensifying their recruiting efforts, encouraging female applicants and employees, altering job specifications, and increasing the flexibility of promotion paths.

Some of the search and recruiting procedures that specifically apply to women include:

1. Job posting to make women aware of promotion opportunities and enable them to make their preferences known.

2. Paid maternity or sabbatical leave for several weeks, combined with the opportunity to work part time temporarily.

3. Expansion of the search effort to include the volunteer sector and women who are seeking a return to work after having spent several years rearing their children.[43]

Women who seek managerial careers need frequent reinforcement of their aspirations. Opening channels of communication among women already in the organization helps provide mutual support and encouragement. Career counseling can also serve this purpose, but male counselors should be sensitized to the specific needs of managerial women.[44]

Bray proposes that the assessment center be used to facilitate the advancement of women in management because of the advantages it offers.[45] First, it would increase the accuracy of woman-manager selection and thus maximize their chances of success when they advance. Second, line managers would be more receptive to assessment-center recommendations than to the opinions of subordinates or staff people. Third, it was found that feedback of assessment center results to successful candidates stimulated them to seek greater management responsibilities. At AT&T the assessment-center approach was also successful in identifying candidates for its "fast track" initial development program.

Women's upward mobility in the management hierarchy can be accomplished, in part, by restructuring career paths. This would include training and/or retraining women who return to work after a period of child-rearing and possibly providing more part-time or assistant-type jobs at lower- or middle-management levels.[46]

In addition to exposures to formal management-training programs, there are some development activities that are peculiar to women. Many women are not as assertive as they would like to be and this has led to a growing demand for assertive-skill training. (Assertive-skill training teaches people to stand up for their rights in such a way that the rights of others are not violated.) **Assertiveness training** serves to: (1) educate women in their personal rights; (2) overcome whatever blocks exist to acting assertively; and (3) develop and refine assertive behaviors through active-practice methods. Assertive-skills development now utilizes a technique called behavioral reversal that involves a special kind of role-playing in which a client practices or rehearses those specific assertive responses that are to become part of his or her behavioral repertoire.[47]

Many organizations have encouraged women managers to attend outside seminars, courses, and degree programs; many of them specifically oriented toward women. One such program is offered at the Minnesota College of Business. In the three-day seminar, participants work at developing a stronger self-concept and managerial skills; they learn to handle the conflict that is likely to occur when moving into a new role; and they prepare career plans to bridge the seminar experience with the real world they are about to reenter.[48] One such program offered in the public sector is the Dynamics of Job Mobility workshop for women employees of the Montgomery County Government in Maryland. The county allows women to nominate themselves for the program.[49]

AT&T sponsors an interesting program called the Womanagement Process. It is a voluntary, ongoing, on-the-job program that provides career planning, educational seminars about the corporation, and workshops in building confidence and practicing strategy. It actually helps women build managerial skills. In one exercise, Alice in Corporationland, participants engage in simulated power plays and learn the rudiments of risk-taking, which is inherent in managerial situations.[50]

Yes, there is much that organizations can do to develop Dagny Taggarts for their management teams.

Minority Development

Many problems of employing *minorities* and laws protecting minorities resemble those for women. There is no need to repeat them here, so the following discussion will focus on the issues pertinent to minorities: blacks, Spanish Americans, American Indians, and Asiatics.

Since the early 1960s organizations have made greater use of minority talent through **minority development.** The impetus to hire and develop blacks and other minorities stems from several sources, the most significant being an awakening of social conscience; affirmative action legislation; skills shortages in professional, technical, and managerial areas; and American business's recognition of a black market.

Organizations that are committed to hiring and developing minorities cite the following affirmative action practices as contributing to their success in minority employment.

EMPLOYMENT

To support a commitment to affirmative action, organizations launch vigorous search campaigns to locate and recruit black talent. To help alleviate the scarcity of black managers, personnel and line executives cooperate with black educational institutions to induce their graduates to pursue business careers. They cultivate other sources of blacks as well, such as special agencies (e.g., the NAACP, Urban League, National Association of Market Developers, the Southern Christian Leadership Conference, and the League of United Latin American Citizens [LULAC]) and their current minority employees who, in turn, can refer candidates and thereby become involved in the recruiting process. These organizations also make a diligent effort to establish and maintain credibility with local minority communities by making them aware of opportunities in the organization. When they can point to patterns of success of minorities within the organization, their chances of attracting other minority candidates are greatly enhanced.

ASSESSMENT

Special assessment methods are needed for screening minorities. The primary criterion for selection should be the ability to learn the job being offered. Hiring the qualifiable certainly does not mean abandoning standards. It does mean, however, that special efforts will be made and the organization recognizes that it may take additional time and effort to develop latent potential.[51] In selecting minority-group members, organizations often emphasize interview results, and if written tests (validated for minority selection, of course) are used, they establish lower cutoff scores. Poor test results are then given less consideration if a candidate's credentials appear to contradict test scores.

TRAINING AND DEVELOPMENT

Despite AA commitments, blacks especially have been almost totally excluded from important positions of responsibility within big business. Although blacks represent 12 percent of America's population, the actual number in management jobs is less than 1 percent.[52] In a study of black management development for the U.S. Department of Labor, the author discovered the following significant differences between black and white managers.[53]

1. Blacks have a poorer opinion of company attitude toward blacks in salaried positions and of advancement opportunities in general.
2. Blacks receive fewer salaried promotions.
3. Blacks are more likely to leave the organization.
4. Fewer blacks are exposed to outside training.

In view of these factors, it becomes particularly important that training for black and other minority managers be tailored to their individual needs. But generally, these employees need an exposure to formal management courses (principles of management, communication skills, dynamic interpersonal relations, and leadership techniques) to orient them to the business world and to help them overcome a possible lack of business orientation in their education and upbringing.

Minorities in organizations may often have an identity crisis, so training efforts can help them realize that they were hired for their qualifications rather than because they are minority group members. In addition, exposure to courses and seminars outside an organization can be beneficial, in terms of both developing abilities and enhancing morale. HRT managers help retain competent black managers by ensuring that after a brief training period, employees are promoted if they meet the criteria. An organization might even *create* promotion openings. To help ensure the success of a program, supervisors of minority trainees need to be convinced of the importance of having minorities in managerial positions and be made aware of their development needs. Many organizations hold supervisors of minority managers accountable, by making the progress of the minority managers a consideration in the performance appraisal of the supervisors. Finally, minority manager trainees can have sponsors assigned to them. The sponsors will maintain close contact with them, encourage them in their development, and assist in the planning of their advancement.

A few of the minorities who have succeeded as business executives include:

1. Gilroye A. Griffin, vice president of staff services at CBS and formerly an executive with Bristol-Myers.
2. Paul G. Gibson, recently Deputy Mayor of New York City, who returned to American Airlines as vice president of marketing projects.
3. James A. Joseph, vice president of corporate action for Cummins Engine Company, who was on leave from the company to serve as Under Secretary of the Interior.

Blacks consider educational credentials important, too. To assist blacks in obtaining MBAs, the Consortium for Graduate Study in Management was formed in 1967 with a grant from the Ford Foundation. It has 180 companies, foundations, and organizations contributing to a fellowship program that places students in participating universities. By 1976 more than 450 fellows had received MBAs with the aid of the Consortium.[54]

COMPENSATION

Despite salary inequities, some organizations offer starting salaries to minorities that are above the area's going rate. It may even be necessary to start minority employees at higher salaries than their white counterparts in order to attract them to an organization.

RETENTION

Challenging work seems to be a primary consideration of minorities (and other employees, too) in remaining with organizations. A technique that is used to encourage retention is to assign to a manager (this is in addition to a sponsor) in each department the responsibility of becoming acquainted with each minority employee. The manager holds conferences with minority employees to review their progress; and makes special efforts to involve them in company affairs and in social and recreational programs.

Development of the Handicapped

People who are not **handicapped** might consider what they could not do if they lost an arm or a leg, or were unable to see, hear, speak, or had some other disability. We can gain greater understanding of the problems of the handicapped if we could imagine ourselves with some sort of physical disability. However, most handicapped people learn to think in terms of what they *can* do.

WHAT IS A HANDICAPPED PERSON?

The Rehabilitation Act of 1973, Section 503 defined a handicapped person as one who: (1) has a physical or mental impairment that limits his or her major life activities; (2) has a record of such impairment; or (3) is regarded as having the impairment.[55] There are approximately 7.2 million persons who fit this definition and who are able to perform some kind of work, but only 5.6 million of them are in the labor force.[56] So, if an employer wants to take affirmative action to hire and develop the handicapped there are a number of steps he can take.

HANDICAPPED AFFIRMATIVE ACTION MEASURES

Today, Affirmative Action for the handicapped is (on a lesser scale) what the 1960s were for blacks and the 1970s were for women. Both EEO regulations and the positive experiences of business organizations in developing handicapped employees indicate certain measures that can be taken. These measures include legal requirements, accommodation, outreach, supervision, and training and development.

LEGAL REQUIREMENTS

Sections 503 and 504 of the Rehabilitation Act and the Vietnam Era Veterans Readjustment Assistance Act delineate the requirements of employers under handicapped Affirmative Action. The following are indicative of the kinds of steps employers must take to assure full opportunity for handicapped people:[57]

1. They must ensure that physical or mental job requirements are valid and do not improperly screen out the handicapped because of their disabilities.
2. Preemployment medical exams must not exclude or limit handicapped people.
3. Reasonable accommodation must be made unless the employer can demonstrate that it would create undue hardship on the business.
4. Outreach efforts must be made to attract handicapped applicants.
5. The Affirmative Action Program should be publicized throughout the company and an executive should be assigned the responsibility for its results.

ACCOMMODATION.   Emphasis is placed on determining what handicapped people can do and attempting to remove dependencies from the work environment that preclude effective performance. For example, the blind cannot be dependent on visual communication, or a wheelchair passenger cannot be dependent upon stairs to get from one location to another. But employers can consider where certain disabilities might be utilized to great advantage. A Southern textile mill, for example, employs deaf people as loom operators. They are not bothered by machinery noises, and they can communicate effectively with hand signals. If employers adopt the attitude that there is no such thing as handicapped people, only people with varied abilities, they can successfully place and retain the handicapped. The key is determining needs on a personal basis, using selective placement, individualized training, and motivational techniques.[58]

Accommodation also means the removal of architectural barriers, and Nathanson suggests that such action need not impose a financial burden on an employer.[59] Raised markers on doorways and hallway signs to assist the blind, and telephones with amplifiers for hearing-impaired workers cost little. For the wheelchair-bound, simple alterations like lowering workbenches, drinking fountains, elevator buttons and telephones; widening doorways, constructing curb cuts in sidewalks and ramps, remove impediments to effective performance for the handicapped. Barrier-free or accessible simply means that all persons—able-bodied and disabled, young or old, short or tall—may move freely, independently, conveniently, and safely throughout the facilities of the organization.

OUTREACH.   Organizations wishing to employ the handicapped can establish a working relationship with one of the agencies that work with the handicapped. An excellent reference source for locating handicapped applicants is the *Directory of Organizations Interested in the Handicapped,* available from the Committee for the Handicapped, People-to-People Program, 1111 20th Street N.W., Vanguard Building, Room 660, Washington, DC 20036. One organization that has been successful in recruiting handicapped people is The Continental Bank of Chicago. It works with such agencies as the (Chicago) Lighthouse for the Blind to pursue its policy of hiring the blind. And the company has taken an active role in the National Alliance of Businessmen (NAB), job fairs, local associations of business and industry, and programs sponsored by rehabilitation agencies to promote its outreach efforts.[60]

SUPERVISION.   The supervision and motivation of handicapped people are no different than those of the nonhandicapped. In fact, studies of handicapped workers show that they have a positive impact on their supervisors and peers. A good work climate and a supportive boss are all that is needed.[61]

TRAINING AND DEVELOPMENT.   In order to ensure the success of employed handicapped people, special programs of development are necessary. The C & P Telephone Company is one organization that reports success with a total approach to the development of the handicapped. Perhaps its experience can serve as a guide for implementing similar programs. In addition to traditional programs of training and skills development, C & P Telephone's approach incorporates these elements:

1. *Handicap awareness program.*   This program concentrates on positive aspects of reasonable accommodation, architectural accessibility, and career opportunities. All company personnel are encouraged to become involved in the program.

2. *Job inventory.*   This inventory is the result of job analyses to update job factors as they relate to handicapping conditions. For instance, a job requirement for writing legibility was reviewed to determine if typing was a viable alternative for an employee with limited dexterity. The

inventory also serves to discover new job opportunities for which some disabled employees were not traditionally considered (e.g., operator positions for blind employees).

3. *Rehabilitation training consultant.* The consultant is retained full-time to oversee the development of special training programs.

4. *Follow-up and counseling.* Counseling is provided on an ongoing basis because of the many challenges that have been generated by this comprehensive approach. Counselors are available for consultation with employees and with supervisors to help them become more comfortable and effective with disabled employees.[62]

The Tennessee Valley Authority's program contains these elements in addition to career assistance through a full-time career development specialist who counsels handicapped employees in their career plans, and TVA also offers sign language courses to enable employees to communicate with their hearing-impaired coworkers.[63]

Cost-Benefit Analysis

The employment, development, and upward mobility of minorities, women, and handicapped people involve the *affirmative* action of employers. Successful special development programs go beyond the law. They reach out in their recruitment efforts to find members of these special groups; they make special arrangements, for example, removal of architectural barriers for the physically handicapped, introduction of training to reduce specific educational disadvantages and so on, in order to accommodate these groups and help ensure their success with an organization.

The costs of these special programs are viewed in terms of the expense of added recruiting efforts, longer training and related adjustment periods, the time of staff and line managers to coach and counsel, and the costs associated with processing and litigating affirmative action suits.

The benefits center around the socially responsible action of an organization contributing to society by employing these special groups. This is an indirect benefit that is difficult to measure. In a negative sense, a benefit of affirmative action accrues in that costly litigation may be avoided. Furthermore, there is direct benefit in seeing development efforts produce dedicated, capable, productive employees.

Organizations can measure the results of special development programs by reviewing employment conditions. The increase in numbers of minorities, women, and handicapped at various levels in each department can serve as hard evidence. And many organizations have established goals for the employment and promotion of these groups; the goals can serve as a basis for comparing progress.

Summary

Working women are fast becoming a significant part of the labor force. They have made the strongest advances in white-collar and professional occupations. Successful business women seem to exhibit common characteristics: a drive to achieve, an orientation to tasks, the desire to be respected for one's abilities, competitiveness, and a capacity to take risks.

Despite their aspirations to succeed at work, and skills and credentials that are equal to those of their male counterparts, women continue to face numerous problems. Their pay is only 60 percent of men's. Traditional feminine roles and masculine prejudices have created stereotypes that cause discriminatory patterns. And even when women rise to positions of influence, they face interpersonal and emotional conflicts in relationships at work and with their family (husband and children) at home.

To remove inequalities for both women and minorities, EEO laws and court rulings have been somewhat effective in producing gains. Individual initiatives of career planning and additional education coupled with organizational efforts such as training programs, flexible work schedules, and redesigned work operations or functions have benefited the cause of women at work.

Minorities, especially blacks, suffer the same inequities as women. But organizations committed to affirmative action have made special efforts to seek, hire, train, and develop blacks for meaningful careers.

Affirmative action for the handicapped includes several measures that help them exercise their abilities. Accommodation emphasizes removal of dependencies from the work environment that inhibit performance. Through outreach programs, relationships are established with agencies that can supply disabled applicants. Once handicapped persons are employed, supervisors must be made aware of their needs and special programs are implemented to train them and develop their abilities.

Key Terms

labor force participation rate
sexual harassment
bona fide occupational
  qualification
Affirmative Action Program
  (AAP)

career goals
networking
assertiveness training
minority development
handicapped

Review Questions

1. What are the characteristics of successful women managers? Do you think any woman with these characteristics would succeed in an organization? Why, or why not?

2. Discuss some of the inequities that women face at work.

3. Describe how an affirmative action program functions. Include each of the steps in AAP.

4. What can women (or minorities) do on their own to help overcome the problems of inequality?

5. Discuss the management development activities within organizations that are common to both women and minorities.

Discussion Questions

1. Under what circumstances could an organization legitimately exclude females because of bona fide occupational qualifications?

2. How can an organization accommodate minorities in an existing management development program?

3. What are the advantages and disadvantages of conducting management seminars that include women (or blacks) only instead of mixed groups?

4. If you were a career counselor, what are some of the needs, emotions, distinctive characteristics, and feelings you should be sensitive to in counseling women? Blacks?

5. What kinds of programs could the federal government sponsor to ensure that future generations of women and blacks have an adequate background in business management?

Case Problem 1

SEX APPEAL

Rita Lancaster had just been appointed Vice President of the Hartfield National Bank and Trust Company. She was the first woman officer in the bank's history. She was forty years old, attractive, and well educated; she held an MBA from Harvard. Yet her education and experience did not prepare her for the business problem she was about to face.

"No sooner did I settle in my new job than I was bombarded from all directions by important bank clients offering me their business if I would go out with them," she recalled.

"My job was to keep and build up our business with these clients. If they stopped doing business with us, my career was washed up," she surmised.

She made light of these propositions at first. Then she ignored them. But the clients persisted in their advances and sometimes she even got phone calls at home. At a business meeting with a group of these clients one of them made some suggestive remarks and Ms. Lancaster lashed out at him.

Finally, she said, "I met with each client individually and I told him firmly that I make it a rule to keep my business and social life separate. I let them know that they could take their business to another loan officer in the bank if they wanted to."

Problems

1. Could the clients' actions toward Ms. Lancaster be considered sexual harassment? What are the legal implications of this case?

2. Do you think Ms. Lancaster acted properly under the circumstances?

3. If you were the client in this case, how would you react to Ms. Lancaster's approach?

4. What would you do if confronted with this situation?

The schools taking part in the Consortium for Graduate Study in Management, which trains minority citizen MBAs are quite proud of their work. One Indiana University professor commented, "Back in 1967, when we got into this minority education work, everyone told us that we would have to lower our standards to find minority students. We decided not to, and we beat the bushes to find fully qualified minority students for our quite selective graduate business program. We found them too—for a while, it was like recruiting football players, except that we did a lot better than our football team. We got some of the best young people in the country to come to Indiana, and the fact that they were black was secondary. Most of them have now moved on to quite successful careers in major business firms."

A director of an organization that consults with minority-owned business in Indianapolis is not so sure that this is a good program. "Certainly IU found some very good talent," he states, "and those young blacks they educated have done very well in white mainstream companies. But one odd result of this new education is the starving of black-owned firms. An IU MBA makes from $20,000 to $25,000 per year to start, and no small black-owned company can afford to pay those rates. As a result, virtually all the Consortium students now work for big companies, while little black companies struggle with limited talent. Perhaps it would have been better if these smart blacks had just gone to work for black companies. At least then they could be part of their own culture, and not have to sell out to the Man."

Case Problem 2

BLACK EXECUTIVES, BLACK FIRMS

Problems

1. What is best for blacks—to work with minority enterprise and struggle, or to get out and compete in the mainstream? Why?

2. Who is right here? Why?

3. Perceptive black observers have pointed out that when successful blacks make it to the big time, that is, when they become well paid executives, they tend to leave the all-black community and behave about like other upper middle class people. Is this good or bad for blacks? Why?

4. Which is more desirable in the future: an integrated managerial world, where about 10 percent of all managers are black, or a world where about 10 percent of all companies are black-owned? Or does it matter?

5. Would you suggest that this Consortium be expanded or contracted? Why?

Notes

1. Ayn Rand, *Atlas Shrugged* (New York: The New American Library, 1957), pp. 54–56.

2. U.S. Bureau of Labor Statistics, *Perspectives on Working Women* (Washington, D.C.: U.S. Department of Labor, June 1980), p. 3.

3. U.S. Bureau of Labor Statistics, *Employment and Earnings January 1981* (Washington, D.C.: U.S. Department of Labor, 1981), p. 180.

4. Mary Green Miner, *Equal Employment Opportunity: Programs and Results* (Washington, D.C.: Bureau of National Affairs, March 1976), p. 11.

5. U.S. Bureau of Labor Statistics, *Employment in Perspective: Working Women* (Washington, D.C.: U.S. Department of Labor, Second Quarter, 1980), p. 1.

6. Anne McDougall Young, "Trends in Educational Attainment Among Workers in the 1970's," *Monthly Labor Review*, July 1980, pp. 1ff.

7. "Women Professors: Where Are They?" *MBA*, September 1977, pp. 40–41.

8. Gary J. Echternacht and Ann L. Hussein, "Survey of Women Interested in Management" (Prepared by Educational Testing Service for the Graduate Business Admissions Council, 1974), pp. 16–18, 29.

9. Margaret Hennig and Anne Jardim, *The Managerial Woman* (Garden City, N.Y.: Anchor Press/Doubleday, 1977), pp. 32ff.

10. *Years for Decisions*, vol. 3 (Columbus: The Ohio State University Center for Human Resource Research, for the U.S. Department of Labor, Manpower Administration, December 1973), pp. 207–9.

11. Leonard A. Lecht, "Women at Work," *Conference Board Record*, September 1976, p. 19.

12. John B. Miner, "New Sources of Talent" in Donald O. Jewell, ed., *Women and Management: An Expanding Role* (Atlanta: School of Business Administration, Georgia State University, 1977), pp. 245–46.

13. Lev. 27:1–4.

14. U.S. Bureau of Labor Statistics, "Earnings of Workers and Their Families: Third Quarter 1980," Wednesday, November 26, 1980.

15. "An Uphill Battle for Female Managers," *Industry Week*, June 23, 1980, p. 33.

16. Eleanor Maccoby and Carol Nagy Jacklin, *The Psychology of Sex Differences* (Stanford, Calif.: Stanford University Press, 1974), pp. 154, 211.

17. Paul S. Rosenkrantz et al., "Sex-Role Stereotypes and Self-Concepts in College Students," *Journal of Consulting and Clinical Psychology*, 32 (1968), pp. 287–95.

18. James E. Haefner, "Sources of Discrimination Among Employees: A Survey Investigation," *Journal of Applied Psychology*, June 1977, pp. 265–70.

19. Virginia Ellen Schein, "The Relationship Between Sex-Role Stereotypes and Requisite Management Characteristics," *Journal of Applied Psychology*, 57 (1973), pp. 95–100.

20. Kay Deaux, *The Behavior of Men and Women* (Monterey, Calif.: Brooks/Cole, 1976), p. 18.

21. L. H. Peters, J. R. Terborg, and J. Taynor, "Women as Managers Scale (WAMS): A Measure of Attitudes Toward Women in Management Positions," *JSAS Catalog of Selected Documents in Psychology*, M.S. No. 585, 1974.

22. U.S. Bureau of Labor Statistics, *Perspectives on Working Women*, p. 1.

23. Theodore Rosenbloom, *A Study of*

Middle Management, unpublished, Iowa State University, 1965.

24. Lynda Lytte Holmstrom, *The Two-Career Family* (Cambridge, Mass.: Shenkman, 1972).

25. Janet Dreyfus Gray, "Counseling Women Who Want Both a Profession and a Family," *The Personnel and Guidance Journal,* September 1980, pp. 43–45.

26. James C. Renick, "Sexual Harassment at Work: Why It Happens, What To Do About It," *Personnel Journal,* August 1980, pp. 658–62.

27. Jeanne Bosson Driscoll, "Sexual Attraction and Harassment: Management's New Problems," *Personnel Journal,* January 1981, pp. 33ff.

28. *Schultz v. Wheaton Glass Co.,* 421 F. 2nd 259 (1970).

29. Oscar A. Ornati and Edward Giblin, "The High Cost of Discrimination," *Business Horizons,* February 1975, p. 38.

30. William J. Kilberg, "Equal Employment Opportunity in the United States: The Affirmative Action Concept," *The Journal of Industrial Relations,* June 1975, pp. 148–55.

31. For a detailed description of an affirmative action program see: *Affirmative Action and Equal Employment: A Guidebook for Employers,* vol. 1 (Washington, D.C.: U.S. Equal Employment Opportunity Commission, January 1974).

32. Neil C. Churchill and John K. Shank, "Affirmative Action and Guilt-Edged Goals," *Harvard Business Review,* March–April 1976, pp. 111ff.

33. Robert H. Flast, "Taking the Guesswork Out of Affirmative Action Planning," *Personnel Journal,* February 1977, p. 71.

34. Churchill and Shank, "Affirmative Action and Guilt-Edged Goals," p. 116.

35. Hennig and Jardim, *The Managerial Woman,* pp. 157ff.

36. Ibid., pp. 158–59.

37. "Women At Work," *Business Week,* December 6, 1976, p. 74.

38. Bonnie Garson, "Views from Women Achievers. A Series of Dialogues From the Management Process," (New York: AT&T, 1977), p. 116.

39. Philomena D. Warihay, "The Climb To the Top: Is the Network the Route for Women?" *The Personnel Administrator,* April 1980, pp. 55–60.

40. Louise Vetter, "Career Counseling for Women" in Lenore W. Harmon et al., *Counseling Women* (Monterey, Calif.: Brooks/Cole, 1978), p. 89.

41. Hennig and Jardim, *The Managerial Woman,* p. 41.

42. Jacqueline Thompson, "How to Find a Mentor," *MBA,* February 1976, p. 35.

43. Francine E. Gordon and Myra H. Strober, *Bringing Women into Management* (New York: McGraw-Hill, 1975), pp. 82–85.

44. Ibid., pp. 79–80.

45. Douglas W. Bray, "Identifying Managerial Talent in Women," *Atlanta Economic Review,* March–April 1976, pp. 40ff.

46. Gordon and Strober, *Bringing Women Into Management,* p. 87.

47. Patricia Jakubowski, "Facilitating the Growth of Women Through Assertive Training," in Lenore W. Harmon et al., eds., *Counseling Women,* pp. 107ff.

48. J. Stephen Heinen et al., "Developing the Woman Manager," *Personnel Journal,* May 1975, p. 285.

49. Susan R. Christen and Frances M. Syptak, "Helping Women to Move Up: A Successful First Step," *Training and Development Journal,* October 1976, pp. 42–45.

50. Gwyneth Cravens, "How Ma Bell Is Training Women for Management," *New York Times Magazine,* May 29, 1977, pp. 12–13ff.

51. Gloria J. Gery, "Hiring Minorities and Women: The Selection Process," *Personnel Journal,* December 1974, p. 907.

52. William M. Young, "Long Road Ahead for Black Executives," *New York Times,* Sunday, July 10, 1977, p. 12F.

53. Donald P. Crane, *Qualifying the Negro for Professional Employment* (Ann Arbor, Mich.: Dissertation Abstracts, 1970), p. 2527-A.

54. Wallace L. Jones and Sterling H. Schoen, "The New Minority Managers: How Far, How Fast?" *MBA,* January 1977, pp. 47–50.

55. This definition appears in the Rehabilitation Act Amendments of 1974, Public Law 93-516.

56. Bernard E. DeLury, "Equal Job Opportunity for the Handicapped Means Positive Thinking and Positive Action," *Labor Law Journal,* November 1975, p. 681.

57. The President's Committee on Employment of the Handicapped, *Affirmative Action for Disabled People* (Washington, D.C.: The President's Committee on Employment of the Handicapped. 1979), p. 7.

58. Gopal C. Pati, "Countdown on Hiring the Handicapped." *Personnel Journal,* March 1978, p. 145.

59. Robert B. Nathanson, "The Disabled Employee: Separating Myth from Fact," *Harvard Business Review,* May–June 1977, p. 8.

60. Gopal C. Pati and John I. Adkins, Jr., "Special Report: Federal Officials Are Stepping Up Their Efforts to Enforce Affirmative Action Requirements," *Harvard Business Review,* January–February 1980, p. 18.

61. Pati, "Countdown on Hiring the Handicapped," p. 151.

62. Ted Brosnan, "There's More to Affirmative Action Than Just Hiring 'The Handicapped'," *The Personnel Administrator,* January 1978, pp. 18–21.

63. Gopal C. Pati, and Edward F. Hilton, Jr., "A Comprehensive Model for a Handicapped Affirmative Action Program," *Personnel Journal,* February 1980, pp. 99–108.

Chapter Sixteen

Performance Appraisal

Perhaps the first known performance appraisal was the efficiency report of the officers under the command of Brigadier General Lewis Cass in 1813. It is reproduced here in Figure 16.1 as it was recorded in the files of the War Department (now the Department of Defense).

Although General Cass's performance appraisal of his officers may not be typical of the approach taken by organizations (including the Army) today, it does exhibit many of the characteristics (variables) of an appraisal situation. General Cass performed the appraisals himself—someone must take *responsibility* for appraising the personnel. The *purpose* of the appraisal in this case appears to be an assessment for promotion. Today, appraisals are conducted for a variety of purposes. The approach or *form* of this appraisal was a free-written, unstructured series of observations. As we shall see in this chapter, there is a wide variety of approaches to performance appraisal. *Criteria* establish an objective basis for evaluating performance. General Cass's observations were based on his own subjective judgment, as evidenced by the blanket condemnation of his Irish 3rd Lieutenants. One might conjecture that General Cass had this same bias toward all Irish people. Generally, the appraisal situation includes an interview during which employees are informed of the evaluator's perceptions and ratings of their performance. It is doubtful that General Cass informed his officers of their ratings. In fact, it was the policy of the Army at that time not to share such information with the troops. However, they were entitled to review their records by visiting the War Department. Each of these variables and their interactions

LEARNING OBJECTIVES

1. To know the purposes of performance appraisal and their relevance to personnel functions.

2. To understand the advantages and disadvantages of the traditional versus developmental approaches.

3. To know the legal standards for performance appraisals.

4. To know how appraisal interviews should be conducted properly.

5. To be familiar with contingency approaches to appraisal interviews.

Figure 16.1
The First Recorded
Efficiency Report in the
Files of the War
Department

Lower Seneca Town
August 15, 1813

Sir:

I forward a list of the officers of the 27th Regiment of Infantry arranged agreeably to rank. Annexed thereto you will find all the observations I deem necessary to make.

Respectfully,
I am, Sir
Yo. Obt. Servt.

LEWIS CASS
Brig. Gen.

* * * * * * * * *

27th Infantry Regiment

Officer	Observation
Alex Denniston—Lt. Col. Comdg.	A good natured man.
Clarkston Crolins—First Major	A good man, but no officer.
Jesse D. Wadsworth—2nd Major	An excellent officer.

Captain Christian Martel
    Aaron T. Crane
    Benj Wood
    Maxwell
	All good officers.

Captain Shotwell (USMC)	A man of whom all unite in speaking ill. A knave despised by all.
Capt. Allen Reynolds	An officer of capacity, but imprudent and a man of most violent passions.
Capt. Daniel Porter	Stranger but little known in the regiment.
1st Lt. Jas Ker Thos Darling	Merely good, nothing promising.

1st Lt. Wm. Perrin
    Dan'l Scott
    Jas. Il. Ryan
    Robt McElworth
	Low vulgar men, with exception of Perrin, Irish and from the meanest walks of life— Possessing nothing of the character of officers or gentlemen.

1st Lt. Jon Hall	Not joined the regiment.
2nd Lt. Nicholas Garner	A good officer but drinks too hard and disgraces himself and the service . . .

2nd Lt. Steward Elder	An ignorant unoffending Irishman.	Figure 16.1 (cont.)
2nd Lt. McConkey	Raised from the ranks, ignorant, vulgar, and incompetent.	
2nd Lt. Piercey Jackob Brown Thos Spicer Oliver Vance	Raised from the ranks, but all behave well and promise to make excellent officers.	
3rd Lt. Royal Geer Mears Clifford Crawford McKeon	All Irish, promoted from the ranks, low vulgar men, without any one qualification to recommend than more fit to carry the hod than the epaulettes.	
3rd Lt. John Scholtz Francis Wheeler	Promoted from the ranks, behave well and will make good officers.	
Ensign Mehan	The very dregs of the earth, unfit for anything under heaven. God only knows how the poor thing got an appointment.	
Ensign Darrow John Brown John Bryan	Of fine appearance Promoted from the ranks, men of no promise or manner.	
Ensign Charles West	From the ranks, a good man who does well.	

in the performance appraisal situation are discussed in this chapter. (Note: The terms appraisal, evaluation, and rating are used interchangeably in this chapter.)

Purposes of Performance Appraisal

Performance appraisal has become an integral part of the personnel function. In federal, state, and local governments, it is universally applied to the evaluation and reporting of job performance for the purposes of determining promotability and for assessing merit for compensation improvements. The Conference Board found in one study that nearly three out of four companies surveyed had formal evaluation programs for lower-level managers and over half of them extended appraisals to top management.[1]

Studies of the applications of appraisals show that they are used for one or more of the following purposes.[2]

1. To provide feedback to employees on their individual performance,

2. To serve as a basis for modifying behavior toward more effective performance,

3. To provide data to management for judging future job assignments, promotions, and compensation,

4. To identify promotable employees,

5. To force managers to relate employee behavior to actual results,

6. To weed out marginal and low-performing managers,

7. To provide data showing both the need for and the effectiveness of training programs,

8. To receive feedback from employees on the effectiveness of the reward structure,

9. To provide the basis for validation of predictors used in selection and placement.

The results of appraisals provide useful input to other personnel activities. Specific training and development plans for the individual being appraised help the employee perform more effectively and prepare him or her for increased responsibility. Collectively these plans become part of the training needs analysis. Predictive information for placement purposes is provided in appraisals. The appraisal measures the employee's achievements in performing the current job; highlights of performance that include the outstanding qualifications or areas needing improvement; an overall evaluation of performance; and potential for advancement. This information can be used to screen candidates for promotion or transfer. The appraisal also provides valuable inputs for human resource planning in that it identifies the strengths and development needs of those who might be placed in future jobs or who might have to be reassigned and/or retrained to strengthen the organization. The appraisal also identifies skills that are included in the skills inventory for planning purposes. Although this chapter emphasizes the developmental nature of appraisals, they are frequently used to administer compensation programs. Employees with higher ratings obviously are awarded higher pay increases when compensation is tied to performance appraisal.

The personnel department is central to the appraisal process. Personnel specialists perform job analyses and prepare the job descriptions that serve as the foundation of the process. They also develop the appraisal instrument and the administrative procedures for conducting the appraisal. Personnel people also train appraisers in the proper completion of paper work, preparation for the appraisal, and the conduct of the appraisal interview. In more enlightened organizations someone from personnel may even assist in preparation by role-playing the appraisal interview with the person who will conduct it. Finally, personnel monitors the appraisal system to ensure that appraisals are properly scheduled and conducted.

Who should perform the appraisal? In most organizations this is not a problem because an *immediate supervisor* performs the function. This makes sense because he or she is closest to the situation and is in the best position to observe an employee's performance and behavior. In the preponderance of appraisals, the supervisor has the sole responsibility.[3] But multiple appraisers, though seldom used, can strengthen the process when all of them know the individual being evaluated. In addition to an immediate supervisor, a committee, the supervisor's boss, and/or a personnel staff member might be involved (the Navy has long reported that peer-group ratings are both reliable and predictive of future performance). Regardless of whether single or multiple appraisers are used, it is generally accepted practice to have the appraisal reviewed by higher authority at some point in the process.

Inverted appraisal or the evaluation of superiors by their employees is common in some European countries and is an integral part of teacher effectiveness evaluations in many colleges and universities. The notion that employees see more of a manager's performance hour-by-hour and day-by-day than does his or her superior gives credence to this approach. It can be of material help to a manager to understand employees' perceptions of his or her own performance and receive feedback on his or her feelings and attitudes. Appraisal by subordinates, however, stops short of control, so it is purely informative.[4] The author has found student evaluations of his performance in the classroom quite helpful. The evaluations are anonymous, and one of the students administers the questionnaires and does not submit the results until after the final grades are recorded. The results have been gratifying; valuable information is provided on teaching style, course content and materials, and student response. Student critiques can be a major factor in the development of a teacher.

Methods of Appraisal

A wide variety of appraisal methods are currently in use. A survey of appraisal practices by Locher and Teel found that the dominant method in current use is some form of rating scale. But organizations use the narrative, Management-by-Objectives (MBO), behaviorally based, or other approaches, too.[5] No single form or method is best for any given organization (criteria for selecting the most appropriate form are presented at the end of this section). A familiarity with the various methods now in use can help personnel managers select the one that best fits the organization. In practice, traditional appraisals tend to be used for hourly employees and developmental ones for managers.

TRADITIONAL METHODS OF APPRAISAL

Traditional methods employ checklists of behavior characteristics (cooperativeness, initiative, and so on) or a standardized format of descriptive phrases with rating or ranking scales. Some of the more commonly used rating forms are described in the following paragraphs.

1. The **graphic scale** is preferred by many organizations because it permits a range in scoring. If supervisors want to rate employees on industriousness, they can find an appropriate level to describe each employee instead of a yes or no response on a checklist. Supervisors can use one of three plans: a bar (Plan 1); standard categories (Plan 2); or descriptive phrases (Plan 3). These are illustrated in Table 16.1. The graphic scale has the advantage of providing a simple format requiring a minimum of time for completion. Yet its very simplicity can detract from its effectiveness because supervisors may check the appropriate ratings but fail to discuss them with employees.

2. **Forced distribution** is a very simple method, perhaps the simplest of all merit-rating systems. Its premise is that job performance is the basic

Table 16.1
Examples of Graphic
Rating Scales

Plan 1
Extremely   Not Industrious
Industrious   at All

(The rater can mark the bar at any point to indicate the individual's industriousness.)

Plan 2 (Standard Categories)
- ☐   Extremely industrious
- ☐   Above average in industriousness
- ☐   Average in industriousness
- ☐   Below average in industriousness
- ☐   Not industrious at all

Plan 3 (Descriptive Phrases)
- ☐   One of the hardest workers in the group
- ☐   A hard worker
- ☐   Works as hard as the next fellow, but no harder
- ☐   Doesn't apply himself as well as he might
- ☐   One of the laziest members of the group

factor in determining an employee's value to an organization, and that other elements (such as cooperation, personality, etc.) are worth considering only insofar as they contribute to performance. This system uses a five-point job performance scale. One end of the scale represents best job performance, the other end, the poorest. Supervisors are told to allocate approximately 10 percent of their employees to the best end of the scale, 20 percent in the second highest category, 40 percent to the middle bracket, 20 percent to the next to the lowest, and 10 percent in the lowest bracket. By distributing their employees in this way, different supervisors will rate them more uniformly. The forced distribution form has the same advantages and disadvantages as the graphic scale. It provides even less substantiation for the basis of rating and, hence, offers less material for discussion with employees.

3. **Ranking** involves rating individuals by arranging them according to merit, from best to poorest, in terms of a specific characteristic or of overall performance. An alternative to ranking is the paired-comparison method, in which pairs of employees are compared with each other so that each individual is compared with everyone in the group. Supervisors indicate the better individual in each pair based on overall performance; then a scoring system gives the highest ranking to the employee most frequently selected as better. Supervisors can rank employees on the basis of each score. Here again, the simplicity of ranking can detract from the appraisal interview because supervisors are not required to develop information to complete the rating.

4. The **free-written rating** is one of the oldest forms of appraisal. Some organizations literally hand a supervisor a blank piece of paper and say, "Give us your overall appraisal of your employees. What are their strengths and weaknesses? What other jobs can they do? How promotable are they? Write down anything special about them that we should know." The appraisal used to introduce this chapter (General Cass's appraisal of his officers) is an example of the free-written form. This appraisal is very flexible; raters are free to appraise their employees in whatever form they choose. When this rating is conscientiously attended to, supervisors make considerable data available for discussion in what will be beneficial appraisal interviews. However, supervisors usually have great difficulty completing this rating.

5. The **forced choice method** developed by the Army is an attempt to make ratings more objective. Statements covering a wide variety of job-performance aspects are grouped together in units of about five or six each. (Table 16.2 shows two units from a forced-choice rating form.) Supervisors mark the one statement in each unit that is most descriptive

Table 16.2		
Forced-Choice Rating	Most	Least	

Most	Least	
A	A	Does not get the facts necessary for making decisions.
B	B	Receives constructive criticism well.
C	C	Can definitely be promoted whenever the opportunity affords itself.
D	D	Makes too many personnel changes.
E	E	Is ready to give credit to others for good work done.

Most	Least	
A	A	Leans over backward in accepting viewpoints of his men.
B	B	Is quick to size up a situation.
C	C	Coordinates the various parts of his work.
D	D	Has little knowledge of the work of other departments.
E	E	Needs time to prove his worth.

of the individual being rated and the one statement that is least descriptive. They know only in a general way if they are rating the individual favorably or unfavorably. Actually, supervisors are reporting the individual's job performance, not rating it. The forced choice approach involves considerable preliminary research on the part of each company using it.[6] While this form does provide objectivity, it affords little opportunity to plan for the improvement of employees.

6. In the **critical incident method,** supervisors list incidents that reflect especially favorable job performance (such as completing a major assignment ahead of schedule) and especially unfavorable performance (such as a high accident rate in the department). Superiors objectively observe the performance of subordinates (referred to as the performance record) and then discuss their strengths and weaknesses to aid in their development.[7] Users of this method sometimes have problems identifying incidents truly important to the success of employees. The very sophistication of the critical incident approach has limited its adoption by industry.

7. The **field review method** represents a very different approach. Supervisors do not make the rating, but they are responsible for it. Specialists from the personnel department discuss a list of employees with supervisors. The specialists take notes and probe for details and concrete evidence of performance. Later, they evaluate their notes and rate each employee. They then show these ratings to the supervisors, discuss them,

and sometimes correct and revise them. The supervisors sign the rating when they are satisfied that it gives a fair picture of an individual. The field review and the free-written method are very similar and thus have the same advantages and disadvantages.

8. **Buddy ratings,** often called peer ratings, are a personnel assessment through co-worker evaluations. Each group member rates every other group member on a recognizable quality (for example, leadership). Group members either assign the others a score, or they nominate a specified number of fellow workers whom they consider high or low in the quality being measured. Both procedures yield an index of an individual's status within the group on specific factors. In practice, peer ratings prove accurate predictors of performance.[8] The major advantage of buddy ratings is that peers are able to observe behavior that superiors do not see.

9. The **group summary appraisal** is the simplest of the many types in use today. If managers want to assess subordinates' performance and possible means of improvement, they invite a group of managers to discuss the matter informally. The points on which all agree constitute the appraisal.[9] Both this assessment and the peer rating involve a series of evaluations that may encumber the process. In addition, some question remains as to the correlation between peer and supervisor appraisals of employees' performance.

10. The **self-appraisal process** lets employees complete their own appraisals. This evaluation enables employees to offer opinions of their own performance and is useful as a vehicle for planning their development. It fits in well with the management-by-objectives approach, which has a strong participative component. Managers have a voice in setting their own objectives and in determining whether these objectives have been met. Studies at General Electric indicate that such participation in the appraisal situation contributes to more effective performance. At least for purposes of management development, self-appraisal does have value.[10]

DEVELOPMENTAL APPROACHES TO APPRAISAL

In addition to rating performance, appraisals can be useful as a tool in developing the capabilities of employees and, thereby, improving the results they achieve. **Developmental approaches** offer specific, goal-oriented, job-related guidelines for performance improvement. They also incorporate a mechanism for identifying, planning, and activating behavior that will most likely yield the desired performance. However, we should recognize that behavior and results are not necessarily directly related. Hence, developmental approaches that are behaviorally based make distinctions between behavior, performance, and effectiveness. Campbell and others point this out in the following explanation:

Behavior is simply what people do in the course of work (e.g., dictating letters, giving directions, sweeping the floor, etc.) *Performance* is behavior that has been evaluated (i.e., measured) in terms of its contribution to the goals of the organization. Finally, *effectiveness* refers to some summary index of organizational outcomes for which an individual is at least partially responsible, such as unit profit, unit turnover, amount produced, sales, salary level, or level reached in the organization. The crucial distinction between performance and effectiveness is that the latter does not refer to behavior directly but rather is a function of additional factors not under the control of the individual (e.g., state of the economy, nepotism, quality of raw materials, etc.).[11]

Developmental approaches attempt to focus on factors within the control of an individual.

Two different yet compatible methods comprise the developmental approach: MBO (Management-by-Objectives) and BARS (Behaviorially Anchored Rating Scales). Both are discussed in this section.

The **MBO appraisal** compares actual performance with individual performance objectives. Variances from objectives indicate strengths and weaknesses. To maintain strengths and overcome deficiencies, employees and their supervisors prepare development plans for implementation and review at the end of a specified period (usually, six months or one year). The MBO process requires three steps. We suggest that readers refer to Table 16.3 as each of these steps is discussed.

The first step is to set objectives (performance planning). The employee and the supervisor mutually establish a list of goals designed to accomplish the needs of the business, further develop the employee, and broaden his or her basic responsibilities. With the aid of job descriptions, supervisors can identify the key result areas of jobs—the essential elements that are critical to performance results. In discussing the employee's responsibilities or key result areas, the supervisor ideally plays the role of a colleague rather than a boss. The purpose is to help employees understand what a specific situation demands of them. This result may take some time, but the employee's full participation in arriving at an understanding of his or her responsibilities is essential to the success of appraisals. The employee and the supervisor complete the responsibilities column in Table 16.3 with key words to describe the employee's job. By this process, performance objectives are clarified and are accepted by the employee.

Next, the supervisor guides the objective-setting process toward a limited number of straightforward, clearly measurable goals to be accomplished in the forthcoming period (usually six months, or one year). These

Table 16.3
Example of a Performance Appraisal and Personal Development Plan

Performance Planning			Evaluation of Performance			
Responsibilities	Priority	Performance Goals	Exemplary	Satisfactory	Marginal	Unsatisfactory
(a brief outline, in order of importance, of key result areas)		(results that employee should achieve in the next performance period)				

Overall Rating

—Accomplishments far exceeded job requirements (exemplary)
—Met all basic objectives. (satisfactory)
—Marginal
—Performance unsatisfactory (ineffective)

Personal Development Plan

1. What on-the-job training methods will you use? _____

2. What development needs can be met:
   a. by training? _____
   b. through self-development? _____
   c. in outside courses (recommendations)? _____

3. What transfers of assignment will help development? _____

How much development is required for incumbent to be completely qualified in present job?

List any more responsible positions incumbent will be qualified to assume:

Position Title	How much development required?
1.	
2.	
3.	

objectives should be related to the employee's responsibilities and be as specific as possible: tasks the employee plans to complete, new projects he or she wishes to undertake, improved standards of performance, the acquisition of new knowledge or skills, changed relationships with his or her own subordinates or peers. Supervisor and employee jointly determine what measurements or judgments to utilize in determining whether the objectives have been met. The idea is to enable employees themselves to evaluate their progress toward reaching their goals. In concluding the performance-planning step, supervisor and employee numerically rank each of the performance goals in order of priority, the supervisor stressing the relative importance of the key result areas.

The second step is **review** (actual performance versus objectives). Periodically, the supervisor and employee should conduct a formal appraisal interview to review the employee's performance. Actual accomplishments are recorded in the column adjacent to the performance-planning section in the table. In attempting to ascertain the actual performance level, supervisors observe employee behavior and note the accomplishments or level of performance. There are causal relationships associated with each level. For instance, marginal performance can stem from a lack of training, low aptitude, improper direction, and so on. The appraisal interview would then include counseling to correct deficiencies. Table 16.4 is a chart of performance levels, their causes, and appropriate managerial actions. It might facilitate a supervisor's review of performance. Informal progress reviews can be conducted prior to the completion of the next formal-review period to assess employees' progress, encourage performance, guide lagging performers, and so on.

The formal appraisal interview itself occurs at the end of a review period. Employees and their supervisors record accomplishments, compare them with objectives, and discuss variances. The interview is conducted in private, and will probably last two to four hours.

The third step of the MBO appraisal process is the **personal development plan** (PDP), prepared jointly by an employee and supervisor for the purpose of improving proficiency and preparing for additional responsibility. PDPs include methods of overcoming deficiencies and building on strengths through specific training measures during a particular time period. Although improving effectiveness and abilities is basically a matter of individual effort, employees should play an active role in the PDP.

After identifying strengths and weaknesses through performance evaluations and the interview itself, an employee and supervisor discuss training methods, for example, on-the-job training, self-development, outside courses, and assignment transfers. The types of training activities depend on an employee's development needs, assessed promotability, career aspirations, and

Table 16.4
Management of Performance

Nature of Performance	Discipline Problem	Zone of Tolerance	Meets Results— Standards	Exceeds Standards
Accomplishment Level:	*Ineffective (unsatisfactory)*	*Marginal*	*Satisfactory*	*Exemplary*
Management Action Through Appraisal:	Discipline: Detail expectations Plan improvements Caution Suspend Discharge	Counsel Correct deficiencies	Review Encourage results/effort Develop competence	Compliment Reward Compensate Analyze potential
Causes:	Personal problems: Emotional Alcohol/drug Mental Intelligence Personality Insubordinate	Lack of training Low aptitude Insufficient knowledge Poor equipment Improper direction	Good Attitude Possesses: Skills Knowledge Ability	Drive Motivation Career orientation Desire to progress Energy Ability Intelligence

Note: Table 16.4 shows the distribution of accomplishment levels. In practice, most employees under established appraisal systems seem to be rated in the highest or next to highest category. This problem of leniency is a major shortcoming of most rating schemes.

personal desires. It is debatable whether supervisors should discuss promotability with their employees. Should employees be told if they are promotable? Should appraisers inform them of the positions to which they are promotable? If they are considered unpromotable, should they be told why? The answers to these questions depend on company policy and on the situation. Many organizations prohibit the discussion of promotion potential with employees; others go so far as to list the positions for which they are being considered.

MBO appraisals have the inherent advantage of focusing on performance results rather than personal characteristics. This method places an emphasis on development rather than rating. Theoretically, through developmental efforts, an employee's performance will improve and commensurate rewards will be forthcoming. However, the performance-reward relationship rarely holds true in the business world. Invariably, financial rewards are not commensurate with an employee's contributions to an organization, primarily because compensation is based more on economic considerations than on performance factors. Therefore, it would seem logical that by divorcing performance appraisal from compensation review, the developmental aspects of appraisal would be enhanced. MBO appraisal has also proven to be a useful vehicle for improving communications between supervisors and employees on job expectations, development plans, and the results of these. Since development rather than rating is emphasized, it reduces the onus placed on a supervisor of having to sit in judgment. MBO is not without its drawbacks, however. The time and effort required to implement the steps in the process are extensive. Supervisors with more than a few employees would be hard pressed to do a conscientious job of counseling with this method. And MBO focuses attention on task results and does little on a formal basis to identify the kinds of behavior necessary to achieve those results. MBO also has at least two types of inherent bias. First, objectives are unequal and may consist of remedying deficiencies that the low (marginal or ineffective) performer should not have had to begin with. It also may penalize the exemplary performer who may already be outstripping the rest of the group. Thus, if he or she merely maintains a given pace there can be little reward if progress is the expected standard.

Behaviorally Anchored Rating Scales (BARS) supplement the MBO approach because they attempt to get at the *how* of performance. The major characteristics that distinguish the BARS appraisal are these:

1. It emphasizes the development goals.
2. It focuses on individual jobs.
3. It identifies definite, observable, and measurable behavior.
4. It differentiates between behavior, performance, and effectiveness (results).[12]

The development of a BARS instrument is accomplished in the following steps:[13]

1. Identify the jobs to which the instrument will be applied. Supervisors over these jobs will develop and use the instrument to appraise their employees' performance.
2. Have each supervisor write five to ten specific statements that reflect both highly effective and ineffective performance. These statements will be actual examples of observed behavior on the job being studied.
3. Translate these statements into scales by sorting them into categories that clearly reflect a common performance dimension, for example, "highly effective" or "ineffective."
4. Have supervisors write statements that fall between the two extremes. Thus, a continuum of job-based behavior is established with descriptions

of behavior ranging from highly effective to ineffective. Only clear and observable statements are included.

5. Finally, retranslate or cross-check. Working from the several homogeneous categories of behavior developed in the initial translation (steps 3 and 4) several supervisors (at least a dozen) sort each specific behavioral statement into the category it most clearly fits. They then scale each statement in its category on a seven- or nine-point scale (one—most ineffective and seven or nine—most effective). When at least 75 percent of the respondents (supervisors) assign a statement to a category, it is retained because consistent interpretation appears evident. In scaling, standard deviations are usually calculated for all items rated by managers and a standard deviation of less than 1.5 is generally the minimum for retention of an item.

Table 16.5 is an example of a completed scale for a single dimension of a particular job (department manager in a retail store).

Administration of BARS is similar to the critical incidents method. The appraising supervisor regularly observes and records job performance behavior. At review time each observed statement is matched with a statement on the scale, and a mean (average) is calculated for each dimension. Specific observed behavior concerning job performance is then available for feedback to an employee.[14]

BARS has many of the advantages of MBO, especially since it is based on observed behavior rather than personality traits. Also, the incidents that were observed for the appraisal represent specific behavior that yielded particular results. Thus, development plans can focus on necessary behaviors needed to improve performance. And the appraisal instrument is being applied by those who developed it, greatly increasing the probability that it will be administered correctly. Much of the problem of employees' ratings being concentrated at one point are overcome by BARS. Millard, Luthans, and Otteman's research suggests that BARS raters tend to spread out their ratings, which indicates greater discrimination in judging performance of the employees being rated.[15]

The drawbacks of BARS are primarily in terms of cost and time. Most organizations do not have the number of supervisors needed to develop these scales. The great expense of designing and constructing them would only be justified for heavily populated jobs so that the cost can be spread. Finally, supervisors using the scales must have an opportunity to observe employee behavior on a systematic basis. Generally speaking, Schwab, Heneman, and DeCotiis concluded that from the standpoint of reliability, ability to provide unique performance information, and susceptibility to leniency

Table 16.5
Department Manager Job Behavior Rating Scale for the Dimension "Handling Customer Complaints and Making Adjustments"

9 — Could be expected to exchange a blouse purchased in a distant town and to impress the customer so much that she would buy three dresses and three pairs of shoes.

Could be expected to smooth things over beautifully with an irate customer who returned a sweater with a hole in it and turn her into a satisfied customer.
8 —

7 — Could be expected to be friendly and tactful and to agree to reline a coat for a customer who wants a new coat because the lining had worn out in *only* two years.

Could be expected to courteously exchange a pair of gloves that are too small.
6 —

5 — Could be expected to handle the after-Christmas rush of refunds and exchanges in a reasonable manner.

Could be expected to make a refund for a sweater only if the customer insists.
4 —

3 — Could be expected to be quite abrupt with customers who want to exchange merchandise for a different color or style.

Could be expected to tell a customer that a six-week-old order could not be changed even though the merchandise had actually been ordered only two weeks previously.
2 —

1 — Could be expected to tell a customer who tried to return a shirt bought in Hawaii that a store in the States had no use for a Hawaiian shirt.

Source: John P. Campbell, Marvin D. Dunnette, Edward E. Lawler III, Karl E. Welck, Jr., *Managerial Behavior, Performance, and Effectiveness* (New York: McGraw-Hill, 1970). Copyright 1970 by the McGraw-Hill Book Company. Used with permission of McGraw-Hill Book Company.

effects (e.g., supervisors tend to give a disproportionate number of favorable ratings), "there is little reason to believe that BARS are superior to alternative evaluation instruments."[16] Nevertheless, BARS can serve as a basis for the creation of appraisal systems that are valid, reliable, and serve to develop employee competence. We must remember that performance appraisals are personnel tools, not panaceas.

THE DEVELOPMENTAL APPROACH IN USE

A good example of a development-appraisal program that combines the elements of both MBO and BARS is the system currently in use at Corning Glass Works. Called the Performance Management System (PMS), it has three distinct parts: MBO, performance development and review, and evaluation and salary review. Evaluation of an employee's current performance, potential, promotability, and salary increase are distinct from MBO and appraisal sections. MBO was designed by each supervisor (manager) to fit his or her own situation. Compensation considerations were purposely kept apart from the other two elements. In performance development and review a supervisor uses a *performance description questionnaire* that contains a series of validated specific behavior items to observe and with which to describe an employee's behavior. Then, with the aid of a *performance profile*, he or she analyzes the employee's strengths and weaknesses. The performance profile is computer generated and helps the supervisor distinguish an employee's strengths and development needs. Finally, through one or more *developmental interviews*, the supervisor helps employees see what changes in behavior are needed, helps them identify areas for improvement, and establishes plans to develop needed abilities.[17]

SELECTING A PERFORMANCE APPRAISAL METHOD

The appropriate method will vary from organization to organization. How can an organization select the most suitable method when so many are available? McAfee and Green[18] suggest several points to consider when selecting an appraisal system that best meets the needs of an organization. We should keep in mind that one appraisal method probably will not suffice for all people in an organization. Different methods usually will apply to executives/managers, professional/technical/clerical, production/maintenance, and sales/marketing. Also, the relative importance of these considerations will vary according to the needs and peculiarities of the individual organization. The recommended considerations include:

1. *Counseling*—how useful the performance appraisal method is for employee development. It includes how well it facilitates feedback on job performance and how well it conveys the organization's goals and expectations to the employee.

2. *Administrative*—how effective the method is in facilitating decision making on promotions, transfers, discipline, training, and compensation.

3. *Personnel*—the beneficial effects of the method on personnel research and test validation.

4. *Economic*—costs of developing and implementing the method.

5. *Other*—comparability of ratings, reliability, tendency to cause: halo effect (evaluator tends to assign same rating to each factor on the scale), leniency errors, and errors of central tendency (evaluators rate all employees within a narrow range).

The actual development of an appraisal method that meets the needs of the organization is best accomplished with a systems view. According to Henderson a systems view of appraisal considers the psychological and emotional impact of each component on the employee.[19] It also is sensitive to the various levels of the organization—the various functional units (marketing, operations, etc.) and different occupational groups. Implementation of the system starts with job analysis. Then performance dimensions and standards are established to measure employee working behavior. The actual selection of an instrument or rating scale recognizes variables such as organizational level, occupational differences, psychological impact, and individual perception.

Standards in Appraisal

Starting in the 1970s performance appraisals came under close scrutiny by the EEOC, OFCC (Office of Federal Contract Compliance), and the courts, which became highly critical of performance appraisals and their utilization. Their tight interpretation of the EEO guidelines maintained that it was the employers' responsibility to prove that their performance appraisals were valid. (See Chapter 6 on selection and placement for a discussion of validity.)

The courts and compliance agencies found that women and minorities might receive low ratings because of a supervisor's prejudices or because, being recently hired, they may have had less opportunity to learn their jobs. Also, appraisal results are often the basis for validating tests and related selection devices that are specifically regulated by the guidelines. Consequently, rating devices are now required to be based on criteria that represent major or critical work behaviors ascertained from job analyses.

Several court cases are noteworthy here because they found that performance appraisal had a discriminatory impact and was, therefore, unlawful. In *Allen* v. *City of Mobile*,[20] the court found service ratings for performance to be discriminatory when several black police officers failed to be promoted to sergeant. Similarly, a municipal fire department's efficiency rating system (performance appraisal) was ruled discriminatory because it could not prove that the ratings were necessary for conducting the business of the department.[21] A statewide cooperative extension service was declared in violation of the law when the court found that its performance appraisal discriminated against blacks because their ratings were lower than whites and the evaluations were based not on objective criteria but on subjective judgments. The appraisals were not based on job analysis, nor was the appraisal instrument validated.[22]

To minimize the chance of challenge, Holley and Feild suggest that the following measures be taken:

1. The performance rating method must be validated.
2. Content of the rating instrument should be developed from thorough job analyses.
3. Raters should consistently observe ratees performing their work.
4. Raters' evaluations should be based on hard criteria.
5. Raters' biases (racial, sexual, etc.) must not influence the ratings.
6. Ratings should be collected and scored under standardized conditions.[23]

And Prien and others suggest these additional measures:

7. Individual employee performance subscores and total scores must be based on a common numerical scale across jobs and departments.
8. The rating instrument must be resistant to rater error tendencies.[24]

Properly constructed appraisal instruments can facilitate their administration, particularly in the interview process.

Appraisal Interviews

Effective appraisal interviews call for conscientious preparation, an application of the concepts and techniques discussed in Chapter 8, "Interviewing and Counseling," and an ability to handle a variety of special situations.

INTERVIEW PREPARATION

In preparing for the interview, the appraiser completes the appraisal form and details an employee's specific accomplishments and performance deficiencies. Part of the preparation involves anticipating problem areas that might cause the interview to falter and planning strategies to handle the problems. Frequently, appraisers will ask a colleague or a member of the personnel staff to review a performance appraisal, especially if it differs from previous reviews or indicates unsatisfactory performance. Another good preparation technique is to request the employee being appraised to complete the evaluation form a few days prior to the interview. The employee's conclusion can then be compared to the appraiser's to provide a basis for discussion. Sometimes appraisers role-play an appraisal interview to get a feel for the situation and discover any areas of potential conflict that may not have been anticipated. Interview preparation can be time consuming, as experience has shown that adequate preparation can take four or more hours.

APPRAISAL AND COUNSELING SESSION

At the beginning of the interview the appraiser puts the employee at ease and explains the purpose of the performance appraisal. Developmental appraisals facilitate this step because employees normally respond favorably to *constructive* efforts to develop their abilities and potential. This is not to say that appraisal interviews are completely devoid of stress. In fact, most of them are viewed as unfair, arbitrary, and capricious by employees, and few appraisers are considered by employees to be competent in this endeavor.

The employee usually participates in the evaluation of his or her own performance, so the appraiser should encourage the employee to do most of the talking. The rating process can be enhanced by reviewing the areas of responsibility (key result areas) with the employee. In this regard, job descriptions are a useful tool. Principles of interviewing suggest that employees be asked their opinions of their strengths and development needs rather than being told what these are. The appraiser should, of course, have in mind his or her own opinion of the employee's abilities and deficiencies. Especially when an employee's performance is not up to expectations, appraisers will want to analyze the reasons in order to explore corrective measures during the interview. A scheme for performing such an analysis is offered by Mager and Pipe.[25]

The analysis first calls for determining whether a skills deficiency exists. If it does, training would be in order. If not, other considerations come into play. Perhaps there are obstacles to performing, for example, conflicting orders, lack of authority, and so on; or the employee may have a misconception of desired performance, viewing it as punitive. Once the employee's job performance has been analyzed, the appraiser counsels the employee to a realization of his or her strengths and weaknesses.

Next, the appraiser explains each element in the appraisal and the reasoning behind the ratings. When criticism is necessary, it is advisable to criticize the performance rather than the person. Employees are more likely to respond positively to the suggestion that their monthly activity reports have been coming in after the deadline than to the admonition that they are unreliable.

At the end of the interview both parties should agree on a plan of action and objectives for the future (particularly in MBO appraisals), culminating in the preparation of a personal development plan. It might be a good idea to have employees cite the major points covered in the interview, thus reenforcing the areas of performance that need to be improved upon in the future.

Table 16.6 outlines the appraisal and counseling interview and also offers some suggestions for conducting the appraisal.

HANDLING SPECIAL APPRAISAL SITUATIONS

Each appraisal interview is a unique situation. It varies with the personality of the employee, the style and experience of the appraiser, and the nature of the appraisal. Some suggestions for handling special interview situations are offered here.

THE OUTSTANDING EMPLOYEE.   This is the most pleasant type of situation. But the obligation of the appraiser is greatest here to explore aspirations and plan career growth.

THE EMPLOYEE WHO HAS NOT IMPROVED.   The appraiser can be frank and discuss whether the employee is in the right job or perhaps should be helped to relocate. The employee should be made aware of his or her performance deficiencies.

UNSATISFACTORY PERFORMERS.   Less than satisfactory performance can stem from a variety of causes such as lack of motivation, poor attitude, improper training, and so on. The appraiser needs to analyze the causes and take corrective action. The steps and techniques are the same as discussed in Chapter 9.

OLDER PEOPLE.   Older, long-service employees deserve special consideration. Their pride may be hurt because younger employees have risen above them. Or they may have anxieties about their future and about retirement. Some of the suggestions on preretirement counseling (Chapter 8) would be appropriate here.

OVER-AMBITIOUS EMPLOYEES.   Ambition and initiative are positive employee attributes, but extremes can create problems for appraisers. Some employees seek raises or promotion before they are deserved. Employees,

Table 16.6
Outline of the Appraisal and
Counseling Interview

Preliminary Steps for Interview
Establish objectives for interview and plan how to say it.
What do you hope to accomplish?
How should the employee feel after the interview?
What should he/she do differently?
Think of ways to ensure communication.
Assess potential areas of disagreement.
Make specific plan of action for improvement.

Appraising Performance
What should he/she have done?
How well should employee have done it?
Did he/she do it?
If not, why not?
What can be done to help improve?
What records or data do I have to appraise performance or support judgment?
On the basis of standards established, support judgment and write instances.

Setting the Stage for the Interview
Friendly atmosphere
Purpose of the interview stated clearly and concisely—the advantage to the employee as an aid in his/her development—where he/she stands, what is expected, areas for improvement.
Ensure mutual understanding of job responsibilities.

Evaluation
Agree on job responsibilities—jobs performed, things employee feels are most important, ways to use time more effectively.
Exchange of views—resolution of differences and agreement on what is being analyzed.
Compliment employee if deserved—do not use false flattery.
Ask employee what he/she thinks are greatest strengths—areas of less competence?
Deal with one item at a time—support judgment with specific instances if possible.
COVER TACTFULLY.
Listen to employee's side.
Lead up to discussion of job standards you expect to be maintained, and show where improvement is needed.
If disagreement, try to find out why.
Did employee get clear view of his/her performance?
Were differences resolved?
Areas for improvement.

Table 16.6
(cont.)

Causes

Search for the reasons why—must be perceived by the employee.
What were the real causes—were they brought out?
Were they understood and accepted by both?

Listing Possible Actions

Encourage employee to make suggestions—reaction to how received.
Were actions practical?

Develop a Plan of Action

Was program of self-improvement completely understood and agreement reached as to who, what, when?
Was plan complete and practical?
Did action plan treat causes?
How do you motivate employee to follow up on plan?
Employee must obtain clear understanding of how performance is regarded by you and feel evaluation is fair.
Employer must recognize need for change in behavior and desire to cooperate.

Summarize to ensure clear understanding, have employee summarize.

Follow up to see if employee taking steps to improve.

To Be Included in Interview Record

Specific objectives and plan for improvement.
Goals and objectives.
Interests and aspirations.
General reaction of appraisee.
Employee signs after review.

---

in these cases, need to be reminded that raises are based on merit—for achieving expected results. The interview then provides an excellent opportunity to explore bases for improving performance so that a raise can be justified. At the same time employee potential and development plans for promotion can be explored. One word of caution—employees should not be given the impression that a promotion will be forthcoming on achieving a certain level of performance or attaining certain competencies. Employees can be encouraged to improve so they will be ready and qualified should an appropriate opportunity become available.

SILENT EMPLOYEES. Sometimes employees are unresponsive—they will not enter into the conversation even when encouraged. Nondirective questioning or asking opinions about something may get them to respond.

ANGRY EMPLOYEES.   They require a lot of listening to and a minimum of arguing. If the appraiser can apply basic counseling techniques and help them to express their feelings and attitudes, it may be possible to determine the source of their anger. At this point the basics of the problem-solving interview (see Chapter 8) come into play.

It should be obvious that to handle appraisal situations properly, appraisers need to be trained in the various aspects of performance appraisal.

TRAINING FOR APPRAISAL

Formal training for performance appraisers is essential to the effectiveness of this process. Studies have shown that very few organizations train their appraisers[26] but those that do indicated benefits such as increased participant appreciation of performance appraisal as a management development tool. Also, well-trained appraisers learn proper administrative procedures and develop interviewing skills that make them more effective in relating to and counseling employees. Lastly, they are motivated to meet target dates for review completion. Appraisal training programs vary, but they generally encompass such basic subject areas as: purpose and importance of performance appraisal; the performance appraisal program of the organization; rating performance (setting objectives, completing forms, reviewing procedures, routing forms); workshops on completing forms; rating standards and guidelines for performance; and interview techniques and procedures.

CAVEATS FOR THE APPRAISER

Objective appraisals based on job-related (validated) standards are ideal and, more significantly, they are required by law. But this ideal is not so easy to achieve. Following are some of the errors or sources of bias that should be avoided in the appraisal process.

1. *Halo effect* results from inappropriate generalizations about an employee from one aspect of the person (i.e., appearance, character, or performance). Thus, an employee who supervises a production crew might schedule work exceedingly well, but be marginal in all other respects of his performance. If an appraiser were to rate the employee outstanding overall on the basis of his scheduling performance alone, the appraiser would be falling victim to the halo effect.

2. *First impression* error is the tendency of an appraiser to judge an employee on first impression. True, first impressions are lasting, but in appraisal

one must be careful not to let first impressions influence long-term judgments.

3. *Central tendency* error is committed by the appraiser who plays it safe by consistently rating an employee at or close to the midpoint of the scale (average) regardless of whether the actual performance warrants a higher or lower rating.

4. *Contrast effect* error arises when an appraiser compares one employee to another rather than rating on the degree to which the employee meets predetermined performance criteria.

5. *Similar-to-me* effect occurs when appraisers judge more favorably those whom they perceive to be similar to themselves.

6. *Negative and positive leniency* errors are committed by appraisers who are too stringent or too easy in evaluating employees. When a manager is too critical (negative) the employee might feel that no matter how hard he or she tries, the boss will never be satisfied. Leniency errors raise unwarranted expectations of raises or promotions in employees.

Cost-Benefit Analysis

Basic analyses of the impact of performance appraisal on an organization can also yield information relevant to human resource planning and development activities. Some organizations maintain central appraisal files in the form of physical records or in computer-data files. These files become the source of information for analyses and the basis for monitoring the system. To ensure that appraisals are properly and regularly conducted, analyses might include: distribution of ratings to see if certain raters or departments rate lower or higher than others; calculations of rating consistency among appraisers and by the same rater from appraisal to appraisal; and the extent to which employees attain positions for which they are being trained.

As an element of control in performance appraisal, managers can be evaluated on how well they evaluate their employees. Some appraisal programs are designed with a high degree of employer-employee interaction. The purpose is to make employees aware of the company's expectations of their performance and thereby improve productivity. In such cases both the degree of employee involvement and the resulting productivity improvements are benefits that can and should be measured.

Direct costs of performance appraisal are the development costs of the system and the time (multiplied by their wages or salaries) of staff, managers, and employees to prepare and conduct appraisals. Indirectly, the costs to train managers in the process might also be included.

Summary

Performance appraisals serve a variety of purposes. They provide feedback to employees on their performance; serve as a basis for improving performance; provide data for making decisions on pay increases, transfer or promotions, or discipline; and compel managers to relate employee behavior to actual results. Appraisals are usually performed by an employee's supervisor, but there are situations in which employees rate themselves or each other (peer ratings) or their supervisors.

A wide variety of appraisals are currently in use. Many utilize scales associated with personal characteristics, others employ written statements of a supervisor's assessment, while some utilize critical incidents that reflect desirable or undesirable performance. Developmental appraisals—BARS and MBO—emphasize the identification, planning, and activating of behavior that will yield desirable performance.

There is no best appraisal system, but a viable one will contain validated rating methods, have evaluations based on hard criteria, provide for consistency in ratings among appraisers, and be resistant to rater-error tendencies. Regardless of the system employed, its effectiveness will be enhanced if appraisers are trained in the underlying philosophy of the system, techniques of rating and forms completion, and the basic skills of appraisal interviewing. The key to performance-appraisal effectiveness is the interview, for it is here that employee and supervisor mutually evaluate an employee's performance; analyze strengths and weaknesses and plan his or her personal development; and discuss the employee's aspirations which, coupled with the needs of the organization, form the basis for career planning (which will be discussed in Chapter 17).

Key Terms

performance appraisal
inverted appraisal
graphic scale
forced distribution
ranking
free-written rating
forced choice method
critical incident method
field review method

buddy ratings
group summary appraisal
self-appraisal process
developmental approaches
MBO appraisal
review
personal development plan
Behaviorally Anchored Rating
  Scales (BARS)

Review Questions

1. How do traditional rating methods differ from developmental appraisals?

2. Describe the elements of an appraisal system that would meet EEOC guidelines.

3. Discuss the advantages and disadvantages of each of the following appraisal methods: a) MBO, b) BARS, c) Forced choice, d) Graphic scale, e) Buddy ratings.

4. Discuss the various steps in the appraisal interview.

5. Describe a scheme for analyzing performance problems. Assuming that a performance problem exists, discuss each of the steps preliminary to deciding on appropriate action.

Discussion Questions

1. Explain why performance appraisal might be considered key to management development.

2. What are the advantages and disadvantages of having an evaluator's appraisals reviewed by his or her immediate superior?

3. Criteria are standards of performance. What criteria would you use to evaluate the effectiveness of an employee's performance on each of the following jobs:

   a. Secretary?

   b. Typewriter salesperson?

   c. Flight attendant?

   d. Heavy equipment operator (bulldozer)?

   e. Cabinet maker?

4. Rater bias is a problem in performance appraisal. What measures can be taken to ensure that appraisals are nondiscriminatory and that ratings are consistent among appraisers?

5. In some organizations appraisal systems may have fallen into a perfunctory and ritualistic pattern. Would the complete absence of a formal appraisal system be better? Why, or why not?

Case Problem 1

THE ROLLING STONE

"Zeke, why on earth do you want another transfer?" Mildred Bailey asked. "Isn't my section good enough for you?"

Zeke looked a bit sheepish. "Aw, Mildred, it's not that—you have nothing to do with it. I got to admit that when they sent me up here to work for a woman, I thought it was the end. But in the past year, you've been about the best boss I ever had."

"I've been trying to keep your assignments as varied as I can, Zeke, because I know how much you detest routine work. And you've come through every time." Mildred was supervisor for United Manufacturing's printing and publications section, which turned out all the printed materials headquarters needed. It was a tough job, working under tight deadlines, and she needed all the good people she could get. Zeke had been one of the best.

"You've been swell, Mildred. Once in a while, like when we had that proofreading to do, I nearly lost my mind, but most of the time I've been learning a lot and even enjoying most of it."

"Well," Mildred said, "you're right on schedule. I got your record from personnel. Just about every year for the past eight years you requested a transfer. Every time your ex-boss said you were okay or maybe even excellent. You do the job, but not for long. And you don't move up much either, Zeke. All that moving around makes everyone nervous."

Zeke stared at the floor. "I know, Mildred, but I get restless. This is a big company, and there's lots to learn. I want to learn it all. Besides, after a while, even tricky jobs, like the one I have with you, get dull. I just have to move on."

"You know that I'm scheduled to move up next year, Zeke. If you stick around, well, maybe. . . ."

"I know that too, Mildred, but somehow I just don't care. I could do your job now, thanks to you. But if I had your job, well, begging your pardon, I think that I'd get pretty bored pretty quick."

Mildred shrugged her shoulders. "So you want me to write up a rating for you, Zeke. How shall I rate you—the way you've been, namely excellent? Or shall I be nervous about your moving around all the time and tell them to lower the boom?"

"You're the boss, Mildred. But you see, I've never been in production-quality control, and that looks really interesting. If I could get in there, and if I could get some training like you've given me, then maybe I'd stay put."

"You've been just about everywhere else in the company—why not quality control? But after that, there's really no place to go."

"I'll make it there, Mildred, I know I will."

She stared at him. "You've only got a high school education, plus a half-year of college, Zeke. You're a very smart guy, but you're not so young anymore, and it's about time you settled down. Lord knows, you've been around the company enough to know everything. If you could only be a bit more patient, you could be a manager pretty soon."

"But I don't want to be a supervisor. I just want to keep on going like I've been."

Mildred shook her head. "Your mind's made up?"

"I just have to have that transfer, Mildred, I really do."

"Okay, I'll approve the request and give you a rating, Zeke. If you have to move on, I suppose that I can't stop you."

Problems

1. What is Zeke's basic problem? Is it what he thinks it is?

2. Why do managers continue to give Zeke good and excellent ratings in spite of his excessive internal movement and transfer?

3. Did Mildred handle this interview properly?

4. Considering the available kinds of performance appraisal, which one would be most appropriate in this situation?

Case Problem 2

THE PERSONNEL MANAGER

Alan Rafferty, an underwriter for Provident Life Insurance Company, was discussing personnel management with Rogers Danville, the personnel manager of the General Insurance Company. Mr. Danville was completing his explanation of his corporation's appraisal system.

"I think that I can fairly state that ours is the most comprehensive evaluation system in existence. Not only that—it is accepted with enthusiasm by both the raters and the ratees. Every six months, we require a formal appraisal of each of our managers by his supervisor. This formal appraisal, of course, is in addition to the daily coaching and appraisal that we encourage.

"Our form for appraisal has two parts, one of which concerns itself with the traits, abilities, and attributes of the person. This section helps us make decisions concerning promotions, transfers, schooling, and the like. The second part has to do with results—statements of objectives set and attained, projects completed, and so forth.

"After the supervisor completes the appraisal form he is required to conduct an appraisal interview, taking as long as he needs to discuss results and the appraisal thereof with his subordinate.

"Each appraisal is reviewed by the rater's immediate superior to insure its fairness and accuracy. And here in personnel, we analyze each form to determine corporate trends and check on the abilities of each manager to evaluate his subordinates."

John Bartlett, Mr. Danville's senior administrative assistant, followed the discussion with interest. When Mr. Danville paused, John made the following statement:

"Rogers, are you sure that we require an appraisal interview? I've been working for you for three years now, and you have never discussed my appraisals with me."

"John," said Mr. Danville, "I am sure you will agree that that hasn't been needed. We work together so closely that I am sure that you always know how I appraise you."

Problems

1. What do you think of the formal appraisal system?
2. Why was John Bartlett never interviewed?
3. What do you think of Mr. Danville's remark, "We work together so closely that I am sure that you always know how I appraise you."?

Notes

1. Robert I. Lazer and Walter S. Wikstrom, *Appraising Managerial Performance: Current Practices and Future Directions* (New York: Conference Board, 1977), pp. 63–65.

2. See Harry Levinson, "Thinking Ahead," *Harvard Business Review*, July–August 1976, p. 30; and Allan Patz, "Performance Appraisal Useful but Still Resisted," *Harvard Business Review*, May–June 1975, p. 75.

3. Alan H. Locher and Kenneth S. Teel, "Performance Appraisal—A Survey of Current Practices," *Personnel Journal*, May 1977, p. 247.

4. Donald Dunlin, "Through the Looking Glass," *Management Review*, August 1975, p. 59.

5. Locher and Teel, "Performance Appraisal," p. 247.

6. A. Zavala, "Development of the Forced Choice Rating Scale Technique," *Psychological Bulletin*, 63 (1965), pp. 117–24.

7. John C. Flannagan and Robert K. Burns, "The Employee Performance Record: A New Appraisal and Development Tool," *Harvard Business Review*, September–October 1957, pp. 95–102.

8. For a more detailed discussion, see J. F. French, P. E. Kuyard, and H. H. Meyer, "Participation in the Appraisal System," *Human Relations*, 19 (1966), pp. 3–20.

9. Ibid.

10. E. P. Hollander, "Buddy Ratings: Military Research and Industrial Implications," in Thomas L. Whisler and Shirley F. Harper, eds., *Performance Appraisal, Research and Practice* (New York: Holt, Rinehart and Winston, 1962), pp. 320ff.

11. John P. Campbell, Marvin D. Dunnette, Richard D. Arvey, and Lowell V. Hellervik, "The Development and Evaluation of Behaviorally Based Rating Scales," *Journal of Applied Psychology*, February 1973, p. 15.

12. William J. Kearney, "The Value of Behaviorally Based Performance Appraisals," *Business Horizons*, June 1976, p. 77.

13. Ibid., p. 79.

14. Ibid., pp. 79–80.

15. Cheedle W. Millard, Fred Luthans, and Robert L. Otteman, "A New Breakthrough for Performance Appraisal," *Business Horizons*, August 1976, pp. 66–73.

16. Donald P. Schwab, Herbert G. Heneman III, and Thomas A. DeCotiis, "Behaviorally Anchored Rating Scales: A Review of the Literature," *Personnel Psychology*, Winter 1975, p. 557.

17. Michael Beer and Robert A. Ruh, "Employee Growth Through Performance Management," *Harvard Business Review*, July–August 1976, pp. 59–66.

18. Bruce McAfee and Blake Green, "Selecting a Performance Appraisal Method," *The Personnel Administrator*, June 1977, pp. 61–64.

19. Richard Henderson, *Performance Appraisal: Theory to Practice* (Reston, Virginia: Reston Publishing Company, Inc., 1980), pp. 19–21.

20. *Allen v. City of Mobile*, 331 F. Supp. 1134 (1971), 4 EPD, para. 7582.

21. *Harper v. Mayor and City Council of Baltimore*, 359 F. Supp. 1187 (1973), 5 EPD, para. 2650.

22. *Wade v. Mississippi Cooperative Extension Service*, 372 F. Supp. 126 (1974), 7 EPD, para. 9186.

23. William H. Holley and Hubert S. Feild, "Performance Appraisal and the

Law," *Labor Law Journal*, July 1975, p. 428.

24. Erich P. Prien, Mark A. Jones, and Louise M. Miller, "A Job Related Performance Rating System," *The Personnel Administrator*, November 1977, p. 38.

25. Robert F. Mager and Peter Pipe, *Analyzing Performance Problems* (Belmont, Calif.: Fearon, 1970).

26. Locher and Teel, "Performance Appraisal," p. 247. See also, Donald P. Crane and Gerri A. Crane, "Performance Appraisal Training" (University of Georgia, June 1970), pp. 1–3.

Chapter Seventeen
Career Planning

"Cheshire-Puss" . . . *said Alice, "would you tell me please, which way I ought to go from here?"*

"That depends a good deal on where you want to get to," said the Cat.
"I don't care much where—" said Alice.
"Then it doesn't matter which way you go," said the Cat.
"———so long as I get somewhere," Alice added as an explanation.
"Oh, you're sure to do that," said the Cat, "if only you walk long enough."[1]

How many of us really know where we are going in life? Or, if we think we do, are we really satisfied with what we are doing, or with what we hope to do? Many successful people *plan* their lives and careers so they won't wander aimlessly through life as Alice seemed to be doing. And today many organizations have formalized programs for the management of careers.

Because Chapters 13–15 covered the development of human resources and other chapters discussed related aspects of career management, this chapter will focus on the individual aspects of careers. We will place career planning in perspective, however, by discussing some of the theoretical aspects of careers and their relationships to organizations.

An Overview of Careers in Organizations

For the purpose of our discussion here, let us make some assumptions about careers. First, they are individual. The degree of success of a person's

LEARNING OBJECTIVES

1. To know why individuals select particular careers.
2. To be familiar with the components of organizational career development programs.
3. To be familiar with the stages of an individual's career.
4. To know the relationships among values, objectives, and plans in career planning.
5. To be familiar with the activities and programs included in an individual (career) development plan.

career is based on his or her own assessment—not someone else's. In today's society there is an increasing recognition of an individual's right to make his or her own life choices. Second, throughout one's career, values, attitudes, and motivation are influenced and changed, and they influence the career choices one makes. Third, a career is viewed from the standpoint of work-related experiences. Thus our view of careers will encompass any type of work (paid or volunteer) a person engages in. Finally, careers span an individual's lifetime—they may even include work experiences during retirement years.[2]

These assumptions fit Hall's working definition of **careers:**

The career is the individually perceived sequence of attitudes and behaviors associated with work-related experiences and activities over the span of the person's life.[3]

This definition implies that careers are developed within organizations. Thus, in an organizational setting, **career development** can be construed as a systematic approach for guiding the entry and movement through an organization. Career development is concerned with the relationship between individuals and their work. The two basic activities associated with career development are:

(1) Career management, which blends individual aspirations with organizational needs in formal programs to develop capabilities (HRT), allocate resources (human resource planning, selection and placement, and career pathing), review accomplishments (counseling and appraisal), and reward desired performance (compensation); and (2) **Career planning,** which is the individual process involving the choosing of occupations and organizations, planning the routes one's career will follow and engaging in appropriate self-development activities.[4]

The relationships among career development, career management, and career planning are graphically depicted in Figure 17.1.[5]

WHY CAREER PLANNING IN ORGANIZATIONS?

In the past few years, organizations have shown a growing interest in career planning. Some of the impetus has come from employees who question their organization's right to affect their lives unilaterally through job assignments, transfers, and relocations. As we pointed out previously, the better educated, new breed of employee views the opportunity for advancement as a key motivator. There is also increasing concern with the trend of executives to drop out to pursue nonbusiness careers. In a similar vein, John B. Miner concludes from his research that the will to manage is dwindling among students, and that this trend will ultimately lead to a

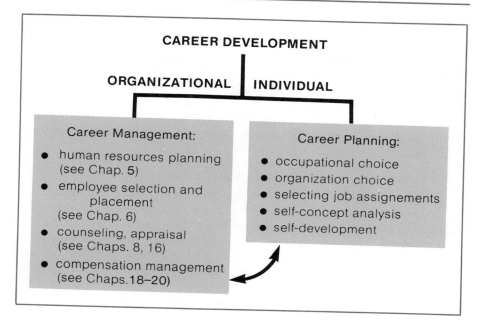

Figure 17.1
Career Development
Relationships

critical shortage of managerial talent.[6] A recognition of this phenomenon has prompted many organizations to initiate career-planning programs that identify and encourage management aspirants. But the primary impetus for career-planning programs is affirmative action. Many organizations have been placing special emphasis on the upward mobility of women and minorities, and they feel a conscientiously implemented career-planning program is the appropriate vehicle for achieving EEO goals. By identifying promotables within an organization, a pool of qualified reserves is created. These organizations subscribe to the principle that each position should be filled by qualified individuals. Through career-planning efforts, they believe a proper balance of minorities and women can be attained.

The economic recession of the mid-1970s reduced the demand for new product development. As a result, the normal work environment did not provide opportunities for employees to upgrade their skills. Without a formal career-planning program to expose these people to new experiences and training, they would soon become obsolete. During economic downturns, organizations have been utilizing career-planning programs to keep their technical and managerial talent vital and interested.

Also, some organizations develop managerial talent through planned cross-training; the versatility that results apparently enhances their managerial effectiveness. The broader exposure gives officials an opportunity to observe managers under a variety of conditions so that the best use can be made of their abilities. An offshoot of this effort is the building of loyalty among managers; the thinking is that they will remain with an organization when they realize there are long-range career opportunities available.

In essence, it seems that organizations are beginning to realize that careers exist within their hierarchies and can be identified empirically. They recognize that there is an advantage to systematically managing and influencing these careers rather than having them operate implicitly within the organization.[7]

CAREER PLANNING—ORGANIZATIONAL RESPONSIBILITY

Managers are in the best position to develop and communicate internal career options to employees, that is, to show them the various career tracks available within an organization. Since they have continuous contact with employees, managers should be aware of their abilities and shortcomings. Also, they know the opportunities that are most likely to become available in the future. Line managers should therefore have direct responsibility for creating a climate that encourages individual career planning. In addition, they can ensure that individuals are taught how to plan their careers.[8]

The personnel department plays a crucial role in career planning, too. It advises and assists line managers in developing or identifying career tracks and helps them understand the relationships among these tracks, for example, how one job can be preparation for others. The responsibility for implementing formal organizational career-planning activities is a primary one of the personnel department.

ORGANIZATIONAL PROGRAMS OF CAREER DEVELOPMENT

Although each organization's career-planning program has unique features, there are enough elements in common to describe a general scheme that is applicable to both large and small organizations.

"We have always believed the growth of the individual employee in competence and responsibility is the source of success of the IBM enterprise." This statement of purpose seems to express the primary objective of many career-planning programs. The major emphasis is on the development of managerial, technical, and professional capabilities for the organization. It stems from a combination of personal aspirations and business needs, with the latter being the primary consideration.

In general, most career-planning programs cover salaried employees, but some have been expanded to include hourly employees.

Figure 17.2 outlines the elements and their relationships in a model program.

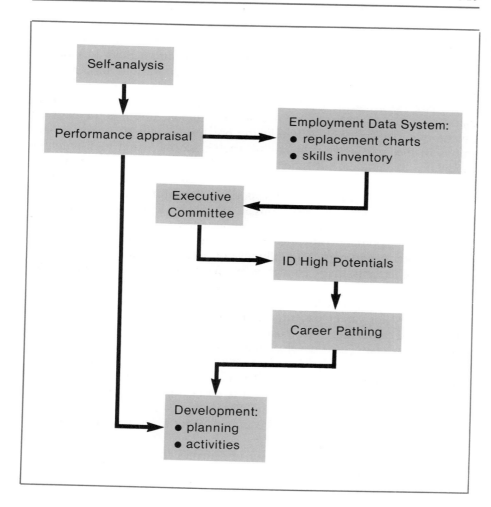

Figure 17.2
A Basic Scheme for
Organizational Career
Planning

An organization's career-planning program stresses the importance of self-analysis and self-development. Although organizational needs are basic to career planning, the individual employee's aspirations also play a major role. Typically, managers are trained to counsel their employees in order to help them analyze their strengths, development needs, and aspirations as well as to appraise their performance and advise them of opportunities within the organization. The General Electric Company seems to be unique in providing instruments to aid employees in self-analysis. A series of workbooks entitled, "Career Dimensions I and II" are made available to employees to help them assess their personal values, their feelings about work, their life, career goals, and desires; these help them to become aware of realistic choices, choose courses of action, guide them in acting on choices and creating future opportunities; finally they encourage them to monitor, evaluate, and readjust plans as they move *through* various life or career stages.[9]

The performance appraisal is key to molding an employee's career plan. It identifies those who are deemed promotable, and it is the basis for inventorying the capabilities within the organization for successors to positions in the management hierarchy. High performers and high-potential candidates are initially identified through the performance appraisal. The final designation of a high promotable or fast-track candidate is generally the responsibility of the candidate's sponsor or mentor and/or that person's immediate supervisor. Such selections are usually made with the concurrence of higher levels of management—sometimes even a selection committee or executive development committee might be involved—and the assistance of the personnel department. The influence of peers, other managers, and organizational variables (e.g., politics, economic conditions, social norms) also plays a part in the designation of "fast trackers."

Once candidates are identified as high potential or promotable they are scheduled for **career pathing.** Based on projected needs of the organization, these candidates are exposed to a variety of work experiences along a career path planned to develop them for the replacement position(s) for which they have been designated. A select few are even placed on a fast track to expedite their preparation. The U.S. Army has traditionally career-pathed individual officers. Figure 17.3 is an example of a career path and depicts the sequence of exposures an officer in the Combat Communications-Electronics Specialty should receive in advancing from lieutenant through colonel.

Organizations utilize a variety of schemes to develop employees in their career paths. The planned assignments are usually with specially trained managers who coach an employee in the art as well as science of performing a job. The Celanese Corporation is one corporation that utilizes supervisors as career counselors.[10] At this point the performance appraisal also serves to give employees feedback on their progress and aids in developing plans for subsequent assignments and development activities. The latter might include special projects to complement job-related activities and formalized training in management skills and other subjects related to job performance.

All employees, high potential and otherwise, are encouraged to participate in self-development activities. Tuition reimbursement plans serve as an inducement to enroll in college or university programs. Some organizations conduct their own formal management training; General Motors even has its own Institute that, in addition to offering accredited degrees, conducts extension programs in various regions to support its career-planning program. To a lesser degree, organizations sponsor mid-level managers and executives to seminars and executive/management programs offered by universities.

Theoretical Aspects of Individual Career Planning

Career planning is an emerging area of study that has a long-standing tradition in the social sciences. Sociologists and psychologists have been studying the bases for individual career choice, the influences on one's occupational selection, the stages of a career, and the methodology for self-management of a career. A basic familiarity with the theoretical aspects of career planning can help the student and the career counselor better understand how careers are developed.

OCCUPATIONAL CHOICE

How does one choose an occupation? Theories of occupational choice fall into two categories: the differentialist view and the developmental perspective.

Differentialist theory places primary concentration upon the talents, abilities, and psychological characteristics of the individual. Occupational choice is viewed as a matching process that balances satisfaction and stability. Differentialists theorize that patterns of ability, interest, style, and disposition are shaped early in life, and they remain fairly constant even though slight modifications might occur.[11]

The **developmental view** suggests that occupational choice does not occur at one point in time but rather represents an evolving sequence of individual decisions. Choice, from this point of view, is a somewhat irreversible process of limiting decisions beginning with a person's first childish fantasies about work and ending with retirement. Occupational identity is considered an integral part of an individual's wide development or what might be termed the confrontation of work in living.[12]

Blau and his colleagues were developmentalists. They viewed occupational choice as being influenced by the social structure in two ways: (1) the social experiences of the individual have shaped his or her personality development (needs, self-concept, orientation, interests, values), which in turn orients him or her toward particular careers; and (2) the social and economic conditions of occupational opportunity influence (help or constrain) the attainment of the individual's aspirations and choices. These factors are interrelated because earlier choices generally restrict the number of future possibilities, thus influencing subsequent choices. Blau and his

Figure 17.3   Professional Development Guide, Personnel Management, Specialty (41)

PHASES of DEVELOPMENT	PROFESSIONAL MILITARY EDUCATION	CIVIL EDUCATION		SPECIALTY* EDUCATION (NOT ALL INCLUSIVE)	ASSIGNMENT OPPORTUNITIES (NOT ALL INCLUSIVE)
		PROGRAMS	SPECIALTY DISCIPLINES AND COURSES		
COLONEL PHASE — Maximum utilization of capabilities in Personnel Management. Full utilization of developed managerial skills and executive talents in either primary or alternate specialty to meet the needs of the Army.				Personnel Management Seminars	HQDA Division Chief** Department Director-Service School Personnel Management Officer Inspector General, Major Command Director, Personnel & Administration** AG Readiness Coordinator** Adjutant General, Major Command** J-1, DCSPER, Director Personnel**
LIEUTENANT COLONEL PHASE — Continued professional development in Personnel Management and alternate specialty.	Army War College Air War College Industrial College of the Armed Forces National War College Navy War College British Royal College of Defense Studies Canadian National Defense College French Ecole Superieure de Guerre Inter-American Defense College Army War College Corresponding Studies Course	COOPERATIVE DEGREE PROGRAM Discipline should be in Personnel Management specialty related area (see Spec Discp and Courses) Normal period of study: less than 6 months Service Obligation: 3 years Normal period of study: Six months immediately after completion of above courses.		Personnel Management Office Course Military Personnel Office Course Race Relations and Equal Opportunity Staff/Instructor Course Race Relations and Equal Opportunity Staff/Instructor Course Army Phase II Alcohol and Drug Abuse Team Training Drug and Alcohol Rehabilitation Training Organizational Effectiveness Staff Officer Course	Recruiting District Commander Personnel Management Officer ACofS, G-1/ACSPER** Adjutant General** Personnel Staff Officer** Labor Relations/Management Officer Organizational Effectiveness Staff Officer
MAJOR PHASE — Continued professional development in entry specialty while emphasizing development in the Personnel Management specialty.	Army Command and General Staff College Air Command and Staff College Armed Forces Staff College College of Navy Command and Staff Marine Corps Command and Staff College School of the Americas	ADVANCED PROGRAM DCP (AR 621-1) Period of Study: 18 months or less Utilization: 3 years ADPRID (AR 621-101) Period of Study: 15 months Utilization: 3 years ROTC Fully Funded (AR 621-1) Utilization Required: None Prerequisites: Attendance at C&GSC or Senior Service College Utilization Required: SSC/CGSC: none	GRADUATE DISCIPLINES Personnel Management Personnel Administration Personnel Management Administration Business Administration General Business ADPS - Business Public Administration Human Resources Management Organizational Development Industrial Management Social Psychology General Psychology	There are numerous correspondence courses available from the U.S. Army Institute for Administration, Fort Benjamin Harrison, Indiana, which support the Personnel Management specialty.	Manpower Analyst Personnel Management Officer Chief, Administration Team, Readiness Group Commander, Personnel Services Company Chief, Personnel Services Division Instructor (Service School)

Phase	Course	Degree Program / Period of Study	Graduate/Undergraduate Disciplines	Positions
CAPTAIN PHASE Continued professional development in entry specialty and commence development in Personnel Management specialty.	Army Command and General Staff College Non-Resident Course	Period of Study: 18 months	A partial listing of the graduate courses which support the Personnel Management specialty includes: Management By Objectives Applied Management Concepts Counseling Communication Analysis Drug and Alcohol Abuse Group Dynamics Effective Decisions Human Behavior in Organizations Race Relations Managing Time Human Relations Managerial Psychology Management Planning and Controlling	S-1 Reserve Component Advisor Recruiting/Induction Officer Reenlistment Officer Personnel Officer Personnel Management Officer Commander, Personnel Services Company Instructor (Service School)
	Advanced Course	UNDER-GRADUATE DEGREE PROGRAM DCP(AR 621-1) 18 months or less Service Obligation: Three years for each year in school or portion thereof, but not more than four years. *Top 5% PRGM for USMA & ROTC DMG (AR 621-1) Utilization: 3 years Service Obligation: Three years for each year in school or portion thereof, but not more than four years.	UNDERGRADUATE DISCIPLINES Personnel Management Personnel Administration Personnel Management Administration Business Administration General Management General Business ADPS - Business Public Administration Human Resources Management Organizational Development Industrial Management Social Psychology General Psychology Statistics Mathematics General Education English Grammar and Composition Banking and Finance Economics Each officer should have an undergraduate degree.	
LIEUTENANT PHASE Commence professional development in entry specialty. Acquire basic military skills and knowledge.	Basic Course	Period of Study: 18 months Utilization: 3 years Service Obligation: Three years for each year in school or portion thereof, but not more than four years. *Effective with the class of 1978 the period of study will occur during fourth through tenth year.		Battalion S-1 Personnel Management Officer, Installation or Division Race Relations, Equal Opportunity Officer

associates also maintain that career choice is actually a composite of two distinct choices: the individual's choice of an occupation and the organization's selection of that individual for the occupation. This process of choosing an occupation is depicted in Figure 17.4.

Essentially, the literature on the theory of career choice suggests that there is an interdependence between personality variables, choice dimensions, and environmental conditions. An individual with a particular set of attributes in a given culture and operating under a specific set of economic circumstances will be confronted with a special set of choices that will lead to a unique sequence of decisions. For example, vigorous, energetic, restless, intelligent young men in nineteenth century America were attracted to entrepreneurial ventures (small shops, manufacturing concerns and so on) as a result of social and economic conditions. Similarly, in the mid-1950s the advent of space exploration motivated such people to pursue technological careers because they represented the same potential for achievement that entrepreneurship provided for their nineteenth century counterparts.[13] But, more realistically what we would *like* to do may be different from what we actually do because of limitations stemming from ability, aptitude, or motivation.

SELF-CONCEPT

Theoretically, individuals implement their self-concepts by pursuing careers that will allow for self-expression. The **self-concept** perspective seeks to answer the questions—Who am I? What is possible for me? Where do I belong? People seek occupations that will be compatible with their self-concepts and will allow these concepts to become reality by permitting them to play the roles they want to play. Basic considerations underlying the self-concept approach were delineated by Super as follows:[14]

As a result of varying interests, abilities, and personalities, individuals may qualify for a number of occupations. And the requirements of occupations are usually flexible enough to accommodate various individuals.

Continuous change and adjustment characterizes people's self-concepts, preferences, and competencies. This process, which constitutes an individual's career pattern, is a function of family socioeconomic level, mental ability, personality characteristics, and opportunities to which the person is exposed. One's career development can be guided partly by nurturing one's interests and abilities and partly by developing one's self-concept. Implementing a self-concept is a compromise between individual and social factors and between perceived self-concept and reality, which is carried out by playing roles. Thus, career satisfactions depend on the degree to which an individual finds outlets for his or her abilities, interests, personality traits, and values.

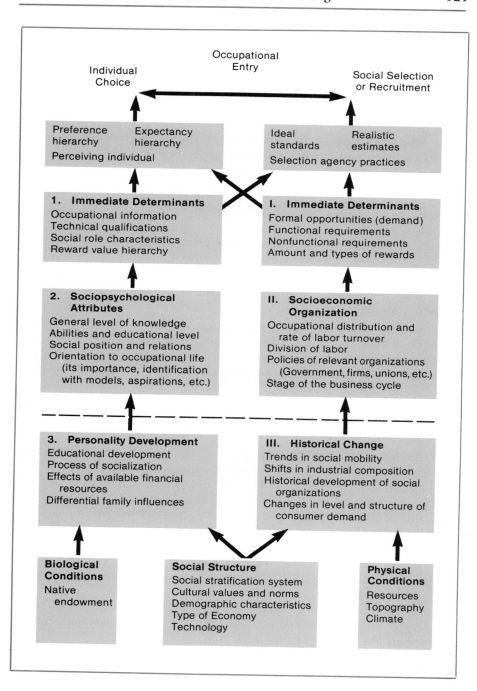

Figure 17.4
A Model of Occupational Choice

Source: Peter M. Blau, John W. Gustad, Richard Jesson, Herbert S. Parnes, and Richard Wilcox "Occupational Choices: A Conceptual Framework," *Industrial and Labor Relations Review, 9* (July 1956), p. 534 Copyright by Cornell University. All rights reserved. Used with permission.

The self-concept approach contends that a person needs to see himself or herself as unique and at the same time be aware of his similarities to others. The individual needs to develop an accurate perspective about his or her abilities and potentials, the ideal self, the discrepancy between the two, and a willingness to change life-style aspirations.[15]

CAREER STAGES

Hall and Nougaim in their study of young AT&T managers found evidence to support a concept of career stages. They described the following career stages:

1. *Pre-work*—when an individual develops credentials and seeks employment.

2. *Establishment*—when initially a new employee gains recognition and becomes established in an organization. The more successful managers, they found, were able, from the outset, to cope effectively with the insecurity and uncertainty in working as a new employee.

3. *Advancement*—the point at which a person is most concerned with moving up and mastering the organization. Achievement and esteem needs are highest at this stage.

4. *Maintenance*—when an attempt is made at stabilization. Once an incumbent had cues that he or she was nearing the advancement limit, there might be less concern to compete, and successful incumbents would help younger people grow in the organization.

5. *Retirement*—when the primary career either ends or is diverted to other endeavors.[16]

Individual Career Planning

Studies of career planning have found that most people are remarkably passive and reactive in letting the work environment determine the course of their careers.[17] But, individuals' values, objectives, and expectations can strongly influence the direction and success of their activities. In other words, as the title of one book admonishes, "If you don't know where you're going, you'll probably end up somewhere else."[18] Most of us are like Alice in Wonderland. We spend so much of our lives working *at* something that we fail to take the time to plan to work *toward* something. In this next section we shall present a strategy for planning a career—a kit of tools for working *toward* something in life.

The author teaches a course in career planning to mid-level managers. As a project students are required to prepare a comprehensive and personal career plan. The elements of the plan appear in Figure 17.5.

The following discussion of each of the elements of this model (career plan) should help students understand how to prepare a career plan and

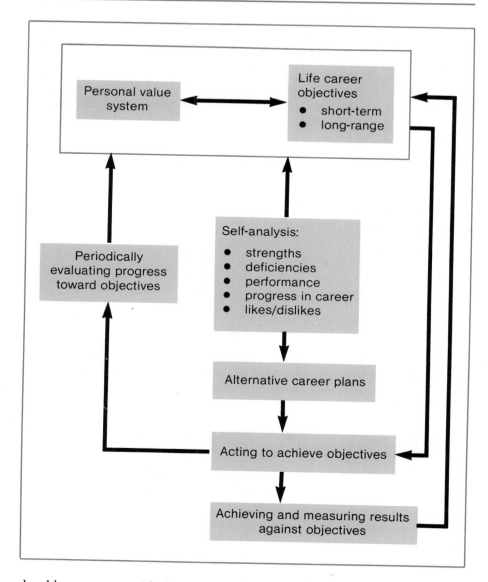

Figure 17.5
Individual Career-Planning
Model

should serve as a guide for personnel staff people to counsel employees in career planning.

PERSONAL VALUES SYSTEM

Values provide a frame of reference that enable an individual to grow. Zaleznik claims they help an individual achieve pleasure and self-respect because the elements of wish and appraisal are united in values.[19] In a broader sense, Rokeach claims that "Values are multifaceted standards that guide conduct in a variety of ways."[20] Although there are values generic to society in general and to a particular time (e.g., patriotism during World War II), value systems are highly individual. Thus it becomes necessary for each person to establish his or her own particular set of values. The process consists of a series of steps: exploration, identification, clarification, and analysis.

EXPLORATION.   In the career-planning course a series of warm up exercises are used to compare and contrast students' perceptions of their values. At this stage the purpose is to stimulate thinking about one's values and produce an awareness that each possesses a complex set of values. By completing sentences like:

> I am . . .
> My most cherished possession . . .
> Success is . . .
> If I died tomorrow . . .

students think about and then discuss their opinions of specific personal values.

IDENTIFICATION.   To identify values specifically, students begin to order them or accord them levels of priority. Rokeach's Value Survey is useful here because it requires the student to rank-order a series of 36 instrumental (idealized modes of behavior, for example, ambitious, capable) and terminal (idealized end-states, for example, a comfortable life, freedom) values.[21] By this process students begin to recognize which of their values are most important to them.

CLARIFICATION.   Clarification of values requires a distinction between a true or full value and a value indicator. **Value indicators** are the same as Rokeach's instrumental values. They include goals, purposes, aspirations, attitudes, interests, feelings, and so on, and they are often confused with our true values. A yardstick for determining whether a person holds a full value consists of the following seven criteria:

Choosing:	1. freely
	2. from alternatives
	3. after thoughtful consideration of the consequences of each alternative
Prizing:	4. cherishing, being happy with the choice
	5. willing to affirm the choice publicly

Acting: 6. doing something with the choice

7. repeatedly, in some pattern of life.[22]

Raths, Harmin, and Simon maintain that *all* seven of these criteria must be met for a value to be a full value. And, if a value has been affirmed as a full value by having met the seven preceding criteria, it follows as a matter of course that the particular value will contribute to and enhance a person's total growth toward the ideals and objectives that he has chosen for himself.[23]

ANALYSIS.   Finally, the student intuitively analyzes those values that were clarified as being full values. At this step, there is an attempt to ascertain the *origin(s)* of the value. Perhaps it was derived from family or religious background, or possibly it was a result of peer influence, or reading. Regardless of the origin, determining the roots of the value produces greater insight into its meaning. Then each student answers the questions: Are my values viable today? Are they compatible with or supportive of my future growth? These values then become the philosophical basis for establishing life/career objectives.

SETTING PERSONAL OBJECTIVES

Personal objectives are stated as short-term (one year) or long-range (five or more years) aspirations. The importance of a thorough exploration of one's values becomes evident at this point. For instance, the individual who values a family relationship, but who seeks high pay through a job that requires extensive travel, may want to reassess the trade-offs. Many students who are disillusioned with their present situation state a job change as being their prime objective. Engineers, especially, who are not doing well in their present jobs are advised by Thompson, Dalton, and Kopelman to relocate before they reach age 40.[24] One researcher pointed out that the half-life (a useful measure for estimating obsolescence of an engineer) has declined from 12 years in 1940 to 5 years today.[25] These factors will force young business people, nonengineers included, to think in terms of serial careers. Anderson predicts that the average business school graduate will change jobs six or seven times during his or her career.[26] Hence, conflicts and decisions regarding what a person is presently doing and what he or she wants to do are the essential first steps in setting personal objectives.

In the career-planning course, students are required to quantify their objectives and include a measure of their attainment. They must also describe how they arrived at their objectives. The objective-setting process requires reducing them to writing. The importance of *written* objectives cannot be overemphasized. By expressing them in writing one becomes committed to their attainment; individuals with written objectives have a harder time rationalizing a failure to accomplish and are more inclined to make an effort to ensure their fulfillment. In recognition of the dynamic nature of the work world, students are asked to develop alternative objectives and to anticipate contingency plans to meet them.

An essential aspect of the career-planning process is the exchange (among students, employees' peers, family, or friends) of objectives, plans, and experience. This is critical to the career-planning experience and has benefits beyond the setting of objectives. Lippitt contends that:

> The "sharing" parts of the design are aimed at revealing one's self to others and through "joint sharing" to generate more self-growth goals than one could achieve through self-insight alone. This gradual revelation of self, during one or more sessions, builds trusting relationships as well as acceptance of self and others.[27]

But what of the individual who has no idea of the direction he or she wants to take in a career? More people than one would suspect face this dilemma. Not only young people seeking to enter their first careers, but plateaued mid-life executives and middle-aged women whose children are grown also seek career information. Fortunately, an abundance of career awareness information is available. A sampling of sources is listed below.

1. *Intuitive exercises.*   Preliminary to consulting available career-information sources a person would be well advised to narrow his or her options. A primary constraint, of course, would be one's educational, physical, and skills limitations. Obviously, a person cannot be a computer programmer without a knowledge of computer languages. But someone seeking a vocation can find some answers in previous work experiences that produced the greatest satisfactions or the greatest dissatisfactions. Some of the author's students have been aided by this simple exercise: they consider the many experiences they have had in their lives and they make two lists. In one they list the experiences they liked (experienced with joy) and in the other the ones they did well (experienced success). Then they compare the "liked" and "did well" lists and isolate any items that appear on both lists. This could give some indication of the direction an individual might take.

2. *Books and periodicals.*   These materials on careers are excellent sources of information. *The Occupational Outlook Handbook* published annually by the Bureau of Labor Statistics (U.S. Department of Labor) describes occupations, entry requirements, projected earnings, and the outlook for employment in each occupation. A similar reference, the *Encyclopedia of Careers and Vocational Guidance,* describes over 600 occupations.

   The Bureau of Labor Statistics also publishes the *Occupational Outlook Quarterly,* which includes articles of interest to job seekers and career counselors and usually includes how-to items. Individual career pamphlets available through the BLS and from specific professional associations (e.g., nursing, legal, sales, information sciences, engineering, and many others) describe particular careers.

Self-help guides are available commercially and are used by a few organizations in their career-planning programs. These guides or workbooks serve to help people decide what career they want to pursue and they aid them in setting objectives along these lines. Following is a sampling:

a. *Career Dimensions I and II* by Walter Storey (Croton-on-Hudson, N.Y.: General Electric Company, 1976).

b. *How to Decide: A Guide for Women* by Nelle Scholz, Judith Prince, and Gordon Miller (Princeton, N.J.: College Entrance Examination Board, 1975).

c. *The Three Boxes of Life—And How To Get Out of Them* by Richard N. Bolles (Box 7123, Berkeley, Calif., 94707: Ten Speed Press, 1978).

d. *The Inventurers: Excursions in Life and Career Renewal* by Janet Hagberg and Richard Leider (Reading, Mass.: Addison-Wesley Publishing Company, Inc., 1978).

e. *Career Planning: Freedom to Choose* by Bruce Shertzer (Boston, Mass.: Houghton Mifflin Company, 1977).

f. *Self-Assessment and Career Development* by John P. Kotter, Victor A. Faux, and Charles McArthur (Englewood Cliffs, N.J.: Prentice-Hall, Inc., 1978).

3. *Counseling Centers.* Counseling centers that serve individuals with career needs now operate in nearly every major city of the country and at many institutions of higher learning. The Catalyst Organization, devoted to providing educational and career information to college-trained women, listed 127 resource or counseling centers in 30 states (as of May 1975). In 1974 an American Institute of Research survey described 367 career-counseling programs nation-wide.[28]

4. *Computerized information.* A U.S. government document, *Computer-Based Guidance Systems*, gives an overview of the computerized information available on career planning.[29] Various systems provide data on selected occupations and the outlook for them, and some even allow an individual to estimate his or her potential for a given occupation.

The Educational Resources Information Center (ERIC), which is coordinated by the National Institute of Education, a division of the U.S. Department of Education, is a clearinghouse for all kinds of educational information including data on careers. Monthly indexes of more than 750 journals list information that is available in microfiche form at more than 600 locations throughout the country.[30]

INDIVIDUAL DEVELOPMENT PLANS

Personal objectives are put into action through an individual development plan. Students (or employees) analyze the strengths that will help them meet objectives and identify shortcomings that will be drawbacks. The next step is specifying what they will do to overcome their shortcomings and preserve their strengths. Reif and Newstrom recommend the development of a set of contingency plans.[31] Too often, in developing career plans, individuals chart only one path because they assume their present employers will move them up a career ladder based on superior performance. Or else they are resigned to being locked into a particular career path. The contingency-planning model for career development describes four phases that help an individual set and eventually attain career objectives. They include: conducting a rigorous situational analysis of self, career opportunities, and career obstacles; setting career objectives; developing realistic plans; and reviewing progress toward their achievement. The career-planning scheme in Figure 17.5 parallels Reif and Newstrom's model.

Finally, there is a myriad of possible activities that individuals can engage in to improve the chances of attaining their objectives. The following checklist can serve as a point of departure for discussing individual development plans.[32]

Checklist—Programs for
Individual Development Planning

_____ Professional reading strategy
_____ Membership in professional associations
_____ Job-related training programs
      _____ Outside seminars
      _____ In-house programs
      _____ Correspondence courses
_____ General development programs
      _____ Advanced degree work
      _____ Professional certification
      _____ Management development programs
_____ Civic and community activities
_____ Personal affiliations (networking)[33]
_____ On-the-job development
      _____ Coaching
      _____ Counseling
      _____ Job rotation assignments
      _____ Special projects
      _____ Observation
      _____ Career ladders

Cost-Benefit Analysis

It may be difficult to isolate the costs of career planning because this activity is integrated with human resource planning and development and performance appraisal. So the direct costs, for example, career counselors, materials, and computer time for plotting career paths, are a small proportion of the total cost.

Benefits may also be indirect. Career commitment; greater competence of people; upward mobility of women, minorities, and handicapped as a result of career planning may also be the consequence of other activities of which career planning is an integral part.

Summary

Careers are individual work-related experiences that span a lifetime. Since they take place within organizations they are managed through programs that select, develop, and move people through the hierarchy. Career planning is the individual process of choosing one's occupation and planning the path one will follow.

The impetus for organizational career-planning programs stems from Affirmative Action and a desire to develop and retain managerial talent. A model program includes employee self-analysis, performance appraisal, identification of potential, and career pathing to balance individual employee aspirations with organizational needs.

Theoretically, individuals choose careers through the influences of personal attributes, culture, and economic circumstances. Each of these creates a unique decision-making situation. They also seek careers that will allow expression of their self-concept. Once in a career, one progresses through the stages of establishment, advancement, maintenance, and retirement.

There is little evidence that individuals attempt to plan their careers or that organizations offer encouragement in this effort. But in recent years people have had second thoughts about their lives and careers. They have become concerned about the lack of promotability or they have been displaced as a result of economic recession and have had to change direction. Students in career-planning programs analyze their personal values, develop life/career objectives that are compatible with their values, and analyze their personal strengths and deficiencies in order to prepare contingency strategies to achieve their objectives.

Key Terms

career
career development
career management
career planning
career pathing

differentialist
developmental view
self-concept
values
value indicators

Review Questions

1. How would you define career? Career development? Career management? Career planning?

2. What is the individual employee's role in organizational career-planning programs?

3. Discuss the basic elements of an individual career plan.

4. What resources are available to a career counselor in advising employees regarding career choice?

5. What are the contributions of career-planning theory?

Discussion Questions

1. How can a small organization with only one or two levels in the hierarchy have a career-planning program?

2. Argue for or against the position that organizational career planning should be confined to managers.

3. In organizational career planning, what organizational needs should be considered? How can employee aspirations be accommodated while ensuring, at the same time, that these needs are satisfied?

4. Develop at least three career objectives for yourself.

5. If organizations decide on the promotions given their employees, how much control can an individual have over his or her career? What are the methods an individual can use to guide his or her own career?

Alice Miller was good, there was no doubt about that. She had an MBA from Stanford, graduating in the top one percent of her class. She was capable, hard-nosed, ambitious, and quite good in her interpersonal job relations. Some men didn't like the idea of a female boss, but Alice could get them to like it.

Her company, Matrix Systems, Inc., was a large conglomerate with over 35,000 employees. They had hired Alice right out of Stanford for two reasons: she was about as good a prospect as the company's recruiters had ever seen; and the company, which had extensive defense contracts, was under court order to cease various discriminatory practices in hiring, one of which was not hiring enough female workers and managers.

Within three months, Alice showed that she was a very high-potential employee. Matrix then quietly placed her on their fast track for promotions, or, in the company grapevine, on the crown-prince track. When Alice got on the fast track, only four young males, all with excellent potential, were on this track.

In her third year at Matrix, Alice was put in charge of a top secret, highly technical government contract involving laser applications. The technology was so advanced that only a handful of scientists really understood what was going on, and about half of them worked for Matrix. Most of the others worked for a smaller and quite aggressive outfit called Trilinear Systems, Inc.

About three months after Alice was put in charge of this project her boss was startled one day to receive seven resignations from key technical people working on the contract. If these people left, there was no way that Matrix could fulfill its contract with the government. Worse, a bit of quick checking suggested to Mr. Baker, the boss, that the seven had all applied for jobs at Trilinear Systems, and this company was seriously thinking of hiring them.

Mr. Baker interviewed all seven employees, all of whom were brilliant and talented people. In the end, he figured out that what they were mad about was the crown-princess problem. They really had no complaints about Alice; indeed, as one of them said, "She's the best boss I ever had!" But what they did object to was the idea that Alice was going to be promoted much faster than they were even though every one of them felt that he or she was equally as competent as Alice. If the company was going to play games with crown princesses, then they would go elsewhere and see if they couldn't become winners too. Two of the seven employees who resigned were women, and one was oriental.

Problems

1. What should Mr. Baker do? Be specific.

2. What should Alice do? Remember, it's hard to stay on the fast track when you're a loser, and she will end up a big loser in this situation.

3. Is it a good idea to have crown princesses and fast tracks for minorities and females? Why or why not?

4. Matrix has 10 levels of management in its organization. If it hired talented people at the lowest level and they spent five years in that level learning the job, it would take 50 years to get to the top. What besides the fast-track/crown-prince option does Matrix have?

Case Problem 1

THE CROWN PRINCESS

Case
Problem 2

THE DISTANT
RESUME

You know by now that everyone has his or her resume. If you don't have one yet, you will soon. This document states what you are and what kinds of training and experience you have had.

Think about yourself carefully, including in particular what you hope to become. Now, prepare your own resume for 20 years from today. Indicate clearly what jobs you have held in these past 20 years. Show what these jobs involved in terms of work and knowledge. Show your salaries for each job as well as your responsibilities. If you took some time off to do something besides work, indicate this, and tell us why you did such things.

Now, in 2000 or 2001, did you achieve what you hoped to achieve? Was it worth it?

Problem

Stick this projected 20-year resume away someplace and forget it. When the 20 years are up take another look at it. If you're within 1 percent of what actually happened, write your old prof and demand an A. If not, you may have learned something older people already know. Life is full of surprises, both good and bad. We hope yours were good.

Notes

1. From Lewis Carroll, *Alice's Adventures in Wonderland* (New York: Random House, 1946), pp. 71–72.

2. Douglas T. Hall, *Careers in Organizations* (Pacific Palisades, Calif.: Goodyear, 1976), p. 4.

3. Ibid.

4. Thomas G. Gutteridge, "Commentary: A Comparison of Perspectives," in Lee Dyer, ed., *Careers in Organizations: Individual Planning and Organizational Development* (Ithaca, N.Y.: New York State School of Industrial and Labor Relations, 1976), p. 39.

5. Figure 17.1 is partially based on research in career planning conducted by Dr. James Walker of Towers, Perrin, Forster and Crosby. See James W. Walker, "Individual Career Planning: Managerial Help for Subordinates," *Business Horizons*, February 1973, pp. 65–72.

6. John B. Miner, "The Real Crunch in Managerial Manpower," *Harvard Business Review*, November–December 1973, pp. 146–58.

7. George T. Milkovich, John C. Anderson, and Leonard Greenhalgh, "Organizational Careers: Environmental, Organizational, and Individual Determinants," in Lee Dyer, ed., *Careers in Organizations*, p. 27.

8. Alfred W. Hill, "Career Development—Who Is Responsible?" *Training and Development Journal*, May 1976, pp. 14–15.

9. Walter D. Storey, "Self-Directed Career Planning at General Electric Company," in Symposium on Organizational Career Development: State of the Practice. (Presented at the Thirty-Sixth Annual Academy of Management Meeting, August 1976), pp. 14ff.

10. Roger E. Hawkins, "Career Planning at Celanese," in Symposium on Experiential Approaches to Career Assessment and Planning (presented at the Thirty-Seventh Annual Academy of Management Meeting, Orlando, Florida, August 1977).

11. John Van Maanen, ed., *Organizational Careers: Some New Perspectives* (New York: John Wiley, 1977), pp. 5–6. For a more detailed discussion of differential theory see: A. Roe, "Early Determinants of Vocational Choice," *Journal of Counseling Psychology*, April 1957, pp. 212–17, and J. L. Holland, *Making Vocational Choices: A Theory of Careers* (Englewood Cliffs, N.J.: Prentice-Hall, 1973).

12. Van Maanen, *Organizational Careers*, p. 6. For a more detailed discussion of the developmental view see: D. E. Super, R. Starishevsky, N. Matlin, and J. P. Jordan, *Career Development: Self Concept Theory* (Princeton, N.J.: Princeton College Entrance Examination Board, 1963), and E. Ginsberg et al., *Occupational Choice: An Approach to a General Theory* (New York: Columbia University Press, 1951).

13. Samuel H. Osipow, *Theories of Career Development*, 2nd ed. (New York: Appleton-Century-Crofts, 1973), p. 297.

14. D. E. Super, "A Theory of Vocational Development," *American Psychologist*, August 1953, pp. 189–90.

15. John J. Pietrofesa and Howard Splete, *Career Development: Theory and Research* (New York: John Wiley, 1972), p. 25.

16. Hall, *Careers in Organizations*, pp. 54–55.

17. Anne Roe and Rhoda Baruch, "Occupational Changes in Adult Years,"

Personnel Administration, July–August 1967, pp. 26–32.

18. David Campbell, *If You Don't Know Where You're Going, You'll Probably End Up Somewhere Else* (Niles, Ill.: Argus Communications, 1974).

19. Abraham Zaleznik, Gene W. Dalton, and Louis B. Barnes, *Orientation and Conflict in Career* (Boston: Harvard University Graduate School of Business Administration, Division of Research, 1970).

20. Milton Rokeach, *The Nature of Human Values* (New York: Free Press, 1973), p. 13.

21. Ibid., pp. 28ff.

22. L. E. Raths, M. Harmin, and S. Simon, *Values and Teaching* (Columbus, Ohio: Charles E. Merrill, 1966).

23. Maury Smith, *A Practical Guide to Value Clarification* (La Jolla, Calif.: University Associates, 1977), p. 13.

24. Paul Thompson, Gene Dalton, and Richard Kopelman, " 'But What Have You Done for Me Lately'—The Boss," *IEEE Spectrum,* October 1974, pp. 85–89.

25. Samuel S. Dubin, "Obsolescence or Lifelong Education: A Choice for the Professional," *American Psychologist,* May 1972, pp. 486–97.

26. Stephen D. Anderson, "Planning for Career Growth," *Personnel Journal,* May 1973, pp. 357–62.

27. Gordon L. Lippitt, "Developing Life Plans," *Training and Development Journal,* May 1970, pp. 2ff.

28. Alan D. Entine, "The Mid-Career Counseling Process," *Industrial Gerontology,* Spring 1976, pp. 105–6.

29. *Computer-Based Vocational Guidance Systems* (Washington, D.C.: U.S. Government Printing Office, 1969).

30. Neale Baxter, "Ask ERIC," *Occupational Outlook Quarterly,* Spring 1977, pp. 18–21.

31. William E. Reif and John W. Newstrom, "Career Development by Objectives," *Business Horizons,* October 1974, pp. 5–10.

32. Checklist based on a paper by Donald P. Crane, "An Experimental Program in Career Planning" in the *Proceedings of the Thirty-fifth Annual Meeting of the Academy of Management.* (New Orleans, La., August 1975), pp. 31–33.

33. Networking is the function of establishing a personal support system (network) of a group of individuals a person recognizes as having some unique ability or talent he or she might have a need of in the future. Generally a network includes people from different professions in different organizations, and from scattered locations. See Richard I. Lyles III, "Networking," *Training,* July 1975, p. 39.

Section Five

MAINTAINING THE WORK FORCE

In this section we consider the necessity for maintaining an efficient and effective work force by rewarding the accomplishment of or movement toward objectives, retaining valuable talent, and sustaining and improving the favorable conditions within an organization.

Pay is important to employees not only for what it can buy but also for the status it represents in society. Because employees frequently measure their relative worth in financial terms, they are concerned about the absolute amount of their compensation and how it compares to that of others doing similar work. Compensation can be a great source of dissatisfaction when employees feel they are underpaid or not recognized for the contributions they make to an organization. Consequently, compensation management maintains personnel effectiveness by attracting needed skills, retaining competent employees, and rewarding performance.

Executive compensation is treated separately because wage rates are essentially based on job requirements rather than qualifications, while salaries (executive compensation) are more a function of individuals' capabilities.

Benefits and services afford employees protection against loss of pay that might result from sickness or injury, compensated time off for leisure pursuits, continued income after retirement, and services that might be too costly to provide for themselves.

Finally, employees function in a safe and healthy work environment under safety and hygiene programs instituted by their union and/or company.

Chapter Eighteen
Compensation Management

Stanley Klibert, attorney-at-law, had just entered his office when he noticed water seeping from under the door of his private bathroom. Something was wrong with the toilet and it was overflowing. He promptly dialed the building superintendent and, with a tone of urgency in his voice, he pleaded, "For goodness sake, get someone up here quick. My toilet won't stop flushing and it's ruining my new carpet!"

Within five minutes a plumber arrived and promptly corrected the problem which, fortunately, was minor. Mr. Klibert profusely thanked the plumber for his prompt response and offered to pay him for his services. The plumber drew up an invoice that read: "Toilet repair—for services rendered—sixty dollars," and handed it to Mr. Klibert. With a look of shock and a tone of exasperation in his voice, he exclaimed, "Good grief, man! This is ridiculous! Sixty dollars for five minutes work is scandalous!"

And the plumber responded, "It's not the length of time, Mr. Klibert, it's knowing what to do that counts. . . ."

Interrupting, Mr. Klibert retorted, "Well, I don't care, this is just a ripoff!"

And the plumber replied, "I can appreciate your position, sir, but this is my normal charge for an office visit."

In utter frustration Mr. Klibert demanded, "How in the world can you justify such a charge?" and the plumber, with little hesitation answered, "Ten dollars is for the labor, and fifty is knowing the right thing to do."

LEARNING OBJECTIVES

1. To be familiar with the purposes of compensation.
2. To be familiar with federal legislation that regulates compensation.
3. To know the various job evaluation methods.
4. To be familiar with the methods for assuring internal and external consistency in compensation.
5. To be familiar with the techniques for administering and controlling compensation plans.

Humorous as this situation may sound it does point out some of the problems associated with compensation management. How are wages determined? Why should one occupation be paid higher than another? Perhaps it isn't realistic to pay plumbers the kind of fees lawyers charge. What, then, should be the basis for assigning wages? Compensation is not the sole consideration in choosing an occupation (we discussed the bases for occupational choice in Chapter 17), but it is an important factor in attracting people to an organization and an occupation. It isn't likely that job knowledge alone justifies high wages for plumbers, but it is a major factor in the better-paying occupations.

Compensation practices affect the entire personnel process. An organization's pay rates must be high enough to attract quality candidates, yet labor costs must remain proportionate to revenues if the firm is to continue to function. Properly administered compensation can provide the stimulus for a dynamic personnel program. Employees who feel they are sufficiently compensated for their efforts are stimulated to achieve more. The true challenge of compensation administration is to provide this impetus.

This chapter will explore the purposes of **compensation management** and the alternative methods for determining and controlling pay rates for various classifications. It will also consider alternative forms of compensation for remunerating, motivating, or rewarding employees.

Basic Purposes of Compensation

Compensation programs enable organizations to attract, maintain, and develop the best available talent. Theoretically, compensation can be designed to achieve these purposes, but in practice it rarely accomplishes complete satisfaction in all three areas. Compensation programs perform the following functions.

OBTAIN QUALIFIED TALENT

Organizations find they must pay enough for each job to attract the best available individuals. They compete in the labor market for needed skills; the shorter the supply of a high-demand skill, the higher the price an organization must pay for it. This is compounded by the fact that the most suitable candidates are often already employed, and organizations must offer them higher pay to induce them to leave their present situations.

RETAIN GOOD EMPLOYEES

Organizations want to retain employees who perform well. When workers earn as much as they could elsewhere and pay scales keep pace with the cost of living, employees are likely to remain with their current employers.

PROVIDE EQUAL PAY FOR EQUAL WORK

Equity in compensation is a controversial area. Workers tend to compare their work and pay to similar classifications in other companies and to other classifications within their own organization. An individual's perception of the fairness of his or her relative pay is a major consideration in determining whether that pay is equitable. But viewpoints differ on the factors that should be considered in evaluating the worth of jobs. One employee might think skill is critical, while another worker might rate physical effort more important. Companies view a classification's contribution to the organization as an essential ingredient in pricing the job. In any event, workers tend to be satisfied with their pay when it compares favorably with that of other workers holding similar jobs.

REWARD PERFORMANCE

Pay plans attempt to provide rewards commensurate with employees' contributions, although in practice compensation rarely accomplishes this goal. Such an objective assumes that organizations have correctly established their goals and can objectively assess the impact of employees' achievements on these goals. It further assumes that there is complete economic freedom to disseminate rewards throughout the organization; this situation never occurs, because pay rewards are contingent on factors beyond the control of individual managers. Organizations cannot provide tangible remunerative benefits in a tight economy, despite the achievements of the employees. Nevertheless the notion of *pay for performance* is a sound one and more and more organizations are adopting schemes to pay employees commensurately with their contributions to the firm's objectives.

PROVIDE INCENTIVE

Under certain conditions monetary gain can motivate people to achieve. When pay is a form of reward or recognition for effective job performance, it can encourage employees to strive for higher achievement. Considerable controversy surrounds the concept of pay as a motivator, but studies continue to reveal that **incentive pay** plans can increase productivity and improve efficiency. For example, piece-work incentive plans are well established as motivators in many industries.

Situational Aspects of Compensation Management

A number of situational aspects affect compensation programs. Legislation and geographic location are beyond the control of the wage and salary administrator, but others, including the type of work and internal pay structure, can be influenced by them.

NATURE OF THE DUTIES PERFORMED

The duties of a particular job classification influence its level of pay. Wage rates tend to increase with higher skill requirements, less desirable surroundings, greater physical effort, and the work's relevance to organizational purposes.

LABOR SUPPLY AND DEMAND

The **market theory** of wage determination maintains that the forces of supply (labor seeking employment) and demand (organizations bidding for this resource) interact in the marketplace. When the available supply equals the demand (this state is called equilibrium), the wage level is established. Consequently, a scarce skill that is much in demand commands a higher wage level. Take, for instance, the example of computer programmers in the late 1960s. As organizations converted to electronic data-processing systems, they required more and more programmers. The demand for programmers far outstripped their availability, and organizations had to pay inordinately high wages for their services. In that the higher compensation attracted more individuals to the field, the result was an increase in the availability of programmers. When the supply increased, salaries declined.

RELATIONSHIP TO OTHER CLASSIFICATIONS IN THE STRUCTURE

Organizations attempt to maintain a relationship among job classifications. After they establish pay differentials they try to maintain the same degree of difference. If an organization determines that it is proper to have a 30 percent pay difference between helpers and mechanics, then it must administer pay increases so that the same relationship prevails. The gap between classifications is narrowed when across-the-board increases are given. When both helpers and mechanics receive the same increase (e.g., 50 cents an hour), the relationship is upset. Classification relationships tend to get out of balance, thus necessitating their periodic reevaluation and restructure.

THE GOING RATE

The amount being paid in the area or the industry for similar work is the **going rate.** In order to attract and retain employees, an organization must pay at or near prevailing wage for each classification. Compensation administrators who want their organizations to remain competitive in the labor market must have a knowledge of customary pay practices in both the industry and the geographic area.

NATURE OF THE INDUSTRY

Some industries always pay higher wages and salaries than the going rate; for instance, aerospace industries traditionally offer higher pay. When government contracts are awarded to an aerospace company, the firm must attract labor quickly. Also, these companies pay a premium for the instability that characterizes aerospace employment.

AREA PAY PRACTICES

There is a relationship between living costs, which vary from area to area, and average pay rates. Generally speaking, both living costs and pay rates are higher in the North than in the South (according to comparative studies of metropolitan statistical areas) and higher in urban centers than in rural areas. It should not, however, be concluded that pay rates are always in proportion to living costs; they only tend to be. But collectively bargained pay schemes often contain provisions for cost-of-living adjustments (COLA) which tie escalation of the wage scale to the increases in the Consumer Price Index (CPI). Sometimes these adjustments are connected to area CPIs to reflect the variations in cost increases (inflation) from area to area.

PRODUCTIVITY

Recent concern with spiraling living costs has focused attention on improved productivity as a justification for pay increases. Increased efficiency, through automation and improved methods, often enables organizations to pay higher wages. For instance, the national agreement between General Motors and the United Auto Workers contains a wage-improvement provision based on the principle that "to produce more with the same amount of human effort is a sound economic and social objective." Accordingly, GM has agreed to increase employees' pay by a specified amount each year because of increased productivity.

BARGAINING POWER

Although there is no conclusive evidence that union activity causes higher wage rates, it is obvious that some unions have successfully bargained for pay increases for their members. The power forces school of wage theory believes that collective bargaining accelerates wage rises in unionized firms. Opponents of this viewpoint, particularly proponents of the labor market theory, contend that differences between union and nonunion wages can be explained on economic grounds, minimizing the importance of union activity in the wage field.

NATURE OF EMPLOYEES

Recent writings have described the changing nature of employees in American business. *Economic man*, individuals who entered the work force in the postdepression 1940s and 1950s, are primarily concerned with material benefits—the financial resources to provide both necessities and comforts.

Their parents, who suffered deprivations during the Great Depression, impressed upon them the importance of attaining financial success as a fulfillment of life's purpose. Consequently, economic employees are money conscious; they measure their achievement in monetary terms; thus, their basic interest is in the amount of remuneration.

During the 1970s a new breed of employee emerged. This generation is concerned with the form of pay (time off, educational opportunities, housing, recreational facilities, etc.) rather than the amount. Success for them is viewed in terms of satisfying higher-order needs such as self-esteem and fulfillment. Their need for money and the things it could buy has generally been satisfied. Because their principal interest is in human relations, this generation is regarded as *social man*. For people working for social reasons, the nature and relevance of the work, and its contribution to society's welfare take priority over affluence. How the philosophy of this new breed will affect compensation administration remains to be seen. However, conjecture points to the probability that social man will emphasize form rather than amount of income.

BENEFITS

The concept of total compensation considers both direct and indirect forms of pay.[1] Fringe benefits (e.g., insurances, pensions, profit sharing) can represent as much as 60 percent of an employee's pay. If one considers the total compensation package, remuneration may be more lucrative than that which the direct wage reflects. The recessions of the 1970s shifted the emphasis toward benefits improvements in lieu of wage increases. Thus, appropriate comparisons of compensation should include benefits. A detailed discussion of benefits is included in Chapter 20.

LEGISLATION

Various laws and federal regulations influence pay scales and the administration of compensation plans. Pertinent federal legislation and government directives concerning compensation are outlined below. State regulations tend to follow federal laws and for this reason they are not discussed.

WALSH-HEALY PUBLIC CONTRACTS ACT OF 1936 (AMENDED IN 1942). The act permits regulation of wages, hours, and working conditions of workers employed on government contracts exceeding $10,000. It influences the general improvement of labor standards. Companies must pay workers covered by the act at least the minimum wage paid employees working in the area in similar jobs and in similar industries. (The Secretary of Labor determines prevailing community rates through public hearings.) The act also requires organizations to pay covered employees time-and-a-half for all hours in excess of 8 in a day or 40 per week (whichever is greater). It prohibits the use of child or prison labor. The government can penalize violators of the act by canceling their contracts and placing them on a blacklist that makes them ineligible for government contracts for three years following the breach.

FAIR LABOR STANDARDS ACT OF 1938. Commonly referred to as the Wage and Hour Act, the Fair Labor Standards Act (FLSA) is aimed at eliminating substandard employment conditions in establishments engaged in interstate commerce. The rationale of the Act is to eliminate labor conditions that are detrimental to the well-being of workers and to eliminate any unfair competition based upon these conditions. Essentially, FLSA is protective legislation that brings the federal government squarely into the arena of employee welfare. It establishes a minimum wage and requires firms to pay nonexempt employees time-and-one-half if they work more than 40 hours in a week. There are also provisions regulating child labor. FLSA is particularly significant legislation in that it covers approximately 43 million workers in over a million establishments.

Initially, FLSA coverage was determined by the nature of the work. If employees were engaged in jobs that affected commerce, they were covered by the FLSA. In 1961 an amendment brought additional employees under its coverage through the enterprise concept. Under this amendment the act covers all firms engaged in a retail, wholesale, or service business with annual sales exceeding a million dollars, or those purchasing goods for resale valued at over a quarter of a million dollars.

Minimum wages are also included in FLSA. Originally, Congress voted a base hourly wage of 25 cents (in 1938), and the figure has been raised more than a dozen times since then, most recently to $3.35 on January 1, 1981.

Compensation managers frequently make a distinction between **exempt** and **nonexempt** salaried employees. This distinction refers to exemption from the minimum wage and overtime provisions of the FLSA. Certain executives, administrators, and professional employees are exempt because of the level of their salaries or the nature of their duties. Employees who manage an establishment or department, direct other workers, hold discretionary powers, and hire, promote, and discharge, may be exempt if they spend no more than 20 percent of their time on nonmanagerial duties. But this rule does not apply if they earn over $200 per week. Administrative and professional exemptions are based on similar rules, except that the nature of the work is, of course, different. The distinguishing requirements of administrators' exemptions are that their work be concerned with management policies or general business operations, that it require discretion and independent judgment, and that it be only generally supervised. The work for professional exemptions calls for intellectual and varied duties that require discretion and judgment and are of sufficient complexity to necessitate prolonged formal study in a scientific field.

FLSA does not have specific record-keeping requirements, but employers are well advised to maintain the following information in the event a wage-and-hour investigation is called:

1. *Personal data*—name, address, birth date if under 19, and job classification.
2. *Time records*—hours worked daily and weekly and absences for each employee.
3. *Payroll records*—dates of payment, pay periods, daily and weekly earnings, bonuses, deductions from wages, and basis on which payments are made.
4. *Other information*—if any employees work at home, additional information on the amount and kind of work distributed to and collected from them.

EQUAL PAY ACT OF 1963.   This act is considered an amendment to the FLSA. It was enacted principally to protect women from discriminatory pay practices, but it affords the same protection to men. This law prohibits employers from paying a lower wage rate to one sex for the same work on jobs requiring equal skill, effort, and responsibility under similar working conditions. However, the act does not preclude paying one sex more than the other when the differential is based on a system of merit, seniority, quantity and quality of work, or any factor other than sex. Yet, the EEOC is not satisfied with this narrow definition of wage determination. It feels that compensation should be determined according to the **comparable worth** of jobs in an organization, based on a set of criteria that are used to measure this value to the organization. An article by Ruth Blumrosen has had significant impact on this issue.[2] Her thesis is that job segregation and wage discrimination are not separate problems, but rather are intimately related. Her thesis is being tested in a series of lawsuits that are working their way to the U.S. Supreme Court. A case in point is a group of Denver nurses who sought to have their work compared to the work of other professionals in (different) male-occupied jobs to establish their relative value (*Lemons* v. *City and County of Denver*). And at Westinghouse Electric's Trenton, New Jersey, light bulb plant 42 female employees along with the International Union of Electrical, Radio and Machine Workers (IUE) charged that the company had set lower wage rates for job classifications predominantly filled by females than for those filled chiefly by males. One example was the female assembly line workers who were paid lower than male truck drivers, even though the jobs were comparable. The final determination of this issue remains to be seen, but those opposed to the Blumrosen thesis contend that the determination of wages by comparison with jobs of entirely different skills would open up a new world in compensation management. This method, they contend, would not be viable without broader legislative mandates than the Equal Pay Act.[3]

MISCELLANEOUS LEGISLATION. The Portal-to-Portal Act, passed in 1947, protects employers against workers' claims for portal-to-portal pay. In 1944, John L. Lewis won for his coal miners a Supreme Court case that recognized the validity of portal-to-portal pay claims. The court's decision led to a flood of claims by workers to collect back portal-to-portal pay. The act stipulates that companies do not have to pay employees for riding, walking, or otherwise traveling to their work place, unless such pay was enumerated in the union-management agreement.

The Classification Act of 1949 established classification grades for civilian government employees—a General Schedule (GS) for professional, scientific, general, and administrative positions; and a Crafts, Protective and Custodial Schedule (CPC) for other positions. The act also created an equitable system for setting and adjusting compensation rates.

The Davis-Bacon Act of 1931 requires that the minimum wage rates paid to employees on federal public works projects of $2,000 or more be at least equal to the prevailing rates and that overtime rates be $1\frac{1}{2}$ times this rate. There are similar provisions relating to government contractors in the Service Contract Act of 1965, and the Miller Act.

In addition, provisions of various titles of the Civil Rights Act and associated executive orders prohibit discriminatory pay practices based on sex, race, creed, color, national origin, religion, or handicap.

STABILIZATION REGULATIONS

During the past several decades compensation practices have been regulated through legislation, directives, and executive orders designed to alleviate adverse economic conditions by deterring inflation and stabilizing living costs.

The Wage and Salary Stabilization Act of 1942 authorized this country's first comprehensive wage and salary controls. Between 1942 and 1947 the act placed upper limits on compensation increases and provided federal policing of the regulation. But the policy did not prohibit promotion or merit increases if they did not lead to price increases.

One of the first policies established by the National War Labor Board was the 1942 Little Steel Formula. Initially applied to workers in the steel industry, it permitted a 15 percent increase in wages that had been previously frozen to stabilize the wartime economy. The policy was later applied industry-wide during the Second World War.

Subsequently, wages have been frozen and/or regulated by legislation or presidential order (e.g., *Defense Production Act of 1950* and *Wage-Price Freezes of 1971–1972*).

With the situational and legal aspects of compensation management in mind, let us turn to the compensation-management process and how it works.

A Framework for the Management of Compensation

Figure 18.1 is a flow diagram of the compensation process. The salary aspects of compensation management are covered in Chapter 19, "Executive Compensation." The following sections of this chapter deal with each element shown in the figure.

JOB DESIGN AND ANALYSIS

Job design is the specification of the job content, methods, and relationships necessary to satisfy organizational, technological, and personal requirements. It is also used to ensure that the work can be performed by

Figure 18.1
The Compensation Process

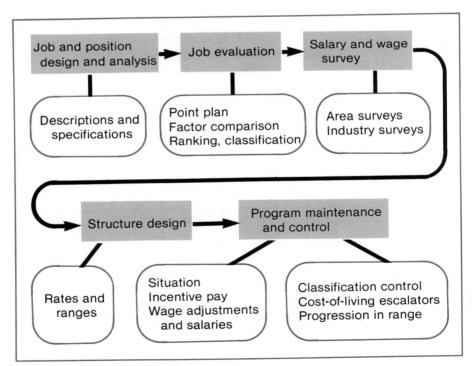

a human being of average intelligence, strength, size, or by a handicapped person (e.g., a blind switchboard operator). Job analysis is the process of identifying (by observation, interview, and study) the significant factors of a job that differentiate it from others. It includes preparing written descriptions of duties, responsibilities, working conditions, and specifications of worker traits necessary for successful job performance. Job analysis as the basis for job description was treated in Chapter 5; here it is viewed as a key element in compensation management.

JOB DESIGN. Organizations use job design to improve the work environment as a means of motivating employees to achieve optimum operation efficiency. This goal may sound idealistic, but there are too many jobs that emphasize only mechanical aspects and inhibit worker effectiveness. Companies must find new approaches to humanize work, especially in production operations. Granted, some tedious tasks cannot be automated and must still be performed by workers, but a scarcity of certain skills and changing employee attitudes toward work are forcing management to find new ways to enrich jobs. When meaningful tasks are added and the job is expanded to include greater responsibility and complexity, job enrichment and, hence, employee satisfaction result. And only redesign can accomplish this objective.

STEPS IN JOB DESIGN. The situation governs the specific approach to job design, but the steps outlined below are generally applicable. Because job design is derived from other personnel functions, job designers vary the order in accomplishing the steps below.

1. Observe job activities (or for new jobs, list the activities to be performed) to identify content, especially the frequency of performance of specific tasks, the relative importance of tasks, and their extent of specialization.

2. Note the job situational factors as described above.

3. Determine workers' psychological and personal characteristics through interviews, tests, and surveys.

4. Analyze methods and procedures necessary to accomplish the job efficiently. Job designers use industrial engineering and operations-research concepts for such analyses.

5. Incorporate job operations into a system.

6. Implement the design. After a trial run, modify the design according to workers' suggestions and then measure the results against a standard.

7. Continuously review the process and encourage worker feedback. These actions form a basis for revision and help assure continued efficiency and employee satisfaction.

JOB ANALYSIS.   Because it provides the basis for job evaluation, job analysis is of key importance in compensation management. One approach, the Position Analysis Questionnaire (PAQ) merits consideration here because it identifies the direct statistical relationship between standardized job analysis data and job values across the world of work.[4] The PAQ is a questionnaire that uses a checklist format to identify 194 elements of job behavior (decision making, public contact, communication) instead of specific tasks or functions. The checklist provides information to determine the extent to which each element relates to the job being analyzed.

Part of the PAQ procedure is the creation of job families described by specific elements of the questionnaire. Job families are groupings of jobs that are homogeneous with respect to job content (e.g., administrative, technical assistance, secretarial, and service positions). The information on the PAQ is computer scored to provide a profile for the job which is, in turn, compared with standard profiles of known job families. In this manner the computer analysis identifies the significant job behaviors and classifies the job. The quantitative characteristics of the PAQ and its feature of grouping jobs by common characteristics and reflecting differences in relative value permit this procedure also to be useful in establishing rates of pay for jobs.[5]

JOB EVALUATION

After completing the job analysis, compensation managers have several important decisions to make. First, they must decide on the **compensable factors** that are pertinent to each job. Then they must decide on the appropriate plan, either ready-made or self-developed, to evaluate the jobs.

DETERMINING COMPENSABLE FACTORS.   In order to develop a basis for understanding the relative value of each job and the opportunity to use the collective knowledge and judgment of other members of the organization, it is necessary to develop a simple and workable procedure. The use of compensable factors that identify certain qualities common to all jobs makes this possible.[6] Patten suggests that the compensable factors be few in number—five or six is ideal—and be sharply differentiated and not overlap.[7] Examples of compensable factors might be knowledge, skill, responsibility, decision making, effort, job conditions. As we shall see in our discussion of evaluation plans, the application of compensable factors varies according to the type of job. Thus different compensable factors would be used for clerical and production jobs.

JOB EVALUATION PLANS.   The purpose of **job evaluation** plans is to achieve and maintain *internal* (within the organization) consistency among classifications. Wage surveys (discussed later in this chapter) serve to attain *external* consistency. Although organizations have used job evaluation plans for many years, opponents continue to voice strenuous objections to them. They are critical of their failure to consider the effect of market forces and employee pressures in establishing wages and their disregard of employee ability and length of service. On the other hand job evaluation has proven to be a consistent method of establishing pay differentials among classifications. Using the same measure to determine the relative worth of each job introduces an element of fairness and objectivity, which helps keep collective-bargaining discussions on a factual rather than emotional basis. Also, with an objective basis for determining the relative worth of jobs, workers have a better understanding of wage relationships and are less confused and disenchanted with compensation programs.

Let us review the basic approaches to job evaluation, which include ranking, job classification, factor comparison, and the point plan. All other methods of job evaluation are variations of these plans.

Ranking Method. Using the **ranking method,** organizations rank jobs from the highest to lowest on the basis of skill, difficulty, contribution to the organization, or any other basis of relative value. The ranking plan is the oldest and simplest job evaluation method, and it is used in small organizations that lack the time and resources to apply more sophisticated methods. Unfortunately, the biases of the evaluators and the personalities of the job holders can influence and distort the rankings.

Job Classification. The **job classification,** or grading method, is a refinement of job ranking. Here organizations categorize jobs by predetermined grades based on the level of skill or responsibility. (The federal civil service system is a typical user of job classification.) Wage administrators assign each job to a class, but they usually organize separate systems for clerical, production, sales, and supervisory jobs. The following grades, for example, might be established for clerical jobs:

Grade I—simple, routine work under close supervision and requiring little initiative or responsibility (examples: file clerk, mail clerk).

Grade II—routine work using simple machines under close supervision and requiring a minimum of independent judgment (examples: duplicating-machine operator, typist, keypunch operator).

Grade III—advanced clerical work involving substantial initiative, discretion, and clerical skill under minimum supervision (examples: clerk-stenographer, payroll clerk, bookkeeper).

Grade IV—supervision of several grade II or III employees, independent judgment in work requiring substantial knowledge of a specialized field such as accounting or complicated calculations (examples: secretary, senior accounting clerk).

Factor Comparison.   Both factor comparison and point plans utilize compensable factors in their operation. To facilitate evaluations utilizing such factors, wage analysts often divide job descriptions into sections that conform to the factors. Generally speaking the factor-comparison method evaluates the monetary value of each compensable factor in a particular job against the established monetary value of the same factor in a benchmark job. Using the job descriptions developed in job analysis, wage analysts follow these basic procedures.

1. They select compensable factors. Compensable factors should reflect the needs and desires of the individual organization and the type of business it conducts. Commonly, organizations use different sets of factors for technical, managerial, clerical, sales, production, and maintenance jobs.

2. They evaluate key jobs. Key, or benchmark, jobs are standards for evaluating all other jobs in the structure, so they must be representative of the duties and responsibilities performed in a cross section of jobs. Once the key jobs have been selected, wage analysts rank them for each compensable factor and evaluate them factor by factor by assigning dollar values to them. The process is more effective if analysts evaluate all key jobs for a single compensable factor before proceeding to the next one. In Table 18.1 several production and maintenance key jobs are evaluated in monetary terms for a single compensable factor on an established scale. The tool-and-die maker rate of $9.60, for example, results from totaling the allocations of $2.55 to mental, $3.26 to skill, $1.10 to physical, $1.83 to responsibility, and $.86 to working conditions.

3. They evaluate remaining jobs. To facilitate this task analysts group jobs by department or by similarity of tasks. They evaluate all jobs on a single compensable factor before evaluating the other factors.

4. They calculate the total value of each job. The rate for each job is the composite of the amounts allotted to all the compensable factors. Even though each job has a dollar value at this point, the procedure should not be confused with job pricing, which is a separate and distinct process. Finally, wage analysts place the evaluated jobs in ascending order, based on total monetary value, and resolve any discrepancies that appear from this ranking.

The Point Plan.   The widely used point-rating method is an extension of factor comparison. After wage analysts establish compensable factors, they assign a weight to each factor based on its relative importance to the eval-

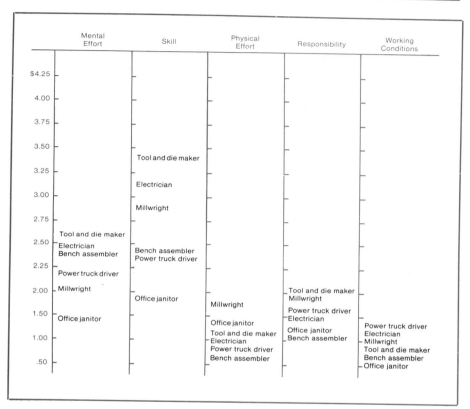

Table 18.1
Factor Comparison—Key Job Evaluation

uation. Then they divide each factor into levels, which are assigned point values. These levels are precisely defined to preclude the necessity for interpolation.

The federal government now uses a system (designated the Factor Evaluation System) that uses a combination of factor comparison and point rating to classify nonsupervisory white-collar jobs.[8] Of all job evaluation plans, the point system has been found to be the most popular. It is generally applied to plant jobs.[9] The United Steelworkers and major steel producers now evaluate production and maintenance jobs below the rank of foreman (a similar method is used for clerical and office jobs) with a plan that considers 12 factors. Each factor, with the maximum number of points, is shown in Table 18.2. This plan was developed by the National Metal Trades Association (now the American Association of Industrial Management) in 1899. It is the oldest and most frequently used point system.

Factor	Maximum Points for Factor
1. Pre-employment training	1.0
2. Employment training and experience	3.2
3. Mental skill	3.5
4. Manual skill	2.0
5. Responsibility for materials	10.0
6. Responsibility for tools and equipment	4.0
7. Responsibility for operations	6.5
8. Responsibility for safety of others	2.0
9. Mental effort	2.5
10. Physical effort	2.5
11. Surroundings	3.0
12. Hazards	2.0
Total possible points	42.2

Table 18.3 shows how the plan defines one of the factors, mental skill, and how it describes each level and assigns numerical classifications. The manual used by the evaluation committee provides the same information on each job. Notice that each factor has a category with a minimum requirement; this base level has no absolute value, because the plan determines only the relative value of jobs.

The job description and evaluation of a mobile crane operator are shown in Figure 18.3 and Table 18.4 as an example of a completed evaluation of a job. Note the structure of the job description; the categorization of information is designed to facilitate evaluation.

WAGE SURVEYS

To remain competitive in the labor market, organizations devise compensation packages with adequate pay levels and benefits that will attract labor and encourage employees to remain with them. Organizations often perform research and wage surveys to determine what adequate pay is. In conducting a **wage survey,** analysts first determine what data to gather. Then they define the labor market and select the sample of firms to survey. Finally, they design and disseminate the questionnaire and compile and analyze the returns.

Consider the mental ability, job knowledge, judgment, and ingenuity required to visualize, reason through, and plan the details of the job without recourse to supervision.

Table 18.3
Point Evaluation Plan
Factor 3—Mental Skill

Code	Job Requires Ability To:	Numerical Classification
A	Perform simple, repetitive routine tasks.	Base (0.0)
	Do simple sorting.	
	Make changes in routine only when closely directed.	
B	Make minor changes in routine or sequence on repetitive jobs involving selection, positioning, and recognition of obvious defects of adjustments where tolerances are liberal.	1.0
C	Perform semi-routine job involving some variety of detail and requiring judgment.	1.6
	Sort material according to size, weight or appearance.	
D	Reason through problems involving set-up and operation of moderately complex equipment. Use considerable judgment in operating equipment.	2.2
	Exercise considerable judgment in selecting and using materials, tools, and equipment in construction, erection, or maintenance work.	
E	Plan and direct the operation of a large complex production unit.	2.8
	Reason through and plan operating problems.	
	Plan work detail from complex blueprints.	
F	Analyze and plan complex nonrepetitive tasks to be performed by skilled workmen.	3.5

PRESURVEY RESEARCH.   Prior to initiating the survey, analysts study the information that is already available. The Bureau of Labor Statistics of the Department of Labor regularly publishes wage data by area, industry, and occupation. Figure 18.2 is a sample page from a BLS Area Wage Survey. Employer associations, state agencies, and private and professional groups (such as the American Society for Personnel Administration) conduct compensation studies and usually publish the results. Local universities and public libraries contain a wealth of information relating to wage surveys;

Figure 18.2
Sample Page From BLS Area Wage Survey

Table A.6. Average hourly earnings of maintenance, toolroom, powerplant, material movement, and custodial workers, by sex, in Atlanta, Ga., May 1980

Sex, occupation, and industry division	Number of workers	Average (mean) hourly earnings (in dollars)
Maintenance, toolroom, and powerplant occupations - men		
Maintenance carpenters	146	8.97
Manufacturing	63	8.70
Nonmanufacturing	83	9.18
Maintenance electricians	537	9.71
Manufacturing	367	9.88
Nonmanufacturing	170	9.35
Maintenance painters	153	8.35
Manufacturing	64	10.22
Maintenance machinists	402	9.71
Manufacturing	306	8.88
Maintenance mechanics (machinery)	705	7.95
Manufacturing	594	7.62
Nonmanufacturing	111	9.73
Maintenance mechanics (motor vehicles)	1,207	9.36
Manufacturing	166	7.90
Nonmanufacturing	1,041	9.59
Public utilities	981	9.64
Maintenance pipefitters	173	10.43
Manufacturing	172	10.42
Millwrights	134	10.84
Manufacturing	126	10.81

Sex, occupation, and industry division	Number of workers	Average (mean) hourly earnings (in dollars)
Material movement and custodial occupations - men		
Truckdrivers	4,100	8.30
Manufacturing	450	5.93
Nonmanufacturing	3,650	8.59
Public utilities	2,029	10.51
Truckdrivers, light truck	437	4.66
Manufacturing	102	5.39
Nonmanufacturing	335	4.44
Truckdrivers, medium truck	1,489	7.12
Manufacturing	167	6.07
Nonmanufacturing	1,322	7.25
Public utilities	454	10.63
Truckdrivers, tractor-trailer	2,042	9.79
Manufacturing	157	5.71
Nonmanufacturing	1,885	10.13
Public utilities	1,443	10.60
Shippers:		
Manufacturing	110	5.66
Receivers	293	6.94
Manufacturing	114	5.81
Shippers and receivers	229	6.31
Manufacturing	196	6.19

Sex, occupation, and industry division	Number of workers	Average (mean) hourly earnings (in dollars)
Material handling laborers:		
Manufacturing	403	5.65
Nonmanufacturing:		
Public utilities	608	8.41
Forklift operators	2,156	6.44
Manufacturing	1,138	6.50
Nonmanufacturing	1,018	6.38
Guards	3,101	3.67
Manufacturing	221	7.55
Nonmanufacturing	2,880	3.37
Guards, class A	177	5.38
Guards, class B	2,924	3.56
Manufacturing	154	7.35
Nonmanufacturing	2,770	3.35
Janitors, porters, and cleaners	4,045	4.03
Manufacturing	718	6.18
Nonmanufacturing	3,327	3.57
Public utilities	163	7.05
Material movement and custodial occupations - women		
Order fillers	1,093	4.41
Manufacturing	285	4.01
Nonmanufacturing	808	4.56

Figure 18.2 (cont.)

Sex,[3] occupation, and industry division	Number of workers	Average (mean[2]) hourly earnings (in dollars)[4]
Maintenance trades helpers	317	6.62
Nonmanufacturing	260	6.35
Public utilities	246	6.41
Tool and die makers	180	10.47
Manufacturing	180	10.47
Stationary engineers	145	8.60
Manufacturing	93	9.83
Nonmanufacturing	52	6.40

Sex,[3] occupation, and industry division	Number of workers	Average (mean[2]) hourly earnings (in dollars)[4]
Warehousemen	623	6.33
Manufacturing	174	5.41
Nonmanufacturing	449	6.69
Public utilities	196	8.11
Order fillers	1,489	8.10
Manufacturing	234	5.29
Shipping packers	612	4.96
Manufacturing	444	4.35

Sex,[3] occupation, and industry division	Number of workers	Average (mean[2]) hourly earnings (in dollars)[4]
Shipping packers	363	4.69
Forklift operators:		
Manufacturing	52	6.35
Janitors, porters, and cleaners	2,923	3.36
Manufacturing	142	4.92
Nonmanufacturing	2,781	3.28
Public utilities	26	6.69

Source: Bureau of Labor Statistics

[1] Standard hours reflect the workweek for which employees receive their regular straight-time salaries (exclusive of pay for overtime at regular and/or premium rates), and the earnings correspond to these weekly hours.

[2] The mean is computed for each job by totaling the earnings of all workers and dividing by the number of workers. The median designates position—half of the workers receive the same or more and half receive the same or less than the rate shown. The middle range is defined by two rates of pay; one-fourth of the workers earn the same or less than the lower of these rates and one-fourth earn the same or more than the higher rate.

[3] Earnings data relate only to workers whose sex identification was provided by the establishment.

[4] Excludes premium pay for overtime and for work on weekends, holidays, and late shifts.

[5] Estimates for periods ending prior to 1976 relate to men only for skilled maintenance and unskilled plant workers. All other estimates relate to men and women.

[6] Data do not meet publication criteria or data not available.

Figure 18.3
Point Evaluation Plan

Reprinted by permission of the
United Steelworkers of America.

Master Job Description and Classification
Bethlehem Steel Company

Department: Mine   Job Title: Mobile Crane Operator   Job Number 815
Sub Division: Date: July 27, 1981

Master Job Description

Primary Function

Operates a powered mobile crane to perform material handling in loading, un-
loading, and construction.

Tools and Equipment

Powered mobile crane and auxiliary equipment such as boom, cables, controls.
Hand tools such as wrenches, hammer.

Materials

Machinery and equipment, structural steel, scrap material, ground, silt, sand,
crushed stone.

Source of Supervision

Mechanical Foreman for work assignment and check on work progress.

Direction Exercised

Determines on-the-job working procedure to those assigned to assist in repairs and
make boom changes when necessary.

Working Procedure

Operates variable hand and foot controls of powered mobile crane to position crane
within plant areas and in operating truck crane over highways with boom detached.

Operates variable hand levers and foot pedals to control the operation of the crane
to perform a variety of work such as:

> Loading and unloading heavy material to or from cars and places
> material in storage area. Working with construction crews and lifting
> and positioning steel, pipe, heavy timber in response to hand signals.

> Using clam-shell bucket or drag line, moving earth on excavation and
> back-fill work and cleaning silt from mill pond.

Rigs up cable as required and uses hand tools such as wrenches, hammer to
mount or detach boom or add section to boom as required.

Figure 18.3 (cont.)

Assists in major repairs to crane or assists by operating crane as required.

Lubricates crane, makes minor repairs and adjustments, and maintains cleanliness of equipment.

The above statement reflects the general details considered necessary to describe the principal functions of the job identified, and shall not be construed as a detailed description of all of the work requirements that may be inherent in the job.

a search of the card catalog or periodical indexes can uncover considerable relevant data. The information gleaned from this preliminary research serves as the foundation for conducting the survey. Table 18.5 lists a number of sources of wage data.

Wage analysts can identify several labor markets. The particular geographic area influences wages because living costs vary from one section or metropolitan area of the country to another. Since these area differentials are a significant consideration in administering compensation, companies usually survey a variety of organizations within their particular geographic area. Some markets may even be international as is the case with scientific personnel.

The industry also influences wage levels, so firms must study their counterparts. For example, synthetic fiber manufacturers located in textile areas with depressed wages must offer significantly higher wages to attract specialized talent from other such producers. The wage patterns within the chemical industry, which produces synthetics, have had more influence on remuneration than area pay practices have had.

QUESTIONNAIRE DEVELOPMENT AND ANALYSIS. To obtain meaningful results from the survey, analysts carefully plan the form and type of data they seek and design the survey instrument to elicit desired responses. Consequently, the jobs they include in the survey must be representative of those in the organization. Analysts can identify job clusters (classifications linked together by technology, process, or custom), lines of progression, or job families (jobs with similar content). If they survey a single job within one of these groups they can obtain information relevant to all other jobs in the group. Also, they need to ensure the compatibility of information among companies. If the same job titles incorporate different duties, their reported rates are meaningless for purposes of comparison. To avoid this pitfall, analysts include a short description of the job's key factors in their question-

Table 18.4
Point Evaluation Plan

Master Job Classification

Job Title: Mobile Crane Operator   Job Number: 815

Factor	Reason for Classification	Code	Classi-fication
1	Pre-Employment Training. This job requires the mentality to learn to:	B	.3
	Exercise judgment in operation of mobile crane servicing construction operations and in loading, unloading and positioning materials.		
2	Employment Training and Experience. This job requires experience on this or related work of:	D	1.2
	13 to 18 months.		
3	Mental Skill.	D	2.2
	Exercises considerable judgment in operating boom-type mobile crane servicing construction operations.		
4	Manual Skill.	C	1.0
	Manipulates multiple variable controls involving a high degree of coordination.		
5	Responsibility for Material.	C	.7
	Close attention required for part of turn to prevent damage to materials such as concrete pipe, structural steel. Breakage or other damage would be variable but would not exceed $100.		
6	Responsibility for Tools and Equipment.	D High	2.0
	Close attention required to prevent damage to crane, cab, cables by lifting loads in excess of equipment limitations or by upset of equipment.		
7	Responsibility for Operations.	C	1.0
	Handles and transports material in construction work. Loads and unloads material in cars, trucks, and storage.		

Table 18.4 (cont.)

Master Job Classification

Job Title: Mobile Crane Operator   Job Number: 815

Factor	Reason for Classification	Code	Classi-fication
8	Responsibility for Safety of Others.	C	.8
	Considerable care and attention required to prevent injury to others in operating powered mobile equipment where others are exposed but probability of accident is low.		
9	Mental Effort.	C	1.0
	Moderate mental and visual application required to operate powered mobile crane involving considerable variety of movement.		
10	Physical Effort.	C	.8
	Moderate physical effort required to operate controls of crane; and to rig cable and to detach or attach boom sections.		
11	Surroundings.	B	.4
	Works outside but protected part of time by cab.		
12	Hazard.	B	.4
	Accident hazard moderate. Exposed to fractures, bruises, and severe cuts sustained in rigging cable or changing boom.		
	Job Class 12	Total	11.8

Reprinted by permission of the United Steelworkers of America.

naires. Many surveying organizations use a *Dictionary of Occupational Titles* (DOT) code number along with their own job title. The DOT code is universally accepted in compensation management circles and helps avoid misinterpretation of job description information.

The basis of pay can be important in interpreting data; high wage rates alone do not assure a competitive edge in the labor market. Consequently, organizations also compare hours of work, availability of overtime,

Source	Type(s) of Data Provided
U.S. Bureau of Labor Statistics	Publishes periodic industry and area wage surveys; occupational wage surveys; average hourly and weekly earnings—establishment data; earnings statistics from current population survey—household data; periodic bulletins, indices; and special bulletins.*
College Placement Council	Quarterly and annual surveys of average starting salaries for college graduates by degree and geographic area.
State Employment Security Commission	Periodic area wage data.
Trade Associations	Industry studies.
Chamber of Commerce of the United States	Special industry and/or area studies.
The Bureau of National Affairs, Inc.	Occasional wage surveys, usually nationwide.
State Department of Industry and Trade	Industry surveys.
Universities—generally in a Bureau of Economic Research	Area and/or industry studies.
Professional societies	Member surveys—ASPA has annual salary study of personnel people.
Local offices of federal agencies	Area surveys—multi-industry—local installations are required to perform comparison surveys.
Various reports of the President, e.g., Employment and Training Report	Usually shows wage statistics for selected occupations.
Private surveys	Data available by industry, area, occupation usually include averages, ranges, quartiles. Examples include: AMA, Endicott Report. Generally available on a subscription basis.

* For a more detailed description of available BLS wage data see: U.S. Department of Labor, Bureau of Labor Statistics: *BLS Measures of Compensation*, Bulletin 1941 (1977) and *A Directory of BLS Studies in Employee Compensation*, 1975. Both are available from the U.S. Government Printing Office, Washington, D.C.

shift-differential pay, premium pay practices, and frequency of pay (weekly or monthly). If they use pay ranges, they usually record the minimum, midpoint, and maximum of the range. Because fringe benefits are a significant part of a compensation package, questionnaires also explore their characteristics, such as the types of benefits and their value (i.e., percent of labor cost).

A thorough survey will inquire into special organizational characteristics that affect wages. Certainly it should record the presence of a union to determine the effect of external influences. Also, the number of hours worked by an organization is a significant factor since it often must pay a premium to offset erratic employment patterns and unstable working conditions. A survey finding confirmed that organizational size and profitability also affect wage scales and must be taken into consideration.[10]

PRICING THE JOB

To establish a wage rate for each job in an organization, wage analysts consider the relative value of the jobs along with external factors such as labor market flexibility. Then organizations establish wage classes on the basis of job evaluations and assign rates or ranges for each class. They use these rates, in turn, as a basis for determining an individual employee's rate of pay.

WAGE CURVES. The relationship between wage rates and job evaluation points can be shown on a curve. Analysts plot the total point value for each job against its proposed wage rate or a current market value as determined by a wage survey. The scattering of points that results has little usefulness to wage administrators, so they draw a simple line or curve that represents a best fit of the points. Figure 18.4 represents a line that shows the relationship between wage rates and point values. Wage analysts can adjust the curve to market rates (from the wage survey), union settlements, legislation, and other situational variables. If companies decide, on the basis of their wage survey, that they are lagging behind their industry, they can adjust their wage rates to become competitive in the labor market. Analysts then modify the slope of the **wage curve** to reflect this adjustment. The broken line in Figure 18.4 depicts a slight adjustment in the wage structure to accommodate changing market conditions.

DETERMINING JOB CLASSES. To facilitate pricing and the subsequent administration of wages, organizations separate jobs into classes, usually on the basis of job evaluation points. All jobs in each class receive approximately equal pay rates or ranges. Management desires or industry practices usually influence the number of classes. Table 18.6 is an example of wage classes

Figure 18.4
Wage Curve

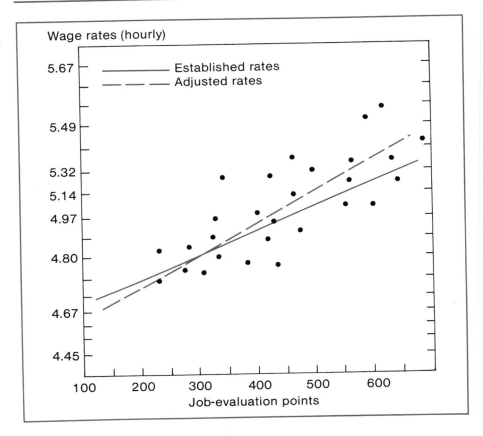

established from job evaluation. Most organizations establish separate job classes for production and maintenance, clerical and office, professional and technical, and sales jobs. Then they determine the hourly rate ranges from existing rates, wage survey data, and various situational variables (e.g., company compensation policy and union influence).

Some aspects of the wage figures in Table 18.6 are interesting to note. First, there is the differential between maximum rates. There is a $.40 increase between class 1 and class 2 maximums. Then through class 5, there is a $.20 increase between classes, $.30 between classes 5 and 9, and $.40 between 9 and 10. There is a fairly wide spread among classes to maintain pay differentials among experienced employees in different job classes. For instance, a class 7 operator at $5.65 working with a class 9 mechanic at $6.25 (both are slightly below the maximum for their range) still have a $.60 per-hour pay difference. (Organizations can create animosity among

Class	Evaluated Points	Hourly Rate Range	
		Minimum	Maximum
1	0.0–1.5	$4.00	$4.20
2	1.6–2.5	4.30	4.60
3	2.6–3.5	4.40	4.80
4	3.6–4.5	4.50	5.00
5	4.6–5.5	4.60	5.20
6	5.6–6.5	4.70	5.50
7	6.6–7.5	4.80	5.80
8	7.6–8.5	4.90	6.10
9	8.6–9.5	5.00	6.40
10	9.6–13.0	5.20	6.80

Table 18.6
Point-Conversion Chart

employees in different pay grades who work in the same area but perform different jobs and receive equal or nearly equal pay.) Of course, the wider difference among pay grades represents a considerable cost to the organization.

Furthermore, the chart gives a minimum and a maximum rate (or range) for each wage class. The **range** permits organizations to award wage increases within classes for seniority, merit, or a combination of these factors. The rate at which employees progress from the minimum to the maximum depends upon company policy, employee performance, and economic considerations. Also noteworthy are the wider ranges in the higher classes. Class 1 has a range of $.20 while there is a range of $1.60 for class 10 jobs. The rationale behind this is that higher-rated jobs are generally held by experienced, skilled employees whom management is particularly interested in retaining. A wider range prevents seasoned employees from reaching their maximum too soon, and it gives management the flexibility to grant these workers increases as a means of retaining critical skills and competing in the labor market. Finally, the overlap in the ranges permits experienced employees to earn as much or more than inexperienced employees in a slightly higher job.

COMPENSATION MANAGEMENT AND CONTROL

The foregoing discussion about wage grades and ranges centered on some basic concerns of wage administration. It is the job of managers to maintain a balance between satisfying employees' financial needs and minimizing labor costs. Managers' problems in striving to achieve this balance are complicated by the following constraints:

1. Organizations must take into consideration the going rate if they want to attract needed skills.
2. Organizations must reward performance.
3. Organizations must make periodic cost-of-living increases.

In dealing with these constraints, organizations often create inequities in the short run. Compensation managers then face the problem of balancing costs with fairness. Some of the considerations in resolving these dilemmas are discussed below.

WAGE COST CONTROL. Many workers become dissatisfied because their job classifications do not represent the actual work they perform, and labor costs are difficult to control when employees are paid more than their duties call for. Recognizing the existence of these problems, Lockheed Aircraft Company instituted a classification control program. Before the company approved requisitions for job vacancies, a wage representative had to verify that the duties to be performed matched the classification to be filled. Managers invariably requested a higher classification than they needed. A manager might request a secretary at $5.80 per hour to perform the duties of a $4.27-per-hour clerk. Without this control procedure, labor costs would have been considerably higher. The program educated managers to the need for classifying employees properly and maintaining a more equitable pay relationship among classifications. As a result of this, underqualified workers were no longer paid the same as higher-skilled employees.

MAINTAINING EQUITY. Once relationships are established between wage classes to produce equity, it takes a conscientious effort to retain these relationships. First, organizations must separate merit increases from cost-of-living adjustments. Wage analysts should base merit raises on objectively determined contributions to the organization. They can make living cost improvements either within the range or through an adjustment of the entire wage structure.

Organizations find they must have a policy on progression within the range so they can apply compensation improvements consistently; they must also establish the same basis for upward movement for everyone. To implement such a policy compensation managers often define rate steps within ranges. They then can award step increases for merit, as a cost-of-living adjustment, or both.

Discrepancies often arise in individual job rates due to wage-structure adjustments or job evaluations. Job rates that fall outside the established structure (either above or below) are called **red-circle rates.** Where they fall below, most companies increase employees' rates to the minimum of the range. Red-circle rates above the job-class structure are a more difficult matter, usually requiring policy decision. To gain employee acceptance of job evaluation, organizations issue a policy statement assuring employees that no job's rates will be reduced due to job evaluation or related wage studies. This policy would determine that red-circle rates above the wage structure would retain their values until the structure caught up.

Inequities are also produced by wage or salary compression, which occurs when new hires receive higher starting pay than the current earnings of incumbents in the same job. Similarly, the earnings spread between crafts persons versus lower level operatives tends to narrow (become compressed) when all classifications are given the same (absolute) increase, for example, $.50 per hour, across-the-board, instead of a percentage increase.

INNOVATION IN WAGE ADMINISTRATION

PAY AS A MOTIVATOR. Research by Donald Schwab[11] reveals that money can be a motivator if workers think that compensation is important to them; higher wages are dependent on their performance; and expended effort will result in higher performance (i.e., they have the ability to perform the task, and the work is designed so that they can achieve their goals). Schwab's research findings indicate that "individually based incentive wages have certain motivational advantages over group and time payment systems."[12] However, the situation must be conducive to such a pay system. Porter and Lawler support this contention with their research findings, which suggest that when an individual can associate personal effort with reward (there is a high probability that effort will yield performance) and the reward is viewed as valuable by the individual, the appropriate performance is likely to result.[13] The effort expended is modified by the abilities and traits of the individual and his or her role perception (the activities the person thinks are necessary to perform the job successfully). An employee then measures the equity of the rewards (perceived equitable rewards) which is the primary determinant of value in the employee's eyes and the determinant of satisfaction gained from effort. These perceived equitable rewards are defined as "the amount of rewards that a person feels is fair, given his performance in the tasks that he has been asked to undertake."[14] It is entirely possible that the types of employees, their attitudes, the nature of the work, and existing pay systems might make wage-incentive plans unsuitable for motivating higher productivity. The subject of incentive pay is still an interesting and controversial one and will be covered later in this chapter.

STOCK OWNERSHIP.   Stock ownership plans attempt to increase the enthusiasm of employees by giving them a sense of ownership in the company. In growth situations, stock values can outpace inflationary trends and contribute to morale. When stock values decline and employees lose money, however, the incentive factor is lost. There is little uniformity in types of plans, but basically, companies offering stock options provide discounts, make partial payment, or guarantee a specified market price for the purchasing of their stock. (A more detailed discussion of employee stock ownership plans is presented in Chapter 20, "Benefits and Services.")

PROFIT SHARING.   **Profit-sharing** plans give employees a current or deferred distribution of a share of the organization's profits. Though profit sharing cannot produce an immediate or direct incentive—the reward does not closely follow achievement—it does produce a mutual interest in the effectiveness of the operation. Then, employee efforts can contribute to production increases and cost savings, which in turn can improve profits.

Perhaps one of the best known cost reduction/benefit sharing plans is the Scanlon Plan, a cooperative union–management program. Companies share the savings that result from suggested improvements and from employee as well as union cooperation. Each month these firms calculate bonuses with a formula that determines a percentage relationship between total sales value (based on a value-added concept) and total payroll. At the end of each year workers receive 75 percent of the improvement from a labor-cost standard as a percentage of net sales.

One of Midland-Ross Corporation's southern plants operating under the Scanlon plan reported some dramatic results. Direct labor efficiency improved 10 percent in one major area and 8.5 percent in another; savings in excess personnel may amount to 12 percent of the work force; grievances have been cut in half; turnover has been drastically reduced; and, overall, the facility is now considered to be the best place to work in the area.[15]

The problem with these productivity sharing plans is that (1) the response is cyclical because the bonus is paid well after the work is done, thus causing a slacking off during a period following a high bonus; and (2) profit-sharing and stock ownership plans work well when productivity and profits are rising. Stable or declining profits are rarely attributable to the work force; yet this group suffers the results of ineffective management.

A NEW ROLE FOR COMPENSATION MANAGERS.   Compensation managers who view their role as clerical probably contribute little to personnel effectiveness. But those who strive to be creative can generate new ideas for solutions to their organizations' problems. They can devise new compensation arrangements that go beyond traditional techniques to support organizational objectives. Specifically, they can recommend job categories in which it would be profitable to raise or lower hiring standards and pay; job categories in which further recruitment efforts should be broadened or curtailed; and skills in abundant supply that could fill shortage areas with minimum retraining.[16]

INCENTIVE WAGE PLANS

Programs relating compensation to productivity are called incentive systems. Their most obvious advantage lies in the direct relationship between individual contributions, and production and reward. Incentive systems automatically recognize differences in ability and motivation. They vary from simple piece rates to sophisticated arrangements that adjust wages according to time saved or level of output, either by individuals or by groups of employees. Some plans are described as premium plans, because they pay a higher rate for production above a standard. Others are classified as bonus plans because they award additional pay for improved efficiency or increased output. Indirectly, profit-sharing and stock option plans are incentives because they reward employees for their contributions while at the same time creating in workers a vested interest in a firm's destiny. Incentive wage plans are becoming less common with advancements in technology because machine paced production has taken much of the control of output away from employees. However, many employees (and unions, too) prefer wage payments that are geared to their performance.[17] Organizations that shied away from pay-for-performance plans to protect employee incomes during inflation periods have reportedly adopted merit arrangements to induce higher productivity.[18]

ADVANTAGES AND DISADVANTAGES OF WAGE INCENTIVES. The most obvious advantage of wage incentives is their direct relationship to output. They are the best means of tying financial reward directly to contribution. In addition, basing pay increases on productivity improvement reduces the unit labor costs because organizations pay more to employees who produce and pay less to those who don't. The inherent disadvantages of incentive plans stem largely from their complexity and imprecision. Complex earnings calculations create misunderstandings and lead to workers' mistrust of the system. This result, in turn, limits effectiveness and can undermine the entire program. The failure of organizations to establish realistic, attainable standards can also frustrate workers.

TYPES OF INCENTIVE PAY PLANS. The plans described in this section include piece rates, standard-hour plans, and sharing incentives such as differential piece rates, task-and-bonus plans, and variations of the standard-hour plan.

The most common incentive plan is the *piece rate*. In its simplest form, organizations pay employees a standard rate for each acceptable unit they produce. They set the rate either by time studies or through product-costing methods. For example, if an employee produced 1,500 acceptable units in a day and the piece rate were $.02 per unit, he would earn $30 for the day.

The *standard-hour plan* is similar to piece rate, except that under the standard-hour plan employees are paid for the amount of time they work plus a bonus for efficiency. The organization calculates a standard time for the task and pays a premium whenever employees complete it in less than standard time. Thus, if an employee whose hourly rate is $4 completes a task in eight hours and the standard is ten hours (125 percent efficiency), his pay is calculated as follows:

Regular pay—8 hours at $4.00	$32.00
Plus efficiency bonus—25 percent	8.00
(Alternative—25 percent of 8 hours = 2 hours at $4.00)	———
Total pay	$40.00

The *differential piece rate*, developed by Frederick W. Taylor, sets and pays a high task standard, with a low piece rate for production below standard and a higher rate (or step) for units produced over standard. The differential in rates above and below the established standard has been criticized for penalizing workers who fail to make production.

The *Gantt task-and-bonus plan* overcomes the deficiency of the Taylor plan by guaranteeing a base wage for production below standard. Instead of units, Gantt used time as the basis of incentive. As an inducement for higher production, the plan uses a low-base guarantee.

The Halsey, Rowan, and Bedaux plans provide for an employee-management sharing arrangement for production efficiency. The *Halsey plan* shares, on a 50-50 basis, the time saved on output above an established standard. The *Rowan plan*, similar to the standard-hour plan, calculates bonuses on the percentage of time saved against a standard. Finally, the *Bedaux plan* expresses standard time in terms of units (60 B units equal one standard hour). Incentive pay is based on the number of B units employees earn in excess of standard.

Cost-Benefit Analysis

Benefits of compensation can be measured in terms of eight criteria proposed by Patten.[19] They are:

1. *Adequacy.* Individuals are paid at least the minimum legal, union, and going rates of pay and benefits.

2. *Equity.* Individuals are paid fairly in accordance with their contributions to the organization consistent with internal and external pay comparisons.

3. *Balance.* The total compensation package is reasonable and adequate in relation to other groups, for example, managers versus hourly employees, private sector versus public sector, and so on.

4. *Control.* Compensation is cost effective; it is commensurate with the organization's ability to pay.

5. *Security.* Employees' incomes are protected through increases against erosion of inflation and other risks or contingencies of modern urban-industrial society.

6. *Incentive.* Compensation induces employees to be productive.

7. *Pay-and-effort bargain.* The pay continues to retain employees at their same level of contribution.

8. *Acceptability.* Employees continue to accept the compensation system as reasonable and understandable.

Obviously, all eight criteria are nearly impossible to attain in any single system. But measures to approach their attainment would include: compensation surveys to determine competitive position of the organization's pay and benefits; control activities that compare pay rates to *actual* job content and adjust discrepancies; and projected ability to pay so that compensation improvements are made only after the organization is assured of improvements in earnings, productivity, cost reduction, and other profit-related factors.

Summary

To provide a compensation program that will attract, reward, and retain employees and at the same time keep labor costs in bounds, wage administrators must go beyond the mere application of techniques. Job design and analysis, job evaluation, and wage determination offer opportunities for compensation managers to make a significant contribution to organizational objectives.

The compensation manager's work with pay rates is complicated by numerous situational variables. Legislation constrains managers by establishing minimum and maximum limits on wages, pay increases, and hours of work. Power forces (labor unions, political groups, and so on) in the organization and in the labor market influence the form and parameters of compensation. Situations also guide compensation plans; practices within the area and the industry establish a going rate, which becomes a benchmark for setting wages.

Imaginative approaches to job design can reduce much of the monotony of the work routine and produce an environment conducive to high motivation and operating efficiency. Properly identified and accurately described jobs help ensure that the duties and responsibilities included in a job description represent the actual work employees perform.

A variety of job evaluation plans are available to maintain equitable pay relationships among job classifications. Each plan considers the relative worth of each job regardless of the individual performing it. The proper evaluation of positions makes it possible for compensation managers to price each job objectively. Wage analysts conduct surveys of their geographic area and of firms within their industry to establish competitive pay rates. Survey results provide data on the going rate for the area and industry and are a basis for establishing wage levels within an organization.

Once organizations obtain area and industry wage surveys and job evaluations, compensation managers can assign a monetary value to each classification and determine workers' rates of pay. Because pay inequity is a constant source of worker dissatisfaction, compensation managers can demonstrate their effectiveness by minimizing such wage inequities. Therefore, compensation managers must use judgment in determining levels of pay rates; amounts of adjustments; the nature of pay (i.e., by the hour or by the unit); the spread of rate ranges; the amount of overlap between job classes; and the basis for employees' upward progression within their range.

Key Terms

compensation management	compensable factors
equity	job evaluation
incentive pay	ranking method
market theory	wage survey
going rate	wage curve
exempt	range
nonexempt	red circle rates
comparable worth	profit sharing

Review Questions

1. What are the arguments for and against comparable worth?

2. Describe the various methods for evaluating jobs.

3. How does federal legislation constrain the management of compensation?

4. In what ways do incentive plans induce higher performance? What are the drawbacks of incentive plans?

5. What methods are available to compensation managers to establish and maintain pay equity?

Discussion Questions

1. Often companies must pay new employees the same or higher wages than outstanding performers with a year or more of service. How can compensation administrators rectify this phenomenon?

2. Why is productivity so often used by management as a justification to give or to refuse wage increases? Is the productivity argument valid?

3. The chapter described social employees as the new breed more interested in nonfinancial gain than in their paychecks. Do you agree? What non-financial reward might motivate the new breed?

4. Why do you think different job evaluation plans are used for production, clerical, and sales personnel?

5. Should organizations pay employees commensurate with their contributions to it? Should this factor be the only basis of pay?

6. Over the years pay increases have reduced the wage differential between skilled craftsmen and ordinary laborers. Many journeymen now feel that the distinction of being an artisan is fading away. To preserve the dignity of craftsmanship what approach would you take to wage increases to preserve or widen the differential?

7. In many companies, outside consultants establish job evaluation programs. Why is it advisable for companies' own personnel staffs to assume responsibility for such programs?

Case Problem 1

THE PAY DIFFERENTIAL

"No way those guys in Chicago are worth $.30 an hour more than we are," Mike Brown said. Mike was the business manager of the Federated Association of Machinists, Local 467.

"You know that the Chicago area is a lot more expensive to live in than Bedford, Mike," Dirk Samson said. Dirk was vice president of labor relations for the Amalgamated Steel Fabrication Company, which had plants in both places.

"So what else is new? We work on the same machines—we produce the same output per worker. We should get paid the same. You guys are taking us."

"No, we're not. You know that our rate is $.10 an hour over any other place in Bedford already."

"So what? That town only has a handful of machinists besides us, and they're nonunion to boot. Come on, Dirk, face up to it. You've got a sweet deal, and I noticed your profits went up 20 percent last year besides. The boys here are upset, and this could get to be a sticky issue when the contract expires next year."

"I've got the figures right here, Mike. The cost of living in Bedford is 96, compared to 107 in Chicago. Actually you fellows are in better shape than those guys up there."

"Whose figures, Dirk—the Bureau of Labor Statistics'? Those things are loaded, and you know it. Try telling one of my boys that it costs less to live here, and he'll laugh at you."

"You used those BLS figures last year to prove that the cost of living went up enough to justify an increase, Mike. They were okay then."

"I still say that we should equalize the rates. We do the same work, so we should get the same pay."

"It costs us more in Bedford."

"I thought that you said it was cheaper, Dirk."

"It is for a family, but not for a company. Look where the place is—way out in southern Indiana. We have higher power costs, bigger transportation expenses, more telex costs—"

"That's your problem, Dirk. Our boys feel that it costs them more to live in Bedford. They're right, too—have you tried to own a house here or buy some groceries? The cost of living is way up."

"It's up everywhere, Mike, but Bedford's a totally different labor market than Chicago. You know that. You just can't compare the two."

"We're doing it, and we don't like what we see. Equal pay, equal work—that'll be the demand in the next contract. You may as well get ready for it."

Problems

1. If you were a mediator (impartial third party) at the next contract bargaining session, what data would you need to work out this differential question? Why?

2. Give all arguments for equal pay for the union's negotiator. Do these seem reasonable?

3. Give all arguments for a pay differential for the company's negotiator. Do these seem reasonable?

4. Who is right?

"It just isn't fair, Mr. Smith!" Beth Little said.

"What isn't fair, Beth?"

"Here I am, doing exactly the same work that the men in the office are doing, and yet I get $.40 an hour less for it. You're the office manager—how can you let this go on?"

"Beth, our salaries are confidential—how do you know that you get less?" Mr. Smith had 20 clerks under him in a small, nonunion insurance office. Four were women.

"Oh, come off it, Mr. Smith—you and I both know who makes what. There are four of us in the programming section, and the three men make more. It isn't fair. I do as much work as they do, if not more."

"Beth, the jobs aren't really the same. You can't do a lot of things."

"Like what—carry in the boxes of punch cards? They weigh 50 pounds each, and no one ever lets me even try to pick them up. I could, you know. Besides, that happens once a month."

"In this state, a woman can't pick up more than 25 pounds."

"In this state, that law is being challenged in court as discriminatory, and the Department of Labor has already announced that it isn't enforcing that part of the law."

"Well, there are other things," Mr. Smith said.

"Like what? I can't go to the men's room? What's that got to do with the job?"

"I mean moving the equipment, things like that."

"We moved some four months ago, and I helped."

"Beth, be reasonable. The men have families—"

"I suppose that my two kids aren't a family." Beth was divorced and the sole support of her family.

"Beth, this is getting out of hand. First, I'm not prepared to admit that you get less. Second, the job descriptions are different. Third, you're not as productive as—"

"Come off it, Mr. Smith. You know that's not true."

"Well, that's all I have to say about the situation."

"That's not all I have to say, Mr. Smith." Beth stalked out of his office.

Problems

1. What should Mr. Smith do, if anything?

2. What can Beth do, if anything?

3. How could you determine if the work done by women was the same as that done by men in this office? What data would you need?

Notes

1. Richard J. Farrell, "Compensation and Benefits," *Personnel Journal,* November 1976, pp. 557–63ff.

2. Ruth G. Blumrosen, "Wage Discrimination, Job Segregation, and Title VII of the Civil Rights Act of 1964," *Journal of Law Reform* (University of Michigan), Spring 1979, pp. 397–502.

3. Karin Allport, "But How About Equal Pay for Comparable Work? Should Housepainters Make More Than Nurses?" *Across the Board,* October 1980, pp. 22–25.

4. P. R. Jeaneret, "Equitable Job Evaluation and Classification with the Position Analysis Questionnaire," *Compensation Review,* First Quarter 1980, pp. 32–42.

5. Richard I. Henderson, *Compensation Management,* 2nd ed. (Reston, Virginia: Reston Publishing Company, Inc., 1979) pp. 160–61.

6. Ibid., pp. 189ff.

7. Thomas H. Patten, Jr., *Pay: Employee Compensation and Incentive Plans* (New York: Free Press, 1977), p. 209.

8. Lawrence L. Epperson, "The Dynamics of Factor Comparison/Point Evaluation," *Public Personnel Management,* January–February 1975, p. 38.

9. Mary Green Miner, *Job Evaluation Policies and Procedures* (Washington, D.C.: Bureau of National Affairs, June 1976), p. 2.

10. Kenneth E. Foster and Jill Kanin-Lovers, "Determinants of Organizational Pay Policy," *Compensation Review,* Third Quarter 1977, p. 40.

11. Donald P. Schwab, "The Role of Compensation in Motivating High Employee Performance" (American Society for Personnel Administration Foundation Personnel Research Study, 1972).

12. Ibid.

13. Lyman W. Porter and Edward E. Lawler, III, *Managerial Attitudes and Performance* (Homewood, Illinois: Richard D. Irwin, and Dorsey Press, 1968), pp. 16–40.

14. Ibid.

15. George Sherman, "The Scanlon Concept: Its Capabilities for Productivity Improvement," *The Personnel Administrator,* July 1976, p. 20.

16. David W. Belcher, "Ominous Trends in Wage and Salary Administration," *Personnel,* September–October 1964, pp. 42–50.

17. Thomas H. Patten, Jr., "Pay for Performance or Placation?" *The Personnel Administrator,* September 1977, p. 27.

18. James C. Hyatt, "Merit Money: More Firms Link Pay to Job Performance as Inflation Wanes," *Wall Street Journal,* March 7, 1977, pp. 1ff.

19. Patten, *Pay,* pp. 8–13.

Chapter Nineteen

Managerial and Executive Compensation

"Please accept my resignation effective two weeks from this date. . . ."

The day Sam Johnson, senior project engineer for World-Wide Construction Company wrote this he was fed up with his situation. He had been doing an outstanding job for the company for the past three years—his performance appraisals stated that he was exceptional—and he even earned a promotion last year. But two days ago Walter Birdseye, who Sam knew at Tech, was hired. Walter had just graduated, had no experience in the field, yet he was offered within $50 a month of what Sam Johnson was earning.

Perhaps you have been in this situation, too. It just doesn't seem fair to hire a new employee at a salary that is almost the same as a proven, seasoned one's. Yet the market price for many management positions outpaces the earnings progression of individuals inside an organization. This is one of the predicaments we face in managing executive compensation. Approaches to this problem and others related to management and executive pay are discussed in this chapter.

An **executive** is a person having administrative or supervisory authority in an organization. Traditionally, executives are the highest ranking officers, but for purposes of discussion, we will include exempt salaried employees in general, and the term executive will frequently be used to describe them.

LEARNING OBJECTIVES

1. To understand how salary evaluation plans differ from wage (job) evaluation plans.
2. To know how positions are priced.
3. To be familiar with various forms of compensation programs for salaried employees.
4. To understand the pros and cons of pay secrecy.
5. To know the methods of administering salary progression.

Salary is affected as much by the individual holding a position as by duties and responsibilities of the classification. FLSA-exempt salaried employees are inherently different from operative and clerical workers. Executives bring a much greater combination of capabilities to their positions; hence, they have greater latitude in the way they perform the work, whereas hourly workers are constrained by the particular demands of their jobs. Consequently, executive compensation must be oriented to the individual. In addition, it is the outcome of an executive's productive efforts that is the measure of success; the operative worker's performance is geared more to the *technique* he or she employs. Salesmen, professionals, and managers therefore have more opportunity to influence the success of their organizations. Hence, executive compensation plans must be responsive to individual contributions. (This is not meant to imply that wage plans ignore individual contributions.)

The executive compensation process is basically the same as that described in Chapter 18. In summary, basic compensation systems include designing positions to meet organizational goals more effectively; analyzing and describing job duties; surveying the area and industry to obtain a basis of comparison; pricing each position by assigning salary ranges to grades; and controlling the entire system. Compensation management maintains as much equity as feasible through periodic review of salaries, maintenance of salary ranges, and control of salary growth.

This chapter covers only considerations that apply specifically to executive compensation: position evaluation, concepts and methodologies of salary progression, and compensation practices for salesmen, professional employees, and executives.

Position Evaluation

In addition to the job evaluation plans described in Chapter 18, organizations use the guideline method and the guide chart-profile method (also called the Hay plan) to evaluate salaried positions. Both of these plans are specifically, but not exclusively, applicable to executive compensation. Although there are a number of other evaluation plans in use, these two appear to be most representative.

GUIDELINE METHOD

The widely accepted guideline approach is essentially an extension of the other evaluation plans (factor comparison, point plans, and so on). However, its basic difference lies in its emphasis on marketplace interpretation of relative job value; salaries established by the guideline method reflect the current prices of positions and are theoretically equitable and competitive. The need for organizations to remain competitive in the job market has been cited by Smyth, Murphy Associates, developers of the **guideline method,** as one of their primary motives for introducing the plan. The particular advantage of this approach over traditional systems became evident in the mid-1960s, when many companies had to create higher salary ranges for electronic data processing (EDP) positions to attract programmers and systems analysts. The surge in demand for these talents accelerated EDP-salary rates to the extent that existing ranges could not accommodate the market price. Organizations who used the guideline method, however, did not run into this problem.

THE GUIDELINE EVALUATION PROCESS.   Evaluating positions under the guideline method has the following unique features.

1. At the heart of the guideline method is a standard scale of salary ranges. The range for each grade in the scale consists of a minimum, midpoint, and maximum. At the lower end of the scale the spread from minimum to maximum is usually 30 percent, with gradual increases to about 60 percent in the higher grades. The reasoning behind the larger spread in the higher positions is that there are fewer openings near the top of the hierarchy, thus leaving less opportunity for the upward movement of key executives. Consequently, the salary ranges of higher-level positions must be wider to provide monetary incentives. To facilitate adjustments in salary relationships, the scale has a built-in tolerance that allows organizations to move positions up or down the scale one or two grades without creating gross inequities. With a large number of closely spaced salary grades with overlapping ranges, evaluators have a margin of error that permits flexibility in administration. The example in Table 19.1 is an abbreviated scale showing the range overlap and the differential in spread for both lower and higher grades. Notice that there are 60 grades in this scale (some have as many as 80).

2. Initially, the evaluation process requires compensation managers to select a substantial number of benchmark positions to compare with outside sources. This is the direct-pricing feature of the plan and the key to its effectiveness.

3. After analysts use area and industry surveys to compare the benchmark positions with the going market rates, they match the average salary for each surveyed position with the nearest midpoint on the salary scale. They then plot each position on a chart or panel to put the job in perspective with the external labor market.[1]

4. At this point, analysts adjust positions to external market rates and evaluate the salaries of existing positions. They also check the relationships

Table 19.1
Guideline Salary Scale
(food products company)

Grade	Minimum	Midpoint	Maximum
1	$ 6,220	$ 7,020	$ 7,820
2	6,644	7,532	8,420
3	7,076	8,012	8,948
.	.	.	.
.	.	.	.
16	10,400	12,400	14,400
.	.	.	.
.	.	.	.
30	20,600	25,000	29,400
.	.	.	.
.	.	.	.
60	89,800	110,800	131,800

between all key positions. Each department then examines the evaluations of its own positions to ensure internal consistency, and analysts review the entire organization for consistency among units.

5. Finally, the salary committee presents the evaluated results to top management for final approval.

GUIDE CHART-PROFILE METHOD

In the early 1950s, Hay Associates developed a sophisticated method for evaluating middle and top management positions. Using the Hay plan, analysts evaluate each position from information contained in position descriptions. They evaluate all positions twice—first through guide charts and again through profiling—against three criteria: know-how, problem solving, and accountability.

Through a correlation process, organizations can convert their evaluations to the Hay control standards, thus permitting direct comparisons of the salary and evaluation practices among organizations. Hay Associates publishes annual surveys showing the compensation practices of selected groups of companies. Because all client organizations use the same evaluation method, participants in the surveys can compare base salaries.

GUIDE CHART EVALUATION.   Similar to the point method of job evaluation, the guide chart utilizes compensable factors, but only three in this case. Each of these factors is, in turn, divided into ascending levels of importance. The guide charts form a grid with ratings of all elements so that salary analysts can consider each factor separately and then fit each one into a numbered slot with a weight for it. The total point value of all three factors is the numerical evaluation for a position. Obviously, analysts tailor guide charts to the individual requirements of their organization. A brief description of each of the factors will help clarify the foregoing discussion.[2]

1. *Know-how* is the sum total of expert knowledge and practical skill necessary for acceptable job performance. It consists of practical and specialized technical, professional, or administrative knowledge; and skills in motivating, appraising, selecting, organizing, and developing individuals and groups. Know-how has two dimensions: breadth (comprehensiveness) and depth (thoroughness). A position may require some knowledge about a lot of things, or a lot of knowledge about a few things. The total know-how is the product of breadth times depth. This concept makes it practical for salary analysts to compare and weigh the total know-how content of different jobs in terms of how much knowledge about how many things.

2. *Problem solving* is the amount of original, self-starting thinking required by a job for analyzing, evaluating, creating, reasoning, and achieving conclusions. The two aspects of problem solving are the kinds of problems and the degree of guidance available to people in solving problems. Problem solving utilizes know-how because people think using what they have learned. The raw material of any thinking is knowledge of facts, principles, and means; people put ideas together from something already known. Therefore, problem solving is a percentage utilization of know-how. To the extent that thinking is circumscribed by standards, covered by precedents, or referred to others, problem solving is diminished and know-how is emphasized.

3. *Accountability* is the measured effect of the position on end results. It has three dimensions:

   a. The freedom to act, which is measured by the existence or absence of personal procedural control and guidance. The degrees of freedom (shown in increasing order of importance) include: prescribed, controlled, standardized, generally regulated, operational direction, oriented direction, top-management guidance, and presidential guidance.

   b. The impact of end results, which is measured in four degrees of increasing effect: (1) remote: recording, informational, or incidental services for use by others in taking action; (2) indirect: interpretive, consultative, or facilitative services for use by others in taking important action; (3) shared: participating with equals in taking action; and (4) primary: controlling impact on end results, where shared accountability of others is subordinate.

c. The magnitude as indicated by the dollar size of the areas affected, ranging from under $100,000 to over $100 million.

PROFILING POSITIONS.   In profiling, salary analysts consider each factor and, on the basis of their expert judgment, assign a percentage or weight to it so that the three factors total 100 percent. In the case of a research scientist, evaluators would emphasize know-how and problem solving, whereas with the vice president's position, they would look at accountability. Then analysts check these profiles against the ratings on the guide charts; where significant variances exist, they reexamine the positions and reconcile their evaluations.

Salary Progression

Effective compensation management will provide clearcut guidelines for executive progression within a particular salary range. Executives functioning within their positions are interested not only in their starting salaries, but also in the expectations they must fulfill to receive salary increases. Although an executive's progress within a range is very much a function of performance, the situation is also a contributing factor. An organization's ability to pay determines starting salaries as well as the size of the ranges and the amounts of increases executives can receive within their range. Generally, compensation managers base nonpromotional increases on length of service and merit. Whatever the basis for salary increases, organizations must periodically review each executive's salary as well as the overall pay structure.

SOURCES OF SALARY DATA

Many of the sources of wage data listed in Table 18.6 (see Chapter 18, Compensation Management) are also useful for obtaining salary information. In addition, Table 19.2 contains specific sources of salary data.

Table 19.2
Selected Sources of Salary Data

Source	Type(s) of Data
Periodicals	
1. *Compensation Review*	Published by AMACOM (New York) quarterly, contains articles and current information on compensation.

Table 19.2 (cont.)

Source	Type(s) of Data
2. *Comp. Flash*	Companion newsletter to the *Compensation Review* includes timely items of interest to compensation-management people
3. *Executive Compensation Journal*	Published monthly by the Bureau of National Affairs, Washington, D.C., includes detailed articles on retirement plans, profit-sharing plans, stock options, and related executive-compensation matters.

Surveys

1. *Business Week Annual Survey of Executive Compensation*	Shows salary and benefits of top executives of leading companies in selected industries.
2. *Dartnell Survey of Executive Compensation*	By Dartnell Corporation (Chicago), surveys compensation practices for various management levels. Includes future trends.
3. *Executive Compensation*	Compiled by Arthur Young and Company (New York) biennially. Survey of current compensation of CEO's and financial and accounting managers by industry and regions.
4. *Forbes* Annual Survey of Chief Executive Officers' Compensation.	Indicates number of years with company, salary, and bonus.
5. *Top Executive Compensation Survey*	Reported annually in the *McKinsey Quarterly*, details findings of McKinsey and Company's survey of 577 large U.S. companies in 31 industries. Shows 10-year company patterns of profits, sales, and CEO compensation.

Analyses

1. *Nation's Business Annual Compensation Study*	Sibson and Company analyzes trends in executive pay by salary level and functional position.
2. *Top Executive Compensation*	By the Conference Board (New York) biennially. Analyzes pay of top three executives of more than 1,000 corporations in a variety of industries.
3. *TPF & C Top 100 Compensation Study*	Issued by Towers, Perrin, Forster and Crosby (New York), profiles 100 industrial firms. Covers ED Cash Compensation and incentive plans.

POSITION PRICING

Organizations can choose from several methods for equitably determining basic salaries. The **top-down approach** fixes a minimum salary for the president and determines the pay of subordinate executives relative to that of the chief executive. When the president's salary is correctly set, the salaries of others are likely to be appropriate. But presidents and subordinates who are paid too low can be lured away. Through its Executive Compensation Service the American Management Association issues reports on executive earnings.[3] These reports provide guidelines on the percentage relationships between the chief executive officer and executive positions below that level. The relationships differ depending on type of business (nondurable or durable goods manufacturing, service), size of the firm, and total revenue. To illustrate, durable goods manufacturers with revenues in the $400 million range annually show the following approximate relationships between the CEO and other executives: CEO 100%, chief operating officer 88%, executive vice president 68%, administrative vice president 53%, marketing vice president 51%, manufacturing vice president 45%, financial vice president (or treasurer) 54%, industrial relations vice president 50%.

When chief executives are overpaid, there is strong possibility of criticism from stockholders, unions, and outside groups. The **bottom-up approach** uses nonmanagerial jobs as a base; it prices higher-level positions according to a fixed-percentage relationship above the base jobs. With this approach, if nonmanagerial jobs are not properly priced, all managers' salaries are out of line. Yet it does have the advantage of ensuring that managerial positions are priced proportionately higher than nonmanagerial ones. In the **budget approach,** firms allocate a proportion of the total payroll to exempt salaried positions. Budgeting offers an excellent means of controlling salary increases. However, with this method, organizations must keep their compensation plans flexible to accommodate a variety of contingencies. For example, when the budgeted amount is insufficient to accommodate high executive performance, firms must make allowances to recognize achievement by supplementing base salaries or through promotion. Finally, the **maturity curve approach** relates salary to age, length of service, or some other measure, and appraised performance. Figure 19.1 is a typical maturity curve for engineers, with whom it has found its most prevalent application.

It graphs an employee's progress in the position based on years in rank and performance. The curve measures annual salary in terms of its relationship to a control point or to the midpoint of the range. Thus, as the figure shows, employees with exemplary performance could reach 125 percent of the control point in seven years, whereas employees rated satisfactory would only reach 115 percent of the control point in the same period. Organizations use percentages, rather than absolute salaries, as a matter of

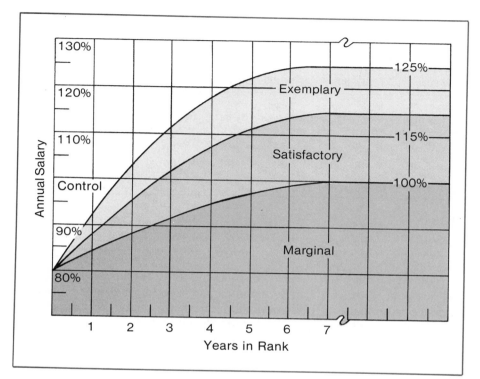

Figure 19.1
Salary Increase Chart
(maturity curve)

expediency; continuously changing salaries would force companies to revise their salaries constantly. When they revise the salary structure they apply the percentages to the new figures. The amount of increase an employee receives under the maturity-curve approach is a function of appraised performance and of the relationship of the current salary to the control point. The salary increase guide shown in Table 19.3 accompanies the salary increase chart (maturity curve) in Figure 19.1. The guide specifies, for example, that satisfactory performers (designated by the letter S) whose salary is 80 to 90 percent of the range's midpoint could receive a salary increase of 6 to 9 percent every 9 to 18 months. Similarly, an exemplary performer (letter E) whose present salary is 90 to 100 percent of the midpoint could be eligible for a 6 to 9 percent increase at 9 to 15 month intervals. Maturity curves not only identify pay rates of employees with a given amount of service, but they also help firms administer salary progressions.

One interesting phenomenon that is worth noting because it creates compensation problems, but has no ready solutions, is the domino principle. The $1 million paid each year to Barbara Walters caused an increase in

Table 19.3
Salary Increase Guide

	Position in Salary Range (percent of control rate or midpoint)									
	Below 80%		80–90%		90–100%		100–115%		115–125%	
Perf.	Intvl. (Mos.)	% Incr.	Intvl. (Mos.)	% Incr.	Intvl. (Mos.)	% Incr.	Intvl. (Mos.)	% Incr.	Intvl. (Mos.)	% Incr.
E	6–12	10–12	9–12	8–11	9–15	6–9	12–21	4–7	12–24	5
S	6–15	8–10	9–18	6–9	12–21	4–7	12–24	5	*	*
M	15–18	6–8	18–24	4–7	24–36	5	*	*	*	*

*Nominal increase

Abbreviations:
Intvl. = interval.   E = Exemplary
% Incr. = percent increase.   S = Satisfactory
Perf. = performance.   M = Marginal

salaries paid to other TV news commentators. The professional sports experience is similar. As Bill Veeck, former owner of the White Sox, has indicated, the problem with salaries today is not that stars are paid a million dollars a year; it is that these high salaries force the earnings of mediocre players to such unrealistic heights that some utility infielder who bats .220 makes $200,000 a year.

MERIT INCREASES

Organizations assign salary improvements on the basis of appraised performance (i.e., merit and length of service). Maturity curves emphasize time in rank, although to some extent they do incorporate merit factors. Organizations generally grant salary increases on the basis of tenure, perhaps because service time is the most objective criterion for justifying raises. There are strong arguments for recognizing performance with merit increases, but in actual practice, the influence of seniority appears to be the guiding factor. One study concluded that "the combination of older employees with longer service beyond the midpoints and younger persons with shorter service under the midpoints indicates that salaries are to some extent dependent upon length of service and age."[4]

Because individual performance is a critical factor in salaried positions, organizations need to consider aspects other than time-in-rank when administering salaries. These other factors are classified under **merit.** Salary increases based on merit are often made difficult because of: (1) the coincidental existence of cost-of-living and across-the-board increases, which camouflage the merit aspects, and (2) the criteria used to determine merit, which vary so much that their application to salary increases is almost impossible. However, there is little argument that, when granting pay increases, salary administrators should consider the factors included under merit—performance, potential, promotability, and position in the range.

Lawler's studies revealed that pay traditionally has not been related to merit.[5] He found that managers considered remuneration a very important incentive to perform because it is a source of satisfying all needs. Lawler bemoaned the fact that the system so rarely made job performance a criterion for determining pay. Nevertheless, for pay to have a positive motivational impact on performance it must be viewed as important by the executive, and its receipt must be seen as contingent on successful performance. Dyer and associates found that organizations did not place as much importance on the link between pay increases and performance appraisals as managers would like.[6] So these researchers suggested that it is essential for organizations to give this criterion more attention when considering merit. A basic prerequisite to the effectiveness of merit systems, thus, is having valid and acceptable measures of performance that executives perceive as related to pay.

Richard Hill's **urgency factor** was designed to provide an objective means of awarding merit increases.[7] His model operates on the premise that the timing of merit increases is critical to the effectiveness of executive compensation. The urgency factor gives compensation managers a method of determining how urgent each executive's salary increase should be before the organization grants the increase. Analysts weigh compensation variables according to management's opinion of its relative value and assign points to the variables. The total score is the urgency factor. Executives with high performance or a long period since their last increase would obviously receive a high score. The model is so constructed that an urgency factor of 100 indicates that an executive is immediately due for consideration; each point more or less than this figure indicates the number of months overdue for consideration or the number of months until it occurs. Hence, an urgency factor of 94 signals that in six months the executive is due for merit-increase consideration.

Another possibility for administering merit increases was indicated by Goldberg.[8] He suggests reserving the upper half of the salary range for merit increases. An executive could progress from the minimum to the midpoint (lower half of range) in regular increments related to the time required to learn his or her job. On reaching the midpoint, however, the salary would be fixed and increases from this point on would be based on performance that exceeded expectations. In this situation, salary increases would be reserved for meritorious performance only. Of course the midpoints would be adjusted in accordance with market conditions to keep salaries competitive.

The basis of merit itself is a matter of individual company policy, and it varies with a situation. Organizations can consider merit along with seniority; they should establish criteria for determining merit, which might include degree of attainment of objectives, ability to perform the job, dollars of revenue generated, new accounts acquired, and many others. They should consistently apply the same measures across the board. Measuring merit has inherent difficulties similar to those of performance appraisal, which have already been discussed.

THE PAY SECRECY CONTROVERSY

Considerable controversy surrounds the issue of pay secrecy versus openness. Under closed systems pay formulas and salaries are not revealed to employees. The feeling is that dissatisfaction will be heightened by revealing salaries and that an individual's salary is a private matter and not something that should be disclosed. Proponents of pay secrecy claim that raw salary figures, when disclosed, lead to misunderstandings because people cannot objectively compare these figures when they do not understand the basis of their assignment, for example, an incumbent's background, starting salary, and special circumstances.

Conversely, supporters of openness on salary matters argue that employees cannot help thinking that secret pay policies are hiding unsatisfactory and inequitable pay. Usually, they claim, resentment stems from not knowing *why* the other person makes more money rather than from the fact that he or she does. The principal advantage of the open-pay system is that the basis and reasons for a person's salary are made known.[9] The trend toward more openness stems from several sources.

First, more information on pay practices is readily available for people to make comparisons (see Figure 19.1, for example). Second, FEPC and EEO regulations require the posting of nonexempt job openings including pay rates under certain circumstances; posting all salaries, or at least the ranges, is just a natural extension of this. It seems that most people in organizations know what other people make despite secrecy rules. Finally, organizations that seek the support and participation of employees find that trust and commitment is gained through openness in all matters, including pay.

PERIODIC SALARY REVIEWS

Whatever method an organization uses to determine the timing of pay raise considerations, periodic **salary reviews** are essential to the success of compensation management. The purpose of reviews is to maintain equity.

Organizations usually consider all the factors that impinge on salary (performance, position in range, etc.). They pay particular attention to potential, because after they have determined that employees have the capacity for growth, compensation managers look for ways to compensate them for potential growth. Salary reviews also help to guard against the eroding effects of inflation on merit increases. Inflation hits middle-manager incomes the hardest. They cannot make up for increases in the cost of living with bonuses and special compensation arrangements that are available to top management.[10] The review process uncovers problems in managers' salaries. When an organization has valued middle-management talent in this circumstance it can make adjustments in salary, promote the individual to a better paying position, or make similar arrangements to improve the salary.

Department heads and compensation managers usually review salaries. In addition, many organizations designate a salary committee to do this and to recommend compensation policies, review position evaluations, and promote equitable compensation management. Most salary committees are composed of the compensation manager and several key executives who head the organization's major units. Prior to the beginning of each fiscal year, the salary committee might establish a merit-increase budget in the form of a percentage of the salaried payrolls or a lump sum allocated to departments for assignment to individuals. The committee would then review the increases to assure conformity to guidelines, consistency among departments, justification based on individual merit, and timeliness of each increase according to the urgency factor or some similar model.

Categories of Salary Compensation

The elements of compensation management discussed above generally apply to salaried employees. There are, however, aspects of compensation management peculiar to specific groups of salaried employees. Firms often make distinctions among compensation methods for salespersons, professionals, and executives. Although these groups are not managerial in nature, their compensation is not a wage. Hence, compensation of these groups is similar to managerial and executive compensation. Each of these categories of salary compensation is considered separately.

SALESPERSON COMPENSATION

Compensation managers apply a number of remuneration schemes to salespeople, including straight salary, straight commission, or a combination of salary plus commission. The type of compensation program varies with the desires of management, the nature of the product, economic conditions, and other factors. The type of plan used should:

1. Be easily understood by the salespeople and be simple to administer;
2. Provide an incentive to sell, but not penalize the salespeople for rigidities in demand;
3. Pay commissions soon after they are earned;
4. Be oriented toward both profits and customer service;
5. Adjust to changing conditions in product lines and the general market;
6. Maintain supervisory controls over account coverage and selling expenses.[11]

COMMISSION PLANS.   Most organizations use **commissions** as a basis for improving salespeople's compensation because they are incentives to sales efforts. Commissions can be based on a fixed or variable amount per unit sold, or on a rate after salespersons meet a set quota. Some organizations base commissions on dollar volume of sales, with either a stable rate or a minimum percentage for a specified volume and increasingly higher percentages for higher sales levels. Too often, however, commission plans fail to account for profitability by offering incentives for selling higher-profit items and new items and for maintaining high sales while holding down expenses. Robertson has proposed a plan that sets a commission rate as a fixed percent of gross profit; organizations pay salespeople a specified portion of the profit margin for all products they sell.[12] They receive a fixed rate, but the amount of commission varies with the profitability of each product.

STRAIGHT SALARY PLANS.   When organizations emphasize product promotion and when the time salespeople spend with customers is more critical than the number of calls they make, a straight salary is the usual arrangement. Straight salary is most acceptable in situations in which salespeople have little direct control over the amount of sales (such as in retail sales) or the factors affecting sales are too numerous and complex to be incorporated into an incentive plan (such as highly technical promotions and some college textbook sales). Organizations that have experienced difficulty in administering commission incentives often return to straight-salary plans.

COMBINATION ARRANGEMENTS.   Some firms use a combination of salary, bonus, commission, and expense account to incorporate the advantages of incentive and income security. They award periodic bonuses on the basis of individual or group accomplishments in profit improvements, account penetration, expense reductions, new accounts, improved customer satisfaction, and increased sales volume.

PROFESSIONAL EMPLOYEE COMPENSATION

Technological advances coupled with an increased emphasis on credentials have, in recent years, expanded the employment of professional workers. From a personnel standpoint, professionals have been less satisfied with their status than other salaried employees. Their association with counterparts in other organizations facilitates salary comparisons, thus giving rise to further dissatisfaction. However, Belcher claims that the compensation plan is one of the basic instruments for creating in professional workers the necessary attitudes, motivations, and behavior.[13] Following are a few practical suggestions for the effective compensation of professionals.

1. Organizations should tailor professional compensation plans to individual employees' needs, work, and desires.

2. Organizations should clearly delineate the relationship between work performance and salary-improvement factors.

3. Pay should be a function of a position's market value, an employee's length of experience, and work performance, with greatest emphasis on the latter.

4. Organizations should not keep salary actions secret, and they should freely discuss the basis of financial rewards with employees.

A few of the larger industrial firms that employ large numbers of professionals have adopted a **double or dual-track** system of salary progression. Under this arrangement there are two distinct but parallel ladders of progression and compensation. The managerial track (or ladder) offers a succession of steps with increasing responsibility for supervision or direction of people. The parallel professional track is ascended through increasing contributions of a professional nature, which do not entail the supervision of people.[14] Thus the professional or technical worker can earn salary improvements comparable to his or her counterpart in management while remaining in a technical or professional capacity.

EXECUTIVE COMPENSATION

A study of management expenditures provides insight for executive compensation. Managers' standards of living do not rise in the same way that average blue-collar workers' do; therefore, it is unrealistic to base executive raises on the cost-of-living increases published by the Bureau of Labor Statistics. Savings, life insurance, and education tend to consume a larger portion of executives' incomes as their salaries increase, until they reach the highest salary levels.[15] These items are important to them, and if management wishes to motivate executives, organizations must supply the rewards that will increase them.

There are a growing number of executives with substantial personal incomes; some have inherited wealth, while others have outside sources of income. Thus, more and more executives have less fear of losing their jobs. Many are interested in capital gains programs because they have the capital to take advantage of them. Finally, some executives may prefer to choose a job they enjoy and find challenging rather than one that pays the most.

Executive compensation programs generally include five basic elements—base salary, short-term (annual) incentives or bonuses, deferred compensation, fringe benefits, and perquisites (e.g., financial counseling, supplemental life insurance, full medical reimbursement, company cars, and physical fitness labs).

EXECUTIVE BASE SALARY.   The most prevalent means of compensating executives is through annual salaries. Executive salaries vary considerably from company to company; it appears that direct compensation levels for executive positions generally correlate positively with the size of a company and the industry; larger companies tend to pay their executives more.[16]

Salary alone is not a true measure of the worth of an executive; therefore, organizations commonly offer inducements beyond salary to motivate executives and to reward performance beyond a position's minimum requirements. Because top managers have the greatest influence on the destiny of an organization, these inducements are a vital ingredient in the compensation system. Compensation beyond straight salary can be financial, nonfinancial, or a combination of these.

Financial incentives include cash bonuses, stock options, and other deferred payments. Nonfinancial incentives take the form of benefits and services that would otherwise represent an expense to executives. They are particularly attractive because they provide tangible benefits for executives without the taxes that take away a substantial portion of other forms of income. Typical of these fringe benefits are insurance, medical care, legal and accounting assistance, memberships in clubs and associations, recreation facilities, vacations and transportation accommodations, and other benefits and services.

The **compensation cafeteria** is attractive to many executives. Here, executives can design their own payment packages by choosing the most beneficial form of pay from a reasonable number of alternatives. This approach to compensation, along with nonfinancial incentives, is covered in more detail in the next chapter. A brief description of the more prevalent financial incentives for executives will provide a better understanding of their relationship to total compensation.

BONUSES. **Bonuses** stimulate performance by rewarding executives with stocks, cash payments, or deferred income. Bonuses are usually awarded in proportion to an executive's impact on profits. The board of directors establishes a formula that links the size of the bonus to the firm's profitability, and also specifies the proportion of profits the company can pay out in bonuses. To be an incentive, executive bonuses must represent a significant proportion of total earnings—at least 25 percent.[17] The *Wall Street Journal* reports a dramatic increase in the adoption of performance share bonus arrangements—41 percent of the nation's largest 100 companies have adopted this arrangement.[18]

DEFERRED COMPENSATION. This type of plan provides additional compensation for executives at a future time when they will be in a much lower tax bracket. **Deferred compensation,** as the term implies, is a portion of salary paid to executives at a specified time after their regular pay ceases, usually at retirement. The advantage of this arrangement is that the tax bite on their income is reduced, and they have additional retirement income.

STOCK OPTIONS. Under **stock option** plans, executives can purchase shares of company stock at a discount for a specified period of time. In recent years, these plans have proven attractive to company officials who could defer purchase of the stock and observe its performance. However, qualified stock options, which provided significant capital accumulation opportunities for many executives in the 1960s because of favorable tax treatment and improving stock market conditions, were virtually eliminated when Congress passed the Tax Reform Act of 1976. Organizations are still utilizing stock options as an incentive, though they are all considered nonqualified (for tax exemptions); that is, the bargain element (spread between the option price—usually a reduced price—and the market price) will be taxed as personal service (earned) income with a present maximum tax of 50 percent in the year exercised.[19] With stock options, the organization benefits because executives have a stake in the company; their efforts in running a successful operation translate into higher market performance of the company's stock, which in turn enhances the value of their shareholdings. Stock option plans vary considerably. Some plans specify the number of shares in the employment agreement, while others gear the size of the purchase to the executive's performance or to the amount of his or her salary. Some plans take the form of bonuses or profit sharing, and a few even stipulate that the executive must sell the stock back to the organization upon leaving its employ.

There are other similar approaches that also tie rewards to an organization's long-range performance. *Performance shares* award stock bonuses with an executive's rights to the shares contingent on achievement of certain goals. The number of shares awarded may vary for achievement above or below a specific goal. The executive is still taxed on receipt of the stock at its current market value. Under *stock appreciation rights* an employer can promise a future cash payment, the amount to be determined by the stock price increase. Through this arrangement, the amount payable per unit awarded equals the appreciation, if any, in the price of stock from the time of award to the time of payment. Closely allied to stock appreciation rights is *phantom stock,* which awards units, each with the full value of a share of stock. When time and any other requirements are satisfied, the organization pays the executive for his or her vested units at the current price of its stock, regardless of whether the amount is above or below the price when the units were awarded. *Participating units* is a scheme that involves the executive directly in the organization's growth and profitability. As with stock appreciation rights, the organization promises to pay according to a formula; but in this case operating results (e.g., return on investment, revenues, or some other predetermined formula) rather than stock price determine the payment.[20] Such pay-for-performance arrangements are especially important in light of the mounting stockholder and public disapproval over current executive pay levels.[21]

COST-OF-LIVING ADJUSTMENTS.   Inflationary trends in recent years have dramatized living cost differentials among geographic areas. Some organizations pay lump sum differentials to employees when they relocate to higher cost areas. One firm, for instance gives $6,000 the first year for relocation costs to people earning $35,000–$41,000 who are transferred from Atlanta to Minneapolis. And an additional $6,000 is paid the second year in quarterly installments to offset the additional living costs.[22] To accommodate accelerating interest costs some firms are also compensating their transferred executives for the difference between their existing mortgage rate and the (higher) rate they will have to pay when they purchase a new home.

Cost-Benefit Analysis

Essentially the same criteria apply to executive compensation as to compensation in general.

Because a manager's pay is more a function of ability and contribution to the organization there should be, theoretically, at least, a high positive correlation between results achieved by the individual and his or her pay. Actual compensation, however, reflects many factors other than contribution and ability—uncertainties of the market and other factors beyond the control of the individual manager.

Nevertheless, some analysis of executive compensation can be performed to show relationships among various classifications and compensation; the distribution of actual salaries relative to midpoints of ranges; correlation of pay and appraisal results; quit rates at various pay levels; and the adequacy of pay ranges (accomplished through surveys) compared to other employers in the same and different industries and geographic areas. In addition, the personnel staff can study the viability of alternative evaluation plans, merit increase schemes and appraisal techniques in an attempt to maintain equity in their compensation system.

Summary

Executives have a considerable influence on an organization's success. The results of their activities determine its destiny, and salaried employees are keenly aware of their value to their organization. Although they tend to be oriented to higher-order psychological needs, they are also sensitive to their value in monetary terms. Therefore, successful salary compensation plans must be responsive to individual contributions.

Compensation managers use several methods to evaluate salaried positions and to establish salaries sufficiently attractive to satisfy individual needs. The guideline method utilizes labor market survey data as a basis for pricing positions. The guide chart-profile, or Hay plan, recognizes specialized know-how, problem-solving capabilities, and accountability for end results required by the position. Analysts conduct annual surveys to keep salaries current and consistent.

In order to reward executives for their accomplishments and length of service, organizations offer them increases within their salary ranges. Firms often base compensation improvements solely on tenure because merit is so difficult to ascertain. However, compensation programs achieve optimum results when they tie salary increases to performance results. In this regard, periodic salary reviews help maintain equity within budgetary limits.

The peculiar nature of sales, professional, and executive positions calls for distinct pay practices for each of these groups. In the case of salespersons, organizations often use commissions to stimulate additional sales, but for maximum benefit, commission rates should be geared to the profitability of the sale. Straight salary is more acceptable when the marketing emphasis is on customer service or promotion, both of which require salespeople to spend more time with each prospect. Compensation plans tailored to individual needs, such as the compensation cafeteria, have proven most effective in their application to professional employees. And the tax bite on executive salaries has led organizations to offer a variety of nonfinancial incentives, deferred compensation, and stock options.

Key Terms

executive

salary

guideline method

top-down approach

bottom-up approach

budget approach

maturity curve approach

merit

urgency factor

salary reviews

commission

double or dual-track

compensation cafeteria

bonuses

deferred compensation

stock option

Review Questions

1. How does the evaluation of executive positions differ from job evaluation?

2. What are the arguments for and against keeping salaries and the plans for their management secret?

3. What are the alternatives for providing compensation incentives for executives?

4. Discuss the relationships between merit increases and incentive.

5. How can the maturity curve be used to help determine salary increases.

Discussion Questions

1. Salary increases are said to have only temporary positive effects; soon after receiving a raise, employees start looking toward their next increase. As a compensation manager what would you do to minimize this frustration?

2. Job evaluation methods are usually concerned with the relative worth of positions, but compensation programs also consider the personal qualities of individuals who fill these. How can compensation managers accommodate both individual contributions and position content?

3. Organizations often keep salaries and salary administration confidential. Do you think it is a good policy? What, if any, are the alternatives? How far would you go in supplying salary information to employees? To outsiders?

4. In establishing a salary for the chief executive officer of a company, what factors would you consider?

5. Who should serve on the compensation committee? Discuss the reasons for each of your selections.

"Did you ever hear of monopsony theory, Al?" Harmon Smith asked. He and Al were young assistant administrators at Barth General Hospital.

Al was in the laboratory. "No, what is it, some sort of new math?"

Harmon was in admissions as an accountant. "No, it's a situation when there is a single buyer. A monopoly is a single seller. And monopsony theory has got us into this pay problem."

"I'm sure the administration has never heard of it, Harmon, so how can it get us in trouble?"

Harmon walked to the blackboard. "Consider the facts. Barth is stuck here in this small city, eighty miles from the nearest metropolitan area, right? Everything is a secret, so you don't know what I make, and I don't know what you make."

"Right," Al agreed. "So what?"

Harmon wrote it down. "Really good young administrators are hard to find and expensive, right?"

"They sure are," Al said. "There are lots of people around, but the top men and women are being paid a lot more than what I got when I came two years ago, and you know that pay raises have been very small."

"This is our situation in admissions," Harmon continued. "Barth has seven assistant administrators. Let's say that each makes $20,000 a year."

"That sounds reasonable from what little I know about pay around here, Al. The secrecy's real tight."

"Now," Harmon went on, "to hire one really good new administrator, Barth has to pay $23,000 a year. If they find a top woman or black, it would be about $25,000. Suppose they find a really good one, and suppose our salaries aren't secret. What would it cost the hospital to hire the new person?"

"Well, $20,000, of course," Al said.

"You flunk economics, Al. It would be $27,000."

Al thought for a minute. "I don't see it."

"The new administrator gets $23,000, that's right. But if everyone in the department knew that, they would scream to get paid the same. Under the present law, they might even have a legal case. The administration would have to raise those seven salaries by a thousand each. And $20,000, plus $7,000 equals $27,000."

Al looked at the blackboard, "Yes, I see that. But why is it necessary to be out in the country? Why did you put that down?"

"The hospital is the monopsony buyer of accountants in this town, Al. If we were in a place where an accountant had other options, he could negotiate the best deal he could with the employer who was willing to pay. If the market price was $20,000, that's what he would get. But if he wants to live in this town, he gets what the hospital pays—there aren't any other options."

"You accountants are great. Now I know why my salary is so low, thanks to monopso—whatever theory. So what? What can we do about it? I have to pay a stiff dental bill next week, and your theory doesn't tell me what to do about that."

Problems

1. Would Harmon's theory explain why executive salaries are kept secret?

2. Suppose Al and Harmon wanted to work toward getting higher salaries. What positive steps could they take?

3. If you were president of a local administrators (collective bargaining) association, and you had just heard Harmon talk about monopsony, would his theory provide ammunition to use in getting better pay for administrators?

4. Why do you think black and female administrators sometimes get higher starting salaries than white males?

"Well, your company is certainly fair enough, Lars—$18,000 a year is right in the ballpark for new accountants."

Lars gulped. He had recommended Jeff himself, because they had been in school together for a while, but Lars had graduated two years ago. Jeff had dropped out for a while, fiddled around, and then gone back to finish. "Ah, $18,000?" Lars said weakly.

"Yeah, not a bad offer. The fringes are pretty good, too. What are they paying you, Lars?"

"Ah, $16,000."

"What? How come? You had better grades than I did."

"Well, two years ago the starting salary was $13,500. I've done quite well, really—gotten two good raises. I guess that the demand for accountants is picking up again."

"Believe me, it is. I had two job offers. One was $17,500, and one was $19,500, but it was a lousy company. I think I'll go with yours."

"You know, Jeff, it just doesn't seem fair. I mean, here I've been working for two years, and I'm not getting as much as you'll get to start."

Jeff smiled. "Remember your economics, Lars. Supply and demand. Supply is up a bit, but demand is up more—and the market is talking. If a company wants a new accountant, they have to pay the price."

Case Problem 2

INEQUITIES

Problems

1. How can the company handle this problem to avoid inequities? Can the problem be solved?

2. What should Lars do?

Notes

1. Anthony M. Pasquale, *A New Dimension to Job Evaluation* (New York: American Management Association, 1969), p. 12.

2. The description of the guide charts was adopted from positive evaluation manuals developed by Hay Associates, management consultants, Philadelphia, Pa.

3. See *Top Management Report,* issued on a subscription basis by the Executive Compensation Service, American Management Associations, 135 West 50th Street, New York, NY 10020.

4. Thomas H. Patten, Jr., "Merit Increases and the Facts of Organizational Life," *Management of Personnel Quarterly,* Summer 1968, p. 36. Patten studied the salary histories of 3,247 employees of the Conglomerco Corporation.

5. See, for example, Edward E. Lawler, III, "The Mythology of Management Compensation," *California Management Review,* Fall 1966, pp. 11–22.

6. Lee Dyer, Donald P. Schwab, and Roland D. Theriault, "Managerial Perceptions Regarding Salary Increase Criteria," *Personnel Psychology,* Summer 1976, pp. 233–42.

7. Richard E. Hill, "The Urgency Factor: A Model for the Administration of Salary Merit Programs," *Personnel Journal,* September 1969, pp. 698–701.

8. Myles H. Goldberg, "Another Look at Merit Pay Programs," *Compensation Review,* Third Quarter 1977, pp. 25ff.

9. Edward E. Lawler, III, "Secrecy About Management Compensation: Are There Hidden Costs?" *Organizational Behavior and Human Performance,* (1967), pp. 182–89.

10. "The Tightening Squeeze on White-Collar Pay," *Business Week,* September 12, 1977, pp. 82–94.

11. Leon H. Robertson, "Profitability Commission Plans Relating Sales Compensation to Profitability," *Management Accounting,* June 1968, p. 40.

12. Ibid.

13. David W. Belcher, *Compensation Administration* (Englewood Cliffs, N.J.: Prentice-Hall, 1974), p. 549.

14. John W. Crim, "Compensating the Non-Supervisory Professional Employee," Doctoral Dissertation, Georgia State University, June 1976.

15. R. E. Sibson, "How Top Managers Spend Their Money," *Business Management,* January 1968, p. 48.

16. William H. Cash, "Executive Compensation," *The Personnel Administrator,* September 1977, p. 23.

17. George W. Torrence states this percentage as a minimum and bases his conclusion on experience with this proportion of bonus over long years. See *Motivation and Measurement of Performance* (Washington, D.C.: Bureau of National Affairs, 1967), p. 36.

18. "More Executive Bonus Plans Tied to Company Earnings, Sales Goals," *The Wall Street Journal,* Thursday, November 20, 1980, p. 29.

19. James J. Sullivan, "Top Executive Compensation: Is It Really Adequate Today?" *The Personnel Administrator,* November 1976, p. 26.

20. James F. Carey, "Successors to the Qualified Stock Option," *Harvard Business Review,* January-February 1978, pp. 143–44.

21. David Kraus, "Executive Pay: Ripe for Reform?" *Harvard Business Review,* September-October 1980, pp. 36–48.

22. Rufus E. Runzheimer, Jr., "How Corporations Are Handling Cost-of-Living Differentials," *Business Horizons,* August 1980, pp. 38–40.

Chapter Twenty
Benefits and Services

In Florida citrus country, disadvantaged farm workers, whose wages would not normally permit it, are able to buy comfortable homes through a special company loan arrangement. A production worker's hopelessly crippled son is rehabilitated through a major medical program. Employees still boast about the great baseball teams sponsored by their company; they recall the 1929 club that even beat a major league farm team. And a shop foreman proudly displays his 25-year service pin exclaiming. "The old man gave it to me himself." Anecdotes like these stem from benefits and services programs for employees. They are an integral part of a compensation package, but the components of benefits and services are so diverse that a separate treatment of these is warranted.

Objectives of Benefits and Services

Benefits and **services** are forms of supplementary compensation because they represent payments (both financial and nonfinancial) over and above wage and salary rates. Today, benefits have become so much a part of the compensation package that they must be administered together. Benefits programs can yield a return to employers and provide advantages to employees if they are part of a plan that supports the objectives of personnel policies. Too frequently, so-called fringes are haphazardly devised and instituted because of union pressure or because other organizations have them. But when organizations initiate objective-oriented plans they can derive substantially more mileage from each benefit dollar they expend. Ideally

LEARNING OBJECTIVES
1. To be familiar with the costs of benefits.
2. To know the principles of successful benefits administration.
3. To know the situational aspects of benefits and services.
4. To know how retirement plans work.
5. To be familiar with various types of employee services.

speaking, organizations should determine their preferences for fringe items and the amount of money available, and then select a mix of benefits most conducive to furthering personnel objectives. Benefits and services programs should provide mutual advantages to employees and employers, offering employees more job and income security, while saving organizations money through reduced employee turnover and higher productivity. Four important objectives of providing benefits and services are described below.

1. *Attract and retain employees.* Candidates considering employment offers evaluate not only salary, but also services, facilities, and benefits. When starting salaries are approximately equal to what other organizations pay, the benefits package can made the difference in influencing applicants to accept job offers. By the same token, it can build employee loyalty, and so reduce turnover; employees feel they have made an investment in the benefit program which they would lose if they left their employer. Retirement benefits accumulate with service time, and after a certain number of years, employees become fully eligible to receive their pensions at a specified age; terminating employment eliminates these accumulated benefits. An additional deterrent to turnover is the increasing length of vacation as tenure increases. Employees are eligible for as much as four or five weeks of vacation after 10 or 15 years of employment, and most workers think twice before relinquishing this benefit—even for a higher-paying job. Similarly, stock purchase plans, profit sharing, special leave arrangements, and savings programs improve as employees' service time increases.

2. *Help employees meet their social and economic needs.* Through group plans, organizations can satisfy many social and economic needs that would otherwise be too expensive for employees to provide themselves. IBM is universally renowned for its benefit plans to help meet employee needs; their employee handbook, *About Your Company,* states their objectives in this area:

The aim of this program is to provide a broad foundation upon which the individual employee can build in providing for the needs and well-being for his or her family. . . . The IBM plans provide a foundation for:

Protection—against temporary loss of income and medical expenses resulting from sickness or accident.
Security—by providing an income for retirement, disability, or in the case of death.
Opportunity—through education assistance, vacations, and holidays.[1]

3. *Reduce operating costs.* The cost of fringe benefits can be justified only when they can be translated into tangible savings or operating efficiencies.

Theoretically, benefits provide income and job security, which means that employees can concentrate their attention on their jobs. Experience has shown that programs of benefits and services help influence and maintain positive attitudes in the work force, and this effect translates into more harmonious employee/employer relations and lower turnover and absenteeism. Though difficult to pinpoint, the ultimate result of such plans is a reduction in operating costs.

4. *Abide by government regulations.* Federal and state laws require organizations to support certain benefits, such as unemployment compensation; old-age, survivors, disability, and health insurance; worker's compensation; and retirement programs. In the late '70's the government imposed a ceiling (7%) on wage/salary improvements. It was not clear which benefit areas were limited by this ceiling, but any improvement had to consider the possible implications of the ceiling.

In summary, benefits and services programs have a number of purposes. Organizations generally regard the costs associated with these programs as an investment. In exchange for the tangible benefits provided for employees, firms expect a return either in the form of operating improvements or a more stable work force. The success of benefits and services programs is contingent upon a planned and objective approach by management as well as an understanding by employees of their value.

Background of Employee Benefits

As far back as the guild system, industry has attempted to provide some relief against worker suffering. In this country, the first industrial retirement and death-benefit plans appeared in the early 1900s. The federal government began to exercise initiative in the area of industrial injury payments following Maryland's enactment of the first workmen's compensation legislation (subsequently declared unconstitutional, but nevertheless a milestone in protective labor legislation). But perhaps the greatest impetus to recognizing the need for employee benefits and services came from the Hawthorne Studies. These experiments concluded that worker job satisfaction led to increased productivity. It was obvious that job satisfaction could be increased through benefits designed to make workers happy. Consequently, during the 1930s, rest periods, vacations, bonuses, profit-sharing plans, holidays, recreation facilities, and similar programs were introduced following publication of the Hawthorne Studies. Thus, the human relations movement was born.

When the War Labor Board froze wages to curb inflation during the Second World War, the dispensing of benefits showed their greatest increase. The Board proscribed wage improvements but allowed increases in noncash benefits, which the board chairman referred to as fringe benefits. Anything not considered a base-pay rate did not directly increase employees' purchasing power and so was not considered inflationary. Companies competing for scarce labor expanded benefits to attract needed skills.

Following the Second World War, labor unions struck for and obtained liberalized fringe benefits, especially in the areas of time-off-with-pay, retirement, and insurance. The greatest gains came in the form of increased company contributions to existing programs. With the advent of automation in the 1950s and concern for workers who lost their jobs due to technological advances, supplemental unemployment benefits and the guaranteed annual wage became popular fringe benefit issues at the bargaining table.

In recent years, attention was focused on reduced and flexible hours and leisure-time activities. Employees have pushed for shorter hours and in some cases have had the work week reduced to 35 hours. The four-day, forty-hour arrangement gained some popularity in the early 1970s; although favored by employees, its feasibility has not yet been empirically demonstrated. Increased holidays, longer vacations (including sabbatical leaves up to three months), and increased free time during the work week have also shortened the number of hours employees spend on the job.

Costs of Benefits

Benefits and services as a proportion of total payroll costs were reported at 36.6 percent in 1979, an increase of 5.8 percent over 1971.[2] At this rate these costs could easily approach 50 percent in the next decade. Table 20.1 offers a breakdown of fringe benefits expenditures as a percentage of payroll. A *U.S. News and World Report* economic study showed that in a ten-year period ending in 1979, the average value of an employee's benefit

Table 20.1
Fringe Benefit Costs

Category	Percent of Payroll
Pension and insurance plans	12.1
Vacation, holidays, sick leave, personal leave, etc.	9.5
Social Security, unemployment and worker's compensation, and other legally required payments.	9.0
Paid rest periods, lunch periods, wash-up time, etc.	3.5
Bonuses, profit sharing, etc.	2.5
Total	36.6

Source: *Employee Benefits 1979* (Washington, D.C.: U.S. Chamber of Commerce, 1980), p. 11.

package soared to $5,560. Between 1969 and 1979 average pay was up 2.2% compared to average growth of 36.8% in benefits (both increases are in constant dollars to eliminate inflationary effect). The magnitude of fringe benefits costs can be realized from the fact that private industry spent $420 billion on them in 1980.[3] We seem to be approaching the limit in the amount industry is willing to pay for benefits and services. Some areas are growing more rapidly than others; for example, medical and pension and certain benefits and services, which represented pet projects of upper management, have had questionable impact on employee morale or well-being. One medium-sized food products manufacturer, for example, found that family picnics and a recreation facility were becoming prohibitively expensive and generated more dissatisfaction than goodwill. So management decided to eliminate both. One compensation manager predicts that there will be a trend toward reducing and/or eliminating segments of the employee benefits package. Organizations, he emphasized, might be well advised to review their benefits and services to see if the costs of the various programs are justified in terms of the benefits received. They might consider self-insurance and/or switching from family to individual employee coverage (with the option of family coverage offered at employee expense) as a means of cutting insurance costs.[4]

Principles of Benefits Management

Experience in managing employee services and benefits has yielded certain precepts to guide those responsible for fringe benefits. The guidelines that follow are not hard-and-fast rules, but their application can help avoid costly errors.

1. *Organizations should allow employees to participate in designing benefits plans.* Benefits must be in accord with employee needs and desires, therefore if organizations involve employee representatives in developing them, the outcome is more likely to satisfy this objective. Unions, when present, represent employee interests in bargaining sessions. In the absence of one, employers must make provisions for an employee voice in administering benefits programs.

2. *Employees should also participate in the cost of benefits-and-services administration to preserve their interest in its proper maintenance.* When employees share the costs of programs they are less inclined to be apathetic about runaway expenses or poor service. The author recalls a certain group of employees who were interested in recreational pursuits and requested that the president of the company provide facilities for a baseball team. Accepting the argument that a ball team would help build employee spirit, the president designated a parcel of land adjacent to the plant for

recreation purposes and had a local contractor lay out a ball diamond, with stands and dressing facilities. The employees solicited interested members to form a team and then made a second request to the president for funds for equipment, which was promptly granted. Following several practice sessions, the team realized that the competing clubs all had uniforms. Once more the team approached the president with the proposition that uniforms would be good advertising for the company and the team would look conspicuous playing without them. Since he had already expended funds for facilities and equipment, he thought a little more wouldn't hurt. But it did. After the team's fourth loss in a row, interest dwindled. One member after another found an excuse to quit, and the team soon folded. The company had provided everything, the employees nothing. Having nothing invested, employees had little incentive to put forth an effort.

3. *The cost of benefits once committed represents a continuing cost to an organization.* After a benefits plan or service is instituted, it continues until it is replaced or eliminated (and eliminating a benefit has adverse consequences that may exceed the cost of administration). Therefore, organizations planning a benefits package should understand that benefits costs are not a one-time expense; they continue indefinitely and generally increase over time.

4. *An organization should not adopt the programs of others without considering the particular needs of its employees.* The same amount of money can buy different combinations of benefits, and options within plans can make benefits more suitable to particular groups of employees. For example, in medical-insurance plans, a small deductible could be applied in return for higher major-medical benefits. If employees' earnings are relatively high, they can usually afford minor medical expenses, but the cost of serious illnesses can prove financially disastrous. These employees would obviously prefer coverage for major expenses instead of insurance for incidentals.

5. *It is difficult to revoke benefits once they are established.* A certain organization had, over a period of years, allowed operating supervisors to use company cars for personal transportation. The use of a company car represented a considerable financial saving in addition to being a prestige symbol. Then one day, in a cost-cutting measure, the company ordered the supervisors to restrict the use of company cars to official business only. The supervisors lost face with their employees, who interpreted the move as a disciplinary measure. The supervisors also had to buy replacement cars themselves. The consequent damage in terms of low morale and resentment toward the company was incalculable.

6. *Organizations should periodically inform employees of their benefits.* Organizations should keep employees aware of the details of benefits and services, the way these are calculated, and the costs of administering them. Because of the variety and complexity of most benefit plans, employee misunderstandings can easily occur. Organizations must not assume that employees understand their benefits package simply because an orientation program discussed it, or because they were given a handbook explaining the details. Continuous communication with employees is critical to the success of a benefits program. The J. C. Penney Company is considered one of the best in providing benefits and communicating them to employees. All associates receive an annual statement that is tailored to their specific situation, showing, in dollar figures, the projected benefits each associate and family members may receive from the program. Assisted by an interview guide, their supervisors review each benefit in the statement with them. They answer any questions associates may have and take the necessary time to assure that they understand all aspects of the benefits program. If they review their benefits statement, employees should certainly have a keen awareness of the size of their investment in the company. And the knowledge that they can accumulate $100,000 in the savings and profit-sharing plan by the time they retire certainly is reassuring.

7. *Organizations should periodically evaluate all benefits and services.* As we previously stated, organizations should revise or possibly eliminate programs that are no longer appropriate. Reviews of costs and the programs' effects on personnel objectives will help ensure that the results support the basic purposes of personnel management.

Situational Aspects of Benefits and Services

Some of the situational variables that affect benefits and services include government regulations, union-management relations, management attitudes, and industry practices. The dynamic interaction among these variables has a positive impact upon benefits and services, which clearly suggests that they will continue to grow in the future.

GOVERNMENT REGULATIONS

Federal and state legislation requires many employers to contribute to programs for Social Security, unemployment compensation, and workers' compensation. Health and safety regulations establish standards for plants and provide the impetus for companies to offer medical facilities and related services. Also, when the federal government institutes wage controls, organizations generally make benefit improvements in lieu of direct pay increases.

UNION-MANAGEMENT RELATIONS

Collective bargaining has had a major influence on fringe benefits. Benefits negotiated between unions and management are usually extended to nonunion employees, and they also act as inducements for other companies to adopt them. Then, too, concessions won by an international union in one location often serve as a pattern for subsequent negotiations with other companies. Very often, union demands for benefits improvements are designed to offset adverse economic conditions or management moves that are considered detrimental to labor. For instance, unions countered technological improvements, which resulted in labor displacement, with demands for a guaranteed annual wage and supplemental unemployment benefits. Of late, unions have proposed extended vacations and sabbatical leaves in an effort to spread the work and avoid lay-offs.

MANAGEMENT ATTITUDES

As more organizations adopt an attitude of social conscience, benefits increase and improve. Organizations are introducing benefits and services to provide satisfactions that formerly came from work itself. They recognize the need for concern about the welfare of their human resources as well as society as a whole. The images of such companies as IBM, Xerox, Delta Airlines, Coca-Cola, and Eastman Kodak have been enhanced through their innovative approaches to employee benefits and services. The good-citizen-in-the-community image influences other firms to look at their own supplemental compensation packages.

PRACTICES WITHIN INDUSTRY

Competitive pressures within an industry are often reflected in the scope and form of benefits programs. Organizations attempt to distinguish their employment offers with an attractive package of benefits and services. Intensive competition for critical skills has prompted many companies to offer generous benefits to prospective employees. For management employees, country club memberships, relocation expenses, bonus arrangements, and company cars are included in this category.

Employee Benefits

Employee benefits, as distinguished from services, are largely financial in nature and supplement regular pay. That is, they are either in the form of money or some means of protecting employees against financial loss. Benefits represent necessary items that would otherwise require a cash outlay by employees. Specifically, any benefit supplemental to wages that is paid for by employers can be considered a fringe benefit. And these generally fall into the following categories: legally required, pay for time not worked, pensions, and insurance.

LEGALLY REQUIRED BENEFITS

OLD AGE ASSISTANCE. The 1935 Social Security Act provided for workers in their old age, their survivors, and disability benefits (OASDI). To be eligible for benefits requires that one have a currently insured status, and the recipient or survivor's dependents must have worked a minimum of six quarters. The 1965 amendments increased the original benefits and made two new ones available to people 65 and over; these are Hospital Insurance (HI) and Supplemental Medical Insurance, which make up the Medicare program. All this aid is financed through payroll taxes shared equally by employees and their employers. These taxes, imposed by the Federal Insurance Contributions Act (commonly referred to as FICA taxes), amounted to 13.30 percent of the first $29,700 of employee's earnings in 1981—6.65 percent is deducted from the employees' pay and an additional 6.65 percent is contributed by the employer. By 1987, the law calls for this 13.30 percent to increase to 14.30. The collected taxes are held in trust for each employee in an account designated by his or her social security number. Employees become eligible to receive full retirement benefits at age 65 or lower benefits at age 62. If an employee dies the family receives survivor benefits regardless of his or her age. Also, workers who become totally disabled before 65 are eligible to receive insurance benefits. Under Medicare provisions eligible individuals receive payments for doctor and hospital bills as well as related benefits and services. Depending on average earnings, the period of contributions, and the nature of the claim, the amount of benefits an individual receives varies.

WORKERS' COMPENSATION. All states now have laws covering the compensation of workers for occupation-related accidents and illnesses. **Workers' compensation** programs are financed through premiums paid either to private insurance companies or to state-operated systems. The amount of the premium is adjusted by a merit-rating scheme based on an employer's accident record or the degree of hazard present in the work environment. Generally speaking, legislation covers the following categories of disabilities:

1. Death, which provides dependents with a lump-sum payment or weekly payments.

2. Permanent total disability or permanent partial disability which provides

a lump-sum payment or weekly payments to disabled employees. The duration and amount of payment is usually dependent on the nature and severity of the disability.

3. Partial temporary or total temporary disability which provides weekly payments for a stipulated period, depending on the type of disability.

Though most states specify the amounts to be paid for various types of disabilities there is still an abundance of court suits filed by employees or their dependents seeking larger awards (in part because judges and juries traditionally are sympathetic to disabled employees). (A detailed discussion of workers' compensation appears in Chapter 21, "Employee Health and Safety.")

UNEMPLOYMENT COMPENSATION. **Unemployment compensation** is a federal/state cooperation program whereby states have passed laws in conformity with the federal law (under the Social Security Act) and pay a portion of their unemployment compensation receipts to the federal government, which is co-insurer. Each state provides weekly benefits to individuals who become unemployed due to specified conditions and actively seek employment. After a short waiting period these individuals receive weekly benefits (which, based on average earnings and length of time worked prior to unemployment, vary from state to state), usually for a period of 26 weeks for each period of unemployment. Some of the provisions require that an employee not be discharged for cause, must be "ready, willing, and able to work, and be actively seeking work." An employer is notified of every claim and may contest it. During the recession of 1975, when unemployment was widespread, several states increased their maximum weekly benefit rate, and Congress passed emergency legislation as a counter-measure. One such law—the Federal Unemployment Benefits Act—temporarily extended unemployment compensation from 26 weeks to a maximum of 65 weeks. The heavy strain placed on state funds by the widespread continued unemployment caused many of them to seek federal loans in order to pay benefits.[5] The weekly stipend is not intended to replace lost income but to help sustain workers while they seek employment. The programs are financed by taxes which are paid by employers and based on a rating of their layoffs (this encourages companies to stabilize their labor force). The Federal Unemployment Tax Act established the maximum amount of tax at 0.7 percent of the first $6,000 of each employee's annual pay. This rate is expected to be cut to 0.5 percent.

Experience with unemployment insurance has not been all positive. Martin Feldstein argues that the economics of unemployment have changed since the program was conceived in the 1930s.[6] He maintains that existing programs provide an incentive to maintain inappropriately long durations of unemployment because the actual cost to an employee of remaining unemployed is small. He also points out that employers pay a relatively small premium for unstable employment practices, and there is little incentive to reduce this. He advocates reforms that would: (1) make unemployment compensation subject to income tax in order to eliminate the possibility that an individual can receive a higher net income from unemployment benefits than from customary earnings; (2) improving employer experience ratings by removing the ceiling on an employer's rate of contribution and by lowering the minimum rate to zero, thereby removing the inequity where stable employers subsidize unstable ones (individual employers would then pay the full cost of the unemployment-insurance benefits of their own employees); and (3) supplement unemployment compensation with unemployment loans, thus increasing protection and introducing a system of individual employee experience ratings.

On the other hand, a Brookings study concluded that ". . . the existing system causes a perceptible, but small, amount of unemployment in the United States—between 0.2 and 0.3 percent of the labor force—that is not a figure that supports the notion of armies of unemployed malingerers and chiselers . . ."[7] Among the various forms of income support for the unemployed, unemployment insurance stands out as the most successful and the least controversial.

PAY FOR TIME NOT WORKED

Time off with pay has become one of the most popular benefits. Numerous studies have concluded that breaks in work time improve productivity, and it is universally accepted that employers should compensate employees for vacation periods, holidays, and other necessary leaves from the job. Modified work hours arrangements have had mixed results in industry, but interest in these programs remains high.

REST PERIODS.   Paid rest periods are quite common in industry today. The coffee break has become the subject of much concern in personnel circles largely because it tends to get out of hand if not closely controlled. Short rest periods, when properly spaced during the work day, can benefit production. However, workers sometimes extend their breaks and frequently take unscheduled breaks from the work routine. The number, placement, and duration of these depend on the type of work, conditions in the work place, and the individual employee. Rest periods are particularly essential in work that involves continuous process, close attention, physical exertion, routine and repetition, or exposure to temperature extremes, hazards, or other undesirable working conditions.

SICK LEAVE. Employees are often unavoidably absent from work due to illness or accidents unrelated to their jobs. Most employers allow **sick leave,** that is, a specified number of days each year for these contingencies without docking pay from employees. But few organizations provide any incentive for employees not to miss work days. A sick-pay provision offers a benefit not only to those employees who must miss work but also to those who feign illness to receive compensation without working. And since the cost of surveillance is greater than blanket approval of benefit payments, violations become widespread. This practice is tantamount to penalizing conscientious employees who have perfect attendance records. To offset this shortcoming some organizations allow employees to accumulate unused sick leave. After an accumulation of a specified maximum number of days, firms pay these employees annual bonuses for additional unused sick leave. Accident and sickness benefits (A&S) are closely allied to sick leave, although A&S is a form of insurance whereby a covered employee receives a percent of his or her weekly pay. Usually this coverage begins after a waiting period and usually when sick-leave benefits have been exhausted. Benefits usually expire after a specified period of illness, for example, 26 weeks. Traditionally, pregnancy has not been a covered disability. In fact, the Supreme Court in 1976 ruled that employers were not required to pay benefits for maternity leaves. However, the practice of covering such leaves under A&S is beginning to take hold, and a number of union-management contracts have been modified to include compensation for pregnancy "disabilities."

LEAVES OF ABSENCE. It is a common practice for organizations to grant employees leaves of absence for specific reasons. However, there is little uniformity in the types of leaves granted and the rules governing leave administration. The most common types of leaves include military duty, union business, maternity, and personal, family, and civic obligations such as jury duty. Organizations strive to apply leave policy uniformly to avoid charges of discrimination. They usually require employees taking leave to give notice, but they grant emergency leave (e.g., for family illness or funeral) with minimum notification. The duration varies with the type of leave needed, type of job or level within an organization, and the latter's policy. Leaves of short duration (under one month) are quite common. Federal legislation (the Selective Service Act) guarantees reemployment to employees who are drafted during national emergencies. Organizations must offer previously employed veterans a position commensurate with the one they would have reached had they not left for military service. (The same rule applies to their seniority rights.) Leave policy usually specifies the status of employees on leave: the length of time their pay will continue during their absence, the status of their insurance, and the accumulation of their seniority and retirement benefits.

HOLIDAYS AND VACATIONS. Paid time off for specified holidays is almost a universal practice. The number of holidays recognized for fringe purposes varies from organization to organization, but seldom are there fewer than 7 or more than 16. With the legal designation of Monday as the day to celebrate Washington's Birthday, Memorial Day, Veteran's Day, and Columbus Day, the long weekend has gained increasing acceptance. A forerunner of this was the practice of many organizations in granting employees the following Monday off when a holiday fell on a Sunday, and more recently, giving off the preceding Friday when a holiday fell on a Saturday. Some organizations offer floating holidays, which are observed on different days from year to year or may be taken at the individual employee's option, such as on a birthday.[8]

It is customary for organizations to pay a premium for employees working during a holiday. The most common practice is to pay time-and-a-half for holiday work hours on top of the regular holiday pay, but some organizations pay double the base rate in addition to holiday pay. To be eligible to receive holiday pay, employees are usually required to complete a probationary period ranging from a month to a year and to work their regularly scheduled shifts immediately preceding and following the holiday. Such a rule is designed to limit holiday pay to full-time employees and to curb absenteeism associated with holidays.

Vacation breaks were offered to permit employees a rest between work periods. It is for this reason that most firms insist that employees take their vacations. However, many organizations allow employees to carry over unused portions or days of their vacations up to a specified number of weeks, after which they must use the time or lose it. Most plans provide for graduated vacations based on length of service, usually 1 week after 1 year of service, 2 weeks after 3 years, 3 weeks after 5 to 10 years, and 4 weeks after 20 years. Under the agreement between the United Steelworkers and the can manufacturers, workers with 20 or more years of service are eligible for 3-month sabbaticals. The underlying purpose of the sabbatical was more to reduce unemployment than to provide therapy through rest and recreation.

MODIFIED WORK-HOURS ARRANGEMENTS. The labor force has historically pushed for a reduction in working hours with no decrease in total compensation. Plans to shorten the work week have gained momentum in recent years. Workers have strongly supported a 4-day work week with 10-hour days or less (the 4/40). Employees who favor working under a reduced work-week arrangement cite the increased leisure time as a prime advantage. They also find it easier to transact personal business without losing work time and wages. With other firms functioning on traditional 5-day schedules, there is the added convenience of less congested travel and easier parking arrangements for workers under this system. Organizations link days off with Monday holidays to give 4-day employees short vacations. Ivancevich and Lyons conducted a field experiment with workers on a 4-day, 40-hour schedule.[9] Their analysis of data after 13 months revealed that workers were more satisfied with their autonomy, personal worth, job security, and pay; experienced less anxiety-stress; and performed better with regard to productivity than did a control group working a normal work schedule. However, their data showed that these improvements lessened or were absent after 25 months on the shortened work-week schedule. Citing the popularity of the 4-day work week, the *Wall Street Journal* estimated that 1.2 million Americans or 2 percent of the full time work force are on the 4-day work week.[10]

Compensation managers also see some drawbacks to the 4/40 and similar arrangements, however. Experience has shown that longer weekends may lead to employee moonlighting. Scheduling can be a headache, especially for those employees who must coordinate their work with 5-day schedules. And supervisors often find themselves working longer hours to keep their areas of responsibility functioning.[11]

Similarly, flexible hours (**flexitime**) arrangements are getting increased attention by organizations. Organizations that have adopted flexible hours offer each of their employees several options for starting and quitting time (each of the options requires the same total number of work hours). There is a base period or core time when everyone must be at work and a flexible band at the beginning and end of each day when employees may elect to arrive or leave at a personally convenient hour rather than the usual specified time. Considerable variation can be established in the flexible-hours arrangements. The length of the core period and flexible band, whether an employee has an option of offsetting fewer hours worked in one day with additional hours another day during the week or month, may vary with the organization or unit (e.g., department, agency).[12]

Although only about 100 corporations report its adoption, experience with flexitime has been generally favorable.[13] Attendance tends to improve and tardiness is virtually eliminated; productivity increases are reported far more often than decreases; overtime hours are usually reduced; utilization of plant and equipment improve; service to clients increases; employees appreciate the freedom to adjust their work schedules to their individual work styles; and they assume more responsibility for their work.[14]

Conversely, not every organization has experienced success with flexitime; in fact, several have abandoned the arrangement because they found it unworkable. Since their total work force is available only during core time, scheduling problems can arise. Another inherent disadvantage results from the fact that employees arrive and depart at different hours, which makes it difficult to conform to wage and hour laws.[15]

Studies of flexitime have been confined to the experience of individual organizations.[16] But a broad-based experiment that could produce empirical evidence for future decisions on the adoption of flexible work schedules was ordered by the House of Representatives in 1976 and placed under the direction of the Civil Service Commission (now the Office of Personnel Management). The study has strong support from women's organizations, which view flexitime as an opportunity for working mothers to improve their chances of getting and holding a job.[17]

Job sharing or worksharing is an alternative form of modified work hours scheduling whereby two people hold responsibility for what was formerly one full-time position. Salary and fringe benefits are prorated according to time worked. But employers worry that most people do not want part-time work or cannot afford the cut in pay, that supervisors' problems would double, and equitable fringe-benefits arrangements become complicated, thus inhibiting the wide use of job-sharing. However, in practice these worries do not seem to materialize. Those employers who have adopted this arrangement find there is more effective use of workers' time; jobs can be restructured so that people work primarily during heavy demand hours and productivity is enhanced. There is also an advantage to employees in trading off hours needed for personal activities with a working partner. This translates into reduced absenteeism and turnover. And permanent part-time employment often enables women and older people to continue to work. Also, cases have been cited of workers currently employed in work-sharing positions who probably would not have been hired within traditional work schedules because of either their inadequate overall experience or intense competition. Take, for instance, the Ph.D. biologist who was unable to find part-time work in her own field and is now working with an electrical engineer on a job-sharing arrangement planning new hospital facilities. Successful job-sharing requires close communication and cooperation between the participants.[18] But not all job sharing is voluntary. Slack workloads create involuntary worksharing and the number of employees affected has remained at or above 1.5 million.[19]

RETIREMENT PLANS

The problems of aging and preparation for retirement appear in Chapter 8. Here we discuss pensions and related retirement benefits plans.

Retirement plans were introduced to add a measure of security to the job by providing income after retirement (pensions, profit sharing, savings, and so on). These plans are based on the philosophy that long-service employees should receive an income from their organization which, in combination with Social Security payments and personal savings, will enable them to maintain a reasonable standard of living during retirement. According to a personnel policies forum study, most organizations have revised their pension plans to meet the requirements of the Employee Retirement Income Security Act (ERISA), particularly as they relate to vesting of benefits, funding, and eligibility for enrollment.[20] Details of ERISA's provisions will be discussed later in this section.

RETIREMENT BENEFITS. The amount of employee benefits retirees receive depends upon the type of plan, their earnings, and their years of service. The retirement plans of some companies supplement pensions (lump sums or monthly payments employees receive upon retiring) with thrift or deferred profit-sharing plans. However, this combination increases the difficulties inherent in the financial aspects of retirement plans. Organizations often cite the depressing effect the economy can have on profit sharing plans and the problem of communicating this effect to disgruntled employees. Just as economic recessions have an adverse affect on profit sharing plans, so inflation erodes pension funds. A combination of inflation, improvements in pension plans, and an increase in the number of people covered has caused payments to climb 307 percent in the past 10 years.[21] Currently, total assets of private pension funds are estimated at $360 billion, but payout demands are surpassing income to the funds. The underlying problem is the increasing number of retirees—10% of the population in 1980 were 65 or over and this figure will jump to 18% by 2025. It is hoped that raising the retirement age to 70 will induce a larger number of workers to remain in the labor force longer.[22]

Organizations require their employees to have a minimum number of years of service before they are eligible to receive benefits. The standard minimum ranges from 10 to 25 years, and obviously, the amount of pension increases with length of service. Employees' earnings also influence the size of their pensions. Because employees generally earn more as their time with an organization increases, many plans have been liberalized by using more recent pay (instead of average earnings over the full term of employment) as the basis for calculating benefits. Further improvements in pensions are realized when employees contribute a stipulated percentage of their total earnings to the fund on either a voluntary or compulsory basis. One pension specialist estimated that an adequate pension should amount to 1.6% of one's final monthly salary for each year of service. This would amount to a pension of 48% of the last year's salary for 30 years of service (1.6 × 30), plus Social Security benefits.[23]

RETIREMENT PRACTICES. A number of practices concerning retirement programs are worthy of mention. Chapter 8 discussed the importance of counseling to ease the transition from active employment to retirement.

Similar in purpose are the tapering-off programs utilized by some organizations. These programs operate on an individual basis to give employees approaching retirement more and more time off through extended vacations, loaned-executive programs, and leaves of absence. Retiring employees gradually learn to manage increased leisure time while their replacements gain practical experience learning the new job.

Vesting is the practice of granting employees accrued credits in the pension plan whether or not they stay with the organization. It is the fixed interest employees earn in a pension or profit-sharing fund with their years of service. After a stipulated number of years, individuals become partially vested. The percentage of their vested rights then increases with service until, usually after 10 years, they become fully vested.

Portability that allows workers to take their accumulated benefits with them when they change jobs is a provision rarely found in plans today, but it is likely to become the norm should Congress add such a provision to existing pension legislation.

The value of private pension plans is universally recognized, but their deficiencies and mismanagement have aroused criticism. Recent regulations have attempted to ensure the financial integrity and fairness of these plans. The Federal Welfare and Pension Plans Disclosure Act of 1958 (amended in 1962) requires bonded administrators and detailed reports. The mismanagement of funds carries severe penalties. Legislation in 1968 established funding standards, required full vesting after 10 years, and guaranteed that pension obligations would be met even when plans fold. Revolutionary changes in pension regulation appeared in 1974 in the form of ERISA.

ERISA.   The Employee Retirement Income Security Act (**ERISA**) was enacted in 1974 to guarantee that employees who are covered by private pension plans receive the benefits to which they are entitled. Prior to the enactment of ERISA many cases of misuse of pension funds and poor management of plans had been uncovered. Consequently, the law sets strict rules for plan administration and specifies penalties for violations of these rules. Although employers are not required to initiate or maintain a pension plan under the new regulations, those that do must comply with complex administrative and reporting requirements.

The protection of employee rights was a principal reason for enacting ERISA. Under the Act pension plan participants and their beneficiaries have a right to:

1. Receive a written explanation of the pension plan in easily understood language so that they can grasp the provisions of the plan.
2. Be informed of any material change in the plan.

3. Receive financial statements of the plan.

4. Receive, on request, a statement of accrued benefits and vesting status.

Fiduciary standards were established by the Act to require investments of a plan's funds according to prudent man standards and limit investment in the employer's own stock or real estate. A fiduciary is construed as a person (or persons) responsible for administering a plan and explaining benefits to employees. He or she can be a pension fund trustee or a compensation specialist. A fiduciary can be sued for failing to be prudent in planning or administering a pension plan.

Employees become eligible to participate in a plan when they are age 25 and have one year of service. According to ERISA a year of service is 1,000 hours of work during a 12-month period. As mentioned previously, employees have rights to benefits at retirement after they become vested. The Act specifies three optional vesting standards, and employers are required to meet any one of them. They are: (1) full vesting after 10 years of service; (2) graded vesting between 5 and 15 years of service, for example, 25 percent after 5 years of service with annual additions of 5 percent over the next 5 years and 10 percent over the following 5, so an employee with 10 years would be 80 percent vested; or (3) vesting under the rule of 45, whereby an employee is 50 percent vested when years of service (at least 5) and his or her age total 45, with a 10 percent increase in vesting for each additional year of service.

Employees who are not covered by a private pension plan are entitled to establish an Individual Retirement Account (IRA) to which they can contribute on a tax-deferred basis up to 15 percent of their earnings or $1,500, whichever is less. A similar tax shelter has been available to self-employed individuals through the Keogh Plan. Under ERISA such a person can contribute the lesser of 15 percent or $7,500 of earned income to his or her own pension fund. This means that if individuals are self-employed on a part-time basis they can set up Keogh plans with the additional earnings, even though they may be covered by a pension plan on their regular job.

Most employers, in response to tax incentives or to spread costs over a period of years, have chosen to fund pension plans by placing money in a special trust fund or by making payments to an insurance company. Internal Revenue Service regulations specify how the plans must be funded, and ERISA established a federally chartered insurance program to protect employees' and retirees' pension rights in case a plan terminates without sufficient assets to pay benefits. Herein lies one of the most troubling aspects of ERISA, in that the insurance fund creates a contingent liability for employers of up to 30 percent of net worth in the event the plan is terminated without sufficient assets. This represents a radical departure from previous practice, which traditionally has limited an employer's liability to the contributions it actually makes to the pension fund.[24]

Both the U.S. Department of Labor and the Treasury Department share in a coordinated effort to administer the law. The Secretary of Labor has been charged with the responsibility of investigating and inspecting plans to insure compliance, writing regulations, and enforcing fiduciary requirements. A new office called the Office of Employee Plans and Exempt Organizations was set up by the Internal Revenue Service to carry out the Treasury's responsibilities of acting on plan applications and reviewing existing ones to see whether they comply with legal requirements.

In addition to furnishing participants and **beneficiaries** with various information, employers must submit these reports annually to the appropriate administrative agencies:

1. Plan Description (Form EBS-1)—gives information on what the plan provides and how it operates.
2. Summary Plan Description—the plan described in simple terms.
3. Annual Report—financial statement showing the current value of plan assets and liabilities and related figures.
4. Registration Statement—nature, amount, and form of deferred vested benefits.
5. Employer's Return for Employees' Pension or Profit-Sharing Plan—number of employees covered and employer contributions.
6. Premium Payment Declaration (PBGC-1)—premium declarations for coverage of basic benefits.

INSURANCE PROGRAMS

LIFE INSURANCE. Companies have long felt an obligation to provide financial protection for their employees. Initially, employers paid the funeral expenses of employees, but as insurance companies began to offer low-cost group plans, these supplanted the less desirable plans covering funeral arrangements. Today the predominant form of company life insurance is term insurance. After passing an employment physical examination and following a waiting period (usually 90 days), employees are insured for the term of their employment. The amount of coverage generally depends on age, earnings, and length of service. Most plans reduce coverage after retirement age, but continue protection without requiring employees to pay premiums. The rationale is that at advanced age, employees have fewer financial burdens, their children are independent, and they have accumulated savings to cover the few financial obligations they may have. Coverage usually increases with earnings up to a stipulated maximum, and executives may be allowed to purchase additional protection by contributing to the premiums. Some plans increase the amount of insurance as service with the company increases (e.g., an additional $1,000 for each year of service). Many plans allow employees to convert from group coverage to individual plans without further physical examination, if they terminate employment. (Former employees would, of course, have to pay their own premiums). Normally, life insurance plans continue in effect, premium-free, if employees become permanently and totally disabled.

A recent innovation in benefits, **split-dollar life insurance** offers employees a large amount of insurance at a low cost and allows employers to provide an important fringe benefit to employees at little cost. Under this plan an employer pays each year's premium equal to the increase in the cash value of the policy, and the employee pays the remainder, if any, of the premium. As soon as the cash value becomes equal to or greater than the annual premium, the employer will pay the entire premium and the employee has no premium payment to make. Should the employee die, the employer would receive the cash value of the policy, and the difference between the face value and the cash value would be paid to the employee's beneficiary.[25]

HOSPITAL, MEDICAL, SURGICAL (HMS), AND MAJOR MEDICAL PLANS.   Serious or extended illness is a burden on an employee's finances. Group insurance plans that offer financial protection against such contingencies—whether absorbed by the organization, the workers, or both—cost substantially less than individual coverage. The HMS and major-medical package consists of the following components:

1. Hospitalization insurance, which covers services rendered to patients confined to a hospital room, equipment use, ambulance service, X-ray and laboratory services, etc., as well as outpatient treatment including emergency care. There are two basic types of hospitalization insurance: cash indemnity plans, whereby the insurance plan pays the insured a daily flat rate for a specified number of days plus an indemnity for other services for each continuous hospital confinement; and service hospitalization plans (e.g., Blue Cross), whereby the plan provides benefits in terms of services rendered by the hospital instead of cash or allowances.

2. Medical care plans, which cover physicians' services outside of the hospital. Benefits include the cost of office visits, physical examinations, diagnostic X-ray and laboratory work not connected with hospital confinement, and possibly even prescription drugs and special equipment, devices, or therapeutic services.

3. Surgical plans, which cover surgical procedures according to a schedule

stipulating maximums for each operation. This component includes post-operative care and the services of a surgeon.

4. Major medical plans, which cover a large share of hospital, medical, and surgical costs above the coverage of the basic plans (1–3 above). Major medical generally stipulates that the insured pay minor costs, say the first $100 to $300, and the plan pays a fixed percentage, usually 75 to 90 percent above the deductible amount. Most major medical plans specify the maximum unit of coverage in terms of number of days of hospital confinement or a total dollar amount, but it is becoming increasingly common not to establish maximum coverage. In the latter case, the plan covers a percentage of the costs up to a set dollar value, 90 percent of the first $10,000, for example, with a reduced percentage beyond that point. The comprehensive plans incorporate all coverage—hospital, medical, surgical—after a deduction (usually $100) for each illness or injury. Recent innovations have specifically included coverage for dental and vision care and psychiatric treatment, items that were previously excluded, and the BLS reports that dental care and vision care have been among the fastest growing areas of employee health benefits in recent years.[26]

Insurance represents a significant portion of a benefits package (approximately 30 percent), and since carriers base premiums on the experience of the insured, efforts to control its costs are in the interest of management and employees alike. In administering HMS, a personnel department can maintain surveillance over the volume and cost of claims. For example, unnecessary claims often result from requiring a doctor's certification of illness or accident during absences if the organization's medical plan covers doctor visits. This is not to say that medical excuses should not be required, but supervisors and personnel staff should realize it is relatively easy to obtain these. A simple review of claims is the best method of establishing and controlling cost effectiveness. It can also uncover duplicate charges which, though inadvertent, occur frequently. Also, reviewing and evaluating benefits may indicate changes that will make the plans more suitable to the work force. For example, an organization might substitute a plan that covers minor expenses such as office calls (which necessitate high premiums) for a comprehensive plan with a smaller deductible. This change would give employees broader coverage with considerably higher limits at the same premium cost (because of the much higher deductible). If employees' earnings are sufficient to pay for incidental medical costs, the comprehensive coverage may be a more desirable alternative.

The Health Maintenance Organization Act was passed in 1973 to stimulate the establishment of Health Maintenance Organizations (HMOs) in an effort to reduce medical costs. As a result, eight million persons are enrolled in 225 HMOs.[27] The basic idea behind HMOs is the prevention and early detection of disease in contrast to conventional plans that reimburse medical expenses. Under these plans employers contract with an HMO to provide prepaid HMS care for a fixed rate. HMOs purportedly offer superior health care at lower cost. But one study found that HMOs did not vary significantly in terms of several variables (e.g., accessibility of care, patient satisfaction) from the conventional fee-for-service arrangement.[28] Nevertheless, HMOs are destined to grow in number if for no other reason than from government requirements that employers offer their workers the option to join an HMO in lieu of HMS insurance coverage.

CAFETERIA-STYLE PLANS

To allow employees some flexibility in choosing their benefits a few companies (TRW, Inc.'s West Coast systems group, and the Educational Testing Service, in particular) have adopted compensation cafeterias. The arrangement requires employees to maintain a minimum core coverage so they will be assured of basic protection, but beyond this they are free to trade off coverage in one area for benefits in another. They can choose from a cafeteria of benefits options, thus tailoring a program to their particular needs. But the complications of administration and the realization that employees are often ill-equipped to judge what benefits are in their best interests have discouraged other organizations from offering cafeteria-style benefits plans.

OTHER BENEFITS

TUITION REFUND.   Many organizations recognize that the continuing education of the work force is a key to progress. To induce employees to seek additional education some firms underwrite a portion of the expenses for courses directly related to their present or future work. Tuition reimbursement plans generally pay a stipulated percentage of the cost of registration fees, tuition, and books, for courses approved by management. The amount of refund ranges from 50 to 100 percent of tuition costs, and many plans even reimburse all educational costs after employees successfully complete degree programs.

DISCOUNTS.   Although discounts are rarely considered a fringe benefit (because employees could conceivably obtain reduced prices at discount houses anyway), the convenience of having merchandise available at the work place for reduced prices is a benefit. In addition, employee discounts encourage workers to purchase goods manufactured or merchandised by their employer.

SAVINGS PLANS. Thrift or savings plans force employees to set aside part of their earnings. Organizations often match a stipulated percentage of employees' earnings that is withdrawn from their paychecks each month for savings purposes. Many firms couple savings plans with investment plans to provide growth opportunities. When withdrawals from the plan are limited, tax laws allow individuals to defer their tax payments until they actually withdraw the money. In such cases, there is usually a provision for borrowing against the account. Savings plans with employer contributions help retain employees in the same way pension plans do.

STOCK OPTIONS. ERISA and the Tax Reduction Act of 1975 endorsed the adoption of employee stock ownership plans (ESOP) by private businesses. Under ESOP employees share in the ownership of corporations and new capital formation is stimulated. To accomplish this the plan borrows money (a loan guaranteed by the employer) to purchase newly issued stock of the employer. The employer makes annual contributions of stock to the plan and also contributes enough cash to permit the trust to retire the original loan. The employees obtain stock at no cost to them, and, legally, they may defer the tax on the stock they acquire.[29] But critics contend that an ESOP is successful only if the company is successful and the amount of stock contributed is meaningful. They point out that "typical ESOP companies often fail to prosper because they are small or in recession prone industries, causing their stock to decline or stagnate."[30] Yet, Congress is enamored of ESOPs and future legislation will undoubtedly encourage their continued growth.

SUGGESTION SYSTEMS. Traditionally, suggestion systems have purported to be systematic procedures to release a flood of beneficial suggestions, provide a sense of participation by employees, and serve as a means of communication between management and the work force. However, research studies fail to support these propositions.[31] But suggestion systems can stimulate money-saving operational improvements by buying good ideas from employees when the following conditions are met:

1. All personnel, including supervisors, are eligible to submit suggestions.
2. Line management determines the value of the suggestions.[32]
3. Companies base awards for suggestions on savings for as long as the savings will be realized. Most plans only pay on the basis of the first year's savings.

LEGAL AID. Prepaid legal-insurance plans have gained popularity in recent years. Spurred by a pilot plan between Chrysler Corporation and the

Auto Workers, similar arrangements are expected to be adopted that will provide a spectrum of legal services (e.g., divorces, legal consultation, wills, representation in suits, and so on) at little or no cost to an employee. Cost estimates of the plan range from $.04 cents to $.15 cents an hour per employee.[33]

NEGOTIATED BENEFITS. Some benefits derive primarily from union-management collective bargaining. Though they may exist in nonunion programs, such items as shift premium, sabbatical leaves (which have already been mentioned), unemployment benefits, guaranteed annual wage, cost-of-living escalators, and supplemental unemployment benefits have usually been associated with labor-management contracts.

A **shift premium** is the additional pay for hours worked on irregular shifts. The second or afternoon shift and the evening or graveyard shift hours are generally compensated above the regular hourly pay rate. This shift premium helps offset the inconvenience and undesirability of having to work other than regular hours.

A **guaranteed annual wage (GAW)** is rare because such a plan binds the company to potentially heavy financial commitments even though the number of employees may be small. The best known of the GAW systems are at Procter and Gamble, the Nunn-Bush Shoe Company, and the George A. Hormel Company. Common characteristics of these plans are:

1. The employer guarantees a certain number of weeks of employment.
2. Emergency conditions, strikes, and natural disasters are excluded.
3. The company restricts the number of employees covered.

Supplemental unemployment benefits (SUB) grew out of efforts by the auto and steelworkers' unions to gain a guaranteed annual wage. In the 1955 negotiations with Ford and later with other auto manufacturers, the United Auto Workers settled on the first SUB plan. Today, more than 2.5 million workers are covered by SUB, which is designed to augment state unemployment insurance benefits. Management usually finances SUB plans at the rate of five cents per hour. A trust fund is set up to disburse funds, and the company's obligation is limited to the amount of the fund. Employees earn one week of SUB benefits for every two weeks of work. Obviously, laid-off workers must qualify for state unemployment compensation before receiving SUB. Payments from both of these sources usually amount to 50 to 80 percent of gross weekly earnings, but the United Auto Workers recently negotiated an arrangement whereby employees could receive up to 95 percent of their regular wages. Also, a steel-industry pact with the United Steelworkers added a new twist to SUB; now workers who have their earnings cut by technological innovation or other reasons, though still employed, may receive pay supplements from the SUB fund to bring their income up to 85 percent of their average quarterly income in the previous year. From a social-welfare standpoint, SUB is subject to some criticism. Such liberal benefits might weaken the incentive of displaced workers to seek other employment, especially when relocation expenses are involved.

Cost-of-living escalators are pay adjustments geared to increases in the cost of living, theoretically to preserve workers' earning power. Union-management agreements with cost-of-living escalators usually designate wage adjustments computed from increases in the Bureau of Labor Statistics Consumer Price Index (CPI). For example, the cost-of-living adjustment might call for adjustments of one cent per hour when the CPI is 249.3 to 249.6, two cents per hour for 249.7 to 250.0, and additional one-cent increases for each upward .03 index-point change. It would seem logical that declines in the CPI would require similar wage reductions, yet few contracts contain such a provision.

Employee Services

Employee services are programs, facilities, activities, and opportunities supplied by or through an employer, which are useful or beneficial to employees. They differ from fringe benefits in that their value is not so easily translated into financial terms. Some services, such as transportation, offer a convenience to employees; others such as recreational and hobby programs are personally broadening or enriching. Still others provide services such as housing and medical-care facilities that might otherwise be unavailable or prohibitively expensive for individual employees. An organization's motivation to provide employee services is based on its philosophy, employee pressure, social consciousness, and community factors. Because most organizations offer some services, such programs tend to be taken for granted; thus it becomes especially important that companies base services on needs as well as interests. And if a service program is to succeed, employees should support it with their own time, money, and effort. Such an investment on the part of employees produces an attitude of ownership and helps assure their continued involvement.

EMPLOYEE CLUBS

Private facilities with membership restricted to employees and their guests range from elaborate country clubs with dining and sleeping arrangements to a modest room with chairs, music, and reading material. An association, governed by elected employee representatives and sometimes employing a full-time administrator, oversees the operation. Employee clubs combine athletic, social, and cultural activities.

RECREATION

Recreation programs build a spirit of teamwork among employees as well as providing a diversion from the routine of work. Theoretically, at least, recreation programs have a beneficial effect on morale.

ATHLETIC TEAMS

An athletic team, especially a winning one, can offer advantages to an organization and its employees alike. Not only does the team advertise the organization, but the spirit of competition improves morale, and the physical activity helps maintain the health of employees. Properly organized athletic programs have a professional coordinator who encourages employees to become active participants. But organizing company teams is no simple matter. Organizations must first answer questions bearing on personnel administration, such as:

1. Will practice and team meetings be on company or employee time?
2. What safety and insurance considerations should the company take into account?
3. What assistance will the company provide?
4. How will the team be financed? (Vending machine receipts and employee dues are usually used to finance recreational activities.)
5. What, if any, relationship should there be with community recreational activities?

SOCIAL EVENTS

Dances, picnics, and Christmas parties are examples of social events that most organizations arrange for employees and their families. To minimize problems, organizations carefully plan the types of activities, food and beverage arrangements, in-plant versus off-site facilities, and the method of financing. Social events are frequently the source of criticism, as evidenced by the notoriety of the office party. It takes considerable tact to curtail excessive drinking and horseplay that could negate the possible benefits of a social event.

RETREATS AND CAMPSITES

Retreats and campsites are often a part of an organization's recreation programs. These facilities bear separate mention to underscore the need to designate land areas for camping. The recent emphasis on ecology has given people an awareness of the rapidly diminishing availability of unspoiled land. Mountain areas for camping, lake shores and stream sites for fishing, boating, and swimming, and wooded areas for hiking and nature walks will become increasingly important to employees.

CULTURAL ACTIVITIES

Hobby crafts, dance groups, music appreciation, and library facilities are just a few of the many cultural activities that organizations can provide for the cultural enrichment of their employees. Behavioral scientists contend that these activities stimulate broad-minded attitudes in people, thus contributing indirectly to more effective job performance. These activities are relatively inexpensive, and industry experience with them has been generally favorable.

Social and cultural clubs frequently appear within organizations to satisfy the need for association or merely for economic reasons. Transportation lines, theaters, and athletic clubs offer discount and charter rates to groups. Employees on vacations and holidays can enjoy low-cost tours, trips, or shows through company-sponsored or company-sanctioned groups.

COUNSELING SERVICES

Chapter 8 covered the concepts and techniques of counseling. The same counseling facilities can provide services to employees. Organizations can make legal aid, financial advice, mental-health assistance, and vocational guidance available to employees through the auspices of a professional counselor. Detailed tax regulations and the myriad of benefit possibilities make financial advice a particularly attractive service to executives.

CREDIT UNIONS

Credit unions are operated for the mutual benefit of their members. They offer small loans at low-interest rates to employee members and also provide savings plans coupled with life insurance. And having a savings and loan institution near the work place is a convenience to employees. Industrial credit unions have experienced phenomenal growth since their inception in the early part of the century; today there are over 24,000 in this country. Federal and state laws regulate credit unions, which may contribute to their acceptability among industrial workers.

HOUSING

Some organizations offer rent-free or low-rent housing to their employees. More recently, organizations have made provisions for employees to purchase their own homes. This service is particularly helpful in areas with many disadvantaged people or in industries employing migratory workers. These people rarely have the opportunity to own decent housing, so programs that enable such employees to become home owners contribute to social welfare and enhance good employee relations. One such example is Coca-Cola's Agriculture and Labor Program, Inc. (ALPI).[34] It includes a home-purchase program for migrant workers in Coke's Minute Maid groves and is part of a system to improve the quality of life among its employees. The project emphasizes worker involvement in policy making and implementation. Worker committees conferred with developers to build the homes; later they administered their planned community, Lakeview Park, near Frostproof, Florida. Disadvantaged black picker families, who were accustomed to a lifestyle of poverty, were finally able to own well-built modern homes. Housing development was not the only aspect of the project. Coca-Cola guaranteed workers stable employment at wage levels sufficient to cover mortgage payments and other living expenses. And the company trained workers, as well as their supervisors, to adjust to the new lifestyle. The company in return rightfully expected, and received, improved efficiency from the pickers. Today, ALPI has a staff of 150 people providing health, housing, education, and social services to more than 1.5 million people.

EXECUTIVE PERQUISITES

Perquisites have traditionally been a source of services-beyond-pay that offered executives status, but recently the list of perks has grown. Organizations provide a combination of perks that relate to their executives' current or future needs and serve to attract or retain their services. Though the possibilities are endless, they include:

1. Company car,
2. Use of company aircraft,
3. Housing—leased company, low interest mortgage, or simple financial assistance,
4. Payment of relocation expenses,
5. Education—advanced study, sabbatical leaves, executive programs,
6. Advice—tax, legal, financial, counseling, estate planning,
7. Country clubs, health spas.[35]

HEALTH CARE

Facilities to administer medical and health care can be sponsored by groups in the plant. Chapter 21 details employee health care and physical fitness programs.

MISCELLANEOUS SERVICES

Organizations offer a great many other services that cannot be described here, but since greater attention is being given to employing minority members and women, several services have received increasing attention. Working mothers with preschool children encounter difficulties arranging for their care during working hours, especially when the work day begins early and ends after dark. To meet this need, organizations provide day-care centers convenient to the work place. In an effort to attract and retain disadvantaged employees many organizations are offering transportation service. One method that has proved effective is a company bus that picks up employees at a location convenient to their homes and returns them at the end of the work day. In many locations, organizations have discovered that the efficiency of workers, particularly the former hard-core unemployed, suffers because of dietary insufficiencies. Employers help overcome this problem by providing in-plant food service, which offers planned, nutritional meals at modest cost. Workers can eat at least two of their regular meals during the work day. Employers usually have to subsidize the cost of operating these cafeterias. The advent of the energy shortage and its attendant high gasoline prices has given rise to company-sponsored car pools and related share-the-ride schemes. Collectively they help relieve the congestion on highways and make riding to and from work more pleasant for the participating employees.

Organizations are also seeking ways to recognize and reward loyalty. Service-award programs are a means for organizations to express their gratitude to employees for their years of service; employees can then display their pins, plaques, and certificates as symbols of their loyalty.

Socially conscious firms are also interested in serving their communities. This attitude encourages employees to give service as well as receive it. In this respect, several companies (IBM and Xerox in particular) are granting paid leaves to some employees to teach retarded children, counsel minorities, quell racial incidents, do research on mine safety, and help communities out of financial crises.

Cost-Benefit Analysis

Benefits and services represent a substantial cost to employers. In some cases they amount to as much as 50 percent of payroll cost. The higher cost does not necessarily produce added benefits. Analysis will indicate that substantial savings on the cost of benefits and services can be realized. Insurance premiums represent the highest cost of benefits, and the amount of the premium is based on experience, for example, more claims lead to higher premiums. Reviews of medical-insurance claims (this should be performed by personnel staff even though an independent insurance carrier may be responsible for a plan's administration) can uncover unnecessary surgical or laboratory procedures, overcharges, and related misuses that would indicate the need for corrective measures. Plotting the trends of the costs of various benefits, for example, worker's compensation, and hospital medical-surgical insurance, will signal those costs that are getting out of line and indicate that changes (different carrier, stringent cost controls, optional plans) are in order.

Benefits surveys are a means of comparing the content and cost of benefits packages with other firms in the industry and in the same geographic area, and with those in other industries and areas. Finding out what others are doing is useful for ensuring that an organization's benefits are competitive and being purchased at a reasonable cost. And studying employee preferences to determine the optimum package for different groups under current conditions (including the organization's needs) can produce beneficial results for both employees and the company. For instance, employees might prefer to add a deductible to the medical insurance plan, if the resulting savings could be used to buy dental coverage.

There is little empirical evidence of the effects of benefits and services on productivity. Unscientific as this may seem, employee opinion of various benefits seems to be the most common method of evaluating benefits and services.

Summary

Benefits and services are forms of supplementary compensation that can provide mutual advantages to employees and employers. While offering workers a greater sense of job and income security, programs of benefits and services can result in cost savings to organizations through reduced employee turnover and possible lower operating costs.

As a proportion of average earnings, fringe benefits have shown dramatic increases in recent years, so that today they represent more than a third of employees' annual pay. Of course, a significant portion of the benefits offered by employers is required by law: social security, unemployment compensation, and workmen's compensation fall into this category. Traditional business practices dictate granting time off with pay for sick leave, holidays, vacations, and rest periods. As organizations become more socially conscious, their benefits increase and improve. Health and life insurance programs help protect the welfare of employees, and retirement plans add security to the job and enable employees to receive an income when they retire. Finally, collective bargaining results in contractual obligations related to benefit improvements, especially those designed to offset adverse economic conditions, technological improvements, or related efficiency moves.

Employee services are less financial in nature than fringe benefits, but they still contain the same mutual advantages to employees and employers. Transportation and child-care services offer convenience to employees and are especially relevant to hard-core employees and women, respectively. Recreational, hobby, and educational programs are personally enriching and broadening. Still other services, such as company housing, health-care fa- cilities, and credit unions, are facilitative since they might not otherwise be available or would be prohibitively expensive for individual employees. The benefit organizations derive from employee services is in healthier, more interested workers who have a high degree of loyalty and esprit de corps.

To derive maximum advantage from supplemental compensation pro- grams, organizations should apply principles of sound benefits administra- tion. Employees should participate in the design, implementation, and fund- ing of benefits and services programs. These programs should be based on the particular needs of an organization, and they should be explained in detail periodically to all employees.

Key Terms

benefits   fiduciary
services   beneficiaries
workers' compensation   split-dollar life insurance
unemployment   insurance
  compensation   shift premium
sick leave   guaranteed annual wage
flexitime   (GAW)
job sharing   cost-of-living escalators
vesting   employee services
portability   credit union
ERISA   perquisites

Review Questions

1. Distinguish between fringe benefits and employee services.

2. How does ERISA serve to protect employees' pension rights? Describe the various reporting and disclosure requirements of the Act.

3. What are the advantages and disadvantages of health maintenance organizations?

4. What can employers do to contain the costs of benefits and services?

5. Discuss the various issues in the unemployment compensation controversy.

Discussion Questions

1. Too frequently, employees are not aware of the benefits they receive from their employer. How can companies inform workers of their benefits? What should they tell workers about their benefits? Is there any infor- mation about benefits that companies should not communicate to employees?

2. Assuming that the orientation of the work force is becoming predominantly social, as opposed to economic, in philosophy, what types of fringe benefits will appeal to these employees?

3. As a benefits administrator for a multiplant manufacturer, you have been asked to evaluate the benefits and services program of your company. How would you accomplish this assignment? If your proposal included cost data, which benefits would you include and which would you exclude from your analysis?

4. If you were responsible for the personnel department and you became concerned about the administration of the benefits and services program, what measures would you take to assure that the results met the department's objectives? What would be the pros and cons of involving worker representatives in administering the program?

5. Should the value of fringe benefits be considered part of employees' wages? If so, should employees select their own benefits package?

"Well, it sure didn't work here, Al," Mitch Baxter, head of data processing, said.

"I don't see why not, Mitch. This four-day work week is going great in all the other departments."

"Two of my women are about to quit, the paperwork has piled up, and we're a week behind in our processing for the tax office," Mitch said. "Maybe it's me, Al, but somehow we can't make this four-day week work."

"Well, I can see one reason why—those punch-card women must get pretty tired working a ten-hour day."

"They're not the only ones—I get pretty beat myself. And then, because we are behind, I find myself coming in the fifth day anyhow, to catch up. Sometimes I put in six days."

"I suppose errors are up?"

Mitch nodded. "Way up—particularly from those last two hours of the day. Besides, we keep getting stuff from other departments on the days we don't work, and it piles up. Have you ever come to work to see a huge stack of stuff to do? You feel beaten before you even begin."

"I notice that you're bringing in people to work on Fridays and Saturdays too."

"We have to, Al. But that doesn't work too well, because lots of times they have a question to ask about keypunching, and their supervisor isn't around to tell them what to do. Then she comes in on Monday to find a big stack of questions on her desk. It's a terrible way to start a week, even a four-day one."

"We can always go back to the five-day, eight-hour schedule."

"I think we should, Al. Maybe the other departments can figure out how to do things in four days, but we can't."

Case Problem 1

DOING YOUR THING, ANYTIME

Problems

1. Why would some operations have trouble with a four-day week? List some other operations that might have real difficulties along these lines.

2. What kinds of work are best suited to a revised work schedule? List a few examples.

3. What key factors would you look for if you were considering going to a ten-hour, four-day schedule? Consider the factors that might make this work schedule successful.

Case Problem 2

DEATH, TAXES, AND BENEFITS

Unemployment for young persons (16–22) has ranged from 12 to 35 percent in recent years. One major reason seems to be the very high cost of the benefits package that companies have to pay employees. The total cost of a new employee is not just the salary, but the benefits too—which amount to an extra 35 percent or more of total compensation.

Hence, many companies appear to avoid new hiring as much as possible. They work present employees overtime rather than employ new people.

Several suggestions have been made to make it easier to hire younger people. One is to minimize benefits for people under 25, on the grounds that young people do not need them as much as older persons. Another suggestion is to have strict limitations on overtime. If this were done, companies might have to hire more young people.

Present workers are not too enthusiastic about either suggestion. Many people like overtime, with its time and a half pay; and if some workers could not be paid benefits, there is a chance that companies would get rid of older employees to save money.

65
66
67
68
69

70
71
72
73
74
75

Problems

1. What do you think about this problem? Is it true that younger people really don't need most benefits?

2. What rights do older workers have here? Why?

3. What rights do younger people have to obtain scarce good jobs? Why?

Notes

1. International Business Machines Corporation, *About Your Company* (Employee Handbook, 1974), p. 16.

2. *Employee Benefits 1979* (Washington, D.C.: Chamber of Commerce of the United States of America, 1980), p. 11.

3. "Why Fringes Have Lost Some of Their Allure," *U.S. News and World Report*, January 19, 1981, p. 66.

4. "Designing a Benefits Package You Can Afford," Summary of workshop comments by Richard Schultz, Assistant Vice President, First National Bank of Chicago, in *Personnel Management Policies and Practices Report* (*Bulletin 1*), (Englewood Cliffs, N.J.: Prentice-Hall, July 12, 1977), p. iii.

5. Joseph A. Hickey, "Unemployment Insurance—State Changes in 1975," *Monthly Labor Review*, January 1976, pp. 37–41.

6. Martin S. Feldstein, "Unemployment Insurance: Time for Reform," *Harvard Business Review*, March-April 1975, pp. 51–61.

7. Stephen T. Mortson, "The Impact of Unemployment Insurance on Job Search," *Brookings Papers on Economic Activity*, 1 (1975), pp. 40–41.

8. The Bureau of National Affairs, *Paid Holiday and Vacation Policies*, (Washington, D.C.: The Bureau of National Affairs, Inc., November 1980), p. 1.

9. John M. Ivancevich and Herbert L. Lyons, "The Shortened Workweek: A Field Experiment," *Journal of Applied Psychology*, February 1977, pp. 34–37.

10. "The 4-Day Week," *Wall Street Journal*, February 16, 1977, p. 1.

11. Ben A. Buisman, "4-day, 40-Hour Workweek: Its Effect on Management and Labor," *Personnel Journal*, November 1975, pp. 565–66.

12. For surveys of the literature on flexitime and related modified work hours arrangements see: William F. Glueck, "Changing Hours of Work: A Review and Analysis of the Research," *The Personnel Administrator*, March 1979, pp. 44–47ff.; and Robert T. Golembiewski and Carl W. Proehl, Jr., "A Survey of the Empirical Literature on Flexible Workhours: Character and Consequences of a Major Innovation," *The Academy of Management Review*, October 1978, pp. 837–53.

13. "The Flexitime Concept Gets a Wider Test," *Business Week*, May 24, 1976, pp. 37–38.

14. Janice Neipert Hughes, "Flexible Schedules: Problems and Issues," *Monthly Labor Review*, February 1977, p. 63.

15. Ibid., pp. 63–64.

16. See for example: William H. Holley, Achilles Armenakis, and Herbert S. Field, "Employee Reactions to a Flexitime Program: A Longitudinal Study," *Human Resources Management*, Winter 1976, pp. 21–23; Warren Magoon and Larry Schnicker, "Flexitime Hours at State Street Bank of Boston: A Case Study," *The Personnel Administrator*, October 1976, pp. 34–37; and Frank T. Morgan, "Your (Flex) Time May Come," *Personnel Journal*, February 1977, pp. 82–85ff.

17. "The Flexitime Concept Gets a Wider Test," *Business Week*, pp. 37–38.

18. Barney Olmsted, "Job Sharing—A New Way to Work," *Personnel Journal*, February 1977, pp. 78–81.

19. Robert W. Bedmarzik, "Worksharing in the U.S.: Its Prevalence and Duration," *Monthly Labor Review*, July 1980, p. 4.

20. Mary Green Miner, *Pension Plans and the Impact of ERISA* (Washington,

D.C.: Bureau of National Affairs, October 1977), p. 1.

21. "Your Pension: Will You Get a Fair Shake?" *U.S. News and World Report,* July 25, 1977, p. 68.

22. "Fringe Benefits and Inflation: How to Pick the Right Package," *Business Week,* April 28, 1980, p. 130.

23. "The Pension Mess," *Newsweek,* February 26, 1979, p. 67.

24. "Private Pensions: Adapting to ERISA," *The Morgan Guarantee Survey,* October 1976, p. 6.

25. Harvey W. Rubin, "Split Dollar Life Insurance, A Unique Employee Benefit," *Management World,* September 1976, p. 6.

26. Donald R. Bell, "Dental and Vision Care Benefits in Health Insurance Plans," *Monthly Labor Review,* June 1980, pp. 22.

27. Virginia T. Douglas, "HMO's: Health Care for the 80's," *HFCA Forum,* June 1980, p. 11.

28. Ernest W. Saward and Scott Flem-ing, "Health Maintenance Organizations," *Scientific American,* October 1980, pp. 47–53.

29. Burton W. Teague, "In Review of the ESOP Fable," *The Conference Board Record,* February 1976, pp. 10–11.

30. "Retirement Issue: Are Stock Plans a Cure-All or a Doubtful Benefit?" *Wall Street Journal,* December 8, 1980, p. 27.

31. James R. Bell, "A Re-examination of Suggestion System Philosophy," *National Association of Suggestion Systems Quarterly,* Summer 1965, pp. 15ff.

32. Ibid.

33. "Prepaid Legal Insurance Is Seen Becoming Unions' Next Big Fringe-Benefit Demand," *Wall Street Journal,* July 29, 1977, p. 28.

34. *Harvest of Hope* (Atlanta, Ga.: The Coca-Cola Company, 1977), pp. 1–24.

35. Hugh Beckwith, "Executive Compensation: An Area of Limitless Options," *The Personnel Administrator,* January-February 1974, pp. 30–31.

Chapter Twenty-one

Employee Health and Safety

It all happened in 10 seconds. The operator raised the guard—"Because it just got in the way, anyhow," he complained—a fellow employee at the next machine asked him a question, he turned his head to answer, in a split second his hand was caught. A scream of pain—men running everywhere—confusion in the department. Someone threw a cutoff switch, and the machinery stopped. The ambulance arrived, and then a frantic rush to the hospital.

An hour later a woman sat solemnly outside the emergency room praying for her husband's survival. Inside, a team of surgeons worked tensely. Two worried employees tried to comfort the wife. Much later the surgeon emerged. With a faint smile—"He'll make it," and then in a consoling voice, "But I'm afraid he'll never be able to use that hand again." What a terrible price to pay for a few seconds of inattention.

Safety and Health: An Overview

Such occurrences are all too common in American industry today. According to the National Safety Council there were 13,200 on-the-job deaths and 2,300,000 disabling injuries (80,000 of which were permanently and totally disabling) in U.S. industry in 1979.[1] In addition, more than 300,000 workers suffer from diseases directly related to their jobs—diseases which in several thousand cases prove fatal.[2]

In 1979 alone, work accidents cost $27.3 billion in lost wages, medical expenses, insurance administration costs, and other related expenses. This represents a cost of $280 for every worker. At a time when productivity is so essential to an organization's well-being, days lost from work become significant. A total of 245 million days were lost in 1979 due to accidents; this is 10 times as many as are lost because of union strikes.[3]

The figures do not present a very rosy picture; they aren't meant to. But statistics overgeneralize. Many organizations have commendable safety and health records, due in large measure to their conscientious efforts to maintain a safe and healthy work environment.

Management's efforts to protect the physical well-being of its employees are a positive indication of its concern for people. In addition, effective safety and health measures usually result in a more efficient work force by reducing absenteeism due to injuries and illnesses. Although line management is primarily responsible for carrying out safety and health programs, the personnel staff also plays an essential role. Safety and health functions that the personnel department might perform include:

1. Training line managers in the philosophies and techniques of industrial health and safety.

2. Conducting meetings and campaigns to influence positive attitudes and desirable behavior about health and safety.

3. Using safety specialists to provide advice on safety, establish standards for safe working conditions, monitor operating conditions to minimize hazards, investigate accidents, and take corrective action.

4. Under the auspices of medical personnel, identifying and correcting sources of occupational diseases, providing advice on physical capabilities of individuals, and treating occupational injuries and illnesses.

This chapter concentrates on the basis for **safety** and health programs, the relationship of **accidents** and illnesses to the personnel process, programs for maintaining a safe and healthy work environment, and the specific nature of the government bodies that deal with health and safety problems. Considerable attention is focused on the Occupational Safety and Health Act, which has had a sizable impact on personnel management. Industrial security and plant protection are also included in this chapter because their activities are so closely related to health and safety.

Situational Aspects of Safety and Health

The nature, extent, and effectiveness of all safety and health programs depend on a number of variables, including management's attitude; location and size of the organization; type of industry; kind of work; make-up of the work force (e.g., percentage of women, proportion of older to younger workers); work-area conditions (e.g., workers, equipment, surroundings);

and the impact of legislation. It is the latter element, legislation, upon which the following paragraphs focus.

The Occupational Safety and Health Act of 1970

The key labor-standards act, the Williams-Steiger Occupational Safety and Health Act (**OSHA**), became effective April 28, 1971. It directed the Secretary of Labor to enforce safety and health standards in 4.1 million business establishments and for 57 million employees. The act requires employers to keep their work places free from recognized hazards and to comply with health and safety standards prescribed by the Department of Labor. The Division of Occupational Health within the Labor Department inspects business establishments on a worst-first priority basis. Investigators penalize violators, although businesses can appeal violations to the Occupational Safety and Health Review Commission, an independent adjudicatory agency. States are encouraged to enforce their own standards based on federal guidelines. In conjunction with OSHA, the Department of Health, Education, and Welfare (now the Department of Health and Human Services) established the National Institute of Occupational Safety and Health (NIOSH) to conduct research under the act. In addition, a commission on state workers' compensation laws began a study of state laws. The act encourages states to assume responsibility for their own programs, which is usually granted when their plan is approved by the Department of Labor. OSHA is considered milestone legislation in the personnel field. Its success depends, to a large degree, on voluntary compliance because safe working conditions cannot easily be legislated. The following discussion of OSHA's basic elements should give readers an appreciation of the regulations.

STANDARDS

The Department of Labor issues detailed safety and health regulations (called standards) which apply to specific industries and have the force and effect of law. NIOSH is undertaking research to help the Department of Labor set standards, especially those relating to hazardous or toxic materials (e.g., coal dust, asbestos, and monoxide gases.)[4]

INSPECTIONS

The Department of Labor uses a cadre of compliance investigators to inspect business establishments within each of 10 regions. Because of the large number of businesses covered by the act, the Department has given regional administrators these priorities in inspection duties:

1. Investigating fatalities and catastrophes.
2. Investigating employee complaints.

3. Investigating target industries on a worst-first basis.

4. Inspecting remaining industries chosen at random.

The OSHA field-check provision that most disturbs management is the one that states that a worker who "believes that a violation of a safety or health standard exists that threatens physical harm, or (who believes) that an imminent danger exists, may request an inspection by giving notice to the Secretary or his authorized representative of such violation or danger." Some managers fear this provision will be misused by disgruntled employees who want to complicate their employers' lives.[5] This appeared to be the case in a grievance that the author arbitrated.

Employees of a common carrier had initiated an OSHA inspection because they felt the protective toe guards being issued by the employer were unsafe. The inspector agreed and ordered safety shoes to be worn instead of the toe guards. The union claimed that the company was obligated to supply the shoes because OSHA required them and because these replaced the toe guards. The author judged that the employees should purchase their own shoes, since they had influenced the inspector to require the safety shoes, which otherwise might not have been necessary. Also, the safety shoes could be used by the employees off the job; they were essentially the same as nonsafety shoes, which the employer normally does not supply.

The purpose of inspections, however, in the words of one compliance officer, "is not to fine people, but to save lives and prevent injury." Inspections usually consist of a thorough investigation above and beyond any complaint that may have been filed. Safety engineers or safety officers (the inspectors' official titles) are equipped with various devices to aid their inspection duties: camera, flashlight, stopwatch, thermometer, air pressure gauge, noise meter, air sampler, velometer (for measuring the speed of air currents near ventilation ducts), and other equipment. During an inspection, worker representatives have a right to accompany federal inspectors on their rounds. At its conclusion, compliance officers conduct a conference with plant management. They ask for management's opinion on a reasonable time for it to correct any observed violations, and they alert company officers to the penalty and appeals procedure. In cases involving imminent danger to workers' health and safety, the compliance officers would, of course, require immediate abatement. Following all inspections the officers send management an official written report of the findings, penalties, and compliance agreements. However, some employers have taken exception to the unannounced nature of inspections, claiming that it violates the Fourth Amendment's protection of privacy. The district court decided that OSHA must now have a warrant to inspect an employer's premises, and the Supreme Court upheld the ruling.[6] Perhaps as a move to appease employers,

OSHA now offers free on-site consultation services to employers who request the service.[7]

RECORD KEEPING AND REPORTS

The new record-keeping system prescribed by OSHA creates, for the first time, a national profile of occupational fatalities, injuries, and illnesses. The system requires employers to maintain an annual log and prepare a summary of specified information. Even if no work time is lost, organizations must record all cases that require medical treatment beyond first aid; or that involve loss of consciousness, restriction of work or motion, or transfer to another job. Figure 21.1 is a guide developed by OSHA to the recordability of cases. The Bureau of Labor Statistics then uses this information as data for reporting accident and illness experience. OSHA Form 200 (which replaced forms OSHA Nos. 100 and 102) is a Log and Summary of Occupational Injuries and Illnesses to help employers maintain records in a simpler format. Also, the form permits recording of permanent transfers and terminations associated with occupational illnesses. This information for injuries is no longer required. Illnesses can be identified in a separate column by type. And yearly totals replace the former requirement of OSHA Form 102.[8]

PENALTIES

Violators of OSHA regulations incur stiff penalties. Inspectors can impose a maximum civil penalty of $1,000 for each standard violation, and a $10,000 fine and six-month jail sentence if a worker dies as a result of a violation.

RESEARCH

The act established the NIOSH, within the Department of Health and Human Services, to advise the Secretary of Labor on research findings. NIOSH handles research on occupational illnesses and conducts inspections concerning these responsibilities. The act also provides for research by independent agencies to aid in its administration of the law.

In conjunction with research activities, the act calls for training programs to increase the number and competence of personnel in the occupational safety and health field. The following research areas come under the jurisdiction of NIOSH:

1. Research to develop innovative approaches to occupational safety and health problems.

2. Exploration to discover latent diseases and to establish causal connections between diseases and the work environment; and other health-related

Figure 21.1
Guide to Recordability of
Cases Under the Occupa-
tional Safety and Health
Act.

Source: Bureau of Labor Statistics,
U.S. Department of Labor, *Occupational Safety and Health Statistics: Concepts and Methods* (Washington, D.C.: U.S. Government Printing Office, 1975), p. 2.

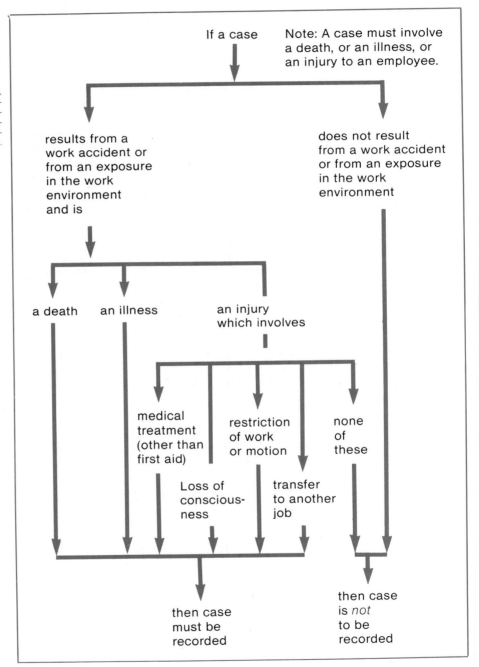

research that recognizes that occupational health standards present problems often different from those of occupational safety.

3. Establishment of medical criteria to insure, insofar as practicable, that employees' health, functional capacity, and life expectancy do not diminish as a result of their work experience.[9]

PROBLEMS WITH OSHA

Although OSHA has unquestionably helped increase the awareness of industrial disabilities, unions, employers, and even members of Congress have expressed dissatisfaction with it. Business is critical of OSHA for having too many trivial, nitpicking rules that tend to undermine the law's basic purpose of protecting the American worker. Critics claim that OSHA has had a history of emphasizing minor safety matters while overlooking major ones, and failing to focus on health standards. Employers complain, too, that the cost—$6.5 billion in 1981 ($1.5 billion OSHA combined budget and $5 billion cost to businesses to be in compliance) is astronomical. Employers don't trust safety inspectors they consider rude and inept. Many of OSHA's standards, they feel, are unrealistic, so these are being attacked in the courts.[10] Yet the decisions heavily favor OSHA, which has been upheld 86 percent of the time.[11] In Congress, OSHA has been upbraided for its poor administration in failing to concentrate on serious violations and in granting employers overly long abatement periods. Similarly, the unions have protested OSHA's laxity in enforcing standards. They maintain that protective equipment has been inadequate, hazardous conditions continue unchallenged, and there are numerous work environments that are unsafe, even to the point of being potentially fatal.[12] And the Reagan Administration, if it doesn't abolish OSHA altogether, will certainly shift its role from the police focus toward a role of a cooperative partner (with business) to reduce illnesses and injuries in most work places.[13]

MINE HEALTH AND SAFETY BILL

In 1977 the Federal Mine Enforcement Safety and Health Act was enacted to combine all existing mine health and safety statutes into a single uniform law. It transferred enforcement and administration responsibilities to the Department of Labor. The Act retains the provisions of the Coal Mine Health and Safety Act of 1949 and strengthens other regulations. It allows the Secretary of Labor to close a mine if there is evidence of a pattern of violations. Many of the provisions parallel those of OSHA.

WORKERS' COMPENSATION

We discussed workers' compensation from a benefits standpoint in Chapter 20. Essentially, it is designed to provide payments to workers who become physically (or mentally) disabled as a result of their jobs. The National Commission on State Worker's Compensation Laws, established by OSHA, set some major objectives that should be achieved by any progressive workers' compensation program:[14]

1. To pay cash benefits promptly and in a reasonable amount to workers injured on the job. Benefits should be no less than two-thirds of the worker's gross weekly wages.
2. To eliminate delays and high costs of personal-injury litigation.
3. To encourage on-the-job safety and allocate the costs of work-related injury and diseases to responsible sources.
4. To provide prompt and adequate medical treatment.
5. To provide rehabilitation for workers unable to return to their former jobs.

In 1979 all but three of the states increased temporary and total disability benefits; some also reduced costs by investigating medical bills, offsetting benefits by other transfer payments, and reducing the effect of disabilities through rehabilitation programs.[15]

Because states vary in their collection of data and the amount of weekly compensation dispensed, it is difficult to make any definitive evaluation of their laws. However, one study did find that it was doubtful that weekly payments were adequate to sustain a worker during a disability. It also concluded that the move from common law courts to state commission has speeded settlements, but it does not ensure fair and just payments of benefits (though this may be the result of a lack of professional administrative directors to handle many of the contested claims). While it may be true that workers' compensation payments alone won't maintain a normal standard of living, most employers have sick leave benefits that supplement such compensation. There is a lack of adequate data, the study found, on reducing accidents. A properly functioning system would encourage accident reduction. The employer who must pay compensation insurance premiums commensurate with accident rate experience would find it in his own interest to maintain a good safety record. Progress in the area of medical treatment appears to be a major achievement of modern workers' compensation laws. Forty-five states provide full medical treatment, that is, the degree of care medically required without legal limitation for a specified time or amount. The study found that rehabilitation for injured workers is probably the least adequately achieved objective because one-third of the state laws have no provision for rehabilitation services (vocational rehabilitation) and most of the others do not deal directly with this problem. The gains derived from rehabilitation are of extreme value both to the individual and society; invariably a disabled worker can be rehabilitated to lead a full and productive life. Compensation payments were also found to be inadequate and discriminatory with regard to where the injury occurs and the seriousness of the disability.[16] The consensus of those studying workers' compensation laws seems to be that they are neither adequate nor equitable. Paul recommends replacing these laws with expanded social disability and medical expense insurance that would cover all illnesses and injuries and would not be tied to a particular employer or insured group.[17] As an alternative to workers' compensation, Kasper suggests a system that would combine universal insurance with a negligence system.[18] By this arrangement workers and employers would be required to insure against the possibility of job injury. The coverage would include income loss, full medical benefits, and contractual incentives to encourage rehabilitation. The negligent party would bear the total cost; the injured, per stipulation, would be paid immediately; and it would be up to the insurers to determine among themselves—through negotiation or litigation—who should ultimately pay the damages.

Employees have begun to take the position that mental problems, for example, emotional disturbances, alcoholism, and drug addiction, are job connected and, therefore, subject to workers' compensation. Though court decisions on this subject are mixed, the evidence points to a trend toward some recompense for mental illness. The plight of air traffic controllers is an excellent example. The high degree of stress associated with their work often causes emotional problems, even breakdowns. There are many cases of successful compensation claims being won by these people as a result of their work-related disabilities.

Analyzing Causes

Accidents are not isolated occurrences, but incidents in a situational process. Technical and human variables (sources of accidents) interact to form an accident situation. The potential victims (or other people who may have been responsible for an accident) have attitudes, work skills, fears, inhibitions, ideas, and other physiological and psychological factors that contribute to causing accidents. Some groups appear to have a disproportionate number of accidents and are considered to be **accident prone.** Studies have revealed a consistent characteristic of the accident prone; that is, social irresponsibility and immaturity, with negative attitudes toward authority, most evident in workers age 17 to 30.[19] Interacting with these human elements are technical aspects: improper lighting; excessive noise, heat, or humidity; defective machinery; improper machine guarding; poor housekeeping; and lack of color coding. Accidents stem from complex causes that go beyond a simple human or mechanical error.

Earlier in this chapter an accident was cited in which an operator caught his hand in a machine. A reexamination of this incident shows that both technical and human factors surrounded the accident situation. The operator's attitude about guards being a nuisance perhaps contributed most to the accident's occurrence. His state of mind was a factor. He could have been under stress—the shop was behind on production quotas, perhaps there were problems at home, or maybe he was daydreaming about an upcoming vacation. The employee next to him momentarily drew his attention away from his work; if the other man had not asked a question, maybe the accident wouldn't have occurred. If the operator had been distracted at another time, possibly after he had fed the material into his machine, the accident might not have happened. And if the machine had been designed so that it could not operate without the guard in place, or if the machine had a shut-off button, the outcome might have been different.

Under the concept of **loss control** safety directors view accidents in terms of injury prevention, total accident control, fire prevention, industrial health, hygiene, and pollution. Hence, loss control not only includes injury to the employees; but loss of time of the injured, other employees, supervision and administration; costs of wages and medical bills; product loss or damage due to the accident; cost of repair or replacement of damaged parts or equipment; and psychological damage of the employees and others affected by the accident. Total loss control also encompasses vandalism, absenteeism, computer fraud, product liability claims, and any other sources of loss to the organization.[20]

If those responsible for plant safety consider it from a situational viewpoint, their approach to accident prevention and correction might be different. Organizations pay little attention to noninjurious accidents or near-accidents. Though these incidents occur frequently, they have little effect on accident statistics and are usually ignored. But organizations can gain insight into the causes of more costly accidents by analyzing noninjury accidents. These incidents are part of the accident process and, but for a slight difference in a single interacting variable, their consequences would have been more severe.

In analyzing accidents, safety directors might attempt to differentiate between technical and human aspects as a means of focusing their attention on specific causes. Many of the technical factors that contribute to industrial accidents can be eliminated, but safety directors must keep the human element in mind when making mechanical changes. In recommending machine locations or design, safety engineers must consider the operators who will use the machines and the workers who will maintain them. Finally, no matter how well engineered a mechanical safety device is, its effectiveness is limited by the people using it; therefore, safety directors must educate employees on the use of safety devices.

Accident Measures

Organizations can evaluate their safety performance by comparing their accident experiences with those of similar organizations or with the entire industry, or with their own previous experiences. To make these comparisons they need a method of measurement that will permit them to compare organizations of different sizes (because an organization having many employees may be expected to have a greater number of injuries than one with few). Furthermore, some injuries are more severe than others; there is little validity in considering a broken arm as being in the same category with a minor scratch. The incidence rate is a mathematical measure which has been developed to facilitate uniform comparisons.

THE INCIDENCE RATE

Starting in 1977 all employers, including National Safety Council members, were required to report occupational injuries and illnesses as prescribed by OSHA record-keeping requirements. The **incidence rate** measures illnesses and injuries combined, and is calculated as follows:

$$\text{Incidence rate} = \frac{\begin{array}{c}(\text{number of lost work days} \times 200{,}000) \text{ or} \\ (\text{number of injuries and illnesses} \times 200{,}000)\end{array}}{\text{total hours worked by all employees during period covered}}$$

200,000 = base for 100 full-time equivalent workers (working 40 hours per week, 50 weeks per year)

OSHA DEFINITIONS

OSHA defines the terms used in the incidence rate formula as follows (see OSHA form No. 200 and Recordkeeping Requirements, Revised 1978):

Occupational injury is any injury such as a cut, fracture, sprain, amputation, etc., which results from a work accident or from an exposure involving a single incident in the work environment. Occupational illness of an employee is any abnormal condition or disorder, other than one resulting from an occupational injury, caused by exposure to environmental factors associated with employment. It includes acute and chronic illnesses or diseases, which may be caused by inhalation, absorption, ingestion, or direct contact.

Nonfatal cases without lost workdays are cases of occupational injury or illness which did not involve fatalities or lost workdays but did result in: (1) transfer to another job or termination of employment, or (2) medical treatment, other than first aid, or (3) diagnosis of occupational illness, or (4) loss of consciousness, or (5) restriction of work or motion.

Lost workdays are those days which the employee would have worked but could not because of an occupational injury or illness. The number of lost workdays should not include the day of injury or onset of illness. The number of days includes all days (consecutive or not) on which, because of injury or illness: (1) the employee would have worked but could not, or (2) the employee was assigned to a temporary job, or (3) the employee worked at a permanent job less than full-time, or (4) the employee worked at a permanently assigned job but could not perform all duties normally connected with it.

NOTE: Not recordable are first-aid cases that involve one-time treatment and subsequent observations of minor scratches, cuts, burns, splinters, etc., that do not ordinarily require medical care even though such treatment is provided by a physician or registered professional personnel.

The Bureau of Labor Statistics has been reporting incidence rates by industry. Figure 21.2 compares incidence rates for 1979. For all industries there were an average of 7.76 *cases* involving days lost from work with an average of 61 *days* away from work for each case (the latter measure is an indicator of the severity of injury, for example, the longer the period away from work, the more severe the injury). According to Figure 21.2, the transit industry is the most dangerous in terms both of cases involving lost time and of severity of injuries.

Accident Control

Successful safety programs are carefully planned in advance of their implementation. The safety function must delineate areas of responsibility and facilitate a coordinated effort toward accident control.

ORGANIZATION FOR SAFETY

SAFETY POLICY.   In organizing for safety, top management first sets and then supports safety policy. Most organizations consider it essential to make their policy statement and its general guidelines known to every employee. The safety policy of the Atlanta Coca-Cola Bottling Company, quoted below in part, is a good example.

Although your company has always tried to provide such job safety, we are taking a new look at our plant and our facilities in order to comply with all the rules and regulations of the law. We shall also review all job procedures to determine if changes are recommended to improve safety,

Incidence Rates *

**CASES INVOLVING DAYS
AWAY FROM WORK & DEATHS**

Incidence Rates *

**DAYS AWAY
FROM WORK**

Figure 21.2

1979 Incidence Rates, Reporters to N.S.C.

Source: National Safety Council. *Accident Facts* 1980 Edition. Adapted with permission.

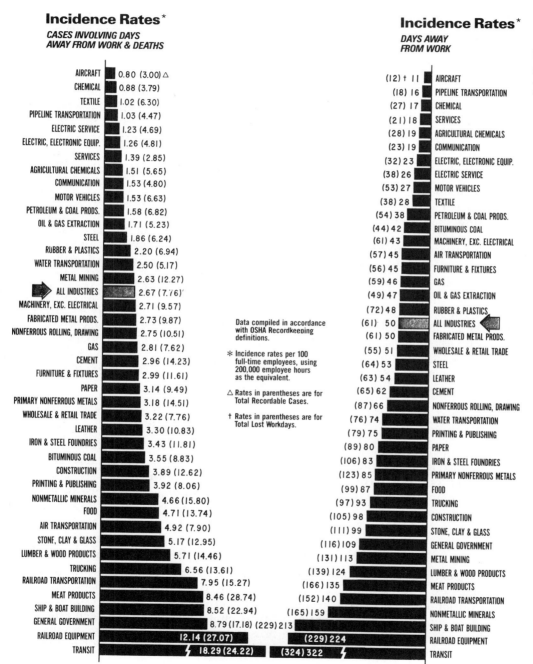

AIRCRAFT	0.80 (3.00) △
CHEMICAL	0.88 (3.79)
TEXTILE	1.02 (6.30)
PIPELINE TRANSPORTATION	1.03 (4.47)
ELECTRIC SERVICE	1.23 (4.69)
ELECTRIC, ELECTRONIC EQUIP.	1.26 (4.81)
SERVICES	1.39 (2.85)
AGRICULTURAL CHEMICALS	1.51 (5.65)
COMMUNICATION	1.53 (4.80)
MOTOR VEHICLES	1.53 (6.63)
PETROLEUM & COAL PRODS.	1.58 (6.82)
OIL & GAS EXTRACTION	1.71 (5.23)
STEEL	1.86 (6.24)
RUBBER & PLASTICS	2.20 (6.94)
WATER TRANSPORTATION	2.50 (5.17)
METAL MINING	2.63 (12.27)
ALL INDUSTRIES	2.67 (7.76)
MACHINERY, EXC. ELECTRICAL	2.71 (9.57)
FABRICATED METAL PRODS.	2.73 (9.87)
NONFERROUS ROLLING, DRAWING	2.75 (10.51)
GAS	2.81 (7.62)
CEMENT	2.96 (14.23)
FURNITURE & FIXTURES	2.99 (11.61)
PAPER	3.14 (9.49)
PRIMARY NONFERROUS METALS	3.18 (14.51)
WHOLESALE & RETAIL TRADE	3.22 (7.76)
LEATHER	3.30 (10.83)
IRON & STEEL FOUNDRIES	3.43 (11.81)
BITUMINOUS COAL	3.55 (8.83)
CONSTRUCTION	3.89 (12.62)
PRINTING & PUBLISHING	3.92 (8.06)
NONMETALLIC MINERALS	4.66 (15.80)
FOOD	4.71 (13.74)
AIR TRANSPORTATION	4.92 (7.90)
STONE, CLAY & GLASS	5.17 (12.95)
LUMBER & WOOD PRODUCTS	5.71 (14.46)
TRUCKING	6.56 (13.61)
RAILROAD TRANSPORTATION	7.95 (15.27)
MEAT PRODUCTS	8.46 (28.74)
SHIP & BOAT BUILDING	8.52 (22.94)
GENERAL GOVERNMENT	8.79 (17.18) (229) 213
RAILROAD EQUIPMENT	12.14 (27.07)
TRANSIT	18.29 (24.22)

Data compiled in accordance with OSHA Recordkeeping definitions.

* Incidence rates per 100 full-time employees, using 200,000 employee hours as the equivalent.

△ Rates in parentheses are for Total Recordable Cases.

† Rates in parentheses are for Total Lost Workdays.

(12) † 11	AIRCRAFT
(18) 16	PIPELINE TRANSPORTATION
(27) 17	CHEMICAL
(21) 18	SERVICES
(28) 19	AGRICULTURAL CHEMICALS
(23) 19	COMMUNICATION
(32) 23	ELECTRIC, ELECTRONIC EQUIP.
(38) 26	ELECTRIC SERVICE
(53) 27	MOTOR VEHICLES
(38) 28	TEXTILE
(54) 38	PETROLEUM & COAL PRODS.
(44) 42	BITUMINOUS COAL
(61) 43	MACHINERY, EXC. ELECTRICAL
(57) 45	AIR TRANSPORTATION
(56) 45	FURNITURE & FIXTURES
(59) 46	GAS
(49) 47	OIL & GAS EXTRACTION
(72) 48	RUBBER & PLASTICS
(61) 50	ALL INDUSTRIES
(61) 50	FABRICATED METAL PRODS.
(55) 51	WHOLESALE & RETAIL TRADE
(64) 53	STEEL
(63) 54	LEATHER
(65) 62	CEMENT
(87) 66	NONFERROUS ROLLING, DRAWING
(76) 74	WATER TRANSPORTATION
(79) 75	PRINTING & PUBLISHING
(89) 80	PAPER
(106) 83	IRON & STEEL FOUNDRIES
(123) 85	PRIMARY NONFERROUS METALS
(99) 87	FOOD
(97) 93	TRUCKING
(105) 98	CONSTRUCTION
(111) 99	STONE, CLAY & GLASS
(116) 109	GENERAL GOVERNMENT
(131) 113	METAL MINING
(139) 124	LUMBER & WOOD PRODUCTS
(166) 135	MEAT PRODUCTS
(152) 140	RAILROAD TRANSPORTATION
(165) 159	NONMETALLIC MINERALS
	SHIP & BOAT BUILDING
(229) 224	RAILROAD EQUIPMENT
(324) 322	TRANSIT

and will be publishing specific new job safety rules for the guidance of all employees. Compliance with such safety rules as are published to you will have to be accepted by all employees as one of the conditions of employment.

However, more important than that is the development of safety-consciousness in our work. The real idea is accident prevention. Our concern is the well-being of our employees, and we all know only too well that it's too late for regret after someone has been hurt on the job.

Although being conscious of safety rules and regulations while trying to get a job done efficiently and effectively seems troublesome at times, it is essential that all of us take the time and trouble necessary to perform our jobs properly from a safety standpoint. Most of our job-related accidents result from carelessness or unwillingness to take the trouble to do the job the right way.

Each of you is asked to cooperate with this program. In addition, we urge you to report to your supervisors or to our Safety Director, any physical conditions or job procedures which you think are or might be a threat to job safety.

It shall be the responsibility of all Department Heads and Allied Plant Managers to familiarize themselves with the Occupational Safety and Health Administration regulations as published in the Federal Register, and as amended from time to time, so as to be aware of the requirements for a safe working place and safe employee practices, and so as to prevent the future modification of the work place or work practices which might be in violation of such regulations.[21]

STAFFING THE SAFETY ORGANIZATION. Many small and medium-sized plants assign the responsibility for safety to their plant superintendent or personnel director. Large plants appoint a safety director who receives assistance from both line and staff personnel. Safety engineers have the technical expertise to recommend machine placement, perform safety inspections, detect unsafe work practices, and design safety-training programs. In addition, the responsibility for meeting hygiene standards (such as those connected with noise and dust control, toxic gases and liquids containment, and heat and humidity regulation) may rest with the safety engineer or might be the function of a separate industrial-hygiene engineer. Large organizations may even employ technicians who assist engineers in performing tests and analyses. The personnel composing the safety and health agencies, trade associations, and workers' compensation carriers frequently offer assistance in locating such people. Finally, OSHA training institutes have been established in all major cities and instructors therein are probably aware of safety personnel who have completed their training. According to McClay there is strong economic justification for making the safety function a full-time position and staffing it with a professional.[22]

Perhaps the most important individual in a safety program is the safety committeeperson already employed by the company. The safety committeeperson represents a department on a company's safety committee; the committee uncovers plant hazards, maintains worker awareness of the need for good housekeeping and safe working practices, and recommends additional safety measures to line management.

BASIC RESPONSIBILITIES OF LINE MANAGEMENT.   Any effort to improve worker safety relies on line management's full support. First-line supervisors have the greatest influence over employees and their working conditions; therefore, supervisors are the key to safety effectiveness. Their responsibilities go beyond those described below because some of these functions are carried out by the staff. But supervisors bear the ultimate responsibility for safety within their departments. In this regard, their basic duties include:

1. *Setting an example.*   There is nothing more effective in impressing the importance of safety on workers than supervisors' attitudes and actions.[23] Effective supervisors can meet production schedules without sacrificing safety measures. To reduce accidents they must be willing and able to communicate with employees about production and safety problems, and to demonstrate the importance they place on safety, wear protective clothing themselves, insist on neat and clean work areas, and stress safe work habits.

2. *Safety orientation and training.*[24]   Safety-conscious line supervisors hold regular, formal meetings with their employees to explain safety rules, equipment, and hazards. Informally, they listen to complaints and encourage safety suggestions.

   Job training should emphasize safe operation. Chapter 13 recommended a job-breakdown sheet as an aid to operative training. For each step on the job sheet, line supervisors should explain to employees the hazard or danger in the step, its remedy, and the safe practice to follow. It is also a good idea to hold refresher training sessions with workers, because workers eventually tend to develop unorthodox habits that can prove dangerous. And in order to avoid damage to both workers and products, supervisors need to retrain employees through regularly scheduled sessions.

   Du Pont's safety training program has been particularly effective. For 32 of the past 35 years (1976 was the last year of record), this company held the National Safety Council's all-time no-injury record. And the safe working conditions are largely attributed to its line-managed safety training. Line managers help design the program and they serve as instructors. Staff develops course materials that require a minimum of preparation and instruction and utilize a multi-media approach, for example, films, programmed instruction, posters, mock-ups, and a variety of other audio-visual aids. And safety-training objectives are built into employee performance evaluations so that managing for safety becomes an integral part of the job, not just course topics to be forgotten outside the classroom.[25]

3. *Cooperating with the safety committee.* Each department's foreman or supervisor appoints a safety committeeperson who checks for work hazards, reports them to the supervisor, and makes recommendations for safety improvements. As committeepersons, employees may become critical of work practices over which their supervisors have jurisdiction. The latter should not take this criticism personally and become defensive; instead they should listen, make objective evaluations, and implement recommendations that will increase plant safety.

4. *Staying informed.* Safety regulations and OSHA standards directly affect line operations. Supervisors should keep themselves informed of the regulations and standards that concern their departments.

5. *Emphasizing safety rules.* Most plants post safety rules in conspicuous places, but this does not mean that they are understood by all who see them. To ensure compliance with safety rules, supervisors need to explain them initially to new employees, and at intervals to all their workers. When supervisors explain the rules and the reasons behind them, employees are likely to obey. When workers violate safety rules, supervisors must use corrective discipline. Since the purpose of safety rules is to minimize accidents, supervisors should emphasize obeying the rule and use punishment as a last resort. This practice does not mean that supervisors should ignore infractions; to the contrary, they should immediately attend to every violation. But supervisors should not make an example of violators by meting out overly harsh punishment.

6. *Recognizing safe practices.* Supervisors have found that recognition of safety efforts and achievements is a powerful motivational force. Recognition not only serves to reward deserving employees, but it also underscores the safety effort through continuous reminders to work, drive, and live safely. Safety incentives include individual awards (safety pins, key chains, pencil sets, decals, or even banquets) to recognize injury-free work over time; departmental or plant awards for reaching a specific safety goal; good housekeeping awards; safety equipment use awards for those who would otherwise have been injured had it not been for the wearing of a safety device (hard hat, glasses, safety shoes, etc.); and safety suggestion awards.[26]

BASIC RESPONSIBILITIES OF THE STAFF. Although safety is mainly the line managers' responsibility, organizations need a centralized authority to coordinate the safety effort and to provide technical and administrative support to the line. Additional safety-staff responsibilities include:

1. *Being informed.* Initially, members of the safety department determine what hazards exist and what safety regulations apply to the plant (as taken from the OSHA standards relevant to the plant site). Members can identify hazards through talking with supervisors, technical people, and fellow committee members; inspecting the plant; and reviewing workers' compensation records. In addition, organizations should maintain a library of safety references, including the state's workers' compensation law; state and local safety codes; chemical and medical dictionaries; and current literature from safety and fire protection groups, insurance carriers, and government agencies. Well-informed safety staffs are in a better position to prevent and correct hazards.

2. *Inspecting plants.* Safety directors (or safety engineers) should make regular, thorough, unhurried safety inspections. They check materials, methods, production flow patterns, and machinery; then they compare their findings against OSHA regulations. They consult with supervisors to determine what production bugs are likely to develop and what physical hazards plague workers. Safety directors ask technical people about the properties of materials being processed. They pay particular attention to plant areas with the highest incidence of accidents.[27]

3. *Reporting to management.* The safety staff should submit periodic written reports to management on the results of safety activities and on recommendations for improvements; these reports should be substantiated with cost figures and supported by references to OSHA regulations. The staff should contrast cost estimates of improvements with medical compensation and injury figures to provide objective support for their recommendations. Since the recommendations will naturally affect line operations, they should consult the supervisors whose areas are involved before submitting their reports. By keeping line managers part of the process, the safety staff can help assure their continued cooperation.

4. *Placing workers.* In conjunction with the employment and medical departments, the safety department sees that workers are placed on jobs they are physically capable of performing. Safety directors need to learn the physical requirements of the job. In preemployment physical exams, the physician lists employees' limitations; safety directors match these physical abilities with job requirements, and place employees with physical limitations on jobs they can handle safely. Figure 21.3 depicts a system that matches physical capabilities with job requirements. It offers

Figure 21.3
A System to Match Physical Abilities with Job Requirements

Reprinted from the Spring Issue 1972 of *Occupational Hazards Executive Report*. Copyrighted 1972 by the Industrial Publishing Company, Division of Pittway Corporation.

SAFETY DEPARTMENT

JOB PHYSICAL CLASSIFICATION SHEET

Dept. No. ________ Foreman ________ Date ________ 194__

Occupational Code No. ________ Occupational Title ________

Job Description ________

Type Machines ________

PHYSICAL DEMANDS

Check		Check	
____	1. Balancing ____	____	17. Standing–100% ____
____	2. Crawling ____	____	18. Standing–Partial ____
____	3. Crouching ____	____	19. Stooping ____
____	4. Climbing ____	____	20. Sitting–100% ____
____	5. Feeling ____	____	21. Seeing–Color Vision ____
____	6. Hearing ____	____	22. Seeing–Depth Perception ____
____	7. Kneeling ____	____	23. Use of right hand–partial use of left ____
____	8. Lifting–10-25 lb. ____	____	
____	9. Lifting–25-50 lb. ____	____	24. Use of left hand–partial use of right ____
____	10. Lifting–50-100 lb. ____		
____	11. Lifting–100-150 lb. ____	____	25. Use of right hand only ____
____	12. Pushing ____	____	26. Use of left hand only ____
____	13. Pulling ____	____	27. Use of both hands ____
____	14. Reaching ____	____	28. Walking–100% ____
____	15. Raising right arm above shoulder ____	____	29. Working Speed–Fast ____
		____	30. Working Speed–Slow ____
____	16. Raising left arm above shoulder ____	____	31. Eye protection needed
		____	32. Work distance ____

WORKING CONDITIONS

Check		Check	
____	39. Dry ____	____	47. Moving Objects ____
____	40. Dusty ____	____	48. Noisy ____
____	41. Exposure to Burns ____	____	49. Outside Work ____
____	42. Hot ____	____	50. Sudden Temperature Change ____
____	43. Humid ____	____	51. Toxic Conditions ____
____	44. High Places ____	____	52. Wet–Soda Water ____
____	45. Inside Work ____	____	53. Wet–Oil ____
____	46. Mechanical Hazards ____	____	54. Wet–Water ____

Place a check mark before the items applying to performance on Code No. listed above.
Use space after items to indicate degree of intensity when excessive.

What is your preference for this job?

Age ____ Height ____ Weight ____ Male ____ Female ____

Special Requirements: ________

Comments: ________

Foreman ________

(Please complete and return to Safety Dept.)

A major company has used these forms for many years to fit new workers to their jobs.

During the preemployment physical examination, the plant doctor fills out the form shown above. He puts small dots in the squares at the upper edge. The dots show what a worker can't do because of physical limitations.

The boxes on the medical form line up with similar boxes at the right edge of the Job Physical Classification Sheet (left). Each foreman makes out a sheet for every job classification in his department. Compare the dotted boxes on the two forms, and you know whether a new man can handle a given job.

A job interviewer can find a place for a physically handicapped applicant very quickly by matching up the new man's medical report with the boxes on a master list of all company jobs and their physical requirements.

1 2 3 4 5 6 7 8 9 10 11 12 13 14 15 16 17 18 19 20 21 22 23 24 25 26 27 28 29 30 31 32 33 34 35 36 37 38 39 40 41 42 43 44 45 46 47 48 49 50 51 52 53 54 55 56 57 58 59 60 61

PLACE A RED DOT • IN EACH BOX DESCRIBING AN ACTIVITY THE EMPLOYEE IS NOT CAPABLE OF DOING UNDER NORMAL HEAVY WORKING CONDITIONS:

BALANCING
CRAWLING
CROUCHING
CLIMBING
FEELING
KNEELING
LIFTING 10 # TO 25 #
LIFTING 25 # TO 50 #
LIFTING 50 # TO 100 #
PUSHING 100 # TO 150 #
PULLING
REACHING
RAISING RT. ARM ABOVE SH
RAISING LFT. ARM ABOVE SH
STANDING – 100%
STANDING – PARTIAL
STOOPING
SITTING
SEEING – COLOR VISION
SEEING – DEPTH PERCEPTION
Use of R.H. & Partial Use of L.
Use of L.H. & Partial Use of R
USE OF RIGHT HAND ONLY
USE OF LEFT HAND ONLY
USE OF BOTH HANDS
WALKING – 100%
WORKING SPEED – FAST
WORKING SPEED – SLOW
GOOD – (20/40)
FAIR – (20/60)
POOR
GOOD – (20/10)
FAIR – (20/5)
POOR
DRY
DUSTY
EXPOSURE TO BURNS
HOT
HUMID
HIGH PLACES
INSIDE WORK
MECHANICAL HAZARDS
MOVING OBJECTS
NOISY
OUTSIDE WORK
SUDDEN TEMP CHANGES
TOXIC CONDITIONS
WET – SODA WATER
WET – OIL
POOR COORDINATION
NERVOUS INSTABILITY
FAINTING OR DIZZY SPELLS

	IS THIS PERSON INCAPABLE OF	VISION Corrected	HEARING	IS THIS PERSON INCAPABLE OF WORKING UNDER THESE CONDITIONS	Does This Person Have

COMMENTS:

NAME | MASTER No. | DEPT. No. | HEIGHT | WEIGHT

DATE OF BIRTH | MALE ☐ FEMALE ☐ | DATE OF HIRE | DATE OF LAST EXAM. | EXAMINING PHYSICIAN

PHYSICAL CAPABILITIES ANALYSIS | SAFETY DEPT.

WHITE COPY — EMPLOYMENT OFFICE BLUE COPY — EMPLOYEE'S MEDICAL FILE PINK COPY — DEPT. FOREMAN the additional benefit of reducing workmen's compensation claims resulting from physical conditions workers had before they were hired.

5. *Coordinating safety committee activities.* Safety committees are composed of representatives from each department, individually striving to reduce hazards; their activities need to be coordinated and directed toward a common goal. The safety director serves as coordinator by holding regularly scheduled committee meetings. Here, he or she instructs the members on their duties, keeps them informed of new developments, and conducts fruitful discussions on the committee's past accomplishments and future activities.

6. *Investigating.* [28] When accident investigations are necessary the safety staff interviews not only the victim but also the supervisor and any witnesses. Questions include:

a. What time did the accident happen?

b. What was the victim doing?

c. Were physical safeguards adequate? If so, were they being used? If so, did they fail?

d. Should protective clothing or equipment be specified for the job? If they were, was the victim using them?

e. Was there anything unusual about the way the victim was doing the job? Did he work according to safe job procedures?

f. Are the job procedures truly safe?

g. Were the supervisor's safety instructions clear?

Before investigators begin their questioning, they should inform workers that they are collecting information not to fix blame, not to relieve the company of liability, but to complete federal recordkeeping requirements and to provide the insurance company and the state with the facts they need to process injured employees' claims and give them their rightful benefits. Investigators analyze the medical reports to determine the nature and extent of the injuries. Their investigations include complete statements from injured employees and physician's opinions about probable recovery time and the chances of ongoing physical limitations that may require job transfers. Finally, organizations should not allow employees to return to work without first getting physicians' approvals and reports on their physical condition.

THE ROLE OF LABOR IN ACCIDENT CONTROL. Labor plays a significant role in the development and administration of safety programs. The BLS estimates that 93 percent of collective bargaining agreements (covering 1,000 workers or more) contain provisions for the health and safety of employees.

About a third of these agreements provide for safety committees that include labor representation.[29] Joint labor-management safety committees are usually advisory, but they are empowered to make or revise safety rules. They recommend the adoption of new practices; review proposed safety and health programs, accident statistics, changes in protective equipment and clothing, and new procedures; and they make appropriate recommendations. Some committees even make safety inspections and have considerable influence on changes in safety policy and physical facilities that will enhance working conditions.

Labor has also become involved in disciplinary matters involving safety. The question often arises, should an employee have a right to refuse to work on an assignment that is abnormally dangerous. Section 502 of the Labor-Management Relations Act and the just cause for discipline criteria offer employees who refuse an unsafe order some protection. In addition, the U.S. Supreme Court in *Whirlpool Corporation* v. *Marshall* ruled that an employee cannot be discriminated against (disciplined) if he or she refused to perform a job because of a genuine fear of death or bodily harm; that the danger was real; that the employee(s) acted in good faith; and that there was no reasonable alternative open to him or them.[30] The Court also concluded that the employee runs the risk of discharge or reprimand should it subsequently be found that he or she acted in bad faith. Thus, when the job is found to be safe, discipline and often discharge invariably result, with the employer charging insubordination. Ferris suggests that unions and employers can avert incidents of this type through negotiated contract provisions.[31] A good example of such a clause appears in the National Agreement between the Steelworkers Union and the United States Steel Corporation. It allows employees who believe that the work conditions they are being required to work under are "unsafe or unhealthy beyond the normal hazard inherent in the operation" to: (1) receive expedited handling of a grievance on the matter, and/or (2) be relieved from the job (he or she may be assigned to another job without loss of pay), with the right to return to it at a later date. If the joint Safety Board determines that the job was unsafe, the employee would be reimbursed for any lost earnings.

Safety Engineering

Safety engineering concerns measures to make work safer through the design of both machines and the work environment, and through the use of protective methods such as guarding, color coding, and protective clothing. It consists of human factors engineering, designing for safety and protective measures, and protecting workers with devices, color codes, and guards.

HUMAN FACTORS ENGINEERING

Since its inception during World War II, **human factors engineering** has been concerned with the interaction between people and machines—and between people and their environment. Its objective is to make controls and machines more comfortable and convenient, and less confusing, exasperating, and fatiguing to users. It is a scientific approach to the problems of designing and constructing things for people to use, so they can become more efficient and less likely to make errors that result in accidents.[32] These results can usually be achieved when organizations integrate the human factors engineering approach with training, protection, and investigation.

In production situations, some tasks are more efficiently performed by people, while others are better suited to machine operation. People's capabilities lie in performing tasks requiring judgment and flexibility, whereas machines are best adapted to routine, repetitive tasks that call for speed and accuracy. One aspect of human factors engineering concerns allocating tasks between people and machines for optimum work performance. Another deals with analyzing the tasks themselves (this aspect, called job design, was discussed in Chapter 18, and showed how tasks can be grouped to enrich jobs and fully utilize an individual's talents). From the standpoint of safety, job design through task analysis can minimize stress from boredom and fatigue and thereby reduce accidents. Finally, human factors engineering considers and applies dynamic and static body measurements to the design of tools, equipment, and materials to improve the safety, facility, and efficiency of their use. Here are some examples of this aspect of human factors engineering:

1. Pliers for electrical wiring were redesigned with contoured handles to eliminate wrist-bending and consequent fatigue.

2. Clock-type dials on meters were changed to digital, direct-reading gauges, thus removing the need for interpretation and thereby reducing errors.

3. The controls on a lift truck were made compatible with its movements to reduce errors associated with its operation. When the lifting controls move left and right instead of up and down, there is bound to be operator error.

4. Controls and dials can be coded by color, shape, texture, location, or symbol so operators do not have to rely on memory for their proper operation; for example, red means stop or off, green is go or on; and an arrow indicates the direction of movement; the shape of control knobs distinguishes lights from a throttle.

PROTECTIVE MEASURES

Organizations have made considerable progress in reducing personal injury by requiring workers to wear protective equipment; guarding machine parts that could cause injury; and color-coding work areas and equipment to alert workers to possible hazards.

PERSONAL PROTECTIVE EQUIPMENT. Engineering and guarding have eliminated many causes of accidents, but these cannot remove all hazards. Under such circumstances, personal protective equipment becomes mandatory; organizations must select the proper type of equipment, and employees must use it correctly. Personal protective equipment (including protective clothing) should be selected on the basis of the protection it affords under varying conditions and the ease with which employees can use it. Specific types of protective equipment and their applications are listed in Table 21.1.

GUARDING. Training, human factors engineering, and protective equipment cannot be relied on to eliminate all hazards, especially where machines are concerned. Machine guards supplement these activities by helping to prevent injury from the following sources:

1. Direct contact with a machine's moving parts: rotating mechanisms that can seize and wind up hair, belts, and loose clothing; rolls and gears that can pinch fingers and flesh; cutting and shearing mechanisms that can cause abrasions, cuts, and even amputations.
2. Work being processed: splashes of molten metal, chips from grinders, and kickbacks from circular saws.
3. Human failure: fatigue, distraction, curiosity, and deliberate risk-taking.
4. Mechanical failures.
5. Electrical failures.

To make guards effective OSHA has specified characteristics for every type of guard used. In general, machine guards should afford the maximum possible protection; they should be permanently affixed to the equipment, and if the guard is movable, it should be interlocked with the machine itself so that the machine is inoperable unless the guard is in place. Also, the guard should be conveniently placed so that it does not interfere with normal machine operation or cause discomfort to the operator.[33]

USE OF COLOR. Organizations use colors extensively in safety programs for several purposes. In general, proper coloring of plant interiors and equipment eases workers' vision problems and thereby enhances safe working conditions. Some colors are better at reflecting light (ceilings are often painted white to give maximum illumination). Also, colors can make interiors more attractive and thus have a favorable psychological effect on workers; tinted shades on lighting fixtures are also recommended. Standard colors identify specific hazards and eliminate confusion. Color coding for specific designations includes: red for fire protection; orange or yellow for danger; green for safety; and bright blue for protective materials. Machinery is usually painted gray. Safety directors also use color coding uniformly on accident-prevention signs so that all employees—even those who cannot speak English or may be color blind—can react correctly.

Loss Evaluation Control

Complete accident prevention systems contain provisions for evaluating their effectiveness and the feedback of data. But first, there must be a means of gathering and recording accident data. Successful accident control includes measurement methods that enable safety directors to understand and predict what could occur and then plan safety controls before losses occur. Idealistic as this may sound, a technique has been developed to evaluate and control accident losses. Gilmore, writing on loss control, emphasizes the importance of applying defensive safety efforts directly to causes, and cites several methods to quantify safety data.[34] Attaching a dollar cost to each loss is one way of comparing individual losses and charting loss trends. An even more meaningful statistic is the probability relationship, that is, the ratio of no-injury, minor-injury, major-injury losses; or the ratio of minor-severity to major-severity accidents.

Health Care Programs

Enlightened health care programs maintain employees' health by providing physical examinations, treating injuries and illnesses, providing sanitation and personal-hygiene services, and diagnosing and treating mental disorders. Health care complements safety programs, and it receives support from fringe benefits programs such as hospital, medical, and surgical insurance.

MEDICAL FACILITIES

The size of the medical staff and the extent of medical facilities depend on the size of the organization and management preferences. Management also decides whether to retain a staff or utilize the services of outside physicians. However, a registered nurse and a medical clerk are considered necessary. In addition to administering first aid and dispensing medicine, the company nurse can provide technical advice to the personnel department on medical matters. In being approachable and available during working

Table 21.1
Applications of Personal
Protective Equipment

Item	Applications
Head Protection	
1. Safety helmets	1. Absorb blows, used where employees are exposed to head injuries.
2. Bump caps	2. Protect against bumps from low head clearances. Not a substitute for safety helmet.
3. Women's caps	3. Protect hair in general factory work. Visor prevents injury from contact with machines and objects.
Ear Protection	
1. Plugs	1. Protect against hearing impairment due to excessive noise.
2. Ear cups and muffs	2. Protect against higher-frequency noises. Used especially by ground crews at airports.
Face and Eye Protection	
1. Spectacles	1. Protect against flying particles.
2. Goggles (flexible)	2. Frontal and side protection from flying particles and chemical sprays.
3. Chipping goggles	3. Maximum protection from flying particles in chipping operations.
4. Face shields (metal screen; chemical resistant full-face; sturdy, nonflammable type)	4. Protect from heat, chemical splashes, sparks, flying particles, and injurious rays.
5. Acid hoods	5. Protect head and face from acids and other corrosive solutions.
6. Laser-protective spectacles	6. Protect from specific wave-lengths.
Respiratory Equipment	
1. Gas masks (various types of air purifiers)	1. Limited protection as specified on equipment label. Purifies air of specific toxic gases.
2. Atmosphere-supplied respirators	2. Provide filtered air to wearers. Prevent foreign matter from entering eyes, ears, nose, or mouth.
3. Air-supplied suits	3. For rescue or emergency repair work in atmospheres extremely corrosive to skin and mucous membranes and dangerous to life.

Item	Applications	Table 21.1 (cont.)
4. Other breathing devices: self-contained, compressed air, etc.	4. Protect from toxic or oxygen-deficient atmosphere.	
Safety Belts		
1. Multipurpose belts	1. Stop wearers after free fall from height, as in window cleaning or linemen's work.	
2. Lifelines	2. Prevent falls or reduce injuries from falls.	
Protective Footwear		
1. Shoes: hard toe, steel insole, instep guards, etc.	1. Protect feet from injuries caused by protruding objects, material falling on top of foot, and hazards of electricity, slime, water, etc.	
Special Work Clothing		
1. Leather clothing, asbestos and wool garments, aluminized clothing	1. Protect against heat and hot metal, as in fire fighting and open-heat furnaces.	
2. Gloves, hand leathers, and arm protection	2. Protect hands and arms against impact and cuts.	
3. Impervious clothing, including gloves, aprons, and pants	3. Protect against dusts, vapors, moisture, and corrosive liquids.	
4. Cold-weather clothing	4. Used for thermal insulation.	
5. High-visibility and night-hazard clothing	5. Used by construction, utility, maintenance, and service people (police, firemen) exposed to traffic hazards.	

hours and having a genuine interest in the well-being of employees, the medical staff can best serve their needs. Under these circumstances, employees are more likely to report injuries and illnesses and seek out medical personnel for counseling. Health service facilities can range from simple first-aid stations to highly sophisticated clinics with extended-care facilities. Whatever the facility's composition, it should be separate from the rest of the organization, provide privacy for treatment and examinations, and be neat and sanitary. The medical facility also needs a place for its confidential records.

MEDICAL EXAMS

It was previously emphasized in this chapter that organizations should place workers on jobs where their physical abilities will permit them to work safely and efficiently. In addition, organizations want to maintain the mental and physical health of their employees in the interest of regular attendance, efficient performance, and even more important, their well-being. Preemployment physicals and periodic reexaminations help achieve these purposes.

Preemployment examinations. The object of the preemployment physical exam is to ascertain applicants' physical abilities so that organizations can match abilities to job requirements and detect existing disabilities for which the firm might otherwise be liable. Physicals should not be construed as a method of screening out applicants; they are an opportunity for employers to discover possible physical impairments. At this point, too, the medical staff can teach employees the importance of physical care and its relationship to their personal well-being. Preemployment physicals should include: a complete medical history; checking pulse rate; tests of breathing, vision, hearing, and reflexes; a chest X ray; and laboratory tests such as blood counts, urinalysis, etc. For heavy-lifting jobs, low back X rays are also needed.

Periodic exams. Sound industrial-medical practice emphasizes the need for annual health (physical and mental) exams for all employees over age 35. A *Fortune* survey revealed that 91.6 percent of the respondents provided annual physicals to some or all of their employees.[35] Organizations should give employees about to retire thorough physical examinations to help prepare them for retirement. These exams also afford an excellent opportunity for preretirement counseling.

Workers who operate special equipment that could endanger their lives or the lives of others should receive periodic medical exams to determine their physical fitness to hold such jobs safely. Organizations should periodically test employees exposed to materials whose ill effects can build up, to determine if toxic materials have accumulated in their bodies. The interval of testing depends upon the nature of the material being handled and the amount of exposure; sometimes companies test employees as frequently as twice a week, but as organizations gain experience, they may extend the interval.[36]

Executives are subject to strains different from those affecting the average employees, and consequently may suffer physical or mental disabilities. Their positions in the hierarchy are vital to the continuity of operations, and executives' absences or diminished effectiveness due to physical or mental impairments can significantly curtail organizational performance. Hence, firms should supervise their executives' health. The best approach is an annual, comprehensive physical examination combined with rest and recreation at a private clinic.

Exit examinations. Before employees are terminated, many organizations examine them and record their findings, particularly when they have been exposed to environments or substances that are hazardous to their health.[37]

PHYSICAL FITNESS PROGRAMS (PFPs)

The number of PFPs has been accelerating in recent years. As early as 1894 NCR provided exercise classes for its employees and today there are about 50,000 firms with PFPs; 300 of them even have full-time physical fitness directors.[38] PFPs range from after-hours employee athletic teams subsidized by the company to fully equipped fitness centers with gymnasium, weight rooms, swimming pools, saunas, lockers, and physiological testing areas. Kimberly Clark's $2.5 million center is perhaps the most lavish one in business. Research studies have offered some insight into the feasibility of adopting a PFP.[39] One conclusion is that employees who are already in good condition are most likely to participate and that there is a weak link between employees initially joining and employees continuing in the program. Similarly, those who most need the program are the ones it is most likely to miss. Study results also suggest that those who stay with the program become more physically fit and healthier and they benefit from increased strength (mental as well as physical), flexibility, endurance, and cardiovascular health. Advocates of PFPs cite their low cost $50–$1,000 per employee as a major plus. But experience with the program also indicates that companies might do just as well with alternatives—such as stay well programs that offer savings to both the employer and the organization in reduced health costs if the employee stays well.

MENTAL HEALTH

A study of automobile workers showed that the lowest level of mental health was found among low and semiskilled operative workers. The repetitive nature of their work probably contributes little to their self-esteem or work satisfaction, and perhaps results in low morale among these workers. The result is a stress situation conducive to mental illness.[40]

Industrial medicine endeavors to place employees in jobs they can handle both physically and mentally, but stress from repetition, monotony, and other pressures may still be unavoidable in some jobs. Outside sources also combine to cause mental stresses. All forms of mental disorders must be viewed and treated as illnesses; industry must take the initiative in recognizing them as such. Until such time as the conditions that produce ill health can be removed (and this may never come to pass), organizations must direct their efforts toward treating the afflicted.

Education about mental illness can help overcome the stigma associated with psychiatric care. The personnel department can teach line managers to identify mental health problems and make appropriate referrals; but the individuals themselves must feel a need for professional assistance and be willing to request help. Beyond this, firms can extend already existing health benefits to include coverage for psychiatric care, psychological testing, and psychotherapy.

INDUSTRIAL HYGIENE AND RELATED SERVICES

Industrial hygiene refers to the work conditions and practices conducive to the preservation of health. The facilities available to employees and the environments in which they work have a direct relationship to safety and health factors. Sanitary facilities, including change rooms, toilets, and showers, should be available in all production facilities. When operations involve contaminants or are particularly dirty, the facility should provide solvents and cleaning agents.

Proper illumination contributes to good housekeeping and also improves the quality and accuracy of work; good lighting must be engineered into a work place. Reducing noise, either at its source or by proper insulation, can cut down hearing injuries and worker tensions. Ear-protection devices can help prevent physical impairment, but because they are uncomfortable and employees resist wearing them, this approach should only be used as a supplement to direct measures, that is, suppressing noise at the source and insulating surrounding areas.

High temperatures and humidity as well contribute to worker discomfort, making work both difficult and unhealthy. Salt loss from perspiration can cause heat cramps or heat exhaustion. If work near sources of heat cannot be avoided, employees should wear protective equipment and perhaps take salt tablets to prevent exhaustion. But the most effective measure in lessening the effects of heat is to reduce temperatures through proper ventilation or air-conditioning.

Two-thirds of occupational disease exposures are attributable to lead, carbon monoxide, and nonmetallic dust—silica and asbestos. The remaining hazards consist of exposure to other dusts, vapors, gases, and fumes. Built-in dust controls often alleviate these conditions, and individual respiratory equipment can provide supplementary protection.

Industrial Security

The protection of employee health and safety extends beyond the programs described above. Theft, sabotage, arson, and riots can be as much a threat to worker security as job hazards. The need for **industrial security** programs has increased, according to an ASP-BNA survey, because of moral deterioration, less respect for authority, and greater instability of today's employees.[41] The 176 respondents (a sample of large and small companies throughout the country) reported theft by both employees and outsiders the most common problem, but bomb threats and vandalism also rank high on the list of security problems.

Two-thirds of the companies in the survey indicated they had developed a formal industrial security program. Investigating applicants and controlling access to the work place are among the new duties of the security function. Receptionists, guards, electronic devices, and ID badges are the techniques most often used. Nearly half of the large companies, but only one-fifth of the small companies, have an executive with the title of security officer. In companies without a security officer, the duties are usually assigned to the personnel director, industrial relations executive, or officer in charge of maintenance or administrative services.

Cost-Benefit Analysis

Cost-benefit analysis of safety programs can be helpful in improving them. Costs are readily measurable. They include the salaries of the safety staff, safety devices, clothing, equipment, and related measures. Fewer and less severe accidents, lower insurance premiums, less damage to plant and equipment, and fewer OSHA citations can be calculated and compared to the costs. Accident data—incidence rates and costs—provide a basis for comparing one organization's experience to others.

Fines for OSHA violations and correction of citations can represent a major safety cost. The main violations (about 70 percent of them) have involved failure to keep walkways and other passages clear of trash and unsafe storage of inventory. For the remainder, trade-offs have to be considered. The monetary trade-off (benefit) is, of course, cost of sick leave, medical and hospitalization insurance, and workers' compensation insurance. Also, where gross negligence on the part of a firm can be proved, it can be held liable in a civil suit in most states. Settlements of these suits are usually in the six-figure range.

The second trade-off is harder to compute, but can be illustrated by asking if we should encourage the manufacture of EDB (pesticide) under conditions that cause cancer, where this can be prevented.

Summary

A safe and healthy work environment is a major contributing factor to the effectiveness of employees. Organizations that keep the work place free from recognized hazards and adhere to health and safety standards experience lower absenteeism and greater efficiency from their employees.

Federal legislation has had a significant influence on the scope and administration of industrial health and safety programs. The 1970 Occupational Safety and Health Act (OSHA) encompasses the major health and safety regulations for industry. It establishes standards for individual industries, provides for inspections of plants and installations to insure compliance, and requires reports on accidents and illnesses. Since the purpose of the act is to save lives and prevent injuries, it also provides for research activities for purposes of devising innovative approaches to improving occupational health and safety.

Effective programs to control accidents and illnesses have a formal organization with line and staff participation. Line managers ensure that all employees understand and comply with safety rules. They stress the importance of safety and hygiene through continuous education and training programs. Their employees undergo periodic physical examinations to determine if they are physically able to perform their work assignments. And at the work place, supervisors make regular inspections in cooperation with the safety committee to see that hazards are not present. In this regard, organizations apply principles from human factors engineering to help workers become efficient and less accident-prone. They also introduce additional precautions through the use of protective clothing and equipment, machine guarding, and color coding.

Staff specialists trained in safety engineering and industrial hygiene support such programs by making inspections, conducting training, providing technical advice and assistance, and maintaining necessary records. Utilizing employee suggestions, safety engineers can implement improvements in the physical work environment. When accidents or work-connected illnesses occur, the staff conducts appropriate investigations, records the information, and files the required reports. For accident analysis and control purposes, incident-related data are particularly useful as a comparative measure of experience among firms and within the plant over a period of time.

Medical facilities complement safety programs by providing physical exams to match employees' abilities to job requirements. They also maintain employee health, diagnose and treat illnesses and injuries, and prepare workers for retirement.

Although safety and hygiene programs protect employees directly, organizations must take additional measures in the form of industrial security to keep plants free from theft, sabotage, riots, fire, and entry by unauthorized persons.

Key Terms

safety	incidence rate
accidents	safety engineering
OSHA	human factors engineering
accident prone	industrial hygiene
loss control	industrial security

Review Questions

1. How is the OSHA incidence rate calculated?
2. What are the ideal qualifications of a safety professional?
3. Describe the elements of an effective accident control program.
4. How can human factors engineering contribute to safety?
5. What types of protective equipment would be most appropriate against each of the following hazards:
   a. Jet engine noise?
   b. Coke oven emissions?
   c. Road traffic (for traffic controllers)?
   d. Falling objects?

Discussion Questions

1. What measures can be taken to improve the treatment of mental illness in American industry? Consider this question from various points of view: legal, intracompany, union-management, other. To what extent do you think employers should accept the responsibility for mental health services for their employees?
2. The talents needed by safety and health programs go beyond those available from the personnel staff itself. Technical expertise in safety, medicine, psychiatry, and counseling services is required. If you were the personnel director of a large plant where these talents were available, how would you utilize them in a coordinated health and safety program?
3. Safety has been characterized as a state of mind. What efforts can the safety staff make to ensure a state of mind conducive to safe working practices? What role do training and performance appraisal play in this regard?
4. What staff services should be available in an accident-prevention system? How can recording statistical data on illnesses and accidents contribute to the system? In what ways might companies modify their fringe benefits to complement safety and health efforts?
5. Discuss the pros and cons of appointing a safety committee. How can organizations most effectively utilize the committee in the safety effort? What steps can organizations take to minimize the possibility of undermining the safety authority of supervisors if their departments' committeepersons become officious?

Case Problem 1

EYE-PROTECTION RULE

The following notice appeared on the employee bulletin board:

As of next Monday, all employees on production and maintenance jobs will be required to wear safety glasses or other suitable eye protection at all times *when they are in the manufacturing area of the plant. This measure has become necessary due to a rash of eye injuries in the past few months.*

The company will provide nonprescription safety glasses to all employees desiring them. The safety department can order prescription safety glasses for all employees desiring them at wholesale cost.

This policy will be strictly enforced and violations will result in discipline.

During the following week, there were numerous complaints from employees who claimed the glasses interfered with their work performance. Several reported to the clinic complaining of headaches and eye strain because the lenses in the glasses made it hard to see their work. And the union filed an official grievance claiming the company violated the contract by unilaterally imposing work rules. In each succeeding week, increasing numbers of employees violated the eye-protection rule, and the incidence of eye injuries remained high.

26
27
28
29
30
31
32

33
34
35
36
37
38

Problems

1. What mistakes did the company make in instituting the eye-protection program? How could the company have convinced the workers to cooperate in the safety effort?

2. What role does discipline play in this situation? How should the company deal with violators of its eye-protection policy?

Trilinear Systems, Inc., a small plant employing 122 people, used a pin-head sized, silicon-chip integrated circuit in its assembly of radar systems. These chips were purchased from an outside supplier at a cost of $21.33 each, and a day's production use could be carried into the plant in a large matchbox. Over 2,000 chips per day were used—the things were really small!

Mr. Acton, the plant manager, noticed that the loss of these chips was increasing. Over 100 per day could not be accounted for. Trilinear's security agent, Plant Protection, Inc., did some quiet investigation and found out why. The chips were in short supply, and unscrupulous buyers were willing to pay up to $25 each for the chips. Apparently some of the employees were walking off with them.

At the suggestion of Plant Protection, Inc., Mr. Acton started a random-search routine at the plant gates at the end of the day. Two or three times a week all employees were thoroughly searched before leaving. The program worked in part—one employee was found with 50 chips on him, and was promptly fired. But searching for such a minute item look lots of time, and the employees objected violently to the searches. Even after one thief was caught, losses continued.

Finally, the employees' union official formally complained to Mr. Acton. He argued that if the company wanted to search everyone, they should pay for it. It took over 20 minutes on search days for an employee to get out of the plant.

Case Problem 2

BIG BROTHER WATCHING

Problems

1. What rights do the workers have here? Why?

2. What rights does Trilinear Systems have here? Why?

3. What other ways might Trilinear Systems impose better security than by searching workers?

Notes

1. *Accident Facts—1979 Edition* (Chicago: National Safety Council, 1980), p. 3.

2. "Safe," *Industry Week*, April 26, 1976, p. 37.

3. *Accident Facts*, pp. 5ff.

4. For a detailed analysis of the major provisions of OSHA and the effect of standards on business establishments, see *The Job Safety and Health Act of 1970* (Washington, D.C.: Bureau of National Affairs, 1971).

5. "The New Job Safety Law: What to Expect," *Occupational Hazards Executive Report*, Spring Issue 1972, p. 8.

6. *Marshal v. Barlow's, Inc.* (No. 76-1143).

7. "On-Site Consultation Agreements," *Federal Register*, Tuesday, August 16, 1977, pp. 41386-41393.

8. For answers to the most frequently asked questions about OSHA record keeping and reports see: U.S. Bureau of Labor Statistics, *What Every Employer Needs to Know About OSHA Recordkeeping* (Washington, D.C.: U.S. Government Printing Office, 1978).

9. *The Job Safety and Health Act of 1970*, p. 66.

10. "O.S.H.A., E.P.A.: The Heyday is Over," *The New York Times*, Sunday, January 4, 1981, Section 3, p. F15.

11. "Industry Batting Poorly on OSHA Challenges," *Industry Week*, September 23, 1974, p. 5.

12. "Staying Alive and Well at the Workplace," *Steel Labor*, September 1975, pp. 8ff.

13. "Labor Transition Team Urges to Switch OSHA Away From Its 'Policeman's Role'," *Wall Street Journal*, December 8, 1980, p. 7.

14. *Report of the National Commission on Workmen's Compensation Laws* (Washington, D.C.: U.S. Government Printing Office, 1972).

15. LaVerne C. Tinsley, "Workers' Compensation Laws—Key Amendments of 1979," *Monthly Labor Review*, February 1980, pp. 19–25.

16. Robert J. Paul, "Worker's Compensation—An Adequate Employee Benefit?" *Academy of Management Review*, October 1976, pp. 112–23.

17. Ibid., p. 119.

18. Daniel M. Kasper, "An Alternative to Workmen's Compensation," *Industrial and Labor Relations Review*, July 1975, pp. 535–48.

19. See, for example: J. B. Gordon, A. Akman, and M. L. Brooks, *Industrial Accident Statistics: A Reexamination* (New York: Praeger, 1971); L. L. LeShan, "Dynamics of Accident-Prone Behavior," *Psychiatry*, March 1952, pp. 73–80; E. J. McCormick and J. Tiffin, *Industrial Psychology* (Englewood Cliffs, N.J.: Prentice-Hall, 1974).

20. Frank E. Bird, Jr., and Robert G. Loftus, *Loss Control Management* (Loganville, Ga.: Institute Press, 1976), p. 52.

21. The Atlanta Coca-Cola Bottling Co., *Employee Safety Manual*, January 1981, p. 1.

22. Robert E. McClay, "Professionalizing the Safety Function," *Personnel Journal*, February 1977, pp. 72–77.

23. Roger L. M. Dunbar, "Manager's Influence on Subordinates' Thinking About Safety," *Academy of Management Journal*, June 1975, pp. 364–69.

24. For guidance in developing safety training to comply with OSHA, see: *Training Requirements in OSHA Standards*

(Washington, D.C.: U.S. Department of Labor, Occupational Safety and Health Administration, 1979).

25. Tita Beal, "Safety Training That Works—And Doesn't Cost an Arm and a Leg," *Training HRD,* August 1977, pp. 47–50.

26. Edward D. Dionne, "Motivating Workers With Incentives," *National Safety News,* January 1980, pp. 75–79.

27. "How to Plan a Safety Program," *Occupational Hazards Executive Report,* Spring 1972, pp. 99ff.

28. Ibid., p. 109.

29. U.S. Bureau of Labor Statistics, *Major Collective Bargaining Agreements: Safety and Health Provisions* (Washington, D.C.: U.S. Government Printing Office, 1976), pp. 1ff.

30. *Whirlpool Corporation v. Marshall,* U.S.C., No. 78-1870, February 26, 1980.

31. Frank D. Ferris, "Resolving Safety Disputes: Work or Walk," *Labor Law Journal,* November 1975, pp. 695–709.

32. National Safety Council, *Accident Prevention Manual for Industrial Operations,* 8th ed. (Chicago: National Safety Council, 1978), pp. 219ff.

33. Ibid., p. 660.

34. Charles L. Gilmore, *Accident Prevention and Loss Control* (New York: American Management Association, 1970), pp. 34ff.

35. Walter McQuade, "Those Annual Physicals Are Worth the Trouble," *Fortune,* January 1977, p. 172.

36. National Safety Council, *Supervisor's Safety Manual* (Chicago: National Safety Council, 1970), p. 99.

37. Ibid., p. 100.

38. John Kondrasuk, "Company Physical Fitness Programs: Salvation or Fad?" *The Personnel Administrator,* November 1980, pp. 47–50.

39. Ibid., p. 49.

40. Pat Greathouse, "Industry's Role in Mental Health," *Journal of Occupational Medicine,* May 1967, pp. 228ff.

41. American Society for Personnel Administration and Bureau of National Affairs, *Bulletin to Management. ASPA-BNA Survey—Industrial Security* (Washington, D.C.: Bureau of National Affairs, March 16, 1972).

Chapter Twenty-two

The Outlook for Personnel

In Samuel Beckett's classic play, *Waiting for Godot*,[1] three characters, Estragon, Vladimir, and Pozzo, meet on a country road. Estragon and Vladimir have been sitting and waiting for Godot, who represents the future. When Pozzo appears they invite him to join them in their vigil. After an anxious hour or so of waiting with no appearance of Godot, Pozzo decides to proceed on his journey in pursuit of his own destiny.

The point of the play is that time (the future) passes by those who sit and wait. We have in our power the ability to shape our own destinies. So it is with personnel management; the future of the function will be influenced significantly by the competence of individuals responsible for its activities; they cannot wait for Godot!

Yet the outlook also depends on forthcoming economic changes, legislative trends, developments in union and management practices, and other dynamic forces acting on organizations in the future. American free enterprise is on the threshold of an era in which personnel management will be essential to the survival of its organizations. Handling personnel problems will shift from maintaining and servicing immediate operational needs to creating a total integrated approach for optimizing the contribution of human resources to organizational objectives. The changing nature of the personnel function in the 1980s will make personnel work more challenging and of greater consequence to organizations than ever before.

LEARNING OBJECTIVES

1. To understand the importance of foresight to the field of personnel.

2. To understand the implications of future developments for personnel.

3. To know the effect of labor force changes on managing personnel functions.

4. To understand the impact of interfaces on personnel.

5. To understand the changing nature of the personnel function in the future.

The Need for Foresight in Personnel Management

Nothing is as constant as change. The ability to manage change will be the key to survival in the remainder of this century. Effective planning requires predicting future problems and their relation to current resources, and then developing resources to meet those problems. This text has stressed the importance of setting objectives and formulating plans to accomplish them. This planning function is based on assumptions and premises about future conditions. Effective planners, then, are those who can think ahead, anticipate obstructions in the way of their plans, and effect the changes that will allow their organizations to accomplish their objectives. Emerging patterns in personnel management signal changes that offer direction for future personnel strategy. The future is not an unalterable fact; by making provisions for it, planners may be able to change undesirable trends and remove obstructions to the efficient performance of the personnel function.

Growing technology in the field of data processing and information systems will make it imperative for organizations to maintain their adaptability to change. As this technology advances, the complexity of personnel-related problems will multiply. Since it will become increasingly difficult to stabilize the work environment, managing change will be the task of all future managers. Personnel directors will need valid information on the pace and direction of future trends, and the techniques of forecasting outlined in Chapter 5 are applicable in this effort.

The National Goals Research Staff observed that the objective of projecting present trends is not only to discover what will happen if nothing is done to change the trends, but to provide an idea of alternative goals so that people can choose the best one. They then can devise and implement policies that will change current trends as necessary, thus working toward a more desirable future.[2]

Areas of Concern for the Future of Personnel Management

Personnel managers would logically consider forecasted developments in their field in general, as well as in each of its functional areas: employment, union-management relations, training and development, benefits and services, and safety. The following projections and prognostications are based on emerging patterns, the author's judgment founded on his first-hand field experience, opinions of other personnel managers, and current writings.

A number of national issues that are outside the scope of personnel management nevertheless have a profound impact on an organization's human resources and the way they are managed.

The demand for higher *productivity* will come from all sectors of the economy as people realize that we must produce goods and services more efficiently in order to compete in world markets. Quality circles and joint labor-management committees will focus their energies on better production methods and machinery. The results to be anticipated are lower costs, higher wages, and less unemployment.[3]

The **ecology** movement will continue to push for changes to improve the quality of life. Programs for cleaner air, better drinking water, more abundant food, improved health and medical care, better schooling, safer products, conservation of energy sources, and so on, are certain to remain at the forefront of citizen demands on all levels of government. The government will continue to respond with programs to regulate industry and to reduce the deterioration of the environment. These programs have a direct cost in terms of increased taxes to both employer and worker, and indirect ones in terms of the higher prices people must pay for goods and services as organizations are required to incorporate government-edicted changes, for example, pollution-abatement systems.

Closely allied to the ecology movement is the *energy* shortage. Shrinking supplies amid escalating demands for fuel, water, and electricity present special problems to the future work force. Transporting goods and services to market and employees to and from work depends on the availability of fuel. And running offices and factories relies on a constant flow of all types of energy. The cost and availability of supplies of energy will have a significant bearing on the future cost and availability of labor.

Inflation will continue to erode the purchasing power of American workers. Hourly compensation improvements are projected to be around 9 to 10 percent for the next several years. Should productivity continue to increase at about a 1 percent rate, the 8 to 9 percent difference would represent a rise in unit cost that would surely be reflected in price increases. This in turn would put further pressure on wages, and the resulting **wage-price spiral** will generate further inflation. It seems inevitable that future economic policy will focus on restraints to slow the acceleration of inflation. But employee demands for improved buying power will continue to be a point of contention.

Security is another major concern of Americans. Unemployment and inflation cause economic worries for employers and their workers. People need to continue to receive and possess the elements essential to their lives, for example, money, food, shelter, and so on, in order to be motivated toward some goal. Hence, it is in the interest of an organization to assure the security of its workers. On a national scale the concern for employment security will lead to the development of new public policy to reduce the jobless rate to 4% by 1984. Undoubtedly, the Reagan administration will seek private initiatives to help solve this problem. The administration's dissatisfaction with the CETA program, the apparent mismanagement of its funds, and its questionable impact on unemployment will likely lead to its early elimination.

Older people have become less secure as those in retirement find their pensions inadequate (primarily because of inflation) to support even a meager existence. But younger employees are becoming concerned that the cost of providing more generously for the growing number of older people, especially those under the Social Security system, may tend to impoverish working people.[4]

An *egalitarian approach* to job opportunity and income will become the norm within the next decade. There will continue to be income differentials among groups, but affirmative action programs in organizations and Equal Employment Opportunity regulations will narrow the gap substantially.

These major policy issues will have a significant impact on the future role of personnel management, and they will obviously bring about changes in the nature of the function.

The Changing Nature of the Personnel Function

In the future, the function of Personnel will largely be determined as it is now, by the attitudes of top management toward employees. Rapid advances in media technology point to the development of highly centralized decision units at the highest levels of organizations; these units will assemble and evaluate data and indicate decisions by applying appropriate information to mathematical models of the firm. If management moves in this direction, its attitude toward employees will probably become impersonal, regarding them as inputs to the production process. Furthermore, rising production costs and increased government regulation will make widespread technological change likely. Intense personnel-related problems will emerge from the impersonal effects of centralized, high-level decision making coupled with the problems of adjusting to change. To compound the difficulty, the nature of employees of the future presents a stark contrast to the circumstances just described. These employees will demand participation in decisions that affect them, jobs that are relevant, and a work environment that is both stimulating and challenging. They will express their strong sense of obligation for public welfare in demands that the organizations they work for meet their responsibilities to society.

QUALITY OF WORK LIFE. Numerous organizations have already addressed this concern with efforts to improve the quality of work life. In general, projects have involved the establishment of sociotechnical systems, a form of organization that enables employees to participate in managing the work. Examples of these include workers' advisory councils, self-managed work groups, employee representation on boards of directors (co-determination), joint labor-management committees, and task forces. Under these systems, jobs are redesigned to enrich the work itself. Work groups set their own goals, and there is open communication on costs, production sales, and other matters relevant to the work. Organizations let employees rotate work assignments even to the extent of moving from production to nonproduction jobs. And pay may even be based on the number of jobs employees can perform rather than the level of skill they attain performing a single function. The future will bring an increase in the utilization of sociotechnical systems to improve the quality of work life.[5]

NEW STATUS FOR PERSONNEL MANAGERS.   Personnel managers can make their greatest contribution by working to resolve the problems employees will encounter as the result of impersonal work situations. They will guide top management's thinking on human resource matters and focus their efforts on innovative means for utilizing personnel. The personnel function, as a consequence, will be elevated in status. Directors of human resources will function at the vice president's level, and rather than assuming a passive, advisory role, they will actively influence major decisions of the organization. And, in the decade of the '80s personnel will be one of the ten fastest growing fields. The accreditation program initiated in 1976 by the American Society for Personnel Administration underscored the importance of professionalism for personnel people. The projected growth of this field (the Bureau of Labor Statistics estimates an average of 20,800 additional personnel job openings each year to 1985) will make it increasingly necessary for practitioners to upgrade their credentials on a continuing basis and seek certification at successively higher levels within the profession.

A CONCERN FOR SOCIAL RESPONSIBILITY.   Future human resource effectiveness will depend on the changing pattern of corporate objectives as profit performance expands to include fulfilling responsibilities to employees and the public welfare. A new social conscience has already begun to emerge. Corporations are assessing their obligations to society by acknowledging the **social responsibility** for solving pollution problems; hiring and training minorities, women, and the handicapped; taking positive action on social problems (e.g., alcoholism and drug abuse); and providing for the education of their employees. Companies will integrate social performance with financial performance, and they will measure, record, report, and audit the results.[6] Accordingly, future personnel issues will have a basis in social conscience.

EXPANDED GOVERNMENT REGULATION. There is a clear trend toward greater regulation of personnel activities. Recent legislation and court rulings on minimum wages, equal employment opportunity, work safety standards, and collective bargaining set limits and demands on the personnel process. For personnel managers, the growing government involvement certainly presents a challenge. Organizations can expect higher minimum wages, an expansion of third-party settlement of labor disputes, more stringent guidelines on equal employment, constraints on an organization's ability to stave off union organizing attempts, and stricter enforcement of health and safety standards. Personnel managers a decade from now may work under a clearly defined, all-pervasive framework of federal legislation of labor practices.

EMPLOYMENT

Forecasted shifts in the composition of the labor force will present new challenges to the personnel function. Aided by personnel research efforts and sophisticated information systems, organizations will develop new methods of dealing with impending changes.

LABOR FORCE COMPOSITION. The Bureau of Labor Statistics estimates that by 1990 the total civilian **labor force composition** will be 199 million. The 1980s will see the largest employment increases in service-producing industries (trade, government, health care, finance, transportation), which will expand to 73.4 million by 1990. This represents a 30 percent increase over the 60.4 million service workers in 1978.[7] The nature of service-industry work presupposes that the workers have a high degree of knowledge. The **knowledge worker** will be more sophisticated and likely to be concerned with job satisfaction. Hence, personnel managers will be challenged to find new ways to motivate a better-educated, more professional, and perhaps more demanding labor force.

In the next decade the work force will get older—the most rapidly increasing age group in the population will be 25 to 44 years old. Its numbers will jump 35 percent to 78 million in 1990 (from 58 million in 1978).[8] The implications of this phenomenon will be significant to personnel managers. First, the fact that during the 1980s an extraordinary number of ambitious young men and women will crowd into the first step of the management ladder means that development programs will have to be initiated to groom them for higher responsibility. And management selection and career development programs will need to find ways to choose the best qualified among the many seasoned junior executives who will opt for the few senior slots available by the 1990s. Second, ways will have to be found to keep the mounting costs of pensions from overwhelming the productive workers.

WOMEN IN THE WORK FORCE.   The increasing participation of women in the labor force seems likely to alter the pattern of future employment. Their growing dissatisfaction with the traditional, limited role of housekeeper and mother has manifested itself in the increase in the number of women in both nonsupervisory and management positions. As more women seek involvement and fulfillment in the labor market, conflicts between the sexes and equal opportunity requirements will demand the attention of personnel managers. They will have to develop work environments that minimize the conflicts and open career opportunities for women on the executive level.

EQUAL EMPLOYMENT OPPORTUNITY.   As organizations gain experience with protected class (women, minorities, handicapped) employment, discriminatory hiring and placement practices will diminish. The new Uniform Guidelines on Employee Selection Procedures will increase the frustration of employment managers as they strive to comply with the law. Until both government and employers gain a feel for the new guidelines, personnel managers will find the hiring process more difficult and time consuming than ever. But, in the long run, the 1980s should witness substantial advances in equalizing job opportunities for all who want to work. Enforcement under the Uniform Guidelines will be aggressive, and compliance agencies will focus on bottom line results, that is, the number of minorities, women, and handicapped actually hired and promoted. Whether because of legislation or social conscience, most organizations will adopt affirmative action programs. Largely because of the expense of validation, they will cut back on the use of traditional selection devices and will resort to interview results, bio-data tests (which evaluate how well candidates have performed in their milieu rather than meeting an absolute standard), and demonstrated ability as a basis for hiring and placement. Interviewing and counseling skills will become essential to everyone who deals with people. In applying these selection skills, employers will be admonished not to discriminate against the majority either. Reverse-discrimination court cases should not inhibit the employment of special groups of people, but they will complicate hiring and selection procedures because *any* form of discrimination, whether it be against minorities or the majority, will be outlawed and subject to court review.

PERSONNEL RESEARCH

Employers in the future will need to know more about the methods of selecting and placing minority groups, training the hard-core unemployed, handling the problems of personnel turnover and evaluating their current employees. In the years ahead, the scope and quantity of personnel research directed toward these problems will increase. Companies will make greater use of researchers trained as behavioral scientists to solve human resource problems.[9] Additional research is likely to center on organizational change and the effects different physical structures will have on the psychological environment in which employees work. The answers to these questions will strongly influence the future direction of organizations.

Human resource accounting, an attempt to quantify previously intangible business assets, is another future development that holds significant promise. Current financial statements evaluate the assets and liabilities of a company and measure the difference between revenues realized and the expenses incurred by a firm. No such analysis is attempted for human resources, however, because they are difficult to quantify. Future research will work to develop a human resource accounting system and formulate a body of generally accepted principles for application. The relevance and usefulness of such a system are easy to appreciate when its potential impact on future financial statements and its value as a measure of a company's potential are considered.

If there is one common element in the areas of research outlined above, it is the scientific and quantitative techniques for dealing with the problems that will plague tomorrow's managers. Relying less on intuition, managers in the future will seek scientific tools of management as both problems and data increase in complexity. While objectivity will not become coldly inhuman, for personal relations will always be an important factor in the work environment, future business problems will almost certainly be solved with scientific methodology.

Widespread computer applications will augment personnel research and record keeping in the future. Programmers are constantly devising quantitative models for personnel decision making and data systems for selection, placement, human resource planning, collective bargaining, job evaluation, and record keeping. There will probably be widespread use of computer-based personnel data systems by the end of the 1980s.

LABOR-MANAGEMENT RELATIONS IN THE 1980s

The future of labor-management relations concerns managers, union members, and citizens alike. Developments in this area affect organizational operations internally, since contract disputes and settlements directly affect the entire organization. And companies that do not bargain collectively with employees are more likely to stay union-free if they are aware of the emerging issues in labor relations.

UNION ORGANIZATION. The decline in union membership in proportion to the labor force should be an inducement for labor to intensify its organizing efforts. The union movement will focus its attention on the relatively unorganized South and on service-industry professionals and white-collar workers. Whether there will be dramatic gains in union membership remains debatable. Public sentiment appears to be running in favor of labor interests. A national Louis Harris poll showed 85 percent of those interviewed agreeing that "unions are needed . . . so that legitimate . . . complaints can be heard and action taken," and 76 percent felt that "most unions in the United States have been good forces working for . . . desirable social needs."[10] Union organizers are certain to meet determined opposition from employers who will mobilize strong union avoidance campaigns. In anticipation of this strategy, unions have countered with bargaining demands for neutrality pledges, in which employers agree to refrain from interfering with union efforts to organize new plants. General Motor's southern strategy to keep their new sun-belt plants union free was blocked when the United Auto Workers got the Company in 1976 to sign the first neutrality pact. Three of the Big Four rubber companies and the United Rubber Workers followed suit in 1979. With more neutrality pacts likely in the '80s, unions are sure to be aided in their organizing attempts, especially in the South.

INCREASED COMPLEXITY OF BARGAINING ISSUES.   Economic factors, for example, inflation, unemployment, aging work force, coupled with the growing influence of young, well-educated, militant union members will raise several issues that will become central in future negotiations. **Job security** has been a central theme in negotiations in recent years. Settlements have increased the protection against layoffs and plant shutdowns for long service employees. In fact, some form of work or pay guarantee is found in a large segment of labor-management agreements. Similarly, unions will likely continue their efforts to provide security, or at least protection, through retraining and relocation allowances, for employees displaced by plant shutdowns. And within the next decade legislation will require employers to give adequate notice of plant shutdowns and to provide assistance to the employees affected.[11]

To alleviate job shortages in the near future, unions will push for a shorter work week. Through bargaining or legislation, or a combination of both, the four-day work week will ultimately become a reality for the American worker. But such a trend could complicate life in the long run because there might not be enough workers in the work force to sustain production a decade or so from now as the baby boom generation enters its mature working years. In this case, we might have to revert to the forty-hour week.

Continuing inflation will lead to almost universal adoption of COLA clauses tying basic wages to the consumer price index (cost of living). Yet economic improvements for workers will be tied to productivity improvements. Toward this end we will see increased emphasis on schemes that tie pay improvements to the company's profit growth (e.g., profit sharing and employee stock ownership plans).

UNION POLITICAL INFLUENCE.   Labor's impact through legislation has grown significantly in the past several years. The labor movement believes it has great influence on Congress and will continue to seek its ends—a higher minimum wage, labor law reform, national health insurance, economic recovery, right-to-work repeal and others—with ever-increasing frequency through the legislature.[12] Unions' concerted efforts to maintain their political influence take the form of lobbying, voter education, and active campaigning (including financial support) for candidates who support labor's position.

MERGERS.   The future will see a trend toward conglomerate unions; a combination of economy and strength will provide the impetus for this. **Union merger** is the expressed desire of AFL-CIO President Lane Kirkland. AFL-CIO officials have encouraged some unions to merge, but they have refrained from taking an activist role. The reason behind the encouragement is that at least 50 AFL-CIO affiliates have less than 50,000 members. This small membership is insufficient to provide adequate services, accumulate the financial resources for effective organizing campaigns, and bargain with management on an equal footing. Prospects point to more mergers. Since the AFL and the CIO joined forces in 1955 there have been more than 20 mergers, and since early 1972 at least a dozen more unions have made advances toward merger. Now that the Steelworkers (the most active union in mergers) has united with District 50 of the Allied and Technical Workers (a former subsidiary of the United Mine Workers), they represent workers in all basic-metals industries from mine to mill. Potentially, teachers could have one of the largest unions in the nation; large units of the National Education Association have been breaking away and affiliating with trade unions, principally the American Federation of Teachers.[13] The merger of the two largest textile unions into the Amalgamated Clothing and Textile Workers Union is another example of a merger to gain power—in this case the purpose will be to organize southern textile plants.

By all indications, the trend to merge will continue. In fact, it is likely that the United Auto Workers union would rejoin the AFL-CIO and even the Teamsters might affiliate. If these events occur, the labor movement would wield even greater political power.

THE HOUSE OF LABOR.   A new attitude pervades the labor movement. Union members today have interests, problems, fears, and aspirations different from those of the 1940s and 1950s. They are younger, of course, and more ambitious and impatient for leadership opportunities. They believe that the union movement should speak for and protect society in general. Not only are minorities exerting more influence in union administration, but women too are demanding their rightful representation—20 percent of union members are women—but there is only one on the AFL-CIO executive council at present. Labor recognizes that it must accommodate the new generation because from it will come tomorrow's leaders.

Douglas Fraser, president of the 1.4 million-member Autoworkers' Union, is one union official who recognizes the need to represent youth. He adds a note of liberal militancy to the union movement, for he supports national health insurance and encourages free and open debate on major issues that affect the union. One such issue focuses on reaffiliation with the AFL-CIO, which is perhaps the most controversial of these. Many of the UAW's leaders fear that reaffiliation would submerge the union in the giant federation, but others feel it would enhance the political and organizational influence of the labor movement.

EXPANDING ROLE OF NEUTRALS.   In the future, the growing threat of legislative action will stimulate free collective bargaining. Labor and management will settle their disputes without resorting to strikes that damage their financial positions and arouse public indignation.

It is unlikely, however, that Congress will enact any restriction such as compulsory arbitration. The nation will still witness some disruptions in both private and public sectors, but more often negotiators will voluntarily rely on third-party intervention to resolve conflicts. In this regard, there will be a dramatic increase in cases referred to mediation and arbitration, and the caseload of the National Labor Relations Board will increase proportionately. Since the present caseload is too great for the board to handle, some basic changes in labor relations procedures under LMRA can be anticipated. It is likely that the NLRB will become more assertive in exercising its authority in new jurisdictions, for instance, expanding its rulings on employee due process.

FOCUS ON THE PUBLIC SECTOR.   Public-sector unionism will continue to grow rapidly, especially among municipal agencies. And as their ranks swell, public-sector unions will push even harder for official sanction of their right to strike. But whether its legality is recognized or not, they will continue to strike when they think it necessary.

The give-away approach to bargaining of inexperienced managers in the public sector will continue to affect the business community detrimentally. When public unions easily win large concessions from government agencies, other unions use these settlements as precedents in negotiations with private-sector management.

HUMAN RESOURCE TRAINING

The major focus of personnel management in the 1980s will be on human resource training. No personnel function is more important in the long run than developing the potential of employees. The success of any enterprise depends on the efficient utilization of its resources, both human and material, in an environment that helps employees fulfill their needs and aspirations.

Developmental efforts will be oriented to the total organization. Personnel managers will emphasize the creation of teams and will seek to improve the collaborative efforts of individuals functioning in groups. The challenge will be in maintaining the cherished value of individual identity. Developmental programs cannot threaten individuality, yet they must influence the efforts of each person toward a common objective. To this end, there will be a major concern regarding the total career patterns of corporate employees, with careful attention being paid to the effects of promotions, raises, and new assignments. Organizations will encourage employees to pursue continuous self-development to keep abreast of rapid change, but they will also recognize that the trend is toward having multiple careers during their lifetime. Enlightened career-development programs will take this phenomenon into account.

The influx of women, minorities, handicapped, and other special groups into organizations will place new demands on HRT managers. Special development programs will be prepared to assure the success of these employees in present and future work situations. As a result of educational and training efforts women should be fully integrated into the work force by year 2000. But the picture for minorities is less promising. One study suggests that until the educational system enables them to achieve equal qualifications, equality of opportunity cannot exist.[14]

Technology will provide some relief to HRT. Video cassettes accompanied by programmed learning manuals will instruct large numbers of trainees on an individual basis. **Computer-based simulation exercises** will teach managers decision making procedures. The simulated business situation lets problem solvers try a course of action without the costly consequences of learning through mistakes in a real situation. Organizations will require HRT managers to substantiate the benefits derived from such training/development programs to ascertain whether their value exceeds their cost. This profit orientation will necessitate extremely conscientious scientific evaluation of all HRT activities.

COMPENSATION MANAGEMENT

Employee dissatisfaction with the monotony of work and with pay inequities will continue to challenge management. Demands of assembly-line workers for the humanization of production work will eventually force managers to design jobs to fit workers and automate those that cannot be enriched. Evidence is conclusive that boredom leads to reduced production.

Likewise, organizations must eliminate the compensation inequities that are a source of worker unrest. To do this they need to centralize compensation administration functions. Furthermore, computer technology will allow firms to analyze job evaluation ratings and maintain these on an up-to-date basis.

The influx of more highly skilled, credentials-oriented personnel will force management to establish harder crtieria for admission to higher level positions. When organizations can appraise employees through specific measures of performance developed from these criteria, they can gear compensation improvements to performance. Merit raises provide greater satisfaction, since recipients perceive the administration of wages and salaries as just and equitable. Similarly, management's concern about a slower productivity growth rate makes pay-for-performance plans seem more attractive. The future should see efforts being made to introduce a variety of pay schemes that tie compensation improvements to increases in productivity.

Inflation will give rise to total compensation philosophies that balance direct pay, incentives, benefits, capital accumulations and other compensation forms to yield a cost effective package. In this respect, incentive programs will add an element of motivation and retirement benefits would be contingent upon economic performance of the firm.

The legal impact on compensation management will be felt through requirements for criterion-based decisions on compensation matters. In this regard, job descriptions will clearly specify what is required of employees, specifications will include valid qualifications (BFOQs), and job evaluation plans (as proposed by the National Academy of Sciences in 1980) will be uniform for all jobs and will utilize job-related criteria determined from job analysis.

Conservative economic growth in the 1980s, less executive mobility, and a growing desire among managers for second careers are factors that will influence the redesign of management compensation plans. Innovative approaches will be taken to accommodate individual needs and desires, reward managerial accomplishment, recognize potential, and retain talent.

WHAT'S AHEAD IN FRINGE BENEFITS

Fringe benefits are moving toward 50 percent of payroll costs, and they are becoming an integral part of total compensation. Added benefits will not lessen employees' insistence on having a voice in matters that affect them. When workers help choose their own benefits, the resulting package is more responsive to individual needs. The ultimate arrangement is the compensation cafeteria, which has had limited exposure at executive levels, but has a chance of gaining acceptance at lower levels in the next several years. The compensation cafeteria gives employees an opportunity to select a base salary and choose the balance of their compensation from a variety of benefits offered by the company. Company-sponsored counseling services will help employees choose the package that best suits their needs. At the same time they can obtain advice on investment, legal, and accounting matters. In fact, prepaid legal insurance, whereby employees are entitled to legal services (wills, divorces, consultation, or even representation in court) will be a major fringe-benefit demand of unions.

Within 10 years, leisure-oriented benefits will be plentiful. They will include more holidays and longer vacations—four to six weeks with pay will be commonplace. Flexible working hours and shorter work weeks, with employees assuming responsibility for their own schedules, will be fairly common. Companies will distribute free concert and theater tickets to employees working four-day weeks, and they will entertain themselves in corporate-owned leisure facilities.

The increased emphasis on education will generate on-site education programs, often for college credit. Organizations will grant sabbaticals for educational purposes and sponsor the education of their employees' children.

By 1985 profit sharing with employees will be the rule, and savings plans with employer contributions will be commonplace.[15]

As health care costs increase, pressures will intensify for employers to institute plans to cover all health-related expenses: hospital, medical, and surgical costs as well as dental and psychiatric care. Organizations will insist that employees share some proportion of the premiums in order to defray the rapidly increasing costs of maintaining coverage.

The cost of pensions is also a growing concern of managers, who are struggling to find ways to pay for the retirement benefits programs that are already in effect. ERISA spelled the demise of many retirement plans that could not meet its stringent legislative requirements. To stimulate the growth of pensions programs ERISA will be overhauled. Tax incentives will be available to organizations as an inducement to create such plans. Employees will have portability rights, that is, they will be able to apply their accumulated service time with a former employer to the pension plan of a new employer. Although the mandatory retirement age has been raised to 70, the tendency to retire early will continue. Many organizations will offer arrangements whereby employees who accumulate a specified number of years can retire with full benefits even before age 60. This will be particularly attractive to knowledge workers and managers who have the propensity to seek second careers. But some workers will also choose to work longer by reducing their hours at midlife or, perhaps by working part-time in later years. This flexible retirement arrangement is destined to become popular during the '80s.[16]

The increasing value and cost of benefits packages mean personnel managers will need to make employees aware of their participation in choosing them. Consequently, a greater number of employers will communicate their benefits programs to employees through annual statements and individual interviews.

SAFETY AND HEALTH

Although OSHA's impact since its introduction has been minimal at best (the number of workdays lost per injury increased 15 percent, but accident occurrences have stabilized), it has helped create an awareness for safety in industry. The future should see the emergence of safety as an integral part of managing. Workplaces will be designed for healthy and safe operations. Employers will seek to reduce hazards on the job out of a desire to operate efficiently rather than from a fear of being cited by OSHA. Even though government inspectors must now obtain warrants before making safety checks, they will intensify their efforts to improve safety and health at the workplace. OSHA will concentrate its efforts on the most hazardous industries, and we should see a significant improvement in the safety record over the next five years, especially as OSHA assumes its new role of partner with business.

Summary

The changing nature of the personnel function in the coming decade will increase the challenge of this work, expand its influence, and enlarge its role within organizations. The complexity of personnel problems will require innovative approaches to elicit maximum contribution of human resources toward organizational goals.

The accelerated pace of technological change will tend to deemphasize the individual. In contrast, employees will assert their right to a voice in management decisions and to influence organizations to meet their social responsibilities. Government influence will pervade all areas of personnel practices through an extensive framework of federal legislation.

Changes in the composition of the labor force—it will be better educated, more sophisticated, and will include more women and minorities—mean that organizations must find new ways to motivate these employees. Personnel research will play a more active role in analyzing problems and seeking better methods of selection, evaluation, turnover reduction, and so on. Although technology may create problems, it will also help solve them. Computer-based personnel data systems will find widespread application in tomorrow's personnel department. Quantifying personnel problems will make more objective decisions possible, and facilitate job matching, selection, performance and training evaluation, compensation administration, and collective bargaining.

An emphasis on economic and social issues will increase the complexity of collective bargaining. Greater sophistication at the bargaining table and widespread efforts to settle labor differences peacefully will limit the number of major strikes. Dispute-settlement methods will rely more on neutrals instead of legislative enforcement, which might interfere with free collective bargaining.

Human resource training activities will have a total organization orientation, directing individual behavior toward a team effort, while still emphasizing continuous self-development. The training will be profit oriented; companies will expect its activities to generate benefits that exceed costs.

Monotonous work and pay inequities will continue to be critical problems. Personnel managers must design jobs that motivate employees and compensation arrangements that pay them according to their contributions. An integral part of compensation will be a wide variety of fringe benefits, with many organizations giving employees compensation menus to choose from.

Key Terms

ecology
wage-price spiral
social responsibility
labor force composition
knowledge worker

human resource accounting
job security
union merger
computer-based simulation
  exercises

Notes

1. Samuel Beckett, *Waiting for Godot* (New York: Grove Press, 1954).

2. The National Goals Research Staff, "Toward Balanced Growth: Quantity with Quality," *The Futurist*, April 1970, p. 113.

3. "A Turn For the Better," *U.S. News and World Report*, February 23, 1981, p. 19.

4. Donald Moffitt, ed., *America Tomorrow* (Princeton, N.J.: Dow Jones Books, 1977), p. 11.

5. For a discussion and examples of quality of work-life projects see: Paul Dickson, *The Future of the Workplace* (New York: Weybright and Talley, 1975).

6. The notion of a social audit was espoused in Raymond H. Bauer and Dan H. Fenn, Jr., *The Corporate Social Audit* (New York: Russell Sage Foundation, 1972).

7. U.S. Bureau of Labor Statistics, *Occupational Outlook Handbook*, 1980–81 ed. (Washington, D.C.: Government Printing Office, 1980), pp. 17ff.

8. "Americans Change," *Business Week*, February 20, 1978, pp. 66ff.

9. William C. Byham, *The Uses of Personnel Research* (New York: American Management Association, 1971), p. 20.

10. "Mixed Views About Unions," *Chicago Tribune*, January 6, 1977.

11. The Bureau of National Affairs, *Labor-Management Relations 1979–2029* (Washington, D.C.: The Bureau of National Affairs, Inc., 1979), p. 2.

12. Daniel D. Cook, "Will Labor Fulfill Its Destiny?" *Industry Week*, March 14, 1977, p. 53.

13. "Why Unions Have an Urge to Merge," *Business Week*, July 15, 1977, p. 94.

14. Fred L. Fry, "The End of Affirmative Action," *Business Horizons*, February 1980, pp. 34–40.

15. T. J. Gordon and R. E. LeBleu, "Employee Benefits, 1970–1985," *Harvard Business Review*, January-February 1970, p. 99.

16. Fred Best, "The Future of Retirement and Lifetime Distribution of Work," *Aging and Work*, Summer 1979, pp. 173ff.

Glossary

Ability to pay (theory). A wage determination concept based on the employer's ability to pay certain wage rates.

Absenteeism. Failure to be in a certain place (e.g., at work) at a specified time.

Accidents. Sudden, unforeseen or unexpected occurrences which result in injury, disability, or death.

Accident prone. One who has a disproportionate number of accidents.

Accreditation. The recognition accorded to an institution or individual that meets the standards or criteria established by a competent agency or association.

Adverse impact (selection guidelines). Effect when selection practices tend to limit groups protected by Title VII of the Civil Rights Act.

Advisory arbitration. A neutral third party hears both sides of a dispute and renders an award that is not binding on either side.

Affirmative action. Federal government contractors are required to give job opportunities to members of minority groups; activities to ensure the job success of minorities, women, and the handicapped.

Affirmative Action Program (AAP). A program to guarantee equal treatment of women and minorities; it takes measures to see that they are recruited, hired, promoted in accordance with their abilities.

Agency shop. A union security provision whereby nonunion members in a bargaining unit pay a sum equal to the union's fees and dues as a condition of continuing employment.

Agreement (collective bargaining). A contract or mutual understanding between a union and company or their representatives setting forth the terms and conditions of employment, usually for a specific period of time.

Alcoholism. A compulsion to consume alcoholic beverages; an addiction to (alcoholic) drink.

Application form. A series of questions, to be completed by the applicant to supply personal history and work-experience data.

Applied research. Study intended to solve immediate practical problems of a limited nature.

Apprenticeship training. A method of teaching skills of a specific trade through a progression of on-the-job experiences supplemented by classroom or correspondence instruction.

Appropriate bargaining unit. A group of employees accepted or designated by an authorized agency (e.g., NLRB) or an employer as appropriate for representation by one union.

Aptitude test. Examination useful in predicting job or training success.

Arbitration. A procedure under which a neutral third party (arbitrator) hears both the union's and the employer's side in a dispute and issues an award that is binding upon them.

Arbitrator. An impartial third party to whom disputing parties submit their differences for decision (award).

Arsenal-of-weapons approach. Threat of use of a variety of measures available to the President and abhorrent to the parties as a deterrent to strikes.

Assertiveness training. Educates women and others in their personal rights and the techniques of "pushing" themselves.

Assessment center. Uses multiple exercises to evaluate individuals and identify promotable candidates.

Assistant-to. An understudy position to develop managers.

Attitude surveys. Questionnaires designed to solicit opinions of employees about various aspects of their jobs and the organization they work for, at a given point in time.

Audio-visual aids. Sensory media (movies, flip charts, displays, etc.) that facilitate learning.

Audit (personnel). A comprehensive analysis of all aspects of personnel work in an organization.

Authoritarian (leadership). Assumes that human relations are irrelevant to getting work done, and that people are necessarily indolent, self-centered, and uncooperative, and that they require strong direction and control if discipline is to be maintained.

Average. Statistical measure of central tendency.

Background investigation. Verifying applicant information and obtaining additional information from references and previous employers.

Basic research. Original investigation for the advancement of scientific knowledge; an investigator may attack any problem anywhere that appeals to his fancy without concern about any practical use of the finding.

Behaviorally Anchored Rating Scales (BARS) (performance appraisal). Identifies observable, measurable performance behavior and feeds back observed behavior to employees in order to improve performance.

Behavior modeling. A method to achieve change in behavior through the individual's involvement (imitation of a role model) in handling real-life situations and receiving immediate feedback on his or her performance.

Behavior modification. Attempting to increase the frequency of desired behavior by rewarding it.

Beneficiary (retirement plan or life insurance). A person other than the employee who is eligible to receive benefits under the plan.

Benefits (compensation). Necessary items that would otherwise require a cash outlay by employees.

Biographical questionnaire. Statistically weighted list of questions about an applicant's personal history.

Body language. Nonverbal communication through which one manages to establish one's roles, intent, and affection.

Bona fide occupational qualification. There is a business necessity for unequal treatment of employees or applicants.

Bonuses. Extra compensation in addition to wages.

Bottom-up approach (position pricing). Nonmanagerial jobs used as basis for setting salaries for higher-level positions.

Boulwarism. Negotiating tactic in which company makes a final offer at an early stage and refuses to accept proposals that would increase the cost of the offer.

Buddy ratings (performance appraisal). Co-workers rate each other on particular qualities.

Budget approach (position pricing). A proportion of total payroll allocated to exempt salaried positions.

Burden of proof. The duty of a party (in arbitration) to substantiate an allegation or issue.

Career. The individually perceived sequence of attitudes and behaviors associated with work-related experiences over the span of a person's life.

Career development. A meaningful progression and achievement of long-run objectives in a person's working life.

Career goals. Specific objectives for future positions in organizations.

Career ladder. Refers to a number of levels that can be defined within the hierarchy of an organization.

Career management. Blends individual aspirations with organizational needs in formal programs to develop capabilities, allocate human resources, select and place, review accomplishments, and reward desired performance.

Career pathing. Exposure of promotable candidates to a variety of experiences designed to prepare them for replacement positions for which they have been designated.

Career planning. The individual process of choosing occupations and organizations, planning the route one's career will follow and engaging in appropriate self-development activities.

Case study. A teaching method that utilizes detailed descriptions of expanded situations for analysis and discussion by students.

Certification (of union elections). Official recognition by the National Labor Relations Board, or a state labor agency, that a labor organization is the duly designated agency for purposes of collective bargaining.

Chemical dependency (CD). A dependency on drugs and/or alcohol.

Civil rights movement. Social movement that sought equal rights for minority groups.

Coaching. Training technique that incorporates demonstration, practice, and encouragement by the instructor.

Collective bargaining. A continuing institutional relationship between an employer (governmental or private) and a labor organization (union or association) representing exclusively a defined group of employees of the employer (appropriate bargaining unit), and concerned with the negotiation, administration, interpretation, and enforcement of written agreements covering joint understandings as to wages or salaries, rates of pay, hours of work, and other conditions of employment.

Commissions. Pay based on fixed or variable amount per unit sold.

Communication. The transfer of commonly meaningful information.

Communication channels. Systems that carry messages from one person or group to another downward, upward, across, or diagonally.

Comparable worth. Compensation based on the relative value of jobs in an organization, according to a set of criteria that are consistently applied to measure this value or contribution to the organization.

Compensable factors. Certain qualities common to all jobs.

Compensation cafeteria. Flexible compensation package design that permits employees to choose the most beneficial form of pay from a variety of alternatives.

Compensation management (wage and salary administration). The development and implementation of policies to ensure that employees are paid fairly for their efforts.

Conciliation. The process of getting a party in a dispute to agree.

Conference method. Training through discussion and sharing of experiences and suggestions on a topic.

Conflict. Sharp disagreement or incompatibility arising out of misunderstandings, perceptual differences, lack of respect, unclear organizational goals, etc.

Computer-based simulation exercises. Generally used in training. Uses computers to generate and/or manipulate data in a game that simulates real-world situations.

Consumer Price Index (CPI). Statistical measure of changes in the prices of goods and services bought by urban wage earners and clerical workers. It is often called the "cost-of-living index."

Contingency theory. There is no one best way to handle problems; concerns the determination of technique or approach that will work best under a given set of circumstances.

Continuing education. College or university sponsored programs that range from skills-building seminars to degree programs.

Control group. Group of individuals similar to the test group (e.g., group of trainees) and used for comparison purposes in scientific experimentation (e.g., training evaluation).

Controlled study. An assumed cause or related "factor" is observed while other conditioning influences are controlled.

Cooling-off period. Provisions of law, federal or state, which postpone strike or lockout action to give mediation agencies an opportunity to settle a dispute.

Corrective (approach to discipline). Counseling attempts to gain employee cooperation; any discipline applied is progressive.

Correlation. An interdependence existing between two sets of data or quantities such that when one changes the other does also.

Correspondence study. Learning by completing written assignments that are mailed to the instructor for grading and comments.

Cost-benefit analysis. Method to investigate costs and benefits in monetary terms and find the alternative for which the benefit/cost relationship best satisfies the decision rule that management has decided to apply.

Cost-of-living escalators. Pay adjustments geared to increases in the Consumer Price Index.

Course outline. Contains objectives for each lesson and details the specific material to be covered along with suggested methodology.

Craft union. Organization of workers in a single craft.

Credit union. Employee-operated mutual benefit organization for savings and low-interest loans.

Criterion. Measure established to judge proficiency, accomplishment, or success on a job.

Critical incident method (performance appraisal). Supervisors list incidents that reflect especially favorable and unfavorable performance.

Cross-validation. The application of a scoring system or set of weights empirically derived in the study of one sample to a different sample (drawn from the same population) to investigate the stability of relationships based on the original weights.

Cutoff score (testing). The minimum score an applicant must achieve to remain in consideration.

Decentralized organization. A type of organization in which a great deal of authority is delegated to lower levels of management.

Decertification. Process whereby the employees in a bargaining unit elect to discontinue having the bargaining agent represent them.

Decision-making interview. Information and related data is gathered, compared to criteria, and a conclusion is drawn or a determination is made.

Deferred compensation. Portion of salary paid to executives at a specified time after their regular pay ceases, e.g., upon retirement.

Dehiring: The process of discharging an employee usually coupled with counseling and assisting the individual in finding other suitable employment.

Delegation. Granting of authority to conduct a particular function.

Delphi technique. A program of sequential interrogations interspersed with information and opinion feedback.

Descriptive study. Explains "what is" rather than "what should be."

Developmental approaches (performance appraisal). Purpose is to identify, plan, and activate behavior that will most likely yield desired performance.

Developmental view (of career planning). Occupational choice represents an evolving sequence of individual decisions.

Diagnosis. Examining the circumstances of a situation in order to make a decision.

Dictionary of Occupational Titles: A compilation of standardized occupational information on job duties and requirements with indexes (for locating classifications) arranged alphabetically by occupational group and by industry.

Differentialist (theory of career planning). Occupational choice is viewed as a matching process that balances satisfaction and stability.

Directive approach (interviewing). Questions and their sequence are determined in advance.

Discipline. A system of rules and regulations that prescribes a desired behavior.

Discrimination. An illegal practice that uses race, color, religion, national origin, or sex as a basis for hiring, firing, or other employment practices.

Distributive bargaining. Negotiations whereby the gain of one party represents a loss to the other.

Double or dual-track (salary progression). Two distinct but parallel ladders of compensation progression for managerial and professional/technical personnel.

Drug addiction. Chronic dependency on drugs.

Dues checkoff. The arrangement whereby employers deduct union dues from the wages of employees and transmit them to the union.

Duty of fair representation. Obligation of both labor and management to ensure that individuals have equal access to the grievance machinery and that their grievances are settled on their merits.

Ecology. The relationship between living organisms and their environment.

Ego states. A system of feelings that motivates a related set of behavior patterns (e.g., parent, adult, and child).

Electronic data processing (EDP). Any systematic procedure for the handling or manipulating of information through the use of high-speed electronic devices.

Employee counseling: The practice of helping an employee identify and solve problems which can be job-related or non-job-related, through a series of interviews.

Employee information systems. A system that provides information regarding the numbers, characteristics, skills, effectiveness, and promotion potential of existing employees.

Employee services. Programs, facilities, activities, and opportunities supplied by or through an employer that are useful or beneficial to employees.

Employment Security Commission. Responsible for two major programs: one is Employment Service, which provides unemployed persons with employment information; the other is Unemployment Insurance, which administers unemployment insurance that is given to qualified unemployed persons until they find work.

Equal employment opportunity. The Civil Rights Act of 1964 prohibits employers and labor unions from discriminating against an individual because of race, color, religion, sex, or national origin.

Equity (in compensation). Fair relationships between the rates of pay for workers and job classifications.

ERISA. Employee Retirement Income Security Act of 1974, enacted to ensure that employees covered by private pension plans receive the benefits to which they are entitled.

Executive. A person having authority to make policy decisions in an organization.

Executive MBA. Master's degree in business programs exclusively for executives who attend classes off-hours, e.g., during weekends, and progress through a program as part of an integrated group.

Exempt (salaried employees). Employees whose rate of pay or position in the organization exempts them from the provisions of the Fair Labor Standards Act.

Expedited arbitration. Arbitrators from a preselected list are instantly available to hear grievances and render quick decisions.

Experiential learning techniques. Training methods in which the students actively participate in the learning process.

Extended injunctions. A national emergency strike remedy whereby a cooling-off period is continued by Congressional action for an additional 30 days.

Extenuating circumstances. Circumstances that make an offense seem less serious.

Fact finding. Actions to investigate, assemble, and report the facts in an employment dispute, sometimes with authority to make recommendations for settlement.

Factor comparison (job evaluation). Monetary value assigned to each job for each compensable factor.

Fair employment practices. Codes regulating hiring and other employment practices that consider race, color, creed, sex, religion, national origin, and other features or characteristics.

Federation (union). A loosely knit league of affiliated national and international unions.

Feedback. The final step in the communication process that involves determining whether the receiver has received the intended message and produced the intended response.

Fiduciary. Person or persons responsible for administering a retirement plan.

Field review method (performance appraisal). Personnel specialists provide ratings of employees from discussion with supervisors.

Final-offer arbitration. Each party submits its final position and the arbitrator selects one of them.

Flexible work hours. A practice whereby workers arrange their starting and stopping times to suit their personal requirements provided that they work a "core time" each day.

Flexible retirement. Arrangements that enable employees to reitre before or beyond "normal" retirement age.

Flexitime. Flexible work-hours arrangement where employees have several options for starting and quitting time.

Forced choice method (performance appraisal). Appraisers must choose the most descriptive statement for each category of performance rating.

Forced distribution (performance appraisal). Allocation of employees' performance on the basis of their contributions on a scale of "best" or "worst."

Forecasts. Giving a statement of what is likely to happen in the future based on considered judgment and analysis.

Formal organization. A group of people working together in some type of concerted or coordinated effort to attain objectives.

Four-day, forty-hour week (4/40). Four 10-hour work days.

Free-written rating (performance appraisal). An overall appraisal that leaves raters complete flexibility on the form of rating.

Games (simulation). Conditions are simulated and trainees make decisions that produce various outcomes; these create new situations requiring further decisions.

Goal-oriented appraisal (MBO appraisal). Actual accomplishments are measured against quantitative objectives jointly established by employees and their supervisors.

Going rate. Amount being paid in an area or industry for similar work.

Graphic scale (performance appraisal). An employee evaluation method that consists of descriptive phrases arranged on a scale, with ratings indicated by checking appropriate phrases.

Grievance procedure. Procedure for the consideration and orderly resolution of disputes.

Group summary appraisal. Managers reach a consensus of assessment of subordinates' performance.

Guaranteed annual wage (GAW). Employer guarantees a certain number of weeks of employment.

Guide chart-profile method (job evaluation). Compensable factors (know-how, problem solving, and accountability) used to evaluate positions.

Guided experience. A variety of approaches to individual development, especially job-rotation assignments.

Guideline method (job evaluation). Salaries are established to reflect the current market prices of positions.

Handicapped. One who has a physical or mental impairment that limits his or her life activities.

Hot cargo agreements. Contract whereby the employer agrees to cease or refrain from doing business with or handling the products of another employer against whom the union is striking.

Human factors engineering. Designing and constructing machines and controls to increase comfort, ease, and simplicity for users.

Human resource accounting. A proposed approach to accounting that involves an attempt to place a value on an organization's personnel.

Human resource planning (manpower planning). Process by which an organization ensures that it has the right number of people and the right kind of people, at the right places, at the right time, doing the things for which they are economically most useful.

Human resource programming. Process of applying employee data and forecasts in the planning of programs to meet future human resource needs.

Human resource. People in an organization.

Human resources inventory. Provides information on employees' past experience with a company, job interests, capabilities, promotion potential, development needs, and other relevant personnel matters.

Human resource training (HRT). A continuous process of teaching and educating employees to improve their effectiveness in present and future jobs.

Hypothesis. A tentative proposition to be confirmed or disproved by research.

In-basket. Simulation of a sample of in-tray or mailbox items of a manager requiring decisions under time pressure.

Incentive pay. Pay as a form of recognition stimulates more effective job performance.

Incidence rate. A measure of illness and injuries combined, relative to total hours worked.

Incident process. A problem-solving training method whereby trainees seek out pertinent details in order to make a decision.

Industrial hygiene. Those aspects of medicine that apply to the environment of the plant or factory and in any way affect the well-being, health, and medical safety of the workers.

Industrial security. Measures taken to guard against criminal or malicious interference with property and protect secrecy of operations.

Industrial union. Organization of all occupations within an industry.

Inflation. Generally rising prices for commodities and factors of production.

Informal organization. The aggregate of personal contacts, interactions, and associated groupings of people working within a formal organization.

Information exchange interview. Involves the simple acquisition or dissemination of information.

Injunction. A prohibitory writ issued by a court to restrain an individual or a group from committing an act that is regarded as inequitable insofar as the rights of some other person or group are concerned.

Insurance. Financial protection against illness, death, or injury.

Integrative bargaining. A joint problem-solving approach to labor-management negotiations. Working toward mutually beneficial solutions.

Interaction. The relationships between or among variables within a situation.

Interest arbitration. Arbitration over the terms of a new contract.

Interest inventories. Measurements of the relative strengths of the applicant's interests in various areas that have vocational significance.

Interview. A medium of exchange of information from one person to another.

Intuition. Direct perception of truth, fact, etc., independent of any reasoning process.

Inverted appraisal. Evaluation of superiors by their employees.

Job adjustment. The process of helping or correcting an employee so that he/she is able to function on the job as expected.

Job analysis. A study of a job (or job cluster) in order to identify distinguishing characteristics and the requirements for successful performance in it.

Job-breakdown sheet. A type of lesson plan which lists all the steps in sequence of operations and the key points of the job that the worker must know.

Job class. Separation of jobs with approximately same pay.

Job classification (job evaluation). Jobs categorized by predetermined grades based on level of skill or responsibility.

Job description. A written description of a job and its requirements.

Job design. Specification of job content, methods, and relationships necessary to satisfy organizational, technological, and personal requirements.

Job enlargement. The addition of meaningless tasks to a job.

Job enrichment. Upgrading a job with factors such as more meaningful work, more recognition, greater responsibility, and increased opportunities for advancement.

Job evaluation. A systematic and objective process of determining the relative value of jobs in an organization.

Job posting. Listing of available jobs, usually on a bulletin board, so that employees may bid for promotion or transfer.

Job rotation. A formal schedule of varying assignments for the purpose of individual development.

Job security. The degree to which employees retain their means of earning a living, that is, protection from unemployment.

Job sharing. Two people hold responsibility for what was formerly one full-time job.

Just cause. What a reasonable person, considering standards of justice and fair dealing, ought to have done under similar circumstances.

Knowledge workers. Employees who rely more on mental skills and abilities than on manual skills; they have a high degree of knowledge.

Labor force composition. Total number of people in the labor force.

Labor force participation rate. Percentage of eligible people who are working.

Labor intensive. A high proportion of labor is used in the production process.

Leadership. A process whereby one person influences the behavior of members of a group.

Leadership effectiveness. The ability to elicit a desired response from others.

Learning curve. Graph of trainee's program of learning (training).

Lesson plans. Tools of the instructor that define objectives of the lesson, list training aids and techniques, and describe how material will be presented.

Level of confidence (statistical). The associated probability of obtaining a value of the test statistic equal to or greater than its observed value.

Line. Functions that are directly involved in producing an organization's goods or services.

Listening. A process that takes place when a person responds to a verbal stimulus.

Lockout. Temporary withholding of work by shutting down an operation or plant in order to bring pressure on workers to accept the employer's terms.

Loss control. Any intentional management action directed at the prevention, reduction, or elimination of the pure (nonspeculative) risks of business.

Maintenance-of-membership agreement. Provides that individuals who were members of a union or who subsequently joined would continue to maintain their membership for the duration of a contract.

Management. The process of accomplishing objectives through the efforts of other people within an organization.

Management compensation. All salaries, incentives, and fringe benefits paid to managers in return for their past, present, and potential services to the organization.

Management development. The continuous process of training and developing selected individuals for present and future positions.

Management information systems (MIS). Systems for providing the information needed to function effectively to all levels of the organization.

Management inventory. An accounting of existing personnel, includes title, age, length of service, promotability, and development needs.

Management-rights clause. Contract language that reserves to management either a specific list of rights or else the general freedom to manage except as restricted by specified items.

Management succession plans. (See replacement charts.)

Managerial obsolescence. A manager is considered no longer up-to-date.

Mandatory retirement. Compulsory retirement at a fixed age such as 65 or 70.

Manpower coefficient. A measure of productivity that indicates the number of employees required per units of product per day.

Market theory (wage determination). Forces of supply (labor seeking employment) and demand (organizations bidding for labor) interact in the marketplace to establish a wage level.

Mathematical models. Variables are expressed quantitatively and logically within functional relationships.

Maturity curve approach (position pricing). Relates salary to position in salary range, length of service, and appraised performance.

MBO (Management-by-Objectives) appraisal. Compares actual performance with individual performance objectives.

Media (communications). Words, pictures, and actions.

Mediation. Third-party assistance in a (labor) dispute to help two parties arrive at their own settlement.

Memorandum of agreement. A brief or informal written note of agreement.

Mental ability test. Measures general learning ability. Used to predict training potential, success in managerial, sales, and some clerical jobs.

Mental alertness test. Measures an individual's ability to comprehend and quickness in reacting correctly to various types of symbols—verbal, mathematical, and visual.

Mental illness. Disorders of the nervous system.

Mentor. Someone in a more senior management position who can serve as coach, advisor, and supporter.

Merit (in compensation management). Pay increases based on performance.

Minorities. Any group that has a small representation in the total work population, e.g., blacks, Chicanos, American Indians, Orientals, and others.

Minority development. The continuous preparation (education and training) of blacks, American Indians, Chicanos, and Asiatics for upward mobility.

Mitigating circumstances. Those circumstances which, while not completely exonerating the person charged, at least reduce the penalty connected with the offense.

Modified union shop. Any deviation from the general standard requiring that all employees become members of the union after a certain period of time following their hiring.

Motivation. An inner state that directs behavior toward goals; goal-directed behavior.

Multiple-management. A method of developing managers through service or decision making committees or junior boards.

National emergency strikes. Circumstances in which a curtailment is likely to cause turmoil within the national economy, create a serious public risk, or endanger the lives of a substantial number of persons.

Need for achievement (McClelland). Need that impels a person to seek out opportunities in the environment and take maximum advantage of these.

Negotiating (in collective bargaining). A process of joint decision making involving bargaining between representatives of workers and representatives of management, with the object of establishing mutually acceptable terms and conditions of employment.

Networking. Intentional communication and contact among individuals for mutual benefit.

Networks (communication). The central nervous system of an organization through which flows information that supplies departments with data upon which decisions are made.

No-furlough policy. No temporary or permanent layoff of a worker because of insufficient work.

Nondirective interview. Guided by how an interviewee sees the situation, encourages expression of feelings, opinions, and perceptions; questions are open-ended.

Nonexempt (salaried employees). Employees who are covered by the Fair Labor Standards Act.

Norm. A rule, a standard, or a pattern for action.

No-strike clause. An agreement by the union not to strike for the duration of a contract.

Null hypothesis. A tentative proposition that is being tested.

Objective. The end toward which activity is aimed.

O.B. Mod. Positive reinforcement strategies are employed in the work situation to accelerate desired behaviors that improve performance and punish undesirable behavior.

Occupational code (DOT). The U.S. Employment Service publishes the Dictionary of Occupational Titles (DOT) which contains the definition of different jobs and a brief description and code for each.

Occupational injury. Injury that results from a work-related accident.

OD interventions. Sets of structured activities — selected organizational units (groups or individuals) engage in a task or sequence of tasks of which the goals are related directly or indirectly to organizational improvement.

On-the-job training. Skills learned at the place of employment.

Open door policy. Encourages employees to express their complaints, ask questions, relate job problems; provides that they be given a fair hearing; and encourages giving them a timely answer if possible.

Operations analysis. Study of actual versus expected performance of employees to help determine training needs.

Opinion survey. Questionnaire to obtain feedback on employee attitudes and opinions of policies, working conditions, wages, and so on.

Organizational analysis. Study of organizational structure, climate, functions, and relationships to help determine training needs.

Organizational development. A continuous and overall effort that increases organizational effectiveness by integrating individual desires for growth with organizational goals.

Organizational effectiveness. Overall performance of the organization which can be measured by various indices (e.g., safety, costs, quality, etc.).

Organizational structure. Boundaries of the formal organization including physical facilities, functions, and human factors.

Organizational projection. A forecast of the organization chart that depicts the ideal organization.

OSHA. Occupational Safety and Health Act of 1970. It constitutes the basic safety and health legislation for industry.

Outplacement. Separated employees for new positions and guiding them in their search for new opportunities.

Partial operation approach. As strike alternative, government intervenes only to the extent necessary to keep minimum goods and services available.

Participative approach. Seeks to achieve an organization's objectives through the involvement of the workers in decision making.

Path-goal theory (leadership). States that the role of the leader in eliciting goal-directed behavior is to increase personal payoffs to subordinates for work-goal attainment, makes the path to payoffs easier to travel while increasing the opportunities for satisfaction enroute, and that the effectiveness of the leader's efforts depends on the particular situation.

Pension. The amount of money paid at regular intervals to a retired employee.

Percentile. Used in reference to a distribution of observations, for example, the 10th percentile is defined as the value below which 10 percent of the distribution of values will fall.

Performance appraisal. Personnel practice which attempts to determine, appraise, classify, and record employees' actual performance and/or behavior on the job; their potential, their need for further training, guidance, incentives, and other related factors.

Perquisites. Services beyond pay for executives.

personal development plan (PDP). Analysis of strengths and development needs with plans to improve performance effectiveness.

Personality inventories. A test or tests designed to measure personality traits, particularly those that have a bearing on a person's effectiveness in handling a particular job.

Personnel analysis. Determination of deficiencies in individual performance, behavior, skills, knowledge, or attitude that training can correct.

Personnel effectiveness. Refers to proper utilization of human resources through understanding why people work and knowing how to get them to perform.

Personnel management. The process of supporting organizational objectives by continually acquiring human resources; integrating employees into an organization; developing employee potential, and maintaining the workforce.

Petition (for certification election). Request for an election to obtain official recognition by the NLRB as the duly elected representative of a group of employees for collective bargaining purposes.

Philosophy (of an organization). Statement of basic purpose and ideals of an organization.

Piecework. Incentive payment based on a price for each unit produced.

Placement. The process of allocating newly selected employees to specific duties and responsibilities in an organization.

Point plan (job evaluation). Weights are assigned to each compensable factor based on its relative importance to the evaluation; factors are divided into levels, which are assigned point values.

Policy making. The process of establishing guidelines for activities.

Policy manual. A manual detailing policies and procedures.

Polygraph (lie-detector). An instrument for detecting and recording the physical reactions that result from emotional stress produced by specific questions asked of respondents.

Portability. Allows employees to take their accumulated benefits with them when they change jobs.

Position descriptions. Detailed definitions of managers' responsibilities, authorities, and cooperative relationships.

Potential. Untested ability that an employee possesses and that may be developed through training or exercise of abilities.

Precedent. What has been done in the past under similar circumstances.

Predictive study. Produces conditional statements from a functional relationship of variables; i.e., if X has a certain value, then according to the functional relationship (regression), Y can be expected to have a certain value.

Preponderance of evidence. In arbitration, the evidence with the greater weight.

Principle. Significant truth that is usually stated as a cause-and-effect relationship.

Privacy of Information Act (1974). Designed to regulate the gathering and dissemination of information on people.

Problem-solving interview. An interview conducted to influence a behavioral change and/or resolve a conflict.

Productivity. Units of output per worker-machine hour or total output/total input.

Professionalism. Engaging in continuing self-education, encouraging research, maintaining high ethical standards, and being willing to police one's own ranks.

Profit sharing. A plan to distribute to employees a share of an organization's profits.

Programmed learning. A learning method that leads students step-by-step toward a desired objective, usually written instructions.

Progressive discipline. A series of disciplinary actions usually starting with an oral warning and followed by progressively more severe penalties (written warning, suspension, discharge) for repeated infractions.

Projective test. A complicated and abstract psychological technique for assessing the unconscious motives, values, attitudes, or traits of individuals by observing and recording their free, spontaneous responses or interpretations of standard, intentionally ambiguous pictures, images, or inkblots.

Project organization. A matrix organization, wherein work is organized around a project rather than around specialized departments as in the typical line organization.

Projects. Small research studies that stimulate students to learn more about a particular subject.

Punitive (approach to discipline). Automatic penalties (punishment) are assessed for any deviation from prescribed standards of behavior.

Pure research. Basic research.

Quality of life. The extent to which the physical and psychological aspects of the environment support improved productivity, satisfaction, and health.

Quality of work life. Enrichment of the work itself.

Quality circles. Small groups of employees that meet regularly and are trained to detect and correct production problems in their areas.

Raiding (union). A term that describes the efforts of a union to bring into its organization individuals who are already members of another union.

Range (wage or salary). Difference between minimum and maximum rate of pay for a job.

Ranking (performance appraisal). Rating performance of individual employees according to merit.

Ranking method (job evaluation). Jobs are ranked from highest to lowest on the basis of skill required, difficulty, contribution to the organization, or any other basis of relative value.

Ratification (of collective bargaining agreement). A vote by union members to accept a contract.

Raw score (testing). The first score obtained in grading a test.

Recruiting. Activities of seeking and attracting a supply of people from which qualified candidates for (anticipated) job vacancies can be selected.

Red circle rates. Wages above the maximum of the pay range that are allowed to remain unchanged.

Reduction in force (layoff). Temporary and indefinite separation from work due usually to slack season, shortage of materials, temporary decline in the market, or other factors.

Reflection. Counseling technique whereby feelings are clarified by their restatement by a counselor.

Reliability (of tests). Individuals taking the same test on several occasions consistently score the same.

Replacement chart. Graphic outline of managers who have been identified as successors to each position in an organization.

Representation elections (union). Secret ballot elections by employees to indicate if they want to be represented by a union.

Retirement. The act of withdrawing from employment following the completion of a specific number of years of service and/or reaching a certain age, or becoming incapable of working.

Retroactivity. In collective bargaining, the terms of the agreement would be retroactive to a specified date, e.g., the expiration of the former agreement.

Review (performance appraisal.) Supervisors and employees compare actual performance to objectives or discuss performance compared to expectations.

Right-to-work laws. Provisions in state laws that prohibit or make illegal any type of union security arrangement between an employer and union.

Rights arbitration. Arbitration of grievances arising out of the interpretation or applications of the contract.

Role playing. A training technique that involves acting, performing, and practicing.

Rule. A specific and detailed guide to action.

Safety. Efforts by management, labor, and government to prevent or reduce the cause of accidents.

Safety engineering. Measures to make the work safer through the design of both machines and work environment and through the use of protective measures.

Salary. The regular money payments, other than by the hour, for services rendered by full-time employees.

Salary reviews. Consideration of individuals for increases in salary (pay).

Sample. A subset of a population having some common observable characteristics.

Scientific method. A rational fact-finding method of research to determine empirically instead of traditionally the right method or approach.

Screening. A process of employment wherein applicants are eliminated who do not fulfill the requirements for a job.

Secondary boycotts. Refusal to deal with a neutral party in labor disputes, usually accompanied by demands that pressure be put upon the employer involved in the dispute to accede to the boycotter's terms.

Seizure. As an alternative to the strike—partial or total government takeover and operation of business enterprises during a labor dispute.

Selection. A process of choosing the individual most likely to perform a job effectively.

Self-appraisal process. Employees complete their own performance appraisals.

Self-concept. An individual's perception of himself or herself.

Self-esteem. A good opinion of oneself.

Seniority system. Method of selecting, promoting, or otherwise considering employees on the basis of their length of service.

Sensitivity training. A group-behavior approach in which participants learn about themselves and how they relate to others.

Services (employee). Programs, facilities, activities, and opportunities supplied by or through an employer that are useful or beneficial to employees.

Sexual harassment. Unwelcome sexual advances, requests for sexual favors, and other verbal or physical conduct when submission is made a condition of employment, is used to make employment decisions, or has the purpose of interfering with a person's work.

Shift premium. Additional pay for hours worked on irregular shifts.

Shop steward. A representative of the union who carries out its responsibilities in the plant at the department level.

Sick leave. A specified number of paid days off because of illness.

Simulation. A representation of the "real world" for purposes of training in decision making.

Situation. The combination and interaction of two or more variables.

Social consciousness. Awareness of social and civic problems and willingness to take positive action.

Socio-technical systems. The molding of people and technology toward the achievement of the organization's objectives.

Split-dollar life insurance. Insurance in which the employer pays a premium equal to the increase in the cash value of the policy and the employee pays the remainder of the premium.

Social responsibility. The obligation of organizations to act in the interests of their employees and the public welfare.

Staff. People whose functions are advisory and supportive in nature and contribute to the efficiency and maintenance of an organization.

Stagflation. An economic phenomenon of the 1970s—a substantial inflation in an environment of stagnating economic activity.

Statistical analysis. A systematic method of arranging and describing data and inferring generalities from specific observations.

Statistics. Systematic arrangement and description of data; a science of inferring generalities from specific observations.

Statutory strike. Production continues, but each side makes monetary forfeitures as a substitute for the strike.

Stock option. Provision for purchase of shares of an organization's stock at a discount for a specified period of time.

Strike. A temporary work stoppage or a concerted withdrawal from work by a group of employees to express a grievance or to enforce demands affecting wages, hours, and/or working conditions.

Styles of leadership. The different processes whereby one person can influence the behavior of members of a group (e.g., autocratic leadership, democratic leadership, laissez faire leadership, etc.).

Subcontracting. A procedure for farming out part of a plant's work on the premise that the work can be performed more efficiently outside the company.

Supplemental unemployment benefits (SUB). Pay to augment state unemployment benefits.

Syllabus. Enumeration of course objectives with an outline of major topics.

Systems theory. Views organizations as a system of components that work in a coordinated manner toward goal achievement.

Take-home pay. The amount of pay that a worker actually receives in his check; gross earnings minus federal and state income taxes, social security taxes, health insurance, etc.

Technology. Refers to new ideas, inventions, innovations, techniques, methods, and materials. Efficiency of technology increases productivity.

Tests. Instruments used in the selection process that provide a sample of behavior, which is used to draw inferences about the future behavior or performance of an individual.

Title VII of the Civil Rights Act (1964). Designed to eliminate employment discrimination in organizations with regard to race, color, religion, sex, or national origin.

Top-down approach (position pricing). Executives' pay set according to that of the chief executive.

Transactional analysis (TA). A rational approach to understanding behavior based on the assumption that any individual can learn to trust himself, think for himself, make decisions, and express feelings.

Transfer of training. The effect of what is learned in one situation on learning in subsequent situations.

Trend correlation. A statistical technique that assumes that the change in a dependent variable can be measured or projected by the change that occurs in two or more independent variables.

Turnover. The ratio of personnel increases and decreases to the total number of employees during a given period of time.

Unemployment. Idleness due to inability to obtain employment; there are four types—seasonal, functional, cyclical, and structural.

Unemployment compensation. Weekly benefits provided by each state to individuals who are unemployed because of specified conditions and who are actively seeking employment.

Unfair labor practices. Certain actions of employers or unions that are prohibited by federal or state labor relations statutes.

Union merger. A consolidation of existing bargaining units into one or more larger appropriate bargaining groups. The joining together of two or more separate unions.

Union organizing campaigns. Efforts of union activists to induce individuals to join a labor union.

Union shop. A form of union security that requires all new employees to become members of the union within a specified period of time, usually 30 days.

Urgency factor (for awarding merit increases). Timing of merit increases based on time since last raise, performance, and other objective determinants for awarding pay raises.

Validate. Demonstrate that a test measures the quality, criteria, predictions, or correlations that it is intended to measure.

Validity. The degree to which inferences from scores on tests or other assessments are justified or supported by evidence.

Value indicators. Goals, purposes, aspirations, attitudes, interests, feelings, and so on as opposed to "true values."

Values. Multifaceted standards that guide conduct in a variety of ways.

Variables. Attributes of the component that take on different values under different conditions.

Variance. In statistics, the degree of difference or deviation about the mean in a frequency distribution.

Vestibule training. Teaching job skills away from the work area in a setting that approximates actual working conditions.

Vesting. Practice of granting employees accrued credit in the pension plan whether or not they stay with an organization.

Vocational rehabilitation. Training the handicapped to enable them to perform useful work.

Wage curves. Total point value for each job plotted against its proposed wage rate or current market value.

Wage-price spiral. A notion (economic) that prices of goods and services increase in response to improvements in wages which in turn leads to the further increase in wages.

Wage survey. Wage studies based on the collection, tabulation, and analysis of data by geographic area or industry.

Weighted application blank. A form of employment application that contains data that has been weighted for scoring to predict job success.

White-collar workers. Nonmanual workers, e.g., office, clerical, sales, supervisory, professional, and technical workers.

Wildcat strike. An unauthorized work stoppage (generally spontaneous).

Work design. A positive, overall study of management systems for the purpose of developing optimum methods of accomplishing a major function.

Workers' compensation (also workmen's compensation). A system that provides for monetary benefits to employees who incur physical injury during the course of their employment.

Work sharing. A plan whereby available work is spread among workers in a group in order to prevent or reduce the extent of a layoff or to make work more available to people who would otherwise not be able to work (e.g, mothers).

Yellow-dog contract. An agreement between an employer and a worker that provides, as a condition of employment, that the worker will refrain from joining a union or resign from membership in one.

Index